CRICKET COUNTRY

PRASHANT KIDAMBI

CRICKET COUNTRY

An Indian Odyssey in the Age of Empire

OXFORD
UNIVERSITY PRESS

OXFORD
UNIVERSITY PRESS

Great Clarendon Street, Oxford, OX2 6DP,
United Kingdom

Oxford University Press is a department of the University of Oxford.
It furthers the University's objective of excellence in research, scholarship,
and education by publishing worldwide. Oxford is a registered trade mark of
Oxford University Press in the UK and in certain other countries

© Prashant Kidambi 2019

The moral rights of the author have been asserted

First Edition published in 2019

Impression: 1

Published in the United States of America by Oxford University Press
198 Madison Avenue, New York, NY 10016, United States of America

British Library Cataloguing in Publication Data

Data available

Library of Congress Control Number: 2019941127

ISBN 978–0–19–884313–9

Printed and bound in Great Britain by
Clays Ltd, Elcograf S.p.A

For
Amma, Appa and Roch

Preface

I

The first time a book entitled *Cricket Country* appeared in print was in the spring of 1944.[1] Its author was the distinguished English poet Edmund Blunden. Published in the midst of a global conflagration, this was an elegiac account of a boyhood spent playing and watching cricket in the Kent countryside. Blunden, as George Orwell noted, wistfully recalled a golden age that had been shattered forever by the First World War.[2] Ostensibly a memoir about cricket, the real subject of the book was England and Englishness. Cricket, for the poet, was an organic expression of a primeval landscape and the rites of male camaraderie that had governed its rural communities from time immemorial.[3] In celebrating this lost pastoral idyll, Blunden reaffirmed the deeply entrenched view that cricket was truly authentic when it was inviolately English. Tellingly, his book had no subtitle: there could only be one *Cricket Country*.

Blunden was drawing on a national tradition that had long regarded cricket as uniquely English.[4] 'The game of cricket,' intoned the Reverend James Pycroft in the mid-nineteenth century, 'is a standing panegyric on the English character: none but an orderly and sensible race of people would so amuse themselves.' Naturally, in this view, it followed that foreigners could not fathom a sport that was 'essentially Anglo-Saxon'.[5] 'Other nations not obsessed by sport are able to hold their own with us at tennis, golf, football, but cricket is incomprehensible to them, a possession or mystery of a clan, a tribal rite,' declared Neville Cardus, a contemporary of Blunden and the most famous representative of this particular literary tradition.[6]

But today even the most ardent English nationalist would concede that there is a new claimant to the title of Blunden's book. 'Cricket,' it has famously been said, 'is an Indian game accidentally discovered by the English.'[7] By a curious historical twist, a sport that defined the identity of the former colonizers is now the ruling passion of the country that they conquered. 'To outsiders, the magnitude of Indians' love for cricket is as incomprehensible as its feverish intensity,' writes a bemused columnist in *The Economist*. 'What was once an English summer game has become in India a celebrity-infused, highly politicised, billion-dollar industry.'[8]

Few would contest that cricket has become an integral part of India's raucous public culture, a unifying force in a land riven by myriad cleavages and conflicts. Indeed, for many Indians, their cricket team *is* the nation. They celebrate its victories as national triumphs, mourn its defeats as national disasters. They regard the Indian team as a symbol of national unity, its social composition as a reflection of the country's cultural diversity. 'In this last decade,' the respected former cricketer Rahul Dravid noted in a public lecture in 2011, 'the Indian team represents, more than ever before, the country we come from—of people from vastly different cultures, who speak different languages, follow different religions, belong to different classes.'[9]

II

Exactly a century before Dravid uttered these words, the first cricket team to represent 'India' made its debut on the playing fields of imperial Britain. This historic venture featured an improbable cast of characters. The captain of the team was a nineteen-year-old prince, the newly enthroned ruler of the most important Sikh state in colonial India. The other cricketers were drawn from across the subcontinent and chosen on the basis of their religion: there were six Parsis, five Hindus, and three Muslims in the squad that travelled from Bombay to London. Astonishingly, the team included two Dalits, who were deemed 'untouchable' by upper-caste Hindus. *Cricket Country* is the story of an extraordinary national team and its momentous sporting journey to the heart of empire.

This book charts how the idea of India took shape on the cricket pitch. Principally, it argues that the nation on the cricket field was originally constituted by, and not against, the forces of empire. Drawing on a range of untapped archival sources, the book documents how the project to put together the first national cricket team was pursued by a diverse coalition comprising Indian businessmen, princes, and publicists, working in tandem with British governors, officials, journalists, soldiers, and professional coaches.[10] Because of this transnational alliance, 'India' was represented by a cricket team long before it became independent.

If the attempt to fashion India on the cricket field reveals the workings of empire, *Cricket Country* also shows how the eventual outcome was decisively shaped by the specific historical contexts within which it was conceived and pursued. The idea of a composite national team was first floated towards the end of the 1890s, when cricket's promoters in India sought to capitalize on the stunning rise of Kumar Shri Ranjitsinhji, the Kathiawari prince whose sublime batting bewitched Britain and the wider imperial world. As it transpired, 'Ranji' (as he was popularly known) was loath to participate in a project that might jeopardize his status as an English cricket icon. In the early 1900s, Europeans in colonial India sought to collaborate with powerful local elites in putting together a national team that would showcase the country's potential as a cricketing destination. Once again, the venture failed; this time because of fierce divisions between Hindus, Parsis, and Muslims over the vexed question of communal representation on the cricket field. A very different set of political circumstances prevailed at the end of the 1900s. The two years between 1907 and 1909 were marked by a wave of violence in which young Indians targeted British officials and their local collaborators. Dismayed by the negative publicity generated by these acts, Bombay's leading business magnates and public men, along with prominent Indian princes, sought to revive the project of sending a national cricket team to Britain. Their aim was to use sport to promote a positive image of India and to assure imperial authorities that the country would remain a loyal part of the British Empire.

Each episode in this narrative underscores how the link between cricket and the nation was neither natural nor inevitable. Equally, it highlights how Indian agency, and not simply imperial imperatives, decisively shaped this cricket country.

III

The making of India as a national cricketing entity, then, is the central theme of this book. But local contexts loom large in my account. The story opens in Bombay, the colonial metropolis where the game first struck deep roots in Indian soil. Long before they invested their energies in fashioning a national cricket team, Parsi promoters, publicists, and players had engineered India's entry into the empire of cricket. The Parsi contests against Europeans in the 1870s, and their tours of Britain in the following decade, laid the foundations of the sporting relationship between colonizers and colonized.

But by 1911, the Parsis were beginning to face a stiff challenge on the cricket field from other Indian communities. Their fiercest rivals were the Hindus, who had come to regard their proficiency in cricket as an index of the community's social and political advancement. The most noteworthy feature of the Hindu team in the first decade of the twentieth century was the presence in its ranks of the Palwankar brothers, Baloo and Shivram, who overcame entrenched forms of caste discrimination to become the preeminent cricketers of their time. Although they first made their mark in the ancient city of Poona (Pune), it was in modern Bombay that these accomplished Dalit siblings consolidated their formidable sporting reputation.

On the other hand, the principal cricketing bastion of the Muslims was the north Indian town of Aligarh. Here, a unique educational experiment, initiated by the prominent reformer Sir Sayyid Ahmad Khan, had resulted in a veritable cricketing nursery that churned out a succession of highly skilled players. The Muhammadan Anglo-Oriental (MAO) College sought to meld together Islamic theology and Western learning. Notably, with the founder's blessings, the college's public school- and Oxbridge-educated faculty made cricket the most important extra-curricular activity within this institution. Cricket at Aligarh thus fashioned Muslim political subjects who were equally fervent about the *Qur'an* and *Wisden*.

The captain of the first national team represented yet another strand in Indian cricket's diverse local cultures. Maharaja Bhupinder Singh of Patiala, a mercurial cricketer, was a troubled prince in the summer of 1911. Only granted full ruling powers the preceding winter, the young man was locked in a deadly tussle with his local British minders. The cricket tour to Britain came at a moment when Bhupinder's hold over his throne was critically in the balance. The book uncovers the intriguing story behind the Maharaja's involvement in this venture and shows how he sought to use sport to rebuild his tarnished reputation in the eyes of the imperial establishment. It thereby illustrates how patronage, politics, and play became mutually intertwined in princely India.

IV

In narrating the history of a pivotal phase in Indian cricket, *Cricket Country* dissents from the deeply entrenched idea that the game's initial appeal in the subcontinent derived primarily from its pre-modern features. For the adherents of this view, the slow pace of cricket, its unpredictability, the lack of direct physical contact between the protagonists, and the significance of its unwritten codes of conduct chimed with the rhythms of an ancient, caste-based, agrarian civilization. Hence, it has been argued, even though cricket was brought to the country by the British, the affinity between its prim Victorian norms and the cultural values of the colonized enabled the game to take root within Indian society.[11]

By contrast, this book affirms that Indians were attracted to cricket because it represented the allure of the colonial modern.[12] From the very outset of its career in the subcontinent, the game was vigorously pursued by Indian middle-class youth residing in towns and cities. Cricket became a site of exclusively male sociability in schools, colleges, offices, and clubs. Acquiring proficiency in the imperial game afforded Indian men an opportunity to savour its kinaesthetic pleasures and assert their masculinity in a context where it was constantly questioned by their colonizers. The proliferating print culture of cricket—both in English and the regional languages—further embedded its vocabulary and rituals in the Indian imagination. Simultaneously, cricket's popularity among the emergent middle classes made it central to debates about race and imperial citizenship within the modern Indian public sphere. Equally, in an intensely hierarchical culture, its rhetoric of equality and fraternity imbued the game with a singular political charisma that fuelled its demotic appeal. In the process, this foreign import became 'a microcosm of the fissures and tensions within Indian society'.[13]

Cricket Country also differs from previous histories of Indian cricket in setting its narrative within a transnational frame. In particular, it shows how the 1911 Indian cricket tour of Britain was part of a regular and well-established pattern of sporting exchanges that had evolved between Britain and the diverse constituent units of her empire. Such visits had come to play an important role in forging international ties within the British world system.[14] Given its exalted status as the imperial game, a majority of these sporting journeys were undertaken by cricketers. 'If historians will examine minutely the doings of either the pioneers or the mainguard of our advancing empire,' declared one late Victorian Briton, 'they will find that cricket and cricket only is the real inspiration of their deeds.'[15] The Indian cricketers' tour needs to be seen in the context of an intensified interplay between sport and imperial cultural diplomacy in the late nineteenth and early twentieth centuries, not least because its promoters and publicists took their own cues from developments occurring in other colonies.

Significantly, the organizers of the venture regarded the formation of a national team as essential if India was to gain entry to the Imperial Cricket Conference, founded in 1909 by the representatives of England, Australia, and South Africa.

At another level, the first Indian cricket tour of Britain was of a piece with the interconnected world created by imperial globalization.[16] From the moment they arrived in the country, the Indian cricketers became part of a singular global moment in the imperial metropolis. The crowning of King George V in the summer of 1911 coincided with an Imperial Conference, a Festival of Empire, a Coronation Exhibition, and remarkably, a Universal Races Congress that sought to question the prevailing racial theories of empire.

Amazingly, the cricketers were not the only peripatetic Indian sportsmen in Britain that summer. This book weaves together the stories of an exceptional bunch of other Indians who landed on British shores in search of sporting glory. In these pages, we will encounter Jamsetji Marker, a thirty-nine-year-old Parsi racquets player, who was the world champion in his sport; a large group of Punjabi wrestlers, who had come to parade their formidable skills in London for the second successive year; and Professor Ramamurti Naidu, the 'Indian Hercules', whose displays of physical strength and endurance enchanted princes and plebeians alike.

Over the course of a blazing coronation summer, dominated simultaneously by imperial pageantry and popular protest, the public reception of these long-forgotten Indian heroes shows how sport forged the imagined communities of empire and nation.

Acknowledgements

This book would not have been possible without the help of a number of individuals and institutions. My biggest debt is to Ramachandra Guha, who first suggested the project, and has been an unwavering source of support and encouragement ever since. His pioneering writings on the social history of Indian cricket are an important point of departure for this study.

The award of a fellowship by the Leverhulme Trust enabled me to undertake the substantive research for the book. This work was carried out in a number of archives and libraries both in the United Kingdom and India. I am grateful to the staff at the following institutions for facilitating my research and permitting me to quote from the records in their possession: the British Library, London; the Bodleian Library, University of Oxford; the Centre of South Asian Studies, University of Cambridge; SOAS University of London; the University of Leicester; the National Library of Scotland, Edinburgh; the National Archives of India, New Delhi; the Nehru Memorial Museum and Library, New Delhi; the Maharashtra State Archives, Mumbai; the Marathi Grantha Sangrahalaya, Mumbai; the Library of the University of Mumbai; the Asiatic Society of Mumbai; and the K.R. Cama Oriental Institute, Mumbai.

Two institutions are indispensable for researching the history of imperial and Indian cricket: the archive and library of the Marylebone Cricket Club, London, and the Anandji Dossa Collection at the Cricket Club of India (CCI), Mumbai. Neil Robinson, the Library and Research Manager at Lord's, dealt patiently with my queries and tracked down rare primary sources. At the CCI, Prakash Dahatonde guided me through that institution's rich holdings of newspaper clippings, books, and journals.

A number of friends contributed to this project by procuring sources, translating documents, and sharing their expertise on specific topics. I thank, in particular, Nandini Bhattacharya, Yug Mohit Chaudhary, Babasaheb Kambale, Aparna Kapadia, Danish Khan, Geoff Levett, Souvik Naha, Dinyar

Patel, Murali Ranganathan, Samira Sheikh, and Carey Watt. In one instance, however, I was the recipient of an extraordinary act of generosity from a complete stranger. Edward Kelvin Storey, whom I never met in person, shared with me his fascinating research on Manik Bajana.

The University of Leicester provided vital institutional support that made possible the pursuit and completion of this book. Equally, my colleagues at the university eased my path through their many acts of kindness. For their friendship and solicitude, I would like to thank Clare Anderson, Bernard Attard, Huw Bowen, Richard Butler, the late Phil Cottrell, Chris Dyer, Lucy Faire, Simon Gunn, Martin Halliwell, Sally Horrocks, Colin Hyde, Richard Jones, George Lewis, Toby Lincoln, James Moore, Mark Rawlinson, Richard Rodger, Kevin Schurer, Keith Snell, Jo Story, Roey Sweet, Deborah Toner, and Ruth Young.

Down the road from the University of Leicester, I have been fortunate to share my ideas with Tony Collins, Rob Colls, and Matt Taylor at the International Centre for Sports History and Culture, De Montfort University. As editor of *Wisden*, Scyld Berry published the early findings of this research; thereafter too, he continued to take a friendly interest in the progress of the book. I have also benefitted immensely from conversations with Kanti Bajpai, Mukulika Banerjee, Neeladri Bhattacharya, Vivian Bickford-Smith, Pratik Chakrabarti, Naresh Fernandes, Matthew Landrus, Peter Oborne, Shalini Sharma, Tony Stewart, Ananya Vajpeyi, A.R. Venkatachalapathy, and Chris Williams.

I am especially grateful to Michael Dwyer, Ramachandra Guha, Samira Sheikh, and Miles Taylor for their incisive feedback on drafts of the manuscript. Tony Morris provided sage counsel at a critical moment. Suresh Menon offered valuable support during the production of the book. He also kindly gave permission to cite some extracts from my essay on Parsi cricket, which first appeared in *Wisden India*.

At Oxford University Press, Matthew Cotton was an exemplary editor. He took to the project with gusto, gave superb advice on the manuscript, and got me across the finishing line. Kizzy Taylor-Richelieu shepherded the book with quiet efficiency through production. I am also grateful to Carrie Hickman, for overseeing the acquisition of illustrations; and Dawn Preston, my copy editor, whose close scrutiny of the text has inestimably improved it.

My family has sustained me through the long writing of this book. For their encouragement and care, I would like to thank especially, Kamala Ramanujachari, the late P.R. Chari, Chandra Chari, Dhiren and Gita Bajpai,

T.C.A. Srinivasa-Raghavan, Jayanti Raghavan, T.C.A. Rangachari, Kokila Rangachari, K.L. Ramu, T.C.A. Ranganathan, Ranjana Sengupta, Divya Chari, Matthew Angus, and Gayatri Rangachari Shah. My brother, Bharat, and sister, Sowmya, have always been at hand with advice and assistance; together with Rachana and Kriti, they remain an invigorating force.

To my parents, Jaya and K.S.V. Krishnamachari, I owe more than I can express, for the quiet comfort of their support and succour. Rochana acted as a sounding board, tolerated my foibles, and made everything possible. This book is dedicated to them.

Contents

List of Figures

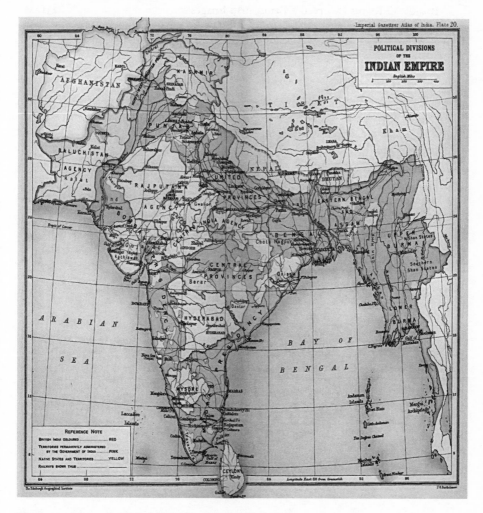

Figure 1. Map of political divisions in Britain's Indian empire, 1909.

An artistic, a social event does not reflect the age. It is the age.

C.L.R. James, *Cricket*

'No one,' Pascal once said, 'dies so poor that he does not leave something behind.'
Surely it is the same with memories too—although these do not always find an heir.

Walter Benjamin, *Illuminations*

I

Parsi Pioneers

I

If the origins of English cricket were decidedly rural, the beginnings of Indian cricket were indubitably urban. It was in mid-nineteenth-century Bombay that Indians of their own accord embraced this alien game, hitherto the pastime of British expatriates in the colonial enclaves scattered across the subcontinent. Notably, it was the Parsi youth of the island who took the lead in adopting the curious sporting pursuit of their foreign rulers.

The passion for cricket among the Parsis of Bombay was part of a profound transformation within the community during the late nineteenth century. At the heart of this process was a distinctive project of self-fashioning on the part of the city's Parsi bourgeoisie that saw them express their 'Britishness' in a range of everyday practices. Their investment in the British connection prompted educated Parsis to embrace the Victorian games ethic with its emphasis on 'civilized' masculinity. And it was their quest for sporting recognition in the imperial metropolis that drove a bunch of young Parsi cricketers to attempt their first cricket tour of Britain in 1878. Had they succeeded in their endeavour, these intrepid Parsis would have arrived on British shores at the same time as the legendary Australian team whose exploits laid the foundation for one of the most famous rivalries in international sport.

But eight years after that failed attempt, the Parsi cricketers of Bombay finally fulfilled their dream. In 1888, a second Parsi cricket team followed in their footsteps. The Parsi forays to the home of cricket took place in a context marked by fractious encounters between Europeans and Indians on the playing fields of colonial Bombay. These tours generated animated public debates about race, community, and imperial citizenship. The attendant publicity magnified cricket's aura and drew more Indians to the sport. The Parsi initiatives thus show how cricket's charisma in the subcontinent was a function of the political significance that it quickly acquired within Indian society.

II

The fire-worshipping followers of Zoroaster, who had migrated from Persia to the Indian subcontinent towards the end of the first millennium, had originally settled along the coast of Gujarat. Over time, the Parsis came to be concentrated in the port towns of Bharuch, Diu, Navsari, and above all Surat, where many of them became artisans or traders. As the commercial fortunes of the Gujarati ports waned in the mid-eighteenth century, there was a growing exodus of Parsis to the English East India Company's settlement at Bombay. They were attracted to this swamp-ridden island both by the commercial security and religious freedom proffered by the company, as well as their own inability to compete on equal terms with well-entrenched business rivals in Gujarat. Colonial Bombay in the early nineteenth century was a town on the make and the Parsis quickly became one of the principal beneficiaries of its growing commercial prosperity. Cultivating close ties with the merchants of the English East India Company and other European private traders, the Parsis gradually attained a pre-eminence in the city's economy and public life that was disproportionate to their tiny numbers.

The Parsi businessmen of Bombay built their fortunes by pursuing a diverse range of commercial opportunities in the first half of the nineteenth century.[1] The most lucrative of these was the thriving export trade in raw cotton and opium with China. But Parsi businessmen 'did not restrict their attention to the China trade' and were to be found in merchant shipping, banking, insurance, retail, and real estate.[2] They also proved to be highly resilient in the face of changing economic circumstances. In the mid-nineteenth century, facing growing pressure from European rivals in the China trade, Parsi merchants quickly transformed themselves into industrialists, establishing Bombay's first cotton mills.[3] Economic affluence brought with it political influence. The Parsi merchant princes were nominated as justices of the peace by the government, which made them a significant element in the administration of the colonial city.

Parsi magnates played a key role in Bombay's public life. As firm supporters of British rule, they swiftly adopted the new 'imperial ethic of improvement'.[4] Leading Parsi merchants undertook lavish acts of philanthropy for the public good. The most notable example was Jamsetjee Jejeebhoy (1783–1859), who built his business empire in the China trade by forging a partnership with the European agency house of Jardine Matheson. This legendary Parsi used his vast wealth to fund a variety of charitable causes and became the first Indian to be knighted by the British Crown.[5]

Parsi merchant princes like Jamsetjee became 'genuinely committed to the project of modernity'.[6] But modern ideas and values were more vigorously espoused by the new, Western-educated Parsi middle class—comprising lawyers, doctors, journalists, teachers, and commercial employees—that rose to prominence in the years after the Great Uprising of 1857. This class was a product of the new educational institutions created under colonial aegis. For those who emerged as its leaders and spokesmen in the late nineteenth century, the engagement with European modernity was a more thorough-going affair. Some pursued projects of social reform within the community. Others, like the activist Behramji Malabari, assumed the role of cultural intermediaries between the rulers and the wider Indian society. And yet others, like the lawyer-politicians Dadabhai Naoroji and Pherozeshah Mehta, became vocal and vigilant critics of the British Raj in India.

The rise of an educated middle class led to severe tensions within the Parsi community. These internal strains manifested themselves over a number of contentious issues: religious reform, gender relations, civic affairs, and, eventually, nationalist politics. On each of these questions, there were heated debates between those of a conservative cast of mind and those who espoused more liberal views. In one respect, however, all sections of the Parsi community were united, and that was in their collective self-fashioning as 'British Indians'. Even the most patriotic Parsi in late nineteenth-century Bombay could not conceive of an India that was not part of the British Empire. British rule in India, Pherozeshah Mehta once remarked, was 'a dispensation so wonderful—a little island set at one end of the world establishing itself in a far continent as different as could be—that it would be folly not to accept it as a declaration of God's will'.[7]

Among the Parsi bourgeoisie of Bombay in particular, the investment in Britishness took different forms. One way in which it manifested itself was in the celebration of the British connection. Take, for instance, the concluding words of Dosabhai Framji Karaka's two-volume history of his community, published in 1884:

> With regard to the present position of the Parsis, it may be said that they are well launched on the path of progress. With the advent of British power in

India better and brighter days dawned for them. With the rise of that power have they risen from poverty and oppression to security and wealth. Upon that power they depend and implicitly rely. It has developed again in their race those high qualities which history attributes to their early ancestors...To it they owe everything, and from it they hope to gain still more. Can it then be wondered at that loyalty—consistent, deep, and abiding loyalty—coupled with a touching reverence and affection for the royal family, has become a part of the Parsi nature, almost a part of the Parsi religion? So that with one consent the whole community daily prays 'God bless the Queen!'[8]

For Karaka, the royal family—and Queen Victoria in particular—was the embodiment of the special relationship that the Parsis shared with the ruling race. But the Parsi investment in the British connection went beyond their professions of loyalty to the Queen. In their everyday practices, too, the Parsi bourgeoisie of the late nineteenth century became highly anglicized. They adopted Western attire, filled their homes with European-style furniture, and imbibed new notions of domestic privacy from the colonial rulers. They were also far in advance of any other Indian community in taking to the English language. One observer wrote in 1899 that, 'The Parsis are most loyal to England, and nearly all the younger generation speak English well.'[9]

Above all, the late nineteenth-century Parsi bourgeoisie sought to cultivate the values of 'civilized' masculinity that they associated with the ruling British.[10] The games ethic was an integral part of the Victorian cult of 'gentlemanliness' and the Parsi middle classes became its most fervent Indian adherents. Eloquent testimony to their passion is to be found in a book published in 1935 by H.D. Darukhanawala. Entitled *Parsis and Sports*, the lavishly illustrated volume is a historical compendium of Parsi distinction in all manner of recreational activities: athletics, aviation, badminton, billiards, bodybuilding, boxing, cricket, cycling, fencing, football, gymnastics, hockey, hunting, jiu-jitsu, rackets, riding, skating, swimming, tennis, and wrestling. 'Thus we see that the Parsi's achievements in sport touch a high level of excellence,' wrote one contributor,

> he has led the way to other communities in manly games and athletics, he has won his spurs on land, in water and up in the air, he has created records in this country and across the waters, and thus he has brought his community to great prominence in the world of sport.[11]

★   ★   ★

Among the 'gentlemanly' pastimes featured in Darukhanawala's book, it was cricket that was most eagerly pursued by the sporting Parsis of colonial

Bombay.[12] This is perhaps not surprising given the moral and political meanings with which the game had been freighted in contemporary Britain. Cricket was extolled by Victorian ideologues as embodying the distinctively British virtues of courage, endurance, self-discipline, selflessness, loyalty, and obedience to rules. For bourgeois Parsis in colonial Bombay, therefore, cricket came to be imbued with a talismanic quality. Demonstrating their devotion to the game became a way of signifying the community's Britishness; proficiency in playing it, a sign of Parsi manliness. Moreover, it was seen as a rational sport: a form of physical recreation that was codified, disciplined, and based on scientific principles rather than chance.

At the same time, the Parsis did not see themselves as mere imitators of their British role models. On the contrary, they sought to proclaim the inherent qualities that made their community uniquely fitted to play this English game. 'The Parsee owes his cricket prosperity as much to the civilizing and inspiring influence of British Rule as to his own innate vigour and adaptability. He is a fine product of Persian pluck and English culture,' declared J.M. Framjee Patel, one of the leading promoters of the game within the community.[13] Others saw in cricketing Parsis the unalloyed martial qualities of their Persian ancestors. 'That the descendants of the ancient Iranians now living in the western capital of India, inspired with all the pride of glorious traditions, should fight the sons of the immortal Alfred on the cricket field and win laurels, is not to be wondered at,' remarked Manekji Kavasji Patel, author of one of the early histories of Parsi cricket. For Patel, it was a matter of regret that 'in these degenerate times they have lost some of those sterling qualities which had distinguished their forefathers'. But he also believed that the reason that 'the Zoroastrians have taken to this game with a keenness surpassing that of the English themselves' was because cricket was the pastime of 'ancient Persian kings and heroes'.[14] Indeed, some chroniclers were in no doubt that the classical Persian texts offered vital clues about the origins of cricket. One Parsi scholar presented a paper to the Bombay branch of the Royal Asiatic Society in September 1890 which began thus:

The modern Parsees of India have made cricket, the national game of their esteemed rulers, their own. But it appears from the Shah-nameh of Firdousi, the great epic poet of Persia, that a game of ball-bat, was known to their ancestors, the ancient Persians. The game was played with great enthusiasm, not only in the later Sassanian period, but also in the earlier times of the Kaiânian dynasty. The young and old, the rich and the poor, played it as a means of healthy exercise and recreation. Even friendly international matches were

arranged under the captainship of the leading men of the rival races...Firdausi
calls this game Chowgân-gui. Chowgân means a bat as well as the ground on
which the game is played. Gui means a ball.[15]

Paradoxically, while these historians entertained few doubts about the
ancient Persian roots of cricket, they were less certain about when precisely
the Parsis of modern Bombay took to it. 'The evidence as to whether the
Parsees knew, in the early part of the present century, even the rudimentary
elements of the game of cricket as played by Englishmen, is all but absent;
and the question must ever remain a matter of vague speculation,' confessed
one writer.[16]

Historical accounts of early Parsi cricket suggest that youths within the
community first began to take up the game sometime in the late 1830s or
early 1840s. According to Framjee Patel, 'one Mr. Boswell, a school master,
was the first to initiate the Parsee lads into the mysteries of the game, at a
school kept by him in the Fort'.[17] But another chronicler, Shapoorjee
Sorabjee, offers a different account:

> Parsee boys began with a mock and farcical imitation of European soldiers and
> officers playing at Fort George, Bombay, their chimney-pot hats serving as
> wickets, and their umbrellas as bats in hitting elliptical balls stuffed with old
> rags by veritably unskilful cobblers. Some enthusiastic boys at first only gleefully
> watched from a distance the game played at Fort George, and then hunted
> after and returned the balls from the field to the players. For such gratis ser-
> vices rendered heartily and joyfully the officers sometimes called them in to
> handle the bat, which was done with extreme pleasure and delight. Thus were
> learnt the initiatory practical lessons in cricket by Parsees.[18]

What we do know with more certainty is that by the mid-nineteenth
century the game rapidly became popular among Parsi school-going
youths who began to practice on the large *maidan* in front of the Fort. The
Esplanade—as the Europeans called it—was a vast open space that had
originally been kept clear in order to provide an unimpeded line of fire for
the military. Over time, as the external threats to the island diminished, the
ground had become a favourite haunt for the Parsi inhabitants of Bombay,
out to 'enjoy the cool and balmy breeze blowing from the western sea'.[19]
Until the mid-nineteenth century, the Parsis who came there tended to
engage in their traditional pastimes: *asookh mahasookh* (a form of physical
exercise), *badshai* (cards), *chopat* (dice), *dam* (draughts), and *gilli danda* (a variant
of 'tip-cat'). But by the 1850s, these customary games began to yield their
place to cricket as the favourite pursuit of young Parsi men.

The early histories of Parsi cricket are notable for their 'whiggishness': the evolution of Parsi cricket was framed as a story of progress from primitive origins to civilized play. 'Just as the "history of the shirt is the history of civilization",' wrote Framjee Patel, 'so the history of Parsee cricket is partly the history of the physical, social and moral progress of the go-ahead and imitative Parsee youth.'[20] Such accounts dwelt with admiration on the pioneering Parsi cricketers who surmounted numerous obstacles in their pursuit of the game. They recounted how the *maidan* that the first Parsi cricketers played on was 'a scene of broken, irregular and rough ground overgrown with coarse grass'. During the day, a vast swathe of the ground was used by Muslim dyers, 'who spread out on the field, for drying, long strips of cloth coloured with indigo blue'. Inevitably, 'scuffles' broke out from time to time between the cricketers and the dyers when the ball 'wandered over the cloth spread out'. Moreover, orthodox Parsis ridiculed the young men for playing a sport 'fit only for children and unworthy [of] the attention of grown-up persons'. But, we are told, 'the pioneer cricketers stood the brunt of all obloquy and prejudice and continued to cultivate the game with the utmost zeal and assiduity'.[21]

These chronicles also suggest that the Parsi youths of the mid-nineteenth century were pioneers in another important respect. They were the first Indians to adopt that distinctively British creation, the sports club, in order to pursue their passion. But, one writer conjectured, such clubs might have also evolved out of the 'old Sadri Fanas (mat and lantern) institutions of a previous generation, where chopat (a native game played with dice) was chiefly favoured'.[22] The first Parsi club on the Bombay *maidan* was the Orient Cricket Club (CC) in 1848, followed two years later by the Zoroastrian CC.[23] Soon thereafter, a number of Parsi cricket clubs mushroomed in the rapidly growing city.

Cricket among Bombay's Parsis began to flourish in the same decade that some of the community's leading merchants anticipated the future by laying the foundations of modern industry in the city. But the cricketing pioneers looked to the past—and a European one at that—for inspiration. The names of the early clubs were frequently inspired by classical Greek and Roman mythology and history.[24] Those who were not so inspired chose instead to celebrate the British connection, naming their clubs after members of the royal family.

Apart from their names, everything else about these early Parsi cricket clubs is a matter for conjecture. The players appear to have been drawn, for the most part, from the Parsi middle classes. The game seems to have become an important element in the patterns of sociability forged by middle-class Parsi youths at this time.[25] The *maidan* became a place where young men from different sections of the Parsi bourgeoisie came together and forged connections that would last a lifetime. At the same time, we also get fleeting glimpses of plebeian Parsis on the cricket field. Clearly, the game allowed for the less well off to rub shoulders with those who were above them in the class and status hierarchy. In turn, the social mixing in these early Parsi cricket clubs generated a distinctive *culture*. Thus, one Parsi cricket historian recalled how 'the players had their peculiar phraseology, strokes, dress and nick-names'.[26]

The last-named feature—their nicknames—is richly evocative of the idiosyncrasies of the early Parsi cricketers. We hear of men like Jamsetji—nicknamed 'Jamsoo Navi' (jamsoo 'the New') 'because he was fond of new clothes and dressed himself elegantly'—a 'highly enthusiastic, light-bodied and nimble-limbed cricketer' who, it is said, 'died fighting the Mahomedans' during the Parsi-Muslim riots of 1874; Hirjibhoy Poncha, known as 'Hirjibhoy Biradar on account of his inveterate habit of styling his cricketing friends as Biradar, a Persian word for brother'; Kharshedjee Dadabhoy, founder of Jupiter CC (1855), who was called 'Thomson, because he was fond of moving in the company of European lads'; Merwanjee Broker, the 'Swift-bowler'; Dorabjee Billia, whose nickname was 'Doloo Faresto' (angel), because of his penchant for 'snow white clean clothes'; Naorojee Shapoorjee Mistree, dubbed 'Navlo Gando, because he was of too jolly a disposition and particularly because he assumed a droll and rollicking gait whilst bowling'; and Fardoonjee Ardeshir Diventry, captain of Zoarastrian CC, better known as 'Fardoon Pasroo' (Fardoon 'the Shirk').[27]

Gradually, Parsi cricket began to attract moneyed patrons in the 1860s. One of the first was the Parsi magnate Sir Cowasjee Jehangir Readymoney, who 'supplied cricketers with kit by the cartload and offered to distribute it through the *Rast Goftar* [an Anglo-Gujarati newspaper], which from the first advocated the claims of the game'.[28] Another generous donor was S.S. Bengalee, an eminent Parsi public figure (and, briefly, the editor of *Rast Goftar*). His biggest contribution was to institute in 1868 'prize matches' between the various cricket clubs on the Esplanade. 'Not only were adequate prizes given away in cricket articles and cash money, but all the expenses in connection with a band kept in attendance, tents pitched for the shelter of the players and the spectators, and dinners and refreshments provided to all concerned were borne by him right cheerfully,' wrote his friend Shapoorjee Sorabjee.[29]

These annual prize matches, which took place on the Bombay *maidan* every December (until they ceased in 1877), generated immense interest within the wider Parsi community. 'It was with the prize-matches,' Sorabjee noted, 'that the beginning was made of large crowds of spectators, mostly Parsees, gathering the whole day long to witness sympathetically and enjoy joyfully the cricket matches.' A perceptive observer, Sorabjee, also highlighted how the change in the Parsi attitude to cricket was mirrored in language: 'For nearly the first twenty years the characteristic word "ball-bat" was the only word most commonly in use for cricket. As years rolled on both the aversion to "ball-bat" and the word "ball-bat" itself were "clean out" for good at the steady and welcome advent of "cricket".'[30]

The prize matches were notable for the intense competition between the participating teams. In particular, the contests between Zoroastrian CC and their fierce rivals, Mars CC, generated immense public interest. Mars CC was an interloper among the Esplanade-based cricket clubs. According to Sorabjee, it 'was the only club that began its existence (about the year 1860) on the Marine Lines Ground'. However, it 'was soon forced to resign [this ground] in favour of the jealous Marine Battalion sepoys and take resort to the east part of the General Parade Ground'.[31] But the change of venue did not affect its performance and under the leadership of Dadabhoy Sorabjee Patel (a.k.a. 'Dady Frith')—a lecturer in English at the Elphinstone College—the club's play 'was characterized by activity and brilliancy' in the late 1860s and early 1870s. Notably, Mars CC successfully took on Union CC, a Eurasian club, as well as a team comprising soldiers and officers stationed in the Colaba cantonment. These matches demonstrated that the Parsis were coming of age on the cricket field, a fact that did not go down too well with some of their opponents. During one fractious encounter between Mars CC and Union CC, 'the parties came from words to blows'.[32]

As with many Parsi clubs of the time, Mars CC was riven apart by internal tensions, and according to Sorabjee, 'ultimately its bier was laid down about the year 1877'.[33] But in its place there swiftly arose a new cricket club that became to Indian cricket in the late nineteenth century what the legendary Hambledon Club had been to English cricket a century earlier. It is this club that single-handedly elevated the status of Parsi cricket both in colonial India and in imperial Britain. Notably, its energetic leader Ardeshir Byramjee

Patel (1855–1902) first conceived and pursued the daring idea of a Parsi cricket tour of Britain.

III

We do not know much about Ardeshir Patel's background, other than that he was a failed medical student who seems to have spent his later years working for the Gujarati weekly newspaper *Jam-e-Jamshed*.[34] But we do know a lot more from contemporary sources about the Parsee CC. Founded in 1876 by Ardeshir Patel, it began life as an offshoot of a football club. According to one chronicler, Patel, as 'the secretary of the Parsee Football Club, with a view to secure regularity of attendance of players and thus to strengthen his club, took it upon himself to form a cricket club in connection with it, and christened it the Parsee Cricket Club'. Ironically,

> the Parsee Football Club languished and died, but what was at first meant to be a strength and support to it happily grew up to be the sturdy main body itself—the Parsee C.C.—and, owing to his [Patel's] fostering and anxiously bestowed care...prospered most enviably, enjoying supremacy over all other native cricket clubs in Bombay.[35]

Although he had 'never handled a bat', Ardeshir Patel was a resourceful organizer.[36] When Mars CC began to disintegrate, he swiftly recruited many of its players to turn out for his newly established cricket club. Importantly, Patel also forged connections with Europeans in Bombay's sporting world. Indeed, from the very outset, Parsee CC made it a point to play European teams.

The new club made its mark very quickly. In January 1877, barely months after it had been formed, Parsee CC defeated a British team representing the Royal Navy.[37] Playing the same opposition two months later, they repeated the feat.[38] News of these victories even reached British shores. After the first Parsi victory, London's *Daily News* informed its readers, 'The honour of our British seamen is tarnished by disaster.' 'This is the first time that the fact of these our Aryan cousins being cricketers has been brought to our knowledge,' confessed the reporter. Although he was appreciative of the Parsi performance, this observer could not quite believe that this was the sole cause of the naval team's defeat. 'Probably the climate, possibly the champagne cup, had something to do with this naval disaster,' he suggested, thereby establishing a precedent that was to be followed by other visiting English cricket teams in India. However, this writer also drew some solace from the sobering defeat: 'While cricket takes root in Eastern hearts, British rule in India is secure.'[39]

These victories appear to have spurred Ardeshir Patel to consider taking a Parsi team to Britain in the summer of 1878. Shortly after Parsee CC's victories against the Royal Navy team, he contacted Charles Alcock, the secretary of Surrey County Cricket Club (CCC), and put the idea to him. Rumours about the proposed cricket tour began to circulate both in Bombay and Britain around this time. 'The Parsee cricketers of Bombay are evidently not content with the triumphs they have achieved over here,' noted the *Indian Spectator* in May 1877. 'They are now about to challenge English players on their grounds. It is not easy to forecast the result, but we may be sure they will astonish English players by their skill.'[40]

Remarkably, at this stage, Parsee CC had not even succeeded in securing a match against the local Bombay Gymkhana, the premier European club in the city, which had refused until then to play any 'native' team. The Gymkhana's racial exclusivity is noteworthy because it kept out the Parsis, who are generally perceived as close allies of the British ruling elite in Bombay. Ironically, the construction of the Bombay Gymkhana had been funded by a generous donation from Sir Cowasji Readymoney.

But Patel was not easily deterred. He turned to his European contacts for help in arranging a fixture with the Bombay Gymkhana. One of his European acquaintances was Michael Wyer, of the mercantile firm Wallace and Co., who played for the Gymkhana cricket team. With Wyer's help, Ardeshir Patel was able to persuade the club to play against Parsee CC.

The 'historic match' was staged in front of a large crowd at the Bombay Gymkhana on 7 August 1877. 'Even at eleven o'clock there were a great number of people present, while by four o'clock there was one of the largest crowds that we have ever seen at a cricket match in Bombay,' reported the *Times of India*.[41] Interestingly, contemporary accounts of the match noted the prominent presence of women—both European and Parsi—at the ground.[42] Batting first, the Europeans got off to a good start. Gradually, the Parsi bowlers found their bearings and restricted their opponents to a total of 167 runs. The sharp underhand bowling of the Parsis attracted much comment in the European press, as did their fielding, which was deemed to be 'first rate'.[43] But the Parsi batsmen were unable to press home the advantage secured by their bowlers and fell short by sixty-two runs.

In order to provide his team with more practice, Patel arranged a series
of fixtures against other European sides. The Parsee CC performed extremely
creditably in these matches, inflicting defeats in quick succession on two
strong European teams. Their first victory was over the 66th Regiment, in
a keenly anticipated match played a few days after the encounter with the
Bombay Gymkhana. Watched again by a large crowd that included the city's
colonial elite, the Parsis won a thrilling contest by three wickets. They
followed this up with a two-wicket win against an outstation military team
in a one-day match at the Gymkhana ground.[44]

Because of their symbolically charged context, both matches turned out
to be contentious affairs. After the match against the 66th Regiment, the
defeated soldiers lashed out at Parsi spectators celebrating their team's
victory. J.M. Framjee Patel, a member of the Parsi team on that occasion,
later wrote how the overzealous sepoys of that regiment, perhaps goaded by
their white superiors, inflicted 'heavy punishment on some of the spectators
by wielding their belts freely'.[45] In the fixture against the visiting military
team, the Parsis, who narrowly emerged as the victors, complained 'bitterly'
about the partisanship of the European soldier who acted as umpire.[46]

The Parsee CC's victories prompted the Bombay Gymkhana to agree to
a second match in October 1877. The two-day match once again drew a
large crowd enthused by the prospect of a local Indian team taking on the
powerful European team. The match was drawn after Parsee CC had led
on the first innings. At the close of play, 'the general opinion among the
Europeans was that it was in their favour and among the Parsees that it was
in their favour'.[47] Some Indian newspapers proclaimed that had time permitted the Parsis would have triumphed in the contest. One of these—the
Calcutta Charivari—reportedly published 'a cartoon styled "Jamsegi [Jamsetji]
Victorious," depicting a Parsee strutting about with a bat and several
Europeans, looking very small, all round him'.[48]

The considerable 'warmth of feeling' engendered by such claims prompted
the Bombay Gymkhana to challenge Parsee CC to a third contest in
December 1877.[49] Although the Europeans won this encounter decisively
by an innings, the match was overshadowed by the contentious decision of
one of the Gymkhana's umpires to repeatedly penalize Rustomjee Katrak,
the Parsi team's opening bowler, for 'throwing'.[50] 'This highly curious opinion of the umpire, who was a soldier, more than surprised the spectators,
most of whom knew Rustom Gargar [so called because he was "rather fond
of his peg"] as the best bowler amongst the Parsees,' remarked one observer.[51]

A furious war of words ensued in the local press. In a letter to the *Times of India*, one incensed Parsi asserted that his compatriots were 'fully equal, if not superior, to their European brethren in this noble game', and alleged that the umpire who had deemed Katrak's action illegal 'did so with the fullest knowledge that the balls were on a former occasion passed by him as fair'. 'These umpires cannot be expected to be impartial to the Parsees, for they (the soldiers) are chosen by the Gymkhana and are of the same nationality,' the letter writer concluded.[52]

For the colonized, then, the theatre of sport presented in a highly dramatic form the racial bias of their rulers. Among the colonizers, on the other hand, this new challenge on the sporting field served to crystallize the antipathy and anxiety evoked by these colonial 'mimic men'. This becomes clear when we consider the attitude of the European elite in Bombay towards the proposed Parsi cricket tour to Britain. When the rumours about the project had first surfaced, the British establishment in colonial Bombay had responded with 'sly civility'. Framjee Patel recounted how, at a farewell reception, Sir Philip Woodhouse, the outgoing Governor of Bombay, 'sarcastically alluded to Parsee cricketers who were just then attracting some attention'. 'While as for cricket,' the Governor is reported to have said to laughter and applause, 'I have no doubt that the Parsees expect to be able in a year or two to encounter an All England XI.'[53]

When it became clear that the Parsis were serious about the venture, sections of Bombay's European press began to openly ridicule the idea. Take, for instance, an extended article in the *Bombay Gazette* entitled 'A New Invention—The Parsee Cricketer of the Period'. 'The Parsee is essentially an imitative animal,' its author declared. 'Where the European leads, the Parsee follows. His imitation of European vices we shall say nothing about; but as for European games, the Parsee has picked them up as patly as if he were to the manner born.' The writer then proceeded to poke fun at the pretensions of the Parsi upstarts who had dared to contemplate a cricket tour of Britain:

> As a commercial speculation, we admit, a Parsee XI in England might pay very well; but then they would have to dress strictly after the manner of their race. Even the wild Red Indians brought over to England from Canada to play lacrosse would have been melancholy failures if they had abandoned their feathers and moccasins and played in tight-fitting tweed trousers and patent leather boots. In like manner, Parsee cricketers would prove failures if they did not adhere to their traditional costume ... English people like shows; they do

not like mock-turtle when they have to pay for the real thing. Parsees playing
in England with patent leather boots, elaborate shirt fronts and flannel trousers,
smoking cheroots, drinking pegs, and talking such good English as 'dammy,
what beastly luck, Pestonjee' would be mock-turtle—no mistake about it.[54]

Such remarks show how the claims to sporting equivalence of the Parsi
cricketers unsettled their European adversaries. In other words, to Bombay's
colonial elites the 'imitative Parsee' became 'at once resemblance and
menace'.[55] The comments also reveal how the colonizers dealt with the
disquiet aroused by these cricketing Parsis who were 'almost the same but
not quite'. One response of the ruling elite was to mock the Parsi attempt
to challenge them on their own turf. Another was to insist that to be anglicized was 'emphatically not to be English'.[56] Hence this writer's unsolicited
advice to the Parsi cricketers that their best chance of sporting recognition
on the imperial stage lay in affirming and enacting their status as the 'Other'.

★ ★ ★

Unfazed by the hostility of the European press in Bombay, Ardeshir Patel
and his associates went about the task of putting together the tour. By
the spring of 1878, Patel and Alcock had finalized a provisional schedule for the
Parsi tourists, and the arrival of the team became a topic of comment in the
British press. 'Early in June next, a team of Parsee cricketers, the champions
of India, will reach England, with the object of playing a series of matches
against English clubs,' reported one London sporting weekly. 'Their first
engagement will be at Lord's against Marylebone Club and Ground and they
have already made fixtures with Prince's and Surrey County Clubs, in addition
to matches at Leeds, Pudsey, Rochdale, Bolton, Birmingham and Nottingham,
Belfast, Brighton, Maidstone, Southampton and other places,' it added.[57]

Many newspapers in Britain could not contain their astonishment at the
news. 'Bombay, of all places in the world, is sending over an eleven to
England, and it is to be—of all the nationalities in the world—an eleven of
Parsees', marvelled the Daily Telegraph.[58] Some dwelt on the incongruity of
a Parsi cricket tour of Britain. 'It will seem strange,' commented the Daily
News, 'after being accustomed to such simple names as Grace, Jupp, Daft and
Walker, to read of a gentleman being out "caught Bhimjeebhoy, bowled
Libuwalla," or that Bhicajee was run out for 36. Lovers of novelty will find
plenty to amuse and interest them in the play of the Parsees.'[59] Others gave
free rein to the prevailing racist stereotypes about Indians. 'An Oriental

wicket-keeper who was also a snake charmer would have great allies,'
ventured one writer. 'He might display a pet cobra at the proper moment.'[60]

However, the public response in the imperial metropolis was not uni-
formly derisory of the Parsi initiative. Notably, an article in the *Daily
Telegraph* deprecated the withering criticism directed at the proposed tour
by the European press in India.

> The Bombay papers, it is true, speak somewhat disparagingly of Parsee cricket.
> The local critics strongly condemn their play. We hope to find these severe
> criticisms not altogether deserved, and in any case they seem excessively harsh.
> The Parsee gentlemen who are about to pay us a visit will, we may be sure,
> discard their native customs. It is impossible to play cricket in a mitre and cas-
> sock, and such is not the costume generally worn on the maidan. A Parsee in
> London usually adopts patent leather shoes, fashionable trousers, a frock coat
> and a smoking cap with a long tassel. The Parsee cricketers will, we may take
> it for granted, don the customary flannels and a head-covering something like
> the rugby football cap. Even now, as all lovers of the game must know, it is not
> many years since cricket was played by veterans such as Mynn in white ducks,
> a linen shirt and a stove-pot or chimney-pipe hat. We have altered all that now.
> But the change is so recent that we have no right to laugh at a Parsee—even
> if he were to play in his national head-gear—and are certainly altogether
> unjustified in comparing a Parsee eleven, as do some of our Bombay contem-
> poraries, to an eleven of schoolboys, or of one-armed or one-legged champions.
> For our own part, we desire to give these gallant Oriental gentlemen from our
> Indian empire every welcome.[61]

These were seemingly generous remarks. Whereas the Bombay newspapers
had poured scorn on the Parsi cricketers, the *Daily Telegraph* had greeted
their efforts with warm words of encouragement. Yet even this newspaper's
sympathetic stance was not without its prejudices. While the Europeans in
Bombay advised the Parsis to showcase their racial difference in order to
appeal to spectators in Britain, the metropolitan newspaper signalled that
these Indian visitors would have to efface all traces of such difference and
play the game just as Englishmen did. Furthermore, the *Telegraph* too cast
the colonized in the role of aspiring pupils requiring the gentle guidance of
their rulers.

But even as it became the focus of press attention, the tour was affected
by an entirely unexpected development. The war between the Russian and
Ottoman Empires had entered a new phase in the early months of 1878.
Britain, fearing a Turkish collapse in the face of the ominous Russian advance

on Constantinople, commenced military preparations to bolster its position in the eastern Mediterranean. As part of these manoeuvres, an expeditionary force consisting of 7,000 Indian troops was dispatched from Bombay to Malta in April 1878. Among those affected by the heightened military threat were two of the Parsi cricketers who had agreed to tour Britain that summer. Their most effective bowler Rustom Katrak, who worked in the Commissariat, and Bhikajee, an employee in the Grand Arsenal, were denied leave by their managers. A third Parsi cricketer, Dinshaw Dadabhai Khambatta (from Karachi), who appears to have been considered as a possible replacement, also expressed his inability to travel for the same reason. Confronted with the late withdrawal of key players, Ardeshir Patel and his associates decided to abandon the tour. They informed the clubs with whom matches had been fixed about their inability to travel to Britain that summer. 'In our disappointment we have one consolation,' they noted in their message, 'and that is, that we are detained to serve our beloved Empress Sovereign in this emergency.'[62]

Their explanation for pulling out of the tour became the butt of jokes in the British press. 'The alleged reason for the non-arrival of the Parsees is a "difficulty of getting leave of absence",' one writer declared,

> but it is well known that the absence of the sun—whom we have only seen three times in London for some weeks—is the real obstacle to their visit. They had been led to imagine that the Object of their Worship was to be beheld in this country throughout the summer. Whereas I write this letter in June, under grey skies, with a north-east wind blowing and beside a roaring fire.[63]

Some wits used the occasion to engage in a contrived bout of punning. For instance, the following snippet, entitled 'DO YOU PARSEE-VE?', was regurgitated in a number of provincial newspapers:

> The visit of the Parsee cricketers has been postponed till next season, in consequence of the leading members of the team having been unable to obtain leave of absence this summer. Parsee-flage, as the French say, apart, the cricketers have every right to appeal against this unworthy Parsee-cution by Parsee-monious employers. If their appeal is disregarded, they must try again; for Parsee-verance conquers difficulties.[64]

Back in Bombay, matters had taken a more fractious turn. The collapse of the tour triggered a fusillade of public recriminations in Bombay's Gujarati press and laid bare the divisions within the Parsi community over the project.

IV

On 30 October 1878, a 'peculiar defamation case' came up for hearing at the Fort Police Court in Bombay. The complainant was Kaikhosro N. Kabrajee, the editor of *Rast Goftar* and president of Parsee CC.[65] The defendants were Manockjee Burjorjee Minocher-Homjee, the editor-proprietor of *Bombay Samachar*, and Ardeshir Patel, the secretary of Parsee CC. At the heart of this curious legal dispute was the role of the two contending parties in the failed Parsi cricket tour of Britain.

Today, it is not particularly unusual to find matters pertaining to Indian cricket culminating in the law courts. But it is astonishing to find that the precedent was set as early as 1878. The defamation case, and the media war in the Gujarati press that it triggered, shows how cricket had become a major preoccupation within the Parsi public sphere by the late 1870s.

The trigger for the clash between K.N. Kabrajee and Ardeshir Patel was the former's opposition to the proposed Parsi cricket tour of Britain.[66] Notwithstanding his position as president of the Parsee CC, the editor of *Rast Goftar* chose to air in public his strident criticism of the venture. He fired the first salvo in May 1878, accusing Patel and his friends of getting above themselves. According to Kabrajee, the Parsi cricketers were inviting ridicule by seeking to take on the mighty English, whose innate sporting prowess and feats of physical endurance they had no hope of matching. That day might arrive in the future, he conceded, but for the moment the Parsi cricketers would do well to avoid such foolhardy schemes. Moreover, he pointed out, although the cricketers were not 'representative' of the community, their actions would nonetheless sully the reputation of all Parsis. Indeed, he declared, the English press had already mocked the pretensions of these upstarts.[67]

The Parsi cricketers rebutted the harsh views expressed by Kabrajee in his newspaper. They contested the charge that their tour was motivated by a desire to challenge the English. On the contrary, they contended, their aim was to watch and learn from English cricketers. Nor was it true, as Kabrajee had stated, that they were unwelcome in Britain. By way of proof, they cited reports in British newspapers that testified to the cordiality with which their efforts had been greeted both by the press and the cricket establishment in that country.

Kabrajee's critics also ridiculed his grasp of the game by citing numerous instances in which the eminent editor had displayed his ignorance of its rules and rituals. They poured scorn on his assertion that cricket in England was only played by professionals.[68] In correcting his errors, they proclaimed their own familiarity with the English game: its history, economics, geography, and sociology. The detailed knowledge that they drew upon in their letters to the press suggests that cricket had become an integral part of the everyday discourse of young Parsis.

When the tour was called off, a fresh round of hostilities commenced between the two sides. In an article in *Rast Goftar*, Kabrajee dismissed out of hand the reasons proffered by the Parsi cricketers for abandoning the venture. 'Cricket was only in name, money in reality was the game,' he claimed. The cricketers, Kabrajee alleged, had used the tour as a pretext to raise a loan from a prominent businessman named Seth Narsinh Keshavji. When that deal fell through, they had sought to travel as the 'paid employees' of an English gentleman. But that plan too had failed and hence these *bahadurs* (bravehearts), Kabrajee declared, had been forced to admit defeat.[69]

Yet again the Parsi cricketers took up the pen to set the record straight. They furnished a note from Seth Narsinh Keshavji denying his involvement at any stage in the organization of the tour. They also pointed out that while an English gentleman had indeed agreed to help them, he had been unable to meet their terms and conditions. The cricketers angrily refuted Kabrajee's charge that their tour was a ruse to extract money from unwary sponsors. On the contrary, they asserted, they had always intended to travel to Britain 'on their own steam' and had even raised Rs. 13,000 for the trip.[70] Indeed, the Parsi cricketers were quick to draw parallels between their own endeavour and that of the Australian cricketers who also travelled to Britain in the summer of 1878, the first white team from Down Under to visit the Mother Country. Like the Australians, argued the Parsi cricketers, they too had sought simply to recover the costs they were likely to incur on the tour. It was this consideration, and not profit, that had guided their actions.[71]

At this point, with both sides having had their say in print, the matter might have ended. But an incendiary letter by the secretary of the Parsee CC in the *Bombay Samachar* escalated the row. Ardeshir Patel alleged that Kabrajee had attacked the Parsi cricketers because they had refused to let him accompany them on their intended tour of Britain. Patel also revealed that a concerted campaign was underway to oust the editor of *Rast Goftar* from his position as president of the Parsee CC.[72]

The publication of Ardeshir Patel's letter stung Kabrajee into taking legal action. After the first hearing, the presiding magistrate 'advised the parties to settle their differences out of Court'.[73] But the irascible Kabrajee rejected the advice and the 'case protracted for months together'. Eventually, however, 'the intervention of mutual friends' resulted in 'an amicable settlement'.[74]

Eight years were to pass before the Parsis were finally able to achieve their dream of sending a cricket team to the imperial metropolis. In the intervening years, a bitter conflict developed between the Parsi cricketers and the European sportsmen of Bombay over the use of the city's principal *maidan*.

V

When Shapoorjee Sorabjee published his *Chronicle of Cricket amongst Parsees* in 1897, he appended to it a densely documented pamphlet. *The Struggle: European Polo versus Native Cricket* shows how the cricket field in late nineteenth-century Bombay became a symbol of the iniquities of colonial rule.[75] Unlike the preceding chronicle, which recounts in an anodyne fashion the institutional history of Parsi cricket, this fascinating supplement recounts the story of how the city's native cricketers took on the European polo players who sought to appropriate their *maidan*. Few were better qualified to write this account than Sorabjee. As Ramachandra Guha has noted, Sorabjee was 'a participant observer, a man who played cricket on the Maidan, who wrote petitions to get rid of polo from the Maidan, and who was a political theorist of some originality besides'.[76]

Sorabjee's narrative focuses on the conflict over the use of the Bombay *maidan*, where, by the late 1870s, hundreds of Indian cricketers practised every day. Towards the end of the decade, the European polo players of the Bombay Gymkhana (which was established in 1875), who had hitherto practised at Cooperage to the south of the *maidan* or at Marine Lines to its west, commenced to play their game on the ground that was used by the native cricketers. Open space was at a premium in colonial Bombay and there was already intense competition among the various local cricket clubs to secure their place on the *maidan*. So, there was general consternation among the native cricketers when they found the Europeans muscling in on their turf.

The cricketers voiced their grievance against the polo players in the ways that other Indians of their class tended to do: they complained in the press and they wrote to the secretary of the Bombay Gymkhana seeking redress. When that official refused to consider their case, 460 Indian cricketers affixed their signatures to a formal petition that they submitted on 27 October 1881 to the Governor of Bombay.[77] In it, they recounted how the European polo players had invaded the *maidan* on which native cricketers had been playing for years, how this was part of a relentless encroachment of land by the Bombay Gymkhana, and how the practice of polo ruined the turf, thereby rendering it unfit and dangerous for cricket.

At first, the Governor of Bombay tried to deflect the matter by turning it over to the military authorities, who brusquely refused to concede any of the Indian cricketers' claims. But the petitioners persisted, and remarkably, were able to prevail over the polo-playing soldiers of the Bombay Gymkhana.[78] On 17 April 1882, a government memorandum permitted 'the Native Cricketers to use the Esplanade Parade ground, when not required by Government for military or other purposes'.[79] Since playing polo could not be construed as a 'military' requirement, the resolution effectively conceded the claims of the cricketers.[80] Five days later, 250 jubilant native cricketers attended a meeting to thank the government and honour those who had campaigned on their behalf. Among these supporters was Dadabhai Naoroji, himself an old hand at petitioning the colonial state.[81]

But the Indian cricketers had celebrated too soon. A year later, the polo players and the Bombay Gymkhana struck back by sending a new petition to the government. Ingeniously, they now claimed that polo was enjoyed by 'a large number' of spectators and that the *maidan* was the only ground in Bombay that afforded the requisite space for the game.[82] They therefore requested that the polo players be allowed to resume practice on the *maidan* on two days of the week. To the dismay of the Indian cricketers, the Bombay government now accepted the polo players' case. A new government resolution in May 1883 overturned the previous order prohibiting polo on the *maidan*.[83]

The triumph of the European polo players emboldened the Bombay Gymkhana to recommence its 'forward policy'.[84] It steadily began to annex an ever increasing expanse of land on the *maidan*, thereby reducing the space available to the native cricketers. Moreover, noted Sorabjee, 'All the near boundaries and "frontiers" having been thus absorbed, they cast their amorous glances around, and found the Marine Lines open ground, "within reach easy enough of the comforts provided by the Gymkhana Buildings".'[85] The Europeans brazenly encroached on this piece of land, which had been thrown open to the public by the government. On being reminded by the Indian press that the Marine Lines ground could not be used without prior government permission, the polo players reacted with petulance. In September 1884, the Bombay Gymkhana's polo secretary went so far as to accuse the Parsi cricketers of wanting 'to monopolize the whole Esplanade to themselves to the exclusion of Europeans'.[86]

In this increasingly bitter conflict, Shapoorjee Sorabjee and his friends had the firm support of the Indian press. One of their most vocal supporters was K.N. Kabrajee's *Rast Goftar*, which had taken a keen interest in the issue from the very outset.[87] In September 1885, the paper called on the newly formed Bombay Presidency Association to take up the cause of 'hundreds of Native youths' whose cricket had been hindered by the colonial government in order to suit 'the convenience of about ten European polo players'.[88]

But there were dissenting voices too among the Parsis. The most prominent of these was Kabrajee's old antagonist Ardeshir Patel, the secretary of Parsee CC. In April 1882, even as the native cricketers were savouring their short-lived triumph, Patel secretly wrote to his friend Michael Wyer categorically denying the involvement of his club and its players in the campaign waged by the native cricketers against the polo players of the Bombay Gymkhana.[89]

The letter provided ammunition to the Gymkhana and the European press in their campaign to reinstate polo on the *maidan*.[90] A year later, when its contents were made public by the *Times of India*, Patel's action generated opprobrium not only within the Parsi cricketing community, but also his own club. There now followed a flurry of accusations and counter-accusations in the pages of the *Times of India* between Patel and his opponents within Parsee CC.[91]

The 'facts' presented by the two sides were utterly at odds with each other.[92] So were the standpoints from which they viewed the anti-polo movement. Because Parsee CC owed its prestige to the recognition bestowed on it by the Gymkhana, Ardeshir Patel and his friends regarded the native cricketers' petition to the Bombay government as an act of 'ingratitude'. Patel's overriding concern was to avoid at all costs 'senseless agitation' that would widen 'the unfortunate breach between Europeans and natives'.[93] From the outset, therefore, he tried to dissuade the 'patriots' leading the anti-polo movement (this was a barely veiled reference to Shapoorjee Sorabjee) from taking on the Gymkhana directly.[94] In his view, the native cricketers would have been better off passing a resolution and leaving matters to the innate 'sense of justice and fairness of such a body of English gentlemen as the Gymkhana'.[95]

For Shapoorjee Sorabjee and his friends, on the other hand, Patel's offer of support to the Gymkhana was 'undoubtedly culpable' as it undermined the solidarity forged by the Indian cricketers.[96] Sorabjee offered the most compelling reason for their struggle against European polo on the Bombay *maidan*:

> Though the European Gymkhana and Parsees have played, and cordially too, many a game at cricket, that circumstance has never been able to induce even a sympathetic consideration from the former, who, carefully keeping their own cricket ground untouched by the shadow of a polo-pony, continue to cut up the turf and make notches and holes in the cricket ground of the latter by polo-playing. Self-interest has too strong a hold upon them and actuates them to act in the manner they do. Where interests clash the struggle is inevitable all the same in cricket as in human affairs... No Government, and no governing class in the world, ever gave to the governed voluntarily, readily, or cheerfully any rights or privileges which in fairness belonged to them: These are always, as history teaches us, obtained after struggles of more or less persistency.[97]

VI

Shortly after this spat, Bombay's Parsi cricketers momentarily suspended their struggle against the European polo players on the Bombay *maidan*. They did so because there now arose a movement to create a new Parsi Gymkhana that would be representative of the entire community. Its leaders assured the local cricketers that such an institution would be better placed to take up their cause with the Bombay Gymkhana and the provincial government.

The idea for a Parsi Gymkhana was first aired at a meeting held in February 1885 at the Ripon Club, which was attended by prominent patrons of Parsi sport. Backed by the leading lights of the Parsi bourgeoisie—men like Sir Jamsetjee Jejeebhoy, J.N. Tata and his elder son Dorab, Dinshaw Petit, Pherozeshah Mehta, Kharshedji N. Seervai, and S.S. Bengalee—the newly constituted gymkhana succeeded in obtaining a grant of land from the government on the Kennedy Sea Face, which lay to the northwest of the contested Esplanade.[98]

Even as plans for the new Parsi Gymkhana began to take shape, an English businessman named Mr Poole arrived in Bombay in August 1885 to explore the possibility of the Parsee Victoria Theatrical Company undertaking a tour of Britain.[99] He was presumably drawn to this venture by the high reputation that Parsi theatre had established for itself in the late nineteenth century. Parsi theatrical companies such as the Victoria were known for their sumptuous production values and spectacular presentation of Persian, Urdu, and Gujarati dramatic tales and texts.[100] During his stay in Bombay, the English visitor attended a cricket match between the Bombay Gymkhana and the Parsis. This fixture had resumed the previous year after having been suspended between 1879 and 1883, the years when the struggle between the native cricketers and the European polo players was at its most intense. After watching the Parsis battle the Bombay Gymkhana on the cricket field, Poole asked Shapoorjee Sorabjee if he could put together a team to tour England the following year. Sorabjee agreed and drew up a draft proposal that he showed to 'two or three men who were thought fit to be included in the proposed team'. But these players considered the terms 'most inadequate' since they believed that 'there was almost the certainty of making a goodly little fortune for each member of the team, after deducting expenses'. Poole too disappeared 'after one or two communications in regard to the proposed cricket adventure'. However, the elusive Englishman's expression of interest in a Parsi cricket tour of Britain 'stirred up again the hitherto dormant ardour of some of those who were prepared in 1877 to undertake such a venture'.[101]

Among those so 'stirred' was Ardeshir Patel, who perhaps saw this as an opportunity to rehabilitate himself in the eyes of the Parsi cricket community. Along with Bamanji Baria, the former captain and treasurer of the Zoroastrian CC, Patel now set about reviving the project of sending a Parsi cricket team to Britain. As before, he contacted Charles Alcock, the secretary of Surrey CCC, who agreed to make the arrangements in Britain. And as in 1878, a majority of the players who were considered for selection belonged to the Parsee CC.[102] Only those who could afford to pay their way were considered for selection. This resulted in the exclusion of a number of good cricketers who either did not turn out for the Parsee CC or else were unable to raise the money for the trip.

To coach the Parsi cricketers who were selected for the tour, the organizers requisitioned, at considerable cost, the services of Robert Henderson, a twenty-two-year-old English professional who played for Surrey. Henderson arrived in Bombay in March 1886 and spent four weeks putting the team through its paces on the Esplanade.[103] Although he was unable to 'make his older pupils unlearn what they had learnt in their younger days', Henderson gave his Parsi wards 'a wrinkle or two in the bowling line and also showed them the advantages of forward play with the bat'.[104] By the end of his stay in Bombay, the Englishman declared that the players had 'improved considerably all round'.[105] The Parsi cricketers too grew fond of their foreign coach, whom they affectionately called 'Framjee'.[106]

Even as Henderson put them through their paces, the community began to rally behind the Parsi cricketers. On the eve of their departure, Jalbhai Ardeshir Sett, one of the city's notable merchant princes, organized a grand dinner—with a volunteer band in attendance—in honour of the team at his opulent Malabar Hill residence.[107] Among the hundred-odd guests present at the dinner were representatives of the major Parsi cricket clubs in the city.

The Parsi cricketers sailed from Bombay on 23 April 1886 aboard the Peninsular & Oriental (P&O) steamer *Clyde*.[108] They were accompanied by Henderson who was given an 'exceptional mark of Parsee respect' at the time of his departure.[109] 'When he was leaving,' reported a British newspaper, 'they decorated him with wreaths of flowers, with a large bouquet in his hand, and provided by the forethought of his hosts with a painted cocoanut to throw into the sea, to ensure calm in the event of it being rough, he was driven through the streets of Bombay to the docks'.[110]

The first Parsi cricket team landed at Plymouth on 18 May 1886. They were not the only colonial cricketers in Britain that summer. A team of Australians was shortly due to commence a cricket tour of the country.[111] Nor was the Parsi cricket team the sole Indian contingent in town. A few months earlier, an exhibition called 'India in London' had opened at Langham Place in Regent Street.[112] Among the forty-two Indian performers on display in this Oriental 'variety show' were Parsi gymnasts and wrestlers, Hindu musicians and snake charmers, Muslim jugglers, and a troupe representing the Parsee Victoria Theatrical Company of Bombay.[113] The Parsi cricketers' visit also coincided with the highly publicized 'Indian and Colonial Exhibition', which was inaugurated in London by Queen Victoria a few weeks before they disembarked at Plymouth.[114]

Like the other artists and artisans from the subcontinent, the Parsi cricketers too were viewed by many in Britain as Oriental curiosities. The tourists kicked off their cricketing campaign with a match against a team put together by the Earl of Sheffield. One spectator, who braved the incessant downpour that prevented play on the first day, put down his impressions of the Indian tourists:

> The Parsees showed at luncheon, and I am bound to say did not win the enthusiastic admiration of certain Sussex veterans of the game who ran the

rule over them. They are handsome young men of the Eastern type, but with more of the cut of students than athletes. Elegance of form—I might almost say effeminacy—rather than strength is their characteristic. The caps they wear are what we call smoking caps. This kind of thatch does not by any means contribute to appearance—as cricketers. One of those caps, by the way, attracted a good deal of attention. It was richly embroidered, and exhibited as part of that form of ornament, a repetition of the word 'God'.[115]

Another Parsi cricketer at lunch that day reportedly 'drank nothing but champagne in honour of his first match at the charming and hospitable seat of the cricketing Earl'.[116] The contest eventually began the following day, but was left unfinished because 'the visitors were anxious to witness the race for the Derby' at Epsom Downs.[117]

Figure 2. The members of the first Parsi cricket team, photographed at Sheffield Park, venue of the opening match of their 1886 tour of Britain. Courtesy of the Roger Mann Picture Library.

The opening fixture set the tone for the rest of the Parsi cricketers' tour. Many of their matches were affected by rain. When they were able to play, the visitors struggled to make an impression on their opponents. Of the twenty-eight matches they played, the Parsis lost half by an innings. One of these resounding defeats came very early in the tour, against a strong team representing the Marylebone Cricket Club (MCC), which included the great W.G. Grace.[118] The sole Parsi victory came against a village team fielded by Sir Thomas Brassey, a prominent railway entrepreneur, at Catsfield in East Sussex.

Some observers were inclined to excuse the Parsi performance on the field, citing in their defence the visitors' unfamiliarity with the conditions. But others were less generous. 'Since the days when the clown cricketers used to perform, no such farce has been seen as the playing of the Parsee Eleven, who for some mysterious reason have visited this country,' scoffed the *Cheltenham Chronicle*.[119] Enumerating the deficiencies in their play, another newspaper commented: 'They cannot bat nor bowl, neither can they field. Even on their own wickets they would not, so far as we could judge, be a match for many an English village club.'[120] Yet another went a step further and asserted that, 'to call these men cricketers is a misnomer. They are a party of rich gentlemen from Bombay, who have come over here for their own amusement, and if they go on as they are doing now they will afford us some amusement also before their return'.[121]

As the tour progressed, the Parsi cricketers began to feel the strain of the relentless schedule, constant bad weather, and endless defeats. 'It will be a relief to them,' one English correspondent reported in early August, 'when, a month hence, they run through the programme of their present cricketing tour.' In a conversation with this reporter, the Parsi captain Dhunjisha Patel lamented 'the accidents that had happened to his team'. They had been 'sixteen strong' at the outset, he informed the journalist, but a series of injuries had reduced them to 'ten efficients'. He was also 'very sore on the hard work his team had to do [sic]'. 'They came over from India to enjoy themselves, and intended to play cricket only half their time, but their agent in London had compiled a programme with not a single break in it,' Patel confessed to his interlocutor. No doubt the captain's own workload in managing the team had increased because their manager, Ardeshir Patel, had been forced to return to Bombay midway through the tour. However, mindful of the fact that his remarks might be misconstrued as 'unmanly', Dhunjisha declared: 'We no like the Americans. They come over, get beat,

and run away; we get beat, no run away; no, we play out all our matches.'
And 'slapping his breast, he said: "British pluck".'[122]

★ ★ ★

While the Parsi cricketers struggled in Britain, back in Bombay their
compatriots took on and defeated the Bombay Gymkhana twice in quick
succession. The victories were particularly pleasurable for Shapoorjee Sorabjee
who had taken on the task of organizing these annual fixtures in the absence
of Ardeshir Patel. Prior to the first match, F.D. Gaddum, the secretary of the
Gymkhana, had written to Sorabjee suggesting that in the absence of their
best-known players in Britain, 'XVI Parsees should meet the Gymkhana XI'.
After the Parsi eleven defeated the Bombay Gymkhana, a red-faced Gaddum
tendered Sorajbee a written apology. 'I ought to have asked if your XI would
object to meeting the XVI of the Gymkhana,' admitted the Englishman.[123]

The victories over the Bombay Gymkhana were achieved by a young
group of Parsi cricketers who mostly belonged to clubs other than Parsee
CC. Buoyed by their triumph, these Parsi cricketers now sought to undertake a tour of Britain in the summer of 1888. Their captain Pestonji Dinsha
Kanga proclaimed that they were especially keen 'to retrieve the honour of
Indian cricketers, which unhappily was lost by the visit of the first team in
1886'. That side, he argued, could not be considered 'representative of the
Parsee clubs in Bombay'. Indeed, it was 'a patent fact that the team referred
to was an inferior one, and was not composed of the cream of cricketers
then in Bombay'.[124] However, the move to undertake yet another cricketing expedition to Britain once again divided the Parsi community, with
some newspapers questioning the wisdom of this venture.[125]

Undeterred by the criticism that was levelled against them in the local
press, Kanga and his friends sought the help of Charles Alcock, who had
played a critical role in facilitating the first Parsi cricket tour of Britain.
Once again, the secretary of Surrey CCC agreed to arrange the fixture list
for the Parsis and negotiated on their behalf with various amateur cricket
clubs in Britain.

The second Parsi cricket team disembarked at Portsmouth on the last day
of May 1888. They began their tour a week later at Leyton against the
'Gentlemen of Essex'. A reporter for the *Sporting Life* provided an evocative
account of the first day's play:

> The Essex County Ground at Leyton, which is 'all very fine and large', was in
> capital trim yesterday, and looked very pretty when the 'Sun worshippers'

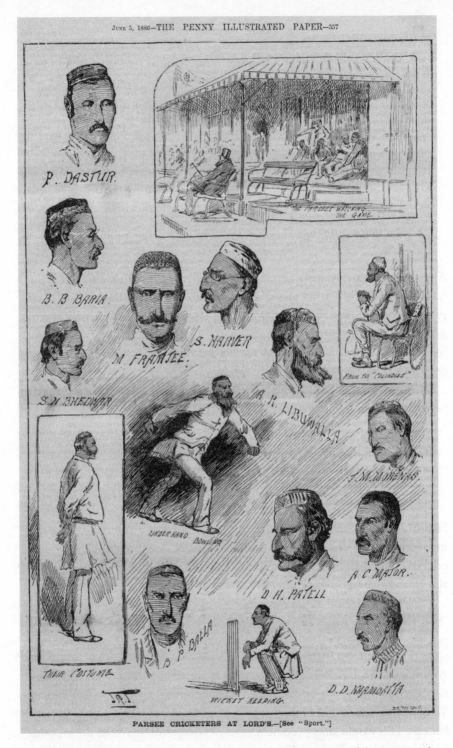

PARSEE CRICKETERS AT LORD'S.—[See "Sport."]

Figure 3. A portrait in *The Penny Illustrated Paper* (5 June 1886) of the Parsi cricketers practising at Lord's during their first tour of Britain. © British Library Board. All Rights Reserved / Bridgeman Images.

made their *debut* against a team of Essex gentlemen. One of the great charms of this rather remote Eastern suburb to a rover's mind is the general somno-lency of the inhabitants, and the singular absence of hurry. No one hurries there. As a striking instance of this, it may be mentioned that Mr. C.E. Green did not hurry (after lunch) to accept a chance, the leathern sphere striking him smartly in the diaphragm. There would be merely a handful of spectators present when the visitors, having won the toss, went to the wickets. The arrival of an old gentleman in a white hat rather stirred the languid curiosity of the spectators, but this was the only feature worthy of note up to luncheon time. During this important interval the rural constable went out, gazed carefully at the wicket, expectorated reflectively on the pitch, and imparted his views to a sad-eyed solitary groundsman, who appeared to be much troubled with the disclosures.[126]

After a tepid start, Kanga's team went on to acquit itself creditably on the field of play. Their batting was of a much higher standard than that of their predecessors, while in Mehalleshah Edulji Pavri they possessed a bowler of great skill. Of the thirty-one matches the team played, it won eight and succeeded in drawing another eleven. In one notable instance, at Hastings, the Parsis won after being asked to follow on.

British observers were quick to laud the team. Some commentators even believed that their performance was

significant as practical evidence of the excellent effects produced by the visit of their predecessors to England two years ago, and cannot fail to be not only satisfactory to the Parsee community but further very encouraging to all those who consider the development of the game among the races of India to be a source of political as well as moral good.[127]

However, others believed that this improvement was an outcome of their interaction with the players of the host nation. 'The example of English cricketers and their own assiduous practice since, have brought about a remark-able change,' remarked the *Northampton Chronicle*.[128]

VII

Although they experienced contrasting fortunes on the cricket field, the two Parsi teams that toured Britain had a number of features in common. To begin with, both tours proved financially costly for their organizers and backers. This would later become a bone of contention between the captains of the two teams. Pestonji Kanga cited the poor performance of the Parsi

Figure 4. The members of the second Parsi cricket team in Britain, *c.* 1888. Courtesy of the Roger Mann Picture Library.

cricketers in 1886 as a key reason why the British public did not turn out in large numbers to watch his own side.

Notwithstanding the racist jibes directed at them in sections of the press, both Parsi cricket teams received a cordial social reception in Britain. At every venue, they were publicly feted by their hosts. The Parsi cricketers also interacted with the upper echelons of British society. We have already noted that the first match of the 1886 tour was played on the home ground of the Earl of Sheffield, a well-known aristocratic patron of the game. It was the first of many such instances during this tour when the Parsi cricketers were recipients of aristocratic benevolence. Thus, Lord Monson, the viscount of Oxenbridge, arranged a visit to the Houses of Parliament for them.[129] The last match of the 1886 tour was played at Cumberland Lodge in Windsor Great Park against Prince Christian Victor's cricket team. The fixture 'was arranged at the express desire of the Queen, and Dr Patell and his comrades had every reason to be pleased with the hospitable welcome accorded to them,' reported the British sporting weekly *Cricket*. 'Carriages were sent to meet them at Windsor and on arrival they were cordially received by His Royal Highness Prince Christian.' During the lunch interval, their host raised a toast to the Parsi cricketers, 'praising the pluck which had induced them to undertake such a trip, in order to acquire a better knowledge of our national game'.[130] In 1888, the Parsi cricketers did not play against a royal team, but Sir Spencer Ponsonby Fane, 'having interested himself in their behalf', arranged a trip to Windsor Castle.[131]

Above all, it is the political significance attached to these tours in the colonial and imperial public sphere that is most noteworthy. Even though both tours were purely private ventures, their organizers and supporters highlighted its public benefits. In particular, they represented the cricketing visits as educational exercises. At the dinner given to the first Parsi cricket team prior to its departure in April 1886, Pherozeshah Mehta, one of the leading lights of the newly formed Indian National Congress, likened their journey to a 'pilgrimage'. Indeed, he declared, just 'as artists go to Italy do homage to the great masters, or as students, in the Middle Ages, went to the great seats of learning in places where science and philosophy had made their home, so now the Parsees were going to England to do homage to the English cricketers'.[132] The point was reiterated by Ardeshir Patel in a public letter to the Bombay newspapers on the eve of the team's journey to Britain. Their principal aim, he stated, was 'to see English cricket so as to profit from it in the future, and at the same time to show the British public that their noble game has admirers even among the natives of India'.[133]

Two years later, in a similar letter to the press, Pestonji Kanga explained that the main objective of the second Parsi overseas tour was to

> improve in cricket, not merely practically, but scientifically, by keenly watching the play of the chief exponents of that noble game, who have from time to time, made names for themselves; and, on the return of the team, to be the means of infusing new life into those devotees of cricket who have not, like ourselves, been fortunate enough to study the game in England.

A second reason for undertaking the trip, he added, was to 'promote an assimilation of taste and habits between the English and the natives of India, by carefully studying the English manners and customs; and, on our return to show our friends the advantages derived by moving in different English circles'.[134]

Yet others saw such ventures as part of a larger political project of shaping British public opinion. The point was made explicitly by Pherozeshah Mehta in his speech on the eve of the first Parsi cricket team's departure:

> Sometime ago, as they all knew, the political associations of India had sent delegates to England. The mission, he thought, had been a great success in bringing closer to the minds of Englishmen the view, the feelings, and if they liked, the prejudices of the people whom they were governing in a distant part of the world. There were many ways in which the object with which the delegates had been sent to England might be secured, and he knew of none more effective than the mission which would enable the Parsee cricketers to mingle with Englishmen on their own play-grounds in the game which was essentially English, for which they had a national liking.[135]

In tying sport to politics, Pherozeshah Mehta spoke from the point of view of the colonized. But in Britain, too, there were many who saw in sport a valuable political tool for strengthening the bond between rulers and ruled. Commenting on these Parsi overseas ventures, *Cricket* remarked:

> The history of cricket fails to furnish an instance more remarkable in its way of enthusiasm and genuine interest in our national game than has been supplied by the presence in England, and twice, too, within the last three years of a team strictly composed of native Indian players...Politically, as well as from the standpoint of cricket alone, the importance of this identification of the native races of our Indian Empire with our own customs cannot be overrated.[136]

However, others in the metropolis regarded such sporting tours as a means of consolidating British cultural hegemony in the colonies. In the interval between the departure from British shores of the second Parsi cricket team and the arrival of a Maori football team, the *Morning Post* observed:

> The test of the power of any race to spread itself in Colonies, is its ability to impress its own character and institutions on the peoples whom it subdues. The Romans possessed this capacity in a marvellous degree. To this day over a great part of Europe the traces of their presence as conquerors still remain in the laws and in the language of the peoples that were once under their sway. This incident of the New Zealand football players—and the Parsee cricketers may be included—shows in its own small way that the English have much of the same colonising aptitude. There is nothing more distinctly characteristic of a nation than its pastimes, and Englishmen not only bring this part of their national training with them wherever they go, but seem to have the gift of establishing the sports of England in strange lands and amid the most untoward surroundings. We are not, of course, sanguine enough to expect that the day will soon come when the sons of the Bengalee ryot will be trained on the village

green to become professional bowlers in Presidency cricket matches, but it may be that little by little the example of the Parsee cricketers will stimulate the young Baboos to devote less attention to crude theories of Radical politics and more to vigorous exercise in the open air.[137]

VIII

As it happened, however, the Bengali *babu* proceeded to marry the 'crude theories of Radical politics' to 'vigorous exercise in the open-air'. The Parsi cricketers, for their part, continued to pursue cricket equally vigorously on the Bombay *maidan*. But the tour of Britain in 1888 was the last undertaken by a Parsi cricket team. Despite repeated efforts, the Parsis were unable to successfully replicate the pioneering ventures of the 1880s. Nonetheless, they had stoked the interest of Englishmen in the possibilities of organizing cricket tours to the Empire's most prized possession. The last decade of the Victorian epoch and the dawn of the Edwardian era saw three amateur cricket teams from Britain travel to colonial India. These Indo-British cricketing encounters in the subcontinent became an important catalyst in spurring the idea of India on the cricket field.

2

Imperial Wanderers

I

A little after noon on the last day of October 1889, the P&O steamship *Bengal* glided out of London's Royal Albert Docks.[1] On board were the members of the first English cricket team to travel to the Indian subcontinent. Led by the Middlesex cricketer George Frederick Vernon, the team was constituted on 'strictly amateur lines'.[2] The players were mostly Oxbridge men, past and present, and none played cricket for a living. On the way to India, the team stopped over at Colombo to play a couple of friendly matches against local European teams, before making its way across the Bay of Bengal to Calcutta. After celebrating Christmas in the capital of British India, the visitors proceeded to take on various European stations in northern and western India before returning home in the spring of 1890.

A second English cricket team visited India in the winter of 1892–3, under the captaincy of Lord Hawke, a cricketing aristocrat who had toured the subcontinent with Vernon two years earlier.[3] There were many similarities between his venture and that of his predecessor. Like Vernon, Hawke picked a team comprising solely of amateurs. His team too had a brief sojourn in Ceylon (Sri Lanka) prior to commencing their tour in the subcontinent. And as they travelled leisurely across India, his side also played mostly against European civilian and military teams. Buoyed by his success in this venture, Lord Hawke sought to organize another tour of India the following year. But he was unable to put together a team and the project was abandoned.

In the second half of the 1890s, colonial India reeled under the combined impact of plague, famine, and earthquakes. These calamities deterred prospective cricketing tourists from visiting the 'Horror-Stricken Empire'. It was not until the winter of 1902–3, by which time the panic induced by these crises had subsided, that an English cricket team once again toured India. The players who undertook this cricketing trip—timed to coincide with King Edward VII's Coronation Durbar at Delhi in January 1903—were members of an amateur cricket club known as the 'Oxford University Authentics'. The club, which typified the idiosyncrasies of Oxbridge life, had been established by a cricket enthusiast named Everard Britten Holmes, who 'being much struck by the number of good cricketers who were never tried in the Parks, jestingly undertook to get together an "Authentic" Oxford team, which should beat the side chosen to give battle to Cambridge'.[4] Unlike the previous visiting English teams, the Authentics commenced their tour in Bombay, the home of Indian cricket, before proceeding on a four-month-long journey that culminated in Kanpur.

The visits to India by English amateur sides form a bridgehead between the Parsi cricket tours of Britain and the creation of the first composite 'Indian' cricket team. Although the English tourists did not play against many 'native' teams during their travels (the Oxford Authentics were a partial exception in this regard), the rare occasions on which they did so served to amplify the popular appeal of cricket in colonial India.[5] In a racially divided society in which there was little scope for Europeans and Indians to interact on an equal footing, engagements on the cricket field held out—even if only theoretically—the prospect of parity and fraternity between colonizers and colonized. Equally, the political charge of such contests enhanced cricket's charisma and emboldened its Indian adherents to assert the principle of equality within an unequal society.

II

On 14 November 1889, even as George Vernon's team was en route to India, there appeared the following comment in a *London* newspaper:

Wherever the Englishman goes he must take the bats and balls with him; in every country where a sufficient number of us can be got together, and where a wicket can be pitched, the game is played. We have sent out touring teams to Australia, the United States, South Africa and Canada, and there is now this Eleven steaming to India. In return, we have received visits from cricketers in all quarters of the globe, and have even seen the dignified Parsee chasing the ball at Lord's and the Oval. In nothing more effectually than in sport has steam annihilated distance... No sooner is the season over in England than some of our men rush off to spend the winter in playing in Australia, in South Africa, or in India. They return in time for the Summer in England, and so they go on from year's end to year's end.[6]

The *Standard* had a point: the late Victorian era was notable for the increasing frequency of international cricket tours from Britain to her colonies. The 1880s had seen as many English tours overseas as the two decades between 1859 and 1879. The decade leading up to Queen Victoria's death saw a doubling in the number of such sporting visits: there were nineteen English overseas cricket tours between 1891 and 1901, as compared to nine in the previous ten years.[7]

The *Standard*'s remarks also attest to the expanding empire of cricket in this period. In the 1860s and 1870s most English cricket tours overseas were either to Australia or North America. But from the late 1880s onwards, English cricket teams began to travel to a number of new destinations within the empire.[8] The year before Vernon took his team to India had seen the first visit by an English cricket side to South Africa. And notwithstanding the political turbulence in the region, English cricket teams regularly visited it throughout the 1890s. The same decade also saw three English cricket tours of the Caribbean.

It is not just the frequency of English cricket tours abroad in the late Victorian and early Edwardian era that is noteworthy. Equally significant was a shift in the imperatives that informed these tours and the social profile of those who organized and took part in them. Notably, the cricket tour as a vehicle for profit yielded to a new vision of its role in promoting the 'imperial game'.

Prior to the last decade of the Victorian era, a vast majority of the English cricket tours overseas had been commercial ventures in which the principal organizers and players were professionals. The template for the cricket tour as a commercial venture had been set from the very outset. Thus, the distinction of being the first cricket team from Britain to travel overseas belongs to the twelve professional cricketers led by George Parr, who set out in 1859 to play a series of matches in Canada and the United States.[9] Inspired by the success of the first venture to North America, Christopher Pond and Felix Spiers—businessmen with 'major catering interests in Melbourne'—arranged for an English cricket team to tour Australia in 1861–2.[10] The enthusiasm with which the Australian public greeted the tourists ensured that 'both the sponsors and the cricketers made much more money than they had expected'.[11]

In the following two decades, barring the occasional amateur overseas tour (primarily to North America), most English cricket teams that went abroad did so primarily to make money. These teams were either fully professional or else had a prominent professional element. Indeed, for the better part of the 1880s, the famous English professional trio of James Lillywhite, Alfred Shaw, and Arthur Shrewsbury were the principal organizers of cricket tours to Australia.[12] Their teams comprised only professionals, as no amateur cricketer would condescend to play under the captaincy of a professional or be part of a side in which the professional element was preponderant.

In the 1890s, however, there occurred a remarkable reversal in the social composition and stated aims of English overseas tours. Such ventures were now organized and led by 'gentlemanly' cricket promoters, out to spread the hallowed gospel of 'amateurism' across the empire.[13] This extraordinary transformation in the nature of English overseas cricket tours in the final decade of the Victorian era reflected the growing amateur dominance of sport within Britain. The games ethic as espoused by gentlemen comprised 'a set of distinctive sporting practices and values, stressing voluntary association, active and ethical participation, and repudiating both professionalism and gambling'.[14] Amateurism was also about a 'contained competitiveness'.[15] The gentlemanly amateur played the game for its own sake and was detached about the outcome. He also played it in a particular style: elegant, and with little sweat. The dominance of the amateur ethos in the late nineteenth century was part of a profound transformation in British elite culture, fashioned in the public schools, in which participation in sport came to be regarded as the supreme expression of 'manliness', 'character', and 'team spirit'.

It was in cricket, a game vested with moral significance and imperial purpose, that the gentlemanly creed of amateurism was most explicitly expressed and enforced. Particularly noteworthy in this context is the role of three key figures within the English cricketing establishment during the late Victorian and Edwardian eras: Lord Harris, Lord Hawke, and Sir Pelham Warner.[16] Typical products of the reformed British public school, all three men were fervent advocates of the amateur ethic in sport and the value of cricket as an 'imperial game'. Crucially, their social connections and business interests straddled metropole and colony and thus predisposed them to act as cricketing proselytizers within the theatre of empire.

George Robert Canning Harris, who first became president of the MCC in 1895 and continued to dominate its affairs until his death in 1932, ardently believed in the value of cricket as the 'imperial game'.[17] Born in Trinidad, where his father had been governor, Lord Harris continued the longstanding family tradition of imperial administration, serving as Under-Secretary of State for India (1885–6) and Governor of Bombay (1890–5). Before he embarked on his career as an imperial administrator, however, Harris had taken a team out to Australia in 1878–9. The team mostly comprised amateurs, though two professionals—George Ulyett and Tom Emmett—were included in the side to make up the required numbers.[18] The tour acquired notoriety on account of crowd disturbances during a match against New South Wales at Sydney. A contentious umpiring decision against one of the local players triggered a crowd invasion of the playing area, during the course of which irate spectators assaulted the English captain.

Chastened by his experience in Australia, Lord Harris never again led an English team on an overseas cricket tour. But as a powerful figure in the MCC, he exerted his influence in expanding the empire of cricket. 'Wherever the flag of old England is raised, wherever two and twenty Englishmen can be got together, there you may be very sure before long the wickets will be pitched,' Harris asserted. He made these remarks in an essay published in 1884, entitled 'Christmas Cricket', which offered a bird's-eye account of the game as it was played in 'far-off lands, where, with un-English surroundings under a tropical sun, with trees and plants that would die in our more rigorous climate, and with races of people who have but little idea of vigorous exercise for the sake of amusement, English muscle and English endurance insist upon some means of displaying themselves'. Surveying the progress of cricket in 'these many lands, so many thousands of miles away from its home', Harris reflected:

> When the English cricketer realizes the mighty work England has set herself to do, of giving to the many millions of races, oppressed for centuries by the horrors of tyranny and misrule, the benefits of many of her own free institutions; of establishing and protecting, until they are strong enough to protect and govern themselves, colonies of Englishmen in every sea, he may well rejoice that the game he loves so well is doing something, it be but little, to unite with the mother country and with each other the peoples of all these lands. It is raising among them a medium of common interest. It is bringing them together, and thus procuring a more intimate knowledge of each other. It is carrying in its wake those blessed results—the eradication of petty jealousies, the discouragement of vicious propensities, and the encouragement of generous, courageous, and amiable feelings, which cricketers believe are more characteristic of their game than of any one among all the sports and pastimes

the world has ever known. Cricket has raised a great bond of friendliness, of charity, and of goodwill among its votaries.[19]

While the fourth Baron Harris pontificated, the seventh Baron Hawke of Towton practised. A descendant of the legendary admiral who had achieved a famous victory over the French at Quiberon Bay during the Seven Years' War, Martin Bladen Hawke became synonymous with the amateur ethic in cricket during the late Victorian and early Edwardian years. After attending Eton and Cambridge, Lord Hawke became captain of Yorkshire CCC in 1883.[20] As the dominant figure in its cricketing affairs, he pursued a policy of benevolent paternalism vis-à-vis the county's professionals, wielding carrot and stick in equal measure. Simultaneously, Hawke became known as the 'Odysseus of cricket', indefatigably organizing and leading a series of cricket tours overseas during the 1890s and 1900s.[21] After participating in G.F. Vernon's tours of Australia (1887–8) and India and Ceylon (1888–9), he took amateur teams to India (1892–3), South Africa (1895–6 and 1899–1900), the West Indies (1896–7), Australia and New Zealand (1902–3), and Argentina (1912–13). 'On the cricket grounds of the Empire,' Hawke once declared, 'is fostered the spirit of never knowing when you are beaten, of playing for your side and not for yourself, of never giving up a game as lost. This is as invaluable in Imperial matters as in cricket.'[22]

The third member of this trio, Pelham ('Plum') Francis Warner, emerged as a prominent figure within the English cricket establishment in the early Edwardian era.[23] Like Lord Harris, Warner was born in Trinidad, where his father had been attorney general. Following his father's death in 1887, Warner moved from Trinidad to Britain, where he attended Rugby School before proceeding to Oxford. Cricket brought Warner into close contact with Lord Hawke, and he became a regular participant in the overseas tours that the latter organized and led during the late 1890s. When the MCC sent out a team for the first time to Australia in the winter of 1903–4, Warner was appointed as its captain. He followed this up by taking teams out to South Africa (1905–6) and Australia (1911–12). A prolific writer, Warner regularly wrote accounts of his overseas cricketing jaunts for the press and in the form of books. In these, he constantly stressed the valuable role played by cricket tours in deepening the 'imperial bond'. Writing in 1900, he noted how the game.

is extending its influence wherever the English Language is spoken, and it is even said by diplomats and politicians that its friendly intercourse does much to strengthen the amity of nations, and to make for international understanding... Cricket, indeed, knits together many interests, and the crown of its influence is the good-fellowship which accompanies it.[24]

But English cricket tours to the colonies were not simply one-sided initiatives undertaken by those who ran the game in the imperial metropolis. On the contrary, the cricketing decision makers at home were responding to the demands of British expatriates in the colonies who clamoured for sporting visits from the Mother Country. Indeed, by the last decade of the nineteenth century, there was enormous interest in such tours. The colonial public eagerly anticipated the appearance of visiting English teams, while the local press devoted reams of newsprint to their doings both on and off the field of play.

More importantly, cricket tours to the white settler colonies in the 1890s became politically significant as an aspect of imperial diplomacy. This development was closely linked to the rise of what John Darwin has called 'Britannic nationalism'. By this, he means that national identity in Canada, Australia, New Zealand, and British South Africa in this period 'was asserted by rejecting subservience to the British government, but by affirming equality with Britain as "British peoples" or "nations"'.[25] Notably, this Britannic nationalism was 'fostered by the growing closeness of educational and sporting connections, the new swiftness of communication, the growth of the press, the convergence between the urban society of the overseas British and their counterparts at home'.[26]

Sporting tours came to play a particularly important role in the political articulation of Britannic nationalism in the white dominions. In Australia, for instance, 'the ideology of imperial union' found practical expression through sport. Anglo-Australian ideals in the sporting realm 'symbolized a belief that Britain and Australia were an integrated, indivisible "Anglo-Saxon" community bound by ties of common cultural activities, not least of which, of course was cricket'.[27]

The role of sporting tours in promoting the ideals of 'Britannic nationalism' was even more apparent in the case of South Africa in this period. Such tours assumed a heightened political significance in a region where an embattled British minority was seeking to assert its social and cultural dominance over the Afrikaner and black population. For instance, the first English cricket tour of South Africa in 1888–9, funded by Donald Currie and led by Major Robert Gardner Warton, not only explicitly promoted the cultural bond between Britain and its settlers in the region, but also 'did much to bring the various political elements together as a single entity in the public mind twenty years before political union'.[28] Importantly, prominent politicians in the Cape Colony regarded Warton's tour as an integral part of imperial diplomacy. At a banquet held in honour of the visitors, 'it was made clear that cricket would be used to help instil the values of British elite culture still further through northern expansion into the African hinterland'.[29]

Sport and politics were especially enmeshed during the two cricket tours of South Africa led by Lord Hawke in the 1890s. Both ventures owed much to the organizational efforts and financial support of James Logan, the Scottish-born 'Laird of Matjiesfontein', who had made a fortune through his catering business in the Cape Colony.[30] The public rhetoric surrounding these tours highlighted the role of cricket in consolidating the imperial union between Britain and South Africa. As one historian notes, 'these early tours were as much (if not more) about imperial propaganda as they were about cricket'.[31]

Unlike South Africa, whose economic fortunes were on the upswing, the West Indies in the 1890s were in the throes of an economic crisis triggered by the declining fortunes of the sugar plantation economy. English cricket tours to the region thus took place at a time of rapid social and political change. Notably, members of 'respectable' white society in the Caribbean used these tours to reaffirm the imperial connection with Britain in a context where their authority had begun to be challenged by the local black and 'coloured' population. Equally, white elites in the islands eagerly solicited such cricket tours in order to tout the region's commercial and strategic significance within the imperial scheme of things and to attract potential investors and tourists from the Mother Country.[32]

But for the players who took part in these tours, their principal attraction lay in the opportunities they offered for sociability and imperial tourism. Warner summed up the relative balance of priorities for the touring cricketer quite nicely:

> To the enthusiastic cricketer there is nothing more enjoyable than a tour abroad with jolly good fellows as companions. Besides, one sees the world—in itself a liberal education. Perhaps, too, these touring teams do something from a political point of view in bringing our cricketing kinsmen across the seas in touch with those of the mother-country.[33]

III

Colonial India emerged as an attractive destination within the expanding empire of cricket around the same time as South Africa and the Caribbean. As with those regions, the visits by English amateur cricket teams to the subcontinent were driven by the urge to escape the bleak winter at home, renew friendships with old school and collegemates serving in the distant outposts of empire, and pursue the opportunities for sport, adventure, and travel in Britain's most prized possession.

But a cricket tour of India also posed a distinctive set of challenges for English visitors. For one, they had to contend with the varied climate of the subcontinent. Reflecting on his experience as a member of the Oxford Authentics, the team's chronicler wrote:

Figure 5. Members of G.F. Vernon's team with their hosts at Calcutta, *c.* 1889: the first cricket tour of colonial India by an English side. Courtesy of the Roger Mann Picture Library.

At Bombay, in November, there was a blinding, baking sun, and exhausting heat; at Bangalore the cold comfort of an English summer's day; at Madras and Trichinopoly the moist, enervating heat of their cold weather, which soaks your tobacco, so that you despair of ever keeping your pipe alight; at Calcutta and Delhi, in December, cold nights and beautiful warm days; at Peshawar and Rawal Pindi 14 degs. of frost at night, and bright, dry days that remind you—with the snow-clad hills in the distance—of the bracing atmosphere of Davos Platz.[34]

Moreover, in India there was no gate money, 'for the reason among others, that most of the Gymkhana grounds are government property, and thrown open to all comers'.[35] The absence of the monetary incentive meant that there was little scope on such tours to include any professionals, who could usually be called upon to shoulder the burden of bowling. At the same time, it was not always easy 'to get together fourteen men of the requisite cricket ability who could afford both the time and money for a tour'.[36] Matters were compounded when a member of the touring party fell ill in the subcontinent—a fairly regular occurrence—and the visitors struggled to make up the requisite numbers. Endurance rather than skill was thus the principal requirement for any overseas cricketer who toured the subcontinent.

Old school and college connections were integral to the organization of these tours. For instance, Lord Hawke's visit to the subcontinent in 1892–3 had much to do with the fact that two of his fellow Etonians—Lord Harris and Lord Wenlock—were governors of Bombay and Madras, respectively, at the time.[37] Likewise, F.H. Stewart, the honorary secretary of the Calcutta Cricket and Football Club (CFC), had played for the Oxford Authentics and it was at his invitation that his old club decided to undertake a tour of the subcontinent in the winter of 1902–3.[38]

Once they arrived in the subcontinent, the English cricketers were treated as privileged guests of the Raj. The Calcutta CFC, the leading Anglo-Indian sporting institution in British India, partially sponsored and supervised the arrangements for all three English cricket tours of the subcontinent.[39] The Indian railway companies offered the tourists generous travel concessions, while the local colonial administration provided them with free accommodation wherever they went. Writing of his experience in 1893, Lord Hawke wrote, 'One of the charms of the tour was that we never saw the inside of an hotel, being put up everywhere, whilst we travelled first-class at the cost of a second-class ticket.'[40] Similarly, Cecil Headlam singled out 'the open-heartedness and kindly disposition of the Anglo-Indians towards their wandering fellow-countrymen' as the most memorable aspect of his 'sojourn in the East'. In particular, he acknowledged a 'special debt of gratitude' to A.L. Rumboll, the cricket secretary of the Bombay Gymkhana and an official in the Great Indian Peninsula (GIP) Railway.[41] This benefactor (and others like him) ensured that the Oxford Authentics received a substantial fare concession, 'which, when you come to journey some seven thousand miles by rail, amounts to a very welcome sum of money saved'.[42]

The hospitality extended by the Raj to the visiting cricketers extended all the way to the top of the official hierarchy. Thus, unlike ordinary British travellers to the subcontinent, the cricketing tourists were often put up in the governor's residence when they visited the major Indian cities. For instance, Lord Wenlock hosted Lord Hawke's team for a week when the latter visited his presidency in November 1892. A few weeks later, Lord Harris, the Governor of Bombay, did likewise when Hawke's men arrived in Bombay. Indeed, Harris spared no effort in lavishing hospitality on his schoolmate and friend.[43] Here is how the *Bombay Gazette* described the official reception he accorded to the visitors:

> The gentlemen comprising Lord Hawke's Cricket Team, fourteen in number, were welcomed on their visit to Bombay at the Victoria Terminus yesterday. His Excellency Lord Harris had sent for them a brake, drawn by four horses with outriders and several other carriages, and had deputed Captain Cox, Captain Poore, and Captain Saiyadoola Khan, *aides-de-camp*, and Dr. Martin, Medical Officer, to receive the members of the team at the station... The gentlemen of the team then drove with Mr. Gould to the cricket ground, and afterwards to Government House, Malabar Point, where they will remain as the guests of H.E. Excellency Lord Harris, who has provided excellent accommodation for them, having rented at a high rent a large bungalow, near Government House, for their special use.[44]

The Governor's extravagant gesture did not go unnoticed in the Indian press. As the nationalist *Mahratta* tartly observed, 'Even the advent of a Viceroy or a three-headed monster could not have created so much interest... Fancy a whole batch of Aide-de-camps and officers of the Government House going to the Railway Station to receive a strolling party of cricketers!'[45]

Nor had things changed much a decade later when the Oxford Authentics travelled across the subcontinent. Thus, Lord Ampthill, the Oxford-educated Governor of Madras, 'showed his interest in his old 'Varsity by putting up several of the team at Government House'.[46] At Hyderabad, their host was Major-General Sir George Pretyman, himself a recent arrival from Kimberley in South Africa.[47] Moreover, even before their arrival in India, the Authentics had deftly 'placed themselves under the aegis of the Viceroy'. The gratified Lord Curzon, an Etonian and Oxonian with cricketing pretensions, accepted 'with much pleasure the honour that was conferred upon him by the O.U.A. [Oxford University Authentics] in electing him an honorary member of the club'. Indeed, 'as an old Oxford man', he also 'expressed his desire to further in any way that he could the interests of the tour in India'.[48] One outcome of Lord Curzon's interest in the team was the inclusion of a fixture between the Authentics and the 'Gentlemen of India' at Delhi during the 1903 Durbar. Arriving in the city for the event, the players were accommodated in the Viceroy's Escort Camp and thereby incorporated into this imperial ritual.[49]

On all three tours, the matches featuring the visiting English teams became the highlights of the social calendar. Stations that were included in the tourists' itinerary eagerly awaited their visit; conversely, venues that were excluded gave free vent to their disappointment. For instance, when Vernon's team made its way to the subcontinent in the winter of 1889–90, the *Madras Weekly Mail* reported that 'much disappointment was felt by Madras folk when it became known that this City had not been included in the tour'.[50] But two years later, when it was announced 'that a visit to Madras would soon be paid by some crack English cricketers, considerable satisfaction was expressed by all lovers of the game in Madras, and the opening match between Lord Hawke's team and the Madras Cricket Club...was eagerly looked forward to'.[51]

The cricket matches between the visitors and the local European teams were 'banner-waving, drum-beating affairs accompanied by military marches and parades'.[52] At some of the smaller venues, the entire resident British population turned up to watch the contests. In keeping with the Raj's obsession with status and hierarchy, the chief guest on these occasions was usually the highest-ranking official in the station where the match was played. In the presidency capitals, this was the governor, who invariably came to the ground accompanied by a large entourage. Occasionally, however, a viceroy on tour could displace the local governor in the order of precedence. Thus, when Lord Hawke's team took on the Madras CC at Chepauk in December 1892, the Governor, Lord Wenlock had to play second fiddle to the Viceroy, Lord Lansdowne, who was on a visit to the city at the time.[53] Not long after, Lansdowne was at the Eden Gardens to witness the match between the tourists and the Bengal Presidency; this time it was the Lieutenant-Governor of Bengal who had to cede his place to his superior.[54]

The cricketing tourists were also made honorary members of the principal European clubs wherever they went, a privilege that was denied even to the most eminent Indians.[55] The visitors thus became a temporary part of the everyday social life of the Raj. At every venue, the local European establishment organized elaborate entertainments—balls, open-air concerts, theatrical performances, and outdoor expeditions—for the cricketers from home.[56] Their participation in such social events no doubt helped the tourists to cope with the tedium of constant travel on a long cricket tour.

In addition to socializing with their own, the English visitors had plenty of opportunities to go shooting, hunting, and fishing during their travels across the subcontinent. Indeed, for many of these 'gentlemanly' amateurs, it was 'sport' in this sense, rather than cricket, which was the principal attraction of an Indian tour. The cricketing tourists who came out with Vernon and Hawke used the time between matches to indulge their passion for pursuing game. For instance, following their match against the Behar Wanderers, a team comprising the European indigo planters of the region, Hawke's men indulged in 'a day's duck and snipe shooting on the "jiels" of Behar'.[57] The Oxford Authentics too came well prepared with their rifles and guns to go hunting in the wilds of India. 'We looked forward to sticking a pig if fortune favoured and to shoot anything from snipe to tigers—and from elephants to Bombay ducks!' wrote Cecil Headlam. However, he lamented, 'cricket and travel occupied most of our time, and did not allow us to go off the beaten track in search of sport'.[58]

Some players stayed back in India after the conclusion of the formal part of the cricket tour in order to go trophy hunting in the mountains and forests of the subcontinent. Thus, after their cricket tour ended in March 1893, Lord Hawke and a few of his teammates 'set off for Nepal in search of tiger'.[59] They bagged thirteen tigers, many of which came to adorn Hawke's home in Yorkshire. Indeed, Hawke had such a good time that he 'saw no reason to return home'. He proceeded to hire a houseboat in Srinagar, which served as 'an ideal base from which to mount hunting forays'.[60] Fortunately for the wildlife of Kashmir, the insatiable hunter contracted fever during his sojourn in Srinagar and was forced to return to England. Likewise, two players—Simpson-Hayward and Williams—who visited India with the Authentics a decade later, 'set out to shoot in far Kashmir' after the conclusion of the cricket tour.[61]

English cricketers visiting the subcontinent also spent their time taking in the sights on the tourist trail. For instance, according to a member of

Hawke's team who published a tour diary, the players divided their time in Ceylon 'between playing cricket and seeing "some new things"'. After quickly wrapping up their matches with the local teams, the tourists immediately set out for the mountain retreat of Newera Eliya. They completed the first part of the journey by train 'through splendid Highland scenery', before being 'carried up to Newera Eliya in chairs, borne by Tamil coolies'.[62] A few weeks later, after their matches in Bangalore, the English cricketers gave themselves 'a holiday, and paid a visit to H.H. the Nizam of Hyderabad'. 'We were entertained royally, and saw all that we possibly could of the wonderful Oriental city in the two short days that we were at Hyderabad,' our diarist recorded.[63] Later in the tour, following their triumph over Calcutta's premier European cricket club, a pleased Hawke allowed his teammates 'a holiday for the purpose of visiting Darjiling'. They were unable to see much on their first day on account of the heavy mist that hung over the hill station and spent their time 'bargaining for various odds and ends in the bazaars, and by playing the station team at hockey'. The next day, however, from their spot on Tiger Hill they 'had the luck to see the snows in all their splendour'. 'Gladly would we have stayed, and have penetrated into these solitary places of the earth,' admitted this writer, 'but *cricket*, not *exploration*, was our mission.'[64] The frequency with which the visiting cricketers gave into the latter impulse during their tour suggests, however, that the order of priorities was not always so clear-cut.

The imperial tourism of the visiting Englishmen was not restricted to the scenic spots of the subcontinent. The cricketers also visited stations that were redolent of imperial heroism and sacrifice. History, as much as nature, was a constant presence in their travels. Thus, passing through the lush Madras countryside with the Oxford Authentics, Cecil Headlam was reminded of 'the beginnings of the British Empire in India'.[65] Likewise, the 'heart-stirring entry of the aged Mutiny veterans' at the Delhi Durbar evoked memories of the traumatic events of 1857. Visiting the carefully preserved ruins of the Residency in Lucknow, Headlam became conscious of 'treading on holy ground, the scene of brave men's successful heroism'. On the other hand, the Memorial Well in the Residency gardens at Cawnpore (Kanpur) was a symbol of 'nameless atrocities, which keeps alive resentment against the butchers'.[66]

★　★　★

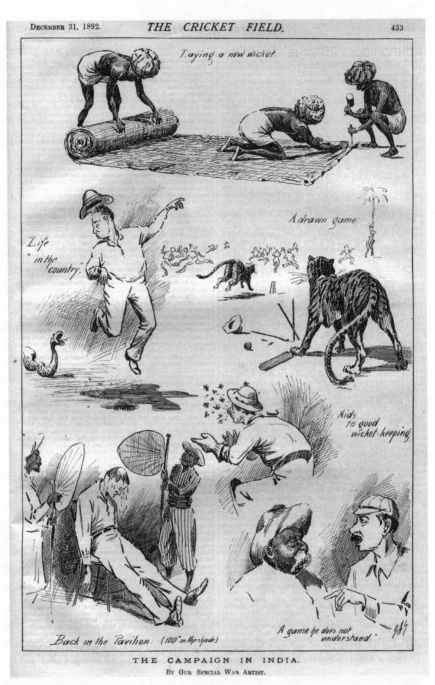

Figure 6. Sketches in a British sporting journal of Lord Hawke's cricket tour of colonial India, 1892–3: note the familiar tropes of Orientalist discourse about India. Courtesy of Marylebone Cricket Club Library.

As they made their way across the subcontinent, English cricketing tourists affirmed the racial prejudices and practices that had become integral to the exercise of colonial power. They not only eschewed any attempt to breach the racial boundaries that sustained the Raj, but also shared with their hosts many of the prevailing cultural assumptions about Indian society. Moreover, not bound by the tacit restrictions that governed the conduct of British officials posted in the country, these visitors dealt more 'freely' with the Indians that they encountered.

Cecil Headlam's narrative of his Indian cricket tour offers a striking illustration of these themes. His book was premised on the fundamental and ineradicable difference between the 'East' and the 'West'. It repeatedly invoked and deployed pejorative stereotypes about Indians that were prevalent among Europeans living in the colony. Moreover, it sought to leave the reader at home in no doubt that the British Empire ought to be regarded as a force for good, holding together an ancient land riven by primordial differences.

Echoing Sir John Strachey, Headlam questioned the very idea of India as a nation.[67] There was, he asserted, 'no such place'. On the contrary,

> There is a huge section of the earth, a vast tongue-shaped peninsula, stretching from the Himalayas to Ceylon, composed of many countries, ranging from the wet, green west and south to the great grey formless land of the Punjab and Central India; countries inhabited by many different peoples of different breeds and creeds and tongues, hating each other; mountain tribes and races of the plains enjoying or disliking many different climates, climates that range from the excessively cold to the excessively hot, from the drought of Pindi to the moisture of Madras; a section of the earth won by the sword and held by the sword, administered under the British Raj.[68]

As for the 'natives', Headlam wrote, 'the impression remains of a very weakly and very patient people living in a poverty-stricken squalor which they seem to enjoy as much as they enjoy anything'.[69] While he was scathing about most of the Indians he encountered on his travels, it was the English-educated ones for whom this Oxford historian reserved the greatest contempt. As a result of misguided colonial education policies, Headlam declared, 'a vain and shifty class of Babus have invaded the offices of Government and of business men; a race of clerks devoid of resources but full of cunning; without moral sense or fibre, but amazingly skilful in keeping and cooking accounts; men who carry to the Nth red-tapeism and petty defalcation'. 'To the sahib nowadays,' he added, 'the ways of these half-emancipated, mis-educated Babus are trying. Placed in authority—and it is part of our system now to give him authority if he can pass his examinations—the native loves to exercise his power in any way which he considers impressive—a way that is usually irritating.'[70]

There was little that was original in these remarks. Headlam was simply regurgitating views about the Indian 'babu' that had become the commonsense of the ruling elite in colonial India at the turn of the twentieth century. Indeed, even as Indian nationalism began to sharpen its critique of the British Raj, the figure of the 'babu'—a part comical, part threatening 'mimic man'—emerged as a constant butt of ridicule, satire, and censure in European circles. Travelling around the country Headlam and his teammates no doubt heard and absorbed the invective directed at these Indian upstarts.

Interestingly, Headlam appears to have enjoyed a greater degree of latitude in his quotidian dealings with Indians than the resident European civil servants who acted as his hosts. By this time, the upper echelons of the Raj had become increasingly wary about the consequences of gratuitous violence against 'natives' (especially the educated classes who were becoming politically conscious).[71] A loss of self-control could sometimes jeopardize the career of an abusive Civilian (a member of the Indian Civil Service). Headlam, on the other hand, aped the European soldiers and planters in the subcontinent, who were notorious for the violence with which they dealt with Indians.[72] He even had a word of advice for the prospective European visitor on the most efficacious way of inflicting corporal punishment on the locals: 'Nearly every native suffers from an enlarged spleen, and any blow on the body is very likely to prove fatal . . . It is best to carry a cane and administer rebuke therewith upon the calves or shins, which are tender and not usually mortal.'[73] Headlam justified his unwarranted aggression by citing the 'offensive' ways of the 'upper class of Babu', who was 'swollen with good living, and a sense of his own importance'.[74]

His encounters with English-educated Indians also confirmed Headlam in his belief that sport was a valuable instrument in the imperial 'civilizing mission'. Cricket, as he saw it, provided 'a moral training, an education in pluck, and nerve, and self-restraint, far more valuable to the character of the ordinary native than the mere learning by heart of a play of Shakespeare or an essay of Macaulay, which is reckoned education in India'.[75] Equally, Headlam argued, cricket was a unifying force that brought together colonizers and colonized. Indeed, he rhapsodized,

First the hunter, the missionary, and the merchant, next the soldier and the politician, and then the cricketer—that is the history of British colonisation. And of these civilizing influences the last may, perhaps, be said to do the least harm. The hunter may exterminate deserving species, the missionary may cause quarrels, the soldier may hector, the politician blunder—but cricket unites, as in India, the rulers and the ruled.[76]

So much for the rhetoric, what of the reality? To what extent did these amateur English cricket tours of colonial India serve to unite the 'rulers and the ruled'?

IV

When the English theatre critic and travel writer Clement Scott arrived in Bombay in December 1892, he 'found that gloriously beautiful city literally cricket mad'. He was 'delighted' to see Indian boys playing the game on every 'square patch' of the commons on the foreshore of the island. For Scott, this suggested that 'one of the fruits of our power in commercial Bombay was an evident love of manly games'. 'It is well,' he reflected,

> that England has induced the rich natives to send their sons to be educated in England, to persuade them to take degrees at Oxford and Cambridge, to go up to the Bar, to walk the hospitals, and so on, and it is as well also that the cricket mania has extended to 'beautiful Bombay'.[77]

Scott's visit coincided with the arrival of Lord Hawke's team, who were due to play a series of cricket matches in the city. Himself a keen cricket follower, the visiting writer was present at the Bombay Gymkhana when Hawke's team took on the Parsis. Seated in the European section of the ground, Scott quickly became conscious of 'a very curious social code existing in Bombay, and doubtless all over India, in connection with the game of cricket'. The Parsi cricketers who had been 'invited to play with Englishmen on the ground of an English athletic club' were nonetheless barred from entering the club 'on any consideration whatever'. 'In fact,' he wrote,

> the cricket field was divided into two sections, one for the Europeans and one for the natives, and no native dared to be seen in the European Section. Joking apart, it was a case of black and white. When the luncheon hour arrived, the English team went into the Gymkhana club-house, and the Parsees went off to their own tents and messed alone.[78]

Nor was this all. During his stay, Scott attended 'a splendid entertainment' in honour of Hawke's team held at the Malabar Hill mansion of the wealthy Readymoney family. All the 'distinguished Europeans resident at, or visitors in Bombay' were invited to this event. But during the course of the evening Scott was taken aback to learn that his hosts 'were not permitted to enter the doors of any club-house in Bombay'. Indeed, even though Sir Cowasji had funded the construction of the Bombay Gymkhana, 'his own daughter and his other children were not allowed to enter the grounds that their father had purchased, because it was an English club and they were Parsees'. When the writer expressed his 'astonishment at this grave inconsistency to Anglo-Indians, they told me that I knew nothing about the subject, that it was far more important than I imagined, and "that a line must be drawn somewhere"'.[79] The issue clearly troubled Scott, for he confessed to his readers back home that the racial divide in colonial India was 'strange to one newly arrived from the London that swarms with Indian students, scholars, barristers, merchants—the London that encourages the Parsee to become educated, to become manly, to become athletic, to become a cricketer, and then sends them home to be snubbed by Bombay society'.[80]

Unlike Scott, the English cricketers who toured the subcontinent did not query the sacrosanct status of the 'colour line' in colonial India. Indeed, as Headlam's narrative of the Oxford Authentics' tour shows, the visiting cricketers actively affirmed the racial hierarchy that underpinned colonial civil society. But for that very reason, the rare occasions when the tourists played against teams composed entirely of native cricketers came to acquire enormous symbolic significance. We can see this most clearly in the tense encounters between the Englishmen and the Parsi cricketers of Bombay in the last decade of the Victorian age.

★ ★ ★

The Parsis of Bombay had made rapid strides in their cricket after their two tours of Britain in the late 1880s. In 1889, they had comprehensively beaten the Bombay Gymkhana and announced themselves as the best cricket team in the country.[81] The occasional reverse apart, the Parsis were to retain that status throughout the 1890s and early 1900s. In recognition of their cricketing pre-eminence, they were awarded fixtures on all three occasions when an English cricket team visited India. On each occasion, the faceoff between the Parsi cricketers and the Englishmen generated immense public interest and came to acquire symbolic meanings that transcended the field of play. In each instance, too, the outcome of the contests generated acrimony and undermined the claim that cricket served to unite colonizer and colonized.

The first of these famous cricketing encounters took place in Bombay over the last two days of January 1890. Vernon's team had arrived in the city after an unbroken run of victories and was widely tipped to maintain its record against the local clubs. The visitors confirmed these predictions by inflicting a humiliating defeat on the Bombay Gymkhana and many expected them to do the same to the Parsis. But their opponents too were fired up, not least because 'every member of the Parsee eleven knew very well that to be successful in exhibiting a good form in such an all-important match was equal to being stamped a first-class cricketer'.[82] The contest was thus eagerly awaited on all sides, and for many it seemed as if normal life in the metropolis had been suspended. As one contemporary noted, 'The match was a struggle for the "Championship of India," and was keenly watched by an anxious crowd numbering over 10,000. So intense was the enthusiasm that merchants, bankers and busy men of all denominations forsook their business to witness the most exciting cricket-match ever played in India.'[83] The Bombay *maidan*, 'the scene of many international contests, presented a most animated and picturesque sight; almost all the varied nationalities of the great city were represented there'.[84]

The match itself turned out to be a tense, closely contested affair. The Parsi cricketers, drawn from all the clubs in the city, put up an outstanding performance. From the outset, the visiting Englishmen 'found that the Parsees could not be trifled with, as both their bowling and fielding testified'.[85] Falling behind on the first innings, the Parsis held their nerve and eventually won the contest by four wickets.

The outcome elicited starkly contrasting responses from the spectators. The Parsi victory electrified their supporters who proceeded to express their joy with gusto. 'Cricket was affected everywhere for some days,' wrote Framjee Patel, 'and the Parsee Team was dined by the leading clubs in Bombay. In short, like Byron, they found themselves famous when they woke the next morning.'[86]

Some Europeans, on the other hand, reacted with barely suppressed fury. Captain Philip Trevor, an army officer who later went on to become a sports journalist, was one of the Englishmen present at the ground and recalled the scene with feeling:

Few of us who saw it will forget that surging, lowing, multi-coloured throng. Its reproduction defied the pen and the brush. But the faces of those who composed it wore, in too many cases, an ugly expression. Of that vast multitude not a thousand knew the name of the thing at which they were looking, not a hundred had even an elementary knowledge of the game of cricket. But they were dimly conscious that in some particular or another the black man had triumphed over the white man, and they ran hither and thither gibbering and chattering and muttering vague words of evil omen. I was in the tent of the Byculla Club when the end came, and the head of one of the largest firms in the city of Bombay said to me, 'I know nothing of cricket and I care less, but I could have collected a lac of rupees on the ground to prevent this, if money could have prevented it.'[87]

This writer was also quick to point to the larger political moral of such sporting encounters: 'We rule in India by conquest, by strength, by prestige, and we cannot afford that these three bonds of empire should be loosened, even through the medium of so trivial an affair as a game of cricket.'[88]

The wider European community in the city no doubt shared that sentiment in private. But in public, the colonial elite had to adhere to the unwritten British code that required losers on the field of play to take their defeat in a 'sportsmanlike' manner. Prominent Europeans in the city were quick to congratulate the Parsi captain and the British newspapers followed suit. 'The Parsees fully deserve their victory, for they played an up-hill game pluckily and well,' declared the *Bombay Gazette*.[89] 'It was hard to see the Parsees beating our Englishmen at their own game,' agreed the *Times of India*, 'but all the more credit to them; they played the game right well, and fairly astonished everyone, including most of those whose money changed hands at the result!'[90] One newspaper even sought to interpret the natives' victory as evidence of successful acculturation. 'If admirers of the game who believe, as we do that, that the English national character and the English national game have a mutually reacting affinity are right, then must the Parsi's excellence as a cricketer be regarded as encouraging proof of his excellence as an English subject,' claimed the *Civil and Military Gazette*.[91]

At the same time, the European press and players could not resist leavening their praise of the Parsi performance with excuses for the English defeat. 'Something, no doubt, is to be put down to the difference between the cold weather temperature of Bombay, and that of the up-country stations where the English team had previously played,' suggested the *Bombay Gazette*. Moreover, it added, the days on which the match had been played 'were exceptionally hot days for the time of the year, and the Parsees, standing on their native heath, had that fact in their favour'.[92]

Likewise, the correspondent for the *Times of India* felt that fortune had favoured the Parsis at critical stages in the match. More controversially, this reporter alleged that R.E. Mody, one of the stars of the Parsi victory, was 'a thrower and not a bowler at all'. He went on to reveal that the legitimacy of Mody's bowling had been questioned by the visiting English cricketers, who were 'best qualified to express an opinion on the subject'.[93] The implications of this accusation were lost on no one, for in the English book 'throwing' or 'chucking' was regarded as a form of cheating.

The slur stung the Parsis into retaliation. In a letter to the *Poona Observer*, a supporter of the Parsi team pointed out that as 'a member of the Bombay Gymkhana, and one of the first eleven', the cricket correspondent of the *Times of India* was scarcely objective in his reportage. This Parsi writer took particular exception to the tendentious remarks about Mody's bowling action. 'The Parsees emphatically won on the square,' he asserted, 'and we hope to see them repeat their success in the return match against the English cricketers, all the carping criticism of amateur journalists to the contrary notwithstanding.'[94] However, there was to be no return match between the Parsi cricketers and Vernon's team. Although the visitors cited logistical difficulties as the reason for cancelling the fixture, the prospect of enduring another defeat against an Indian team no doubt influenced this decision.

Beyond the boundary, too, the Parsis invested their victory over the Englishmen with political significance. 'It is quite on the cards that the imaginative and emotional Parsee youth felt for a day or two that he was the victor of the victors of Waterloo,' wrote Framjee Patel.[95] Nor were older members of the community immune in this giddy hour of triumph. So elated by the Parsi achievement was S.S. Bengalee, the man who had first instituted the prize matches on the Bombay *maidan*, that he proclaimed that it was the community's greatest hour since the Battle of Navahand (which took place in the seventh century between the Zoroastrians and the Arabs).[96] 'We rejoice over their success,' said the *Rast Goftar*, 'not so much from a momentary feeling of quite pardonable pride, as on account of the fact that the virtues which are necessary for success on the cricket field are some of the same virtues which go build up the physical and moral character of a nation.'[97] The paper also alluded to the recent decision of the colonial government to admit 'selected Parsees' into the Poona Volunteer Corps, whose commandant, it hoped, would now 'see in the performance of the Parsees on our Esplanade a vindication of his choice, and an earnest of what may be expected from their co-religionists in Poona as Volunteers'.[98]

At the same time, mindful of the optics of their actions, leading lights of the community sought to assuage the injured pride of their European opponents by couching their celebration in the soothing language of empire loyalism. At a dinner organized in honour of the Parsi cricketers at the prestigious Ripon Club, one speaker averred that Parsis 'were indebted to the English for education, and were beholden to the same people for teaching them self-reliance, independence, and public spirit'. He also viewed the 'instinctive fondness of the Parsees for the national game of Englishmen as proof of their aptitude for cultivating the national spirit of Englishmen—i.e., their courage, their manliness, their perseverance, and their coolness under adverse circumstances'. Another speaker at the event reminded his audience that the Parsi cricketers 'had learnt a great deal in England, and by their practice and perseverance had turned their knowledge to the best account'.[99]

★ ★ ★

Notwithstanding the Parsi avowals of loyalty, the European cricketers of Bombay continued to simmer with resentment towards their rivals. A few months after Vernon's team had returned home, the Bombay Gymkhana informed J.M. Framjee Patel, the Parsi captain, that they no longer wished to play their annual fixture against his side. 'You are aware,' wrote the honorary secretary of the Bombay Gymkhana's cricket committee,

> that there has been a great deal of feeling displayed in our matches with you during the past year or two. This has made the match an unpleasant one for players on the Gymkhana side, and the existing tension has been brought to a head by a combination of circumstances culminating in the display of feeling during the Bombay Poona match.[100]

The incident that the secretary of the Gymkhana referred to had involved some Parsi schoolboys who had cheered their own team vociferously. In his response, Framjee Patel acknowledged that 'every well-behaved Parsee cricketer deplores the incident alluded to in your letter'. But, he pointed out, 'You are no doubt aware all over the world much partisan spirit is manifested by the spectators at big matches, when especially played between different nationalities; and I have never heard that on the score of this alone cricket matches were ever given up.'[101] Patel identified an entirely different reason for the Bombay Gymkhana's decision. He had been informed by a member of the Gymkhana that 'the matches would not come off, unless we consented to appoint European umpires'. However, the Parsis 'could not agree to so objectionable a proposal, not warranted by precedent or practice' and would 'be tantamount to a reflection upon ourselves'. Patel ended by appealing to the very values that the colonizers ascribed to the imperial game. The 'abrupt termination of a great annual sporting event', he wrote, 'which has for many years been the means of bringing us more closely together, and also the source of giving pleasure to thousands, cannot but be looked upon by true lovers of sport in this Presidency with feelings of much regret and disappointment'.[102]

The Bombay Gymkhana's decision to cancel the fixture against the Parsis was made just days before it was due to take place. Even its supporters in the Anglo-Indian press were rendered uneasy by this unilateral step. 'We can fully appreciate the annoyance that has been suffered by the members of the Gymkhana eleven,' observed the *Times of India*, 'but we are sorry in common with most of our readers that it has been thought necessary, at this eleventh hour, as it were, to put off the match.' Uncharacteristically, the paper also sided with Framjee Patel over the question of appointing European umpires in the matches between the Gymkhana and the Parsis. The repercussions of such a move, it argued, would be 'felt far outside the small arena of the cricket field'.[103] The Bombay Gymkhana did not budge from its stance and there were no cricket matches that year between the city's Europeans and Parsis.

Rebuffed by the Gymkhana, the Parsis set out to make 'a bold bid for the championship of India'.[104] They travelled across north India, playing a series of cricket matches against teams put up by native princely states and European civil stations.[105] Their triumphant cricketing peregrinations forced the European establishment in Bombay to rethink their cricketing boycott of the Parsis. In 1892, shortly before the cricket season commenced, Lord Harris informed Framjee Patel that 'he and some of the leading English cricketers thought the time had come when the Parsees should be asked to play a combined team of Englishmen selected from the Bombay Presidency'.[106] This was an astute move by the Governor of Bombay. It had become increasingly apparent to the Europeans that individual clubs such as the Bombay Gymkhana had little chance of winning against the Parsi team. Hence, they would have to combine forces if they were to defeat their opponents. Lord Harris' initiative paved the way for the annual Presidency-Parsi cricket matches, which laid the foundations for what later became the famous Bombay Pentangular tournament.

According to Framjee Patel, these matches 'served a good purpose in promoting, in some measure, social intercourse between the rulers and the ruled'.[107] But a closer scrutiny of the historical record suggests that, more often than not, these contests stoked tensions between the European cricketers and the Parsi players. Indeed, not long after they had been initiated there occurred one of the most fractious episodes in the cricketing relationship between the two sides. The trigger for this confrontation was the visit of Lord Hawke's cricket team to Bombay in the Christmas week of 1892.

Hawke's men were scheduled to play three matches in the city, one against the Europeans of the Bombay Presidency and two against the Parsi cricketers. But without a doubt, it was the latter contests that were the principal focus of public interest. In the days prior to the first match between the Parsis and the visitors, the air was thick with anticipation. 'From the reports we have had of the bowling capacity of Lord Hawke's team,' declared one European, 'I can say, without the fear of contradiction, that the Parsee's sun on the cricket field is about to set.' This observer was convinced that the Parsis would be undone by their 'over-confidence in their own skill which, to say the least, is not of a high order as far as batting is concerned'.[108] Others dismissed such fears as groundless. One Parsi journalist reassured his compatriots that they 'need not be anxious about the coming match with their new rivals, in spite of what the Anglo-Indian journals have been saying to the contrary'. 'If the seven or eight Parsee bowlers come off,' he assured his readers, 'the Parsees will give them a licking.'[109]

Old wounds were also reopened in the run-up to the match. A fortnight before the encounter between the Parsis and Hawke's men, the veterinary surgeon Manekji Kasvaji Patel gave a public lecture on the history of Parsi cricket at the Framji Cowasji Institute. Reflecting on the strides made by the Parsi cricketers, Patel reminded his listeners of the fraught conditions in which they had to practise.

> Let anyone imagine an extensive three-cornered rough field, with patches of short coarse grass, and he will get some idea of the ground on which Parsee cricketers have to train themselves in the science of batting. They do not find a single good plot of ground for a wicket anywhere on the wide field, as the English polo-players of the Bombay Gymkhana insist upon playing their favourite game upon the cricket-field, and spoiling it in spite of repeated remonstrances to the contrary of all the native cricketers of Bombay. The ground

is so rough and bumpy that the ball kicks and twists in a marvelous manner, and often gets up so high that the players have much ado to save their eyes and noses from severe injury...Englishmen are famous in the world for their love of freedom, are ever ready for asserting and maintaining their rights, to do battle either with the tongue, the pen or the sword as the case may require; even women in England have discovered that they have what are called rights, and yet the Gymkhana polo-players have been depriving native cricketers twice a week of their right of utilizing the Esplanade ground for cricket.[110]

The politically charged build-up ensured that a large crowd of around 15,000, was present at the ground when the two sides finally faced each other.[111] The Parsi cricketers silenced their detractors with a robust performance, easily outclassing the visitors. 'I have seldom seen,' admitted Clement Scott, 'a better eleven than that of the young and active Parsees who beat Lord Hawke's team in the first match at Bombay. They batted well, they bowled well, and in the field they were active as cats.'[112]

Predictably, the Parsi team's victory was greeted with jubilation by their supporters. 'Pluck, energy, prudence, and abiding confidence in their own strength, coupled with that healthy spirit of rivalry, which animates the breast of fair-minded competitors—it was these which achieved the victory and bound the brows of the victorious with bays and laurels,' exulted the *Kaiser-i-Hind*.[113] 'The Parsee cricketers' success we consider a national success,' opined the *Indu Prakash*.[114]

The outcome stunned both the visiting English cricketers and the city's resident Europeans. 'At a dinner given to my team at the Yacht Club, Lord Harris, the Governor, as Chairman, told us he had prepared a speech for the winning team, to which I replied that I, too, had prepared one without a thought that we could lose,' Lord Hawke later wrote.[115] Back in Britain, news of the Parsi victory was greeted with incredulity. 'What would the ancient heroes of our cricket fields—those veterans of the past, Pilch and Mynn, Lillywhite and Felix—have thought, if it had been predicated in their time that a picked and crack British eleven would be defeated by a team of fire-worshippers?' wondered the *Daily Telegraph*. 'How scornfully they must have rejected the prophecy! Yet the thing has happened, and Lord Hawke's travelling company of first-class English batters, bowlers and fielders has been handsomely defeated at Bombay by the Parsee local club.'[116] Another British newspaper saw the Parsi victory in more portentous terms. The Parsis, remarked the *Liverpool Mercury*, 'are quite harmless in their most militant moods; but if they begin to beat Englishmen at cricket it will not be long before they will be successful in their demand for some voice in the government'.[117]

The Parsi team's victory raised the political stakes in their second match against the visiting Englishmen. 'The return match between the Parsees and Lord Hawke's team was talked about everywhere,' recalled Framjee Patel. 'It is no exaggeration to say that public interest was excited to the very highest pitch as to the probable result.'[118] As before, the match brought the city to a standstill. 'Never has a cricket match in India been watched with more interest or by a larger and more enthusiastic crowd than was present on the Gymkhana cricket ground when play began,' wrote the *Times of India* correspondent.[119]

This time around it was the Englishmen who prevailed, winning a thrilling contest by the slim margin of seven runs. The outcome once again produced very different responses from the supporters of the two sides. 'The result of the "clash of arms" was hailed with intense delight by the European section, who cheered the triumphant party to the echo,' reported the *Bombay Gazette*.[120] None was more delighted than the Governor of Bombay. 'I'm awfully glad about it: for they were very down poor boys,' exulted Lord Harris to his old school friend Baron Wenlock, the Governor of Madras.[121] On the other hand, the Parsi spectators could not hide their surprise and disappointment at this reversal in their team's fortunes. 'When the end came they were quite unprepared for the blow, and quietly left the field,' wrote Framjee Patel.[122]

Their opponents seized on the crowd's reaction as proof that the Parsis had not imbibed the necessary qualities of 'sportsmanship'. 'The Parsee ladies cried like babies, and the crowd did not take the result in good spirit,' Lord Hawke later alleged. 'I confess I felt that, and the Press was very severe in their notice of the lack of sportsmanship.'[123] 'The capacity to acknowledge and receive defeat, however unexpected, with a good grace and the generosity to allow merit in the victors even in the moment of disappointment is part of the *code d'honneur* of European players at all games,' commented the *Asian*. 'We feel that the Parsees have done themselves scant justice and it argues some degeneracy from the glorious traditions appertaining to the race from which they spring.'[124]

★   ★   ★

The dust had scarcely settled on this *contretemps* when there erupted an even bigger controversy about Parsi 'sportsmanship'. Its origins lay in an informal agreement between the Parsis and the Bombay Presidency to play a match against each other after the conclusion of their fixtures with the visiting Englishmen. Buoyed by the victory of Hawke's men over the Parsis, and encouraged by their own strong showing against the visitors at Poona, the local European cricketers eagerly looked forward to settling scores with their opponents. Accordingly, they assembled a strong team, including some fresh arrivals known for their cricketing ability. Their supporters also questioned the Parsi claim to cricketing supremacy by asserting that the Bombay Presidency team was 'much better prepared to meet the Parsees than Lord Hawke's men, who may be experienced cricketers for aught we know, but certainly inexperienced in India so far as cricket is concerned'.[125]

The Parsis, for their part, were plagued by injuries following the two strenuous games against Hawke's side and had begun to have second thoughts about putting a team in the field against the Presidency. But the Europeans would have none of it. 'If the Parsees really wish to say that they are fairly deserving of the laurels they have won,' declared one letter writer in the *Bombay Gazette*, 'they ought to take up the challenge, and not show a disinclination to play as they do.'[126]

On the eve of the match, however, the Parsis informed the Presidency cricketers that 'four of their number were ill or absent and that they could not play'.[127] The match was therefore abandoned. There now followed an angry war of words. 'Failure to produce an eleven to meet an engagement is an offence against the rules of cricket etiquette so serious as to be practically unknown in England,' raged Captain Newnham (known locally as the 'Demon'), the skipper of the Presidency team, in a letter to the *Bombay Gazette*. 'In failing to keep their engagement,' he expostulated, 'the Parsee cricket authorities have committed a most serious offence against all the best traditions of the game, and one which will make it extremely difficult, if not impossible, for English cricketers to meet them again.'[128]

Newnham's threat provoked outrage among the Parsi cricketers and their supporters. One of them pointed out that 'the Presidency match was forced upon the Parsees, and forced in a downright methodical way'.[129] Another Parsi letter writer went further and revealed what had transpired behind the scenes. 'I know as a fact,' asserted 'Vox Populi',

> that some of the Anglo-Indians who air themselves as the exponents of English cricket here had the gentlemanly instinct of sending a message to Mr. Pavri or to Mr. Patel . . . that if the Parsees failed to play a match with them on the 2nd instant and the following days they would not meet the Parsees any more on

the cricket field. I think Lord Hawke can bear testimony on this point. What does Captain Newnham think of this sportsmanlike message? If not for anything, for this message the Parsees ought to have refused to play a match.[130]

Yet another Parsi writer also used the occasion to remind the captain of the Presidency team of the occasion two years earlier when the Bombay Gymkhana reneged on its commitment to play the Parsis. He went on to add:

> It is quite certain that the Parsees enjoy a decided superiority over Englishmen in India. But very few people out of Bombay know one thing, and I hope they will sympathise with the Parsees when they come to know about it. Does the cricketing world know that no Parsee umpire is allowed? Why not, I ask emphatically? Are they not good judges? Have they not given satisfaction formerly? Have they not acted as such? What would the cricketing world think if they were told that the Bombay Gymkhana have made it a rule to have their own umpires for any matches played on their own ground. I say it is a shame to say so. Fancy in Lord Hawke's match against the Parsees men who acted as umpires were those who were deadly against the Parsee cricketers being defeated by them year after year.[131]

In the face of this Parsi protest, the Europeans in Bombay closed ranks.[132] The lead was taken by Lord Harris, who issued a public rebuke to the Parsi cricketers for not adhering to the 'etiquette of play'. 'I think that the eleven ought to have put themselves in the field, however weak the team may have been,' he thundered.[133] For other British commentators, the actions of the Parsis furnished further proof that in cricket, as in everything else, the 'Orient' was radically different. Indeed, it was this supposedly fundamental cultural difference that prompted one Anglo-Indian newspaper to question the decision of their compatriots to cease playing cricket with the Parsis. 'The position taken up by the Parsees would, no doubt, be indefensible in England,' observed the *Madras Times*,

> but when we consider the different conditions under which the game is played in this country, we cannot think it is either wise or proper to enforce this unwritten law against them. That they are wrong, and very distinctly wrong, in failing in their agreement is a matter about which there can be no two opinions; for, as Captain Newnham pointed out, it is part of the duty of a cricketer to keep his promise, and there can be little said in defence of the manner in which the Parsees 'sold' their opponents at the last moment, after the latter had been put to both expense and trouble to arrange the match. But it must be remembered that the Parsees are not only not Englishmen, but they are Orientals and therefore unable to appreciate to the full the etiquette which is a natural law to English cricketers.[134]

V

A troubling aspect of Hawke's tour for some Anglo-Indian observers had been the way it had stoked 'native passions' by blurring the boundary between sport and politics. One European newspaper expressed its concerns in a lengthy editorial. 'It is more than possible that cricket may be destined to play no inconsiderable part in the future history of India,' admitted the *Bombay Gazette*.[135] 'Its rapid development among a large section of the native community, the high pitch of excellence that one race has already attained, and the budding enthusiasm which is noticeable in other quarters, are without doubt important factors to be considered in working out the problem.' 'But,' it cautioned,

> even cricket has its dangers. It is most valuable as a means to an end, but as an end in itself it is purely valueless. To be a good 'animal' may be a requisite of success, but it is nothing more; and if there is reason in the complaints of such as are in authority over the Parsee youths of today, the mark has already been overstepped, and what should be merely a pastime is coming to be regarded as the business of life. Such ideas may, perhaps, have derived encouragement from the extraordinary interest which was aroused by the last match Lord Hawke's eleven played in Bombay. But, without question, they are fatal to the truest interests of the game, and the sooner they can be checked, the better chance will native cricket have of maintaining its prestige.[136]

For some Indians, however, cricket had become the 'business of life'. 'All thoughtful persons and all who hate national prejudices and jealousies,' wrote Manekji Patel, 'unhesitatingly declare that there is no natural inequality between natives of India and Anglo-Indians. The Parsis have proved that Indians possess physical and moral qualities which, under given circumstances, stand favourable comparison with those which Europeans themselves possess.'[137]

The tensions generated by the visits of the English amateur teams showed that the cricket field, like other arenas of social life under the Raj, served to affirm rather than abolish the 'colour line'. Far from deepening the cultural bond between rulers and ruled, the imperial game in India became yet another site of racial estrangement in the 1890s. But matters were shortly to take a surprising turn.

3

Elusive Quest

I

In the decade that elapsed between the visits to the subcontinent of Lord
Hawke's men and the Oxford University Authentics, cricket struck
deeper roots in Indian soil. 'Cricket, to use a slang phrase, has "caught on"
for some years now in India, and whether in Calcutta, Madras or Bombay,
or on *maidans* multitudinous in the mofussil, the game is a source of delight
and recreation to thousands,' reported the *Asian* in 1896.[1] A view corroborated by Cecil Headlam, who was struck by the fact that 'all over India from
Peshawar to Tuticorin, from Bombay to Calcutta, cricket at one season or
another is played ... not by Europeans only, but by natives.'[2] Indeed, declared
one Indian writer, 'cricket is fast becoming the national game of Indians,
just as the English tongue is fast growing into the *lingua franca* of all educated people'.[3]

The 1890s marked a watershed in the evolution of Indian cricket.[4]
Historians have explained this as an outcome of the visits of the English
amateur cricket teams and Lord Harris' patronage of the sport in the Bombay
Presidency. Arguably, however, it was the emergence of an incipient popular
cricketing culture in many towns that was responsible for the indigenization
of cricket across the subcontinent. The pattern was often similar to the one
we have already seen at work in Bombay. Young boys, exposed to cricket in
their educational institution or imitating the resident Europeans, would get
together and form a club. The implements were often rudimentary, for
proper cricket equipment was expensive, and improvisation was the norm.
And because they rarely had access to a playground of their own, the budding cricketers tended to invade the urban commons. 'One can see brown
little brats, dressed in six inches of cloth, and a smile, playing cricket with a
slat off a packing-case and a bit of rag rolled into a ball, on almost any vacant

plot of land in towns where Europeans indulge in the national pastime,' an English newspaper informed its readers.[5]

The members of the early cricket clubs were usually drawn from the same caste, community, or neighbourhood. But where the teams were based on the friendships formed at school or college, youths from different communities and castes might sometimes play together in the same side. Most cricket clubs had an ephemeral existence. However, the material support of a rich Indian benefactor or a benevolent Englishman and the exertions of a dedicated organizer enabled some clubs to flourish. The proliferation of clubs gradually led to regular competitive matches. A few clubs even took to organizing tours in which they took on teams from other towns and cities. The successful clubs were usually the ones that were able to recruit the best talent. In turn, the fierce rivalry that emerged between the most powerful clubs nourished the sport's growing folklore.

Bombay remained the centre of this evolving cricketing universe. By the end of the 1890s, the city's Parsi cricketers had established themselves as the undisputed 'champions of India'. With a large pool of talent that was drawn not only from Bombay and its environs but also cities and towns in Gujarat and Sind (most notably, Karachi), they were a formidable force on the cricket field. Notably, they regularly triumphed over the Bombay Presidency team in the 'international matches' played between the two sides. Indeed, many in the community would later come to regard the late Victorian and early Edwardian era as the 'golden age' of Parsi cricket.[6]

Meanwhile, other Indian communities in Bombay had also begun to invest their energies and resources in this foreign sport. The first 'Hindu' cricket club in the city—the Bombay Union CC—had been established as early as 1866.[7] According to one source, this club comprised 'elegant youths of the Prabhu caste' whose enthusiasm for the game waned after a few years.[8] By the 1890s, however, there were numerous castes and communities bunched together under the elastic category of 'Hindu cricket'. Towards the end of that decade, these clubs had started to compete spiritedly against their Parsi and European opponents. As with the Parsis, the establishment in May 1894 of a new gymkhana on the Kennedy Sea Face gave a fillip to 'Hindu' cricket. Characteristically, the move to establish a Hindu Gymkhana was triggered by the colonial administration's recognition of 'Muslim' cricket. In September 1892, Lord Harris had approved a petition by prominent Muslims in the city to provide land for an 'Islam Gymkhana' adjacent to the Parsi Gymkhana on the Kennedy Sea Face.[9] The three sectarian gymkhanas began to play each other on a regular basis, thereby consolidating a 'communal' cricketing culture in the city.

Yet even as cricket began to acquire a popular base in India, an elite network simultaneously coalesced around the sport and sought to direct its future. This network comprised Indian businessmen, princes, and publicists, as well as British officials, soldiers, journalists, and professional coaches.[10] Increasingly, these Indian and imperial elites began to exert their influence over the game in the subcontinent. Here again, Bombay played a pivotal role. For it was in the famed 'city of gold' that the alliance between money and power first began to have a decisive impact on the organization of cricket. It was this coalition of interests that conceived and pursued the project of sending a composite Indian cricket team to the imperial metropolis.

However, constructing India on the sporting field was easier said than done. Twice in the late 1890s and early 1900s, the proposal was put forward and pursued, only for the venture to come unstuck along the way. Nonetheless, these aborted attempts cast fascinating light on a formative phase in the history of Indian cricket. Each episode in this story shows how cricket was subsumed by elite agendas in colonial India. Equally, these failures also suggest that the idea of India on the cricket field was not preordained. On the contrary, it was the contingent outcome of the interplay between the game's emerging patrons and its evolving politics.

II

In October 1898, the following brief news item appeared in the British press:

The suggestion has been made in the Anglo-Indian papers that an Indian team should visit England next summer. Indians have taken very kindly to the game, and many of them display great proficiency in it but all lack style. This is chiefly attributable to want of instruction. Indians never have the chance of seeing the finest exposition of cricket and thus it is that however good they may be, they all fail to reach a really first-class standard. In 1886 an eleven of Parsees visited England, and again in 1888. These elevens only played second-class matches, and made no notable scores. But the improvement they gained during the tour was immense. The Parsee community furnishes the finest players in India, but Mahomedan, Sikh, and Hindu also have skilful champions with bat and ball. If the suggestion now put forward were to bear fruit it would, it is believed, receive support here in England. On the cricket ground many kindly sentiments are bred and new bonds of union forged and any reasonable proposal that helps to bring us nearer to the peoples of our great dependency is to be encouraged.[11]

This is the first time that the idea of sending an 'Indian' cricket team to Britain appears to have been aired in public. It is surprising that such an initiative was even contemplated at this moment, for the subcontinent was reeling under the impact of a devastating epidemic of bubonic plague. To account for this curious development, we need to turn our attention to the presence in the subcontinent in 1898, after a decade spent in England, of the most famous Indian of the day. This was, of course, Kumar Shri Ranjitsinhji, the Cambridge-educated cricketing aristocrat from Kathiawar, whose sensational batting exploits had made him a celebrity within the British Empire.

Given the central place that 'Ranji' came to occupy in the late Victorian and Edwardian imperial public sphere and how important he became to the project of constructing an Indian cricket team, it is necessary to consider his extraordinary career up to this point. Indeed, Ranji's career in England and India cannot be viewed in isolation from each other.[12] His return to India in 1898 is particularly significant in this regard, as it was the first serious attempt by Ranji to use his celebrity status in England to pursue his political agenda at home. And as we shall see, on more than one occasion, this princely aristocrat was to play a decisive role in undermining the project to fashion a composite Indian team.

★ ★ ★

Born on 10 September 1872, 'Ranji' belonged to a subsidiary lineage of the ruling Rajput family of Nawanagar, a princely state in the Kathiawar peninsula. Vibhaji, the ruler of Nawanagar, who had disinherited his only son and hence lacked an heir, had adopted Ranji when he was very young. But it was a short-lived arrangement. Not long after his adoption Ranji was swiftly cast aside when one of Vibhaji's Muslim wives gave birth to a son.[13] Despite the loss of his status as crown prince, Ranji was allowed to continue his education at the Rajkumar College in Rajkot. This was one of the select institutions established by the colonial authorities in the late nineteenth century in order to educate the offspring of the Indian princes. Here, under the watchful eye of Chester Macnaghten, the Cambridge-educated headmaster of Rajkumar College, Ranji acquitted himself creditably as a student and a sportsman. It was here, too, that he first learnt the basics of cricket from a

Parsi named Cowasjee Desai, a fact that was subtly elided in later accounts of his career.[14]

In March 1888, the sixteen-year-old Ranji, chaperoned by Macnaghten, was sent to Britain to pursue his higher education at the University of Cambridge.[15] It was at this ancient institution that the young Indian aristocrat first made his mark on the English cricketing scene. In the summer of 1892, his beguiling batting skills began to attract attention within the university. But despite scoring heavily in local club matches, he was unable to break into his own Trinity College team. This was because the team's captain, Francis Stanley Jackson, was not persuaded that the Indian was good enough to merit such a coveted mark of recognition. However, that winter Jackson toured India with Lord Hawke's team and the experience appears to have changed his views regarding the cricketing ability of Indians. In the summer of 1893, Ranji got his long-awaited chance to play for Trinity and performed well enough to become the first Indian to be awarded the prestigious Cambridge 'Blue'. His cricketing success prompted Ranji to postpone his return to India on the completion of his studies at Cambridge. By this time, he had developed a close friendship with Charles Fry and William Murdoch, both amateur members of the Sussex county cricket team. The duo worked behind the scenes to ensure that Ranji was inducted into their side. His move to Brighton in the summer of 1895 marked the beginning of a remarkable three-year run that saw the Indian become one of the most pro-lific batsmen in the history of English cricket.[16]

In turn, Ranji's success as a cricketer and the air of mystery that surrounded him captivated the British public. He became a major draw and large crowds flocked to watch him play for Sussex in the English county championship. 'At the present time,' noted the *Strand* magazine in July 1896, 'it would be difficult to discover a more popular player throughout the length and breadth of the Empire. The roar of welcome that goes up from the throats of the assembled thousands as "K.S." steps upon the field is equal to the outburst of enthusiasm that greets the champion immortal "W.G."'[17] Advertisers used his image and endorsement to market all kinds of products, from cigarettes to cricket bats.[18] The press, too, could not get enough of him. Newspapers constantly sought interviews with the 'Prince' and kept up a steady stream of reportage on his activities, while popular journals regularly published poems and cartoons featuring him.

It was not simply Ranji's sheer skill that accounted for the massive public adulation that was showered on him in Britain. At the heart of the Indian cricketer's popularity, as Satadru Sen perceptively noted, was a 'Romantic pleasure in possessing and displaying exotic artifacts'.[19] In other words, many British observers regarded the enchanting Indian's batting exploits as yet another marvellous possession thrown up by their vast and varied empire. Ranji's presence as a cricketing star in the very heart of the empire also allowed liberal Englishmen to trumpet their 'cosmopolitan generosity' as imperial hosts and to celebrate visions of an inclusive and meritocratic empire.[20] More conservative-minded observers, on the other hand, saw him as a symbol of imperial unity. One contemporary remarked:

> In spite of recurring and present hints that our dominion in India is always threatened in one or other outlying quarter, and that our best efforts cannot reconcile the Oriental masses to all our western ways it is of hopeful augury for the eventual if slow development of a consolidated and contented India that so manly and sympathetic a spirit should be found among its native aristocracy.[21]

Although he swiftly became an imperial celebrity, Ranji's presence in English cricket raised vexing questions about his national identity.[22] His supporters sought to portray the Indian Prince as an English cricketer, whose skills had been honed after his arrival at Cambridge. They also saw Ranji as manifesting the prized qualities of self-discipline and physical courage, both seen as essential traits of the English 'gentleman'. But others were less inclined to regard Ranji as an Englishman and, therefore, questioned his eligibility to play for England. One of those who took this view was Lord Harris, who used his influence over the MCC's selection committee to deny the Indian cricketer the chance to make his international debut for England against Australia at Lord's in 1896. However, the MCC's decision to overlook Ranji led to a popular outcry. Responding to the dominant public mood, the selectors of Lancashire CCC included him in the English team for the next test match at Old Trafford. Ranji justified his selection with an outstanding batting performance.[23]

The controversy over Ranji's selection for England mirrors in interesting ways the ambivalence about Dadabhai Naoroji's election to the House of Commons four years earlier.[24] In both instances, the presence of Indians in British public life became a matter of concern to those who viewed race as the defining feature of 'Britishness'. Equally, it points to the double standards that governed the actions of the cricket establishment at Lord's. For a number of white cricketers from Australia had represented England in international cricket without any questions being raised about their eligibility to do so.

Indeed, as one supporter of Ranji noted, had place of birth been used consistently as a criterion for inclusion in the English cricket team, 'Lord Harris would have been ruled out; he was born in the West Indies'.[25]

Public discourse in Britain about Ranji's achievements also manifested deeper anxieties about their implications for the racial hierarchy within the empire. For some observers, his rise portended an imminent Indian conquest of English playing fields. One 'pessimist' in the *Daily Mail* openly expressed his fears. 'As the Indian newspapers attest,' he wrote,

> the success of an Indian cricketer in England has stirred up the better class natives, but especially the Bengalese [sic], to an intense pitch; and as I see by a paper to hand, four other Indian cricketers, two from Patna and two from Calcutta, are coming to England in time to play next season. All of these players are declared to be superior to Ranjitsinhji, but one of them is said to be a phenomenon, although he has only been playing three or four years.

Unnerved by this prospect, he posed a question that no doubt resonated with his readers: 'So where will be our Graces and Stoddarts if our cricket field is invaded by Indians who devote sixteen hours a day to specialising with bat and ball?'[26] A visit to Earl's Court to watch an exhibition by Indian jugglers from Bombay only served to confirm the writer's worst fears about this looming threat:

> The juggling was marvellous, and I watched the performance with great interest and a sinking heart. For when I came to speak with these jugglers themselves, it was as I expected. They were all anxious to become cricketers. Heretofore, one of them explained, they supposed only Indian princes were allowed to play cricket—and that it was all done for nothing... Ten pounds a day for juggling with bat and ball! Oh, the prospect made their mouths water. When the exhibition closes many of the troupe will remain in England, or if obliged to go back they will practice cricket all the winter. Next year Earl's Court will have to go elsewhere for new jugglers. These nimble gentlemen will doubtless only be seen at Lord's.[27]

The correspondent's imagination was clearly working overtime, for it is hardly credible that an Indian troupe arriving from Bombay would labour under the impression that cricket was a game solely played by princes. But the remarks show how Ranji's feats generated fears about the breach of the 'colour line' at the very heart of empire.

Nor was this writer alone in locating the Indian cricketer within a broader narrative of changing race relations. Others, too, saw the advent of Ranji as the harbinger of a fundamental reversal in the power dynamic between the Orient and the Occident. The 'Oriental', declared a European stationed in colonial India, had 'very special advantages' on the cricket field. The 'best conjurors', he asserted, came 'from the East, and not from western climes such as England, where everything, climate, temperature, temperament and a thousand and one other things cause eyes to be less quick and muscles less lithe than in the case of one reared in the shiny, supple East!' To this writer at least the conclusion was inescapable. 'The game will, if Indians and Orientals take it up and excel at it, pass through such a process of evolution . . . that the old-fashioned sort of game as now played will appear barbaric in its primitive ways, relying so much on mere strength and physical advantages.'[28] Cricket, in other words, would no longer remain the sacrosanct Anglo-Saxon game that it had been since time immemorial. Its future would be dominated by the wily 'Asiatic', whose suppleness and agility was bound to overcome the 'mere strength' of the plodding Englishman.

For his part, Ranji proved remarkably adept at negotiating the complexities of his public reception in England.[29] He actively fashioned his public image through the print media and by his comportment on and off the field. In particular, he constantly highlighted his status as an Indian prince.

In keeping with this princely status, Ranji cultivated a flamboyant lifestyle in Cambridge, engaging in conspicuous acts of consumption and display.[30] Not surprisingly, this profligacy quickly landed him in financial difficulties. Ranji's allowance from Nawanagar was sufficient to cover the costs of his education, but not substantial enough to lead a life of princely extravagance. Predictably, he piled up large debts and was pursued by irate creditors whose dues he had failed to clear. Fortunately for Ranji, timely remittances from Vibhaji saved him from public embarrassment. But he became increasingly frustrated by the constraints on his expenditure and the precariousness of his financial situation. He had, moreover, never come to terms with the loss of his regal status as the crown prince of Nawanagar.

The heightened public scrutiny which he was increasingly subjected to as a cricketing celebrity made it even more incumbent upon Ranji to secure his future. In his press interviews in Britain, he had deliberately perpetuated the fiction that he was the lawful heir to the Nawanagar throne.[31] That stand would be hard to maintain once it became known that he had been passed over in the line of succession. It was also likely to make it harder for him to secure any future loans from creditors in Britain, and thereby allow him to lead the lavish lifestyle to which he had become accustomed. Hence, when Vibhaji passed away in April 1895, Ranji resolved to press his claim as the rightful successor.[32] Over the next two years, even as he lit up the cricket fields of England with his incandescent batting, the Prince started to correspond with local British administrators in Kathiawar. In his letters to these officials, Ranji not only sought a clarification regarding his inheritance but also asked for a raise in his allowance from the Nawanagar court. But he quickly realized that real progress on these fronts could only be made in India. Accordingly, in the spring of 1898, Ranji stopped off in the subcontinent on the return leg of his first cricket tour of Australia.

III

It was the first time in a decade that Ranji had visited the land of his birth.[33] Princes and plebeians alike were eager to catch a glimpse of the returning hero and large crowds greeted him wherever he went. But Ranji did not let the public adulation distract him from the main purpose for which he had come back to India. During his year-long stay in the country, he single-mindedly used his fame as a star cricketer to prosecute his campaign for the Nawanagar crown. He adopted a twin-pronged strategy to this end. On the one hand, he met and corresponded with colonial officials stationed in Kathiawar to persuade them to review his case. On the other hand, he cultivated close ties with the major Rajput princely states of central and western India, whose support was crucial if he was to succeed in attaining his goal.

The British authorities in the Bombay Presidency, who had long been anticipating Ranji's reappearance in Kathiawar, closely watched his every move. A division of opinion soon emerged between the local British officials in Kathiawar, no doubt enamoured by the presence in their midst of an international sporting celebrity, and the upper echelons of the Government of Bombay, who were concerned that Ranji might emerge as a 'potentially disruptive and dangerous influence in the state'.[34] The key figure in the first category was Lieutenant-Colonel Willoughby Kennedy, the British administrator of Nawanagar, who lobbied on Ranji's behalf with the government and secured a raise in his allowance. Kennedy's superiors acceded to his request but were disinclined to reopen the vexed question of the Nawanagar succession.[35]

Even as he kept the lines of communication open with sympathetic British officials in Kathiawar, Ranji simultaneously deployed his cultural capital as a celebrity to cultivate close ties with the rulers of Indian princely states. In particular, he actively solicited the support of the local Rajput chieftains in Kutch and Kathiawar in his quest to displace Jassaji, the new Jam of Nawanagar.[36] Significantly, towards the end of the nineteenth century, the Rajput aristocracy in western India had begun to emphasize the purity of its racial origins. As a result, there was a growing attempt to distance itself from those Rajput clans—like the Jadejas of Nawanagar, for instance—whose members took on Muslim wives. Ranji's attempts to cast aspersions on Jassaji's Muslim parentage and his assertion of a pure Rajput identity thus found support among the rivals of the Nawanagar ruler.[37]

At the same time, Ranji also recognized that in order to get a favourable hearing from the imperial establishment in British India, he needed more powerful backers than the relatively minor chieftains of Kutch and Kathiawar. He thus set about buttressing his connections with prominent Indian princely houses in north India. Their support proved critical in allowing Ranji to gain access to the highest levels of the Raj. Two Indian princes, in particular, played an important role in this regard.

The first was Sir Pertab Singh, the regent of Jodhpur, who had become something of a legend in his own lifetime. Famously, he was prone to exaggerated expressions of loyalty that had passed into imperial folklore. His proximity to the British royal family and his influence with the colonial authorities gave Pertab Singh great clout among the Indian aristocracy. He acted as a mentor to several young princes, guiding them in their dealings with the British officialdom. Shortly after his return to India, Ranji sought out Pertab Singh, whom he had briefly met when the latter had travelled to Britain for Queen Victoria's Diamond Jubilee celebrations. Ranji began to refer to the older man as his 'uncle' and quickly became one of his favourite protégés. In return, Pertab Singh inducted the Kathiawari prince into the Jodhpur court and supported him financially.[38]

It was through 'Sir P' that Ranji met his second major benefactor, Maharaja Rajinder Singh of Patiala, in the summer of 1898.[39] Rajinder and Ranji hit it off from their very first meeting in Simla (Shimla), the summer capital of British India, and the Patiala prince offered the celebrity cricketer an honorary position in his royal establishment. At one level, the close friendship that developed between the two men probably had to do with the fact that they were both of the same age and shared a mutual passion for sport. But at another level, it was also a relationship based on mutual need. For Rajinder Singh, Ranji was a role model for the kind of anglicized princely identity that he was seeking to forge. Ranji, too, had much to gain from his association with the ruler of Patiala. The funds that he received from Rajinder Singh shored up his precarious financial situation. More importantly, though, being stationed at Patiala gave Ranji easy access to the imperial officials in Simla who had the power to decide his fate.

Ranji spent the better part of his time at Patiala in pursuing his case against Jassaji at the highest levels of the imperial administration. In September 1898, he submitted a petition to the Secretary of State via the Government of Bombay.[40] In this, he claimed that he was the lawful heir to Vibhaji and sought to discredit Jassaji's right to the Nawanagar throne. He also stressed that Vibhaji had legally adopted him, whereas Jassaji was born to 'low and irregular' Muslim women, who were not entitled to be regarded as legitimate wives. But Ranji made no headway with the authorities at Bombay, who dismissed his petition.[41] He was playing cricket in Patiala when he learnt of the Bombay government's decision. Shortly thereafter, Lord Elgin came to

Page 113.
*Ranjitsinhji and the late Maharajah of Patiala.
India, 1898.*

Figure 7. Kumar Shri Ranjitsinhji and Maharaja Rajinder Singh, *c.*1898–9. This photograph of the two cricketing princes was presumably taken during Ranji's stay at the Patiala court. Courtesy of Prakash Dahatonde, India.

Patiala on a state visit and Ranji lodged an appeal about his petition. On his return to Calcutta, the Viceroy asked the Bombay authorities for Ranji's file. Before he could act further, however, Elgin was replaced by Lord Curzon. The new Viceroy loved cricket and this, no doubt, predisposed him to be sympathetic to Ranji. In February 1899, the Viceroy's Executive Council overrode the Bombay government and forwarded the prince's petition to London.[42]

While Ranji used his time in India to further his private political agenda, his presence galvanized cricket promoters in the subcontinent in their bid to send an 'Indian' team to Britain. 'The agitation which has long been afoot in Bombay to enlist the sympathy and support of cricketers in India of an invasion of England by a cricket team composed of pure Indians appears to have achieved some sort of definite result,' reported the *Indian Sportsman* in April 1899. The credit for conceiving the project was claimed by 'Old Rossalion', the Bombay correspondent of the *Asian*. This journalist suggested that it was his 'powerful pleading' that had prompted J.M. Framjee Patel, the former captain of the Parsi cricket team, 'to forward the scheme with all his influence and energy, and not a little of his wealth'.[43] Framjee Patel, for his part, did not require much persuasion and took with relish to the role of cricketing impresario. As a member of the Parsee CC, he had been closely associated with the organization of the 1886 Parsi tour of Britain.[44] Moreover, in 1897 he had tried, in vain, to mobilize his cricketing compatriots to undertake yet another cricket tour of the imperial metropolis.[45] The failure of that venture made it amply clear to Patel that any future cricketing visit from India to Britain would need to include the other cricket-playing communities. Before he set to work, Patel made sure that the new scheme had the approval and support of both Lord Harris, the former governor of Bombay, and Lord Sandhurst, the current incumbent of that post.[46]

At the outset, the organizers decided to buy themselves more time by postponing the proposed tour to the summer of 1900. This had the added advantage that the Indian cricketers would tour in a year when there would be 'no Australian team in England to distract public attention'.[47] Charles Alcock, the secretary of Surrey CCC, who had helped the Parsis during their tours a decade earlier, and Francis E. Lacey, the MCC secretary, promised to arrange a provisional fixture list for the Indian tourists.[48] 'Framjee Patel's Indian Eleven', as the team was to be known, was to take on the MCC, the first-class counties, and the universities.[49] Messrs Thomas Cook

& Son were entrusted with the travel arrangements and 'asked to reserve accommodation for the Indian team by the first mail in April 1900'.[50]

Meanwhile, rumours about the composition of the proposed Indian team lent a keen edge to competitive cricket in Bombay. 'Cricket in the native communities has been watched with great interest during the past season,' observed the cricket correspondent of the *Times of India* in November 1899, 'as it had been proposed to send an eleven of Indian cricketers to England during the coming summer.'[51]

Given the timing of the initiative, it is more than likely that the organizers proceeded on the assumption that Ranji would lead the venture. Moreover, it was clear to everyone that the financial viability of the tour hinged on the participation of the star cricketer. 'An Indian team without the famous player would be like the play of "Hamlet" without the chief character,' remarked the *Times of India*.[52] As soon as the plans began to be laid, therefore, Framjee Patel wrote to Ranji offering him the captaincy of the prospective Indian team.

But to the disappointment of his many Indian admirers, the Kathiawari prince showed little enthusiasm for the proposed tour. At the end of March 1899, shortly before he departed for England, Ranji told the *Indian Sporting Times* that because he had come to the country on 'special business' he had not had much time or interest in matters pertaining to cricket. Pressed for his views on the Indian tour of England, Ranji suggested that the visit was premature. He insinuated that the future prospects of Indian cricket might be harmed if the project were to prove a sporting and financial failure. The prince also pointedly refused to offer a public commitment that he would take up Framjee Patel's invitation to captain the Indian team.[53]

One reason for Ranji's indifference towards the venture was that he was preparing to bring over a team of English amateurs over to the subcontinent that coming winter. He had made known his intentions in a telegram to the English sporting press in February 1899.[54] Indeed, in his interview with the *Indian Sporting Times*, Ranji was far more enthusiastic about his own scheme than he was about the prospects of the first Indian cricket team. His English side, he informed his interviewer, would come out to India in October and return home in March after playing twenty matches across the country. His aim, he announced, was to 'teach' Indian cricketers how to play proper first-class cricket.[55]

But at a deeper level, Ranji's reluctance to participate in the proposed Indian cricket tour of Britain stemmed from his sharp awareness that such a step would inevitably reopen the debate over his national identity. He knew that influential figures in the English cricket establishment—notably, Lord Harris—regarded men like him as 'birds of passage'.[56] If he agreed to lead an Indian team, these critics were likely to question Ranji's right to represent England. Moreover, he may have also calculated that his status as an English cricketer was crucial to his bid for the Nawanagar *gaddi* (throne). It is also worth noting that Ranji had constantly declared that he saw himself as an *English* cricketer. As he saw it, it was in England that he had learnt how to play the game properly and acquired the skills that had made him famous. To play for an Indian team would thus undermine Ranji's claim to Englishness and put at risk the social capital that he had acquired as a cricketer.[57]

Some of the opinions that were expressed in the Anglo-Indian papers suggest that Ranji was prescient in anticipating the likely fallout of his leading an Indian team to England. For instance, a contemporary writing in the *Indian Sportsman* in April 1899 assailed the proposed tour, arguing that the 'present condition of cricket in this country does not justify the ambition of an invasion of England any more than it would an invasion of Australia'. This writer could not see how an 'Indian team can hope to draw the shillings of the British spectator any more than did the Parsee tour of 1886'. 'If Mr. Patel or any other wealthy Indian gentleman wishes to take an Indian team to England and disport himself about the country, let him by all means do so,' he added, 'but for goodness' sake do not bring more ridicule on this poor country by attempting to give that holiday jaunt the colour of a national invasion.'[58] As for Ranji's participation in such an enterprise,

> The idea is preposterous, and we think the young Rajput is very wise in declining to identify himself with it. Then, again, Ranjitsinhji is not an Indian cricketer. His education in the game has been purely English. His great performances have been on English ground. In India he was a comparative failure, and his sympathies are all English. His nationality from a cricketer's point of view is a pure accident. The idea of taking an Indian team to England with any hope of prevailing against representative county cricket, or of immortalising some of the members in the way Prince Ranjitsinhji has been immortalised, is ridiculous, and the sooner it is dropped the better.[59]

Ranji's unwillingness to sign up effectively scuppered this first attempt at putting together an Indian cricket team. Without the famous Indian cricketer on board, Framjee Patel and his associates were unable to raise the necessary funds and were forced to jettison the tour. But they do not seem to have entirely given up on the idea. In April 1900, *Cricket* reprinted a report from the *Indian Sporting Times*, which stated that 'a good many cricketers in India are talking of the chances of getting up a team of fifteen to twenty cricketers in India to tour in England'. Interestingly, this team was 'to consist of Europeans as well natives, regardless of creed or caste'. The report also noted that the idea had much to do with 'the fact that the West Indies are sending a team of no less than eighteen members over to England this summer, and... that South Africa will do likewise'.[60]

The talk of sending a racially 'mixed' cricket team to England is intriguing. It was by no means an entirely inconceivable idea. Local cricket matches in Bombay sometimes featured combined sides comprising Europeans and Indians. Even the racially exclusive Bombay Gymkhana had sometimes included Parsi cricketers in its ranks (presumably to make up numbers). Notably, too, in January 1893, Lord Hawke's team had played a match at Allahabad against a predominantly European 'All-India' side that included three Parsi cricketers. Interestingly, the first West Indian team that toured England in the summer of 1900 was also a 'mixed' one. But the prospect of a combined team to the Mother Country in which the rulers and ruled played side by side appears to have held little appeal for the European elite in colonial India. 'It is easy to argue,' the *Indian Sporting Times* noted defensively, 'that what the West Indies can do, so can the East, but the thing must be gone into a little more below the surface before its real difficulties appear.'[61] The rumours died a natural death, for nothing more was heard of the scheme.

IV

Three years later, as the tour of the Oxford University Authentics drew to a close, talk once more revived of a potential Indian cricket tour of Britain. In January 1903, the *Indian Sporting Times* published a long article by the English cricketer and journalist E.H.D. Sewell, who argued that the time was ripe for such a venture. Born in India, where his father was an army officer, Sewell completed his schooling in England and then returned to the subcontinent in the 1890s as a civil servant. A keen sportsman, he played a great deal of his cricket in south India. Notably, in January 1893 he represented 'All-India' against Lord Hawke's visiting team. Sewell moved back to England in 1900, and briefly played cricket for Essex County in the early years of the new century. He then commenced a career as a newspaper columnist, writing mostly on rugby and cricket. Because of the length of time he had spent in India, he acquired a reputation as an expert on Indian cricket.[62] A man of robust opinions, Sewell took to the role with enthusiasm, frequently contributing informed articles on the subject in the British press.

In his article in the *Indian Sporting Times*, Sewell wrote that he could 'see nothing but Jupiter Flavius standing between a thoroughly business-like undertaking and great success'.[63] He began by noting 'the success of the home forces' against the touring Oxford University Authentics. He had in mind not only the usual Parsi victory over a visiting side from England, but also the promising displays by the Hindus at Bombay and the Muslim students at Aligarh. But Sewell was also quick to declare that these performances did not warrant the 'wild conclusion that Indian cricket, Native or Anglo-Indian or the two combined is superior to English first-class cricket'. There were more substantive reasons, he argued, why an Indian cricket tour of Britain was likely to prove a success. First, there was the 'intense interest in India and all things Indian that exists throughout this country'. This would ensure that the tourists would generate 'full and plenty' gate receipts. Moreover, the Parsi tours of late Victorian Britain had long since been forgotten and the public now had a 'larger interest in India and natives thereof than it can ever have in one particular sect or creed'. Second, the cricket-watching public had been 'glutted with Australian, South African and West Indian cricket…and would therefore welcome a new lot of cricketers'. An Indian cricket team would thus satisfy 'the craze for novelty that exists nowadays'. Third, it was time for Indian cricket 'to pay her debts' to English cricket. In other words, 'One return visit for three paid to Indian cricket is not so much to expect'. Finally, 'a representative native side under an experienced captain', Sewell asserted, would acquit itself 'quite fully well over here against the average first-class counties and would be too good for all the second'. He ended with a ringing exhortation:

> It is time Indian cricket took its proper place in the world. A country that has produced a Ranjitsinhji 'must' have several more articles of the same brand up its sleeve somewhere. The world-wide fame of the native of India for keenness of eye, suppleness of wrist, and, when at all athletically inclined, agility and speed of movement, ought to be turned to some account, and not most wickedly allowed to rot or turned to no better account than plugging holes through thrown rupees with a Quackenbush, or scoring centuries off Tommies' bowling, or chasing a chunk of bedaubed bamboo root about a dusty maidan…In conclusion, let the 'Cricket Tour in England' be your 'Durbar' for 1904.[64]

The gusto with which Sewell made his case stood in stark contrast to his views three years earlier, when he had cast doubt on the viability of an Indian cricket tour of Britain. On that occasion, he had dismissed the idea on the grounds that Indians did not 'know enough about the game yet'.[65] Nor was Sewell the only European to change his mind on this issue. The *Indian Sporting Times*, previously rather lukewarm about the proposal, now enthusiastically set about mobilizing public opinion in favour of it. The paper averred that the idea of sending a mixed native team to England was 'distinctly feasible' and only needed 'some courage, much energy and perseverance to be successfully and triumphantly carried through'. It also echoed Sewell's view that the proposed team had to be a combined one featuring Parsis, Hindus, and Muslims. 'A Parsee team or a Hindu eleven, though strong enough in India, would count for little in England,' the paper argued, 'and it is because we have a firm belief in the forces and resources of Indian cricket if united, that we would emphasise a united policy.' Were the different communities to come together, there would be 'little difficulty in getting together a representative eleven' to tour Britain. In turn, a strong representative team would be 'a magnet in attracting the curious crowds to the famous English grounds'.[66]

Other Anglo-Indian newspapers in Bombay added their voice to the chorus orchestrated by the *Indian Sporting Times*. 'Considering the great progress made by cricket in India during the last score of years,' noted 'Young Ebor' in the *Times of India*, 'it seems extraordinary that no representative team of Indian cricketers has ever left these shores to take part in English first class cricket. Apart from the merits of the best Indian native cricketers the trip would have been a worthy one merely from an educational point of view.'[67] The *Bombay Gazette* pointed out that 'the visit of a mixed native team to England would not be without some political importance'. 'The South Africans have done it and also the West Indians, and why not the Indians whose all-round cricket is certainly of the same standard and probably higher', the paper added.[68]

Members of the visiting Oxford University Authentics cricket team also lent their support to the venture. Interviewed by the *Indian Sporting Times*, Cecil Headlam was cautiously optimistic that a 'well-backed and carefully managed' tour would be a 'great success'. But much would depend, he added, 'upon the way in which the members of it play together and stick steadily to hard work'.[69] Others were more enthusiastic that the tour would be an attractive proposition because of the interest in India and Indian cricket. 'Avoid being the second attraction, travel as much as possible, and a successful tour should result,' one player told the same newspaper.[70]

The European enthusiasm for sending an Indian cricket team to Britain at this juncture raises interesting questions. Why did the colonial sporting establishment seek to orchestrate such a project? After all, the Anglo-Indian newspapers that extolled the virtues of 'unity' on the cricket field among the native communities were also the same ones that constantly disavowed claims that Indians could ever transcend their primordial attachments and forge a nation. Even more intriguingly, why did these newspapers become fervent supporters of a scheme that some of them had earlier opposed? The political context was hardly propitious, given the growing estrangement between the Raj and the Western-educated Indian middle classes. Nor was the sporting realm exempt from racial tensions between Europeans and Indians.

Indeed, as we have seen, cricket had frequently served to divide, rather than unite, colonizers and colonized. A particularly noteworthy instance of racial antagonism between the European and Indian cricket community was furnished by the Oxford Authentics' tour of the subcontinent. When the visiting Englishmen played against the 'Gentlemen of India' at Delhi in January 1903, not one Indian cricketer was included in the home team. The optics of this exclusion was readily apparent to Sewell, who believed that it was a 'big mistake, particularly on such an occasion to exclude natives from the team' and that the match had 'done the game in India almost irreparable damage'.[71]

Sewell's enthusiasm for a purely Indian cricket tour of Britain stemmed perhaps from a desire to make amends for the racial insensitivity of the European sporting establishment in India. If so, his response suggests that notions of benevolent paternalism prompted some Anglo-Indian cricketing enthusiasts to promote the cause of Indian cricket. These sympathetic Europeans saw it as their duty to guide Indians, now that the latter were beginning to make progress on the cricket field. Indeed, even though colonial civil society was racially divided, there were several individual Europeans whose encouragement and support had provided an impetus to indigenous cricket. This was not only true of the presidency capitals like Bombay and Madras, but also of smaller urban centres elsewhere in the subcontinent. One might surmise, then, that the attempt to construct an 'Indian' team was the same paternalist impulse writ large.

But the Anglo-Indian sporting campaign to send a composite 'native' cricket team to Britain might also be read differently. Arguably, the movement was a direct outcome of the dwindling strength of European cricket in the subcontinent. One index of this decline was the growing frequency with which European teams began to lose to Indian ones by the end of the century. Importantly, it was not only the Parsis who triumphed over the cricketing representatives of the ruling race: Hindu and Muslim cricket teams also began to defeat their European opponents in widely followed local matches.[72]

As a consequence, the late 1890s and early 1900s were notable for a grow-ing sense of crisis in Anglo-Indian cricketing circles. 'Cricket in India, as far as European players are concerned, has, during the last two years, shown very visible signs of deterioration, and at the present time the number of really good players in the different provinces is lower than it has been any time during the last thirteen years,' rued the *Bombay Gazette* in 1901.[73] Cecil Headlam, too, reported that he heard the same lament wherever he went in the subcontinent: 'men do not keep up their cricket out here as they used to do'.[74]

In his book, Headlam dwelt at length on the reasons for the decline in the standards of European cricket in colonial India. To begin with, he sug-gested, cricket did not suit Europeans in the subcontinent because it was 'too long a game'. What Europeans in India needed was a 'game which is both violent and short', because India was 'a land of work—of increasingly hard work'. Moreover, unlike other games, cricket required standing in the midday sun for long hours. 'Compared with the advantage of polo,' for instance, 'which is over after a few "chukkas", and at which you can get a station game two or three times a week, a short day's cricket once a week has not much to offer.' Again, in polo, 'if you miss your ball once, you can recover; at cricket, if you are out first ball you must wait a whole week for another possible chance, and then perhaps not get an innings'. Nor were the playing conditions in India particularly congenial. Thus, at Bombay where a lot of cricket was played during the monsoon,

> the wickets, baked by a hot sun after heavy daily rain, are just a bit of glue, and give the batsman no fun, while the bowlers feel the effect of the burning, exhausting sun, and quickly modify their run, lose their sting, and, as the phrase goes, soon bowl only twelve annas to the rupee.

In the cold weather, on the other hand, 'you cannot, without very great expense and trouble in watering, provide a tolerable grass wicket at all'.[75]

Headlam also pointed to factors beyond the boundary that made European cricket in India increasingly unviable. Both British soldiers and civilians were being moved around more often and hence 'the days when every little station had its ground and regular team as a matter of course, are over'. Moreover, he noted, India was

> a large country; men are all busy here, and they are separated by vast distances. That means that at most places there is little chance of a match with any out-side team, except, it may be, with a regiment on the march. There are no touring clubs, and cricket with the same people every week becomes monstrously monotonous.[76]

However, Headlam believed that the visit of the Oxford Authentics had provided a shot in the arm to European cricket in colonial India. Their visit, he argued, had 'supplied for this past cold weather the needed incentive to play and practice, and has given undoubtedly a great fillip to the game'. In turn, these reflections prompted Headlam to suggest that if 'some such tour, either of English or Colonial cricketers or of an Indian team, could take place frequently, cricket among Europeans in India would rapidly revive'.[77]

But, as Headlam recognized, notwithstanding the generous hospitality on offer, cricket teams from Britain would have little incentive to visit India if, in addition to the absence of gate money (which deterred the professionals), the quality of the opposition was deemed too mediocre. Since there was little hope of an immediate revival in the fortunes of European cricket, advertising the virtues of Indian cricket was one way in which the Anglo-Indian establishment could attract teams from home. In turn, if Indian cricket was to attract English attention, it was necessary to send a combined team out to Britain in order to showcase its skills.

The quest to form a composite Indian team might thus be seen as a function of the rapidly diminishing vitality of European cricket in the subcontinent. That such considerations were at play in the chorus of European voices supporting an Indian cricket tour to the Mother Country can be discerned in the opinions expressed in the European press. Deprecating the 'tendency to under-rate the strength of Native Indian cricket', 'Major Max' of the *Indian Sporting Times* argued that 'for this reason, if for no other, if it is only to show home cricketers that the game out here has progressed to a far greater extent than they suspect, it is high time that a representative team should follow the example of the South Africans and West Indians and visit England'.[78]

V

Yet a scheme floated by the Anglo-Indian newspapers would have remained a non-starter without the participation of influential Indians. In sport, as in much else, colonial authorities depended on Indian resources and intermediaries to give effect to their plans. However, in this instance, they did not have to make much effort. The idea of sending an Indian cricket team to Britain resonated with indigenous elites, who had increasingly begun to exert their influence over the organization of cricket in the sub-continent. Significantly, two different types of local patronage had begun to shape the world of Indian cricket in these years.

In the first category were businessmen, propertied magnates, and wealthy professionals, whose financial support was crucial in sustaining cricket at the grassroots. In Bombay, we have already seen how Parsi cricket benefitted from the keen interest that merchant princes of the community took in the game. Funded by the Tata, Petit, Jeejeebhoy, Readymoney, and other prosperous business houses, the Parsi Gymkhana became one of the most well-endowed cricket clubs in the country.[79] Their lead was followed by wealthy Gujarati Hindu and Muslim businessmen in Bombay. The Hindu Gymkhana, for instance, was named after its principal benefactor, the Bhattia merchant Goverdhandas Parmanandas Jivandas. Other Gujarati businessmen—among them Gokuldas Tejpal, Mulraj Khatau, Tribhowandas Mungaldas, Jivandas Mulji, Vijbhukhandas Atmaram, and Dwarkadas Dharamsi—also made generous contributions to the construction of the gymkhana.[80] Likewise, the Muslim bourgeoisie of Bombay readily opened its purse strings to build the Islam Gymkhana. Among the prominent patrons of the new club were Khoja merchants and mill owners—men like Ibrahim Rahimtulla and Currimbhoy Ebrahim, for example—as well as Bohra mercantile and professional families such as the Peerbhoys and the Tyabjis, who did much to nurture cricket within the community.

Indian men of wealth played a crucial role in sustaining local cricket in other towns and cities in western India. Take, for instance, the port town of Karachi, the capital of Sind after the British conquest of the province in 1842. During the American Civil War, this region emerged as an important centre for cotton cultivation and much of it was exported through Karachi. Moreover, after the Suez Canal opened in 1869, it was the first port of call for ships arriving from Europe. The presence of British regiments in the town also generated a large demand for a variety of imported goods. Karachi thus became a magnet for a wide range of commercial interests that included, in addition to the European trading agencies, a sizeable number of Parsi, Hindu, and Bohra merchants. Some of these men became patrons of cricket, which had become the most popular sport in the town by the early 1900s. Moves to establish a cricket club for their community commenced among members of the emergent Parsi bourgeoisie as early as 1883. The selection of three Parsis from Karachi—Dinshaw Dadabhai Khambatta, Pestonji Dastur, and Burjorji Balla—for the pioneering 1886 tour of England provided a further impetus to their project. Funded by donations from the leading lights of the community, the Karachi Parsi Institute was founded in 1893 and went on to become one of the strongest cricket clubs in the city.[81]

The first Hindu cricket club in Karachi also owed its existence to the munificence of a businessman. This was the Sahta Sports Club, formed in 1889 by Ladharam Khimanmal, who was probably a Sindhi merchant.[82] A decade later, another propertied Hindu, Moolchand Kauramal, founded the Young Hindu CC, which went on to produce a string of famous Karachi cricketers.[83] The Bohras of Karachi, too, were enthusiastic cricketers, no doubt inspired by their brethren in Bombay and by Hindu and Parsi rivals in their hometown. A Bohra Gymkhana was founded in 1898, funded by the leading businessmen within the community.[84] But, as in Bombay, sectarian divisions did not preclude cross-communal interactions on the cricket field. For instance, we learn that Seth Visoomal Pahelajrai Sahta, a prominent Karachi businessman, took the lead in establishing the Young Cricketers' Association in 1900, which organized regular matches between the different communities of the Old Town.[85]

Undoubtedly, Bombay and western India were ahead of other regions in the extent to which indigenous capital facilitated the organization of local cricket. But elsewhere, too, cricket had begun to attract the patronage of the Indian bourgeoisie. In south India, for instance, one might cite the example of Modhavarappu Venkatamahipathi Nayudu (better known as 'Buchi Babu'), whose wealth and patronage laid the foundations of native cricket in Madras.[86] A maternal grandson of the legendary M. ('Dare House') Venkataswami Nayudu, a *dubash* (interpreter; but here, broker) in the European firm of Parry & Co., Buchi Babu 'was brought up in the English manner'.[87] He was a keen hunter and horse rider and maintained a large stable for this purpose. And as an anglicized Indian, he developed a deep love for cricket. Affronted by the racial exclusivity of the European sporting clubs, Buchi Babu invested the considerable wealth he inherited from his grandfather in promoting native cricket. Notably, he became the founder and principal patron of the Madras United Club, established in 1888, which soon came to rival the Madras CC, the bastion of European cricket.[88] By the early 1900s, the new club was easily one of the best in the country. It also made Buchi Babu a recognized name in the world of Indian cricket. Indeed, in the summer of 1898, when Ranji stopped off briefly in Madras on his way to Rajasthan, he readily accepted an invitation to visit Buchi Babu's palatial residence, where he proceeded to demonstrate his cricketing skills against the latter's trained syces.[89]

In eastern India, it was football rather than cricket that had captured the imagination of the indigenous middle classes. But even here, the last two decades of the nineteenth century saw the emergence of Indian cricket clubs. In Calcutta—where the organization of cricket was controlled by British expatriates—members of the city's Bengali *bhadralok* (the 'respectable' middle classes) formed, successively, the Boys' Club (1880), the Howrah Cricket Club (1880), the Wellington Club (1881), the Presidency Club (1883), the Town Club (1885?), and the Sovabazar Club (1887). Of these, the Town Club eventually became the principal rival of the Calcutta CFC.[90]

By the end of the nineteenth century, a second type of indigenous patronage began to play a crucial role in the spread of cricket across the subcontinent. Prior to this, Indian royal houses had mostly pursued traditional Indian sports: polo, wrestling, archery, sword fighting, and *shikhar* (hunting). But from the mid-1890s onwards, a growing number of princely states began to promote and support cricket. Two factors spurred royal interest in the game. First, some of them had studied in the new anglicized educational institutions for the scions of Indian royalty that were founded in the last quarter of the twentieth century. These included the Mayo College, Ajmer; the Rajkumar Colleges at Rajkot and Raipur; Daly College, Indore; and Aitchison College, Lahore.[91] Although the Indian princes funded these institutions, the headmasters and teachers were mostly Englishmen, who laid an emphasis on physical education. They accorded particular importance to cricket, which they saw as a valuable instrument for developing 'character' and leadership skills among their aristocratic students. As a result, their royal wards continued to invest their energies in the imperial game even after they became full-fledged rulers. Second, Indian princes also became aware of the premium placed on cricket by the British ruling elite. They realized that playing cricket could allow them to forge connections with the highest levels of the imperial state in India and Britain. Notably, the Indian princes had before them the startling example of Ranji, a product of the Rajkumar College at Rajkot, who had succeeded in becoming an imperial celebrity through his cricketing achievements.

The lead here was taken by Rajinder Singh, the pleasure-seeking Maharaja of Patiala. Following his accession to the throne as an eighteen year old in 1890, Rajinder pursued all manner of sport with flamboyant zeal. The Anglo-Indian establishment, which benefitted from his sporting largesse, lauded him as an 'all-round sportsman'. European newspapers described him as 'a daring rider and a splendid shot', the 'best polo-player in India, a second Ranji in cricket...and the finest amateur billiardist of the day'.[92] Cricket was a relatively new interest for Rajinder: it was only in the mid-1890s that he began to pursue the game seriously.[93] The timing suggests that the rapid rise of Ranji as an imperial sporting hero had something to do with Rajinder's conversion. But once he took to cricket, the Maharaja poured vast resources in promoting the game in his state. At Chail, in the Simla Hills, which served as his summer residence, Rajinder fashioned the world's highest cricket ground by levelling the top of an 8,000 feet mountain. He also transformed Patiala into a cricketing powerhouse by recruiting players from far and wide. Some, like Jack Hearne and William Brockwell, were English professionals who spent the winter months in Patiala, playing for the Maharaja's team and coaching their princely patron in return for handsome pay and perks. Others, like K.M. Mistry, the Parsi player from Bombay (about whom more anon), were imported from within the subcontinent. Even the great Ranji himself played for the Patiala eleven during his stint in the state in 1898.[94]

By the end of the 1890s, a number of other princely states had begun to patronize cricket: Baroda, Bikaner, Bhavnagar, Cooch Behar, Dhar, Kapurthala Kashmir, Mysore, Natore, and Wadhwan.[95] Some princes—among them, the Maharaja of Kashmir—quickly became the butt of ridicule among Anglo-Indians for their cricketing idiosyncrasies.[96] But others were more systematic and serious in their commitment to the game. For instance, Sir Nripendra Narayan, the ruler of the medium-sized state of Cooch Behar in Bengal, built up three competitive cricket teams (two at Calcutta and one at Darjeeling). Following the Patiala model, Cooch Behar had racially mixed cricket teams comprising English professionals and Indian imports.[97] However, the ruler of Natore, who sought to rival Cooch Behar, appears to have been a notable exception in this regard. Formed in 1900, the Natore team was entirely made up of Indian cricketers, many of whom were hired from outside Bengal.[98] Long before the arrival of the Indian Premier League, then, the maharajas had pioneered the tradition of using the game as a vehicle for their status or political aspirations, creating cricket teams that were notable for their cosmopolitan ethos.

The project of sending an Indian cricket team to England that was initiated in the wake of the Oxford Authentics tour thus brought together two very different worlds of elite sporting patronage within the subcontinent. On the one hand were the Anglo-Indian publicists, officials, and sportsmen keen to attract visits to the subcontinent from the Mother Country. And on the other were the growing number of Indian aristocrats and moneyed elites, who saw in cricket a way of registering their presence in the eyes of the British Raj.

VI

In February 1903, an informal gathering of the leading lights of Bombay's cricketing world was held at the city's Parsi Gymkhana. The purpose of the meeting was to explore the possibility of sending a 'mixed' Indian cricket team comprising Hindus, Muslims, and Parsis to tour Britain in the summer of 1904. The Parsis were represented by three of their stalwarts: J.M. Framjee Patel, Dr Mehallasha Pavri, and J.M. Divecha; P.K. Telang (son of the well-known Bombay jurist Kashinath Trimbak Telang) and S.G. Velinker spoke for the Hindu Gymkhana; while Hadi Tyabji (a scion of the famously liberal Bohra family) was the voice of the Islam Gymkhana. But significantly, there were also four European participants, of whom two were journalists associated with the newspapers that had originally suggested the idea: Albert Sidney Galtrey, editor of the *Indian Sporting Times*, and R.S. McGregor Shepherd of the *Bombay Gazette*. The meeting unanimously agreed that the idea of sending an Indian team to England 'was a most admirable one and that every endeavour should be made to carry into practical effect'.[99] The proceedings concluded with the formation of a committee—comprising all the members who had attended the meeting, as well as the Aga Khan, Gokuldas Vithaldas (the president of the Hindu Gymkhana), the industrialists Dorab Tata and Ibrahim Rahimtulla, and four other Europeans (among them M.R. Jardine, father of the future England captain, Douglas Jardine)—to oversee the project.

Although Bombay's cricketing elites were the principal protagonists, a leading nationalist newspaper in Calcutta was quick to express its support for the venture. 'The project that has just been started in Bombay to organize an Indian cricket team, with a view to be sent out to England, deserves the sympathy and co-operation of the entire Indian community,' noted the *Bengalee*. 'We are glad that Bombay has taken the lead in this matter.'[100] The British press too responded favourably to the news of the proposed Indian cricket tour. 'Needless to say,' remarked the *Athletic News*,

> we shall be heartily pleased to see these Oriental potentates. Nowhere is cricket pursued with keener enthusiasm than among our Indian dependencies. Our dusky friends have taken to England's national game with infinite gusto since the days when deeds of derring do on the part of Ranjitsingji [sic] stirred two hemispheres, and we bid them welcome.[101]

Back in Bombay, the tour organizers had to deal with three pressing imperatives as they set about their task. To begin with, they had to secure support for the idea from the game's imperial administrators in Britain. They also had to raise the necessary finances to pay for the team's expenses and cover any losses on the venture. And last, but not least, the squad needed to be suitably 'representative' of the three major cricket-playing communities in the subcontinent.

Negotiating the first challenge proved relatively easy. Francis Lacey, the MCC secretary, and Charles Alcock, the secretary of Surrey CCC, once again responded positively to the idea of an Indian tour of England. In his letter to the organizing committee, Lacey wrote that the MCC would not only 'welcome a visit from native cricketers of India' but also 'be prepared to do anything we can to contribute to its success'.[102] As the *Bombay Gazette* was quick to acknowledge,

> To have sent them [the Indian cricket team] without the powerful cooperation of the M.C.C. would only have meant failure in both a financial as well as a cricket and social sense. In the welcome extended by the M.C.C. we fancy we can detect the influence of Lord Harris who had promised to assist in every possible way to further the project.[103]

The paper was right in surmising the role of the ex-Governor of Bombay, who by this time, was the dominant figure within the MCC. Adopting his most paternal manner, Lord Harris wrote to the organizers offering his unstinted support for the tour. 'You may be perfectly certain that I will do my best to help you,' he declared, 'and if can be done I shall be delighted to see the team over here, if for no other reason, because you have been able to sink caste and religious differences, and therefore able to get together, or so I hope, the best team possible.'[104]

Securing the necessary finances proved to be a more challenging task for the organizers. When the idea was first mooted in the pages of the *Indian Sporting Times*, Edward Sewell suggested that a team comprising sixteen members (including a manager) would be well advised not to 'sail from Bombay without Rs. 30,000 in solid cash at its back, with the prospect of course of "half-gates" at home adding to the amount'.[105] He also noted that the team would be able to recoup £500 in gate receipts in England. The rest of the tour expenditure would have to be covered by subscriptions raised in India.[106] The *Indian Sporting Times* contested this line of reasoning, arguing that Sewell's estimate was 'rather a modest one', and that he had 'altogether underestimated' the gate receipts and subscriptions that the Indian cricket team was likely to generate. 'To state that £500 in subscriptions and half-gate receipts is all that the team could with certainty look forward to as a result of four months' cricket is, indeed, to take the lowest possible figure in this connection,' the paper opined.

> The interest at home in Indian cricket has increased largely during the last few years and it is not too much to expect that the four matches in London against the M.C.C., Middlesex, Surrey, and London County C.C. would realise in the shape of half-gate receipts more than Mr. Sewell regards it as safe to reckon on for the whole tour.[107]

At the outset, many observers were confident that raising the money required for the tour was unlikely to prove an insurmountable obstacle. 'We think that if the proposal to send a native mixed team home were properly put before those of the native princes who are fond of cricket and other rich and influential supporters of the game out here, there should be no difficulty in raising a sufficient sum to ensure the team against loss,' noted the *Indian Sporting Times*.[108] Other contemporaries echoed this view. As one writer averred,

> There should be no difficulty in raising the Rs. 38,000 required as a guarantee fund. If the Fiji Islanders are able and willing to open their purse strings to finance the visit of a team to England...surely the Indian Princes will not be hesitant about lending their support to a movement which not only promises to be a financial success so far as the return of the money is concerned, but will elevate Indian cricket to a higher status in the cricket world.

And he went on to add that 'There are thousands of sportsmen who risk large sums on horse racing, and of this number I am convinced that some will be found who will not be backward in supporting the present movement.'[109] 'The moral effect of a tour like this would be very great,' agreed the *Bengalee*, 'and in view of it we are sanguine that our richer classes will not be slow to subscribe to such a fund.'[110]

The fundraising campaign for the Indian cricket tour got off to an encouraging start and the *Bombay Gazette* reported at the end of March 1903 that Rs. 10,000 had 'already been promised by various gentlemen in Bombay'.[111] The most prominent of these donors was J.N. Tata, who it was said, had agreed to give 'anything between three and five thousand rupees towards the guarantee fund'.[112] Two other Bombay business magnates, Sir Dinshaw Petit and Bomanjee Petit, were likewise said to have 'promised to give handsome sums towards the guarantee fund'.[113] Nor was it only the moneyed men of India's cricketing capital who sought to open their purse strings. Notably, the committee received promises of financial help from B. Baliah Naidu and M. Buchi Babu, the principal Indian patrons of the game in Madras.[114] Furthermore, the *Bombay Gazette* anticipated that 'a large sum, probably amounting to Rs. 10,000 will be forthcoming in the shape of a subscription from a well-known ruler'.[115]

As it transpired, however, the most generous princely donor, in terms of actual contribution, was Sir Nripendra Narayan, the Maharaja of Cooch Behar, who offered Rs. 3,500 to the cause. An equally sizeable contribution of Rs. 3,300 was forthcoming from the Aga Khan. Other Indian rulers who contributed to the guarantee fund, though on a smaller scale, were Patiala (Rs. 1,500), Bikaner (Rs. 1,000), Mysore (Rs. 500), Kapurthala (Rs. 500), Bhavnagar (Rs. 500), and Kolhapur (Rs. 300). The organizers also received offers of financial assistance—of a more token kind—from some of the leading figures of the imperial establishment in India: Lord Curzon (Rs. 200), Lord Ampthill (Governor of Madras, Rs. 150), and Lord Northcote (Governor of Bombay, Rs. 150).[116]

In order to broaden the scope of the appeal for funds from the public, the organizers sent out a letter in July 1903 to prospective subscribers to the scheme. The purpose of the guarantee fund, they explained, was 'to enable the Committee to feel secure in the event of there being any excess of liabilities over subscriptions and gate money'. On the other hand, they assured prospective subscribers that if the trip was profitable, 'a sum representing that profit will be applied to pay off the guarantors "pro rata" so far as it goes'.[117]

But the tour organizers' assurances had little effect on the public. By the autumn, only Rs. 15,000 had accrued to the guarantee fund. 'The committee which has in hand the arrangements,' observed the *Bombay Gazette* in September 1903, 'must...feel disappointed at the comparatively poor response from local cricket-lovers up to date to the appeal for funds to carry the project through.' 'The project is, one which should strongly appeal to the patriotism of all classes and communities in India, cricketers and non-cricketers, and we are at a loss to account for the poor interest evinced in it,' the paper admitted. 'If every cricketer in India subscribed a small sum, according to his means,' it went on to suggest, 'the greater proportion of the money still required would be forthcoming and we venture to think that subscribers to the fund would find themselves taking a prouder and more personal interest in the goings of the team which, they would be able to reflect, they had a share in sending to England.'[118]

Yet again, the organizers sent out 'printed circulars for subscriptions or guarantee of subscriptions to the public of Bombay and several parts of India generally'. This time around, the call elicited a more enthusiastic public response. In November 1903, the *Bombay Gazette* reported that 'The scheme to send a team of native Indian cricketers to England next summer is slowly but surely maturing and the difficulties which at one time seemed likely to crop up in connection with the financial side of the question have happily been overcome in great measure.'[119]

The drive to recruit players for the proposed tour also began on a promising note. At the outset, the committee wrote to the leading Hindu, Muslim, and Parsi players in the country inviting them to become a part of the Indian team. The *Bombay Gazette* reported in March 1903 that the promoters of the scheme had 'every reason to be satisfied with the results of their efforts'. All the players in India contacted by the organizing committee immediately agreed to join the touring party.[120] 'It is satisfactory to find the selected candidates enthusiastic,' commented the *Times of India*. 'Not a single refusal has been received since the proposed tour was mooted. This being the first representative tour, there will necessarily be a good deal of honour attached to those whose skill will entitle them to places.'[121]

By the winter of 1903, however, unease about the composition of the team began to surface in Bombay's Parsi press. This was triggered by the news that two leading Parsi cricketers—K.M. Mistry and A.H. ('Johnny') Mehta—would not be taking part in the proposed tour. There followed a raucous debate in the Gujarati newspapers about the 'representative' character of the Indian team. 'Some of the local Guzerati papers seem to have deliberately set themselves out to throw cold water on the scheme to send a team of native cricketers to England next year,' reported the *Bombay Gazette* in December 1903. The tour organizers were forced to issue a public statement rebutting the 'misleading and unfair reports in circulation'. A unanimous resolution of the 'Committee for the Indian Cricket Team for England' stated that it had 'no intention of sending a native cricket team to England in 1904 if such combination be not strong and fairly representative'.[122]

As a sign of their continued commitment to the project, the organizers proceeded with the preparations for the tour. Acting on their behalf in London, Sewell arranged an ambitious fixture list for the Indian team, commencing at Crystal Palace on 9 May 1904 and ending at Harrogate in late August.[123] Of the twenty-five matches they were scheduled to play, fifteen were to be against 'first-class' teams 'including Surrey, Yorkshire, Kent, Middlesex, Leicestershire, Warwickshire, Derbyshire, Worcestershire, Cambridge University, MCC, London County, and the South Africans'.[124] 'Despite the croakings of the vernacular press and the doubt that exists about the services of one or two of the selected players being available, everything promises well for the scheme,' remarked the *Bombay Gazette*.[125]

A series of trial games was scheduled in Bombay over the Christmas holidays of 1903. The finale to the cricket week was a 'test match', featuring players from across the subcontinent who were in contention for selection to the Indian team. As one witness later recalled, in addition to the local stars there gathered in Bombay on this occasion, 'a greater galaxy of cricketing talent than Western India has ever seen before or since'.[126] A noteworthy feature of these matches was the participation of two of Ceylon's best-known cricketers, Tom Kelaart and Douglas de Saram. Their presence in Bombay was presumably dictated by the fact that Ceylonese cricket clubs had subscribed to the tour fund in return for the inclusion of their players in the Indian team.

★ ★ ★

As a new year dawned, the first ever Indian cricket tour of Britain seemed to proceed on schedule. Places for the team had already been reserved on the P&O steamer *Caledonia*, scheduled to depart from Bombay on 2 April 1904. All that remained was the announcement of the final squad and a last push to raise the funds that were still needed to cover the costs of the tour. But at the end of January 1904, at a meeting held in camera, its promoters voted to abandon the tour.

It was an astonishing *volte face* given the bullish public statements that had emanated from the committee in the preceding weeks. According to an 'Old Timer', who wrote about the event a quarter of a century later:

> At that fateful last meeting of the Gymkhana Club House, after nearly a year and a half's work in connection with the scheme, it was a fearful blow to the members to discover that the composition of the side was likely to cause so much dissension among Parsi, Hindu and Mahomedan supporters that the only thing to do was to call the tour off. The committee were not altogether unanimous in coming to this decision, and it required the casting vote of the president to carry the resolution. But it was realized that the danger of sending a mixed Indian team to England without perfect harmony between the members of the different communities composing it was one which could not be over-looked and some members feared that were the tour allowed to take place it would end in disaster on account of the quarrels on the tour.[127]

'Two factors were the main cause of the trouble that loomed up a month or so before the abandonment of the tour,' he recalled, 'and they were the appointment of a Parsi to captain the side and what the Hindus and Mahomedans regarded as too great a preponderance of Parsi players in the team.'[128]

Interestingly, however, the final resolution of the tour's organizing committee made no mention of the vexed question of representation. Instead, it simply stated: 'That the finances being in the condition disclosed by the honorary treasurers, it was not expedient in the opinion of the committee that the scheme for sending an Indian team to England should be further considered, and that, therefore, it should be abandoned.'[129]

The committee's explanation for aborting the venture was greeted with consternation in some quarters. 'Having collected in subscriptions and guarantees over two-thirds of the sum required it may appear strange to those who are unaware of the underlying influences that were at work that such drastic step as the abandonment of the scheme would have been necessary,' remarked the *Bombay Gazette*.[130] This newspaper attributed the failure of the project to the disunity among its organizers. 'Had perfect harmony prevailed in the Committee and the members all worked together from the outset to further the interests of the scheme, there can be no doubt that it would have been successful,' it argued.

> But unfortunately a certain section of the community represented on the committee regarded the available team as being weak and not representative of native Indian cricket, owing to the inability of two or three well-known players to make the trip and opposed the carrying out of the project so successfully as completely to cripple the finances.[131]

These remarks were pointedly directed at Framjee Patel and his Parsi compatriots, who were implicitly accused of having put their own selfish interests over that of Indian cricket.

Other members of the European sporting establishment expressed similar sentiments. Edward Sewell, who had spent the previous months working on the arrangements for the tour, vented his fury in the press. 'The Parsees began to realise that only three or four of their cricketers would be chosen, and did not care about the bitter pill that lies in the fact that Parsee cricket is not now synonymous with native cricket in India,' he alleged. Indeed, 'the best native cricket in India now is undoubtedly Hindu and Mahommedan'.[132] His remarks elicited an agitated response from a Parsi named Cooverji Ghodadalal, who sought to defend his community's cricketing representatives. Sewell's tirade, this correspondent suggested, was based on 'second-hand information, and animated, moreover, by a sense of some personal financial loss' that he had sustained on account of his involvement in the project. 'Indian cricket does not stand in need of Mr. Sewell's strictures,' declared Ghodadalal.[133]

Framjee Patel too strenuously 'defended the attitude taken by some of the leading Parsi sportsmen in connection with the scheme'. He argued that 'for the scheme to be successful it was necessary to have sufficient funds at their disposal and to raise a team perfectly representative of Indian cricket'. But, Patel noted, 'months after the scheme had been started, they realized that both were not possible, and the sportsmen he had referred to were, therefore, perfectly justified in taking up an attitude against the scheme which action of theirs had been very ungenerously criticized by certain parties in the newspapers'.[134]

Notwithstanding Framjee Patel's rebuttal, however, the role of the 'Parsee element in Bombay' was clearly a significant factor in the implosion of the project to put together the first Indian cricket team. Indeed, a few days before the formal public announcement, a report appeared in the Anglo-Indian press anticipating the abandonment of the tour to Britain. This paper noted that the Parsis, unhappy about the composition of the proposed Indian cricket team, were 'moving heaven and earth to defeat the plans of the committee which has in hand the arrangements for the tour'.[135]

But it was not only the representatives and publicists of Parsi cricket who were responsible for the collapse of the project; their actions were encouraged and abetted by the most charismatic cricketer in the world.

From the moment the idea of sending an Indian cricket team to England was floated, Ranji had deployed the tactics that had served him so well in 1899. As on the previous occasion, the Kathiawari prince refused to make a public commitment to the venture despite being invited by the tour organizers to be a part of the Indian team. But rumours about his role frequently surfaced in the press reports on the venture. In February 1903, the *Times of India* reported that Ranji 'would most probably assist the team in five or six matches in the Metropolitan district'.[136] The Indian star neither confirmed nor refuted such reports, thereby fuelling the rumours about his participation in the tour. Later that year, news arrived in India that Ranji had resigned the captaincy of Sussex CCC. This gave rise to renewed press speculation that he might 'have been influenced by other reasons in taking the step he has taken and perhaps the fact that an Indian team will be touring in England next summer, and that he will be expected to assist it, may to some extent have contributed to his resignation'. But Ranji, the report admitted, 'has not been credited with any great keenness to identify himself with the movement to send a team of native Indian cricketers to England, and although several times sounded as to his views by the committee which has in hand the arrangements, he will not commit himself to any expression of opinion'.[137]

In December 1903, Ranji arrived in Bombay. Five years earlier, his return to the subcontinent had triggered the first attempt to put together a composite Indian cricket team. This time around, however, his arrival in the city became the occasion for spurring the political manoeuvres that eventually led to the unravelling of the project.

Publicly, Ranji maintained his non-committal stance towards the proposed Indian cricket tour of Britain. In an interview to the *Indian Sporting Times*, he claimed that 'he knew very little about it [the Indian cricket tour of England], and only knowing one or two of the players mentioned as probable members of the team, he should not like to express an opinion'. Pressed by his interviewer if he would consider assisting the Indian team in Britain, Ranji stated that the matches in the forthcoming English cricket season had already been arranged and that it would therefore 'not be fair to my county to devote my services to the Indian team when the county is engaged in the important fixtures'. When the reporter persisted with the question, Ranji irritably replied that he might consider playing for the Indians 'occasionally'. The interview suggests that the prince continued to shy away from any involvement with Indian cricket lest it raise awkward questions about his status within English cricket. Moreover, as in 1899, Ranji made it clear that he favoured an altogether different kind of cricket tour. What he wished to see, the prince told the reporter, was yet another English cricketing visit to India. 'A lakh of rupees subscribed in the whole of India to entertain an English team,' he remarked,

> would be a very small sum and good cricket would be witnessed. If you worked up in Bombay alone, I am sure you could get it. It might also be probable for the team to be entertained by some of the Native Princes. It would be a splendid trip for any English cricketer to look forward to.[138]

During his stay in Bombay, Ranji repeatedly sought to undermine the ongoing efforts to put together a composite Indian team. The most notable instance of this was at a dinner organized in his honour at the Ripon Club, a prominent Parsi institution in the city. The imperial cricketing superstar used the occasion to tear to shreds the idea of an Indian cricket tour of Britain. 'Why, Indian cricketers do not yet know the A.B.C. of the game, and an Indian team would find that in England there is no county so weak that it could not score 500 runs against Indian bowling and in turn dismiss the Indian team for 30 or 40 runs,' he scoffed.[139]

Evidently, Ranji's opposition to the idea of an Indian cricket tour of Britain proved popular with his Parsi audience. According to one newspaper account, at the behest of 'certain members of the Parsee Gymkhana', the Kathiawari prince wrote a letter to their cricket committee 'ridiculing the idea of sending an Indian team to England'.[140] In all likelihood, too, his views provided much needed ammunition to the Parsi representatives who attended the final meeting of the committee that pursued this ill-fated venture. 'By Ranji's discouraging observations the development of the game in India has been retarded for many years,' rued one commentator in the *Indian Field*.[141]

VII

The sudden abandonment of the Indian cricket tour of Britain plunged into deep gloom the Hindu and Muslim sections of the cricketing community in the subcontinent. One Muslim cricket lover wrote to the *Bombay Gazette* to express his deep disappointment at the manner in which the Parsis had wrecked the venture. 'To draw a moral from it,' wrote 'Fez',

> an All-India XI with Parsees in it is an impossibility now and for a very long time to come. Those who knew the peculiar attitude of Parsee cricketers towards the game had many misgivings when they heard that the Committee was located in Bombay. How far these misgivings were justified need not now be discussed when we know that the All-India Team is a thing of the past.[142]

This letter writer went on to propose that the project to send an Indian cricket tour to Britain be resurrected by altogether excluding the Parsis.

But the European sporting press was inclined to draw an even more pessimistic conclusion from the botched attempt to construct a composite Indian cricket team. In a lengthy editorial entitled 'Love's Labour Lost', the *Bombay Gazette* observed:

> We consider that the failure of the scheme has wrought immeasurable harm to native Indian cricket, and we doubt if the home clubs will, for some years to come at all events, be willing seriously to consider a visit from an Indian team. The abandonment of the Fijian visit to England last year, after all the fixtures had been arranged, created a very bad impression in home cricket circles, but the feeling evinced there will be nothing to what will be felt when it is known that the Indian team is not coming. We cannot agree with those who opposed the carrying out of the scheme on the ground that the available team was not representative. It was perhaps not thoroughly representative . . . but we should ask if ever in the annals of the game a touring team has been thoroughly representative? This ending to a project which at the start promised to be so fruitful of success will cause great disappointment to those who really have the interests of Native Indian cricket at heart.[143]

'Judging from the experiences of the past twelve months,' the paper declared, 'we see no hope whatsoever of a Native Indian team visiting England in the near future as Parsee, Mahomedan, and Hindu cricketers will never be got to combine to make up a representative team.'[144] But the *Bombay Gazette* was to be proved wrong.

4

Reviving the Dream

I

On the evening of 30 September 1909, an unusual meeting took place at Navsari Buildings, located on the busy Hornby Road in the Fort district of Bombay. Gathered in the office of Ratan Tata, younger scion of one of India's preeminent business families, were the leading representatives of European, Hindu, Muslim, and Parsi cricket in the city. They had been invited there to consider reviving the idea of sending an Indian cricket team to Britain. In the chair was Ibrahim Rahimtulla, a prominent Ismaili industrialist, civic leader, and leading patron of the Islam Gymkhana, who kicked off the proceedings by calling upon J.M. Framjee Patel to address the meeting. Patel began his speech by quoting from a letter he had recently received from the Private Secretary to Sir George Clarke (Lord Sydenham), the Governor of Bombay. Promising official support to the idea of sending an Indian cricket team to England, the letter went on to state:

> His Excellency looks upon such a game of cricket as an excellent means of promoting mutual understanding among the different races and communities of India. At the present time the happy relations which exist between Indians and Englishmen in many forms and many places are in danger of being overlooked. It is best to emphasise these kindly relations as much as possible and His Excellency is sure that the visit of Indian cricketers to England would be most beneficial. They as good sportsmen, would meet other good sportsmen who would thoroughly appreciate them, while the people at home would be led to understand a side of the Indian character which in present circumstances they may be tempted to forget.[1]

The 'present circumstances' alluded to in the letter points to a new moment in which cricket and politics in the subcontinent once again became intertwined. For the meeting that day took place against the background of deepening political conflict between the Raj and its subjects. Notably, in the preceding two years, the growing resentment of a rising generation of Indians towards the autocratic policies of the British in India had begun to express itself in instances of physical violence directed at individual European officials. The zealous young men who perpetrated these acts saw the bomb and the gun as the only answer to India's subjugation by a foreign power.

The renewed attempt to put together a composite Indian cricket team to tour the imperial metropolis needs to be set within this wider historical context. Significantly, there was a far more explicit political rationale at work in this instance than had been the case in 1899 or 1903. Although the role of sport as a means of showcasing the bonds of empire had previously been acknowledged in a general fashion, this political imperative had come to acquire a new urgency at a time of intense racial discord between Britons and Indians.

The revival of the idea of India on the cricket field owed much to the exertions of J.M. Framjee Patel. As we have seen, Patel was widely blamed for the failure of the 1903 project to put together a combined Indian team. Gallingly for this aspiring international sporting impresario, the criticism of his actions emanated not only from those who championed the interests of Hindu and Muslim cricket, but also from the European sporting establishment and press. In the years after 1904, the project of sending the first Indian cricket team to Britain became a burning personal quest for Patel. Indeed, he became the principal mediator in the diverse coalition of interests that came together to achieve the goal that had proved so elusive. Importantly, Patel played a key role in effecting an uneasy truce between Bombay's warring Parsi and Hindu cricket clubs, without whose support his dream could not be realized. Simultaneously, attentive to the evolving international politics surrounding the imperial game, Patel saw that an Indian tour of Britain was essential if the country was to gain formal recognition within the empire of cricket.

As before, the organization of the tour drew together the Indian and European elites whose interests had coalesced around cricket in the subcontinent. However, the project also heralded a shift in the balance of power between the Anglo-Indians, on the one hand, and the Indian big bourgeoisie and native princes, on the other. Whereas the Europeans had been a significantly vocal element at the time of the 1903 venture, they played a secondary role when the idea was resuscitated six years later. This reflected the precipitous decline of European cricket in the subcontinent even as it signalled that Indian elites had begun to take charge of the country's cricketing future.

II

A few minutes past 11 p.m. on 1 July 1909, a series of revolver shots rang out in the Imperial Institute in London's South Kensington district. The sound of the firing brought to an abrupt end the annual 'At Home' organized by the National Indian Association for Indian students residing in the United Kingdom. Startled guests in the institute's Cowasji Jehangir Hall rushed out to ascertain the source of the noise and encountered a grisly sight. In one corner of the adjacent landing lay the slumped body of an Englishman, his face shattered by the four bullets fired at him from close range. A middle-aged Indian man, who had been shot in the chest, was sprawled beside him. A few feet away, a group of Englishmen and Indians had pinned to the ground a swarthy, bespectacled young man, who had ceased to resist his captors.[2]

Even as the police were summoned, those present on the spot identified the victims and perpetrator of the attack. The dead Englishman was Sir William Hutt Curzon Wyllie, political *aide-de-camp* to the Secretary of State for India. The second victim was Kavasji Lalkaka, a forty-six-year-old Parsi surgeon based in Shanghai, who succumbed to his bullet injury on the way to hospital. The man who carried out the attack was Madan Lal Dhingra, a Punjabi student pursuing an engineering degree at University College, London.

At the Westminster Police Court where his case was first heard, Dhingra astounded the press reporters with his studied coolness in the dock.[3] One reporter noted that he did not show 'the smallest trace of nervousness, his general demeanour giving one the impression of complete callousness and indifference'.[4] When he was finally allowed to speak, Dhingra read out a defiant statement that savaged British rule in India and asserted that it was 'perfectly justifiable to kill the Englishman who is polluting our sacred land'.[5]

Two weeks later, Dhingra was put on trial at the Old Bailey. The jury's verdict was swift: he was pronounced guilty and sentenced to death. Asked by the judge if he had anything further to say, Madan Lal replied: 'You can do what you like. You can pass sentence of death upon me if you like. It is perfectly illegal. You are all-powerful and can do what you like, but remember we shall have our time. That is all I have to say.'[6] He then offered a 'military style' salute and left the courtroom with the words: 'I am proud to have the honour to lay down my humble life for my country.'[7] On the morning of 17 August 1909, Dhingra was executed at London's Pentonville Prison.[8]

The assassination of Curzon Wyllie was the latest in a series of acts of revolutionary violence that had commenced two years earlier in colonial Bengal. This development was a direct outcome of the *Swadeshi* movement, which profoundly transformed Indo-British relations between 1905 and 1908.[9] As is well known, the movement was triggered by the politically motivated decision of Lord Curzon's administration to partition Bengal. When the plans for partition were first made public in December 1903, it caused an immediate outcry in that province. At first, the moderate nationalists of Bengal sought recourse to their traditional methods of prayer and petition in opposing the proposals. But after the official announcement of the Partition in July 1905, these forms of protest soon gave way to overt anti-colonial mass protests. In Calcutta and other parts of Bengal, massive public meetings were organized in which pledges were taken to boycott British-made goods. 16 October 1905, the day the Partition came into effect, was marked as a day of public mourning all over Bengal, with thousands of people parading through the streets of cities and towns singing patriotic songs and tying coloured wristlets symbolizing Bengali unity.[10] Outside Bengal, too, there was an intense upsurge of popular patriotism in Maharashtra, Punjab, Delhi, and the Andhra and Tirunelveli districts of the Madras Presidency.[11]

Over the next two years, the *Swadeshi* movement came to express itself in diverse forms of 'constructive nationalism': the establishment of indigenous schools and colleges, industrial enterprises, retail stores, and newspapers and journals. Even cricket felt the effects of the new cult of *swadeshi* as local manufacturers of bats, balls, pads, and gloves touted their nationalist credentials.[12] Some 'extremist' nationalists also called for a rejection of 'Western' sports and a return to indigenous games and pastimes.

Towards the end of 1907, however, the *Swadeshi* movement had begun to falter. On the one hand, the moves to boycott foreign goods and engage in a systematic campaign of 'passive resistance' had failed to develop and sustain mass support. On the other hand, colonial repression brought the popular movement to heel.[13] To make matters worse, the Indian National Congress was rent apart by internal divisions, resulting in an acrimonious split at its Surat session in December 1907. All this contributed to a growing mood of frustration, especially among the English-educated youth, with the existing methods of effecting political transformation.

It was in this context that some educated youth in colonial India came to espouse violence as a political tactic against the British Raj.[14] At its heart, this form of resistance was based on a philosophy of 'exemplary action' that held that the sacrifice of a brave few would inspire others to follow suit.[15] The radicals who embraced the new cult of violent action believed that foreign rule was illegitimate and that it was morally justified to deploy violence against its symbols. Accordingly, they targeted individual British officials and Indian collaborators.

From the outset, Bengal was the epicentre of the revolutionary movement, which coalesced around the secret societies called *Anushilan Samitis* based in Calcutta and Dacca.[16] The core members of the Calcutta organization founded the revolutionary weekly *Yugantar* in 1906 and launched an unsuccessful assassination attempt on Bampfylde Fuller, the highly unpopular Lieutenant-Governor of the newly created province of East Bengal. In October and December 1907, they tried in vain to blow up the train carrying Sir Andrew Fraser, the Lieutenant-Governor of the Bengal Presidency. When the revolutionaries finally succeeded in taking European lives, they got the wrong victims. On 30 April 1908, a bomb hurled at a carriage believed to be carrying Douglas Kingsford, the 'sadistic' district judge of Muzaffarpur, instead killed two European women. The police swiftly apprehended Khudiram Bose and Prafulla Chaki, the two perpetrators of the attack. In turn, this led to the discovery of the Calcutta Anushilan Samiti's 'bomb factory' located in a garden house in the city's Maniktala suburb. There now followed a further round of bloodshed. On 31 August 1908, Satyendranath Basu and Kanailal Dutta assassinated Narendranath Gossain, an accomplice turned state approver, inside Alipore Jail. Nandalal Banerji, a police subinspector who had helped to trap Prafulla Chaki, was shot dead on 9 November 1908. Three months later, Ashutosh Biswas, the public prosecutor in the Alipore conspiracy case, was killed in Calcutta. The police investigation of these events revealed the existence of several active revolutionary groups in and around the city. Meanwhile, the *Dacca Anushilan Samiti* in East Bengal had also begun to undertake daring operations against the colonial state and its Indian agents, beginning with the Barrah dacoity in June 1908.[17]

Revolutionary violence in Bengal was greeted with admiration and approval by the radicals in Maharashtra, the other bastion of political extremism in colonial India. Writing in the *Kesari*, the Maharashtrian firebrand Bal Gangadhar Tilak sought to defend the actions of Khudiram Bose and Prafulla Chaki and praised the bomb as a 'weapon of offence against unpopular officials'.[18] His articles on the Muzaffarpur murders prompted the colonial authorities to prosecute and sentence Tilak to six years' transportation to Mandalay in Burma. In the days that followed his conviction on 22 July 1908, Indian shops and markets in Bombay downed their shutters and popular anger exploded into violence on the streets of the city.[19]

★ ★ ★

Simultaneously, London became the principal base for a number of Indian radicals.[20] The key figure here was Shyamji Krishnavarma, a native of the princely state of Kutch, who emerged in these years as one of the leading Indian nationalists in Europe.[21] Krishnavarma had first come to Britain in 1879 to study at Balliol College, Oxford. He subsequently went on to pursue law at the Inner Temple in London. In 1883, Krishnavarma returned to India and took up service in a succession of princely states. However, his career as an administrator stalled in the mid-1890s after he was turned out of Udaipur, a move that was orchestrated by its British Resident, Colonel Curzon-Wyllie. This personal humiliation rendered Krishnavarma receptive to Bal Gangadhar Tilak's brand of militant nationalism. But following the government's crackdown on seditious activities in India, he left for Britain.[22]

Soon after his arrival in London, Krishnavarma became friendly with an assortment of British socialists, Irish republicans, and other political activists opposed to imperial rule.[23] In 1905, he took a series of initiatives that established his radical nationalist credentials. At the suggestion of the British socialist Henry Mayers Hyndman, Krishnavarma started the Indian Home Rule Society in January that year. The aims of the society were to secure 'home rule' for India and to carry out 'genuine Indian propaganda' in Britain in the pursuit of this cause.[24] By the end of its first year, the Indian Home Rule Society had attracted more than a hundred members.[25] Its meetings passed resolutions criticizing colonial policies in India and also sought to commemorate the anniversary of what they termed the 'Indian national rising' of 1857.[26] The ideological mouthpiece of the society was a monthly journal edited by Krishnavarma called the *Indian Sociologist*. In its inaugural issue, the journal declared that it would 'remind the British people that they can never succeed in being a nation of freedom and lovers of freedom so long as they continue to send out members of the dominant classes to exercise despotisms in Britain's name upon the various conquered races that constitute Britain's military empire'.[27]

In July 1905, Krishnavarma established 'India House'—a hostel for students and other political visitors from the subcontinent—at 65 Cromwell

Avenue in the Highgate district of north London.[28] Towards the end of that year, he also endowed six lectureships to enable 'authors, journalists and other qualified Indians to visit Europe, America and other parts of the world beyond the limits of India'.[29] One of the recipients of these travelling fellowships was Vinayak Damodar Savarkar, a twenty-two-year-old Chitpavan Brahmin from Nasik. Savarkar, who had graduated from Poona's Fergusson College, had been deeply enmeshed in radical nationalist politics in Maharashtra prior to his departure for London in June 1906. In particular, he was one of the founders of *Abhinava Bharat*, a revolutionary secret society modelled on Mazzini's Young Italy Society, which played an active role in the *Swadeshi* movement in western India.[30]

By the summer of 1907, the political activities at India House began to attract public attention in Britain. Official surveillance and public scrutiny had prompted Shyamji Krishnavarma to move to Paris.[31] Savarkar now emerged as the leader of India House.[32] He established the London branch of the Free India Society at 65 Cromwell Avenue and began to actively engage in revolutionary propaganda. Savarkar led regular Sunday meetings that met to discuss the political situation in India and to consider strategies and tactics for the overthrow of British rule in the subcontinent. He began the practice of celebrating Dussehra and Diwali and commemorating the lives of Indian martial heroes like Shivaji and Guru Gobind Singh. The annual 'Martyrs' Day' in honour of the 1857 Indian Uprising was also scaled up and began to attract Indian students from across Britain.[33] Simultaneously, Savarkar frenetically worked on a history of the Great Rebellion, which he regarded as the first nationalist 'war of independence'. Chapters from his manuscript were avidly read and discussed at the weekly gatherings at India House.[34] Unlike Krishnavarma, moreover, Savarkar did not restrict himself to preaching. On the contrary, he constantly kept in touch with the world of Indian politics, clandestinely sending a steady supply of revolutionary literature and arms to the subcontinent. He also despatched to Paris one of his accomplices, Pandurang Bapat, to learn the art of bomb making.[35]

Among the young men who had gathered around Savarkar at this time was the twenty-five-year-old Madan Lal Dhingra, a regular participant in the Sunday meetings at India House.[36] The well-dressed Punjabi, who came from a prosperous professional family based in Amritsar, already nurtured deep resentment against the British.[37] He had begun to chafe at the constant revolutionary talk at India House, and yearned to undertake an act of violence that would inspire others to follow suit. In the spring of 1909, the Punjabi student began to stay aloof from his old associates at India House and instead began revolver practice at an establishment called *Funland* on the Tottenham Court Road. By late June, he had acquired considerable proficiency in the use of his newly purchased 32-calibre Colt automatic pistol.[38]

At this point, Dhingra appears to have been goaded into action by Savarkar, who was highly inflamed by the conviction of his brother Ganesh in a sedition case at Nasik.[39] Their initial target for assassination may have been Lord Curzon, but in the end the Indians settled on Curzon Wyllie.[40] Late in the afternoon of 1 July 1909, Dhingra went to the revolver range at Tottenham Court Road and, as usual, fired twelve shots with his pistol. At a quarter to nine that night he left his lodgings at 108 Ledbury Avenue, Bayswater, and made the journey by taxi to the Imperial Institute where the National Indian Association was holding its annual social reception.[41] Savarkar had prudently left London for Reading, but one of his acolytes—a Maharashtrian named Koregaonkar—is alleged to have accompanied the would-be assassin to the Imperial Institute to stiffen his resolve.[42] Dhingra had forgotten to carry along his invitation to the event, but as a registered member of the association he was allowed to enter the venue without hindrance. Inside the Cowasji Jehangir Hall, Dhingra mingled with the mixed crowd of British and Indian guests, none of whom were aware that the turban-clad young man in their midst had concealed two automatic revolvers and a dagger in his dark lounge suit. Sir Curzon Wyllie and his wife were late arrivals at the reception, having spent the earlier part of the evening dining at the Savoy Hotel with Sir Currimbhoy Ebrahim, the prominent Khoja industrialist from Bombay. The proceedings were scheduled to terminate at midnight, but by eleven o'clock the party had begun to peter out and the Wyllies made their way out of Jehangir Hall. Sir Currimbhoy escorted Lady Wyllie to the cloakroom. Her husband was about to follow, when a young man wearing large gold-rimmed spectacles intercepted him.[43]

III

The double murder at the Imperial Institute and the trial of Madan Lal Dhingra created a public sensation in Britain. For a society that prided itself on its liberal political culture, the assassination of Curzon Wyllie came as a rude shock. The spectre of sedition in colonial India acquired a new prominence in metropolitan political discourse. Dhingra's act crystallized sharply in the public consciousness what came to be known as the 'Indian Unrest'. Since Savarkar was as yet unknown, many British observers chose to see in these events the shadowy machinations of Shyamji Krishnavarma. 'He has caught the young Oriental at an impressionable age and persuaded him that the short cut to Paradise is through a pool of Anglo-Indian blood,' thundered one newspaper.[44] Interviewed in Paris, Krishnavarma refrained from expressing any views on Dhingra, but argued nonetheless that political assassinations were not a crime in the ordinary sense.[45] The press promptly construed his statement as irrefutable proof that the founder of India House was behind the killing of Curzon Wyllie.

Tabloids in the British capital also gave free rein to the wildest speculation about fanatical Indian secret cells that were supposedly plotting dastardly deeds. Thus, the *Daily Express* declared that Dhingra's action proved 'beyond doubt the existence of a dangerous Indian terrorist organisation in London'. The Indian, it was claimed, 'belonged to a band of young men who have associated themselves together under the name of the "Sons of Siva"'. The paper helpfully reminded its readers that Siva was a Hindu deity 'with wild and terrible attributes'. The 'Sons of Siva' were said to meet secretly in the backrooms of Bayswater and Bloomsbury, 'seldom twice in succession at the same place'. And since no outsider could gain admission to these meetings, the 'difficulty of obtaining direct evidence against these terrorists is very great'.[46] Of course, such allegations did not need any firm basis; in fact, it was enough to deploy the familiar tropes of Orientalist discourse. 'When they work abroad it is with Orientalist insidiousness,' asserted the *Daily Express*. 'A little poison poured in the ear of a young student whose mind is inflamed with ideals about liberty and the wrongs of his own race, is in their view far more effective and far less dangerous to themselves than the holding of meetings to advocate Home Rule for India.' These Indian conspirators were also alleged to have spewed their venom 'in the form of insulting and scurrilous communications sent to distinguished Anglo-Indians and signed "The Sons of Siva"'.[47]

The events of 1 July 1909 also led many in Britain to declare that the liberal project of 'civilizing' the native had proved to be an utter failure. In this view, the brutal murder of Curzon Wyllie showed that Western values had failed to take root in an inherently 'primitive' society. In the words of the *Penny Illustrated Paper*:

The people are intensely conservative and intensely ignorant, wedded to every ancient custom to an extent difficult for Europeans to understand, and between their customs and religion no line of distinction can be drawn. We often deceive ourselves with regard to the changes that are taking place. We believe that our Western knowledge, our railways, and our telegraphs must be break-ing up the whole fabric of Hinduism, but these things have touched only the merest fringe of the ideas and beliefs of the population of India. The vast masses of the people remain in a different world from ours. They hate every-thing new, especially hate almost everything we look up as progress and they live for the most part in blind ignorance of the aims and ideas of their practice. The average 'native of India' in the country districts is as much a savage as the average European at the time of the Roman Empire.[48]

The assertion that British and Indian values were radically incommensurable led the conservative press to call for new restrictions on the free movement of people between the two countries. From this perspective, their exposure to Western culture and mores had served to accentuate rather than dispel the antipathy of the colonized to British society. In an extended reflection on the presence of Indian students in Britain, the *Daily Telegraph* noted:

The old friendly relations in England have been disturbed, and the question by which we are now confronted involves hardly less than a complete recon-sideration of our policy in this matter. If this easy welcome into English life is becoming the source of ultimate dissatisfaction to the Indian student and danger to ourselves, it seems clear that some modifications will have to be introduced into the present system. The Indian Government has for some time past set its fact against the frequent presence in England of the native chiefs. It is hardly logical, therefore, for us to encourage the sojourn here of other natives, whose capacity for doing good or harm is often greater than that of the ordinary chief.[49]

For other conservative commentators, the assassination of Curzon Wyllie demonstrated that the only effective means of dealing with Indian 'sedition' was through an unalloyed use of force. 'Orientals are not deterred from murder by that fear of death which pre-eminently characterises Christian nations,' an old Madras Civilian wrote in the *Fortnightly Review*. For all the veneer of Western learning, he argued, the 'educated classes in our Oriental Empire...are still Orientals, and have deep down in their inmost hearts an ineradicable feeling that a ruler who does not exercise absolute power has not got the one essential attribute of sovereignty.' As a consequence, the Indian *babu* had 'grown to doubt whether the British Government have the power to punish sedition since they have so long allowed the serpent to raise its head unchecked in different parts of the thrones, dominations, princedoms and powers included in that spacious whole which for convenience sake we call India'.[50] Such views conveniently glossed over the extraordinary augmentation in these years of the colonial state's powers of political surveillance and repression.

Equally, the belief that outright force was the only viable strategy of governance in India led such observers to question even the barest concessions to educated Indian opinion. Indeed, they attacked ferociously the modest dose of constitutional reform piloted through parliament earlier that summer by the Lord Morley, the Secretary of State for India, working in tandem with the Viceroy, Lord Minto. The Indian Councils Act of 1909 introduced a heavily circumscribed elective principle in legislative councils, more powers to discuss the budget, the entry of an Indian into the Viceroy's Executive Council, and most controversially, the principle of separate electorates for Muslims. These measures were intended to defuse 'Indian unrest' and 'rally the moderates' in the Congress. Yet the old India hands sought to portray them as a sign of weakness and attacked the Liberal government for its alleged pusillanimity in tackling 'sedition'.

The fulminations of the conservative press in Britain echoed the views expressed by influential sections of the bureaucratic establishment and European press in colonial India. As the Aligarh politician, Mohammed Ali wrote, for the reactionary sections of the British Raj, 'every concession made to the people is a sign of weakness incompatible with the glory of the imperial race of rulers to which they belong'. 'Liable to scares, whether cholera be the cause or mango-tree daubing,' he acerbically added, 'they would like to issue ball cartridges to the troops twice a year to suppress another mutiny.'[51]

IV

It is against this fraught political backdrop that we need to view the revival of the proposal to send an Indian cricket team to Britain. Its principal backers regarded the tour as a way of affirming the imperial bond at a time of intense mutual antipathy and antagonism between the rulers and the ruled. Equally, they sought to promote a reassuring image of India in Britain and thereby counter the pervasive rhetoric of ineradicable colonial difference.

The men who gathered in Ratan Tata's office on 30 September 1909 saw themselves as 'British Indians'. That is to say, they believed in the providential nature of the British connection and viewed with concern the growing political chasm between the representatives of the Raj and the new generation of radical nationalists. On the one hand, they were highly critical of the racial arrogance and exclusivity of Anglo-Indian officialdom. On the other hand, they opposed the violent methods deployed by the Indian revolutionaries. In the face of this polarization, these Indians called for fraternity in the public sphere. 'Political expansion can wait; participation in administration may be ushered in by degrees; the drain to Europe may continue,' declared Mohammed Ali. 'But the reform that cannot wait but must come, now and to-day, the account in which India is exacting, and the drain which she cannot tolerate any longer, is the Social one. Unprepared for unrestricted liberty, unqualified for absolute equality, India has always been ready and ripe for genuine fraternity.'[52]

Framjee Patel, in particular, saw sport as ideally suited for promoting fraternal feelings between the imperial rulers and their Indian subjects. Notably, in the spring of 1905, he published a history of Indian cricket—dedicated to his 'guru' Lord Harris—whose final chapter dwelt on the game's significance for imperial politics.[53] Here, Patel observed that 'the social gulf in India is every day widening, owing to the many antipathetic influences at work'. However, he argued, cricket was 'one of the most effectual means of bringing the rulers and ruled closely together'. Although he acknowledged that there had been 'friction' on the field of play—recalling, no doubt, the ill-tempered exchanges between Parsis and Europeans in the 1890s—Patel nonetheless believed that cricket was an 'effective peace-maker, and the men who are engaged in honourable and keen rivalry for a while cannot but be friends in the end, when the discordant notes have died away owing to the healthy influences of the game itself'. 'In the end,' he declared, 'cricket will heal racial antagonism.'[54]

Equally, he suggested, fraternizing on the playing field could forge shared values between the colonizers and the colonized. The history of the imperial game in the subcontinent, he contended, showed that it wielded 'an influence, even beyond its social, physical and disciplinary value, in breaking down artificial barriers and knitting all races and classes into a common citizenship'. Moreover, like many Anglophone Indians of his generation, Patel also believed that Britishness was a cultural acquisition, not a racial identity. The values represented by cricket, in his view, were integral to Britishness, and since Indians had shown real passion for the game, they too were no less British than the white settlers of Australia and South Africa. He therefore implored the official representatives of the Raj to draw appropriate lessons from the Indian adoption of this quintessentially English game. 'Educated Indians,' he asserted, 'are quite alive to their Imperial destiny and yearn to share with their white fellow subjects the rights and privileges of their great heritage, along with the burdens.'[55]

Framjee Patel had welcomed the Morley-Minto reforms as a sign of the 'liberal' intentions of the British government.[56] Like other empire loyalists, he no doubt viewed with alarm the assassination of Curzon Wyllie and the damage it was likely to inflict on Indo-British relations. A few days before the meeting in Ratan Tata's office, he travelled with a team of Parsi cricketers to Poona to play the annual match against the Governor of Bombay's side. It is more than likely that on this occasion Patel discussed with Sir George Clarke his intention to resurrect the project of sending an Indian cricket team to Britain. Such a visit, Patel probably reasoned, would offer an opportunity to present India in a light that would appeal to British opinion and thereby counter the pervasive discourse about 'Indian sedition'. 'In fact,' the *Bombay Gazette* noted some months later, 'it may safely be asserted that this was the prime motive of the whole project. If the tour assists towards removing to some extent at least, the misunderstanding between the ruling nation and the governed, it will have done an immense service to both England and India.'[57]

V

But Framjee Patel's attempt to revive the idea of India on the cricket field was as much a personal quest for exoneration as it was a political project to improve Indo-British relations in the fractious climate of the late Edwardian era. As we have seen, Patel had been vociferously attacked by sections of the Anglo-Indian and Gujarati press for his role in scuppering the venture to send an Indian cricket team to England in 1904. These critics had refused to accept Patel's explanation that it was a lack of sufficient funds that had led the organizers to abandon the project. Dark rumours had swirled of how Patel and the other Parsis on the organizing committee had deliberately sought to sabotage the tour because they were unhappy about the Hindu and Muslim claims for parity in the team's composition.

The insinuation that he had placed loyalty to his community over the greater good of Indian cricket appears to have stung Patel deeply. In his book, he sought to refute the allegations about the role of the Parsis in the affair. Noting that the Parsis 'were blamed for the failure of the trip by certain infatuated enthusiasts', he argued that they had been 'actuated by honest motives in opposing the scheme'.[58] 'Though nobody was more anxious to send an Indian team to England in 1904 than I,' Patel wrote, 'still my humble opinion is that to send a weak team and without the requisite sinews of war would be a fatal mistake, inasmuch as instead of helping Indian cricket it would throw it back many years.' However, he assured his readers, the dream of sending an Indian team to England would someday 'be an accomplished fact'.[59]

In April 1906, Framjee Patel travelled from Bombay to Britain. The trip was ostensibly for medical reasons, but prior to his departure Patel made known his intention to arrange, with the support of Ranji, 'the preliminaries for a visit of a representative team of Parsee, Hindu, Mahomedan and Ceylonese cricketers'. The scepticism with which the news was greeted by the Anglo-Indian press showed how Patel had lost a great deal of goodwill amongst his erstwhile supporters in the European sporting establishment. A correspondent for the *Englishman* was swift to express his doubts:

> I am afraid that the very mention of raising sinews of war by public subscription spells failure for the scheme as the various communities are so jealous of each other that it is hopeless to look for a spontaneous response to such an appeal. Apart from the question of finances there is the even more important one of the personal influence of the organisers of a project such as that under discussion. Mr. Patel's influence in the Indian cricket world is confined to his own community, while K.S. Ranjitsinhji far from identifying himself with native Indian cricket has systematically declined to be in any way associated with the hopes and ambitions of native cricketers.[60]

However, Framjee Patel was greeted with greater warmth in Britain. He was invited by Lord Harris to stay at his home at Belmont. He also met Lord Hawke, who had returned from a winter visit to India earlier that year. The support of the most influential cricketing aristocrats in the land ensured that Patel was made an honorary member of the MCC and Surrey CCC. Furthermore, his presence in Britain attracted the attention of the British sporting press. *Cricket*, the premier journal dedicated to the imperial game, ran a cover story on him in June 1906 in which he was described as the 'Nestor of Parsi cricket'. His interviewer was none other than Charles

Alcock, the man who had helped facilitate the Parsi cricket tours of Britain two decades earlier. Alcock took the opportunity to laud the 'work the Patels have done to acclimatise and consolidate the greatest of all games in Western India'. In particular, he lamented the death of A.B. Patel, 'under whose personal guidance...the pioneer team of Parsee cricketers came to England in 1886—beyond a doubt the most enterprising and ambitious cricket mission so far recorded in the history of the game'.[61]

Framjee Patel clearly revelled in his role as Indian cricket's principal spokesman. In his press interviews, he described the rapid progress that the sport had made among the different communities in India. He took care to praise the role of 'sporting Anglo-Indians', especially the patronage and support of successive British governors of the Bombay Presidency. Above all, he used these interviews to drum up public interest in a future Indian cricket tour. Aware that the botched venture of 1904 had not been forgotten in Britain, Patel stuck to his usual line of defence. The tour, he smoothly

Photo by Bholenath.

J M. Framjee Patel.

Figure 8. J.M. Framjee Patel, *c.* 1905. By the mid-1900s, this influential Parsi had emerged as the principal spokesman for Indian cricket. Courtesy of Marylebone Cricket Club Library.

explained, had been abandoned owing to 'the fact that several of the best players could not go that year, and, what was of even greater importance, that the finances were not in a condition to warrant the risks incidental to such a tour'.[62] Drawing a veil over the bitter infighting that had marred the project, Patel portrayed the decision to jettison it as a consensual one, arrived at by 'the majority of the committee which was representative of Anglo-Indian as well as of native cricket'. However, Patel was quick to assure his British audience that Indian cricket was getting its act together. Thus, he declared confidently that 'such a visit will take place in the near future in spite of many and obvious difficulties'. And, as usual, he proceeded to invoke the name of Ranji, 'who has shown great interest in the matter'.[63] For, as Patel well knew, the most effective way of arousing public interest in Britain in an Indian cricket tour was to draw on the magic of Ranji's celebrity.

Even as Patel was talking up the prospect of an Indian cricketing visit to Britain, a West Indian cricket team was already touring the country. This was the second time—the first occasion was in 1900—a combined squad representing the nations of the Caribbean travelled to Britain. Organized by the West Indian Club in London, the tour sought to promote intercolonial union as well as closer ties with the Mother Country. The team included both whites and blacks, and 'racial inclusivity' was a key theme in the way the tour itself was promoted by its backers. At a welcome dinner for the cricketers organized by the West Indian Club in London on 10 June 1906, its vice-president, Sir Cavendish Boyle, referred to them as 'West Indian Anglo-Saxons' who would 'add another link in the chain friendship, the chain of oneness and whole-heartedness, which binds the sons of Great Britain with the children of the Greater Britains in that undefeated, aye, undaunted whole—our United Empire'.[64]

Sir Cavendish's words would no doubt have resonated with Framjee Patel. Two weeks later, Surrey CCC hosted a dinner at the Kennington Oval in honour of the Caribbean cricketers. Also present on this occasion was Framjee Patel, in whose honour the assembled guests raised a toast. Dwelling on the imperial value of cricket, Patel expressed his hope that before long 'a third Indian team would visit England, consisting not only of Parsees, but other sections of the country'. Ranji, he reminded his audience yet again, 'had kindly promised to act as captain'.[65]

Given Ranji's track record in the matter, however, it is hard to believe that this was a promise that he intended to keep. As it transpired, a few weeks after Patel had made his speech at the Oval, the prince's floundering bid for the Nawanagar throne was reinvigorated by an unexpected development. On 14 August 1906, Jassaji, the reigning Jam Saheb, died in mysterious circumstances. Although typhoid was officially stated as the cause of death, many suspected that he had been poisoned by one of the factions at his intrigue-ridden court.[66] As the twenty-four-year-old Jassaji had left no heirs, the succession to the Nawanagar throne once again became a bone of contention. Ranji, who had been in India since November 1904, swiftly seized his chance. On 11 September1906, he submitted a new petition to the colonial government staking his claim as the rightful heir.[67] He was not the only one to make his case: Lakhuba, a grandson of Vibhaji, and Jassaji's widows, too, had petitioned the ruling authorities to the same end.[68] Confronted with these competing claims, the Raj took time to arrive at a decision. As the agonizing wait continued through the winter of 1906, it is unlikely that Ranji had much appetite for cricket.

Ranji's preoccupation with his struggle to become the new Jam of Nawanagar ruled out the prospect of his involvement in Framjee Patel's scheme. Nonetheless, rumours continued to circulate about an impending Indian tour of Britain. 'The reader would remember that for some time a proposal is before the public of fitting and sending out a representative Indian team to compete with Englishmen in their national game of cricket,' the *Amrita Bazar Patrika* stated in December 1906. 'We hear in this connection that a patriotic Indian gentleman of Bombay has promised Rs. 20,000, several English counties too have promised subsidies, so that the proposal appears to make headway.'[69] It is the last we hear of the venture.

VI

While nationalist newspapers eagerly anticipated the day when an Indian cricket team would play against the colonizers on their home turf, the most reactionary sections of the European press had begun to regard this aspiration with a jaundiced eye. 'The experiment, if it is ever made,' noted the *Asian* in August 1906,

> will simply bring ridicule upon the game in India. We feel confident that no Indian team would be equal to the task of making a hundred runs against the weakest of the first-class counties under the ordinary English conditions and while admitting that Indian bowlers would perhaps do better than the batsmen, we doubt if they would get a first-class county eleven out in a full day's play.

The paper added that while it was not averse to the idea of an Indian cricket team touring Britain, 'the time for this is not yet ripe, and never will be unless the leading Indian cricketers put aside all jealous feelings and work together with the common object in view of improving their play'.[70] This was by no means a lone view. Even Lord Harris, a longstanding patron of Framjee Patel, declared in an interview to *Cricket* in November 1906 that 'caste custom, caste prejudice and racial prejudice' made the prospect of a composite Indian team highly unlikely.[71]

Such pejorative remarks about the hold of caste and community on the Indian mind were, of course, the staple fare of colonial discourse about the subcontinent. Nonetheless, it is undeniable that in the early 1900s cricketing encounters in cosmopolitan Bombay were increasingly marred by communal animosity. In particular, the cricket field had emerged as a site of conflict between the Parsis and other Indian communities. 'Talking of envy versus emulation,' the *Indian Spectator* remarked in August 1898,

> it is with pain that we have noted the increasing tendency amongst all the other classes of Natives to gloat over the defeats of the Parsis by the Europeans. It is said that this is the result of bitter memories of the past—of the days when the Parsi was irritatingly proud of his championship of cricket in India and when he took no pains to conceal his contempt for Hindu and Mahomedan cricket.

'Paying back of old scores may be sweet, but it is not noble,' the paper remonstrated. 'Nor is it the way to progress onward. It will not be by the fall of the Parsis that Hindu or Mahomedan cricket will rise. The time is come for a friendly spirit amongst all.'[72]

However, few appear to have paid heed to such sentiments. In particular, local cricket matches in Bombay between the Parsis and the Hindus came to acquire a keen edge as players and partisans on either side sought to needle the other. In October 1901, a closely contested match between the Hindu Gymkhana and Baronet CC, one of the strongest Parsi sides in the city, ended in a violent clash between the supporters of the two teams. The match was played on the Hindu Gymkhana's home ground at Marine Lines and was marred by contentious decisions by the umpires nominated by each side. The most controversial of these came when the Parsis were fifteen runs short, with only two wickets in hand, of the Hindus' total of 119. At this critical juncture, the Hindu umpire upheld an appeal for leg before wicket against Bapasola, the Parsi batsman who appeared to be steering his team to a famous win. 'The decision of the umpire was considered to be erroneous,' reported the *Bombay Gazette*, 'and appeared to have so worked upon the minds of a portion of the spectators, that they rushed into the field and questioned the umpire's decision. The Hindus opposed them and a scuffle ensued in which several persons are said to have been hurt.'[73] There now followed the inevitable letters to the Anglo-Indian newspapers by representatives of both sides, each accusing the other of deliberately misrepresenting the facts.[74]

The controversies generated by such intemperate sporting encounters vitiated relations between the two communities. For example, when the Hindus played against the visiting Oxford Authentics in November 1902, the match was notable for the ill feeling between the Parsi and Hindu spectators. Recalling this contest in his book, Cecil Headlam referred to 'the unseemly behaviour of a large section of the Parsee crowd, who displayed their jealousy of the Hindus by "barracking" them disgracefully when in the field or at the wicket'. 'We had had some warning of the jealousy that exists between the two races of cricketers, and which is, one could not help feeling, a little too keen to be quite healthy, during the Presidency match,' Headlam remarked.[75]

The promoters and supporters of Hindu cricket also grew increasingly frustrated that the Parsis sided with the Europeans in disregarding their claims to parity. 'The Hindus have a grievance and a very real one, too, in that neither the Parsis nor the Presidency will give them a chance of figuring in representative cricket,' noted the sports correspondent of the *Bombay Gazette* in August 1902. It was the perceived perfidy of the Parsis, in particular, that rankled with the Hindus. 'The committee of the Hindu Gymkhana,' the *Gazette* reported, 'have tried hard to arrange a fixture which should become an annual one, between teams representative of Hindu and Parsi cricket in the Presidency, but on each occasion that the subject has been brought up, the Parsis have raised all kinds of obstacles.'[76]

The tensions between the Hindus and the Parsis on the organizing committee were an important factor in the decision to abandon the project of sending the first Indian cricket team to Britain in 1904. The rancour generated by the collapse of this venture drove a further wedge in Hindu-Parsi cricketing relations. The conflict between the elite patrons and administrators of the game was mirrored at the grassroots in the everyday cricketing encounters between the two communities. Cricket matches involving Bombay's Hindu and Parsi clubs became sullen affairs. Matters took a turn for the worse in September 1904, when the Hindu Gymkhana unilaterally passed a resolution cancelling all cricket fixtures with Parsi clubs. It justified this sudden move by pointing to the increasingly unruly behaviour of Parsi spectators during club matches. In April 1905, all the Hindu clubs ratified their gymkhana's decision and agreed not to play against *any* Parsi cricket club.[77]

The retaliation was swift in coming. At a meeting held at the Parsi Gymkhana in May 1905, a call was issued to all the Parsi clubs in the city to refrain from initiating any fixtures against the Hindu Gymkhana without prior approval of their cricketing co-religionists.[78] Some Parsi newspapers welcomed their response. The decision of the local Parsi cricket clubs to boycott the Hindu Gymkhana was 'not arrived at, a day too soon', declared *Rast Goftar*. 'It is a matter of regret that the supremacy of the Parsee on the cricket field in India, should be the cause of some heart-burnings in some native communities.'[79]

Other observers called for a truce. 'We are dismayed by the narrow-mindedness displayed by both sides in the matter,' stated the *Kaiser-i-Hind*. 'The game of cricket should increase unity and not deepen discord.' The paper urged the warring parties to 'forswear conflict' and show 'broad-mindedness and generosity'.[80] 'It is very regrettable,' agreed the *Praja Bandhu*, 'that a high feeling between the Parsees and the Hindus should be a normal feature of Bombay, and that anything should be done to increase the existing tension.'[81]

But such strictures were to no avail. In the months that followed, the city's Hindu and Parsi cricket clubs ceased to play against each other. 'It is a pity that the Bombay public should have been robbed of the pleasure afforded by the most interesting cricket matches between the Hindus and the Parsees,' lamented one contemporary to the *Times of India* in September 1905. 'Games are played to bring different communities into closer contact and not to create inimical feelings between each of them.'[82]

In February 1906, the Hindus finally achieved their long-cherished goal of playing a cricket match against the Bombay Presidency. The historic victory of the Hindus in this encounter, which took place on the Bombay Gymkhana's ground, showed that the Parsis could no longer treat lightly the Hindu claims for cricketing parity. A few days after the match, the Bombay Gymkhana attempted to broker a truce between the Parsi Gymkhana and the Hindu Gymkhana.[83] The meeting, which was attended by Framjee Patel and other leading figures from both gymkhanas, appeared to have thawed the ice between the two sides. 'We have learnt with much pleasure that the little misunderstanding between Parsi and Hindu cricketers has been settled and that they are to hold a match next September between themselves,' reported the *Indian Social Reformer*. 'There are so many excellent reasons why Hindus and Parsis should pull on well together that we, for one, have never been able to understand why there should ever arise any misunderstanding between them,' it added.[84]

Matters appeared to be progressing smoothly when the Hindu Gymkhana formally passed a resolution in April 1906 rescinding its earlier decision not to play against the Parsis.[85] To the surprise of many observers, however, the local Parsi cricket clubs responded coldly to this move. At a meeting held at the Parsi Gymkhana the following month, a majority of its members voted against the withdrawal of its previous resolution. They justified this response on the grounds that the Hindu Gymkhana had not shown sufficient contrition for the 'abrupt way' in which it had previously cancelled its fixtures with the Parsi cricket clubs. Interestingly, the official cricket committee of the Parsi Gymkhana had called for a more conciliatory response and 'dissented from the resolution passed by the majority of the representatives of local clubs'.[86] In other words, while the elites within both communities were ready to come to an understanding, the bitterness between the ordinary cricketers on both sides was not so easily dissipated.

A few days after the local Parsi clubs' decision became known, the Hindu cricketers of Bombay held a meeting at the Hindu Gymkhana and resolved that they too would make no further attempts to reach out to their opponents. 'A further deadlock has thus been created,' observed the *Times of India*, 'and there seems to be no immediate prospect of a representative match between the two communities.' 'Even at this hour,' the paper added, 'an amicable settlement and reconciliation should not be difficult to arrive at, for the present misunderstanding ought easily to be cleared by the exercise of a little broad-mindedness and common sense on both sides.'[87]

★ ★ ★

When he returned to Bombay in the autumn of 1906, Framjee Patel would have undoubtedly regarded the Hindu-Parsi conflict as one of the key impediments to achieving his goal of assembling a composite Indian cricket team. He now set out to make peace between the two sides. J.M. Divecha, the honorary secretary of the Parsi Gymkhana, and M.E. Pavri, the Parsi captain, supported Patel in his efforts to reach out to the Hindu Gymkhana. On 28 March 1907, a crucial meeting took place at the Parsi Gymkhana between the representatives of the leading Parsi clubs and the Hindu Gymkhana. Its aim was 'to take preliminary steps to rescind the former resolution passed by the Hindu Gymkhana as well as by the Parsee local clubs against playing match [sic] with one another, and to restore the old fixtures between the two communities'.[88] Framjee Patel acted as the chair and 'in a few impressive words urged the meeting to do their duty by Indian cricket—the Hindus by withdrawing their resolution, and the Parsees doing the same. They would thus open the door for a reconciliation honourable to both sides, and it would be in the true interests of Indian cricket.' Next, Divecha took to the floor 'and pointed out that triangular contests between the Presidency, Parsees and Hindus would provide a cricketing carnival for the public during the coming seasons, and that desirable object it was necessary that the former resolutions should be rescinded'. The Hindu representatives, for their part, said that 'they were quite willing to restore the friendly relations between the two communities, but were afraid of the feeling that the crowd might show during local matches'. The meeting ended with a joint statement by both parties in which they agreed to rescind their former resolutions and once again arrange matches with each other.[89]

Both sides kept their word. At their annual general meeting two months later, the Hindu Gymkhana withdrew 'their previous resolution prohibiting cricket matches with the Parsi cricket clubs and a copy of that resolution was duly communicated to the Bombay Parsi Gymkhana'.[90] The latter returned the compliment by authorizing their fixtures committee to arrange matches with the Hindu Gymkhana. Framjee Patel presided over a meeting of the local Parsi cricket clubs and entreated them 'to let bygones be bygones, and act in the common interest of the game with amity, unity and good sense'.[91]

The Bombay press responded ecstatically to the news of this *entente cordiale* between the two parties. 'The clouds hovering over Parsi-Hindu matches have lifted and the rays of brotherhood have shone through. This should cause great satisfaction among the well-wishers of Indian cricket,' declared the *Kaiser-i-Hind*. The paper blamed 'unscrupulous individuals of both communities' for 'sowing the seeds of bitterness between Hindu and Parsi cricketers'.[92] 'We have no desire to refer to old misunderstandings,' said the *Times of India*, 'except to congratulate both the Parsis and the Hindus on the sporting manner in which they have settled their disputes, and in this connection the thanks of all cricketers are due to those gentlemen who assisted in the task of reconciliation.'[93]

The *Times of India* made these remarks in the run-up to Bombay's new Triangular cricket tournament featuring Hindu, Parsi, and European teams. The historic inaugural match between the Hindus and the Parsis, held at the Bombay Gymkhana in August 1907, attracted 'an immense crowd of spectators'. 'The seating accommodation in the Gymkhana pavilion and Byculla and Bombay Club tents was well patronised, and the tents erected by the Parsi and Hindu cricket clubs were packed with enthusiastic supporters,' reported one Bombay newspaper. 'The behaviour of the crowd was excellent,' it added, 'there were no signs of barracking, and all good play was impartially applauded.'[94]

For Framjee Patel, the reconciliation between the Hindu and Parsi cricketers represented a major step forward in achieving his goal of an Indian cricket team. But it was a fragile peace and the prospect of a clash between rival supporters could never be ruled out when the two sides met on the cricket pitch. Indeed, in late August 1909, only weeks before the momentous meeting at Navsari Buildings, we come across the following report in the *Tribune*:

> An unfortunate incident occurred between the Hindu and Parsi spectators on the conclusion of the match between the Hindu Gymkhana and the Baronet Cricket Club on Sunday. Widely different versions are given as to how the fracas originated. One version of the story is that the unfavourable decision of the Hindu umpire incensed the Parsi spectators, of whom the lowly element made a rush towards the Hindu pavilion, intercepted the Hindu umpire and belaboured him with sticks and umbrellas, as well as other Hindus who came in the way with sticks. Another version is that only a few youngsters made a rush for the Hindu pavilion to give vent to their enthusiasm for the fine bowling of their co-religionists and consequent collapse of the last Hindu batsmen, and that it was a few low caste Hindus that started the trouble by making a rush at the Parsi crowds and flourishing sticks at them, that the Parsis fought merely in self-defence and that the injury received by the umpire might have been inflicted with Hindu sticks as the fight had soon turned into an indiscriminate melee. About half a dozen persons on both sides received injuries and some were removed to the hospital. Information was given to the police who promptly turned [up] and dispersed the crowd.[95]

Reflecting on the affray, one 'Native Thinker' wrote, 'Cricket and other sports are rightly recommended as great levellers. But I doubt whether their claims to promote brotherly feelings can be unreservedly accepted. The intense desire of each nationality for the success of its own representative degenerates on occasions into passionate partisanship leading to discreditable scenes.' This writer therefore welcomed the revival of the project to put together a composite Indian cricket team to tour Britain. 'In an eleven consisting of Hindus, Parsis, and Moslems,' he remarked, 'each one will instinctively feel that he is an Indian first, and a member of their own race afterwards; and all being animated by one common impulse, it will result in co-operation and also as surely in the promotion of cordiality.'[96]

VII

Even as Framjee Patel devoted his energies to the task of creating fraternal relations between communities in the domestic sphere, he closely followed international developments that were concurrently transforming the empire of cricket. In particular, the Parsi impresario watched with keen interest as South Africa made a brazen attempt to become part of 'an imperial crick-eting triumvirate of Test playing countries' organized under a new 'Imperial Board of Cricket Control' based in London.[97] This development owed much to the initiative of the powerful Transvaal-based mining magnate, landowner and press baron Abraham ('Abe') Bailey (1864–1940), who was primarily responsible for South Africa's growing cricketing prominence in the late Edwardian era.[98]

After the end of the Anglo-Boer War, Bailey sought to use cricket to promote a South African national identity based on close ties with imper-ial Britain. Notably, he deployed his resources to hire talented British players to play for the Transvaal cricket team, transforming it in the process into the 'stronghold of South African cricket' by the mid-1900s. In the same years, Bailey acquired 'enormous influence' over the South African Cricket Association on account of his willingness to fund its international ventures.[99]

In 1906, an MCC team led by 'Plum' Warner visited South Africa to play the first official test matches between the two countries. The tri-umph of the South Africans in this contest prompted the MCC to invite them for a series in England the following summer. Bailey bankrolled the 1907 tour, which saw the South African cricketers 'wearing for the first time the Springbok emblem on their blazers and caps'.[100] Although it narrowly lost a hard-fought series, the team became 'an advertisement for the success of [post-war] reconstruction, and the importance of the mining industry'.[101]

Bailey now seized the moment to press the case for South African parity with Australia and England at cricket's imperial high table. In November 1907, he wrote to Francis Lacey, outlining his idea of an 'Imperial contest', to be held in England or South Africa. To this end, Bailey suggested the formation of an 'Imperial cricket board'.[102] The move, as Rowland Bowen noted, 'was an early illustration of the power of South African gold in influencing policies in Britain'.[103]

To canvass the support of the MCC and the local county cricket clubs in England, Bailey deployed the services of two well-established English amateurs, C.B. Fry (Sussex) and E.G. Wynyard (Hampshire).[104] More importantly, he secured the backing of Lord Harris, the most influential figure in the MCC, who expressed his wholehearted support for the idea. This cricketing lord was not only a firm believer in cricket's imperial role, but also, as chairman of the Consolidated Goldfields of South Africa, a close business associate of Bailey's. Indeed, Bailey 'acted virtually as Lord Harris's alter ego both in the mining industry in the reconstruction period and in the cricketing world'.[105] At a meeting held on 27 January 1908, Harris ensured that the representatives of the county cricket clubs gave their assent to the idea of an imperial cricket contest featuring England, Australia, and South Africa. A few days later, the MCC too approved the scheme and recommended sending out invitations to Australia and South Africa.[106] Accordingly, the MCC despatched a draft scheme, largely devised by Wynyard, to both countries in April 1908, which stipulated that a triangular cricket tournament would be held in England in the summer of 1909. England, Australia, and South Africa were each to play six test matches and take 'one third of the gross gate' at every venue.[107]

The South African Cricket Association immediately cabled their acceptance of the scheme. However, the Australians, who were scheduled to tour England in the summer of 1909, were against the idea. As the recently formed Australian Board of Control for International Cricket saw it, a triangular tournament involving the South Africans would eat into their profits. Moreover, the Australians also looked askance at the brazen intrusion of the South Africans into the traditional 'Ashes' fixtures. Accordingly, in May 1908, the Australian cricket board informed the MCC that it would not take part in the proposed imperial cricket contest.[108]

By now, the triangular cricket tournament had begun to stir passions in England and Australia. At a meeting held in London on 3 July 1908, the Advisory County Cricket Committee, persuaded of the merits of the scheme proposed by Wynyard and Fry, asked the MCC to inform the Australians that they would only be welcome if they took part in the tournament.[109] This 'needlessly curt' resolution elicited a stern rebuke in the *Times* from F.S. Jackson.[110] The Australians, too, were put out by the intransigence of the English counties. A few days after Jackson's letter, *The Times* published a letter from Dr Leslie Poidevin, the official Australian representative, who pointed out that the MCC's attitude would have an 'unfair and destructive effect' on the authority of his country's new cricket board.[111] These were strong words and had their intended effect on the English authorities. The Advisory County Cricket Committee held another meeting at the end of July 1908, wherein it resolved 'to request the MCC to invite the Australians to tour England alone in 1909'.[112]

The MCC's decision to act on this advice was a setback for Bailey's ambitious bid to remake the empire of cricket. However, his disappointment at this outcome was more than offset by the MCC's decision to convene a 'British and Colonial Cricket Conference' in England during the Australian tour of 1909, 'to discuss arrangements for a triangular tournament and other issues relating to international cricket'. This was an outcome that Bailey had sought from the very outset of his campaign for an imperial cricketing contest.[113]

The inaugural meeting of the Imperial Cricket Conference was held at Lord's on 15 June 1909 and was attended by the representatives of England, Australia and South Africa. The new body unanimously agreed to stage a 'Triangular Cricket Contest' in England in the summer of 1912. The three contestants were to play one another three times, with the gate money to be equally shared in each instance. Simultaneously, the Imperial Cricket Conference approved a draft scheme featuring international cricket visits between England, Australia, and South Africa. And perhaps most importantly, it ratified the new hierarchy within the cricketing world. 'Test' matches were now defined as contests between representative teams chosen by the recognized national boards of the imperial cricketing triumvirate.[114]

Framjee Patel was clearly galvanized by these developments. This is amply clear from a speech he made at the annual general meeting of Bombay's Parsi Gymkhana in May 1908. On this occasion, Patel reflected on the eventful year gone by, which had seen the Parsi and Hindu cricket clubs settle their differences and the birth of a new triangular tournament in Bombay. 'Just as they had their triangular contest,' Patel pointed out, 'so for the first time had they been inaugurated in the home of cricket.'[115] He therefore 'pleaded for Indian participation in the triangular cricket contest between England, Australia and South Africa'. 'The question had,' Patel added, 'an imperial side to it, and in future India need not be excluded from taking part in the English international matches because an Indian representative eleven, led by the Jam Sahib Ranjitsinhji would not fail to render a good account of themselves on the cricket fields of England.'[116] As Patel was quick to recognize, if India was to stand any chance of being recognized as a possible contender for future 'test' status, it was imperative to send a representative cricket team as soon as possible to Britain. It was this awareness, too, that spurred him on to convene the historic gathering at Navsari Buildings.

VIII

'We are glad to hear that the scheme for sending an Indian cricket team to England has again been revived and that a representative eleven will probably go West for a tour in the summer of 1911 or 1912,' observed the *Times of India* in an editorial entitled 'Imperial Cricket' on 20 September 1909. 'Apart from the warm sporting interest which a tour would be sure to arouse, the visit should also have an educational and political result which in these days would give it special value.' The paper paid a fulsome tribute to Framjee Patel, whom it described as 'one of the earliest and keenest promoters of the game amongst Indians', and hoped that 'his countrymen of all classes' would 'back him up in forwarding this latest scheme'.[117]

The timing of the editorial shows that Framjee Patel had begun work on his pet project well before the first formal meeting of the leading lights of Bombay cricket. He was, thus, well prepared when he addressed the gathering in Ratan Tata's office that September evening. After he read out the Governor of Bombay's letter, Patel proceeded to inform his audience that he had already been in touch with the imperial cricket authorities at Lord's about the proposal to send an Indian cricket team to Britain. Once again, he repeated his claim that the 'chief reason' their project had failed in 1904 was 'the want of funds'. This time, he declared, they could 'expect great financial support from Mr. Rutton Tata, one of the promoters of the project, as well as from some of the Princes of India'. In particular, Patel revealed that he had already received a telegram from Maharaja Sayaji Rao III of

Baroda, promising his support for the venture. The Gaekwad's keen interest in the Indian cricket tour is particularly interesting given his increasingly nationalist leanings in these years.

Patel estimated that a tour of Britain involving fifteen players and a manager would cost around Rs. 40,000 (£3,000). The 'gate money from various counties and clubs' would enable them to recover these costs. Meanwhile, as on the previous occasion, they needed a guarantee fund to ensure that the costs were covered in case the gate money did not live up to their expectations. He therefore suggested that they once again form 'a representative committee' to collect funds, which would 'approach all those gentlemen and many more who were good enough to help us on the last occasion'.[118]

Patel's suggestions were unanimously accepted by all present and a thirty-strong 'Indian Cricket Team for England Committee' was instantly formed. Its composition reflected the commercial clout and famed cosmo-politanism of Bombay's elite society. The members included, among others, the Tata brothers, Dorab and Ratan, Jamsetjee Jeejeebhoy, Dinshaw Manekji Petit, Shapoorji Bharucha, Bomanji Dinshaw Petit, Jehangir Petit, Dinshaw F. Mulla, D.R. Chichgar, N.G. Chandavarkar, Govardhandas Khatau, Narotamdas Morarji Gokuldas, Ibrahim Rahimtulla, Ibrahim Adamji Peerbhoy, Amiruddin Tyabji, and Fazulbhoy Currimbhoy.[119] Many of these individuals had long dominated Bombay's public life and had been closely involved with the city's principal gymkhanas.

The composition of the committee points to the shifting power equations within Indian cricket. There were only four Europeans in its ranks, a stark reflection of the diminishing significance of Anglo-Indian cricket. Moreover, unlike the previous occasion when the project had been pursued, this time around the Europeans on the committee had little or no role to play in the key decisions regarding the organization of the Indian cricket tour of Britain. The representatives of the Raj may have encouraged the idea, but control of the game had passed decisively into Indian hands.

★ ★ ★

The prominent part played by the Tatas in making the tour possible shows how powerful Indians now shaped the game's fortunes in the subcontinent. Significantly, their involvement in the project to send an Indian cricket team to Britain came at a time of frenetic activity for the two sons of the legendary J.N. Tata. The upcoming Tata iron and steel works at Kalimati were on the verge of completion and would shortly commence operations. They had also launched an ambitious hydroelectric project in the Western Ghats, designed to supply power to Bombay. And last but not least, they were about to bring to fruition their father's vision for an indigenous scientific and technological research institute in India. In May 1909, their plans for a new Institute of Science, endowed with money generated from Tata properties and jointly developed in partnership with the princely state of Mysore and the government of India, received official sanction. 'The Tatas,' remarked one contemporary English journal, 'are to Hindustan what the Mitsuis are to Japan, the Rothschilds to Europe, the Vanderbilts and the Astors to America.'[120]

Following in the footsteps of their father, Dorab and Ratan Tata sought to promote *swadeshi* enterprise. And this was as true of sport as it was of other spheres of activity. As we have seen, J.N. Tata was the most generous contributor to the guarantee fund for the failed Indian cricket tour of Britain in 1904. When the venture was revived five years later, the two Tata brothers were the leading subscribers. However, the Tata contribution went beyond funding. All the meetings of the organizing committee for the Indian cricket tour were held at Navsari Buildings, with the times of meetings being publicized in the Bombay newspapers. Both the Tata brothers regularly attended the meetings of the committee and played a leading role in its deliberations.

Although Ratan Tata was fond of tennis and horse riding, it was Sir Dorab Tata (he was knighted in January 1910) who was the keener sporting enthusiast. As an undergraduate at Cambridge in the late 1870s, he had taken part in athletics, cricket, football, and rowing. On his return to Bombay, he continued to nourish his love for cricket. One of the founders of the Parsi Gymkhana in 1885, Dorab Tata regularly participated in cricket matches in Bombay during the 1890s.[121] Indeed, his devotion to the imperial game was such that on one occasion he remarked to a friend that he 'would much rather be the president of the Marylebone Cricket Club than be the Viceroy of India'.[122] More importantly, Sir Dorab had impeccable connections at Lord's, not least because Francis Lacey, the MCC secretary, was an old college friend from his days at Cambridge.

In some ways, the Tata brothers were comparable to Abe Bailey. Like the latter, they were members of a new global capitalist elite in the age of empire. As with Bailey, the Tata's business interests, especially the need to access the London capital market and canvass imperial policy makers, took them frequently to Britain. The name 'Tata', one contemporary declared, 'acts like a charm in high political circles in London'.[123] Significantly, Ratan Tata and his wife Navajbai became a notable fixture on the metropolitan social scene in the late Edwardian era. In 1906, the younger Tata scion purchased York Place, once owned by James II, in the leafy southwest London suburb of Twickenham. Thereafter, the Tatas travelled to the British capital every summer and hosted lavish parties attended by the city's aristocratic, financial, and imperial elite. Furthermore, just as Bailey sought to cement the bonds of union between Britain and South Africa, the Tatas too were proud 'British Indians' who greatly valued the imperial connection.[124] Not surprisingly, then, both saw sport as a means of cementing the bonds between metropole and colony.

However, there was one crucial difference between Bailey and the Tatas: they were on opposite sides of the 'colour line' that increasingly became manifest across the British Empire in the 1900s. 'I am for the white race being on top of the black,' Bailey had once insisted. 'On the native question I am Boer to the backbone.'[125] This was no empty boast. In 1906, Bailey 'arranged to send 150 volunteers of the Transvaal Lancashire and Yorkshire Association, of which he was president, to assist the Natal colonial forces put down the Zulu rebellion'.[126] The previous year, he had torpedoed a request from the Transvaal Indian Cricket Union to watch matches at the Wanderers Club.[127]

The Tata brothers, on the other hand, were increasingly incensed at the ill treatment meted out to 'British Indians' within the empire.[128] Indeed, in December 1909, India's leading liberal leader, Gopal Krishna Gokhale, publicized a letter he had received from Ratan Tata regarding the Indian fight for civil and political rights in South Africa. 'It is a struggle of which the people of this country have every reason to be proud,' Tata wrote.

> I have watched with unfeigned admiration the undaunted and determined stand which our countrymen in the Transvaal—a mere handful in number— have made and are making against heavy odds, and in the face of monstrous injustice and oppression, to assert their rights as citizens of the Empire and as freemen, and to validate the honour and dignity of our motherland.

He contrasted favourably the 'perfectly legitimate and constitutional character of the resistance' offered by the Indian protestors in South Africa with the 'occasional acts of violence and crime which we deplore nearer home'. Tata also went on to express his 'surprise and disappointment' that no steps had been taken to offer financial aid to the protest movement in South Africa. 'For myself,' he told Gokhale,

> I feel I should lose no more time in doing my duty by our brave and suffering brethren in the Transvaal, and I have, therefore great pleasure in enclosing a cheque for Rs. 25,000, which I shall feel obliged by your forwarding to Mr. Ghandhi [sic], the money to be spent in relieving destitution, and in aid of the struggle generally.[129]

IX

Backed by the financial heft of the Tatas, the project to send an Indian cricket team to Britain progressed far more smoothly than it had on previous occasions. Importantly, this time around, the finances for the tour posed no insuperable difficulties. Within three months of the first meeting, the organizing committee had secured over Rs. 26,000 for the guarantee fund. That amount more than doubled in the following six months, and by June 1910, the committee informed the press that the 'monetary position of the project has been made perfectly safe, as about Rs. 53,900 have already been subscribed towards the Guarantee Fund'.[130] As before, Indian princes or business magnates were the principal donors to the venture. 'The generous support that has been extended to the project has exceeded the most sanguine expectations of the Committee,' admitted the *Bombay Gazette*.[131]

The imperial cricket establishment at Lord's was also quick to offer its support to the project. Their attitude was no doubt influenced by the news that the Tata brothers were the principal backers of the tour. At a meeting of the MCC Committee on 9 November 1909—at which Lord Harris was present—the members welcomed Framjee Patel's proposal to send an Indian cricket team to Britain. Because the imperial triangular cricket series had been scheduled for 1912, the MCC asked the Indians to consider sending their team over in the summer of 1911. The MCC also offered a guarantee of £200 for their match at Lord's.[132] In a subsequent letter to Framjee Patel, Francis Lacey promised to 'arrange an attractive programme' for the Indian cricketers and seek a minimum guarantee of 'half the gross gate money' from the English county cricket clubs. With the South Africans abandoning their proposed tour of England in 1911, he pointed out, the Indian team would have 'no counter-attraction in the cricket world'. 'There is no doubt,'

Lacey declared, 'that the visit will do much to remove prejudices and promote friendship.' He assured Patel that 'everyone with Imperial views...will cordially welcome the All India team in England'.[133]

In June 1910, nine months after its first meeting, the 'Indian Cricket Team for England Committee' informed the MCC that it had 'definitely decided' to send a 'representative' side to the United Kingdom in April 1911.[134] The die had been cast and this time there was no turning back.

5

Men in White

I

Shortly after 6 p.m. on 28 February 1911, the 'Indian Cricket Team for England Committee' held a crucial meeting at the Tata headquarters. Addressing his compatriots, J.M. Framjee Patel announced that the time had come to pick the team that would represent India on the playing fields of imperial Britain.[1] The organizers nominated a seven-member selection committee to undertake this task. In order to balance the interests of the major cricket-playing communities, Bombay's three sectarian gymkhanas were each allowed to put forward two representatives. The following evening, the members of the selection committee got down to the task of choosing the men who would make the historic journey.

The composition of the committee reflected the changing balance of power within Bombay cricket since 1904: the Muslim representation was augmented, while the Parsis had to accept parity with the other two communities. The Parsi Gymkhana was represented by its longstanding leaders Framjee Patel and Mehellasha Pavri; the Hindu Gymkhana by its captain, the future business magnate Chunilal Vijbhukanas Mehta, and its secretary, H.S. Naik; and the Islam Gymkhana by the Khoja industrialist Ibrahim Rahimtulla and Hadi Tyabji, who had been the sole Muslim representative seven years earlier.[2] As before, the committee was presided over by a European. Major John Glennie ('Jungly') Greig was the military secretary to the Governor of Bombay. He knew Indian cricket well, having regularly played for the Bombay Presidency against local teams. But his nomination as the chairman of the selection committee had less to do with cricket and more to do with politics. He was entrusted with this task in order to break any deadlock that might emerge among the representatives of the three communities.

In the months leading up to the final selection meeting, there had been intense speculation about the composition of the first Indian cricket team. At the very outset, Framjee Patel and his associates contacted around forty leading Indian cricketers in different parts of the country inquiring about their availability for the tour of Britain.[3] As in 1903, the tour organizers considered the possibility of including 'two or three Ceylon players in the combined Indian team'.[4] But mindful of the complexities of team selection, they eventually decided to play it safe and restrict their choice to players from the Indian subcontinent.

As the time for choosing the final squad drew closer, some critics began to question the lack of transparency in the selection process. In September 1910, one letter writer in the *Tribune* demanded to know on what basis the first ever representative Indian cricket team was to be chosen. 'I quite understand and believe in the individual merits of some players,' wrote H. Golaknath, 'but that alone is not the test on which the composition of an all-Indian team can be decided. Cricket is a game in which not only the individual but group merit as a unit counts.' This correspondent argued that a team selected purely on individual merit—even if it included Ranji himself—would 'make no stand whatsoever against a tried first-class English team'. This defect could be remedied, he suggested, by constituting provincial teams that could 'compete for an All-India Championship'. In the process, 'not only the true composition of an All-India Team will come in view, but with it the whole heart of India will throb in unison, a consummation...much to be wished for'.[5] But the plea for provincial contests fell on deaf ears. The tour organizers in Bombay were unable to conceive the possibility of a composite Indian team chosen on the basis of region rather than religion.

Meanwhile, with the requisite funds for the venture secured, Framjee Patel and his associates hired an English coach to help identify the best players, and to train those who were finally selected for the tour. On the recommendation of Lord Harris, the job was entrusted to John Alexander Cuffe, an experienced Australian professional cricketer who represented Worcestershire in the English county championship. Cuffe arrived in Bombay in November 1910 and stayed on in the city until shortly before the Indian team's departure for Britain.[6] A few days after his arrival, a committee comprising representatives from the Parsi, Hindu, and Islam Gymkhana was formed 'to fix the number of those cricketers who would be allowed to practice at the nets and take advantage of the coach's instructions'.[7] Under the watchful eye of the Australian coach, trial matches were held in Bombay to gauge the form of the Indian players who were under consideration for selection. As in 1903, these featured mixed teams, with cricketers from different communities playing side by side.[8] Their performance in these matches, and the form they had exhibited in the previous two years, informed the final decision of the selection committee when it met on 1 March 1911.

After a long meeting, the selectors announced the names of the sixteen men who had been chosen to represent India.[9] The list was as follows:

> Maharaja Bhupinder Singh of Patiala (Captain), Major K.M. Mistry, Maneck Chand, Dr H.D. Kanga, P. Baloo, J.S. Warden, M.D. Pai, H.F. Mulla, K. Seshachari, Salamuddin Khan, Shafqat Hussain, Syed Hasan, M.D. Bulsara, R.P. Meherhomji, B. Jayaram, and Noor Elahi.
>
> *Reserves*: P. Shivram, M. Parekh and K. Tamboowalla

Undoubtedly, the biggest surprise in this team was the choice of the young and inexperienced Maharaja of Patiala as its captain. Chapter 6 will look more closely at how this troubled prince became entangled with the first Indian cricket tour of Britain. But first, let us consider the stories of the forgotten men, drawn from different religions and regions, whose lives were to become intertwined over the course of a momentous summer. Threading together their diverse individual trajectories are two broad themes.

First, the urban middle classes had emerged by 1911 as the principal adherents of the game in the subcontinent. We have already noted how educational institutions in urban India provided the institutional framework within the game had flourished. It was in schools and colleges that young Indians were socialized in the ways of the game.[10] Many who took to the game in school tended to pursue it in college. Here, the encouragement offered by cricket-loving college teachers and administrators played a part in nurturing the game. Indeed, the best college teams had taken to organizing cricket tours to other parts of the country.[11] These contests diffused new cricketing techniques and practices, cemented sporting relations between different provinces, and led to the discovery of new stars. This growing middle-class takeover of the game was reflected in the fact that all but one of the sixteen cricketers named in the first Indian cricket team had been to college.

Significantly, more than half the team was from Bombay, a city where the game was deeply embedded in an extraordinarily dense network of institutions. By this time, India's cricket capital had already developed the highly competitive ethos that later came to be seen as its defining feature. Bombay's cricketers pitted their skills against each other at every level. The Harris Shield (established in 1897) and the Giles Shield (established in 1901) were responsible for unearthing fresh talent in the city's schools; the competition for the Northcote Shield (established in 1900) helped to identify the best college cricketers. In 1907, the city also became the first to host a competitive urban league involving government agencies and private firms.[12] By 1910, notwithstanding the constant struggle for space on the *maidan*, the Bombay Cricket League had twelve 'office' teams that regularly played each other every Saturday afternoon during the monsoon.[13] The older tradition of club and gymkhana cricket continued to flourish too, ensuring that a promising Bombay cricketer had no dearth of opportunities for displaying his talent.

Second, in the 1900s, cricket became implicated, in different ways, in debates about community. For the Parsi bourgeoisie of Bombay, these years were marked by a growing crisis of the ethos of civilized masculinity that had long defined their identity. The catalyst here was the publication of the decennial Indian census, which showed a distinct stasis in the Parsi population in comparison with other communities. The cricket field thus came to acquire a new significance at a time of deepening anxieties within the community about its putative racial degeneration. As the Hindus and Muslims became more competitive on the *maidan* and elsewhere, the Parsis began to fret about their racial decline. Among north India's Muslims, too, cricket and the attendant cult of 'manly games' came to signify a new relationship with the political order established by British rule in the subcontinent. Notably, the game was an integral feature of the most important educational initiative in colonial India to forge a new Muslim political identity. Of the four Muslim players named in the first Indian cricket team, three came from Aligarh, the town which became inextricably associated with this ambitious experiment in reconciling Western learning and Islam. And finally, cricket also became a prism through which Hindu society was forced to reassess the insidious effects of the caste system. At the heart of these debates was the stirring example of an extraordinary Dalit family, whose cricketing ability and accomplishments called into question the pernicious system of inequity and exclusion practised by the Hindu upper castes.

II

On 5 March 1911, a well-attended ceremony was held in the Parsi Gymkhana to commemorate the silver jubilee of Dr Mehellasha Pavri's contribution to Indian cricket. An oil portrait of the doctor, funded by a subscription drive within the Parsi community, was duly unveiled. After eulogistic speeches from his compatriots, it was the guest of honour's turn to address his audience. Thanking his well-wishers, Pavri proceeded to reflect aloud on the state of cricket within his community. His message was a sombre one: Parsi cricket was no longer what it was. Their cricketers were 'simply resting on their oars, calmly seeing other communities running a dead-heat with them, nay, even overtaking them in the race for advancement in cricket'.[14] Pavri's remarks anticipated a collective theme and a mood that was to become ever more pervasive within the community as time went by: the decline of Parsi vitality and its gradual decline in the face of external competition.

Nor was Pavri alone in expressing such fears. Six years earlier, the renowned Anglo-German physical culture exponent Eugen Sandow, during a visit to Bombay, had cast doubt on the much vaunted sporting prowess of the Parsis. 'I have been a fairly keen observer of the Parsis during my stay in this city,' Sandow wrote in the very first issue of a new journal called *The Parsi*, 'and the result of my observation is that the proportion of well-built, strong men and women is very small indeed. The majority are small in stature, and weak in limbs.' Worse still, Sandow declared, Parsi men lacked 'the firm and manly tread of the European'. And in a bid to plug his own patented techniques, he suggested that Parsi parents ought to 'compel' their children 'to have physical culture taught by a properly certified inspector'.[15] The fact that Sandow's essay was at all published suggests that his views resonated with growing concerns among his readers about the community's future. A few months later, an essay in the same journal examined the census figures of the Parsi population and concluded gloomily that 'the community with all its prosperity has so far shown no vitality of growth'.[16] As it happened, the first decade of the new century saw a small numerical increase in the size of Bombay's Parsi population. But for a community that numbered a little over 50,000 in a city with close to a million inhabitants, the spectre of racial extinction loomed large.[17]

Anxieties about their decline elicited a range of proposed solutions from within the community. Some Parsis advocated the cultivation of closer links with their original homeland in order to rediscover the well springs of vitality that had nourished their robust Persian ancestors. Indeed, in the mid-1900s influential commentators even considered seriously proposals to establish a Parsi colony in Iran, as a way of counteracting the racial ener-vation that they regarded as an inevitable consequence of India's tropical climate.[18] Others sought to police the boundaries of Parsi conjugality even more fiercely in a bid to maintain racial purity. And yet others campaigned for a greater emphasis on physical culture as a way of reversing the com-munity's perceived racial degeneration. It is against this wider backdrop that we need to interpret Pavri's speech.

★   ★   ★

Yet fears about racial degeneration were curiously discordant as far as the cricket field was concerned. Notwithstanding the advance of the Hindus and Muslims, the Parsis remained a formidable cricketing force in 1911. This is reflected in the preponderance of Parsis in the first Indian cricket team. In all, seven Parsis were to represent India during their tour of Britain: Mistry, Kanga, Meherhomji, Bulsara, Warden, Mulla, and Bajana. All of them (with the possible exception of Bajana, whose origins are shrouded in mys-tery) had learnt their cricket in Bombay. Most of them had followed an established pattern of cricketing advancement: conspicuous success in school cricket, followed by stellar performances for their college and club sides, leading to a much coveted place in the Parsi team.

Kekhashru ('Keki') Manikji Mistry, Rustomji Pherozesha Meherhomji, and Hormasji ('Homi') Dorabji Kanga, formed a powerful batting triumvirate that was responsible for the continued cricketing success of the Parsis. The oldest, and most accomplished, of this trio was the thirty-six-year-old Major Mistry. Said to be in a 'class by himself', Mistry had first made his mark as a bowler for the long-established John Bright CC in Bombay.[19] Pitchforked as a teenager into the Presidency match of 1893, he was, thereafter, a regular member of the Parsi team for this prestigious match. But it was while playing for the famous Patiala side in the late 1890s that Mistry developed into a truly great batsman.[20] This left-handed Parsi was adept at playing strokes all around the wicket, 'attaining the maximum of power with the minimum of power'.[21] In May 1899, a profile of Mistry appeared in *Cricket*, which began thus:

> There has been much discussion of late in Indian newspapers as to the position which K.M. Mistri ought to take in the native cricket world, and for that mat-ter of that, in the world of cricket at large. His warmest admirers claim for him

that on the past season's form he is better than Ranjitsinhji; critics who possess less enthusiasm place him on a level with the Prince; while other critics say that for a native cricketer he is good, although he could not hold a candle to any first-class batsman in England or Australia. Whether he is all that the fancy of his admirers paints him, or whether he is not a 'second Ranji', it is certain that against the best bowling that India can produce he has made a rare lot of runs.[22]

One man had little doubt where Mistry stood in the pantheon of Indian cricket. Mehellasha Pavri, the captain of the Parsi team, firmly believed that Mistry was the only Indian batsman who could measure up to Ranji. 'If he only had a chance of coming to England,' Pavri told one British newspaper in 1909, 'he would make a name for himself second only to Ranji.'[23]

Younger than Keki Mistry by two and a half years, the elegant Rustomji Pherozesha Meherhomji had established his batting reputation while playing for the renowned Baronet CC. 'One finds it difficult whether to award the palm to him or to Mistry as the most graceful batsman of the present time,' wrote Framjee Patel in 1905. Like his senior, the right-handed Meherhomji possessed the ability to time his strokes 'to a nicety' and therefore make them look effortless. Patel was inclined to give Mistry the slight edge but observed that 'in back play Meherhomji stands alone'.[24]

The youngest member of this batting trinity, the thirty-one-year-old 'Homi' Kanga, belonged to a Bombay Parsi family with a distinguished cricketing pedigree. 'The Kanga family has always influenced Parsi cricket considerably,' noted one writer. 'So large a family were they,' he added, 'that a Kanga team once played a match, every member of which belonged to the same family tree.'[25] Two of Homi's uncles were a part of the second Parsi tour of Britain: Pestonji Kanga as captain and M.D. Kanga as a player. His elder brother, Dinsha Kanga, had also regularly played as a wicket keeper in the Parsi team. If Mistry was a bowler-turned-batsman, Kanga was a batsman who could also bowl. A wielder of a heavy willow, Homi was said to possess 'nerves of steel' and play 'a scientific game'.[26] By the mid-1900s, these qualities had made this Wilson College graduate one of the most prolific batsmen in the Parsi team. 'He is one of those brilliant cricketers who can bat against all kinds of bowling as calmly as possible and make runs freely,' wrote one contemporary on the eve of the Parsis' encounter with the Presidency in September 1905.[27] As if to prove this writer's point, Kanga proceeded to score a double century, thereby becoming the first Parsi player to achieve this feat in the Presidency match.[28] 'He is sure to make a name for himself if he ever goes to England with the Indian team,' Framjee Patel wrote in the same year, 'as to-day he is as great in the batting line as Mistry or Meherhomji.'[29] Not long afterwards, Kanga travelled to Britain to pursue a degree in medicine. During his stay in the country, he played for the famed Hampstead CC for two seasons.[30]

As with the batting trinity, the selection of the two Parsi bowlers in this team was uncontentious. Maniksha Dadabhai Bulsara and Jehangir Sorabji Warden were renowned for their bowling skills. This bespectacled pair presented a study in contrast: Bulsara, a burly figure with an expanding waistline; the gangly Warden, at six feet two inches, easily the tallest member of the Indian cricket team. Bulsara was the older and more experienced of the two, having played for the Parsis for close to a decade. Born in Daman on 2 September 1877, he had studied at the Fort and Proprietary High School in Bombay, an institution that had turned out some of the best-known Parsi cricketers of the time. A 'fast round-arm bowler of exceptional merit', he was said to be 'the only man in India who can make the ball "swerve"'.[31] Although Bulsara was regarded as the workhorse of the Parsi cricket team, he nonetheless had his wiles and could deliver a vicious leg break 'that would beat the most wary of batsmen'.[32] In his prime, this Parsi bowler had possessed 'a fine physique' and was said to be 'worth his place in any team for his fielding alone'.[33] As his agility on the field waned, Bulsara increasingly compensated with useful contributions as a lower-order batsman.

The Bombay-born Warden, described by his captain Pavri as 'a magnificent fellow', was a relatively new find for the Parsis.[34] This talented twenty-six-year-old slow bowler—reputedly 'one of the best in India'—was said to send down 'balls which would beat the most wary of batsmen'.[35] In some respects, his cricketing trajectory was similar to that of his illustrious compatriot Keki Mistry. Like the latter, the left-handed Jehangir first revealed his potential as a bowler while playing for the formidable Bharda New High School cricket team. Unlike Mistry, however, Warden did not make an impression at first.[36] 'Then he suddenly leaped into fame by securing some magnificent analyses against the best batting combinations in Bombay,' remarked one reporter after his selection to the Indian team was announced, 'and he has maintained the position which he then secured, by making still better efforts in subsequent years.' Indeed, this journalist prophesied, 'if there is any bowler of the team who is likely to set England agog with his bowling it is he'.[37]

But public opinion was divided about the inclusion of the relatively inexperienced Hormusji Fardoonji Mulla in the Indian cricket team. Born in Bombay on 4 May 1885, Mulla had first burst onto the cricketing scene as an undergraduate at Elphinstone College. His brisk batting had swiftly earnt him a devoted following on the Bombay *maidan*. Even half a century later, one observer nostalgically recalled the 'fabulous Homi Mulla... whose very turn to go in was the signal for us small boys to rush out of the tent or shamiana so as to be able to follow the ball as it became a tiny speck in the very clouds'.[38] This flamboyant batsman was said to have 'more than once pulled his side from a tight place by his unorthodox style'. In addition to his quick scoring, the young Parsi was also a competent wicket keeper. It was the latter ability that may have persuaded the selectors of Mulla's value to the Indian side. However, not everyone was convinced about the merits of his selection.[39]

The seventh Parsi cricketer to play for the Indian cricket team in Britain was not named in the original list of players.[40] Manikji Pallon Bajana only joined the Indian cricketers in Britain shortly before the first match of their tour. Born on 14 September 1886, the enigmatic Bajana had spent the early part of his cricketing career representing the Bombay, Baroda and Central India (BB & CI) Railway Company's famous 'Carriage' Department Recreation Club at Ajmere. A photograph with his teammates taken in the early 1900s shows a slim youth with an intense gaze.[41]

'There is no better occupation on earth than playing cricket,' a well-known English writer on the game once declared.[42] But as far as the Parsi cricketers were concerned, none of them could solely depend on this activity for their livelihood. Some pursued professional careers in Bombay. Homi Kanga, who returned to his home town in early 1911 after completing his medical training at the Royal College of Surgeons in London, had embarked on his career as a doctor; Hormusji Mulla was an articled clerk in his own family's legal firm; and Jehangir Warden was employed as a French teacher in a local school.[43] Yet others, however, used their cricketing skills to find employment outside Bombay. Thus, Mistry moved to Patiala in 1896 after he was hired by Maharaja Rajinder Singh to play for his cricket team. Two other Parsi cricketers in the Indian team also found employment in princely states. One of these was Bulsara, who in the early 1900s coached the Nawab of Rampur's cricket team.[44] But it must have either been a short-lived stint or an occasional commission. For in 1911, Bulsara lived in Delhi and appears to have worked as an official for the BB & CI Railway.

Manikji Bajana was the other Parsi cricketer whose cricketing skills took him to a princely state. A regular player for the Cooch Behar cricket team, he sailed to Britain in the summer of 1910 as a part of his employer's royal entourage.[45] The fact that Maharaja Nripendra Narayan had made a generous donation to the guarantee fund may explain why Bajana was called to assist the Indian cricket team in 1911.

Finally, there was one other Parsi sportsman who, unlike Bajana, travelled with the Indian cricket team to Britain, but not as a player. This was Jijibhai Manikji Divecha, the longstanding secretary of the Parsi Gymkhana, who was appointed as the manager of the Indian cricket team. Divecha was one of the links between the Parsi overseas tours of Britain in the 1880s and the first Indian cricket tour of that country. He had been a part of Pestonji Kanga's team in 1888 and it was this experience, in addition to his close involvement from the outset with the organization of the 1911 cricket tour, that prompted his appointment as manager. In some ways, Divecha had the most challenging role on this tour: he was expected to look after all the travel arrangements, ensure the comfort of his players, deal with the organizers, press, and public at every match venue, and last but not least, ensure that harmony prevailed within the Indian team.

III

On 19 December 1910, there appeared in a number of Indian newspapers a letter signed by the Honorary Secretary of the Old Aligarhians CC. The letter informed 'Old Boys and other lovers of Aligarh that a cricket team of past and present Aligarhians will shortly be going to Bombay to play the Hindus, the Parsis, and the Bombay Gymkhana'. Although the main purpose of the Aligarh cricketers' trip was to take part in the trial matches to select the Indian cricket team for the forthcoming tour of Britain, the letter expressed their desire to 'meet many old friends and brothers and to make new ones too'.[46] The signatory was Shaukat Ali, better known to posterity as one half of the Ali brothers' duo, who famously joined hands with Mahatma Gandhi to launch the Khilafat movement in 1920. In the winter of 1910, however, the future Maulana was involved in the circumscribed domain of college politics. And here, cricket was to play a crucial role in Shaukat Ali's bid for influence, for the game had been integral to the public profile and internal ethos of his *alma mater* from the very outset.

If Bombay was the longstanding bastion of Parsi cricket, Aligarh had emerged by the dawn of the twentieth century as the principal stronghold of 'Muslim' cricket. Unlike the cosmopolitan port city with its myriad schools, colleges, and clubs devoted to the game, the cricketing reputation of this town, eighty miles east of Delhi, stemmed from the remarkable concentration of sporting talent in a singular educational institution. The *Madrasat-ul-'ulum Musalmanan-e-Hind,* or the MAO College, as it was more familiarly called, had been established in 1875 as a residential school and college. Its founder, Sayyid Ahmad Khan, had drawn inspiration from the British public schools and the ancient universities of Oxford and Cambridge in seeking to create, in an Indian setting, an educational institution that would impart Western education in a manner that would be compatible with the tenets of Islam. In his view, this was the only way in which Muslims in the subcontinent could overcome their 'backwardness' and find an honourable place for themselves in the new imperial dispensation that had emerged after the suppression of the 1857 uprising. The result was a unique place of learning that embodied in its design, buildings, and curriculum a new vision of the role of education in fashioning public-spirited individuals who would serve their community. Although it opened its doors to students from every religious denomination, the college quickly became synonymous with the education and political advancement of the Muslim *qaum* (community). The students who enrolled at the MAO College lived, studied, dined, and prayed together. And importantly, they also *played* together. For the founder's insistence on hiring Oxbridge graduates as teachers resulted in the infusion of the British ethos of 'manly games' as an integral element in the college's evolving student culture.

★ ★ ★

Cricket at the MAO College began with the creation of a club on 9 February 1878. Interestingly, in the light of its subsequent history, it was a freshly appointed Hindu professor of mathematics, Pandit Rama Shankar Misra, who is said to have started this club.[47] At first, the club was 'limited to twenty-two dues-paying members', who were required 'to pay three rupees in advance'. The aspiring cricketers were also required to wear a distinctive uniform: a 'blue flannel coat, shirt, knickerbockers and cap'.[48] Although the college founder was its patron, the future prospects of the club did not at first appear very promising. Rama Shankar Misra departed from the college very soon after he had initiated the venture, and the funds needed to keep the club afloat were hard to come by. In 1881, an attempt was made to introduce a regular subscription for its members, but this met with little success.[49]

However, a dramatic transformation occurred in 1883 with the arrival of a new Cambridge-educated European principal. The legendary Theodore Beck regarded himself as a 'complete duffer' when it came to cricket. But he accorded the imperial game a central place in the life of the college.[50] Cricket, as we have seen, was viewed by many late Victorian Britons as the sport par excellence in inculcating the appropriate moral values required of an educated 'gentleman'. Under Beck's stewardship, the game began to receive systematic and sustained institutional support within the college.[51] The principal himself showed the way, taking an Aligarh team on a keenly followed cricket tour of the Punjab during his very first year in charge.[52] On this occasion, the team, comprising mostly schoolboys wearing their new cricket uniform—'white flannel shirt and trousers, red kamarban, and fez'—was seen off at the railway station by the venerable Sayyid Ahmad Khan himself, who 'with a quotation from the Koran wished them success'.[53]

Thereafter, Beck silenced critics who queried the Aligarh college's emphasis on sport, by pointing to its role in fostering a culture of 'civilized masculinity'. He was particularly proud of the reputation that the college had developed throughout the North-West Provinces and Punjab for its proficiency in the 'noble and manly game of cricket'.[54] Indeed, Beck reportedly asserted that Ranji was a far better role model for his students than Dadabhai Naoroji.[55] Moreover, he stressed the value of cricket in fostering 'bonds between Aligarh and significant groups outside'.[56] By travelling to different cities and hosting visiting teams from distant places, Beck argued, Aligarh students would forge social networks that were vital to the college's success.[57] Equally, he believed that success in sport would generate publicity for the college and thereby attract more students. Sport, and not mere bookish learning, was thus at the heart of Beck's vision of Aligarh's future.[58] His vision was praised by the Anglo-Indian press. One newspaper commended the college's cricketing tours, and had little doubt that 'this experience of travel in a different province, with the many sights of interest it afforded and the opportunities it gave of coming in contact with different men, has had a higher educational effect on the students than if they had spent twice the time at their books'.[59]

As the college rapidly grew in size and numbers in the 1880s, Beck entrusted the cricket club to an English colleague. Professor Wallace introduced a new honours board for the college's first eleven, which was displayed in the Union Room. He also added flourish to the cricketers' uniform—'an elegant black jacket with a border made of red satin' with the college monogram prominently displayed—that marked them out as a privileged elite.[60] In thus elevating the cricketers within the institution, its British teaching staff made the game the focal point of its social life and an essential part of its public identity.[61] As one alumnus remarked, 'The first impression of the College on the mind of a visitor is that it is an institution for cricketers, for most of what he sees in the course of his perambulations has something or other to do with Cricket'.[62]

Notably, too, the college's cricket captain became a prominent presence within the Aligarh student community.[63] 'The room of the Cricket Captain,' it was said, 'was the venue of a royal durbar where appeals of freshers and younger boys were heard, decisions given and enforced.'[64] In the early 1890s, the boisterous Shaukat Ali, personally recruited by Theodore Beck, was undoubtedly one of the most well-known figures on the campus on account of his cricketing skills.[65] As a batsman, he was reputedly 'a fine slogging player'.[66] And under his captaincy, the Aligarh cricket team 'played to win'.[67] But some of its most notable victories came after Shaukat's departure from the college. In late December 1896, the MAO College team visited the capital of British India to take on the Calcutta CFC.[68] On the eve of the match against this much vaunted European club, a dinner was held in honour of the 'National Mahomedan cricket team of India'. On this occasion, their supporters expressed a desire to see the Aligarh cricketers defeat the 'conquerors of India' on the sporting field.[69] When the college team duly achieved this feat, they were enthusiastically feted by the Muslims of Calcutta. At a celebratory event organized by the city's Mahomedan Sporting Club, their success was deemed a matter of 'national pride'. 'I assure you the next time I meet an European, I shall look him in the face more courageously than I did before,' the Club President declared.[70]

As the century drew to a close, the Aligarh team went from strength to strength. In 1897 and 1898, the college cricketers defeated in quick succession a formidable visiting Parsi side from Bombay as well as Maharaja Rajinder Singh's powerful Patiala eleven on its home turf.[71] These triumphs enhanced the college's cricketing reputation. Indeed, the Aligarh college cricket team became so famous that it even found a mention in Rudyard Kipling's *Kim* (1901).[72] As a result, European teams became wary of playing against them. 'The number of foreign matches played in Aligarh has unfortunately declined of late years owing to the reputation which our XI has established; on this account, regimental teams passing through and the XIs of neighbouring stations are less ready than formerly to challenge our XI,' noted the Aligarh college magazine at the beginning of the new century.[73]

But as the Victorian era ended, some within the college believed that its cricketers had become complacent and careless. In 1901, the Aligarh team suffered defeats against the European CC at Simla and the Government College, Lahore.[74] The same year, an article appeared in the college magazine criticizing the state of the game within the institution. Its author foresaw 'a serious danger threatening the athletic reputation of Aligarh either through mere carelessness or as a result of the exclusive and disastrous system of cliques and parties that has been allowed to pervade the management of games recently'. The cricket squad, this critic alleged, was 'weaker than it has been for years, and depends for success largely on one or two members of the School team'.[75]

However, notwithstanding such criticism, the Aligarh team was still widely acknowledged as the best in north India. As a result, when the Oxford Authentics toured India in the winter of 1902–3, a match against the college was scheduled at Aligarh. 'There are few more interesting movements in modern India than that which has resulted in giving an eleven composed of the past and present members of the Mohammedan Anglo-Oriental college at Aligarh a claim to be considered one of the best eleven in India,' noted Cecil Headlam.[76] During his stay at the college, Headlam attended a debate at the 'Union' where the students discussed 'whether it was desirable for Mohammedans to adopt European customs'. Reflecting on what he had witnessed, Headlam concluded, 'cricket and purdah ladies, education and Mohammedanism—do these not suggest somehow that eternal contrast and communion of East and West which is the very flavour of modern India?'[77] As for the cricket itself, the rain-interrupted encounter ended in a draw, but not before the Aligarh bowlers gave the visiting Europeans a proof of their redoubtable skills. Their best bowler, Ali Hasan, wrote Headlam, 'came down like a wolf on the fold', bamboozling the Authentics with his variations of pace and length.[78]

In December 1903, an Aligarh team travelled to Bombay to take part in the trial matches that were held in the city to choose the side that would tour Britain the following summer. Comprising both past and present players, this team took on the Elphinstone College as well as the Parsi and Hindu Gymkhanas (but not the Islam Gymkhana, who were their hosts).[79]

Figure 9. The Muhammadan Anglo-Oriental (MAO) College cricket team, *c.* 1905. The Aligarh college was the principal bastion of 'Muslim' cricket in the years 1894–1914. Courtesy of Marylebone Cricket Club Library.

The presence of the Aligarh cricketers in the city attracted 'a considerable amount of interest both among the local cricketers of all communities and the large number of Mohamedans who have come up to Bombay from various parts of India for the Mahomedan Educational Conference'.[80] Six members of the Aligarh contingent also participated in the 'test match' that was organized between mixed teams comprising Hindus, Muslims, and Parsis.[81] One of these teams was captained by Dr Pavri, while the other was led by Ahsan-ul-Haq, a talented Afridi cricketer from Jullunder (Jalandhar). Ahsan had first been selected to play for the Aligarh college team by Shaukat Ali. After the latter's departure, he quickly established himself as the best batsman in the college. Following his graduation, Ahsan travelled to Britain to pursue a degree in law. But he continued to play cricket, representing Hampstead CC and Middlesex CCC, before returning to his home town in the autumn of 1902.[82]

The failure of the campaign to send an Indian team to Britain in the summer of 1904 was felt most acutely by the Aligarh alumni. In March 1905, there appeared a letter in the Indian press from one Khwaja Mahomed

Yahya, a 'rais' (notable) of Aligarh, who suggested that the college 'send out a team to play matches in England and the Colonies like the Authentics of Oxford'. Were such a tour undertaken, Yahya declared, 'the fame of Aligarh outside India would no longer be a hearsay but a matter of actual experience'. The college, he added, could draw on a large pool of rich donors who would be able to finance such a venture.[83] The suggestion was greeted with approval by some observers. 'Aligarh College is not only the nursery of Mahomedan cricket, but is probably the principal institution in the country for the game,' concurred the *Bombay Gazette*. Had the scheme to send an Indian team to England not failed, the paper noted, 'at least five Aligarhians would have accompanied it'.[84]

But the idea did not take off. This may have been because of the turmoil that beset the college in the years between 1905 and 1910. There was growing friction between the European teaching staff and the students, resulting in a strike by the latter in February 1907.[85] The European professors were convinced that their students secretly harboured nationalist sympathies. There were also tussles for control between William Archbold, a newly hired principal from Britain, and the trustees in matters pertaining to the college's administration. Simultaneously, these years saw bitter infighting among the Aligarh 'Old Boys', in which the Ali brothers, Mohammed and Shaukat, were central protagonists.[86] For the latter, in particular, cricket became a vital means of shoring up support among the Aligarh alumni.

By the time Shaukat Ali led the 'Aligarh Past and Present' team to Bombay in December 1910, most of the cricketers who had vied for selection seven years earlier were past their prime. Indeed, Shafqat Hussain was the only member of the 1903 Aligarh squad to make it to the Indian team in 1911. When he had first played in Bombay as an eighteen year old, this fast bowler from Meerut had captivated the spectators and press alike. The *Bombay Gazette* reported that he had 'been a revelation to local cricketers' and commended his ability to bowl at varying speeds and lengths. 'He scarcely bowls two balls alike in an over and we have seen no fast bowler in India who more admirably works with his head,' the paper added.[87] Indeed, even Ranji, who watched him play against the Parsis, was said to have formed 'a very high opinion of him'.[88] But by 1910 even this Aligarh fast bowler had visibly slowed and was no longer the man 'who trundled so magnificently half a decade ago'.[89] Shafqat's selection did not go down well in cricketing circles in Bombay, where many felt that the principle of communal representation had deprived the Indian team of a more qualified candidate.[90]

The other two Aligarh cricketers were both three years younger than the twenty-six-year-old Shafqat, but like him, they hailed from small urban centres. Salamuddin Khan was a Pathan from the Basti Sheikh Darwesh district of Jullunder. His compatriot Syed Nawab Hasan, born in the same year, was from Moradabad.[91] While their cricketing abilities meant that they were a part of the Aligarh elite, both men came from a social background— the north Indian service gentry—that was more typical of their fellow students. Not surprisingly, the two men pursued a degree in law. The main difference between these two was in their cricketing specialisms. Salamuddin was an all-rounder, who was said to have 'favourably impressed the Committee with his batting and bowling during the Bombay tour of the Aligarh team'.[92] Syed Hasan, on the other hand, was regarded as a reliable batsman-wicket keeper.

The cricketers of Aligarh may have dominated the sport in north India. But in the early years of the new century there emerged another educational institution that would eventually supplant it as the nursery of cricket in the region. This was the Government College, Lahore, which, as we have noted, announced its arrival on the cricketing stage with a surprising victory over the MAO College in 1901.[93] Playing in that match for the Lahore team were Noor Elahi and Maneck Chand, both of whom made it to the first Indian cricket team a decade later. Unlike the Aligarh college, the Punjabi side was a mixed one comprising both Hindus and Muslims.[94] One of the members of that Government College side was Mela Ram, the scion of a wealthy Punjabi Hindu merchant and founder—sometime in the early 1900s—of the famous Frontier CC in Peshawar. This keen cricket enthusiast was 'said to have spent more money on his team than any other cricketer of his time'. Notably, he recruited Noor Elahi and Maneck Chand to his club, which included 'nearly all the leading cricketers of North India'.[95] Towards the end of December 1903, the Frontier CC, with Noor Elahi and Maneck Chand in its ranks, arrived in the capital of Indian cricket, where they took on the Hindu and Parsi gymkhanas.[96] While they were in Bombay, Maneck Chand was selected to play for the mixed side led by Ahsan-ul-Haq in the 'test match' that was organized to choose the Indian team for the tour of Britain the following summer. The *Bombay Gazette* described the Punjabi as a 'fast right hand bowler' who could prove 'very deadly' if the conditions were favourable.[97] Some even considered him the quickest bowler in the entire country. Noor Elahi, too, was regarded as a fine batsman and a useful bowler.[98] Following the untimely death of their club founder and captain,

Mela Ram, this Punjabi duo was hired by the Maharaja of Kashmir, who aspired to build a cricket team that would rival the famed Patiala Eleven.[99] And it was while they were playing in Kashmir that they were invited to take part in the Indian cricket tour of Britain.

IV

In February 1906, there appeared in the pages of the *Indian Social Reformer*, a leading liberal journal of the day, an article simply entitled 'Hindu Cricket'.[100] Its author was not named, but the immediate occasion for its publication was the Hindus' famous victory over the Bombay Presidency team a few days earlier. In the days prior to the match, the Hindus of Bombay had worked themselves into a state of feverish excitement in anticipation of this encounter. As the *Bombay Gazette* noted, it was the first such 'contest between the Europeans and a community which forms, if not the bulk of the population of the Presidency, a very large part of it'.[101] Thus, when play began on the morning of 8 February 1906 at the Bombay Gymkhana's ground, the 'northern, southern and western boundaries were lined with tents and shamianas, which, as the game advanced, became crowded to their utmost capacity, while the eastern side of the square was thronged with a surging crowd representative of every community'.[102] In a tense, keenly fought match, the Hindus gradually demonstrated their superiority over the European team. One of the star performers with the ball for the Hindus in the Europeans' first innings was a bowler called Erasha, who had been specially summoned from Poona for this game.[103] But in the decisive second innings, it was another bowler, Palwankar Baloo, who won them the match. Notably, too, Baloo's younger brother Shivram produced two crucial batting performances that showcased his talent and grit. The most astonishing feature of the Palwankar brothers' performances was that they were allowed to play for the Hindu team. For the two men were born into a caste of leather workers, traditionally regarded by upper-caste Hindus as 'Untouchables'. 'The admission of these chamar brothers in the Hindu Gymkhana,' noted the *Indian Social Reformer*, 'is a credit to all and has done far more to liberalize the minds of thousands of young Hindus than all other attempts in other spheres.'[104]

The author of the article cited the example of the Palwankar brothers to illustrate the progress that had been made in the cause of Hindu social reform. In this self-congratulatory narrative, the presence of two Dalits in the Hindu team was presented as evidence of the tolerance and broadmindedness of the upper castes who had set aside their reservation about pollution and countenanced free social interaction between the cricketers. This 'conscious voluntary change' among privileged Hindus, the journal suggested, was infinitely preferable to the 'compulsory' social interaction between different classes and communities fostered by the railways. What this account did not acknowledge, of course, was Palwankar Baloo's *struggle* to achieve recognition on the sporting field.[105]

However, it was precisely his tireless toil on the cricket pitch in the face of deep-seated caste prejudice that defined Baloo's long cricketing career. Equally, it was his exceptional skills and the recognition bestowed upon him by his European and Parsi opponents that prompted the leaders of Hindu cricket to overlook Baloo's caste status. Indeed, the *Indian Social Reformer* admitted as much when it noted that the Hindu sportsmen of Bombay and Poona had 'shown in different degrees that, *where national interests required* [my italics], equal opportunity must be given to all of any caste, even though the offer of such opportunity involved the trampling of some old prejudices'.[106] In other words, it was collective self-interest rather than a change in social consciousness that prompted reluctant upper-caste Hindu cricketers to include a Dalit in their team.

★ ★ ★

Palwankar Baloo (or 'Baloo Babaji Palwankar', if we go by some contemporary newspapers) was born on 4 July 1875 in the south Indian town of Dharwad. By virtue of his birth, he had to confront the iniquities of the Hindu caste system from the very outset. Scattered all across India, members of the caste known as *Chambhar* (the north Indian term was *Chamar*) had traditionally occupied 'a well-defined place' in the social order as leather tanners, dyers and shoemakers.[107] 'Ill-clad...badly housed, and insufficiently fed, they belong to the poorest in the land,' noted one colonial ethnographer in the early twentieth century. Moreover, in many parts of the country they were a predominantly rural community, who lived 'at the beck and call of others' and were thus 'obliged to do a great deal of work for which they receive no pay whatever'.[108] But far more than their material exploitation, it was the everyday forms of discrimination that they were forced to endure which reinforced the degraded status of the *Chamars*. Castigated as consumers of beef and vermin, they were excluded from

Figure 10. Palwankar Baloo, *c.* 1905. The Dalit bowler was undoubtedly the 'first great Indian cricketer'. Courtesy of Marylebone Cricket Club Library.

upper-caste Hindu spaces. Indeed, it was widely believed by those who claimed a superior status that 'the very touch of a *Chamar* renders it necessary for a good Hindu to bathe with all his clothes on'.[109]

Given this social background, how does one explain Baloo's appearance in a cricket team comprising upper-caste Hindus? We might begin by noting key factors that rendered the *Chambhars* in the Bombay Presidency *relatively* better off than their brethren in other parts of the country. Here, there were castes, such as the Mahars and Mangs, who were ranked even below the *Chambhars* in a finely graded hierarchy of degradation.[110] Moreover, colonial rule in the nineteenth century had begun to transform the social order with important consequences for the prospects of upward mobility among the lower orders. First, the *Chambhars* of late nineteenth-century Maharashtra not only occupied an important place in the agrarian economy but were also able to use their skills as leather workers in gaining 'entry into the towns and cities'.[111] Second, along with the more numerous Mahars, the *Chambhars* of this region found employment in the armies of the English

East India Company and its successor state. Until their recruitment in the
British Indian army ceased in the early 1890s, this was to prove a significant
source of social mobility for these communities. Third, the provision of education for the lower castes was a key feature of the vigorous proselytizing
activities undertaken by European missionaries in western India. In turn,
this contributed to the emergence of a new strata of intellectuals among
the lower castes, who now began to challenge Brahmin dominance.

Notably, the late nineteenth century witnessed the rise of a powerful
non-Brahmin movement in Maharashtra, whose most radical strand argued
that the elimination of all forms of Brahmin power was 'the prerequisite for
the liberation of the lower castes'.[112] The *Satyashodhak Samaj* was established
two years before Baloo was born. Its founder, Jotirao Phule (1827–90),
belonged to the lowly Phul Mali caste, whose members were mostly garden-
ers, cultivating flowers, fruits, and vegetables. But even though he was not
an 'untouchable', Phule tried to forge an alliance between the diverse sections of Maharashtra's lower castes and those who had been cast outside the
pale of Hindu society. The ideas of equality and fraternity that he pro-
pounded were to prove highly influential in stirring the political consciousness of the communities that later came to identify themselves as 'Dalits'.

It is within this wider social and political milieu that we need to situate
Baloo's extraordinary career. An autobiography in Marathi penned by his
younger brother Palwankar Vithal, who went on to become a famous
cricketer in his own right during the 1920s, provides us with valuable information about the early life of this subaltern cricketer.[113] Here, we find a
brief but stirring description of how Baloo overcame caste prejudice over
the course of his cricketing journey. Vithal's account begins by highlighting
the highly peripatetic existence of the Palwankars, who originally hailed
from the Ratnagiri district in the Bombay Presidency. Their father (and
before him, their grandfather) was employed in the 112th Native Infantry
regiment and as a consequence the family moved regularly from place to
place within western and central India. Baloo was educated in schools established for the children of Indian army employees. The schoolboy became
transfixed by the sight of European soldiers in the Poona Gymkhana playing
the alien game of cricket. Enamoured by the sport, he soon became part of
a cricket club comprising the sons of pensioned soldiers. The boys played
with the discarded equipment of the European cricketers. It was in these
circumstances that Baloo first learnt to bowl. Before long, he was hired as a
member of the ground staff by the local Parsi Gymkhana, which paid him

Rs. 3 a month for his exertions. Over the next five years, Baloo developed his skills as an 'underhand bowler' at this club. Thereafter, he moved to the Poona Volunteers' Club, which paid him Rs. 4 a month to bowl regularly to the European cricketers who used its facilities.[114]

It was during his stint as a 'net bowler' at the Volunteers' Club that Baloo caught the eye of Dr Trask, a member of the Indian Medical Service and the cricket captain of the Poona Gymkhana. With a crucial match coming up, Trask ensured that his club secured the services of the talented Indian bowler at a salary that was three times what he had previously been paid.[115] At the Poona Gymkhana, Baloo watched closely a famous European left-handed slow bowler named Captain Barton, who was known 'for his accuracy', and began to model his own technique accordingly. But, as Vithal was quick to point out, Baloo was no mere imitator. On the contrary, he began to work out different ways of bowling to different batsmen. The presence of many well-known European batsmen of the day in the Poona Gymkhana helped the diligent plebeian develop his bowling repertoire as well as his stamina. The most well known of these cricketers was 'Jungly' Greig, who soon began to arrive an hour ahead of all his compatriots specifically in order to hone his own skills against Baloo's bowling. Greig, so the story goes, paid the young bowler eight annas every time the latter got him out.[116] But his interaction with European army officers appears to have also had a bearing on Baloo's prospects outside the cricket pitch. In the early 1890s, he secured employment as a clerk in the Second Grenadier regiment of the Bombay Native Infantry.[117]

In the mid-1890s, Baloo's caste status became a matter of public controversy in Poona. The Young Men's Hindu Club had emerged in these years as a prominent cricketing institution in the town. This club had within its ranks a number of promising young cricketers but pointedly chose to ignore Baloo. 'Jungly' Greig wrote a letter to one of the local newspapers criticizing the Hindu club for excluding a promising cricketer on account of his caste status.[118] Greig's tirade in the press stirred the Young Men's Hindu Club into action and a special session of its members was convened to discuss Baloo's admission. On this occasion, a majority of the club membership favoured his exclusion. It was only the stern intervention of some of the Telugu-speaking, non-Brahmin cricketers that forced the club's organizers to reluctantly override the majority and admit Baloo.[119] His stellar performances in the months that followed no doubt gave the club's leaders much cause for self-congratulation. The Poona Young Men's Hindu Club trounced its local Indian rivals with ease. Ironically, too, Baloo's bowling enabled his team to inflict stinging defeats on the Poona Gymkhana in 1896 and 1897. By this time, Baloo, working in tandem with a bowler called Bhide, had become the club's most successful wicket taker.[120]

His achievements earnt Baloo the admiration and praise of some of Poona's leading Indian politicians. On one occasion, after a spectacular performance against the European Gymkhana in Satara, the liberal Maharashtrian social reformer Mahadev Govind Ranade shook hands with the young spin bowler at a public function held in the latter's honour. On another occasion, the nationalist firebrand Bal Gangadhar Tilak felicitated Baloo by garlanding him with flowers and praising his achievements on the cricket field.[121] Yet a majority of the Poona Hindus found it hard to stomach the presence of a low-caste cricketer in their midst. Moreover, even at his own cricket club, he was served refreshments separately during cricket matches and often forced to sit on his own.

Nor did such caste prejudice cease when Baloo shifted from Poona to Bombay in 1899. According to Vithal, this move was occasioned by the transfer of his brother's regiment.[122] As in Poona, Baloo's entry into club cricket in Bombay was met with resistance by orthodox Hindus. Moreover, even after he began to play for the city's Hindu Gymkhana at the invitation of the club's captain, he continued to face myriad forms of caste prejudice designed to remind him of his status as an 'Untouchable'. But Vithal's narrative also makes it clear that Baloo was by no means a passive recipient of such disparaging treatment. On the contrary, he made it clear in no uncertain terms that he would not put up with discrimination. Fearful of losing the services of a match-winning bowler, the leaders of the Hindu Gymkhana were forced, by degrees, to mend their ways and treat Baloo in the same way as they did his upper-caste teammates. As Vithal noted, it was because of Baloo's willingness to contest the humiliating behaviour directed at him that considerably eased the path of the other Palwankar brothers who followed him.[123]

In other respects, however, the young man must have found the cosmopolitan atmosphere of the big city liberating after the conservative ethos of Poona. With a bigger stage on which to display his bowling skills, he soon began to make a mark on the local cricket scene while playing for the Hindu Gymkhana against European and Parsi clubs.[124] In 1901, Baloo's cricketing career in Bombay was briefly interrupted when he was forced to move to Mhow with his regiment.[125] But he had taken to his life in Bombay and before long quit military service and returned to the city. In 1902, Baloo was recruited by the BB & CI Railway Company as a clerk in their engineering department, a place where he would work for the next thirty-one years.[126]

Thus far, we have considered Baloo's life within the political and social context of his times. But what of Baloo the cricketer? Any consideration of his career would be incomplete without reckoning with the specific skills that Baloo displayed in his chosen specialism, that of slow, left-arm spin bowling. The best practitioners of this art have certain features in common: they can control the pace and flight of the round, leather-encased projectile they direct at the batsman, deceive their opponent with subtle variations in line and length, and sustain long spells of accurate bowling. Baloo, by all accounts, not only possessed all these qualities in ample measure but had also perfected them to the point where he was indisputably one of the finest practitioners of the art in the *entire* cricketing world.

The views about Baloo expressed by his contemporaries and colleagues offers eloquent testimony to his bowling skills. In its assessment of the first Indian cricket team, the *Bombay Gazette* called Baloo the country's 'premier bowler', who could 'bowl unchanged through an innings, rarely sending down a loose delivery'. Moreover, the paper added, his ability to withstand 'punishment much better than his colleagues' rendered him 'invaluable' in a crisis.[127] Mehellasha Pavri, who saw a good deal of Baloo in his prime, had little hesitation in comparing the Indian to Wilfred Rhodes, the great contemporary Yorkshire and England slow left-arm bowler.[128] The Poona cricketer D.B. Deodhar, who played alongside Baloo in the Hindu team, went a step further. 'In the art of bowling,' he wrote, 'Baloo was a genius. The ease, grace, the rhythmic and fluent movements which characterised Ranjee's style, in the use of the bat, were equally visible in his work on the ball. There was no laborious, awkward, jerky action anywhere and it was a pleasure to watch his easy, smooth and graceful style.'[129] In his autobiography, Vithal echoed Deodhar's remarks about Baloo's fluent bowling style and the infinite variations in line and length at his command. At the same time, he also stressed that Baloo was a 'head bowler', who constantly sought to out-think batsmen by paying close attention to their distinctive foibles.[130] It was an opinion vociferously seconded by Jehangir Warden, a fellow practitioner of the art of slow bowling, who declared that Baloo's 'great virtue lay in fooling the batsman, getting him in two minds, dropping the ball on that fabled "eight anna bit"'.[131]

Baloo was at his best as a bowler in the first decade of the twentieth century. The BB & CI Railway Company had a highly regarded cricket team and Baloo soon became the spearhead of its bowling attack. He turned out one match-winning performance after another in these years. As Vithal proudly recalled, Baloo not only achieved the much coveted 'hat-trick' regularly in local club matches, but also bowled out the entire opposition on one occasion.[132] So impressed were Dorab Tata and Pavri by Baloo's feats that in the early 1900s they even sought to send him to Britain to play a season's county cricket for Surrey. However, for reasons that are not entirely clear, the proposal never went beyond the discussion stage.[133] But his growing fame led some princely patrons to seek Baloo's services for their cricket teams. Vithal notes that his brother was regularly invited to play for the Maharaja of Natore's side every December. Interestingly, playing for the Natore eleven in the winter of 1910, Baloo came up against Ranji, who had turned out for the Maharaja of Jodhpur's team. It was only the third time that the two had faced off, and as on the previous occasions, the prince succumbed to the plebeian.[134]

This was entirely in keeping with Baloo's uncanny ability to rise to the big occasion. When the Hindu Gymkhana played against the Oxford Authentics team at Bombay in November 1902, he produced an impressive spell of bowling against the English tourists. As we have already noted, Baloo was the match winner for the Hindus when they defeated the Bombay Presidency team in the historic match at the Bombay Gymkhana ground in February 1906. Against the same opposition the following year, his exceptional bowling performance once again allowed the Hindus to gain a decisive victory.

The heavy workload that Baloo shouldered as a bowler took its toll on his body. In the late 1900s, he sustained an injury in his left shoulder. Vithal records in his autobiography that his brother was afflicted with 'synovitis', an inflammation of the membrane lining the shoulder joints.[135] As a result, Baloo struggled on occasion to turn his bowling arm over with the old ease and fluency. Indeed, during the cricket season of 1908, there were rumours that the best Indian bowler had lost form and was no longer the destroyer of old.

But Baloo bounced back in the following two years and remained a formidable bowler at the time of his selection for the Indian cricket tour of Britain. Notwithstanding his injury, he had been the leading wicket taker for the Hindus in the Triangular matches held between 1907 and 1910.[136]

His performances in these contests left an indelible impression on those who watched the ageing Baloo bowl on the Bombay *maidan*. A.F.S. Talyarkhan, who as a thirteen-year-old boy witnessed the legendary bowler display his wiles against the Parsis in September 1910, recalled the memory forty-five years later:

> The gloss is off the ball and the skipper throws it to a flannel-clad player, a quiet, unassuming sort of chap, looking the least deadly of all on the field. But a ripple of cheering would burst forth because that was the signal for things to happen. 'Baloo!' would be heard on all sides of the ground as the wizard of the slower delivery took charge of the attack. It all happened many years ago, but if I have perfect recollections of all this, even as a teenager, it is because P. Baloo was a name to conjure with in those seasons of long ago . . . One can see Baloo even now, that short, easy run, that very facile delivery as the left arm came over, always the unbuttoned cuff of his flannel shirt dangling at the wrist, always the batsman dangling in his mind where to play the ball and when.[137]

★   ★   ★

Even as he extolled Baloo's exploits, Talyarkhan recalled the other Palwankar brothers: 'Shivram, he of thick and broad leather belt round his waist, Vithal, he of the wristy elegant strokes, and Ganpat, dynamic all-rounder who died at very early age'.[138] His words serve to remind us of the sporting achievements of this remarkable Dalit family. Astonishingly, four of the Palwankar brothers *simultaneously* distinguished themselves in two sports: hockey and cricket. Accomplished hockey players, they regularly represented the 'Bombay Pioneers' in competitive tournaments. In 1908, their team won the prestigious Aga Khan All-Indian Hockey Championship. Equally, in the years between 1913 and 1919, all four Palwankar brothers turned out for the Hindus in the Bombay Quadrangular tournament.[139] Indeed, even before 1911, they had begun to receive regular collective invitations from princely states keen to strengthen their cricket teams. Importantly for our story, both Shivram and Vithal were in contention for a place in the first Indian cricket team.

Born in Bhuj on 6 March 1878, Shivram was eight years older than Vithal.[140] The early part of his career was spent in Baloo's shadow, both on and off the cricket pitch. Shivram had taken to cricket while studying at the same military school as his elder brother, and like the latter was employed on the ground staff of the Poona Volunteers' Club on a salary of Rs. 3 a month. He also followed Baloo into the Second Grenadiers as a clerk, moving with the latter to Bombay when their regiment was stationed in that city. However, unlike Baloo, Shivram did not resign his job after their regiment shifted to Mhow. Indeed, he even travelled with his unit to Hong Kong, where he worked for a couple of years. But eventually, ill health prompted Shivram to give up his job in the army and return to Bombay. Here, he secured employment in the GIP Railway, and resumed his cricket.[141] In the mid-1900s, we find him playing both for his office team and the Hindu Gymkhana. One match, played in January 1905, is particularly noteworthy. Representing the Hindu Gymkhana against a visiting Lahore Gymkhana side, Shivram scored a century and took five wickets.[142] In the opposing team were the Punjabi trio we have already encountered: Melaram, Noor Elahi, and Maneck Chand.[143] Such stellar performances with the bat and ball, as well as his agile fielding, clearly impressed the Hindu selectors, for a year later Shivram was drafted into the team for the historic match against the Bombay Presidency. Over the next four years, Shivram became an integral part of the Hindu side in the Triangular tournament. Like his elder brother, he developed a reputation for reliability in a crisis and was thus an automatic choice for the trial matches that took place in Bombay prior to the final selection of the Indian team. Had the selectors not adopted the principle of communal parity, Shivram might well have found himself in the main squad, instead of being relegated to the status of 'first reserve'.

In his autobiography, Vithal was deeply critical of the way the first Indian cricket team was chosen. The principle of selecting teams on the basis of community, he argued, had vitiated the process and led to the exclusion of meritorious players.[144] He had good reasons for venting his anger at the selection process. In the two years preceding the 1911 tour, Vithal had made a strong case for his inclusion in the Indian team. Vithal had been identified as a rising star during his time at the New High School, long regarded as one of the nurseries of Bombay cricket. Shortly after leaving school in 1905, Vithal was recruited to play for the Royal Indian Marine Dockyard by its captain, a man named Wilson, who was eager to strengthen his team. His high scores in local cricket led to Vithal's selection in a combined team representing all the Bombay office clubs which travelled to Delhi and Agra to play a series of matches. Here, too, Vithal showcased his talent with a string of good scores. Before long, his burgeoning cricketing reputation yielded him a job as a clerk in the GIP Railway. Thus, he came to play for the same office club as Shivram.[145]

In 1908 and 1909, Vithal scored heavily against some of the strongest cricket teams in Bombay. As a result, he received an invitation to take part in the selection trials for a place in the Hindu team for the prestigious

Triangular tournament. But, much to Vithal's disappointment, the Hindus' captain, C.V. Mehta, deemed him too young for a place in the team.[146] Taking the setback in his stride, Vithal continued to perform consistently in every type of local cricket until the Hindu selectors had no choice but to include him in their squad for the Triangular tournament of 1910. That winter, he was also invited by the Hindu Gymkhana to participate in the selection trials for the forthcoming Indian cricket tour of Britain. Notably, the foreign coach brought in to train the Indian cricketers was highly taken with Vithal's distinctive batting style. Indeed, Vithal noted in his autobiography that John Cuffe strongly urged the selectors to include him in the Indian cricket team. However, he remarked, his 'inexperience' and the principle of communal representation resulted in his exclusion from the squad.[147] What made the blow even harder for Vithal was that, twenty-one years later when an Indian cricket team next toured Britain he was considered too old to make the trip. His autobiography makes it clear that this missed opportunity was one of the great regrets of Vithal's cricketing career. Reflecting on this episode, the third Palwankar brother ruefully quoted a friend who once quipped that, unlike the great Marathi poet-saint after whom he was named, '*this* Vithal never had a chance to go on *his* pilgrimage to Pandharpur'.[148]

V

The three other Hindu players in the first Indian cricket team came from the opposite end of the social hierarchy. This should come as no surprise, given the alacrity with which Brahmins had taken to Western education in colonial India. In the light of their numerical preponderance in schools and colleges, one would expect to find Brahmins well represented in an Indian cricket team. One of these cricketers was a figure whom the Palwankar brothers knew well, by virtue of having played alongside him both for the Hindu Gymkhana and the Natore princely team. Notably, Palwankar Baloo and Kilvidi Seshachari had long been a deadly combination at either ends of the cricket pitch. The Madras-born Tamil Brahmin, six months older than the Dalit slow bowler, was the Indian selectors' first choice as wicket keeper.

Intriguingly, according to one source, Seshachari had been educated at Dulwich College, 'where he soon became a favourite, and his prowess as a wicket-keeper was not long in becoming known'.[149] This raises the tantalizing possibility that the Tamil Brahmin and one of the great English prose-stylists of the twentieth century—P.G. Wodehouse (who joined Dulwich in 1894)—might have run into each other in school. However, a detailed profile of Seshachari in *Cricket* in June 1906 makes no mention of his education at Dulwich.[150] The writer of this article began by noting that it was 'not a little remarkable to find an Indian, a Brahmin by birth, dwarfing all his competitors in the country'. He then proceeded to offer an account of how Seshachari had come to be 'recognized by veteran and novice alike' as the finest stumper in India. According to this account, the Tamilian's wicket-keeping abilities had first attracted public attention when he was as yet a teenager playing club cricket in Madras. Consequently, 'he found himself elected as a member of the Premier Hindu Club of Southern India'. Here, Seshachari 'settled down to regular practice, continuing to play for the Hindu Club at Madras, his *alma mater* of cricket, for several years together with marked success'. But his 'real cricket career', we are told, began in 1900 when he moved to Ootacamund, 'whose sweet half-English air is most exhilarating and congenial to the cricketer. In this bracing climate, and with experienced European cricketers, among them Mr. C.T. Studd, giving him the benefit of their invaluable advice, Seshachari continued to make progress with the bat as well as with the gloves'.[151] Now, Charles Studd, the pastor of the local church in Ootacamund, was one of the most well-known cricketers of his time. The youngest of three cricket-playing brothers, all of whom represented Eton, Cambridge University, and Middlesex, he was a member of the English team that lost to the Australians in the famous Oval test match of 1882.[152] Seshachari was thus fortunate in being able to hone his cricketing skills under the tutelage of this accomplished English cricketing missionary.

Soon, the results began to show. When the Hindus took on the Oxford Authentics at Bombay in November 1902, Seshachari 'kept wicket for his side so brilliantly as to earn the unanimous opinion of the Englishmen that he was the best stumper they had met in India'. Nor was it just his wicket keeping that earnt plaudits in that match; he also made a dogged contribution with the bat to help his team secure a creditable draw. 'In recognition of this fine effort,' it is said, 'he was presented with a gold watch and chain by an admirer.' Thereafter, 'Seshachari's services were always in demand'.[153]

Photo by *Wiele & Klein.*

K. S. Sehsachari.

Figure 11. Kilvidi Seshachari, *c.* 1905. The Tamil Brahmin was reckoned by many of his contemporaries as the best Indian wicket keeper of his time. Courtesy of Marylebone Cricket Club Library.

It was not only the Hindus who called upon his services. Some months before the match against the Oxford Authentics, *Cricket* reproduced the following story from the *Indian Sporting Times*:

> While in Madras, Seshachari was a constant guest at the Ordnance Cricket Club, which was then one of the best organised institutions of its kind in the city. A cricket match was on the day's card, the match being against a strong regimental team. In the second innings the Ordnance wicket-keeper was unable to continue behind the sticks owing to a bruised finger, and Seshachari's services were requisitioned, the regimentals being ignorant of the local crack's proclivities in this particular direction. But to their chagrin and discomfiture he proved so detrimental to the Tommies that no less than six men were sent to the 'right-about'—which presumably is the largest number of dismissals to any wicket-keeper's credit.[154]

'If ever an "All India" team should cross the seas to England, it is believed that his presence in it will be a tower of strength,' one observer presciently

remarked of Seshachari after watching his performance against the Oxford
Authentics at Bombay.[155] Indeed, he was included in the team that was due
to undertake that journey in the summer of 1904. 'His wicket-keeping is
quite first-class and brilliant enough for any county; in fact many people
think that he is one of the best wicket-keepers in the world,' noted *Cricket*
in 1906.[156] Five years later, the *Bombay Gazette* declared that the Madras man
was still the 'best wicket-keeper in India' and that his presence in the national
team was 'simply indispensable'.[157]

Eight years before Seshachari was profiled in its pages, *Cricket* had run a
feature on another Brahmin cricketer from south India. Accompanying the
article was an illustration showing a moustachioed man wearing the outfit
common to many contemporary upper-caste Indian professionals: a coat
worn over a shirt in the Western style with a white turban wrapped around
his head. While admitting that it would be 'rash in the extreme' to compare
this south Indian with his famous compatriot Ranji, the author of this
article nonetheless ventured to suggest that 'given the opportunities, he will
develop into one of the finest cricketers of the day'.[158] Over the next few
years, 'Bangalore' Jayaram amply fulfilled this writer's prediction, prompting
many contemporaries to declare that he was on his day as good a batsman
as the Kathiawari prince.

Born in the same year as Ranji, Jayaram had to overcome more obstacles
than the former in learning to play this alien sport. 'As a "Native" in Madras
Presidency,' noted *Cricket*, 'he met with absolutely no encouragement in his
early boyhood when he began to watch the cricket played on the Bangalore
Gymkhana ground, and there seemed no hope for him to excel in the
game.'[159] At the city's Central College, where Jayaram was a student, cricket
was not pursued seriously nor was it easy to procure the necessary equipment. Undaunted, 'the coming cricketer induced a few companions to
explore the outskirts of the game, as it were, by means of a ruler and a racket
ball'. His regular forays to the Bangalore Gymkhana to watch the European
cricketers at play also prompted him 'to imitate the style of the better known
batsmen and their manner of making their strokes'. Gradually, cricket
became the principal sport at the Central College. Jayaram, whose fame as
a batsman had 'spread through the district', soon became its cricket captain.
He played a number of match-winning knocks, both for his school team
and the Hindu Star Club, against a variety of Indian and European teams. In
1891, he scored his first century against a European team, the Yorkshire
Regiment, which attracted 'widespread attention'. Under his leadership,

the Bangalore team won the provincial intercollege trophy four times between 1889 and 1895. By the latter date, Jayaram had come to be regarded as a cricketer 'worthy to take his place among the best of the Englishmen'.[160]

After Jayaram finished college in 1895, he took up a job in the Mysore state's Geological Department. Meanwhile, his cricketing reputation continued to burgeon and by the time *Cricket* featured him in March 1898, the Bangalore batsman was said to be 'a household name in India'.[161] In September 1901, Jayaram joined a select band of Indian players to have scored a double century.[162] This achievement was particularly noteworthy because it refuted the entrenched opinion among many Europeans that Indians lacked the physical endurance to play a long innings.

By this time, Jayaram had acquired a large fan following in south India. One of his admirers was the young Chakravarti Rajagopalachari, who would later go on to become one of the leading figures in the Indian anti-colonial struggle.[163] But a more consequential supporter at the turn of the century was Edward Sewell, who had played against the south Indian many times in the 1890s. The Englishman described Jayaram as a 'pleasant featured, square shouldered lissom Bangalorean, who speaking English fluently, is a very genial companion, and very popular wherever he goes'. 'There is not a shot that he does not possess,' he added, 'but cutting is his forte and he is always a dashing bat, never scoring slowly.'[164] Indeed, Sewell angrily defended his friend after a member of the Oxford Authentics team publicly disparaged Jayaram's batting for being too risky.[165] The Indian's style might be 'restless and jumpy', he wrote in the *Athletic News*, 'but no writer can lay down the law about one particular style being the only first-class one'. Sewell then drew a comparison calculated to silence this critic: 'Jaya Ram, when I knew him was a very respectable imitation of the Victor Trumper of 1902. And did the incomparable Victor Trumper never take a risk?'[166]

Sewell not only ranked Jayaram above Keki Mistry, but also believed that if he had been given similar opportunities, the Bangalorean would have been as accomplished a batsman as Ranji. Hence, when the south Indian travelled to Britain in the spring of 1903 to pursue an engineering course at the Royal School of Mines,[167] the Englishman 'at once put W.G. on his track'.[168] Grace, who captained London County at this time, immediately inducted Jayaram into his team. In one of his newspaper columns, Sewell recounted what happened thereafter:

Jayaram scored a century in his first innings on an English wicket, and is perhaps the holder of a unique record in doing so. His few appearances for

London County were not startling, but the surroundings were scarcely in his favour, especially when in his first first-class match a bitter east wind with occasional falls of snow made him long for the ruddy East or to be anywhere else but the Oval. Even then he made one cut off Lockwood which, as a chronicler wrote, 'ought to have been put in a glass case'. But, on the whole, I never remember seeing a more miserable object than Bangalore Jayaram was that winter day at Kennington.[169]

Had an Indian cricket team toured Britain in the summer of 1904, Jayaram would no doubt have played for it. His employer, the ruler of Mysore, had even granted him special permission to remain in London for the purpose. Returning to the warmer climate of his homeland the following year, the Bangalore player rediscovered his touch and once again began to score heavily in local cricket.

By the time the selectors announced the Indian team in 1911, Jayaram was a few days short of his thirty-ninth birthday. Notwithstanding the limited amount of cricket he had played in the years immediately preceding the tour, he was regarded as an automatic choice on account of his experience of English playing conditions. 'Although he is no longer quite in the front rank of Indian cricket,' admitted the *Bombay Gazette* in its appraisal of Jayaram, 'he is still a reliable bat and should make useful contributions to the scores of his side.'[170]

Remarkably, the third Brahmin player in the first Indian cricket team was also profiled in *Cricket*. But the article appeared in November 1912, more than a year after Mukund Damodar Pai had returned home with his teammates.[171] Born in Bombay on 29 July 1883, this Gaud Saraswat Brahmin had emerged in the early 1900s as one of the rising stars of Hindu cricket. His early career was typical of the successful Bombay cricketer: tons of runs for school and club leading to a place in the premier Gymkhana team.[172] In the winter of 1902, Pai was nominated as a reserve player for the Hindus' match against the Oxford Authentics, 'but many considered that he should have had a place in the team'.[173] The following December, he took part in the trial matches that were held to select the Indian side for the tour of Britain in the summer of 1904. In one of these matches, he scored a big hundred against the Aligarh 'Past and Present' team.[174]

Over the next three years, Pai consolidated his cricketing reputation in Bombay's competitive environment. As with the Parsi cricketers and the Palwankar brothers, he played simultaneously for different clubs. These were defined by caste (Gaud Saraswat CC), religion (Young Hindu CC, Hindu Gymkhana), occupation (Jacob Sassoon CC), and sociality (New Shivaji

CC, Friends Union). Pai was a certainty to play in the historic fixture between the Hindus and the Bombay Presidency in February 1906. But he missed that match due to ill health. However, the following year, he was one of the stars of the Hindus' second successive victory over their European opponents.[175] And although his performance in the Triangular tournament was relatively undistinguished, Pai remained a key player for the Hindu team. Hence, many observers regarded him as a safe choice for the Indian cricket tour of Britain in 1911. The *Bombay Gazette* described Pai as a 'fast run-getting bat, though...not quite of the hurricane type'; besides, he was said to be 'a brilliant field'.[176]

VI

In October 1935, that indefatigable commentator on imperial cricket, Edward Sewell, published a column in the *Times of India* entitled 'Indian Cricket Memories: The Best Pre-War Side'. This was written a few months prior to the selection of the Indian cricket team due to tour England the following summer. The veteran journalist issued a challenge to his readers:

> I ask any judge of cricket in India who has seen all the players concerned whether he would back for one anna any of the elevens who played against the M.C.C. in the Tests of 1933–34 against the following eleven of Pre-War players, assuming, of course, all 22 players were between the ages of 20 and 30.
> Maharajah of Patiala (Capt.), K.M. Mistry and Buta Ram (all of Patiala), B. Jayaram (Madras), Ali Hassan and Salamuddin Khan (Aligarh), N.C. Bapasola, R.P. Meherhomji, D.N. Writer and M.E. Pavri (Parsees), and Baloo (Hindus). I am not suggesting this is the 'best' Pre-War side, but it would beat any of the 1933–34 Test XIs every time, on turf and matting.[177]

Perhaps the ageing Sewell had fallen prey to a misty-eyed nostalgia. Nonetheless, his remarks are a reminder that the men we have encountered in these pages were regarded by their contemporaries as the finest cricketers in the country.

However, at the time that the first Indian cricket team was put together, it is Sewell's crucial *caveat* that prompted sceptics to query the judgement of the selectors. The journalist's imaginary eleven comprised players 'between the ages of 20 and 30'. In the months preceding the selection of the 1911 Indian team, some observers were inclined to look askance at the fact that half the side was in its thirties. Indeed, one English writer declared that a team of 'past celebrities' stood 'no chance of success in England'. These players, he argued, 'simply could not now stand the strain of a cricket tour in a strange climate'.[178] If the English first-class counties put their best sides in the field, this writer prophesied, 'the Indian team will not win a match'.[179]

6

The Captain's Story

I

The pacified remnants of a once fearsome warrior elite, the rulers of India's 600-odd princely states have been portrayed in two, mutually opposed ways.[1] An older tradition of writing often tended to excoriate them for their sybaritic proclivities and spendthrift ways. They were regarded as weak individuals who had free rein to indulge in sensory pleasures, utterly oblivious of their responsibilities towards their impoverished subjects. Their loyalty to the Raj and opposition to Indian nationalism was construed as evidence of their reactionary tendencies as a class. More recently, the Indian princes have come to be seen as active historical agents who played a key role in the making of empire. They are regarded as exemplars of enduring indigenous political traditions that predated colonialism. Moreover, the more enlightened among them are extolled for their patronage of the arts and their efforts to enhance the economic and social infrastructure of their principalities.[2] These conflicting representations of princely rule—as exemplars of reaction or reform—are not easily reconciled. Undeniably, however, some princes manifested both aspects in their comportment and conduct. And none more spectacularly so than Maharaja Bhupinder Singh, or, to give him his full title: *Farzand-i-Khas-i-Daulat-i-Inglishia, Mansur-i-Zaman, Amir-ul-Umara, Maharajadhiraja Rajeshwar, Sri Maharaja-i-Rajgan Bhupinder Singh, Mahindar Bahadur of Patiala.*

In popular accounts, Bhupinder Singh is the archetypal Indian maharaja because of his unbridled pursuit of the high life. The legend owes much to the outpourings of Jarmani Dass, a former employee of the Patiala state, whose lurid revelations about his sovereign's alleged sexual peccadilloes fuelled the sales of his best-seller, *Maharaja*.[3] Sympathetic biographers and sober scholarly accounts, on the other hand, have pointed to Bhupinder's political acumen as well as his generosity as a patron of art and culture.[4] But in the spring of 1911, neither image had as yet taken firm root. At this time, Bhupinder was a callow prince seeking to test the boundaries of his sovereignty vis-à-vis the Raj.

The elevation of the Maharaja of Patiala to the captaincy of the Indian cricket team was symptomatic of an era when it was taken for granted that the princes were 'natural leaders' of society. But he was by no means the organizers' first choice to lead this team. Indeed, as far as Framjee Patel was concerned, there was only one man who had an incontrovertible right to be accorded that honour. 'Every effort will be made to induce H.H. the Jam Saheb to skipper the team,' Patel assured his colleagues at the very outset. In his view, there were several reasons why Ranji's participation in the tour would ensure its success.[5] At the very least, it would swing any 'waverers' among the Indian cricketers who had not yet made up their mind to join the touring party. Beyond that, 'the Jam Saheb's presence would attract the attention of the cricket public of England in a greater degree than would be possible in his absence'. Finally, with Ranji as captain, the rest of the team 'could enter upon the tour with no small degree of confidence'.[6]

However, India's best-known sporting celebrity once again displayed a lofty indifference towards the venture. A dramatic transformation had occurred in Ranji's life since the winter of 1906, when Framjee Patel had last entreated him to lead an Indian cricket team to Britain. On 20 February 1907, the Government of India formally ratified the prince's claim to the Nawanagar *gaddi*. This sudden change in his status was the outcome of a confidential report submitted to the government of Bombay by Percy Fitzgerald, the Political Agent in Kathiawar. Fitzgerald was well acquainted with the dispute over the Nawanagar succession, having served in Kathiawar between 1878 and 1884. Now, as the Political Agent, he sided with Ranji on the grounds that all the documentary evidence substantiated the latter's claim to be Vibhaji's rightful successor.[7] The pressure brought to bear on the colonial administration by notable Rajput princes, led by his old mentor Sir Pertab Singh, also swung the decision in Ranji's favour.[8] Once the official decision was made public, the wheels of government moved swiftly. On 11 March 1907, Ranji was formally installed as the new ruler of Nawanagar at a hastily arranged ceremony in Jamnagar.[9]

Following his unexpected elevation, Ranji actively set about cultivating his public image as an Indian king. He outlined ambitious civic schemes to tackle the plague in Jamnagar as well as plans to develop the natural resources and transport infrastructure in his state. Very soon, however, Ranji's inadequacies as an administrator were exposed. Even as his state was simultaneously assailed by plague and drought, he devoted his energies to extracting more resources from his impoverished subjects. And like many of his princely peers, Ranji exercised his discretionary authority in a quixotic fashion. Moreover, he quickly began to indulge his penchant for luxury. This trait was amply on display during an extended visit to Europe in December 1907. The trip, undertaken on medical grounds, following a bout of typhoid, became a year-long sojourn, during the course of which the new Jam Saheb lavishly entertained his old friends in England. But Ranji proved to be an elusive customer when it came to settling his bills. His increasingly irate creditors sought recourse to the law courts to recover their outstanding dues. Gallingly for the prince, the India Office was drawn into these disputes as his opponents began to raise questions about his status in Britain.[10]

Given his onerous responsibilities, one might think that the new Jam Saheb would have very little time for sport. However, Ranji did not let his official duties impede his pursuit of cricket. Thus, during the English summer of 1908, he frequently represented Sussex in the county championship. Although he was no longer the player of old, the prince occasionally showed flashes of his legendary skills. Nor did his interest in cricket cease when he returned to India after his year-long stay in Britain. Indeed, he had a new cricket pavilion built near his palace in Jamnagar and sought 'to have all the young men playing the game'. His aim, Ranji proclaimed, was 'to lead a team of Rajputs into the field that would rival even the Parsees'.[11]

But the Jam Saheb kept aloof from all forms of organized cricket in British India.[12] Indeed, when the organizers of the Indian cricket tour to Britain wrote to him, Ranji did not immediately respond.[13] When he finally deigned to send a reply, it was through his English private secretary. In his letter to the tour committee, Ranji expressed his 'cordial sympathy' for the venture and offered Rs. 1,000 towards the guarantee fund. But he pointedly refused to commit himself to playing for the Indian team, let alone serving as its captain. And although he promised to do 'anything for the success of the undertaking', the prince took little interest thereafter in its progress.[14]

Ranji's refusal to lead an Indian cricket team to Britain left the selector committee in a quandary. On the basis of ability and experience, the captaincy ought to have gone to Major Mistry. Instead, the selectors plumped for his young princely employer, whose only previous experience of the role was as captain of his college team. Intriguingly, in an interview after the conclusion of the 1911 Indian tour, one of the selectors—Mehellasha Pavri—revealed that the reason for picking Bhupinder as captain was to secure the services of his private secretary. Mistry, it will be recalled, had pulled out of the Indian cricket team in 1903 on account of his official duties. This time around the selectors did not want to take a chance, Pavri suggested, and therefore offered Bhupinder the captaincy in order to ensure Mistry's participation in the tour.[15]

This may well explain why two other cricket-playing royals, both pursuing their studies in Britain, were not considered for the captaincy of the Indian cricket team. The first was Rajkumar Shivaji Rao, third son of Maharaja Sayajirao III of Baroda. An undergraduate at Christ Church College, Oxford, this prince was in contention for a regular place in the university's first eleven. His progress was eagerly followed in India by those who sought to find a successor to Ranji. One cricketing enthusiast—drawing on colonial stereotypes—declared that Shivaji Rao looked 'more like the tall and graceful Rajput than the sturdy little Mahratta'.[16] In 1910, the prince played for the Hindus in the Triangular tournament and made an instant impression on spectators. Indeed, no less a figure than A.C. ('Archie') MacLaren, one of the giants of the Edwardian cricketing scene, had come to form 'a very high opinion of his abilities'. On a visit to the subcontinent in the winter of 1910, the Englishman told reporters that if there was 'a better player in India at the present time I should like to see him'.[17]

However, the imperial establishment feared that this scion of the Gaekwad family had begun to follow in his father's footsteps in exhibiting 'extremist' views. By this time, government officials in India had come to regard Baroda as a hotbed of sedition and Maharaja Sayaji Rao as an actively 'disloyal' ruler. The Gaekwad, they alleged in their correspondence with London, was secretly supporting Indian revolutionaries seeking to overthrow British rule. As a consequence, colonial authorities became increasingly concerned about the political leanings of the princely cricketer in Oxford. But unaware of the official disquiet about Shivaji Rao, the Indian selectors requisitioned his services on behalf of their cricket team in Britain.

The other princely cricketer whose name was regularly mentioned in the press was the Eton- and Cambridge-educated Rajkumar Hitendra Narayan of Cooch Behar. Many contemporaries believed that 'Prince Hitty', who had played for Somerset in 1910, ought to have been an automatic choice for the Indian team.[18] His absence from the Indian team is especially

curious given that his father, Maharaja Nripendra Narayan, had been a
prominent contributor to the guarantee fund for the cricket tour of Britain.

At any rate, it was Bhupinder Singh who was finally called upon to lead
the first Indian cricket team. No doubt the Indian selectors hoped that his
royal status would enable the prince to command this socially diverse group
of cricketers. However, the Maharaja's involvement in the tour of Britain
was inextricably linked to his own attempts to negotiate the challenging
political environment that confronted him as the newly enthroned ruler of
the most prominent state in the Punjab. This chapter thus highlights an
enduring theme in the early history of Indian cricket: the intersecting
worlds of princely politics and play.

II

A little after midnight on 8 November 1900, Maharaja Rajinder Singh of
Patiala died in his palace after a violent episode of *delirium tremens*.[19] The
European doctors attending on him attributed the twenty-eight-year-old
prince's untimely demise to his heavy drinking. Rajinder's death was
reported widely both in colonial India and imperial Britain. The Anglo-
Indian newspapers dwelt on his skills as a sportsman and a soldier and their
views were echoed in the glowing obituaries that appeared in the British
press. Sections of the Punjabi press, on the other hand, took a less sympathetic
view of Rajinder's rule. One newspaper declared that 'the late Maharaja was
a spendthrift of the worst type' and that the principal beneficiaries of 'this
waste of money were almost exclusively low-born European and Eurasian
vagabonds, who induced the deceased to indulge in European forms
of pleasure'.[20]

The mandarins of the Raj, for their part, viewed Rajinder's death with
mixed feelings. 'In physical courage and energy he was assuredly not lack-
ing,' wrote one colonial official shortly after his demise, 'in moral courage
and force of will he was deplorably deficient. The last man who had his ear
could sway his mind in any direction he pleased, and as his courtiers were a
crew of unprincipled revellers and debauchees, no good resolution was ever
allowed to bear fruit.'[21] It was not the first time that such criticism had been
directed at Rajinder. For throughout his short-lived reign, the Patiala ruler's
behaviour had frequently exasperated his British minders. A particularly
irksome episode for the imperial establishment occurred in April 1893

when the Maharaja suddenly married Florence Bryan, the sister of his Irish stable superintendent. Colonial authorities in the late Victorian era frowned on Indian rulers entering into relationships with European women, and the Viceroy himself warned Rajinder when rumours of the liaison first surfaced.[22] But it was to no avail, and the *Civil and Military Gazette* reported that the British government 'received no intimation of the Maharaja's marriage until some days after it had taken place'.[23] As a result, British officials ignored Rajinder's marriage and refused to recognize the child that was born out of this union four months later.[24]

The veneer of indifference masked official anxieties about the entry of a European wife into the Patiala seraglio. With a total area of over 5,400 square miles—'about the size of Yorkshire', one official report noted[25]—a yearly revenue of about ninety-six lakhs and a mixed population of Hindus, Sikhs, and Muslims numbering 1.5 million, Patiala was the premier princely state in the Punjab.[26] Moreover, its ruler had come to be regarded as the natural leader of the Sikh community, from whose ranks half the British Indian army was drawn. The Government of India thus took a close interest in its affairs, fearing that 'disorder and mismanagement in Patiala may involve disturbance and unrest in the Sikh population'.[27]

In the aftermath of Rajinder's marriage to 'Florence Maharani', official fears about the state of affairs at Patiala appeared to be justified by the circulation of rumours that the two-year-old Bhupinder Singh, the recognized heir to the throne, had been 'purchased at Sirsa in the Hissar district'.[28] Soon thereafter, his mother, the official queen of Patiala, passed away, consumed by tuberculosis and grief. Bhupinder himself was despatched to the princely state of Dholpur, a move that was presumably intended to minimize the threats to his life at the intrigue-ridden Patiala court. The heir apparent—'a delicate child of nine', as one British official described him[29]—only returned to Patiala at the beginning of 1900, just months before his father's death.[30]

In the intervening years, the relationship between the British and Rajinder Singh had grown increasingly tetchy. The death of Florence Maharani in rather mysterious circumstances in 1895 had prompted Rajinder to drown his sorrows in alcohol, women, and sport. In any case, the marriage to Florence had been a tumultuous and ill-fated affair, with the Patiala ruler's kinsfolk refusing to accept his Irish wife as a legitimate queen. Their child was poisoned to death in October 1894, presumably by a disaffected insider at the court.

By the end of the century, Rajinder's erratic personal conduct and his neglect of state affairs had begun to draw public criticism and arouse official concern.[31] 'I hear he is clever, but very hostile to us,' remarked Secretary of State George Hamilton in a letter to the Viceroy, Lord Curzon, in February 1899. 'As he is practically the head of the Sikh community, such hostility, if true, is a matter of some consideration.'[32] But Patiala was also one of the three Phulkian States—besides Nabha and Jind—with whom the British government had signed treaties that promised to respect their internal autonomy.[33] Notably, these states did not have a resident Political Agent. Moreover, they had considerable latitude in the authority they exercised within their territorial boundaries. Nonetheless, under pressure from Calcutta, the Punjab government belatedly sought to circumscribe Rajinder's autonomy by prevailing on him to introduce administrative and financial 'reforms' in his state.

However, the inability of the local government to exercise effective control over the Patiala ruler caused considerable annoyance to Curzon, who favoured a more interventionist approach towards the princely states. In October 1900, the Viceroy stated in an official note that after 'a most careful study of the character, dispositions and careers of the various Native princes', he was convinced that the 'instances of capacity, or brilliancy, or devotion to public duty, are not on the whole in a majority'. In the Punjab, Curzon argued, the 'want of opportunity for exercising personal influence' over the princes had 'resulted in complete and disastrous disappointment'. By way of an example, he pointed to the Maharaja of Patiala who had been 'left alone, with no adviser at the most critical epoch of his life, to drift into the society of stablemen, jockeys, and panderers of every description'.[34] The Viceroy was therefore keen to bring the three Phulkian States under the direct control of the Government of India through the creation of a new, specially qualified Political Agent to manage them.[35]

Rajinder Singh's sudden death offered the Raj an opportunity to intervene directly in the affairs of a state that had hitherto been able to evade close supervision and surveillance. In the hours following the Maharaja's demise, colonial authorities swiftly moved in to take charge of the succession. Key Patiala officials, some of whom were blamed for fuelling Rajinder's excesses, were placed under house arrest and asked to hand over state papers and possessions. Worried about his security, British officials also sought to confine Bhupinder in a secure location within the sprawling Moti Bagh palace.[36] Although they felt obliged under their treaty obligations to acquiesce in the creation of a three-member Council of Regency comprising Patiala officials, the colonial authorities nonetheless had the decisive say in the appointments. A new Political Agent was appointed to take immediate charge of the Phulkian States. In instructing him 'to guide and to advise the Council of Regency', the job description made it clear that henceforth this British official would call the shots at Patiala. 'What Patiala requires for the next ten years is the superintendence in every department and in regard to all details of an experienced British Administrator,' declared Lord Curzon.[37]

The first Political Agent sent to the Phulkian States was the Viceroy's choice. Major James Dunlop Smith, Curzon observed, had shown a 'marked aptitude for handling Native Chiefs and Durbars'.[38] Dunlop Smith took a close personal interest in matters concerning the Patiala prince, which led the Viceroy's Private Secretary to note with approval that he 'is just what a Political Officer should be—a friend and adviser, and not a dictator'.[39] At the same time, the new Political Agent sought to get rid of Rajinder's old cronies. The one exception was the Parsi cricketer from Bombay, K.M. Mistry, whom the deceased Patiala ruler had appointed as Bhupinder's guardian. British officials regarded Mistry as 'sound' and trustworthy and hence allowed him to continue in this important role.[40] The young prince too became very attached to the Parsi cricketer.

Colonial authorities not only tightened their grip over the administration of Patiala, but also took charge of Bhupinder's education. Indeed, the boy soon became an experiment in fashioning 'a real fine Chief'.[41] British officials agreed that the task of training the prince could only be entrusted to an Englishman. However, they also acknowledged the need to appoint some Indian tutors, to ensure that Bhupinder learnt 'to identify himself with the interests of his subjects and State'.[42] In 1904, following discussions between the Government of India and the Punjab administration, the prince was sent to Aitchison College, Lahore. He was the first in his family to travel out of Patiala for his education.[43] In taking this decision, colonial officials hoped that the exposure to a liberal institution intended for the Indian aristocracy would transform Bhupinder into an 'enlightened' ruler.

III

But as his eighteenth birthday approached, Bhupinder's personal behaviour increasingly belied the expectations of his British minders. In December

1908, anonymous petitions about the prince's alleged sexual misconduct reached the Lieutenant-Governor of the Punjab. The petitions began to arouse official anxieties that Bhupinder was following in the footsteps of his father. 'The late Maharaja began to go wrong under very similar conditions and when he was about as old as his son is now,' noted the chief secretary of the Punjab government in December 1908. 'When once they begin to go wrong the men of this family ruin themselves rapidly.'[44] At play in such judgements were evaluative notions that were the staple fare of late nineteenth-century Victorian discourse.[45] Thus, successive Patiala rulers were deemed to have lacked the self-restraint and steadfast devotion to duty that were regarded as the essential prerequisites of a 'sound character'.

In Bhupinder's case, colonial authorities became increasingly concerned that he had fallen under the influence of 'the same clique which were his father's boon companions'.[46] Their attention centred, in particular, on Bakshi Pritam Singh, commander-in-chief of the Patiala State Force, who, rumour had it, was 'procuring women for the Maharaja'.[47] Pritam Singh had been one of the Patiala officials whom the Punjab government had removed from his post following Rajinder's demise. He was also implicated in an embezzlement case, involving jewels purloined from the Patiala treasury.[48] The colonial authorities thus took a dim view of Pritam Singh's growing proximity to the young prince.

By convention, power was to be transferred from the Council of Regency to Bhupinder Singh after he had turned eighteen. As that day drew nearer, an animated internal debate ensued within the British imperial establishment about the merits of such a move. Notwithstanding the persistent rumours about his personal conduct, the Political Agent for the Phulkian States was inclined to give Bhupinder the benefit of the doubt. 'He has lots of common sense and for one so young seems to have an almost marvellous insight of human character. I am confident he will take a keen interest in the management of his State,' wrote Major Powney Thompson.[49] But Sir Louis Dane, the Lieutenant-Governor of Punjab, was inclined to take seriously the reports about Bhupinder's behaviour. Dane, therefore, sought to 'deprecate any undue haste in giving him too much power'.[50] The matter was referred to the Viceroy.

Since taking over from the meddlesome Curzon, Lord Minto had sought to change the Government of India's policy towards the princely states. He believed that his predecessor's wrong-headed approach had resulted in 'too much petty interference with the personal affairs and administration of Native Chiefs'.[51] More importantly, he believed that it was necessary to treat the princes as allies, especially to quell the challenge posed by nationalist revolutionaries.[52] Working in tandem with Harcourt Butler, his new foreign secretary, Minto developed a doctrine of non-interference in the internal affairs of the princely states.[53] The Patiala case offered a chance to test the new official approach. Minto was particularly invested in Patiala affairs on account of his family's connection with the Phulkian States. A century earlier, his great-grandfather had signed the crucial accord with King Ranjit Singh that brought the Cis-Sutlej states under British protection. Now, Minto reviewed Bhupinder's situation and concluded that 'the risks of post-poning the gift of full powers' were 'greater than the risks of any alternative proposal'. Moreover, the Viceroy considered it 'natural that the Maharaja should want to have full powers'. He therefore sided with the Political Agent in seeking to 'show trust in the young man' and granting his wish.[54] Minto's view prevailed and Bhupinder was given 'full powers without any reservation' in October 1909. At the same time, the Maharaja was 'privately' informed that these powers were 'given to him on trial, and on the under-standing that he should consult the Political Agent in all important matters'.[55] If he acquitted himself well, Bhupinder was told, he would be formally invested by the Viceroy at a ceremony in Patiala in the spring of 1910.[56]

Events in Patiala swiftly brought home to the imperial establishment the pitfalls of pursuing a policy of non-interference vis-à-vis the princely states. A new Political Agent to the Phulkian States had taken charge in the winter of 1909. Colonel Dallas soon began to file alarmed reports to his supervisors in the Punjab government about Bhupinder's alleged escapades involving 'wine and women'.[57] Like his predecessor, he held Sardar Pritam Singh and his relatives responsible for leading the prince astray. While admitting that the Bakshi had 'no doubt done excellent work as Commander-in Chief', Dallas argued that Pritam Singh's 'bad influence' necessitated his removal 'from such close intimacy with the Maharaja'.[58] The Political Agent was equally concerned about the manner in which the prince had come to rely excessively on the official advice of his *Wazir*, Sardar Gurdit Singh. A member of the famous Patiala polo team in Rajinder's time, Gurdit Singh had grown close to Bhupinder by virtue of having been his erstwhile guardian.[59] Dallas' reports prompted the Lieutenant-Governor of the Punjab to write to James Dunlop Smith, now the Viceroy's private secretary, about the behaviour of his former ward. The Maharaja, he told Dunlop Smith, had 'taken to Polo and the old gang have reappeared. Naturally drinking has recommenced and the boy has been led into it... There are also rumours of a third marriage besides other excesses.'[60] In February 1910, the Punjab government accordingly advised the Viceroy that it would be best to postpone the formal investiture ceremony.

The news emanating from Patiala unsettled the Viceroy. Minto accepted the need to postpone Bhupinder's investiture and sanctioned the Punjab government's decision to warn Pritam Singh about his conduct. But the Viceroy also expressed his irritation at the inability of the Political Agent to establish 'personal influence' over the prince. The role of the Political Agent, as Minto saw it, ought to be 'that of a friend giving friendly advice whenever required'.[61] He therefore advocated the appointment of a British officer as a companion to the Maharaja. This officer, Minto stipulated, ought to be 'young and fond of sports, especially cricket, and a man on whom the Maharaja could lean as a friend. He would have nothing to do with the Political Agent, but might be called a Private Secretary.'[62] Clearly, the Viceroy believed that adhering to the values enshrined in the imperial game would awaken Bhupinder to his princely responsibilities.

The Punjab government agreed that if the Maharaja did not act according to the Political Agent's advice, it would consider replacing the latter with 'an officer who is a good cricketer, an Oxford Blue ... in the hopes that he might be able to keep His Highness to cricket and tennis at which he is good, the L-G being afraid his excursions in the direction of polo were the beginning of trouble'.[63] The person selected for this post was an Englishman named Short, employed in the Punjab police force, who was regarded 'as a fair cricketer and a fine lawn tennis player'.[64]

Bhupinder did not take too kindly to the colonial government's proposal that he hire a European private secretary.[65] He had, no doubt, swiftly intuited that such a 'friend' would be yet another cog in the wheel of imperial surveillance. In June 1910, the prince wrote a defiant letter to the government, which sought 'to point out that this appointment may not be made contrary to the treaties and agreements of the British Raj with the Patiala State, and that it should not be considered a precedent for the future'.[66] The petulant tone suggests that Bhupinder had increasingly begun to chafe at the treatment meted out to him by the imperial establishment.

IV

Ever since he had been provisionally granted full powers in October 1909, the Patiala prince had become sharply aware of the precariousness of his situation. He had adopted a variety of tactics in response to the actions of the colonial government. In his meetings with the Political Agent, Bhupinder defended himself strenuously against the allegations about the impropriety of his political conduct. On more than one occasion, he denied outright any charge of wrongdoing on his part. At the same time, he also sought to dispel insinuations that his court had begun to manifest distinct anti-British sentiments.

It was perhaps the urge to demonstrate his loyalty that led Bhupinder to overplay his hand in dealing with a so-called 'seditious' plot apparently being hatched by a group of Arya Samaj activists in Patiala.[67] The alleged anti-British conspiracy was uncovered in August 1909, following which the overzealous inspector-general of the Patiala police, John Warburton (supposedly the inspiration for Rudyard Kipling's 'Strickland Sahib'),[68] peremptorily arrested eighty Arya Samaj members. The prosecution case soon turned into a farce as thirty-seven suspects had to be released for lack of evidence. In February 1910, the remaining forty-three prisoners applied to the Maharaja for a pardon and the trial was summarily terminated, with all the charges against the accused being withdrawn. But Bhupinder, perhaps anxious that his actions might be misconstrued by the British government, banished them from his state. The Punjab government was unimpressed by the Maharaja's handling of the case.[69] Luckily for the Patiala prince, the Government of India was more inclined to blame the Political Agent for this 'fiasco'.[70]

Presumably chastened by the bungled sedition trial, Bhupinder sought to convince British officials that he was committed to the responsible discharge of his duties. 'For the last two months or so the Maharaja has been going through his budgets; he has gone into most of them very thoroughly and has worked hard,' reported Colonel Dallas in May 1910. Bhupinder, he added, had been talking to him 'more freely and frankly' and was 'now anxious to turn over a new leaf'. 'He is himself intelligent and with a little more experience I am sure he will make a wise and sympathetic Chief,' the Political Agent concluded.[71] He also sought to convince his superiors to reconsider their decision to force the Maharaja to employ a European private secretary. Bhupinder, he wrote, was 'very much opposed to the appointment of an European officer'. The Political Agent feared that the move would 'embitter the Maharaja and make him discontented'.[72] Convinced by the colonel's arguments, Minto agreed to drop the proposal. But in return the Viceroy demanded that the prince 'make radical changes in his official and personal staff'.[73]

Bhupinder, recognizing that any further truculence on his part would jeopardize his position, agreed to the Viceroy's conditions. In late July 1910, he sacked Gurdit Singh as *Wazir* and reorganized his administration. He also offered to change his personal staff in line with the government's wishes.[74] In turn, these moves persuaded his British overlords that the time had come to confirm Bhupinder's formal accession to the Patiala throne.

However, there now followed a series of official flip-flops that suggests that imperial decision making was driven, more often than not, by rumour rather than reason. Early in September 1910, the Punjab government hastily requested the Viceroy to defer the investiture ceremony. Their decision was based on a report from a new Political Agent at Patiala, which stated that Gurdit Singh still controlled the Maharaja.[75] The Punjab government ordered their man on the spot to interview Bhupinder at once 'regarding this matter, and certain allegations of a vigorous pro-Sikh policy'.[76] After the interview, however, the Political Agent sang a different tune. He told his superiors that there was not much to be gained by deferring Bhupinder's formal installation. 'After all we have at present very little more control over him than we shall have if he is confirmed,' he argued, 'and if he is installed at once he is more likely to feel that the British Government is really his friend and the Political Agent not a school master and spy to be deceived and cajoled.'[77] Minto, himself due to depart shortly from India, promptly agreed. Bhupinder was informed at the end of September 1910 that the Viceroy would shortly install him on the Patiala *gaddi*.[78]

Yet days before the Maharaja's formal investiture ceremony, colonial authorities once again developed cold feet about the transfer of power. Fresh allegations about Bhupinder's sexual misconduct surfaced and resonated with the suspicions of British officials. As before, their anxieties centred on Sardar Gurdit Singh and Bakshi Pritam Singh, who were held responsible for the prince's actions.[79] Based on a new report from his capricious Political Agent, Sir Louis Dane, the lieutenant-governor of Punjab, informed the Viceroy that the state of affairs at Patiala were 'very bad and the Maharaja's immoralities scandalous and open'. While the former *Wazir* could be 'dealt with more easily', he argued, there was no alternative but to make Bhupinder's investiture conditional on the dismissal of Pritam Singh.[80]

It was a view shared by all the European military officers stationed at Patiala. A febrile letter from Major E.J.M. Molyneux, the inspecting officer of the Punjab Imperial Service Cavalry, mounted a devastating attack on the commander-in-chief of the Patiala State Force.[81] It accused Pritam Singh of recruiting close relatives into the force, receiving bribes in return for dispensing favours in the internal distribution of posts, and flouting rules regarding the procurement of supplies. Molyneux also claimed that Pritam Singh's overweening ambition was to 'get the Maharaja under his power' and thereby become 'King in Patiala'. He suggested, on the basis of informal testimony from local court officials, that Pritam Singh had engineered the departure of his rival Gurdit Singh. Now, Molyneux darkly alleged, the Bakshi was bent on encouraging Bhupinder 'in every kind of dissipation that will shorten his life or render him inefficient to carry on State business'. But the well-meaning Maharaja, he insinuated, had been unable to take action against his commander-in-chief out of fear that Pritam Singh would reveal incriminating details about his personal conduct to the British government. Molyneux therefore urged his superiors to act 'before the installation of His Highness sets the seal of official approval on what has already happened'.[82]

Informed of these developments, the Viceroy weighed his options. Minto had no desire to humiliate Bhupinder by cancelling his state visit to Patiala, not least because it 'might create sympathy for him amongst the Sikh Chiefs'.[83] At the same time, he was also unwilling to rely on the Maharaja's verbal assurances that he would henceforth keep a distance from Gurdit Singh and Pritam Singh.[84] Eventually, Minto insisted that Bhupinder meet four conditions if he wished his investiture ceremony to proceed as planned. First, Pritam Singh would have to be immediately dismissed and turned out, along with those of his relatives who were mentioned in Molyneux's report, from Patiala territory. Second, Gurdit Singh was to be 'summarily dealt with and not permitted to come near the Maharaja in future'. Third, Bhupinder would have to undertake 'to appoint no new men in the place of those dismissed without consulting the Local Government'. And lastly, he had to 'consult the Political Agent informally in future in all important matters'.[85]

A desperate Bhupinder, fearful for his throne and increasingly conscious of the public ignominy that would follow yet another postponement of his investiture ceremony, reluctantly complied with the Viceroy's demands. Pritam Singh was removed from his post and, along with all his relatives in the Imperial Service Troops, turned out of Patiala. Gurdit Singh was also forced to go out of the state.[86] Satisfied with the pound of flesh that he had extracted, Lord Minto attended the investiture *durbar* in Patiala on 3 November 1910.[87]

V

This, then, was the political context within which Bhupinder chose to participate in the first Indian cricket tour of Britain. There is a misconception that the Maharaja of Patiala 'organised, financed and captained' the venture.[88] But, as we have seen, nothing could be further from the truth. Preoccupied as he was with securing his position as ruler, Bhupinder had little time to devote to the cause of Indian cricket. Indeed, in the eighteen months that went into the organization of the tour, the Maharaja's only tangible contribution was as a subscriber to the guarantee fund.

However, unlike Ranji, the Patiala prince was quick to accept when the tour organizers invited him, sometime in the spring of 1910, to join the proposed Indian cricket team. Indeed, from then on, Bhupinder's name regularly began to appear in the list of players who were considered certainties for the cricket tour of Britain. Interestingly, the prince was not required to attend any selection trials: he was an automatic choice. This is not to insinuate that his cricketing skills were negligible. On the contrary, from his childhood, Bhupinder had been coached by some of the best cricketers of the day. After all, under his father the Patiala cricket team was one of the finest in the subcontinent. And even after Rajinder's death, Bhupinder continued to benefit from the coaching of his Parsi guardian K.M. Mistry. In 1909, the prince also hired the famous Australian and Middlesex professional cricketer Frank Tarrant to hone his skills.[89] Thus, by the time he was invited to play for India, Bhupinder had become renowned as a powerful striker of the cricket ball. He played in a manner that befitted his regal status: short, sharp bursts of flamboyant batting before boredom set in and induced a fatal error. Nonetheless, it was a style of play that left an indelible impression on teammates and spectators alike.

Bhupinder's eagerness to travel to Britain as a member of the Indian cricket team is significant. In 1909, he had rejected a proposal from the Lieutenant-Governor of Punjab to undertake a tour of Ceylon, the Straits Settlements, and Japan. On that occasion, colonial authorities had hoped that a foreign sojourn would keep the Maharaja from idling in Patiala while awaiting news about his future. Besides, Punjab officials believed that travelling out of his state would widen Bhupinder's horizons and yield educational benefits.[90] However, the prince refused to go abroad, citing his recent marriage as the reason for his unwillingness to leave Patiala.[91] Yet he showed no hesitation in accepting the invitation to travel with the Indian cricket team to Britain.

Was Bhupinder's move a means of evading, even if only temporarily, the relentless scrutiny and surveillance of the Punjab government? If not, did it perhaps stem from a straightforward desire to see and experience *vilayat*?[92] Or did he seek glory at the home of cricket of the kind that had made Ranji an imperial celebrity? Then again, was this a canny bid to forge personal connections at the highest level of the imperial hierarchy in Britain and thereby gain powerful allies whose influence he could deploy against the officials who harried him at home? The historical record does not yield any clear-cut answers: all these calculations may have been at play in Bhupinder's decision to participate in the Indian cricket tour.

What is clear, however, is that Bhupinder knew that he could not travel to Britain with the Indian cricket team without the official sanction of the Raj. He first appears to have made his intentions known to his British interlocutors in June 1910. The news came as a surprise to the Government of India. 'This is the first I have heard of the Maharaja going to England with the cricket team,' exclaimed the Secretary of the Foreign Department when he learnt the news. 'I daresay it will do him no harm, but it is a dangerous experiment.'[93]

As time went by, Bhupinder grew increasingly anxious about securing the government's permission to travel to Britain. The Political Agent in Patiala reported in January 1911 that the Maharaja had asked him 'to obtain the permission of Government' for the visit. 'He hopes to play cricket for the All-India team and also to see something of England,' he noted.[94] The Political Agent, who felt that Bhupinder had lately been leading a healthier life, recommended to the government that the Maharaja be permitted to undertake the trip. The move, he believed, would 'do much to cement the Chief's loyalty and friendship and to help him to adhere to his resolution of abstaining from liquor'.[95] However, in the light of the recent troubles at Patiala, the Political Agent suggested that the official sanction for the visit be made conditional on Bhupinder meeting two requirements. First, he would only take with him attendants and companions approved by the government. Second, he would make 'arrangements satisfactory to Government for the administration of the State in his absence'.[96] The Punjab government agreed and informed the Government of India that 'it would be well to allow the Maharaja to visit England, especially as he has set his heart on going'.[97]

Colonial officials had determined that because of the forthcoming royal visit to India, no ruling chiefs, except the King's honorary *aide-de-camps*, were to be formally invited to London for the impending coronation of George V.[98] Bhupinder's participation in the Indian cricket tour thus confronted the imperial establishment with intricate issues pertaining to protocol. Was it appropriate for the Maharaja to travel with the tour as a private individual? And, if he visited Britain, would it be necessary to invite him to attend the coronation ceremony? The Punjab government thought 'it would be awkward to allow him to go as a private individual and member of a cricket team, as he is politically one of the most important Chiefs'. Furthermore, it noted, 'if he were not invited to the Coronation our action might be misinterpreted, while if he were invited other Chiefs to whom such permission has been refused might perhaps feel that they had a grievance'.[99] One way to get around the difficulty, the Lieutenant-Governor of the Punjab suggested, would be to appoint Bhupinder as an *aide-de-camp* to the King-Emperor. Such a move, he ventured, 'might prove a considerable influence for good'. At the same time, the Lieutenant-Governor worried that 'the past conduct of His Highness since his unhappy investiture with powers in October 1909 has hardly been such as to entitle him to so signal an honour'. In these circumstances, the Punjab government was inclined to suggest that the Maharaja 'be allowed to visit England as a private individual'. Further, if he behaved himself during the trip, 'His Majesty might be asked to appoint him a special aide-de-camp for the Coronation'.[100] The Government of India refused to entertain this idea. But it agreed to issue Bhupinder 'an invitation to the Coronation ceremony in London, should he go to England with the cricket team'.[101] At the same time, the new Viceroy, Lord Hardinge, made it clear that the Maharaja would only be allowed to accompany the Indian cricket team to Britain if he complied with the requirements specified by the Political Agent.[102]

Meanwhile, colonial officials continued to nurture misgivings about Bhupinder's conduct. The Political Agent reported that even after his formal investiture, the Maharaja appeared to find it 'too difficult' to overcome 'his resentment of Government interference'. He also alleged that Pritam Singh and Gurdit Singh retained their influence at Bhupinder's court. Moreover, the Maharaja was 'always accompanied by half a dozen young men, idlers, most of whom are called *Aides-de-Camp*'. 'If he only takes a few attendants with him to England and lives for a time in the society of English gentlemen his tastes may improve,' the Political Agent observed. He therefore deemed it necessary to limit the size of Bhupinder's entourage and only select companions who were of 'good character'.[103] His remarks had the necessary effect. The colonial government insisted that Bhupinder supply them with the names of those who would form part of his entourage to Britain.[104] Eventually, the Maharaja agreed to travel with a small party comprising K.M. Mistry, his new private secretary; his father-in-law; two *Aides-de-Camp*; and two 'body servants'.[105] This was considerably less than the thirty-strong entourage permitted to the prominent princes who were invited to Britain for the coronation.

But even after they had granted Bhupinder formal sanction to take part in the cricket tour, colonial authorities sought to keep up their surveillance of the prince. To this end, the Punjab government recommended the appointment of a political officer to watch over Bhupinder during his stay in Britain.[106] 'A very great deal depends on the effect which his tour will have on the young Maharaja,' wrote one government official. 'His family instincts will attract him to an undesirable class of society, and his Political Officer must endeavour not only to keep him out of that but give him every possible of getting into the right society.'[107] In keeping with Bhupinder's wishes, the selection of this officer was entrusted to Sir James Dunlop Smith, who was now the political *aide-de-camp* to the Secretary of State for India in London. The Government of India requested that the political officer chosen for this task 'should be a man of 30 to 35 years of age, of steady character, well at home in good society, and good at games'. The Viceroy, in particular, regarded 'the last quality essential if the Political Officer is to have a good influence over the Maharaja'.[108]

Lord Hardinge, an ex-Harrovian devotee of the imperial game, had one further, if inadvertent, impact on Bhupinder's participation in the Indian cricket tour of Britain. According to the Political Agent stationed at Patiala, Bhupinder had vacillated over the captaincy.[109] At first, he accepted the offer, only to change his mind shortly thereafter. But at the very end of March 1911, the Maharaja travelled to Lahore to attend a viceregal durbar to commemorate the formal British annexation of the Punjab by Lord Hardinge's grandfather in 1848. When the two men met, Hardinge, unaware that Bhupinder had turned down the captaincy, reportedly congratulated the Patiala prince on the honour accorded to him by the Indian selectors. Perhaps the interest taken in the tour by the Viceroy alerted the Maharaja to the political possibilities of the captaincy. It may have also dawned on Bhupinder that colonial officials in Patiala would be unable to raise any last-minute objections to his trip if he became captain. In any event, according to this particular version of events, the prince hurriedly cabled the selection committee in Bombay and expressed his willingness to lead the Indian team to Britain.[110] The news was not welcomed in all quarters. 'We thought he was going for political education and for studying English and European institutions,' remarked the *Tribune*. 'But he is merely going out as the captain of a cricket team!'[111]

The Political Agent, for his part, offered the following assessment of Bhupinder's prospects:

> Personally I should rather have preferred that he were not Captain, but it should be alright if he has a good officer with him in England and is kept out of second-class hotels. I do not think that the Maharaja will play much cricket in England. There will be so much else to do and he hates sitting about doing nothing. If he begins well and makes big scores he may remain keen, but if, as equally possible, he does badly, he will soon give up cricket.[112]

VI

At the beginning of May, Bhupinder set out for Bombay. On the eve of his departure for the metropolis, his subjects assembled at the Moti Bagh palace 'to give him a hearty send off'. The Maharaja used the occasion to express his pride at being 'the first Chief of this State to participate in the celebration of an auspicious event which symbolizes the heartfelt rejoicings of the numerous millions of His Majesty's subjects'.[113] Such public affirmations of loyalty were no doubt meant to dispel any misgivings that his imperial minders might have harboured about the prince's foreign visit.

By the time Bhupinder's entourage disembarked in Bombay, the other members of his team—with the notable exception of Maneck Chand and Noor Elahi—had already arrived in the city from different parts of the country.[114] The three Aligarh students had recently sat for their annual examinations and the cricket tour of Britain was a welcome break from their studies. On the other hand, Manik Bulsara might well have had mixed feelings about the impending journey, as his wedding had taken place only the previous week.[115]

Meanwhile, public fervour about the 'national' cricket team reached a fever pitch in the city in the days immediately preceding their departure. 'Bombay is largely occupied the last day or two of this week in wishing farewell to the All-India Cricket Team,' noted one newspaper.[116] Some of the Bombay players were felicitated by their clubs and offices. E.D. Sassoon & Co., a firm run by the city's most prominent Baghdadi Jews, organized an office function at which Mukund Pai was presented with a purse.[117] The Baronet CC held an event in honour of Meherhomji and Mulla. Both these club stalwarts were congratulated and each was presented 'with a watch as a souvenir of the occasion'.[118] One private firm was also quick to use the departure of the Indian cricket team as an opportunity to publicize its goods. Messrs Jhanda Singh Uberoi & Sons of Sialkot presented each member of the Indian team with their company's 'high class Perfecta' cricket bat. This 'recent introduction' was said to be 'made of English Willow by an expert who for many years made Cricket Bats for England's leading Professionals, including such champions as Dr W.G. Grace and the late Arthur Shrewsbury'. Its makers therefore felt confident that 'finer bats have never been placed in the hands of Professional cricketers'. Moreover, the manufacturers asserted, these indigenously made bats were proof 'that Indian can now successfully compete with the imported articles'. The company announced that one of the bats with the signatures of the leading Indian players would 'be sold by auction for the benefit of poor cricketers'.[119]

On the morning of 4 May 1911, Bhupinder, along with the other Indian cricketers, was photographed at the Bourne and Shepherd studio on Hornby Road.[120] A grand function to felicitate the Indian cricketers was held later that evening at the city's Orient Club. Formally inaugurated in January 1910, this club was one of the few in the city that enabled Indians and Europeans to socialize with each other.[121] Present on this occasion were all the well-known figures in Bombay's high society: captains of industry and commerce, prominent lawyers, journalists, and politicians.[122] But there is one name in this gathering that is of particular interest to the historian: Mohammad Ali Jinnah was, at this time, one of the rising stars of Bombay politics. Known for his razor-sharp intellect and highly anglicized ways, this urbane lawyer was a familiar figure in the city's elite social circles.

That evening, however, Jinnah was a mere onlooker. For it was J.M. Framjee Patel who took centre stage, revelling in his role as the principal spokesman for Indian cricket. Addressing the gathering, the cricket impresario began by announcing that the Governor of Bombay had sent him a telegram expressing his support and best wishes for the venture. 'I am sure they will show good cricket and good fellowship, thus helping to strengthen the ties which unite India with the Empire,' wrote Sir George Clarke.[123]

Figure 12. The members of the All-India cricket team, photographed in Bombay on the eve of their departure to London, May 1911. Courtesy of Prakash Dahatonde, India.

Framjee Patel began his own speech by echoing the sentiments expressed by Pherozeshah Mehta on the eve of the first Parsi cricket's team departure for Britain. 'As artists go to Italy to do homage to the great masters, or as pilgrims to Jerusalem to worship at shrine, so now our representatives visit the land that has inspired most of our ideals and to acquire greater proficiency in the natural [sic] game of England,' he proclaimed. Reviewing the personnel in the Indian team, Patel expressed his confidence that 'we are sending a fine side to England to represent us in the Coronation year' and hoped that 'given a fine and bright summer our representatives may be counted upon to win at least half the matches in their ambitious programme'. 'Only one great name is missing from the list selected,' he told his audience, 'it is that of H.H. the Jam Saheb Ranjitsinghji [sic]. All I can say is that I have left no stone unturned to secure the greatest cricketing asset of the country for team, but unfortunately without success.' However, keen to avoid causing any offence to the Patiala prince, Patel called Bhupinder 'one of the best sportsmen in India'. As for the players who were bound for Britain, Patel had one word of advice: 'I hope that every member of the team will go on training and practice regularly and thus try to be worthy of the trust reposed in him by his countrymen.'[124]

Reminding his audience that cricket had 'an imperial side to it', Patel concluded his speech with a ringing endorsement of the role of sport in promoting fraternal relations between rulers and ruled: 'Let cricket be one of the many links to unite the citizens of the greatest Empire the world has ever seen. Let the providential alliance of Ind and Britain be cemented with the lasting and enduring ties of one peace-loving King-Emperor, one beautiful language, one victorious flag, and, last but not least, one grand Imperial game.'[125]

There is no way of knowing what effect these rousing words had on the Indian cricketers. Their young captain, however, took the opportunity to praise his British overlords and thanked the organizers for electing him captain of 'this friendly cricketing mission'. Echoing Patel, the Maharaja declared that the cricketers' visit would 'bring closer together India and the British Empire'.[126]

The farewell function at the Orient Club was widely reported in the Indian press. Prominent Anglo-Indian newspapers, too, devoted editorials to the impending departure of the Indian cricketers. The *Bombay Gazette* called it 'an event without a parallel in the history of cricket'. The two Parsi cricket tours of Britain, the paper noted, 'were only representative of a single community, and had no claim to stand for Indian cricket as a whole'. By contrast, 'the present team, is an All-India combination, representative of the best cricketing ability of the country'. The paper also highlighted the political value of the tour. 'Indeed, the one ideal, that has all along been kept in view by the organisers of the tour and which might without exaggeration be described as the prime motive of the tour, has been the promotion of friendly feelings between the people of the two countries, of bringing various classes more closely together,' it observed.[127] The *Times of India* regretted that Ranjitsinhji and Framjee Patel could not make the journey to Britain but agreed that 'the eleven may be trusted to acquit itself well in the field, to gain honour for India, and to make lasting friends of its opponents'.[128]

Other Europeans, however, were unimpressed by the publicity accorded to the departing cricketers. 'As to the Indian cricket team,' said the Bombay correspondent of the Calcutta newspaper *Capital*, 'well, they should have a good time, but I am afraid they will not set the Thames on fire. If they toured Ireland instead of England, they would win a lot of matches. Cricket is not a national game in the step-sister Isle.'[129]

One does not know if the Indian cricketers read the newspapers in the hectic days immediately preceding their departure. What can be inferred with more certainty is that the team was distracted by the news that two of

BUMPERS, GENTLEMEN!

Mr. Punch—(To H. H. the Maharaja of Patiala, the Captain of the All India Team, and the Vice-Captain, Dr. Homi Kanga, and Secretary, Mr. Divecha)—Friends, all success to you and the members of the Team! And more power to your elbow and their !

[The All India Team, which started yesterday (6th May) for England under the best auspices, w s entertained at the Orient Club on Thursday (4th May). H. E. the Governor sent the following telegram to Mr. J. M. Framjee Patel :—" My best wishes to His Highness and members of All India Team for a most pleasant and successful tour. I am sure they will show good cricket and good fellowship, thus helping to strengthen the ties which unite India with the Empire."]

Figure 13. A cartoon in *Hindi Punch* depicting the farewell ceremony arranged for the departing Indian cricketers at the Orient Club, Bombay, on 4 May 1911. © British Library Board. All Rights Reserved / Bridgeman Images.

its members—Maneck Chand and Noor Elahi—had withdrawn from the tour.[130] It is not entirely clear why the two Punjabi players suddenly decided to abandon the journey at this late hour. According to one account, the men were unable to travel because their eccentric employer, the Maharaja of Kashmir, rescinded his earlier decision to let them travel abroad as part of the Indian cricket team.[131]

The telegrams from Kashmir prompted the tour organizers to hurriedly requisition the services of Palwankar Shivram. In his autobiography, Vithal recalled that his brother was informed of the selectors' decision on the eve of the team's departure. Caught unawares, Shivram had to scramble to get together the necessary papers and baggage for the journey.[132]

As it transpired, he was the only reserve to be called up, for the organizers inexplicably decided to restrict the touring party to sixteen members.

VII

On the morning of 6 May 1911, the Indian cricketers assembled at the Parsi Gymkhana. The team, *sans* Bhupinder, proceeded to Ballard Pier, where it was greeted by a surging crowd.[133] Enthusiastic supporters cheered and garlanded the cricketers. Only the two Dalit players remained unacknowledged in the midst of these farewell rituals: neither Baloo nor Shivram received any garlands.[134] Oblivious to their feelings, the rest of the touring party clambered onto the launches that ferried them to their ship. Their captain, meanwhile, travelled separately to Apollo Bunder, where the organizers had arranged a luxurious boat to transport him to the waiting P&O liner.

Shortly after noon, the *S.S. Arabia*, with the first Indian cricket team on board, ventured into the grey-green waters of the Arabian Sea.

7

The City of the World

I

On 21 May 1911, a fortnight after their departure from Bombay, the Indian cricketers made an unobtrusive entry into London's Victoria Station, having covered the last leg of the journey by train from Dover. Their two-week sea voyage to Marseilles on the *SS Arabia* had been a difficult one. A newspaper correspondent who interviewed the players in France revealed that a number of them 'did not enjoy the trip at all'. Indeed, towards the end of their voyage, some were so seasick that they had not even stirred out of their cabins.[1] Their onward journey from Marseilles to London via Paris was an equally trying affair. The *Times of India* reported that the players had 'travelled for twenty-four hours without sleep'. To make matters worse, 'The carriages placed at their disposal in France defied any attempt to find within them a measure of comfort.'[2]

Their princely captain had a very different experience. Bhupinder Singh and his entourage travelled separately by a 'deluxe' train from Marseilles to Dover. Their journey to London, in the newly designed Pullman carriages of the South Eastern and Chatham Railway, was equally luxurious. The carriages were said to 'excel not only in comfort but artistic design, being treated in the styles of distinctive periods, so that the traveller may choose between Adamesque, Georgian, Renaissance and Louis XVI decorations, carried out in fine paneling of maple, oak and mahogany'.[3] The prince and his entourage created a stir when they disembarked at Charing Cross Station. The *Daily Mail* reported:

> His Highness was gorgeously arrayed in rich flowered silk of bright hue, and attracted a great deal of attention as he strode down the platform to his motor-car wearing about his neck and upon his chest a garland of red roses. Very many Indians resident in London and Indian visitors who had previously reached England were at the station to welcome the Maharajah.

The imperial officials who had come to receive Bhupinder and his 'distinguished-looking suite' whisked the visitors away to a specially chosen private residence.[4]

Meanwhile, the Maharaja's teammates made their way to the hotel that Thomas Cook had arranged for them.[5] It was half past eight in the evening by the time they arrived at their final destination. The weary Indians 'sought their bedrooms and gave instructions that they were not to be called until the following afternoon'.[6] The next day the Indian players were much in demand with reporters eager to interview and photograph them. 'It would be very difficult to imagine a more interesting lot of men,' noted one journalist. 'They differ in every way from the ordinary cricket team. They shun publicity, and to look at them one would never think for a moment that they were athletes.'[7] Another correspondent informed his readers that the players had spent their first morning taking a 'stroll through London, the city they have all been longing to see'.[8]

The Indian cricketers had landed in a city that was described by a contemporary as 'the world's clearing-house, the world's springboard, the home of lost causes, the death-chamber of the past, and the birthplace of the future'.[9] It was also, he might have added, an imperial metropolis at the zenith of its glory. Indeed, the arrival of the Indian cricketers coincided with the start of an extraordinary summer in which the city played host to what one observer breathlessly touted as 'the greatest imperial spectacle ever witnessed in the history of the world'.[10]

II

For the Indian cricketers, the impress of empire would have begun with their hotel. Designed by Charles Fitzroy Dell, the Imperial Hotel on Southampton Row was a striking red brick building suffused with decorative motifs that exalted empire. Four 'life-size statues of the emperors Charlemagne and Julius Caesar, and Edward VII and his consort, Queen Alexandra' dominated the front elevation. Other imperial symbols included the 'two hemispheres of the globe, executed in mosaic' representing British territory.[11]

But there was a subtler imperial sporting resonance in the choice of this hotel for the cricketers' stay. Among the Imperial's earliest occupants when it opened in 1907 was the South African cricket team that toured Britain that year. The visit had been explicitly organized to demonstrate that

South Africa was an integral part of the British Empire, at a time when its political future was at stake. In London, the organizers made every effort to underscore the 'imperial bond'. For their part, the proprietors of the Imperial were so eager to host the South African team that they hastened the completion of the hotel in order to register the cricketers as the first guests.[12]

In the vicinity of the Imperial Hotel were landmarks—many of which did not exist when the Parsi cricketers had visited the city a quarter of a century before—testifying to London's status as the first city of the British Empire. Sauntering down Southampton Row towards the Thames embankment, the Indians would have traversed the newly developed Kingsway, conceived as a suitably imperial riposte to London's continental rivals with their broad thoroughfares, magnificent boulevards, and spectacular vistas. Built at a cost of 5 million pounds and inaugurated by King Edward VII in 1905, large stretches of this grand avenue were as yet unoccupied at the time of the cricketers' visit.[13]

On either side of Aldwych, in an arc extending from Westminster Bridge to Tower Bridge, the Indians would have seen further evidence of London's imperial identity, visibly inscribed in stone. The prevailing imperial architectural style was Edwardian Baroque, whose ornate classicism dominated the public buildings of inner London in the first decade of the new century.[14] Even hotels, departmental stores, company offices, and restaurants adopted the 'Grand Manner' of the neoclassical revival.[15] These buildings 'reflected and reinforced an impression, an atmosphere, celebrating British heroism on the battlefield, British sovereignty over foreign lands, British wealth and power, in short, British imperialism'.[16]

Baroque classicism was also the preferred style of Sir Aston Webb, the architect selected by the government to design a national memorial for Queen Victoria, which was completed a few days before the Indian cricketers arrived in the city.[17] Its two most striking elements bookended a redesigned Mall, now transformed into a regal and imperial processional route from Buckingham Palace to Charing Cross.[18] The three symmetrical archways of Admiralty Arch framed entry into the Mall from Trafalgar Square. At the other end, Thomas Brock's ornately sculpted Victoria Memorial was placed in front of Buckingham Palace. Described by its creator as 'a great imperial and national ideal', the marble monument was unveiled on 16 May 1911 by the new King-Emperor in the presence of a large gathering that included his cousin, Kaiser Wilhelm II of Germany.[19]

But imperial intimations could also be discerned in the more prosaic features of London's built environment. Nowhere was this more so than the docks, wharves, and warehouses lining the Thames riverfront from Tower Bridge to Tilbury, whose 'smudgy detail' had once reminded Henry James of 'nothing less than the wealth and power of the British Empire at large'.[20] Within their capacious precincts were housed a staggering array of commodities that testified to the global reach of the imperial metropolis.[21] 'A visit to the docks is profoundly interesting,' a contemporary guidebook noted,

> and perhaps nothing will convey to the stranger a better idea of the vast activity and stupendous wealth of London than a visit to the warehouses of the London Docks... filled to overflowing with interminable stores of every kind of foreign and colonial products; to the enormous vaults with their apparently inexhaustible quantities of wine; and to the extensive quays and landing-stages, cumbered with huge stacks of hides, heaps of bales, and long rows of casks.[22]

Had they followed the suggestion in the guidebook, the Indian cricketers might well have been reminded of home, for the air in the docks was 'more or less fragrant with the products of Eastern and other climes'.[23]

And here, too, they might have glimpsed something of London's fabled ethnic diversity. In the immediate vicinity of the docks lived transient groups of sailors, 'lascars', and labourers from Africa, Asia, and the Caribbean. In and around Canning Town, Limehouse, St George in the East, and Southwark, there had developed by the early twentieth century a cluster of boarding houses, brothels, cafes, clubs, shops, restaurants, and taverns catering to their needs. But migrants fleeing persecution in other empires vastly outnumbered this floating seafaring population. Of these, the most notable were the Ashkenazi Jews, who had arrived in London in large numbers from Russia during the last two decades of the nineteenth century, fleeing state-sponsored anti-Semitic pogroms in their homeland. Settling in the districts of Whitechapel, Bethnal Green, and Stepney, these East European migrants constituted 'the biggest immigrant community since the Irish influx of the 1840s'.[24]

This, then, was the notorious East End, lurid tales of whose exotic aliens and Oriental vice dens offered a frisson of pleasurable dread to the propertied classes of the West End. Increasingly, however, the popular press was beginning to show a propensity for stoking latent anxieties about immigrants into full-blown moral panics. The tendency was exemplified by the *Evening Standard*, which ran a series of articles in January 1911 about the growing 'menace' of 'foreign undesirables' who, it claimed, were taking over parts of east London. One member of the Stepney Borough Council told the newspaper's special correspondent that

> if you start at London Bridge, you can go to Stoke Newington and Hackney, and round by Stratford back to London Bridge without knowing you are in England at all...The whole atmosphere is unmistakably foreign...the people in the streets look at a Christian stranger out of the corners of the eyes with suspicious curiosity, and the stranger notices how un-English they are.[25]

The Indian cricketers are unlikely to have ventured into the East End. But wandering around central London, they would have run into their fellow countrymen. As early as 1896, an Indian visitor to London observed that it was 'quite common' to see other Indians on the city's streets. When he went to see England take on Australia in a test match at the Oval, this writer counted 'nearly fifty Indians' among the spectators, all eagerly present to watch Ranji play.[26] The Imperial Hotel itself was located in the heart of Bloomsbury, described by a contemporary as 'the adopted home of the economical American visitor and the Hindoo student...whose myriad boarding-houses give the lie to the poet's statement that East and West can never meet'.[27] But most middle-class Indian visitors tended to reside in Bayswater, popularly known at the time as 'Asia Minor'.[28]

By 1911, the South Asian community in the imperial metropolis had grown more diverse. 'The Indian community in England,' reflected the *Hindoo Patriot*, 'is not now a handful of men, but is now a pretty little colony. The members are not all students as they were just a few years before.'[29] We have already noted the presence in the city of the Indian revolutionaries. Following the arrest of V.D. Savarkar in March 1910, their numbers in the capital had dwindled to a mere handful.[30] The vast majority of Indians in the capital pursued more mundane ends. There were businessmen eager to profit from the opportunities that were available in this mecca of global capitalism; lawyers and doctors honing their professional skills; and Indian students, who came to acquire the educational qualifications that would launch their careers back home. In addition, the capital attracted other kinds of temporary sojourners from the subcontinent: Indian princes in search of pleasure; intellectuals eager to learn about the ways of the West; lascars toiling on the steam ships that made their stately entrance into its docks; and the cooks and servants who accompanied the rich.

One indicator of the growing South Asian presence in the imperial metropolis was the rise of cafes and restaurants that served Indian cuisine.

Most of these were dotted around Holborn and frequented by Indian students out to get a cheap meal. But there were also other Indian restaurants that catered to a richer clientele. Two of these—the Coronation Hotel and Restaurant on Gray's Inn Road and the *Salut-e-Hind* in Holborn—opened in 1911.[31] Perhaps the Indian cricketers stopped by to sample the fare.

III

On 24 May 1911, the *Manchester Guardian* published a photograph of the British prime minister Herbert Asquith and his secretary on their way to the opening session of the Imperial Conference at the Foreign Office. Immediately below it was another photograph: the Indian cricketers at Lord's. The juxtaposition of the two photographs in a leading national daily is richly suggestive of the ways in which the Indian cricket tour became part of a coronation summer suffused with imperial events and themes.

'The presence of the Prime Ministers from the Dominions coincides with the visit of a team of Indian cricketers,' announced the *Graphic* on 27 May 1911.[32] The premiers of Australia, Canada, South Africa, and New Zealand had come to London to participate in the Imperial Conference. The *Daily Mail* declared that the arrival in the imperial metropolis of these leaders of 'the Britains Beyond the Seas and the thousands of over-sea Britons now visiting England' was proof that in the Dominions there was 'a real love for the land they call "home".'[33] 'Our colonies,' mused a British diplomat,

> have been largely built up by Scottish shrewdness and Irish imagination, and have absorbed highly important French and Dutch elements. So it seems as right as it is interesting that the doyen of the Colonial Premiers, Sir Wilfred Laurier, should be a Frenchman; the head delegate of South Africa [General Louis Botha] should be Dutch; that the chief spokesman for Australia should be a Scottish mechanic; and that Sir Joseph Ward of New Zealand, who was born in Tasmania, should be the son of Irish parents.[34]

It was the first time that the word 'imperial' was used to designate this gathering of the Dominions' premiers; previous meetings had been called 'colonial conferences'. 'The word "colonial" indicates a certain inferiority,' remarked one writer, 'and that description as applied to the self-governing Dominion has to be dropped.'[35] Moreover, noted the *Manchester Guardian*, the shift in nomenclature was 'not one of words merely' and showed that the Dominions were now 'equal partners in the duties and responsibilities of Empire'.[36]

Figure 14. The arrival in London of the first All-India cricket team aroused great interest in the British press. This image is from *The Illustrated Sporting and Dramatic News* (3 June 1911). © Illustrated London News Ltd/Mary Evans.

But there was one glaring absence at this imperial get-together. 'Is India, for the first time to be heard speaking with her own voice, or is her Government once more to resign its rights to an instructed spokesman out of touch with Indian views?' *The Times* queried a few days before the start of the conference.[37] As it soon transpired, however, India was not directly represented at the event. The omission was keenly felt by Indian nationalists, not least because of the increasingly hostile attitude of the white Dominions towards immigrants from the subcontinent. 'What India therefore needs and what must be accorded to her sooner or later,' stated the Lahore-based *Tribune*, 'is direct representation on an adequate scale in the constitution of the conference.'[38]

The month-long conference of the Dominions' premiers concluded on the eve of the coronation. They had spent much of their time making a strong case for the right to determine their own immigration laws. But the formal political discussions done with, the leaders remained in the capital to participate in a fresh round of festivities to mark the set-piece event of the imperial summer. They were joined by a global assortment of visiting dignitaries. Some represented those regions of the British Empire—the crown colonies and protectorates strung across from Southeast Asia to the Caribbean—that had been excluded from the Imperial Conference. Others were aristocratic representatives of various European royal houses, related to the British royal family through dense webs of kinship, who would find themselves on opposite sides in the cataclysmic conflict that erupted three summers later. Yet others represented nations across the Atlantic: Argentina, Bolivia, Brazil, Chile, Colombia, Costa Rica, Cuba, Ecuador, Guatemala, Honduras, Mexico, Paraguay, Peru, Salvador, Uruguay, and the United States.

Representatives of Oriental royalty also arrived in London to participate in this orchestrated display of imperial power. These included Prince Youssouf Izzedin Effendi of Turkey; Prince Mirza Mohammed Ali Khan of Persia; Prince Mohammed Ali Pasha, brother of the Khedive of Egypt; Dejazmatch (General) Kasa, a cousin of the Ethiopian ruler, Menelik II; Prince Sayyid Khalifa of Zanzibar; Prince Higashifushimi of Japan; Prince Tsai-Chen of China; the sultans of Perak and Kedah; and Prince Chakrabongse Bhuvanath of Siam. However, there was some disappointment in the local press that even though London was 'so full of Orientals' there was 'a singular absence of Oriental costume'. 'The Japanese, for example,' complained one correspondent, 'have adopted European garb.' He contrasted this with the previous coronation, when 'it was quite a common sight to see turbaned gentlemen promenading the streets and other Orientals wearing their flowing robes as far east as St. Paul's'.[39]

The charge that the 'Oriental' was failing to display the difference that was called for in the theatre of empire did not apply to the Indian maharajas who had come to attend the coronation. 'Many of the Indian princes by reason of their picturesque costumes and the flashing jewels in their headgear were eagerly watched for by spectators as they drove through the crowded West End,' the London correspondent of the *Hindoo Patriot* informed his Indian readers.[40] But there were some old India hands who felt that the maharajas deserved greater public recognition. 'We welcome with enthusiasm the Prime Ministers from overseas, but what of the Princes from overseas, who are now moving amongst us, a little silent, a little unguarded?' asked one Anglo-Indian.[41] This writer also sought to highlight the role of these royal visitors in buttressing the British Raj. 'Next to the Army,' he declared, 'the princes and chiefs are the best bulwarks of British rule in India. Their interests and ours grow closer every year.'[42]

The maharajas were not the only Indians who were accorded a formal role in the coronation. Also present in London for the event, were representatives of the Indian army, the lynchpin of British imperial power across the globe. These consisted of 'a native officer (accompanied by an orderly) from every unit of the Indian Army, with a special representation in the case of the King's regiments, and a proportionate admixture—about one to ten—of British officers'.[43] The Indian contingent, numbering around 500 soldiers—'Sikhs, Gurkhas, Punjabi Mussulmans, Hindus, Jats, Baluchis, and many more', noted the *Manchester Guardian*—was stationed at Hampton Court, where its presence quickly became a tourist attraction.[44]

The Indian maharajas and soldiers were the most eye-catching element in the 'Royal Progress' through the streets of London. Held the day after the coronation, this newly invented ritual was designed as an explicitly imperial affair and included, in addition to the Indian princes and soldiers, the Dominions' and other colonial premiers, representatives of the crown colonies, and several detachments of colonial troops. 'The prominence of the Dominions and the Indian Empire in this Procession is one of the features making the coronation of George V an imperial landmark,' averred an editorial in *The Times*.[45]

Alongside these royal rituals, dominated by the elites of the empire, the coronation also became the occasion for staging popular exhibitions and entertainments that struck 'an Imperial note of unparalleled volume and significance'.[46] The grandest of these events was the Festival of Empire and Imperial Exhibition, inaugurated by King George V on 12 May at the Crystal Palace in Sydenham, site of the iconic exhibition held there six decades previously. 'In these beautiful grounds framed in the Surrey hills and the fair English landscape now in the dawn of its verdant summer beauty,' rhapsodized one writer, 'has sprung, as though under the spell of a magician's wand, an epitome of Empire, even as that Empire has radiated from the little island mother kingdom.'[47]

Within the vast grounds of the Crystal Palace loomed massive replicas of the parliament buildings of the white Dominions. India, which had no comparable institution, was represented in a suitably 'Eastern' fashion by 'a lofty dome-crowned palace' containing 'an interesting and valuable collection of Oriental works of art'.[48] Linking together these imposing buildings was the 'All-Red Route', a mile and a half electric railway that was 'cunningly designed to give the spectator a bird's-eye view of the British Empire'.[49]

This was the 'world-as-exhibition', that is to say, 'the world conceived and grasped as though it were an exhibition'.[50] Accordingly, the organizers of the exhibition sought to combine pleasure and pedagogy. Guides, who provided information about the sights on this imperial journey, accompanied travellers on the 'All-Red Route'. 'To the stay at-home-Britain the fifteen minutes journey in the comfortable observation cars is a telling object lesson, while to the travelled Britain it is full of pleasures of retrospection,' one observer declared.[51]

The other major highlight of the Festival of Empire was the Pageant of London, a spectacular theatrical epic that presented the city's imperial past through a series of dramatic historical vignettes.[52] The pageant was conceived and executed by Frank Lascelles, who had staged similar events in places as far apart as Oxford, Quebec, and Cape Town. A 'complex and ambitious undertaking' involving 15,000 volunteers, the Pageant of London presented the story of the imperial metropolis 'in over forty scenes organised in four roughly chronological parts, with the performance spread over three days'.[53] Like the Imperial Exhibition, the pageant sought to instruct its audience: the aim was to show how London had shaped empire and, in turn, come to acquire its imperial status. Commencing with 'The Dawn of British History' in Roman London, Lascelles recreated notable episodes in the history of the 'Empire City' before concluding with a 'Masque Imperial', which highlighted significant events in the intertwined histories of Britain and its Dominions and was enacted by volunteers from Australia, Canada,

South Africa, and India. These subjects from the colonies, noted one newspaper, had 'come to London at their own expense, and of their own accord' and had sought 'to show their loyalty to the Throne and their love of the Mother Country in this practical manner'.[54]

The ties of kinship that bound the Mother Country to the overseas Dominions were constantly reiterated in events such as the Imperial Exhibition and the Pageant of London. But such occasions also served to showcase the economic and commercial advantages of empire. The Imperial Exhibition, enthused one observer, was 'the most elaborate advertisement of the resources of the British Empire that has ever been devised'.[55] Housed within the hundreds of buildings that dotted the Crystal Palace complex were exhibits of varied colonial landscapes, economies, and populations.

Given the scale on which it was organized, one might imagine that the Festival of Empire was a singular affair. However, it was not the only exhibition that summer to showcase the riches of Britain's global empire. Across town, in the White City at Shepherd's Bush, a rival Coronation Exhibition was simultaneously organized by Imre Kiralfy, a Hungarian Jewish impresario responsible for conceiving and staging a series of spectacular events including the London Olympics of 1908.[56] Designed as an exercise in 'imperial stock-taking at the commencement of the new reign', the Coronation Exhibition sought to showcase the arts, industries and architecture of Britain's imperial possessions.[57] Newspaper reporters who were given a preview of the White City complex on the eve of its opening on 18 May 1911 were dazzled by the display. In the words of one writer:

> The fantasy of the Arabian nights has been brought into modern London. Now you know what the Empire means; you have seen it stage by stage; you have girdled the globe. The native workers, sitting cross-legged in their huts and bazaars, have been brought before you: you have touched the fringes of all the races of the world who swear allegiance to the British flag.[58]

But not all those who had gathered in London that coronation summer were there to affirm the world fashioned by empire. In the last week of July 1911, there took place at the University of London an extraordinary global event that queried the dominant imperial theories of race. This was the Universal Races Congress, 'a rich and compelling episode in modern world history'.[59] Whereas imperial exhibitions cast the colonized peoples as exotic 'others' marked by their essential and eternal cultural difference, participants in the congress asserted 'the biological unity and racial intermixture of mankind, and were committed to ideas of inter-racial and international understanding and civilizational parity and progress'.[60]

The Universal Races Congress drew its supporters from across the globe. This impressive list included:

> thirty-five Presidents of Parliaments, the majority of the Members of the Permanent Court of Arbitration and of the Delegates to the Second Hague Conference, twelve British Governors and eight British Premiers, over forty Colonial Bishops, some hundred and thirty Professors of International Law, the leading Anthropologists and Sociologists [among them Max Weber, Emile Durkheim, Georg Simmel, and Patrick Geddes], the Officers and the majority of the Council of the Inter-Parliamentary Union, and many other distinguished personages.[61]

In the last category were some of the wealthiest men in the world: Lord Lever, George Cadbury, Lord Rothschild, Joseph Rowntree, Andrew Carnegie, and the Tata brothers, Dorab and Ratan.

No less remarkable was the global array of writers who authored the pre-circulated papers that formed the basis for the discussions at the congress. Prominent among these were the British radical liberal critic of imperialism, John A. Hobson; the German-American pioneer of modern anthropology, Franz Boas; the German sociologist, Ferdinand Tönnies; the Anglo-Jewish writer, Israel Zangwill; the African-American political theorist and activist, W.E.B. DuBois; the ex-president of Haiti, François Denys Légitime; the Nigerian pan-Africanist, Mojola Agbebi; the founder-editor of the first Bantu-language newspaper in South Africa, John Tengo Jabavu (who had sought many years earlier to bring the first black African cricket team to Britain); the Persian educationist and reformer, Hadji Mirza Yahya; the Turkish philosopher-politician, Riza Tevfik Bölükbaşi; the Chinese diplomat, Wu Tingfang; and the Japanese sociologists, Tongo Takebe and Teruaki Kobayashi. Two eminent Indians were also among the contributors to the conference volume: Gopal Krishna Gokhale, the leading moderate congress politician of the day, and the astonishingly versatile scholar Brajendra Nath Seal, principal of the Maharaja's College in Cooch Behar. Gokhale, whose paper was titled 'East and West in India', did not travel to London to attend the congress. But his compatriot did and was accorded the honour of delivering its opening lecture on the 'Meaning of Race, Tribe and Nation'.[62]

The wide publicity accorded to the Universal Races Congress in the press attracted a large number of visitors to its sessions. A sizeable British audience was leavened with attendees from over fifty countries across Europe, Asia,

Africa, and the Americas. The eight sessions of the conference were marked by intense debates, although there were tetchy comments in the press about the faulty acoustics that rendered these inaudible. Outside the formal meetings, there were serendipitous encounters and animated conversations among the participants that cut across the boundaries of class, race, and nationality.[63]

Even in this unprecedented age of imperial globalization, one doubts if such an 'extraordinarily polychrome and polyglot' gathering could have taken place in any other contemporary city.[64] Indeed, it was precisely because London in 1911 was, in the words of W.E.B. DuBois, 'the metropolis of the modern world' that its organizers chose to hold the conference there.[65] As one observer remarked, 'That city more than any other capital is in intimate touch with all the different quarters of the globe'.[66]

IV

On 9 July 1910, even as the preparations for the Indian cricket tour were underway in the subcontinent, the following news report was published in the *Leader* (an Allahabad newspaper):

> It appears that some wealthy Bhatia merchants of Bombay are chartering a steamer to take them to witness the performances of the Indian Cricket Team, and also the King's Coronation. It is stated that the steamer is being chartered to protect caste. That is not in the spirit of the go-ahead social reformer, but still we should not fight these Bhatia millionaires. It is bold enough for them to undertake the voyage, and a caste that can live on the broad expanse of the sea and the wide, wide world of Europe, must be something better than a caste which withers away the moment it comes into contact with a stranger or a Hindu returning from foreign lands.[67]

The Bombay Bhatias' initiative received a great deal of publicity over the following months. One reformist journal noted that 'there can be no doubt that such a project, if carried out, will have an important effect on that community and on the Hindoo community generally'.[68] It transpired that the idea had been floated by Govardhandhas Gokuldas Tejpal, a leading merchant prince within this prosperous trading community, who sought to take to Europe a 'large party of about 400 orthodox Hindu gentlemen of high caste, all vegetarians and collected from different parts of India'. The 'special steamer' chartered for this purpose was to have 'up-to-date conveniences and appliances' as well as 'complete arrangements' that would 'ensure the strict observance of High caste Hindu custom and manners in regard to diet and general conduct of life'.[69] That this was a seriously pursued venture can be gleaned from the following advertisement that appeared regularly in a number of Indian newspapers that winter:

RARE OPPORTUNITY FOR TRIP TO EUROPE
Specially arranged for High-Caste Orthodox Hindus Only
Under the Management of Sheth G.G. Teizpal

Food strictly VEGETARIAN prepared by BRAHMIN COOKS only, all arrangements on Orthodox principles.

Trip timed for four great events:—THE CORONATION, VISIT OF INDIAN CRICKET TEAM, the DERBY horse-race, and the IMPERIAL EXHIBITION.

Facilities will be given to visit COMMERCIAL CITIES IN EUROPE besides NOTABLE PLACES EN-ROUTE.

The Trip is arranged to extend to THREE MONTHS commencing about the last week of April 1911.[70]

The move divided the Bhatia community. Those of a more orthodox disposition cavilled at the prospect of the loss of caste involved in crossing the *Kala Paani*;[71] reformers within the community touted it as a necessary step to embrace modernity. To assuage the misgivings of the conservatives, the promoters of the venture made it known that every step would be taken during the sea voyage to preserve the purity of their caste brethren.[72] It was to no avail. A few weeks later, a cartoon in the *Hindi Punch* depicted the leader of the scheme, Govardhandas Tejpal, as a rider thrown off his horse and floundering in the sea. The accompanying caption, entitled 'A Catastrophe in the Indian Sea!', stated: 'Owing to the failure of the scheme for carrying the Orthodox 400 Hindus to England at the time of the Coronation, the Hindus, who had resolved to take the opportunity of breaking caste restriction, have been disappointed and abandoned the idea of going to England.'[73]

The fate of the aborted Bhatia venture is curious, for by this time, a growing number of propertied Indians had begun to travel to the imperial metropolis. Indeed, the summer of 1911 saw a spike in the number of travellers from the subcontinent to Britain. In addition to the usual traffic of those who were going abroad either to study or on business, there were a number of individuals who made the journey because of the attractive prospect of simultaneously witnessing the coronation, the attendant imperial events, and the first Indian cricket tour. The surge had been anticipated by an Indian writer who noted in September 1910 that 'some hundreds of individuals of both sexes are likely to pay a visit to Europe on the occasion of the King-Emperor's coronation'.[74] Many of these Indians applied for 'certificates of identity' in order to undertake the journey. Those who stated as their principal reason for travel a desire to witness the coronation comprised an eclectic mix of minor aristocrats, businessmen, and professionals drawn from different parts of India. In many instances, friends from the same town decided to make the trip together.[75]

As it happens, two travellers from the subcontinent wrote accounts of their trip to the imperial metropolis in the summer of 1911. Both were Brahmins from South India. One was Thottakadu Ramakrishna Pillai, a writer based in Madras; the other, Nyayapati Ramanujaswami, a lawyer from the coastal town of Berhampore (Brahmapur). Their travel narratives give us a vivid idea of what it was like to be an Indian subject in imperial Britain that coronation year.[76]

In writing about their visit to Britain, the two South Indians were representative of a growing trend. In the preceding two decades, many Indians travelling to the heart of empire had begun to put down their impressions in print. Aimed at the growing middle-class public in India, some of these accounts were written up in the form of diaries, while others were straightforward narratives of their experiences in the 'West'. Irrespective of their format, however, the writings in this genre had some common features. First, even though many of the writers travelled extensively in Britain, their accounts tended to focus on London. The imperial metropolis dominated their imagination and their reflections. They were transfixed by its dense crowds and unsettling speed; its enchanting mixture of antiquity and modernity; its beguiling promise and hidden perils. Second, these narratives sought to inform and enlighten their readers on what it was like to navigate the spaces of the imperial metropolis. In the process, they suggested ways in which colonial subjects travelling to London could experience its pleasures and avoid its pitfalls. Third, for many writers, travel triggered reflections on the relationship between India and Britain and prompted them to compare and contrast the two societies.[77]

The travelogues penned by Ramakrishna Pillai and Ramanujaswami exhibit many of these features. Both men set out, separately, on their journey to London via Colombo within days of the Indian cricketers' departure from Bombay. Both writers dwelt at length on the places they traversed and the people they encountered during their sea voyage. Indeed, both men found themselves travelling to Britain alongside a large transnational group of passengers, many of whom were also going to witness the coronation. Of these, a majority were from Australia and both Pillai and Ramanujaswami quickly forged friendships with their antipodean fellow travellers.

The two texts also show how the ship was a transient imperial 'contact zone' that offered opportunities for unexpected cross-cultural encounters.[78] After hearing him hold forth 'on our history, our ancient civilization, our social and religious life', his new Australian friends confessed to Ramakrishna Pillai that they were unaware that 'Hindus were so civilized'. They hastened to assure him that although their government had passed 'immigration laws against the Asiatics for fear of the cheap labourer wiping out of existence their own', they would welcome Indian tourists like Pillai 'with open arms'.[79] Ramanujaswami, too, observed that the Australians onboard his ship mixed with the Indian passengers 'in a free and social manner'. 'Whether this present virtue of social equality on board the ship has been created out of necessity is another matter, and is a debatable point,' he mused.[80]

Both men wrote feelingly about the moment of arrival in Britain. It was past three o'clock in the afternoon when Ramanujaswami first glimpsed the chalky outlines of Dover. 'The sight of the English shore, longed after with devout expectation,' he confessed, 'sent a thrill of joy through me, and although the surrounding atmosphere was chill, I was kept up by the warmth of my pleasure which the sight of Dover produced in me.' But arriving later that evening at Charing Cross, he did not find the station 'very striking or grand'.[81] Ramakrishna Pillai described how as his train approached London at sunset, 'the dim outline of the city rose before me, and it seemed to me as if it were set up in mid air'. Outside the station, he became an 'infinitesimal part of humanity caught in the whirlpool of a vast maelstrom'.[82]

The desire to witness the coronation was an important factor in prompting both writers to travel to Britain that summer. Ramakrishna Pillai attended the solemn ceremony in Westminster Abbey. Looking around, he noted the presence in the abbey that day of 'nearly six thousand persons distinguished men and women from all parts of the globe, representative of foreign potentates, members of both Houses and their wives and men distinguished in literature, science, and art'.[83] Ramanujaswami, on the other hand, had to rest content with viewing the event from afar. He was among the crowds that gathered at Hyde Park Corner to cheer the royal procession as it made its way back to Buckingham Palace after the coronation. He arrived on the scene only to discover that the state carriage carrying the King-Emperor and his consort 'had passed into Constitution Hill just five minutes previously'.[84] The following day, Ramanujaswami made sure that he reached his allotted place at St James Palace well in time to witness the Royal Progress. He was particularly pleased that the colonial contingent was 'most lustily cheered from beginning to end' and observed that the spectators 'seemed to be attracted no less by the fine appearance of Indian Maharajahs and Maharanees than by the rich and coloured costumes worn by the Indian troops'.[85]

Ramakrishna Pillai and Ramanujaswami also took part in the Universal Races Congress. Pillai participated in the crucial preparatory meetings that were held prior to the opening of the conference. Here he 'came in contact with representative men who left their distant homes to meet in London in pursuance of a common object—to bring the East and the West together'.[86] Ramanujaswami also took a keen interest in the Universal Races Congress and met Gustav Spiller, its principal organizer.[87] 'Any congress or organization that has, for its object, the accomplishment of the desired end of creating or furthering harmony among the different races of the world has my fullest sympathy and good wishes,' he declared. It was therefore with the heartiest of feeling that I became a member of the First Universal Races Congress.'[88]

But there are also significant differences between the two travel accounts. Ramakrishna Pillai was in London for a short duration, departing for Edinburgh immediately after the coronation. His narrative was mostly given over to reflections on the cultural and political affinities between Scotland and South India. Ramanujaswami, on the other hand, was based in London throughout his two-month stay in Britain and recounted his experiences in the form of a diary. Perhaps taking his cues from the contemporary travel guides and other literature for tourists, he provided an extraordinarily detailed picture of his daily activities and routines. He explored London on foot, from the top of buses, and by train, constantly describing the places he visited and the people he encountered along the way.

The two South Indians differed, too, in their attitudes and approach towards the West. Ramakrishna Pillai had nurtured a desire to visit Europe since his youth, but only made the journey after he had turned sixty. When the time came, he decided that he would travel as 'a staunch Hindu, live in England as a thoroughly orthodox Hindu and return "untainted"'.[89]

He took along his own cook and appears to have eschewed the material pleasures of the imperial metropolis.

Ramanujaswami's decision to travel to Britain was an impulsive one, the result of a chance conversation with a fellow lawyer in the Vakils Room of the Ganjam (now in Odisha) Bar Association.[90] And unlike Ramakrishna Pillai, he showed an eagerness to taste the fruits of Western modernity. In London, Ramanujaswami savoured the sensory delights of its art galleries, concert halls, exhibitions (including the Festival of Empire and the Coronation Exhibition), libraries, museums, and theatres. Equally, he enthusiastically partook of the metropolitan culture of consumption by shopping in the city's famed department stores. His purchases during this trip included, among other things, a pair of boots, a bicycle, and 'a trumpetless gramophone with a dozen records and a leather case'.[91]

As an anglicized middle-class Indian, Ramanujaswami also displayed an interest in sport, the ruling passion of the host nation. Thus, at the end of May he travelled by coach to Epsom Downs to witness the Derby. The traffic along the route—with its 'double-horsed and four-horsed coaches, motor cycles, cycles, not to speak of numberless pedestrians'—reminded him of 'the procession of people to Jami Festival on Tarinamma Hill in my district'.[92] He also paid a visit to the National Sporting Club, the home of British boxing.[93]

But more relevant to our story is his diary entry for 8 June 1911:

After breakfast... I proceeded to the Lords cricket grounds, where M.C.C. (Marylebone Cricket Club) played the All-India Team. I gained entrance into the ground paying 6 d. at the gate, and occupied a seat on the very first row of seats just abutting the boundary line of one side. The whole play could be easily be seen from where I was seated... All-India batted from 12 noon to 2 P.M., when there was a three-quarters of a hour interval for lunch, and they batted again till 4 P.M. when they were all out with 204 runs. M.C.C. began batting at 4.10 P.M. and at 6 P.M. when I left, they had scored 190, three wickets being down.[94]

8

Indian Summer

I

The Indian cricketers were not the only international sportsmen on show in Britain that summer. They formed part of an extraordinary conjunction that saw the arrival in London of athletes from across the world. The simultaneous presence in the city of these sportsmen was a function of the increasingly transnational character of sport in the age of imperial globalization. In a world on the move, sportsmen too were now able to parade their skills outside their homelands. And for many of them, as we shall see, London was the centre of the sporting world.

Around the same time as the Indian cricketers, sporting contingents from the 'white dominions' came to Britain to take part in the first ever intra-imperial sports championships.[1] Held in late June as an adjunct to the Festival of Empire, teams representing Great Britain, Canada, and 'Australasia' (a combination from Australia and New Zealand) competed against each other in track and field, ring, and swimming events. The organizers had originally intended to include India and South Africa in these imperial games. But Australia was opposed to the participation of 'non-whites' in the competition and the idea was jettisoned. The Canadian contingent emerged as the victors and took home the newly established Lonsdale Cup.

The press coverage of the Festival of Empire games was tepid; the event aroused little public interest. In sharp contrast, the arrival on British shores of the controversial African-American boxer Jack Johnson generated an intense buzz in the press. The optics and ramifications of Johnson's visit differed significantly from the other sportsmen who came to Britain in the summer of 1911. The previous July, Johnson had demolished Jim Jeffries—the American 'Great White Hope'—and retained his status as the world's first black heavyweight champion.[2] Staged in the 'Sin City' of Reno, Nevada, the Jeffries-Johnson encounter was the most eagerly anticipated sporting event of its time. Billed as the 'battle of the century', the contest brought to the fore a new type of 'commercialized racial spectacle' whose profitability was directly proportional to its publicity. The fight generated more news over the wires than 'the fall of Port Arthur during the Russo-Japanese War'.[3] Johnson's fight with Jeffries was also filmed and the prints and images made their way around the world. This triggered a backlash among white communities across the United States, the British Empire, and Europe. A transnational alliance of conservative white politicians, pastors, reformers, bureaucrats, newspaper editors, and concerned citizens launched a vociferous campaign to ban a film that threatened to undermine the established racial hierarchy.[4]

It was against this fractious backdrop that Johnson travelled to Britain in the first week of June 1911. In London, the world's greatest boxer put on a display of choreographed extravagance.[5] He also attracted large crowds wherever he went. On Coronation Day, his car was mobbed by spectators outside Westminster Abbey.[6] After the imperial festivities ended, Johnson 'became a sellout sensation in London's music halls', entertaining audiences with his boxing routines and his beloved bass viol.[7]

Predictably, Jack Johnson's presence in Britain dominated the newspaper headlines. It thereby overshadowed a remarkable bunch of Indian sportsmen whose feats also captivated the public in the imperial metropolis that coronation summer. Their presence and reception in London points to the diverse ways in which sport, power, and identity came to be intertwined in the age of empire. Equally, it shows how cricketers were not the only sportsmen to vie for public attention in colonial India and imperial Britain.

II

On the day the Indian cricketers boarded the *SS Arabia* in Bombay, the *Times of India* published an article—reproduced from London's *Morning Post*—about a sportsman from the subcontinent whose presence in Britain was attracting a great deal of attention in the imperial metropolis. Entitled 'Style of Jamsetji', it had this to say about its subject:

> There is no denying that Jamsetji's style is a thing apart; nearer to theoretical perfection than the method of the great players of the nearer or further past, and as manifestly *sui generis* as the style of the Jam Sahib's batting on a lightning

fast wicket. It has been said that the great Indian cricketer, whom we had all hoped to see again this summer as captain of the Indian team, was able to make strokes which no other batsman—with the possible exception of Victor Trumper on his day of days—dared even attempt, because he saw what the ball was doing some fraction of a second sooner than the average Test Match player...Racquets is not a spectacle for the multitude: courts are few and far between (even Oxford does not possess one), and the number of those who can see below the surface of the game is necessarily limited. But it is not necessary to have played racquets (which is not a difficult game to follow), in order to appreciate the Ranjitsinhji of the game when his unquestionable genius is contrasted in action with mere talent, howsoever carefully cultivated. Any tyro can appreciate the style of Jamsetji and that, after all, is the highest compliment that can be paid to the athletic specialist.[8]

A century later, these words are oddly poignant. Ranjitsinhji is today accorded an honoured place among cricket's immortals, but his racquet-wielding compatriot—equally a genius, in the eyes of many contemporary observers—has long been obliterated from public memory. Few today have heard of this remarkable middle-aged Parsi from Bombay, who was the *world champion* in his chosen sport during the first decade of the twentieth century. And it was to defend his world title that Jamsetji went to Britain in the spring of 1911.

A forerunner of squash, racquets is based on the simple principle of hitting a ball against a wall. First played in open courtyards in London's debtors' prisons, it had gradually been transformed into a respectable recreational sport played in enclosed indoor courts.[9] The sport came to colonial India in the early nineteenth century, around the same time that it became popular in Britain. As British rule spread across the subcontinent, 'the game followed it'.[10] 'When I first went to the East in 1892,' one veteran army officer wrote, 'the most popular "bat and ball" game was undoubtedly Rackets.'[11]

Jamsetji Merwanji belonged to a family that had long been associated with racquets in western India. His grandfather, Cursetji, was possibly one of the first Indians to pursue a sport that was largely the preserve of European soldiers and civilians.[12] From 1870 onwards, he was a 'marker'—an official who combined the duties of linesman and scorer—at Bombay's Byculla Club.[13] The designation became the family name. Cursejti's sons, Merwanji and Dhunjibhoy, followed in his footsteps and served as markers for European clubs in the Bombay Presidency. Both were also very fine racquets players. Indeed, in 1885 Merwanji was 'considered good enough to be sent to England to compete for the World Championship'. Unfortunately, eye trouble prevented him from undertaking the trip.[14] Given this family background, it should come as no surprise that Jamsetji and his siblings took to the game at an early age.

In 1890, the eighteen-year-old Jamsetji was engaged as a racquets marker by the Bombay Gymkhana, thereby perpetuating the family tradition begun by his grandfather.[15] Watching and playing with the best European players in the city further sharpened Jamsetji's racquet skills. His first major triumph on the national stage came in 1899 when he won a professional racquets tournament featuring fourteen of the top players in the subcontinent. The same year, he also defeated the north Indian champion Abdul Majid in an encounter at Murree.[16]

At the beginning of the new century, Jamsetji repeatedly underlined his status as the best racquets player in colonial India by winning a series of tournaments. In February 1902, a correspondent for the *Times of India* noted that 'this Bombay marker has never found any one in this country to get near him, no one has even "stretched" him'.[17] Among his growing band of supporters was 'Jungly' Greig, who was convinced that the Parsi player was 'very nearly as good as Peter Latham', the reigning world champion.[18] This was high praise indeed, given that Latham was regarded by many as the greatest player of all time. He had first won the world racquets championship in 1887, just months after turning twenty-one, and proceeded to retain his title uninterruptedly for the next fifteen years.[19]

In December 1902, Jamsetji travelled to England to pit his skills against the legendary Mancunian. The *Manchester Sporting Chronicle* noted that the Parsi from Bombay had been able to come to Britain 'through the generosity of the English players out there and the members of his own caste, who, although not racket players themselves, take a great interest in his performances, and quickly subscribed half the cost of sending him over'.[20] Two influential Europeans in the Bombay Gymkhana—'Jungly' Greig and F.B. Shaw—had contacted the principal racquets clubs in Britain to arrange fixtures on his behalf.[21] Dorab Tata contributed £100 to the venture and took care of the travel arrangements.[22] Without their assistance, it would have been virtually impossible for the Parsi champion to undertake the journey.

But upon arriving in Britain Jamsetji learnt, much to his disappointment, that Peter Latham had retired from racquets in order to concentrate solely on his tennis career. The world title had in the meantime passed by default to Gilbert Browne, a professional marker at the Prince's Club in London. Brown was the last rival Latham had defeated prior to his retirement.[23]

The Indian champion now challenged Browne for the world title. The challenge was accepted, and the two players signed an agreement to play the best of three matches. The first match was to be staged at the Queen's Club, Jamsetji's choice; the second at the Prince's Club, Browne's home turf; and the third, if required, at a neutral venue.[24] In addition to the prestige of the world title, there was also £100 at stake in the encounter. But there was one noteworthy stipulation in the pre-match agreement. If Jamsetji were to win, he would have to undertake to play the next championship match—if challenged—in Britain. If he failed to defend his title within six months, he would forfeit it.[25]

Jamsetji prepared for the championship matches by playing a series of exhibition games in London and Manchester. Even though he had struggled to adjust to the cold English weather, the Parsi player quickly demonstrated his formidable skills. When they eventually met on court, Browne was no match for Jamsetji. The first match on 23 May 1903 was watched by a relatively small crowd at the Queen's Club.[26] The *Times of India* informed its readers that it 'was practically a walkover for the Parsee', who won the match by four games to one.[27] The score line was identical when the two players met again five days later in front of a much larger crowd at Prince's Court. The Parsi player was in top form and once again trounced his rival. 'Jamsetji,' noted one British newspaper the day after he had been crowned world champion, 'is without a doubt a very fine player and completely out-pointed his opponent.'[28]

The relative ease with which Jamsetji defeated Browne led to talk of Latham coming out of retirement to reclaim the world title. The retired racquets champion was impressed by the Parsi player but refused to return to the court for anything less than £500.[29] By this time, the original sum raised on Jamsetji's behalf had been spent. At this point, two generous Parsi businessmen in Bombay—Shapoorji Barucha and Dadiba Dalal—offered to put up the money for the match.[30] But for reasons that are opaque, the proposed fixture between Latham and Jamsetji never took place.

Interestingly, unlike the interracial boxing matches of this decade, the prospect of a Latham-Jamsetji match had aroused anticipation rather than anxiety among white sports fans. Racquets was not a mass sport, and the Parsi champion was no hell-raiser. More importantly, although they were unable to spell his name correctly and remained confused about the basic details of his background and identity, the British press approved of the decorous and unthreatening Jamsetji. In their descriptions of the Parsi racquets player, one can discern the same fascination for the 'Oriental' that was a ubiquitous feature of contemporary writings about Ranji. As with the cricketing prince, descriptions of Jamsetji tended to focus on his distinctive physical characteristics. 'He is possessed of a wonderful eye, and he uses a great variety of strokes, some of them, indeed, are such as no one else could attempt with any hope of success. He hits the ball, too, with enormous force, seeming to put a great deal of wrist, arm, and body work into every stroke,' remarked *The Times*.[31] Press accounts also dwelt on the simultaneously mysterious and simple qualities of this Indian sportsman.[32]

One writer expressed the hope that Jamsetji would 'get some permanent appointment in England, so that he may help to infuse new life into the game'.[33] But there was little prospect of the Parsi champion staying on in Britain. With his funds running out, he chose to return to Bombay. Although he had been unable to achieve his ambition of playing against Latham, Jamsetji had become the world racquets champion. He was to retain the title for the next eight years.

Surprisingly, no challenger even appeared on the scene for the first six years of his reign.[34] It would appear that professional racquets went into decline after Jamsetji's departure from Britain. In 1909, *The Times* noted that 'even an exhibition game was of the rarest occurrence'.[35] But in that year the sport experienced a revival of sorts with a series of fixtures between the best professional racquets players in the country. Most of these professionals were employed by the great British public schools and it was from their ranks that there now emerged a new contender for the world title.

A racquets coach at Harrow, the twenty-year-old Charles Williams announced himself by winning the English professional championship in 1909.[36] Shortly thereafter he secured the national open title in January 1911, with a victory over his principal amateur rival.[37] Fresh from these triumphs, the precociously talented Williams proceeded to challenge Jamsetji for the world title.[38] He had tried unsuccessfully to do so once before, just after he had become the English professional champion. A fund had even been started in Bombay to send Jamsetji to Britain but fell short of the amount required. The proposed fixture thus remained a non-starter.[39] In February 1911, however, matters moved more swiftly. Jamsetji immediately accepted the Englishman's challenge and this time around the money for his journey was quickly raised.[40]

The Bystander, April 19. 1911   147

GAMES AND PASTIMES

The Last of the Hockey Internationals: England v. Ireland. The English Goal in Jeopardy

There is great rejoicing in Ireland over the result of this match, which was played at Park Avenue, Dublin, on the 8th, for the Irishmen, contrary to expectation, managed to make a draw of it, and were perhaps a little unlucky in not winning. The score was 2 goals all. Ireland is the only International team which has scored against England this season

RACKETS

A "Line" for the Championship The exhibition match at Queen's Club on April 8 between Mr. E. M. Baerlein, the English Amateur Champion, and W. Jamsetji, the World's Champion, was quite a momentous affair in view of the fact that Jamsetji has come over to England from Bombay to defend his title to the Championship against Charles Williams, the English Champion, who has challenged him. For Williams won the English Championship recently by defeating Mr. Baerlein, and accordingly students of form were afforded an opportunity of comparing the results of Williams v. Baerlein and Jamsetji v. Baerlein, and so "getting a line" as to the probable issue of the big match between the two professionals which is to begin towards the end of this month. The line that is now forthcoming indicates that the Parsee will retain his title.

W. Jamsetji, World's Rackets Champion

Williams has challenged Jamsetji for the Championship of the World, and the match will be played in two instalments, at Queen's Club and Prince's, on April 29 and May 13. Jamsetji, who is nearly twenty years older than his rival, beat Gilbert Browne, who claimed the title on the retirement of Peter Latham in 1903, and has since held it unchallenged until now

C. Williams, English Rackets Champion

Mr. Baerlein played Williams level, whereas Jamsetji had to give him three aces in every game. In each case the amateur was the loser, and of the two Jamsetji beat him more decisively. Hence, on form, Jamsetji ought to beat Williams. But we all know that collateral form is unreliable. If it were not there would be far less excitement in sport than there is.

"Jam" for Short "Jam"—to use the inevitable abbreviation which his admirers have adopted when applauding him—is really a very wonderful person, for he has reached the age at which players of games are irreverently styled veterans. But there is very little of the veteran about him. Every man loses something in actual activity after the age of thirty or thereabouts, and "Jam" is not actually as quick about a court as he used to be, or as some younger men, including his chief rival, now are. But he makes up for this in other ways. He possesses, in the first place, that power of anticipation which is so valuable in all ball games, and this, coupled with his experience and thorough knowledge of the game, enables him to reach the ball just as easily as a man of half his age and perhaps nearly double his activity. In fact, instead of him going after the ball, the ball seems to come to him, while his opponent is tearing all over the court after it. Prior to his last match with Mr. Baerlein, the amateur had always beaten him at the odds. He naturally took some little time getting back his form after his voyage from India, and the cold weather has, of course, handicapped him; but he has got it back now, and in beating Mr. Baerlein he gave one of the finest displays

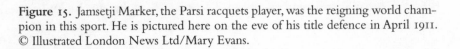

Figure 15. Jamsetji Marker, the Parsi racquets player, was the reigning world champion in this sport. He is pictured here on the eve of his title defence in April 1911. © Illustrated London News Ltd/Mary Evans.

The world racquets championship was scheduled to begin in London at the end of April 1911.[41] Jamsetji set out from Bombay in early February so as to reacquaint himself with British conditions and prepare for the most daunting challenge of his career.[42] As before, he played a series of exhibition matches in London and Manchester. His presence aroused immense curiosity among fans. 'The galleries were crowded, and the Indian's victory was enthusiastically applauded,' wrote the *Manchester Guardian* correspondent after witnessing one of these games. Connoisseurs of the sport were effusive in their praise of the ageing Parsi master. 'Jamsetji is getting in years for a racquets player, but he has not yet put on weight and is playing the same beautiful game that was so admired in 1903,' noted *The Times*.[43] 'No one interested in racquets should miss seeing him play,' the paper urged.[44]

Jamsetji had been in good form in the practice matches leading up to the championship. Many observers believed that he would successfully defend his world crown and take home the £400 prize money that came with it. But the pre-match predictions of a close contest between the two players were widely off the mark. Seventeen years younger than his Parsi rival, Williams proved too swift and strong on court for Jamsetji. Tactically, too, the English challenger repeatedly wrong-footed the world champion. Interestingly, Williams was coached for this match by Peter Latham, an indication of the strong patriotic feeling aroused in Britain by the contest.[45]

The first match was played at the Queen's Court on 29 April 1911. 'Not since Peter Latham defeated George Standing in New York in 1897 has such widespread interest been shown in a racquets match,' reported the *New York Times*.[46] The spectators' gallery was filled to 'its utmost capacity with past and present players both amateur and professional'.[47] Among the audience were a number of Parsis in London who had turned out to support their hero.[48]

On court, noted the *Daily Mail*, the two players 'presented a wonderful contrast of style and appearance—Williams short, thick and square-jawed, every inch a fighter; Jamsetji, almost lethargic in his pose, graceful and lissome, and capable of some strokes whose beauty Williams cannot ever hope to attain.'[49] 'The Parsee showed all his old skill in placing the ball, and when it came his way he frequently finished the rally with a beautifully low stroke,' added the *Sporting Life*, 'but the match had not progressed far before it became apparent that he had lost much of his old mobility.'[50] Williams won the encounter decisively by four games to nil.[51] He thus needed to win only one game in the second fixture, two weeks later, to wrest the world title from Jamsetji. The spectators at the Prince's Court did not have to wait long: Williams won the opening game in nine minutes and settled the matter.[52]

Although Jamsetji had lost his world title, his courage on court was acclaimed by many observers. 'The "Jam" was never beaten for lack of heart; again and again he made great efforts, and looked as if he might pull the game out of the fire,' wrote the special correspondent of the *Daily Mirror*.[53] 'Everyone will sympathise with the loser,' agreed *The Times*.

> He was giving away nearly 20 years—he is 39 and Williams 22; he has come 3000 miles to play the match; he has in practice given keen delight to players and spectators alike; and it was hard to lose without showing the beauty of his game. And he was not lucky, in that he was constantly having to change his racquets owing to breakages.[54]

But some observers in Britain were more interested in reading political meanings into Jamsetji's defeat. After the first championship match, the following comment appeared in one British newspaper:

> We have been told lately that the heavy Englishmen must prepare in almost every sport for defeat by Orientals—that the lithe Hindoo and the wiry, cool-headed Jap were bound in time to excel our best cricketers, wrestlers, tennis players; perhaps even our boxers. But young Williams of Harrow, found support against the great Parsee racquet player, Jamsetjee, called him over from Bombay, met him yesterday at Queen's Club, and in eye, judgment, speed and strength proved his superior in almost every part of the game. The West has not yet lost all its athletic virtue.[55]

One does not know what Jamsetji made of such statements. He rarely gave press interviews, and on the few occasions that he did speak to journalists, confined his remarks to the world racquets championship. In his manner and conduct, then, Jamsetji was like his self-effacing cricketing compatriots. Interestingly, in his only surviving press interview from that summer, Jamsetji dwelt at length on the forthcoming Indian cricket tour of Britain. A 'keen cricketer', it should perhaps come as no surprise that the Parsi champion spoke knowledgeably about the team that was shortly to follow him to the imperial metropolis.[56] But even as this interview appeared, the British public was transfixed by the arrival in London of another group of Indian sportsmen who were far less publicity shy about their competitive skills.

III

Three days after their arrival in London, the Indian cricketers—led by the Maharaja of Patiala—visited the famous Crystal Palace. But they did not go there to view the Imperial Exhibition that was drawing vast crowds. Instead, Bhupinder Singh and his teammates made the trip to watch a very different kind of exhibition: a highly publicized wrestling bout featuring Ahmed Baksh, a little-known Punjabi, and Maurice Deriaz, a formidable Swiss strongman.[57] The encounter between the two wrestlers that warm May evening had come to acquire immense public significance. 'The future of wrestling as a public attraction,' the *Sporting Life* declared before the fight, 'depends wholly upon the contest at the Festival of Empire.'[58] To understand why this was so, we need to consider the extraordinary historical context of this event.

Ahmed Baksh was part of a troupe of nine Punjabi Muslim *pehelwans* (wrestlers) who had arrived in London earlier that summer. This was, in fact, the second successive year that he had travelled from his homeland to the heart of the empire. In 1910, he had been part of a formidable cohort of Indian wrestlers whose feats had created a stir in Britain. Their tour was a result of the combined efforts of R.B. Benjamin, a British sporting impresario who was the principal promoter of the venture, and Sarat Kumar Mitter, the scion of a wealthy Calcutta landed family who sponsored it.[59]

The partnership between the Briton and the Bengali is intriguing but by no means inexplicable. From the late nineteenth century, there had developed in Bengal a vigorous physical education movement that drew on British 'inspiration and support'.[60] What is distinctive about Benjamin's role in this venture is that he was not a member of the civilian or military establishment in colonial India. Instead, he appears to have been one of those elusive private entrepreneurs who circulated between metropole and colony, seeking to profit from the exotica of empire.

Sarat Kumar Mitter's support, on the other hand, points to the growing investment of nationalist Indians in 'traditional' physical culture. During the late nineteenth century, educated middle-class Indians had begun to chafe at the 'self-image of effeteness' that had become an integral part of their identity. They sought to counter the negative stereotypes about their physical degeneration and lack of manliness and courage, which had first been propagated by the British colonizers but came to be internalized by Indians.

As a sharper political consciousness began to crystallize, some middle-class nationalists actively began to promote sporting traditions that were authentically Indian in origin and untainted by contact with the West. They elevated indigenous wrestling, gymnastics, and yoga over British sporting imports such as cricket and racquets. And they enrolled in *akharas* (gymnasia) dedicated to physical culture in order to cultivate the martial attributes and values necessary to fight against the colonizer.[61]

But the principal patrons and performers of these indigenous sporting traditions were mostly drawn from other social classes. This was especially the case with wrestling, an ancient sport that flourished in the numerous princely states of the subcontinent. Among the more prominent royal patrons of wrestling in the early twentieth century were the rulers of Aundh, Baroda, Bharatpur, Bhopal, Darbhanga, Datia, Gwalior, Indore, Jodhpur, Kashmir, Kolhapur, Patiala, Rampur, and Rewa. The wrestlers employed by these princes were fed, clothed, and housed at state expense, their sporting performances a matter of royal prestige. As for the wrestlers, they were drawn either from the ranks of the peasantry or the urban working classes. Wrestling was deeply embedded in the daily life of rural and small-town India. For those who were endowed with talent and had honed their technique to a high degree of perfection, the sport offered a route to secure employment and fame in the wider world. Wrestlers employed in royal courts were able to showcase their skills in major tournaments organized by princely patrons. The rapid growth of the press brought to national attention the victors in such tournaments.[62]

From the 1890s onwards, Indian wrestlers began to make a name for themselves on the international stage. The first to do so was a twenty-year-old Punjabi plebeian named Karim Baksh Pehrewala who defeated Tom Cannon, an English professional wrestler, in 1892. Cannon, an ex-miner and ex-policeman from Lancashire, had come to the subcontinent after a decade spent touring the globe, frequently taking part in fixed matches on the professional wrestling circuit.[63] His bout against Karim was staged at Calcutta, with the rulers of Cooch Behar and Darbhanga acting as referees. Karim was one of twenty wrestlers put up by the Jodhpur court to take on the Lancastrian fighter and, much to the glee of the Bengalis present, comfortably won the contest.[64] The same decade also saw the rise to prominence of Ghulam, widely acknowledged as the first truly great Indian wrestler. Renowned for his strength and suppleness, this legendary Punjabi fighter accompanied the Allahabad lawyer Motilal Nehru to Paris in 1900. There he took part in a wrestling bout held against a well-known Turkish strongman named Cour-Derelli.[65]

Not long after he returned from Europe, Ghulam succumbed to cholera. In his place there now emerged a man who was to become the most internationally renowned Indian wrestler of the early twentieth century. Gama Baksh was born into a family of well-known Punjabi wrestlers. He was introduced to the sport at a very young age by his father, Aziz Baksh, who was engaged as a fighter by the ruler of Datia. Following the sudden death of his father when he was still a child, Gama was brought up by a maternal uncle, Ida Pahalwan, who is said to have vowed to make Gama 'the champion wrestler his father had wanted him to be'.[66] Determined to fulfil his father's wish, Gama adhered to a punishing exercise regime that enabled him to become the most fearsome fighter of his time. As a teenager, he reportedly performed 'three thousand *bethaks* (sit-ups) and fifteen hundred *dands* (push-ups) and run one mile every day with a 120-pound stone ring around his neck'.[67] To nourish his body for such strenuous physical activity he consumed copious amounts of *yakhni*, a broth extracted from meat and bones, in addition to 'twenty liters of milk, half a litre of clarified butter, ¾ of a kilogram of butter, and four kilogram of fruit per day'.[68]

In the early years of the new century, Gama was engaged as a court wrestler at Datia and made a name for himself by successively vanquishing the champions of other princely states in a series of famous encounters. His most notable triumph was over Gulam Mohiuddin, an equally promising contemporary. The only fighter who stood up to Gama in these years was Rahim Sultaniwalla, the most accomplished of Ghulam's disciples.[69] The two wrestlers grappled for supremacy on three occasions between 1907 and 1909, but neither was able to emerge the outright winner. Nonetheless, by the end of the decade, most observers had come to regard Gama as the premier wrestler in India.

It was at this point that R.B. Benjamin, backed by Sarat Kumar Mitter, approached the 'Lion of the Punjab' with an offer to take him and a select group of his fellow wrestlers on a tour of Britain. Gama readily accepted the challenge and embarked on the journey along with three members of his *akhara*. Among the chosen ones was Ahmed Baksh; the others being Imam Baksh, Gama's younger brother, and Gamu Jalandhariwalla. The tour was a momentous event in the life of these Punjabi *pehelwans*, none of whom had ever travelled abroad before.

The Punjabi contingent, which also included a cook, arrived in London in April 1910. The four Muslim wrestlers settled down to a rigorous training routine at the Royal Oak Hotel in Surbiton, a suburb of southwest London. Meanwhile, their manager issued a challenge to prospective opponents through the sporting press. Benjamin announced that Gama ('Champion undefeated wrestler of India, winner of 200 legitimate matches') and his compatriots ('Imam Bux, Champion of Lahore'; 'Ahmed Bux, Champion of Amritsar'; and 'Gamu, Champion of Jullundhur')—'The Sensation of the Wrestling World'—would take on 'all comers' irrespective of their nationality. They would also pay out £5 'to any competitor, no matter what nationality', whom any of them failed 'to throw in five minutes'. 'The wrestlers,' Benjamin stressed, 'were all British subjects.'[70]

THE GAME OF GAMA.

Figure 16. Gama Baksh is widely regarded as one of the greatest Indian wrestlers of the twentieth century. He travelled to London along with a group of Indian *pehelwans* in the summer of 1910. This image appeared in the British journal *Health and Strength*, which sent one of its reporters to interview the wrestlers. © British Library Board. All Rights Reserved / Bridgeman Images.

The impresario may have felt compelled to differentiate his own wards from the other strongmen then present in the imperial metropolis. London at this time was a magnet for professional wrestlers from across the globe. Many of them came to take part in an annual wrestling championship that had been started in 1908 by the National Sporting Club.[71] On any given day during the competition, Londoners could watch an eclectic mixture of the familiar and the exotic at the city's famous Alhambra Theatre. Fighters from Australia, North America, and the Caribbean rubbed shoulders with Lancastrian wrestlers from Wigan, Icelandic *glima* exponents, Swiss *schwinger*, Turkish *yagh güres*, and Japanese *sumotori* and *jujutsu-kai*.[72] The wrestling itself was in the hybrid 'catch-as-catch-can' style that had rapidly grown in popularity over the previous two decades.[73] This was an amalgam of old folk wrestling and new fighting techniques that had developed on either side of the Atlantic in the late nineteenth century. Unlike the 'Greco-Roman' form of wrestling prominent in Europe, 'catch-as-catch-can' was a no-holds barred form of 'freestyle' grappling that permitted fighters to attack their opponents below the waist.[74]

The Punjabi *pehelwans* were latecomers to London's cosmopolitan wrestling scene and the mongrel form that was its currency. But they appear to have been unfazed by 'catch-can' wrestling and adapted quickly to its rules and requirements. Indeed, Benjamin even claimed that 'the style was born in India thousands of years ago'.[75] What the Indians did not grasp, however, was that professional wrestling in the city was closely linked to the world of music hall entertainment. 'Match fixing' was pervasive and there were few contemporary professional bouts that were entirely untainted by it. For Gama and his compatriots, on the other hand, wrestling was not simply a sport; it was a way of life governed by a code of ethical personal conduct that precluded the pursuit of illicit material rewards. 'Throwing' a wrestling contest was thus simply inconceivable for these *pehelwans*. Sensing that matches with the Indian interlopers would be risky for their reputations, many of the professional wrestlers in the city avoided an encounter with them.

By early July, even as the impending Jeffries-Johnson fight across the Atlantic gripped the public imagination, the Indian wrestlers became increasingly restive at their own inactivity. Their predicament attracted the attention of the British press. The *Sporting Life* observed dryly that 'Gama's advent has synchronised with an extraordinary exodus of champions from England'.[76] The editor of *John Bull* also weighed in on behalf of 'our Indian subjects':

For some time past there have been suspicions that most of these wrestling matches have been simply a question of £ s. d. and that there have been no sport in them, the winner having been declared upon before entering the ring. Of these things we personally know nothing, but we are told that these Indian wrestlers could have had scores of matches and made a pile of money had they only fallen into line and wrestled to order. This they refused to do. Their reply has always been: 'We have to go back to India.' They wish to return victorious.[77]

A despairing Benjamin meanwhile issued a fresh challenge on behalf of the 'Lion of the Punjab'. Gama offered to fight against the world's best wrestlers for a prize stake. He also announced that he would take down within an hour of wrestling time every one of the thirty Japanese wrestlers whose exploits were mesmerizing visitors to the Japan-British Exhibition at the White City in Shepherd's Bush.[78]

Finally, Benjamin Franklin Roller, a professional strongman who had recently arrived in London from the United States, stepped forward to fight Gama. An ex-football player and all-round athlete who also possessed a degree in medicine, 'Doc' Roller was an unlikely prize fighter.[79] Although it was rumoured in some quarters that he feigned injuries, the American had given a very good account of himself against some of the prominent wrestling champions of the day—notably, his compatriot Frank Gotch— and fancied his chances against a man who was relatively unknown in London's wrestling world.[80] The bout between the two wrestlers was arranged by the *Sporting Life* newspaper. Both sides agreed beforehand that the contest would be decided, as was the norm in 'catch-can' wrestling, on the best of three falls. The winner was to take home a £200 stake as well as two-thirds of the proceeds.[81]

As the day of the fight drew closer, Gama's manager sought to heighten public interest in the event by proclaiming that his man was 'the greatest wrestler ever born'.[82] A reporter from *Health and Strength*, who went to watch Gama and his compatriots train at their hotel, was highly impressed with the physical prowess of what he took to be upper-caste 'Hindoos'. 'They are superbly built—no forced, bulging muscles, but just smooth, hard, thick, sinuous strength,' he wrote admiringly. He was particularly struck by the fact that these Indian fighters only ate flesh 'from animals which they have killed themselves'.[83]

There was, thus, an intense air of anticipation as Gama and Roller squared off at the Alhambra Theatre on 8 August 1910. 'Every part of the house was filled, while a large crowd assembled outside to hear the result,' noted *The Times*.[84] The result of the fight was also 'eagerly awaited in all parts of the Indian Empire, where Gama's name is a household word and his deeds are told with pride'.[85] The compere attested to the *bona fide* nature of the event by announcing that 'not all the money in England' could buy the Punjabi *pehelwan*.'This man,' mused a journalist present in the hall, 'merits the title of "The Incorruptible" more than the great French revolutionary, Robespierre, upon whom it was conferred.'[86]

Another reporter who covered the event was eager to see if 'the proceedings would throw some light on the question much discussed of late years, of the relative merits of the Oriental physique and that of the Occidental strong man'.[87] He penned a vivid account of the event as it unfolded that afternoon:

> When he was stripped for the first bout, Gama set about loosening his muscles in the quaint fashion favoured by nearly all Oriental wrestlers...It was clear that some of the spectators did not take him very seriously because of these curious genuflections and the fact that (like Cyrus on a memorable occasion) he smote his thighs as he went into action, presumably with the idea of intimidating his gigantic opponent...With his small hands and feet and compact though loose build...Gama looked small, almost puny, in comparison with the American wrestler. When, however, the wrestling began it was at once evident that the Oriental was not only the swifter but also the stronger man. He has the surprising agility and grace of the great *Felidae*, and in a minute threw Roller between the mat and the footlights, the fall not counting. Here the supple conscious Oriental leg came into play. On returning to the mat, and receiving the advantage of the hold to which he was clearly entitled, he threw Roller with what appeared to be a chest-stroke and promptly pinned him, winning the first bout in 1 min. 40 sec.[88]

In the second round Roller tried to dodge Gama. But he 'could not escape his leonine opponent for long, and went to the mat with the worst of the position'. Watching him in action, this writer concluded that, 'Except, perhaps, in Japan, there is probably nobody to throw Gama.'[89]

One person in the audience watched the proceedings with keen interest. This was 'Stanley Zbyszko', one of the professional wrestlers whom Gama had challenged earlier that summer. After the match had ended, the Galician shook the Punjabi *pehelwan* 'warmly by the hand and congratulated him on his triumph'.[90] It transpired that the two men were to fight each other in a contest arranged by the *John Bull* newspaper the following month in London.[91]

Gama's victory over Roller finally drew public attention to 'the great troupe of Indians who have come to England in the hope of meeting the best white exponents of the art'.[92] The immediate beneficiary was Gama's younger brother Imam Baksh, who now received an offer to take on John Lemm, a well-known professional wrestler in London. A former mountain guide from Switzerland, Lemm was said to be 'one of the most gifted of modern wrestlers'.[93] Unlike other European fighters, he also 'displayed a readiness to tackle the best'.[94] The fight was staged at the Alhambra on 6 September 1910 in front of a large crowd.[95] The two rivals were utterly dissimilar in their physique: Lemm, 'broad, stocky, and compact'; Imam, 'supple and tall, quite 6 ft in height, with very powerful thighs'.[96] The Indian, who had prepared assiduously for this encounter, entered the arena wearing his 'favourite amulet' and proceeded to outclass Lemm.[97] Although he began nervously, Imam soon had his opponent 'struggling like a stranded fish underneath the chairs of the privileged spectators on the stage'.[98] And in 'less than four and a half minutes of actual wrestling', noted one newspaper, the Swiss wrestler 'was twice fairly and squarely nailed to the floor'.[99]

Imam Baksh's victory whetted the public's appetite for the clash between Gama and Zbyszko that was to take place four days later at the Olympic Stadium in Shepherd's Bush. But it also raised the stakes in the impending contest. The editor of *Health and Strength* claimed that the wrestling feats of the 'astounding Sikhs' had prompted letters to the journal from worried British readers in India, 'pointing out that if they kept on winning their victories would give a dangerous fillip to the seditions amongst our dusky subjects that menace the integrity of our Indian Empire'.[100] As it turned out, the match was to prove highly controversial but for a very different reason. At the centre of the storm was the most intriguing strongman in Edwardian London.

Born Stanislaus Cyganiewicz in Krakow, Poland, the erudite and multilingual 'Stanley Zbyszko' first made his name as a wrestler in Europe, fighting in the traditional Greco-Roman style. In the early 1900s, however, he was spotted by Charles Cochran, the manager of the great Russian wrestler George Hackenschmidt, who persuaded him to move to London.[101] Here Zbyszko plied his trade in the world of music hall entertainment, taking part in arranged wrestling shows that he was paid to lose. Occasionally, though, Zbyszko was involved in competitive bouts with other professionals. One such contest brought him great notoriety. In January 1908, he took on a Turkish fighter called Kara Sulaiman, supposedly the 'Champion of the

Bosphorus'. To the chagrin of the crowd, Zbyszko made little attempt to defeat his opponent. A rematch was held and resulted in a scrappy victory for Zbyszko. It later emerged that 'Kara Sulaiman' was in fact a Bulgarian named Ivan Offtharoff, who had been put up by his opponent.[102] The incident sullied Zbyszko's reputation as a fighter.

The match against Gama was Zbyszko's first major engagement since his return to Britain. Aware that he was up against a highly skilled practitioner, Zbyszko appears to have concluded that his best chance of success lay in stonewalling his fleet-footed opponent. As soon as the two wrestlers came face to face in the fighting arena at the Olympic Stadium, the Polish fighter took to the floor and abjured all attempts at wrestling.[103] Despite Gama's best efforts and the jeers of the 8,000 spectators in the stadium, he refused to budge from this recumbent position. Finally, after a little over two and a half hours, the (non-)contest was called off. With the light rapidly fading, the proceedings descended into chaos as sections of the irate crowd invaded the fighting arena to remonstrate with Zbyszko. The police were called in to protect the two wrestlers and usher them out safely.[104] In order to procure a result, a rematch was scheduled for the following Saturday. But while Gama came to the stadium at the appointed hour, there was no sign of Zbyszko.[105] Gama was thus declared the victor and picked up the winner's cheque of £250. He was also presented with a gold belt on behalf of *John Bull* by the member of parliament Horatio Bottomley.[106]

The 'fiasco', as the press came to refer to the Gama–Zbyszko match, led to a public backlash against professional wrestling in London. 'A more miserable, more disappointing match than this,' raged the *Sporting Life*,

> has fortunately seldom if ever taken place. To expect that the public will again waste their time and pay their money for the privilege of seeing a so-called champion wrestler lie flat on his chest, or lie on his hands and knees for two and a half hours, and to make no attempt at genuine wrestling, is to insult their intelligence and over-estimate their credulity.[107]

Much of the criticism was directed at Zbyszko, who had left the country after the fight.[108] But, rather uncharitably, Gama too was blamed by some for his inability to dislodge the Galician.

A few weeks later, the Punjabi *pehelwans* returned home. One newspaper reported that the Indian wrestlers had taken this decision because they could not 'obtain any matches'. It added that 'the financial results of the Gama- Zbyszko were so unsatisfactory that Mr. Benjamin, despairing of getting anything to recoup his troupe and himself for all the expense and trouble already entailed, made arrangements to leave England immediately after the affairs were settled up'.[109]

★   ★   ★

The public criticism of his match with Zbyszko seems to have stung the 'Lion of the Punjab'. For when R.B. Benjamin brought over another troupe of wrestlers to Britain the following summer, Gama was a notable absentee. It is not entirely clear though why Benjamin organized this venture, given the losses that he claimed to have sustained on the first tour. Even more intriguingly, the Indians arrived in England in two batches. The first led by Ahmed Baksh and Imam Baksh arrived in April 1911; they were joined in early June by a second group, which included Gama's old rival Ghulam Mohiuddin.

The reputation of professional wrestling in London had yet to recover from the damage inflicted by the 'fiasco' of the previous year. But the arrival of the Indians prompted the *Sporting Life* to launch a public campaign to promote 'clean' wrestling, untainted by 'match fixing'. The bout between Ahmed Baksh and Maurice Deriaz at the Crystal Palace on 24 May 1911 was publicized as the first step in this direction. The newspaper, which arranged the fight, was determined to proscribe the tactics that had 'brought wrestling into disfavour'. In particular, the referee for the contest was given the power to disqualify a contestant who deliberately avoided wrestling. 'The sport is a healthy one, a manly one,' the paper declared, 'and all that is needed...to bring it back to the position it should hold is for the public to have confidence that matches are genuinely conducted and carried through. The public may feel reassured of the point with regard to the contest between Ahmed Bux and Maurice de Riaz.'[110] In order to signal a break with the 'theatrical trappings' that had marked previous wrestling bouts in the imperial metropolis, the organizers of the contest decided to link the Baksh–Deriaz match to the Festival of Empire. They promoted the fixture as a charity event and announced that one third of the gate receipts would go to the festival fund.[111] In return, the festival officials permitted them to stage the fight in the great concert hall, which could hold up to 8,000 people.[112]

The *Sporting Life* trumpeted the support it had received from the British establishment in its efforts to revive 'healthy wrestling'. As chief patrons of the event, the paper had roped in Lord Minto, the former Viceroy of India;

Lord Desborough, chief organizer of the 1908 London Olympics; and Lord Lonsdale, one of the founders of the National Sporting Club.[113] On the eve of the bout, it also publicized a message of support from the new King-Emperor.[114] At the same time, the paper highlighted the keen public interest in the event, especially among the Indians in Britain. 'The Maharajah of Patiala and the members of the Indian team of cricketers, together with the Indian population now in London,' it reported, 'are keenly interested in Ahmud Bux, among whom his chances have been and are being openly discussed.'[115]

Not all observers were ready to be swept along by the *Sporting Life*'s enthusiasm. Writing in the *Daily Chronicle*, 'Corinthian' cast doubt on the quality of the fighters and expressed his reservations about the presence of 'foreign wrestlers' in Britain.[116] The *Sporting Life* would have none of it. 'Bux and De Riaz are wrestlers of the highest repute: exactly what their ability is may be accurately gauged from their respective records'.[117] The Indian, it pointed out, 'is at least as good a man as Imam Bux, and not greatly inferior to Gama. Mr. Benjamin would certainly not have troubled to bring novices with him.'[118] And as for the charge that Ahmed Baksh was a 'foreigner', the paper retorted, wasn't 'an Indian a British subject?'.[119] Baksh, it asserted, was 'only a foreigner to defeat'.[120]

The heat generated by these debates led many to expect a sell-out crowd on the day. Much to the surprise and disappointment of the organizers, however, there were not more than 3,000 people present at the start of the match. One reporter noted that 'the vast extent of the building caused the assembled spectators to look somewhat like a few cherries in a bowl'.[121] 'A conspicuous feature of the attendance,' he added, 'was the number of Hindoos present, and—this seems somewhat extraordinary to Western ideas—an appreciable number of them were ladies, so that the emancipation of women in Hindustan would seem to have advanced appreciably during the past decade.'[122]

Shortly before 9 o'clock in the evening, both fighters made their appearance. Deriaz was the first to enter the arena, wearing 'a blue bath robe, followed within a minute or two by Bux, who was clad in something that looked like the fur robe an Indian trapper wears in the Far North-West'.[123] The two men were a study in contrast: Baksh, 'tall, stately, silent in his movements'; Deriaz, 'a brick wall of a man, all square'.[124] But the first round 'was over almost before it had begun'. It took the lithe Indian just over a minute to throw his muscular European adversary for the first fall. Deriaz retired from the arena for the stipulated fifteen-minute break, while 'Bux remained in his chair calmly waiting for his man's return smiling and chatting with Mr. Benjamin as though such summary victories were of every day occurrence'.[125] The next round lasted a little over three minutes, before Baksh deployed a decisive 'half-nelson' that 'brought the burly Swiss flat on the ground'.[126] 'In quickness and subtlety of movement, agility, coolness, and sureness, and knowledge of balance and equilibrium, Ahmud Bux was far superior to his opponent,' wrote one observer after the fight.[127]

'Evidently it will be difficult to find heavy-weights good enough to beat these Indians, who have the look of all-round athletes, possessing long elastic muscles, great pace, and quickness of vision—qualities generally absent in the Continental wrestler, who is a product of the gymnasium,' The Times concluded.[128] Others concurred. 'Is there a man in England or anywhere else who can stand up against Bux in a straight match with any chance of success? We are convinced there is not,' declared the Sporting Life.[129] The assessment had some merit in it, for none of the prominent professionals of the day showed any inclination to accept the challenge thrown out by the Indian wrestlers. It was mid-July before Benjamin was able to fix another bout for Ahmed Baksh. This was staged at the Oxford Music Hall in London on 10 July 1911 against a Swiss wrestler named Armand Cherpillod.

The thirty-four-year-old Cherpillod was regarded as a 'strong and scientific wrestler'.[130] But once again, the outcome was a quick, one-sided victory for Ahmed Baksh. According to The Times' report of the fight:

> Cherpillod was utterly outclassed in speed and science and also in strength, although he was only 6 lb. lighter than his opponent. He was a babe in the embrace of Ahmed Bux, and what surprised the spectators most, a squalling babe; several times he emitted frenzied ejaculations while his friends raised cries of 'Foul' in the French of Switzerland. These appeals were very properly ignored by the referee; there was nothing approaching unfair or unduly rough play in the Indian's methods.[131]

The first round barely lasted four minutes. During the break, Cherpillod claimed that Baksh had injured his wrist and refused to return to the fray.[132] The Indian was, thus, declared the winner of the contest. But to give the small crowd its money's worth, Baksh and his fellow Punjabi wrestler, Kala Partapa, agreed to put on an exhibition of their wrestling skills. The latter, noted The Times correspondent, was 'a darker and a broader and a shorter person, with a smile resembling Jack Johnson's'. He then proceeded to describe what followed:

> It was a most exhilarating show while it lasted. The two big men did not spare one another, and their pace was equal to the little indiarubber men who are produced in the Lancashire coal-pits. They worked maniacally like thorough sportsmen; there was nothing of the mere exhibition in their display. It was clear to the expert critics present (1) that the European heavyweights are slower in every way than these invaders; and (2) that their repertoire of stratagems is much more varied than that of the best Western wrestler, even Hackenschmidt, whose inventiveness seemed unsurpassed. In the first place, the Indian's muscles are readier to obey his brain than is the case with European wrestlers. Secondly, they have the advantage of traditions which have evolved themselves through many generations of athletes, each adding something to the stock of practical knowledge to be passed on from father to son.[133]

Others went further and freighted the sporting comparison with the politics of race. These observers yearned for a British 'white hope' who could take on the Indian wrestlers. 'It is certainly time some white man came forward to extend the Indians,' wrote the despairing editor of *Health and Strength*. 'Is there none to be found? Surely—surely there must be someone who could do it. In this great game of chess, will the dark pawns sweep the board all the time?'[134]

But the impassioned call for a home-grown champion went unanswered. The two preeminent white wrestlers of the day who might have taken on the challenge—George Hackenschmidt and Frank Gotch—were preparing to fight each other in Chicago for the 'catch-can' world title that September. Neither had responded to the repeated challenges issued by the Indians. Finally, frustrated by their lack of engagements in Britain and keen to try one last time for a bout with the Russian and the American, some of the Indian wrestlers crossed the Atlantic in late August. A brief news item on 22 August 1911 cast tantalizing light on their future plans: 'They hope to arrive in Chicago...and Mr. R.B. Benjamin, the Manager of the troupe, will then use his best endeavour to bring about a meeting between Ahmed Bux or Karla [*sic*] and Hackenschmidt or Gotch.'[135]

As it transpired, the intrepid Indians waited in vain for the 'Russian Lion' and the Iowa strongman. But at this point we must leave them and turn to the story of another intriguing figure from the subcontinent who had arrived in London earlier that summer.

IV

On 1 June 1911, exactly a week after Ahmed Baksh defeated Maurice Deriaz at the Crystal Palace, the Indian and his fellow wrestlers made their way to Charing Cross Station. The person they went to greet that day was no ordinary figure. Dubbed the 'Indian Hercules', Professor Kodi Ramamurti Naidu was widely known for his astonishing displays of strength and endurance. Ahmed Baksh and his compatriots had frequently performed in his travelling shows and were eager to pay their respects to a man they regarded as a mentor. When the 'Professor' alighted from his carriage, 'in accordance with Eastern custom, they hung around his neck a garland of newly-cut flowers'.[136] Accompanying him was the ubiquitous R.B. Benjamin, who made the arrangements for his visit to London, and a fresh batch of Indian wrestlers.

Yet, unlike his acolytes, Ramamurti was not after sporting glory in the conventional sense. The extraordinary physical feats that he performed were not directed against any opponents. Although some contemporaries described him as a 'weightlifter' and a 'bodybuilder', he made a living by enchanting spectators with wondrous, reason-defying exploits. A photograph of the Indian wrestlers with Ramamurti—it is not clear when it was taken—is revealing in this regard. The bare-bodied fighters, stern exponents of an ancient art, stare solemnly at the camera; but the professor, resplendent in a shiny tunic and splendid turban, looks more like a magician than a professional strongman.[137]

Much like the Maharaja of Patiala ten days earlier, Ramamurti's flamboyant presence made a deep impression on the reporters who had gathered at Charing Cross. The *Sporting Life* described his arrival at the station thus:

> Quite a stir did the appearance of Rama Murti make, dressed in a most elaborate costume of red velvet, lavishly trimmed with gold. He is not what you would call a big man, perhaps he would be best described as unusually square, with great shoulders, deep chested; a man with much charm of manner, and striking carriage. The professor is 27 years of age, stands 5ft. 6 ½ in. high, and weighs 14st. 6lb.[138]

An editorial in *Health and Strength* invested Ramamurti's arrival in London with a wider imperial significance:

> Who knows but he and the Indian wrestlers, for whose visit to our land he is very largely responsible, may not lead to a better understanding between our

Indian Empire and the Mother Country! Who knows but that it may do far
more than drastic legislation to extinguish the embers of sedition that are
smouldering in that far off land![139]

Present-day retellings of the story of the 'Indian Hercules', which tend to be
in the mythic register, have erased the complexity of his encounter with the
colonizer. Ramamurti's biography has been deftly annexed by nationalist
narratives of the anti-colonial struggle in coastal Andhra, his astounding
achievements extolled as unambiguous acts of physical self-assertion against
the foreign rulers. But his life was more fascinating than the legend.

Fortunately for the historian, two contemporary essays by Saint Nihal
Singh, a peripatetic Indian journalist, provide a detailed first-hand account
of the professor's career and times. The first, entitled 'The Story of India's
Hercules', appeared in June 1912 in the *Indian Review*. The subject clearly
possessed a wider public appeal, for three years later, the writer penned

Figure 17. The arrival in London in the summer of 1911 of Professor Ramamurti
Naidu, the 'Indian Hercules', was widely anticipated by physical culture enthusiasts.
Like the Indian wrestlers, many of whom regarded him as their guru, he too was
featured on the cover of *Health and Strength*. © British Library Board. All Rights
Reserved / Bridgeman Images.

yet another essay on the remarkable strongman in the prestigious *Strand Magazine*.[140] Both essays drew on the author's personal interviews with Ramamurti and were undoubtedly inflected by their subject's self-representations. Nonetheless, the biographical details they provide, used in conjunction with the newspapers of the day, tell us a great deal about the professor's life.

According to Nihal Singh, Ramamurti was born in 1883 in Viraghatam (Veeraghattam), a small town in the princely state of Vizianagaram, in the northeastern corner of the Madras Presidency. His mother died when the child was two years old, and his early upbringing was overseen by his father, a police inspector. 'Both of the parents were common place, mentally and physically,' noted the writer, 'so the "Indian Hercules" did not inherit his great strength from them.'[141] Indeed, he was a 'sickly youth, and suffered from asthma'. Nor did he take much interest in his studies. Although his father had enrolled him in a school in Vizianagaram, 'the boy did not make much progress in his studies, often retrogressing from a higher to a lower form'.[142] Worse still, he took to loafing about town. One day, however, he ran into some wrestlers, who took him under their wing. A few years in their company 'transformed the boy's physique'.[143] Although Ramamurti continued to attend school—in order to please his father—'his heart was in physical culture, and not in academics'.[144] Soon, he became proficient in wrestling and gymnastics, both Indian and foreign. Remarkably, the thirteen-year-old Ramamurti was hired in 1896 as a physical instructor at the newly established Provincial High School in Vizianagaram. Here, he worked in a voluntary capacity since the school management 'was not prepared to pay any salary to the boy-instructor'. Importantly, the experience 'afforded him ample opportunity to engage in manly sports and develop his physique'.[145] To pursue his passion in a more systematic manner, he enrolled in 1899 at the Saidapet Physical Training College in Madras. He successfully completed the twelve-month course of study, graduating 'with high honours'.[146] Returning to Vizianagaram, he resumed his honorary position at the Provincial High School. But possessing 'a great deal of animal spirits', he soon became involved in local brawls.[147] At this juncture, a 'severe reprimand from a police magistrate made him realize that if he wanted to keep out of jail he must stop wandering about and take life seriously'.[148]

Ramamurti's subsequent career alerts us to an interesting aspect of the Indian physical culture movement in the first decade of the twentieth century. Alongside the *akharas* and physical culture institutions dedicated to physical and spiritual self-strengthening, there emerged a world of popular entertainment in which strongmen earned a livelihood by parading their prowess in variety acts.[149] In some instances, the stalwarts of particular gymnasia diversified their portfolio by setting up travelling circuses that toured across the subcontinent.[150] Ramamurti's career in the early 1900s followed this trajectory. As he told Nihal Singh, 'the only vocation he could follow was to obtain a situation with a circus'.[151] In November 1902, he joined the 'Raja of Tuni Circus Company'. Recognizing his talent, the proprietor of the circus 'at once made him the manager of the concern'.[152] However, the circus was disbanded in 1904 and Ramamurti 'was once again thrown on his own resources'.[153]

An encounter in May 1905 with Eugen Sandow, who had arrived in Madras during his tour of the Indian subcontinent, transformed the south Indian strongman's life.[154] As Sandow went about his dumbbell routines, Ramamurti is said to have challenged him to a contest. But the German celebrity refused to 'pit his strength against that of a mere "native"'. Nonetheless, watching Sandow on stage kindled a new idea in Ramamurti. 'Now he began to entertain notions of large audiences witnessing and applauding his performances,' wrote Nihal Singh.[155] Accordingly, Ramamurti decided to perform as a solo act. His first public show took place in Madras in December 1905, and was patronized by Lord Ampthill, the governor of the presidency. So wildly successful was Ramamurti's debut that he was invited to perform for the Prince of Wales and his wife when they visited Madras in January 1906. The pleased royal couple presented him with a special 'gold medal as a token of their appreciation'.[156]

Following this spectacular triumph, Ramamurti formed his own company and began to tour across India. 'In 1906 and succeeding years he performed in a number of Indian cities, winning laurels wherever he went,' recorded Nihal Singh.[157] The statement is corroborated by a report in the *Times of India* in 1908, which noted that in the preceding two years the professor's 'athletic troupe and company of wrestlers' had performed in 'Belgaum, Hubli, Dharvar, Bijapur, Sholapur' before arriving in Bombay.[158] In 1909, Ramamurti 'took a fast trip through some of the countries of the Far East, and was received with acclaim everywhere he exhibited his strength'.[159] After his return, he travelled all over north India, visiting a number of towns in the Punjab and the United Provinces.

In these years, Ramamurti performed 'seven days a week and usually twice a day'. His takings ranged from 'Rs. 1000 (£66 13s. 4d.) to Rs. 5000

(£333 6s. 8d.) at each performance'.[160] But an even more telling sign of his popularity was the public adulation showered on him wherever he travelled. 'In many towns the young people have shown their admiration for the man by unhorsing the carriage in which he was riding and dragging it themselves,' wrote Nihal Singh.[161]

It was not simply the masses who were enchanted by Ramamurti. The rulers of many princely states also showed 'their gracious appreciation of the professor's talent by awarding him gold and silver medals and valuable gifts'.[162] Indeed, some of the maharajas even 'treated him as if he was a Prince'.[163] Among these was Bhupinder Singh, who on more than one occasion invited the south Indian strongman to perform in his state.[164]

★   ★   ★

As a public performer, the 'Indian Hercules' constantly claimed that his feats of strength and endurance were based on ancient Indian bodily techniques and exercises. According to Nihal Singh, Ramamurti derived his inspiration from 'the great Hindu traditions attributing almost unbelievable feats of strength to various heroes'.[165] Even as a child, he had been fascinated by the tales of derring-do in the ancient Indian epics. Fuelled by these stories, 'his overpowering craving was to become as strong as the legendary strong men'.[166] But now he looked for more specific lessons in these myths and concluded that they 'showed the way to a complete mastery of the will'. Thus, 'Hanuman and the other Hindu heroes had performed what appeared to be miracles to the moderns, not through extraordinary physical strength, but through a wonderful power to direct and control the will'.[167]

Armed with this insight, Ramamurti 'devoted himself to the cultivation of an absolutely inflexible will-power, that would render him insensible to all pain'. Nihal Singh noted that the professor had learnt 'the secret of going into a trance whenever he wished to do so, and thereby rendering himself unconscious of all feeling'. In particular, he had 'cultivated the ability to concentrate all his life forces at one or more points in his body, so that great weight imposed upon them will not crush his bones or strain his muscles'.[168] Indeed, Ramamurti generally prefaced his act with a speech in which he told the audience that his feats 'would not be accomplished by physical strength, but by spiritual power'. 'He had acquired that power,' he declared, 'by holding communion with the Unseen—or practising yoga.' The professor was also keen to stress that 'he was a vegetarian, did not eat flesh of any kind, and abjured even eggs and fish'. Further, he 'did not drink liquors of any kind, and took no drugs'.[169]

Ramamurti's words were perhaps meant to counter the suspicion lurking in the minds of his audience that his feats were a sleight of hand, that they were somehow 'Eastern magic'. Equally, his pronouncements might have been dictated by the need to differentiate himself from his Western counterparts. By highlighting the uniquely Indian provenance of his techniques and diet, he sought to draw attention to alternative traditions of physical culture. Significantly, Ramamurti claimed that he had tried Eugen Sandow's methods 'for some length of time', but eventually gave them up in favour of *Hathayoga*.[170] This points to the Indian strongman's affiliation with contemporary nationalist attempts to resurrect ancient Hindu traditions of physical culture.[171] The emphasis on vegetarianism and spiritual purity was integral to this project of remaking the Indian body as a site of authentic national values. It is not surprising, therefore, that Ramamurti soon became a totemic figure among nationalists eager to promote indigenous forms of physical culture.[172]

Yet, while he claimed that his methods were based on traditional 'Hindu' principles and practices, Ramamurti was undoubtedly a modern showman. His public shows were driven by the commercial imperatives that made his profession a part of the emergent world of mass entertainment. Notably, he fashioned his own performances along the lines that had been pioneered in the late Victorian era by strongmen like Sandow.[173] On the occasion that Nihal Singh watched his show in Bombay, the 'Indian Hercules' made his entry onstage to the strains of 'See the Conquering Hero Comes', performed by an Indian brass band. Singh noted that Ramamurti 'wore evening clothes, and looked as if he might have strolled out of a club in Pall Mall'.[174]

By the time he arrived in London in the summer of 1911, tales of the Indian Hercules' exploits had preceded him to the imperial metropolis. 'He is a wealthy man, and has come to Britain not merely as a "strong man," but as a Physical Culture missionary,' the suitably impressed editor of *Health and Strength* informed his readers. 'He assured me that his great idea is to gather ideas from the West, and so weld them with the Oriental systems as to produce as nearly as possible a perfect scheme of physical development.'[175]

But that may have not been the only reason for the professor to undertake the trip to Britain. London at this time, as we have seen, attracted strongmen from across the world. The city was at the forefront of a unique conjunction of physical culture and popular entertainment during the late

Victorian and Edwardian period. Strongmen were the new stars of the metropolitan showbusiness world in these decades. Their presence in the city's music halls and vaudeville theatres drew vast audiences eager to watch them perform their wondrous deeds. For Ramamurti, who had scaled the peaks of popularity in his own country, parading his prowess in the bastion of imperial power was simultaneously an irresistible challenge and an attractive commercial proposition. Evidently, too, there were sporting entrepreneurs in the city who regarded him as a potentially profitable investment. In the months preceding his departure for Europe, one Indian newspaper claimed that the professor had been 'invited by a sporting club in England on one thousand pounds a day'.[176]

On 20 June 1911, Ramamurti made his first appearance at the London Palladium before a 'select company of connoisseurs'.[177] In the audience that evening was Jack Johnson, 'who, on the introduction of Mr. R.B. Benjamin, came upon the stage and shook hands with him'.[178] Thereafter, the 'Indian Hercules' proceeded to thrill the audience with the remarkable repertoire that he had assiduously developed over the preceding six years.

The editor of *Health and Strength*, who was one of the special invitees to the show, penned a detailed account of the event. Ramamurti began by lying prone on his chest, 'whilst a stone weighing 2,000 lb., was placed by some twenty attendants upon his back'. A dozen men—'Indians and whites'—clambered on to the stone. But Ramamurti 'never flinched'.[179] Nor did he show any trace of discomfort when workmen armed with pickaxes smashed the stone to smithereens. 'This scene reminded me of the Death of Porthos, only that Rama Murti did not die,' remarked the writer. Another massive stone was now placed on the Indian superman's chest and on this once again stood 'a number of men'. This time, Ramamurti 'by his own unaided efforts, contrived to extricate himself from beneath the stone'. The professor's next two acts were designed to showcase his muscular power. In one instance, he shattered an iron chain by expanding his neck muscles; in the other, he slipped out with ease from a rope tightly wound around his upper body by contracting his chest. The *Health and Strength* representative did not regard these two stunts as particularly original, since they had 'been performed at various times by many of our British strong men'. 'But,' he added, 'though these feats did not impress me very much, the remaining two in the great man's repertoire unquestionably did.'[180]

These acts required Ramamurti to 'turn himself into a human cart track'. To begin with, two bullock wagons carrying around fifty men passed over him: 'the wheel of one went over his neck; that of the other over his legs'. The Indian strongman 'bore this mighty burden without flinching'. Finally, there came the famous elephant act that had made Ramamurti a public sensation in the subcontinent:

> The elephant is, prior to the exhibition, led several times over a swinging platform. Then Rama Murti, with his head bandaged, comes on to the stage and lies down on his back. A square-shaped velvet cushion, or to be strictly accurate a mat, is placed upon his chest, and the platform is fixed upon it, fitting into grooves. Then the ponderous elephant walks slowly over this 'Bridge with a Human Keystone'. Rama Murti ought, by all accepted physical laws, to be crushed to pulp, but he isn't. He rises, as before, and retires.[181]

His appearance at the Palladium was an unqualified triumph for the Indian Hercules. Afterwards, the world's most famous boxer expressed 'his astonishment that such a man existed in the world'.[182] Others looked forward to his next public performance and expressed the hope that he would display his 'famous feat of stopping with his body a motor car which is running at full speed'.[183]

After that spectacular opening performance, however, Ramamurti's trip to Britain did not go quite according to plan. Although some of his subsequent shows were successful, he appears to have become bogged down in fruitless negotiations with the owners of London's music halls. Ramamurti 'refused to give his exhibitions on the music-hall stage unless he was paid £1000 a week'. This, he told Nihal Singh, was 'much less than what he normally earned in India', but the London managers, while willing to pay a high salary, could not afford to give him the amount he asked for. 'As a consequence,' Singh wrote, 'the capital of the Empire lost the opportunity of witnessing the most marvellous feats ever exhibited on the stage of a variety theatre.'[184] But a perusal of contemporary newspapers also indicates another reason for the professor's disappointing trip. On 20 July 1911, the *Amrita Bazar Patrika* reported that Ramamurti had been injured in London during a performance.[185] Two and a half months later, the Indian strongman departed for India from Marseilles. 'He was exhibiting his feats in London but his success was marred by an accident,' stated a report in the *Tribune*.[186] Notwithstanding the tame end to Ramamurti's British sojourn, his visit was accorded an important place in subsequent histories of Indian physical culture. In the words of S. Mazumdar, author of a chronicle about India's strong men published in 1942, the professor had 'rendered a great service to India' in taking with him to England 'a number of reputed Indian wrestlers who convinced the European world that the Indians stood supreme in the game'.[187]

V

Even as sportsmen from the subcontinent were making their mark in Britain, the most historic sporting event of this Indian summer took place thousands of miles away in their homeland. On 31 July 1911, a number of British papers reported the startling news that Mohun Bagan, a Bengali football club, had defeated in succession two military teams—the Middlesex and East Yorkshire Regiments—to win the Challenge Shield of the Indian Football Association.[188]

A few weeks later, the *Manchester Guardian* carried a long report by its Calcutta correspondent on the match and its aftermath. This account described for the benefit of British readers the symbolic charge of this extraordinary encounter in the imperial capital:

> For a week Calcutta, even European Calcutta, has been discussing the victorious career of the Mohan Bagan football team, and amongst the Indian community little else has been talked about. The excitement was intense. The military teams have hitherto been looked upon as invincible. At any rate, they have never been defeated by an Indian football club. A certain section of Europeans deplored the victory, not because they grudged the success of an Indian team, but because they feared that a political moral would be read into the event. Others hoped that Mohan Bagan would be defeated on Saturday, when they would meet the redoubtable East Yorkshires, pointing out that the Middlesex goalkeeper had been injured at an early stage in the game. When Saturday came, half the city flocked to the football ground and those who could not enter sat down in their thousands to listen. Alas! for European hopes, Mohan Bagan, in a clean and well-fought game, won by two goals to one.[189]

However, the writer hastened to reassure his British readers that the Indian team's triumph had served to promote racial amity:

> This victory has had the most excellent effect. From the moment when the captain of the East Yorkshire men ran across the field and shook hands with the captain of the Mohan Bagan, every European worth his salt has joined in the congratulations showered on the winning team. And the Indian community has undoubtedly been touched by the feeling of good-fellowship thus mani-fested. The success of the Mohan Bagan and its reception by Anglo-Indians have done much to obliterate the tension between the races.[190]

Matters were not quite so straightforward. The extraordinary achievement of the 'Immortal Eleven', as *Amrita Bazar Patrika* called the victorious team, was variously interpreted in Bengal and the rest of India.[191] The responses, both among colonizers and colonized, ranged from expressions of outright hostility—an Englishman slapping a Bengali Christian in a railway carriage; an Indian who saw in the European defeat on the football field an imminent lowering of the Union Jack fluttering over Fort William—to cordial calls for racial fraternity.[192]

But quite apart from the diverse sentiments triggered by this politically charged event, there was a sense among many Indians that their country had finally arrived on the international sporting stage. 'At the present time Indian sport of all sorts is booming not only in this Empire, but in the wider field of the British Isles,' declared one writer. 'Perhaps no previous year has afforded so complete an example of the prowess of the various races of India in many different classes of outdoor and athletic pastimes.'[193]

Cricket would one day triumph over its rivals in establishing itself as India's de facto national sport. However, its success in this regard was by no means preordained. With that caveat in mind, let us return to the first Indian cricket team and follow its progress on the playing fields of imperial Britain.

9

Lost and Won

I

On 11 June 1911, Leonard Woolf arrived back in London after spending six and a half years as a civil servant in Ceylon. In his autobiography, Woolf recalled the journey to the family home in Putney 'in a London summer afternoon of perfect sunshine'. 1911, Woolf wrote, 'was one of those rare years, an unending summer of the snakeless meadow—a summer which began in early spring and gently died away only in late autumn'.[1] In the Weald of Kent, another budding writer spent that summer playing cricket for the Tunbridge Wells Blue Mantles Club. For Siegfried Sassoon, too, 1911 was one of those 'specially remembered summers, from which one evolves a consistent impression of comingled happiness'.[2]

To the reminiscences of the writers, we can add the assessments of the scientists. 'The summer of 1911 has been remarkable in so many ways that without doubt it will receive the special attention of meteorologists and will in course of time be dealt with thoroughly,' noted Charles Harding in a talk delivered to the Royal Meteorological Society in London later that year. He reminded his readers of the 'unusual amount of bright sunshine throughout the summer'. The 'aggregate duration in the three months June to August was 819 hours'; this was '189 hours more than the average for the last fifteen years'. The mean temperature for the three-month period from June to August was '4.9° in excess of the average for the past seventy years'.[3] On seven occasions, the temperature exceeded 90° F, equalling a record set forty-three years earlier.

The year 1911 ranks as the one of the hottest English summers since the mid-seventeenth century. The 383.9 hours of sunshine experienced that July by the residents of Eastbourne, Sussex, remains the 'highest monthly total ever recorded in the UK'.[4] The intense heat wave in early

August is also considered an early record setter in the twentieth century. The temperature of 98° F (36.7° C) recorded at Raunds (Northamptonshire), Canterbury (Kent), and Epsom (Surrey) on 9 August 1911 was not surpassed for eighty years.[5]

Vast swathes of southern and eastern England experienced drought as the continuously sunny, dry weather of May and June gave way to the prolonged hot spell from mid-July to mid-August. As the *Daily Mail* reported on 22 July 1911, 'In the agricultural districts pastures are burnt up. Rivers and streams are at the lowest they have been for years. A blazing sun smote upon the parched land, and refined the torture which all living things are undergoing, while heath fires occurred in many places.'[6] 'Positively at the moment,' declared a London correspondent of the *Times of India*, 'one would be better off in India than in England, for it could not be hotter in the tropics.'[7]

A vast majority who lived through this heat wave, one writer cattily remarked, simultaneously 'suffered excruciating agony and enjoyed it immensely'.[8] Thousands of town dwellers took advantage of the affordable railway fares to flee to the seaside.[9] Those who remained behind in the cities congregated in parks and other sun-drenched pleasure spots. Londoners, in particular, 'rediscovered' their city. 'And what a London it was,' noted one contemporary, 'no shops and no business, but such a delightful variety of open-air enjoyment in the parks and on the commons, at the exhibitions and on the river.'[10]

But the heat wave also enhanced the mortality rate, and the death toll began to be reported on a daily basis in the newspapers. In London, there were 4,000 more deaths between July to September 1911 than there had been for the same period the previous year. Among those who were felled by the heat was one Mr Ganter, a member of the Hampstead Liberal Association CC, who was said to have died as a result of 'over-exertion and the heat', following a match against the Kilburn Liberal Club.[11]

Newspapers also reported 'strange effects of the heat' across the country. On 14 July, for instance, a 'remarkable shooting' was reported at Tunbridge Wells. According to the *Manchester Guardian*, a young man named Arthur Tutt, who was said to be 'affected by the heat', entered at midnight the shop where he worked and fired at his manageress with a revolver. His victim escaped with an injury, but Tutt 'then ran along the road firing at himself and fell about 50 yards from the premises mortally wounded'. The heat that day was also said 'to have driven a man insane on the Colchester main road between Romford and Brentwood'. Having steadily discarded all items of his clothing en route to his destination, the man was found 'in a nude condition' by the police. He was promptly charged and confined in the Brentwood Police Station.[12]

One might discount the wider significance of individual instances of rash, heat-induced behaviour. But historians have discerned in the events of this time evidence of a new mood of insubordination within British society. George Dangerfield famously argued that the years between 1910 and 1914 marked the 'strange death of liberal England'.[13] As he saw it, this dramatic period witnessed the simultaneous convergence of four rebellions that threatened to rip apart the complacent liberal order of the previous century. The aristocracy, ensconced in the House of Lords, sought to prevent the Liberal government of the day from curtailing its privileges even at the risk of undermining longstanding constitutional norms; the Suffragette movement, which demanded the immediate enfranchisement of women, took a militant turn under the Pankhursts and increasingly engaged in spectacular acts of violence; workers began to organize more systematically in trade unions and undertake nation-wide collective strikes for better wages and working conditions; and the question of Home Rule for Ireland returned to the centre stage of British politics, making ever more likely a prolonged civil war.

Dangerfield's 'dazzling impressionism' has been questioned by scholars.[14] But there is a general consensus that the years between the death of King Edward VII and the assassination of Archduke Ferdinand witnessed a significant political conjuncture in British history. The summer of 1911, in particular, was a critical moment. Although the question of Irish Home Rule and the vote for women was momentarily put on the back burner, the country was plunged into a crisis by the Tory peers' revolt against the Liberal government's Parliament Bill and the simultaneous eruption of country-wide labour protests.

The 'Tory rebellion' in the summer of 1911 marked the bitter climax of a political drama that had been played out over the preceding two years.[15] The first act commenced with the 'People's Budget' that Lloyd George introduced in April 1909. The chancellor's bid to tax unearned increments on landed wealth and enhance death duties was a direct challenge to aristocratic power. In an unprecedented move, the Tory-dominated House of Lords refused to ratify the budget. Their intransigence triggered a political crisis that remained unresolved even after two successive general elections during the course of 1910. When the Liberals took up the reins of office for an unprecedented third successive time, the confrontation between the two Houses of Parliament entered its decisive phase. The government's new Parliament Bill sought to entirely dispense with the power of the Lords over all finance bills, and give them a circumscribed two-year veto over all other legislation. The Tory grandees—led by Lord Curzon—immediately adopted a recalcitrant attitude when this contentious bill first came up for discussion in May 1911. As the debate in parliament grew increasingly vituperative, Prime Minister Asquith played his trump card. In late July, he informed Arthur Balfour, the leader of the opposition, that he had already secured a constitutional guarantee from the monarch to create 500 new Liberal peers in the House of Lords. He also made it clear to his opponents that his government would take this step if the Lords rejected the Parliament Bill. Asquith's move split the Tory aristocrats into two camps: the 'Hedgers' (among them, Curzon), who advocated cautious compromise, and the 'Ditchers', who wanted to fight until the bitter end. Fittingly, the final debate in the Lords began on 9 August, a day when the Royal Observatory at Greenwich announced that it had 'the doubtful honour of reporting for the first time in its history, a shade temperature officially returned as 100 degrees Fahrenheit'.[16]

Even as the peers raged in parliament, a very different scene was unfolding across town in the East End. London's dock workers had been on strike since the beginning of the month demanding higher wages. By 9 August they had been joined by coal porters, watermen, lightermen, carmen, and stevedores employed in the vast port. One tabloid reported that the 'strike fever seemed to have entered the blood of the whole of the East End'.[17] Thousands of workers thus participated in a general strike the likes of which had not been seen in the capital since 1889. Remarkably, even though the demands of the dock workers were swiftly met, they refused to return to work until the grievances of their comrades had been redressed. Newspapers noted how a 'strange and frightening silence' descended on the city as the strike paralysed all activity in the port.[18]

The London dock strike was the latest episode in a sustained wave of workers' protest that had convulsed the country since mid-June. The 'great labour unrest', as it came to be known, began on 14 June 1911, a week before the coronation. On that day, seamen in all the major ports embarked on a strike with the bursting of rockets and the unfurling of banners declaring war on their employers.[19] Southampton, Goole, Liverpool, Hull, Manchester, and Cardiff became the leading centres of resistance. The seamen demanded higher wages, overtime pay, and better working conditions.[20] Their ranks were swelled by dock workers and other labourers who also simultaneously went on strike. At many places, massed ranks of protestors clashed with the police. The bloodiest confrontation was in Liverpool, where a massive labour rally organized by the National Transport Workers' Federation on 13 August ended in unprecedented scenes of rioting and retribution.

Some observers attributed the strike wave to the heat wave. The *Lancet* even wondered if 'the potent sun' had 'altered the energies of the body and mind of the workers, as in the case of the would-be coloniser in the unsuitable tropics?'[21] Others saw in the labour upsurge the sinister hand of foreign doctrines. 'It is now clear that the French development known as Syndicalism has caught many of the rank and file of workmen,' declared the *Graphic*.[22] But irrespective of their diagnosis of the 'unrest', contemporary observers agreed that their world was being turned upside down.[23]

In the face of this subaltern uprising, the government and local authorities reacted with panic-stricken heavy-handedness. Civilian authorities, unable to cope with the protests on the streets, called for military assistance. Winston Churchill, the trigger-happy Home Secretary, was only too happy to oblige. In a number of cities that summer, it appeared as if a civil war had broken out, with troops manning barricades and patrolling the streets. The most dramatic show of strength came after the Liverpool riots in mid-August. Convinced that 'a revolution was in progress', local notables appealed to the government for help. Churchill responded by sending a warship to the Mersey, 'where it anchored off Birkenhead with its guns trained on Liverpool'.[24]

It is against this tumultuous backdrop that the Indian cricketers travelled the length and breadth of the United Kingdom. And in one way or another, these events impinged on their tour. The unusual weather that summer meant that the Indians were favoured with playing conditions that were far more congenial than they might have anticipated at the outset of their tour. On the other hand, they had to compete for public attention in a context where the newspaper headlines were dominated by the sizzling heat, the parliamentary crisis, and the dramatic civil unrest.

But it is the challenge on the cricket pitch that is likely to have been uppermost in the thoughts of the Indian cricketers. To boost the attractiveness of the tour, the MCC had designated their fixtures against the English counties as 'first class'. However, as with the West Indians in 1900 and 1906, the imperial cricket establishment did not deem the Indian team worthy of 'test match' status. Hence, the Indians did not take part in an international contest with a representative English side: there were no 'test matches' that provided a focal point of public interest. Instead, in the twenty-three matches that they were scheduled to play, the tourists were pitted against county teams in England and representative sides in Wales, Scotland, and Ireland.

As they made their way across the country, the Indian cricketers were incorporated into the local rhythms and rituals of one of the most extraordinary summers of the legendary 'Golden Age of Cricket'. The phrase is often used to describe the two decades spanning 1894–1914, when the game is said to have acquired its recognizably modern form and reached a level of unsurpassed popularity. English cricket, in particular, was retrospectively portrayed as a dazzling spectacle in which an extraordinary cohort of batsmen and bowlers paraded their skills with panache.[25] However, as with any 'golden age', the reality was more complex. The Indians' visit came at a time when cracks were beginning to widen within the structure of English cricket. Significantly, there had emerged a glaring contradiction between the amateur ideology that governed the game and the requirements of a modern spectator sport. As a result, patrons, pressmen, and sections of the public increasingly expressed their anxiety and frustration about the state of the 'national game'.

Yet for a team representing the subject people of a colonized nation, an encounter with the renowned cricketers of the ruling race represented a daunting prospect. How would the first Indian cricket team fare?

II

On 20 May 1911, the day before the Indian cricketers arrived in London, an astonishing feat was recorded at Hove. On a grey Saturday, a rare occurrence that summer, the sparse crowd at a county match between Sussex and Nottinghamshire was treated to a mind-boggling performance by an unheralded player. When Edward Boaler Alletson walked out to bat on the final morning of the game, Nottinghamshire in their second innings were ahead by nine runs with only three wickets in hand. The result seemed a foregone conclusion and not many deemed it worthwhile to make their way to the ground.

The son of a wheelwright on the Duke of Portland's estate, the twenty-seven-year-old 'Ted' Alletson was 'over six feet tall, deep chested, wide

shouldered and remarkably long-armed'. A medium pace bowler and a
lower-order batsman, this professional cricketer had struggled for six
years to find a secure place in the Nottinghamshire team. So, no one was
prepared for the mayhem that unfolded over the next few hours. In his
first fifty minutes at the crease, Alletson made a brisk forty-seven of the
seventy-five runs that were scored. But the real fireworks began when
play resumed after the lunch interval. In forty frenzied minutes, Alletson
scored 142 runs, with eight sixes and twenty-three fours. His last eighty-
nine runs came in just fifteen minutes, during the course of which he
reserved his fiercest punishment for an unfortunate Sussex slow-bowler
named Tim Killick. Hit for thirty-four runs in one particularly brutal
over, the nervous bowler feared for his life as he delivered each ball.
A Nottinghamshire player at the ground later recalled that the ball 'fizzed'
through the fielders 'as if they were ghosts'. One ferocious stroke 'smashed
the pavilion window and wrecked the bar'; another 'went through the
clock face'. Five balls disappeared outside the ground, never to be
recovered. One lodged itself in the soft wood of a newly built stand and,
'no chisel being available', much time was wasted in prising it out. John
Arlott, whose writings on cricket eschewed hyperbole, called it the 'most
remarkable innings ever played'.[26]

'Alletson's innings,' as it came to be known, was a one-off; the rest of his
career was pedestrian by comparison. But the manner in which he played
that May afternoon at Hove captured the spirit of what was retrospectively
characterized as cricket's 'Golden Age'. Alletson had set about the bowling
with carefree gusto, intent on enjoying himself and uncaring about the
outcome. Ironically, Alletson was a 'professional', for this attacking style of
batting was more commonly associated with the 'amateurs' who dominated
English cricket in these years. Taught in their public schools that cricket
was a game meant to be played for pleasure, the amateur batsmen of the
Edwardian era transformed batting into a display of calculated and crowd-
pleasing aggression.[27]

The new technologies of photograph and film offer us tantalizing images
of these Edwardian batsmen. But their cricketing immortality owes a great
deal to the First World War and the purple prose of Neville Cardus.[28] Those
who survived the war looked back with nostalgia on the years that preceded
the catastrophe. It is precisely this sense of a world that was lost that the
music-loving cricket correspondent of the *Manchester Guardian* captured in
a series of articles and books. In his copious writings on cricket, Cardus

vividly described the cricketing heroes of his boyhood, vesting them with a glow that grew ever brighter as the Edwardian age receded in time. The years 'extending from 1890 to 1914 witnessed the Golden Age of batsmanship', he asserted in *English Cricket* in 1945.[29] 'Never since has such batsmanship been seen as this for opulence and prerogative; it was symbolical of the age's prestige.'[30]

Significantly, the sumptuousness of Edwardian batsmanship was built on prosaic foundations. The widespread use of marl in cricket pitches, in tandem with the heavy roller, produced glass-top smooth playing surfaces that allowed batsmen to flourish as never before.[31] As Cardus wrote, 'A great batsman could now on fine days give his mind to the display of his arts, free of incalculable and unscientific misconduct caused by a rough and entirely unscientific pitch.'[32] Outfields too were tended with greater care and designed in a manner that allowed excess water to drain away after rain. The introduction of boundaries maximized the returns on scoring shots. Protective equipment for batsmen grew more sophisticated, while the investment in practice nets and indoor matting allowed them to hone their techniques. The result was a spectacular increase in the volume of runs that were scored by Edwardian batsmen. Before the 1870s, a score of 250 was regarded as a match-winning one; by the late 1900s, teams frequently posted totals in excess of 500.[33] The declaration law, which until 1910 stipulated that teams could not terminate their innings before the halfway point in a three-day match, encouraged such high scores.

But good batting in the Edwardian era was not simply about the sheer volume of runs. It entailed 'a profusion of runs, handsomely scored', by batsmen who sought to dictate terms to the bowlers.[34] The most extraordinary exemplar of this approach was Gilbert Laird Jessop. 'No man has ever made cricket so dramatic an entertainment': that was the plain verdict of one of his contemporaries, Charles Fry, himself regarded as one of the most accomplished batsmen of the day.[35] Remarkably, in his career of 855 innings, the 'Croucher' (a nickname that he acquired on account of his unusual stance) batted longer than two hours only on ten occasions. And he occupied the batting crease for more than three hours only once, 'this in a "slow" innings of 240 which lasted for 200 minutes!' By the time he retired in 1914, after two decades of first-class cricket, Jessop 'had scored the two fastest hundreds yet known, and the two fastest double centuries'.[36] On fifteen occasions, he stroked his way to a century in an hour or less; eighteen times he made a fifty in twenty-five minutes or less.[37]

'Jessopus,' as his teammates called him, was only one of a cluster of amateur batsmen whose style defined cricket's 'Golden Age'. It is a roll call that features, among others, Ranji and C.B. Fry at Sussex; 'Archie' MacLaren and R.H. Spooner at Lancashire; F.S. Jackson at Yorkshire; Lionel Palairet at Somerset; R.E. ('Tip') Foster at Worcestershire; K.L. Hutchings at Kent; and J.N. Crawford at Surrey. With the exception of the uniquely gifted Ranji, none of these batsmen attained individually the preeminence of W.G. Grace, the greatest cricketer of the Victorian age. But collectively, they left an indelible impression on the Edwardian cricketing scene. Indeed, as Alletson's innings showed, even the professional cricketers were influenced by their quick-scoring amateur contemporaries. 'Johnny' Tyldesley at Yorkshire, Tom Hayward, and the young Jack Hobbs at Surrey, and the promising Frank Woolley at Kent, and many others batted more like these carefree stylists than the professional grafters of a previous age.[38]

For some, however, it is not so much the sheer style of individual players as the institutional transformation that the game underwent in the period between 1894 and 1914 that make it 'the Golden Age of Cricket'. In England, two developments were crucial. First, the MCC emerged as the central decision-making body for the administration of the game, overseeing test-match selection at home through a new board of control and (after 1903) for overseas tours. Second, the county championship doubled in size with the inclusion of eight new teams between 1894 and 1905, while clubs that were not deemed 'first class' participated in a new 'Minor Counties' competition. This expansion of organized cricket vastly increased the opportunities for batsmen, bowlers, and fielders to create new records on an unprecedented scale. 'Cricket was borne up onto a plateau in this period, and we are now far below it,' remarked Rowland Bowen in his magisterial global history of cricket.[39]

Others have seen the Edwardian years as the 'Golden Age' of *English* cricket. The sport at this time is seen to have captured the spirit of the wider society of which it was a part. The vigour and versatility of Edwardian cricketers, in this view, reflected the confidence of a country that dominated the globe. It is also seen to represent the values of a society whose elites regarded the pursuit of pleasure as a desirable goal. 'Edwardians practiced enjoyment as Victorians had practiced self-denial,' it has been said.[40] Thus, the amateur emphasis on stylish play, unencumbered by practical considerations of achieving victory and avoiding defeat, is regarded as an expression of this pleasure-centred elite ethos.[41]

Yet others have also pointed to the prestige and popularity that cricket enjoyed in the Edwardian years as the nation's unrivalled summer sport. Between April and September, the game was played in a variety of settings from ancient village commons to the manicured grounds of opulent country houses. Every kind of social institution—school, college, church, factory, office—either had, or aspired to have, its own cricket team. 'Never, before or since, were there so many active cricketers in England,' wrote John Arlott. Moreover, there was 'virtually no other summer spectator sport: long columns in the press, green squares in every town and village, country-house weeks, and the talk of the clubs and pubs declared that cricket came into its kingdom with the first warmth of the English sun'.[42]

★ ★ ★

'First-class cricket is a valetudinarian invalid': thus began an article entitled 'The Problems of Contemporary Cricket', published in the *Fortnightly Review* in 1911. Its author, Home Gordon, a well-known aristocratic commentator on the game, argued that cricket's current state was comparable to that of the country's parliament. 'When all was well, those in authority would not make judicious remedies which would have modified the game according to the exigencies of modern tendencies, exactly as the Conservative Cabinet would not amend the Upper Chamber during Mr. Balfour's long tenure of office,' he rued. Now, as with the Liberals' reform of the House of Lords, there was 'an epidemic of tinkering with the rules of cricket'. 'Still the present situation is sufficiently serious,' he added, 'and those in authority oscillate so publicly between one reform and another that the game is endangered—like a patient with too many physicians, and the Man-in-the-Street has become hopelessly confused.'[43]

Home Gordon's remarks are a salutary reminder that golden ages are retrospective constructions. Most observers who wrote about cricket in the Edwardian era did not consider themselves to be living through a 'golden' period.[44] On the contrary, by the late 1900s there was a growing chorus of opinion in the press that first-class cricket in England was in decline. Reviewing the English cricket season of 1910, the editor of *Wisden* noted that 'a good many people have come to the conclusion that first-class cricket is losing its hold on the public'.[45]

Lamentations about decline were by no means new in English cricket. Even in the 1880s, there had been recurrent complaints about falling standards and the loss of the bucolic idyll of the game's mythical past.[46] But there is little doubt that the language of crisis surrounding cricket in the Edwardian era did acquire a new urgency. Between 1900 and 1904, almost 40 per cent of first-class matches in the county championship yielded no result. Restrictions on the preparation of pitches in the mid-1900s effected a reduction in the proportion of inconclusive matches. Still, more than a quarter of all county matches between 1907 and 1911 ended in a draw.[47] The monotony induced by high-scoring draws was probably an important factor in the steadily declining attendance at county games.[48] However, it was not the only factor in diminishing spectator interest. By the late 1900s, many of the 'star' cricketers of the late Victorian years had faded away. Worse still, gate receipts were affected by a succession of inclement summers between 1907 and 1910. As a consequence, many county cricket clubs struggled to stay solvent.[49]

Contemporary explanations of the crisis afflicting first-class cricket attributed it to the way the game was played on the pitch and organized off it. Many observers blamed overprepared cricket pitches, which were said to have robbed cricket contests of their competitive edge. But this was not all. These critics identified and attacked a number of contemporary cricketing practices for being antithetical to the traditional 'spirit of the game'. They excoriated players for time wasting, slow play, and engaging in 'safety-first' cricket. Such negative tactics were attributed to the championship system, which had made cricket teams and their administrators excessively concerned about the county's place in the league table. Commentators were especially critical of counties that imported players from the colonies or poached them from their rivals. They claimed that such practices had weakened the locally rooted character of county cricket and dampened popular enthusiasm for the game.

Running through such accounts was an inherently ideological conception of cricket's place within British society. Cricket was regarded as a traditional English sport whose values had been sullied by 'hard utilitarianism and commercialism'.[50] A representative sample of such views is to be found in a book entitled *The Problems of Cricket*, published in 1907 by the English sports journalist Major Philip Trevor.[51] It will be recalled that we last encountered this ex-army officer at the cricket ground in colonial Bombay, digesting with silent rage the Parsis' historic victory over Vernon's team in 1890. After his return to England, he took to writing a column in the *Sportsman* under the pseudonym 'Dux'. A recurrent theme in Trevor's book was that artifice and commerce had eroded the authentic qualities of this pure English game. 'Reality is the essence of county cricket, and directly commercial manipulation makes that word a farce,' he argued.[52] Equally, he was vehemently critical of any cricketing practice that smacked of a risk-averse mentality. 'The life of cricket,' he wrote, 'depends upon incident and variation.'[53] Indeed, he asserted, 'cricket would never have got its hold upon the Englishman had it not contained an element of personal risk'.[54] But it was precisely this daring, risk-taking element, he railed, which was being erased by the encroaching forces of standardization and 'point-scoring' competitiveness on and off the cricket field. 'A variety of circumstances, have now combined to make first class cricket no longer a game, but an exhibition,' he complained. 'The paid attendance of the public proves this face. We play a game, we watch an exhibition. And that being so, one foresees in pessimistic moments a decline in much that is best in cricket.'[55] Moreover, Trevor suggested, the consequences of the increasingly risk-averse forms of play went beyond the cricket field. 'The traits which are now too distinguishable in it are rather un-British. Stolidity in practice with business result in prospect smacks of the German,' he declared.[56]

Such views were widely shared by all those who believed that the national game was in crisis. The solution that commentators proffered was invariably the same: a drastic curtailment of the 'professional' element in first-class cricket. As Home Gordon noted in 1910, 'the fact remains that there is an increasing preponderance of the professional element in county elevens, and this preponderance must be in the inverse ratio to the more sporting aspects of the game; because the paid element cannot afford to run those risks which are the elixir of cricket.'[57] 'The moment that the strength of a county depends on its professionals, its kudos depends on strangers, and its success upon finance,' added the *Illustrated Sporting and Dramatic News*.[58] Conversely, these critics called for an increase in the amateur presence in, and control of, cricket. 'The best remedy I can suggest for the evils that exist is that committees should, as far as possible, encourage the amateur element,' wrote the editor of *Wisden* in 1910. 'Amateurs are never prone to accept a draw when there is a chance of winning, and as a natural consequence the matches in which they take a prominent part are seldom open to the charge of being dull.'[59]

The deeply entrenched ideology of amateurism coupled with the widely shared belief that cricket was the last refuge from the inexorable advance of modernity accounts for the 'peculiar economics' of the game in the Edwardian period. As historians have pointed out, first-class cricket in

England before 1914 was not 'profit-oriented', nor did the county clubs under the stewardship of the MCC act as a conventional sports cartel.[60] There was no attempt to improve or diversify the product that was offered to spectators, nor equalize the playing strengths to make contests more even and exciting. Proposals to divide the championship into two divisions were rejected out of hand. Significantly, the counties were not even required to play the same number of matches: they only had to play eight 'home' and 'away' fixtures each season with opponents of their choice. A reluctant leader, the MCC mostly confined its role to tinkering with the points system in the county championship. Even at the level of individual clubs, there was little sustained or systematic attempt to maximize profits. The balance sheet of a county cricket club was dependent on match attendances. This, in turn, was determined by its performance in the county championship. Winning teams registered a significant increase in gate receipts, while losing teams found to their cost that there was a sharp decline in their takings at the turnstiles. Six county clubs—Yorkshire, Lancashire, Surrey, Kent, Middlesex, and Nottinghamshire—dominated the competition before 1914 and were thus financially secure. On the other hand, weak performers like Essex, Somerset, Hampshire, Derbyshire, Leicestershire, and Worcestershire were caught in a vicious cycle in which falling gate receipts and rising operational costs adversely affected their viability. But even clubs in a precarious pecuniary position did not attempt to cover the shortfall by arranging more games, raising the standard entry fee of six pence and making more profitable use of their fixed assets.[61] 'County cricket clubs naturally like to make ends meet,' remarked Pelham Warner, 'but they are not possessed with an unholy idea that profit is everything and that the game is nothing.'[62]

III

'In spite of wearisome discussion about the decay of country cricket and the urgent need of prescribing strong tonics for the invalid, the coming season is looked forward to with quite the average measure of public interest,' noted the *Manchester Guardian* in its preview of the cricket season in April 1911. 'If one could only be sure of decent weather, without which cricket can never be quite itself, it would be fairly safe to predict a satisfactory year.'[63] But as the season began in glorious sunshine, tentative hope turned into unalloyed optimism. *The Times* stated that conditions had 'rarely been better in the last few years for the opening of the cricket season'.[64] 'One begins to think that the cause of the despondency that has arisen in recent years ought to be found in the succession of bad summers,' wrote another journalist. 'We get a fine week in May and the crowds "roll up" to see the counties at play.'[65] This writer also detected a new spirit in the air. 'The county elevens seem to have shaken off their sloth,' he remarked.[66] The *Daily Mail* agreed:

> If the Clerk of the Weather continues to supply us with samples of last week's sunshine and players continue to 'oblige' the spectators with such interesting cricket I fancy that the croakers whose delight it is to hymn the doom of cricket in dismal measures will be very effectively silenced, if not for ever at least for the present season.[67]

These remarks were borne out by the results in the first fortnight of the season, which saw a number of exciting matches. Notably, minnows like Essex and Warwickshire inflicted defeats on stronger teams like Yorkshire and Lancashire. Many observers attributed the entertaining quality of the matches to the new points system for the county championship that had been introduced that season. Teams were now awarded five points for a win in completed matches and three for gaining a first innings lead in a drawn game. Matches in which no result in the first innings was obtained were to be ignored. The new rules, one cricket watcher noted, were 'infinitely better than the old, as it practically means there is a decisive result to every game, whereas in the old way a three-day match ending in a draw meant nothing to either side'.[68]

The cricket season was thus well under way by the time the Indian cricketers arrived in Britain. The sporting headlines in the days after their arrival were dominated by the extraordinary match between Sussex and Nottinghamshire at Hove. 'Alletson's amazing hitting has formed the topic of conversation in many a pavilion during the week,' reported the *Globe*.[69] 'Many wonderful scoring feats have been seen in club and country house cricket of recent years, but one knows of nothing in a first-class match to equal this performance,' admitted *The Times*.[70] 'We who advocate the quickening of cricket must bow to Alletson,' said London's *Daily News*. 'His method of reform is more effective than any legislation could be.'[71]

But the press also devoted a great deal of attention to the Indian cricketers. 'For some time past one of the chief topics of discussion in cricket circles has been the prospect of the All-Indian XI,' noted the *Observer* on the day of their arrival.[72] These remarks prefaced an interview with Sir Dorab Tata, who was in the imperial metropolis for the coronation, about the prospects of the Indian team. Asked to compare the strength of his side vis-à-vis English county teams, the Indian tycoon parried the question. He pointed out that the Indians had 'never played together, and their success depends so much upon the trend of circumstances which cannot possibly be forecasted [sic]'. A prudent businessman, Tata also played down public expectations about the Indian team. 'I do not expect to beat such sides as Surrey and Yorkshire, but I think we shall give the weaker counties a good game,' he told his interlocutor.[73]

During their first week in London, the MCC provided practice facilities at Lord's for the visiting cricketers and also made them honorary members of the club. This drew an interested crowd of reporters, photographers, and onlookers to the home of cricket. 'The "vim" they put into their work is remarkable and there is no doubt about their eagerness to get fit for their coming fixtures,' commented one observer.[74] Individual players were singled out for comment in the press reports. Warden was described as a 'great stylist', the hard-hitting Mulla as the 'Alletson of the team', and Pai as a 'dapper little bat'. Others stood out because of their perceived idiosyncrasies: Shafqat Hussain's 'peculiar style' of bowling attracted 'considerable interest', while Jayaram, to his consternation, was said to bear a striking resemblance to Lloyd George.[75] However, for the first three days neither Bhupinder nor Mistry appeared at the practice sessions. In their place, J.M. Divecha and Homi Kanga, the team's manager and vice-captain, respectively, served as its principal spokesmen.

Journalists who watched the Indian cricketers go about their routines at Lord's differed in their estimates of their abilities. The reporter for the *Evening News* thought they looked 'short of practice, and would make a poor show if called upon to meet a first class county'.[76] The *Daily News* felt that the team had 'capable batsmen', but preferred to reserve judgement about their prospects 'until they have become more accustomed to our wickets'.[77] Writing in the same paper a few days later, 'Old Shako' was more effusive in his praise. 'From what little I have seen of the Indians at practice at Lord's I should say they will interest the British public better than any of our county sides,' he declared. 'They have come over without any attempt at booming themselves, and the consequence is they are in need of a little advertisement.'[78]

One English journalist, however, lost no opportunity to advertise the attractions of the Indian cricket team. In a series of newspaper articles, Edward Sewell sought to acquaint the British public with these visitors from the subcontinent. He also urged his readers neither to assume that the team contained 'half a dozen Ranjis' nor to 'under-rate them'.[79] A few days after they had arrived in London, Sewell was included in the Indian side in a friendly fixture against H.D. Kanga's old team, Hampstead CC. Ironically, playing for the north London club in this match was Manikji Bajana, who struck Sewell as being 'more like a *pailwan* [wrestler] than a typical Parsi'.[80] Ironically, a daring batting performance by Bajana allowed the London team to win a closely fought match. 'That their cricket will be interesting to watch is certain,' Sewell declared after the Indians' first appearance on an English cricket field. 'Their fielding is capital, their bowling varied and full of resources, and their batting replete with cases of men who repeatedly take the big risk which compels attention. I shall be surprised at nothing that they do.'[81]

Sewell had entered into an arrangement with a number of newspapers in India to provide regular reports on the progress of the Indian cricketers' tour. In his first letter, the Englishman commented on the curious absence of the Maharaja and Mistry. 'Clearly cricket is not His Highness's sole objective on this trip, or something would have been done ere this to try to get used to the light and strange surroundings,' Sewell concluded.[82]

He was not wrong. Bhupinder's attention was focused on an entirely different kind of performance, with stakes that went beyond the cricket field.

IV

The Maharaja's tour began on his very first day on British shores. On arrival at Dover, Bhupinder was greeted by Sir James Dunlop Smith, who had taken Curzon Wyllie's place at the India Office. In a secret report, the British official described his meeting with his former ward:

> I had a long talk with him on the train on the way to London, and explained to him what the situation was and how anxious the authorities were regarding himself and his future with perfect frankness. We know each other very intimately, and I think he was as open with me as I was with him. Even as a child, and I have known him since he was born, he could never be driven, but I have rarely known an appeal to his affections or to his honour fail, provided he felt sure he would be trusted.[83]

The India Office had reasons to be worried about the arrival of the Patiala prince in London. The Edwardian years had seen the dramatic transformation of the staid Victorian city into what one observer called the 'metropolis of pleasure'. The tone had been set by the extroverted Edward VII, whose colourful reign was in stark contrast to the austerity of the Victorian age.[84] Known for his extravagant tastes, Edward inaugurated an era of conspicuous consumption in the imperial capital. In the first decade of the twentieth century, London also became the playground of a new breed of plutocrats, financiers, and entrepreneurs who had fattened on the spoils of imperial globalization. This moneyed elite was eager to splurge its wealth on the pursuit of pleasure. Novel sites and practices of elite sociability were fashioned in the city's West End: luxury hotels, restaurants, theatres, clubs, and department stores catering to the rich.[85] The *public* display of wealth and status was an essential feature of all these spaces. Activities—courtship, dining, entertainment, networking—that had been carried out in gated estates and private residences now took place in the full glare of publicity. The attendant rise of mass-oriented tabloids simultaneously marked the birth of a celebrity culture focused on the doings of these wealthy elites. Imperial officials were therefore fearful of potential scandals involving the pleasure-loving Maharaja.

No doubt the India Office was equally concerned about how the young prince would conduct himself in London's high society. Every summer, the elites in the imperial capital participated in a series of collective rituals familiarly known as 'the Season'.[86] Its highlights were the presentations at Court of prominent visitors and society *debutantes*, balls and dinners organized by leading aristocratic families, as well as a series of famous annual events: Derby Day at Epsom Downs, Royal Ascot, Wimbledon, and the Oxford-Cambridge and Eton-Harrow cricket matches at Lord's. The coronation that summer meant that the Season was even more crowded than usual on account of the imperial festivities. Given what the India Office had been told about Bhupinder's bibulous tendencies and his roving eye, it is not surprising that Dunlop Smith cautioned the young prince.

The Maharaja of Patiala was one of a select group of Indian princes who took part in the coronation of King George V in London. As we have seen, the Government of India had decided to ignore the precedent set in 1902 by not inviting any Indian royals, other than the King's honorary *aides-de-camp*, to this event. However, the imperial authorities in Delhi and London concurred that any princes from the subcontinent who happened to be in the imperial capital at the time would be included in the coronation rituals. Bhupinder belonged to this category, which also included the rulers of

Baroda, Bhopal, Gondal, Indore, Jodhpur, Pudukkotai, Rajpipla, and Shahpura.
The Maharaja thus spent the better part of his time performing the role of
an Oriental feudatory on the imperial stage. As such, he participated in a
very different kind of tour from the one that had been envisaged by Framjee
Patel and his associates.

The maharajas' visit to London for the coronation was organized and
overseen by the India Office.[87] The key figure here was James Dunlop
Smith, whose responsibility it was to arrange for the stay and entertainment
of these royal visitors in the capital, present them at court, and chaperon
them during the coronation. Princes who were guests of the treasury 'were
provided with servants in Royal liveries, and each was given a Royal Carriage
and a motor-car'.[88] Others were expected to make their own arrangements
for accommodation and travel. But in practice it was the India Office that
carried out these tasks. For the ruler of Patiala, the officials selected a 'fine
house' in South Kensington, which came fully equipped with a retinue of
trained staff and servants.[89]

But Bhupinder was annoyed and alarmed to hear that he would have to
share his house with the political officer assigned to cover him. The prince
remained unconvinced by Dunlop Smith's assurance that this official was
there 'not as a spy to report to Government, but as a friend and helper'.[90]
However, Bhupinder chose not to press the issue and abided by the India
Office's decision. No doubt, it had become clear to him that he was still on
probation, and that even the slightest misstep on his part could cost him the
support of key allies at the highest levels of the imperial establishment.
Bhupinder, therefore, set about using his visit to create a favourable impression on the imperial stage.

The young Maharaja's first big opportunity came four days after his
arrival in the capital. On 25 May 1911, he was presented by Dunlop Smith
at the fourth royal court of the Season held in Buckingham Palace. It was a
grand occasion, with over 900 guests, including 'several of the great leaders
of society'.[91] Bhupinder, along with the Aga Khan, was accorded a pride of
place at this gathering. Prior to his public appearance at the court, the
Maharaja had a private audience with the King. It was the second meeting
between the two men: the first had occurred at Lahore six years earlier,
when George V had toured India as the Prince of Wales. On that occasion,
it is said, the British royal presented the young prince with a toy.[92] This time
around, however, the meeting was more formal. The King expressed his
deep interest in the Indian cricket tour and promised Bhupinder that he

would attend the match against the MCC at Lord's.[93] He also invited the Maharaja to lunch in the royal pavilion at Ascot.

In the days following his meeting with the King, Bhupinder was a prominent presence at various coronation-related ceremonies. For instance, on the afternoon of 27 May, he attended the Trooping of the Colours, watching the proceedings from a specially erected stand for visiting dignitaries. The same evening, he was a guest at a lavish banquet hosted by the Secretary of State for India to mark the King's birthday. These occasions gave the prince a chance to hobnob with the senior-most figures in the imperial government and thereby cultivate allies who might come in handy in future tussles with his detractors in Patiala.

In other ways, too, his London sojourn was a key moment in Bhupinder's political education. This was the first time since he had been elevated to his throne that he was thrown together for a prolonged period with his fellow maharajas. The Patiala ruler had the opportunity to rub shoulders with the other princes at various imperial events leading up to the coronation. The visiting ruling chiefs also attended official engagements at the India Office. They were received by the Secretary of State 'with the usual ceremonies' and met 'the Under Secretaries of State and other high officials' in the department.[94]

But equally important was the informal socializing that occurred during excursions and entertainments. For instance, in mid-June, the Indian princes travelled as a group to the races at Ascot, where they were admitted into the Royal Enclosure 'and a special refreshment tent was set apart for their use'.[95] On 24 June, the maharajas and their families were conveyed from London to Portsmouth by special trains to attend the King's Naval Review. That night they stayed on board a luxurious liner as guests of the Secretary of State for India. On 26 and 27 June, they attended 'gala performances' at the Royal Opera House at Covent Garden and His Majesty's Theatre at Haymarket.[96] At Covent Garden, 'the Chiefs had front seats in the Royal box on the ground floor immediately under that occupied by their Majesties'. At Haymarket, 'the whole of the dress circle was fitted up as the Royal box and the Chiefs were given excellent seats'.[97] It is more than likely that his interactions with fellow royals sparked off Bhupinder's lifelong interest in princely politics. As a newly enthroned ruler, however, the Patiala ruler had to defer to the senior maharajas who had come to London for the coronation. Among these seasoned chiefs were men like Sir Pertab Singh of Idar and Sir Ganga Singh of Bikaner, both of whom were honorary *aides-de-camp* to the King and thus had great influence at the highest levels of the imperial establishment.

Bhupinder assiduously cultivated the thirty-one-year-old Ganga Singh as a mentor. 'Patiala is devoted to Bikanir and admires him more than anyone else,' noted Dunlop Smith, 'and the latter likes the former, and his influence all for good.' He reported that Bhupinder's 'general behaviour was excellent' and credited Ganga Singh 'for the good reputation which Patiala has made in England'.[98]

Importantly, Bhupinder made a favourable impression on the Secretary of State. After his meeting with the Maharaja, Lord Crewe wrote to the Viceroy that 'Patiala talked sensibly about himself and his State'. Indeed, the only time that he betrayed his age was when, *apropos* of the forthcoming imperial Durbar, he asked the Secretary of State 'whether it would still not be possible to have an elephant procession at Delhi, as so many of the Princes would like it'.[99] Hardinge, for his part, was relieved to hear that Bhupinder had acquitted himself well. 'He is a young man who requires watching over and is very susceptible to friendly encouragement,' the Viceroy wrote back to Crewe. He also reminded the Secretary of State that Patiala was not only 'by far the most important of the Phulkian States', but also had 'the best Imperial Service Troops'. Moreover, he assured Crewe, Bhupinder was 'honestly trying at the present moment to get his State into proper order'.[100] The Maharaja was still on trial, but the official wind was beginning to blow in his favour.

Bhupinder also made his presence felt in London society. In popular writings, the sunlit 'perfect summer' of 1911 is portrayed as the apogee of the Edwardian elite and its luxurious way of life.[101] Every day of the week there were lavish *soirees* featuring royals, aristocrats, politicians, plutocrats, foreign ambassadors, prominent overseas visitors, and leading figures in the country's public life. The Indian princes were much sought after by society hostesses. 'The lady who can secure the attendance of a Maharaja at one of her parties considers that her social reputation is firmly established,' noted one journalist.[102]

After his presentation at Buckingham Palace, Bhupinder was inundated with invitations to banquets and balls. But he was not free to accept any invitation that came his way. The India Office carefully vetted each one and the prince was only allowed to attend events that were hosted by aristocrats and plutocrats with unimpeachable credentials. One of these gatherings was a garden party hosted in honour of the Indian princes by Mrs Ratan Tata at

York House.[103] On such occasions, the turbaned Maharaja commanded attention because of his ornate attire and his stately comportment. He had, of course, come well prepared for this purpose, carrying with him jewels worth 'half a crore of rupees'. Among these fabulous jewels, Dunlop Smith confided to his former colleagues in India, were 'the Empress Eugene diamonds with the famous Sancy diamond as a pendant', which was 'once included in the Regalia of England until it was sold by James II'.[104] A series of iconic Carl Vandyk photographs from that summer, currently in the National Portrait Gallery, show Bhupinder in his full regalia. The portraits suggest that the Patiala prince played the role of the richly bejewelled, but mysteriously opaque, Oriental potentate in a manner that would have undoubtedly satisfied the expectations of his society hosts.

★   ★   ★

But what about the expectations of the cricket-watching public? Even before Bhupinder's arrival in the country, there was a great deal of interest in the British press about the man who had been chosen to lead the Indian cricket team. 'A very interesting young fellow is the Maharaja of Patiala, who is captaining the team of Indian cricketers which is to play in England during the summer,' commented one newspaper on hearing of Bhupinder's appointment as captain. The *Manchester Guardian* dwelt on the tragic circumstances in which the callow prince had ascended the Patiala throne. 'He is an open-hearted boy with all the Sikh impulsiveness and abandon of manner where field sports and fighting are concerned,' the paper stated.[105] But not all newspapers were discerning enough to identify Bhupinder as a Sikh. After the team's arrival in Britain, Edward Sewell noted wryly that many of the tabloids referred to the prince as the 'Parsee Potentate'.[106]

Bhupinder's imposing presence attracted a great deal of media attention when he finally appeared on the imperial cricket field. 'The Maharaja is a magnificently set-up young man, with eyes like black diamonds,' observed the *Manchester Guardian*. 'With the black burls round his chin and his high white turban he looks forty; in reality he is only nineteen.'.[107] More than one newspaper was intrigued by the revelation that the prince did not cut his hair and that he intended to play cricket wearing his turban. 'The Maharaja of Patiala,' the *Daily Mirror* informed its readers, 'will be the first turbaned player to appear in English first-class cricket.'[108] Observers were suitably impressed by the raw power exuded by the powerfully built Bhupinder. 'A man of splendid physique, one can quite believe the report

THE MAHARAJAH GOES A-CRICKETING.

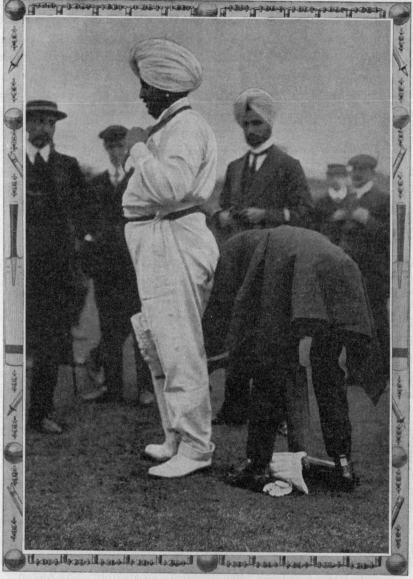

HARNESSED FOR THE FRAY BY A TRUSTY HENCHMAN: THE MAHARAJAH OF PATIALA
HAVING HIS PADS ADJUSTED BEFORE GOING IN TO BAT.

The Maharajah of Patiala, who has brought over an all-Indian cricket eleven, is one of the most interesting of the Indian potentates at present visiting this country. He is not only a keen cricketer, but an enthusiastic all-round sportsman, and is very popular both among his own people and his British friends. He is only in his twentieth year, and was invested with full powers as Maharajah in October 1909. He is entitled to be received and visited by the Viceroy of India, and enjoys a salute of seventeen guns. Patiala is one of the Phulkian States of the Punjab, whose ruling families are descended from Phul, successor of Baryam, whom the Emperor Baber in 1526 made Revenue Collector of the lands north of Delhi. The Maharajah's all-Indian eleven began their match against a team of the M.C.C. and Ground at Lord's on Thursday last, when the Prince of Wales and Prince George were among the spectators. Nothing is more likely to promote Anglo-Indian goodwill than these friendly contests on the cricket field.—[*Photograph by C.N.*]

Figure 18. Cricket was not one of Bhupinder Singh's priorities during his first visit to imperial Britain. Nonetheless, he attracted photographers every time he stepped out on to a cricket ground during his short-lived stint with the first All-India team. © Illustrated London News Ltd/Mary Evans.

that when he is set he hits like a horse kicking,' remarked the *Athletic News*.[109]
This paper also reminded its readers that the Maharaja had been coached by
some of the best English professionals like Jack Hearne and Frank Tarrant.
Others who watched him practise admired Bhupinder's batting style. 'He
keeps his bat wonderfully straight, and stands at the wicket comfortably and
well,' gushed one reporter.[110]

At the outset, the Indian team's tour committee had informed the
press that the Maharaja of Patiala would take part in fourteen matches. As
it turned out, however, Bhupinder only took part in three fixtures. Two
of these matches were against the universities of Oxford and Cambridge,
while the third was against the MCC at Lord's. The prince's most impressive performance came at Oxford, on the opening day of the Indian
cricketers' tour. Staged at the Christchurch ground, rather than the parks
where no gates could be collected, the match commenced on 1 June in
'perfect cricket weather' and watched by a 'big crowd'.[111] Not far away,
there was another kind of gathering that morning at the Oxford Union,
where Lord Curzon, the university's chancellor, inaugurated a new wing
of the buildings housing the famous undergraduate society. The self-
regarding former Viceroy of India was informed, to his chagrin, that the
motion for debate that evening was 'the British nation is degenerating'.[112]
However, there was evidently no sign of decline in the quality of Oxford's
cricketing elite. The university team, which included in its ranks Prince
Shivaji Rao, was more than a match for the Indian cricketers. The visitors
began on a disastrous note and half their team was out for thirty-seven,
when the white-turbaned Maharaja walked out to bat. After a shaky start,
Bhupinder struck some lusty blows and top-scored with forty-seven in
his team's paltry total of 193. The 'delightful vigour' with which the prince
essayed his strokes made him quite popular with the spectators.[113] But
even a fine bowling performance by Palwankar Baloo could not prevent
the undergraduates from easily vanquishing the visitors. 'Oxford people
were very disappointed with their display,' wrote one reporter, 'and the
general opinion seemed to be that they would fare badly at the hands of
the first-class counties.'[114]

Bhupinder's next appearance was against the MCC at Lord's on 8 June.
He had skipped the intervening game at Cardiff, where his team was once
again defeated. But he was well aware of the importance of leading the
Indian cricket team in the most prestigious fixture of the tour. The *Manchester
Guardian* described at length the Maharaja's spectacular entry on the

THE ALL INDIAN TEAM.

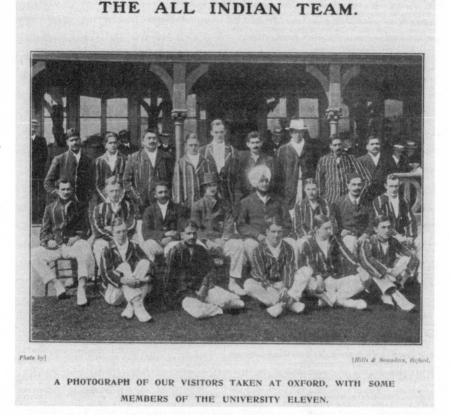

Photo by] *[Hills & Saunders, Oxford.*

A PHOTOGRAPH OF OUR VISITORS TAKEN AT OXFORD, WITH SOME
MEMBERS OF THE UNIVERSITY ELEVEN.

Figure 19. A rare photograph of Maharaja Bhupinder Singh with members of his cricket team, Oxford, June 1911. Courtesy of Marylebone Cricket Club Library.

opening day of the match, which began in 'Indian sunshine tempered by a delightful "seaside" breeze'.[115] The prince 'arrived at St. John's Wood in great state in a mighty motor-car. He was attended by his suite of curly-bearded young Sikhs, each with a different coloured turban on his head—yellow, white, mauve, black and blue.' His striking appearance made 'an impression on the crowd, who looked in vain for the diamond and ruby studded bat His Highness is credited with having brought over with him'.[116] But the audience was even more disappointed with his performance: the prince was dismissed for a 'duck' in the first innings. Nor did Bhupinder do much of note when the Indians batted again after the MCC had posted a huge total (with Sewell scoring a century). The visitors crumbled against the English bowling and lost the match by an innings.

After the match had ended, the Maharaja became the focus of a public controversy. Awaiting his turn to bat in the second innings, the prince had been summoned to the India Office by the Secretary of State. It is not quite clear why the imperial officials scheduled this meeting on a day when it was known that the prince would be playing cricket at Lord's. At any rate, by the time Bhupinder returned to the ground most of his teammates were back in the pavilion. In order to give him a chance to bat, the organizers extended the tea break to over forty minutes. Moreover, the MCC captain instructed his bowlers to direct some friendly deliveries at the Indians in order to ensure that the visitors were not bowled out before the prince was back at the ground. Many spectators, unaware of the reason for the delay, saw the extended tea break and the contrived bowling effort as being contrary to the spirit of the game. In particular, they argued that the Maharaja should not have been treated differently from an ordinary cricketer. 'These auto-cratic and overbearing ways even at Lord's, are out of date,' fulminated one irate letter writer.[117]

Bhupinder's last appearance with the Indian team was at Fenner's in Cambridge, the ground where Ranjitsinhji first made a name for himself. But unlike his illustrious cricketing compatriot, the Maharaja did little of note. The university team posted a big first innings score and inflicted another innings defeat on the Indians. The Patiala prince played in his usual swashbuckling manner, but did not unduly tax the scorers. Once again, the visitors failed to impress the crowd that had come to watch them play.

Bhupinder's subsequent disappearance from the touring party was the subject of comment at every venue visited by the Indian cricketers. In public, the spokesmen for the team cited his duties in connection with the coronation as a reason for his absence from their ranks. But well after the imperial festivities had ended, the Maharaja showed no inclination to return to cricket. Intriguingly, in one of his reports, Sewell reported that Bhupinder was 'spending some of his time at the Sandow Institute, in St. James Street'.[118] Earlier that summer, this 'world renowned exponent and founder of scien-tific physical culture' had secured a royal appointment from the new king.[119] One wonders if the remarks in the press about his girth prompted Bhupinder to undergo the strenuous Sandow course in physical training. 'Anything worse for cricket than the making of a lot of muscle cannot be imagined, but the famous strong man does athletes so much good in other ways that one can pardon him if he removes some of the Sikh prince's priceless lissomness,' wrote Sewell, tongue firmly in cheek. But he also pointed out that the Indian cricket team was 'seriously handicapped by the absence of the Maharajah and the accomplished Mistri'.[120]

However, if there was a sporting reason for Bhupinder's enrolment in the Sandow school, it was evidently not cricket. Instead, the prince pursued his other passion: polo. Like his father, he had become an adept at this ancient game that had been remade by the British in India. Immediately after their arrival in the capital, Bhupinder and his entourage were spotted by pressmen at the Ranelagh Club and the Hurlingham Club, the principal venues for prestigious polo tournaments.[121] And in the following days the Maharaja spent a great deal of time in both places, either watching or taking part in matches.

Bhupinder devoted more time to polo than to cricket during his British sojourn for two reasons. Ranelagh and Hurlingham were sites par excellence of elite sociability. They were frequented by the *crème-de-la-crème* of society during the London season. In these rarefied settings, representatives of the upper classes engaged in the untrammelled pursuit of sport. By 1911, both London clubs also put on a variety of other shows that attracted the rich and famous, notably, 'driving competitions, croquet tournaments, aeroplane flights, pony and horse shows, gymkhanas'.[122] Like a number of other prestigious clubs in the city, Hurlingham and Ranelagh had temporarily incorporated the Indian maharajas into British high society by according them honorary memberships. The visiting princes, for their part, used these occasions to socialize with the imperial elite and impress them with their sporting prowess. Bhupinder sought to use his access to the elite polo clubs to interact with his fellow princes, in particular Sir Ganga Singh of Bikaner, as well as display his skills in a game that was cherished by the British aristocracy. 'The Maharaja must be a fine all-round sportsman, for there are not many Indian princes who can play back and captain their polo team, and can captain a cricket team as well,' commented one admiring contemporary.[123]

But there was another reason why Bhupinder became more invested in polo on this tour. The Ranelagh Club had instituted a new competition that summer to mark the ascension to the throne of George V. The King's Coronation Cup, remarked one observer, was 'the largest piece of silverware that has ever been competed for in athletics'.[124] It was to be open only to winners of the Inter-Regimental Tournament, the Hurlingham Champion Cup, the Ranelagh Open Cup, 'and approved teams representing India, and the Colonies and Dominions of the Empire'.[125] Scheduled for the second week of July, the competition was to mark the finale of that season's polo events in the capital. Given the presence of many polo-playing officers serving in the subcontinent, both in the British Army and the Imperial Service troops, the Indian Polo Association decided to enter a team from the subcontinent in this tournament. Among the top contenders for a place in the side was Colonel Chanda Singh, a member of Bhupinder's entourage, who was regarded by contemporaries as 'one of the outstanding figures in modern Indian polo'.[126] A week before the tournament, the Patiala man was part of an entirely Indian team that inflicted a stinging defeat on the Ranelagh Club. Bhupinder took a close interest in Chanda Singh's practice sessions and regularly took part in polo sessions with his *aide-de-camp*.[127] Perhaps he hoped to derive some reflected glory as the patron of one of the Indian players taking part in this prestigious tournament. However, to the disappointment of many observers, three of the four players chosen by the Indian Polo Association were European officers. The only Indian to be picked in this side was Captain Shah Mirza Beg from Hyderabad, who was 'generally acknowledged to be the best native player in India'.[128] Some observers of the game 'considered that Colonel Chanda Singh should have been included in the team'.[129] As it turned out, the King's Coronation Cup 'fell somewhat flat' because two premier sides withdrew from the tournament.[130] The 'Indian' polo team defeated the 4th Dragoon Guards by ten goals to four to win the prized trophy.[131]

The final was played in front of a large crowd at the Ranelagh Club. But the Maharaja of Patiala was not among the spectators. On 8 July, he had been forced to undergo an operation on his troublesome adenoids. Dunlop Smith was at hand to facilitate matters and the doctor who performed the surgery told him that 'it was as bad an operation of the kind as he had ever done'.[132] Assured by the doctors that Bhupinder was making a satisfactory recovery, Dunlop Smith left London for the weekend. But he was recalled to the city 'that same night by telegram, as violent haemorrhage had begun, and it was some time before the doctors could stop it'. 'We had an anxious time for some days afterwards,' he added, 'as the medical men expected that pneumonia would set in.'[133] However, the fears proved unfounded and in mid-July the Maharaja was allowed to leave for Harrogate. By the time Bhupinder returned to London on 1 August, the Season was almost over in the increasingly deserted imperial metropolis. Three days later, the prince departed for Paris. But he did so secure in the knowledge that he had made a favourable impression on the royal family and imperial officialdom in

London. 'We allowed the Maharaja to go to Paris without any Political
Officer,' Dunlop Smith informed the Government of India, 'and, His
Highness justified the confidence placed in him.'[134]

V

On 13 July 1911, even as their captain was recovering from his operation, the
Indian cricketers began the twelfth match of their tour against Leicestershire
CCC. In the weeks that had elapsed since the Maharaja and Mistry had
abandoned the tour, the Indians had sustained seven consecutive defeats.
Without exception, they were defeated by large margins in every match.
Against the 'first-class' teams, the visitors lost to Yorkshire by an innings,
Warwickshire by ten wickets, Lancashire and Kent by nine wickets, and
Surrey and Northamptonshire by six wickets. But their most ignominious
defeat was against 'second-class' Staffordshire at Stoke-on-Trent, where they
were beaten in a single day.

A chronicle of the Indian cricket tour of 1911, published a few months
after the event, reminded its readers that 'in the earlier fixtures the Indians
had all the conditions against them, totally new and, to them, inexplicable
conditions of turf, weather, climate, atmosphere and light, not to speak of
the personal discomforts experienced by every new arrival in Britain'.[135]
Undoubtedly, the playing conditions affected the way the Indian cricketers
played at the outset. J.M. Divecha recalled how in the weeks after their
arrival it had taken the Indians time to get used to the alien conditions. The
light had been 'disconcerting' and had 'affected the initial matches'.[136]
But as the tour went on, it was the heat that began to bother the visitors.
The Parsi manager admitted that 'at one or two centres the heat was
more oppressive and distressing than what we were even accustomed to
in India'.[137] Indeed, Mukund Pai had to retire during the match against
Yorkshire on account of heat-induced exhaustion. 'One would have thought
that our visitors from India would revel in such hot weather conditions as
we are experiencing,' wrote 'Old Ebor'. 'Yet the contrary is the case. The
heat of India is drier than that now being experienced in England, and this
is the explanation given as to why the change is felt by our visitors.'[138]

Undoubtedly, the weather conditions and unfamiliar playing surfaces dis-
comfited the Indian cricketers. But it was not the principal reason for their
poor showing during the first half of the tour. The abject performance of

Figure 20. The members of the All–India team with their hosts at the Kent County Cricket Club. Palwankar Baloo is seated next to the legendary W.G. Grace, the greatest cricketer of the Victorian age. Courtesy of the Roger Mann Picture Library.

the Indian team was a function of the power dynamics that were at work both on and off the pitch.

On the field of play, the Indian cricket team encountered English sides that were technically superior because of a remarkable transformation in the art of bowling in the previous decade. 'We can say of any of the arts and pastimes of man that it is in its Golden Age when every technical part and potentiality of it are being explored and exhibited, with a masterly exponent for every conceivable manifestation of style,' wrote Neville Cardus.[139] This was certainly the case with bowling in the Edwardian era, which saw two key innovations that remain an integral part of cricket to this day.

First, bowlers began to use the seam of the cricket ball to control its movement in the air. In the nineteenth century, bowlers had relied on the pitch to get rid of batsmen. But with marled pitches increasingly favouring the latter, they began to experiment with new grips that allowed them to 'swerve' the ball. This innovation is credited to the Yorkshire professional George Hirst, but ironically its originator was John Barton King, an

American fast bowler who toured England in 1897 with the 'Gentlemen of Philadelphia'.[140] In favourable atmospheric conditions, this form of bowling became a highly effective weapon against attacking batsmen. Following a change of the rules in 1907, which allowed a bowling team to claim a new ball after their opponents had passed 200 runs, a premium was placed on the effective use of its original shine.[141]

Second, slow bowling, too, underwent a revolution with the discovery of the 'googly', a leg break which spun the 'wrong way' after pitching. Its inventor was the Oxford and Middlesex amateur cricketer Bernard Bosanquet, who discovered it accidentally while playing with a tennis ball.[142] Although he first used the googly in July 1900 in a match between Middlesex and Leicestershire at Lord's, it was during England's tour of Australia two years later that its full potential became apparent. In that series, Bosanquet mesmerized the Australian batsmen with his new weapon. Before long, spin bowlers in Australia and South Africa had incorporated the googly (or the 'bosie', as it was called Down Under) into their repertoire. Notably, in 1906 the South African spin quartet of 'Reggie' Schwarz, Gordon White, Albert 'Ernie' Vogler, and Aubrey Faulkner used the delivery to devastating effect against a visiting MCC team. The following year, these googly specialists made a collective mark on the Edwardian cricketing scene in Britain.[143]

Both fast-paced swerve as well as the googly had become widely diffused within English domestic cricket by the end of the Edwardian era. Every county team had a fast bowler or two who could use the seam to make the ball move in the air. Many teams also possessed exponents of the 'wrong-un'. 'There are now many votaries of the art of "googlie" bowling all over England,' reported one observer of the game in 1909.[144]

However, to the Indian cricketers these innovations were as yet a mystery. 'They are quite innocent of any of the modern bowling embellishments,' commented the *Athletic News*.[145] In fact, their difficulties had been anticipated at the outset by Sir Dorab Tata, who admitted that the googly was 'quite unknown in India' and that only Bulsara had some knowledge of how to make the ball 'swerve'. Moreover, the Bombay businessman added, the Indian batsmen had never before encountered 'really fast bowling on fiery wickets'.[146] Thus, it is hardly surprising that the colonial visitors were all at sea against the new metropolitan innovations in the art of bowling. In the early weeks of the tour, H.D. Kanga revealed in a press interview that his teammates were clueless about how to counter the 'googlie workers' and the 'swerver wallahs'.[147] 'The fast bowling at the outset, with swerves and googlies thrown in later, upset the nerves of our batsmen who took long to settle down,' agreed Divecha.[148]

Utterly disoriented by the bowling that they encountered, the Indians alternated between wild slogging and overcautious defence. The former approach occasionally yielded results. But when it failed to come off, such bravado invited ridicule. Following on against the MCC at Lord's, the Indian batsmen tried to hit their way out of trouble and were bowled out for ninety-six in under two hours. 'One after the other the members of the side gave one the impression that they went in with the idea to do or die. They did—they died,' wrote one bemused correspondent.[149] Chastened by the manner of their defeat, the Indians batted with exaggerated caution in the following matches.

But either way, the Indian batsmen failed to counter the English bowlers. The figures tell their own sorry tale. In their first eleven games, the visitors were bowled out eight times for a total score of less than a hundred runs. In twenty-two innings, the Indian batsmen passed fifty only ten times, and not one of them went on to make a century. Moreover, on forty occasions an Indian batsman failed to open his account.

Occasionally, however, some of the Indian batsmen came good. Against South Wales at Cardiff, Mulla blazed his way to an audacious ninety-eight. At Lord's, in the following match, K.M. Mistry played a dazzling innings of seventy-eight, which one reporter thought 'was well worth going miles to see'.[150] His compatriot Meherhomji showed glimpses of his batting skills against South Wales at Cardiff and Kent at Catford. Shivram, drafted into the side in place of the luckless Pai, scored a chanceless ninety-one in the Indians' second innings against Warwickshire at Edgbaston. And both Kanga and Jayaram, after a series of poor scores, recorded half-centuries in the first innings of their match at against Surrey, the best Indian display up to that point in the tour. This creditable effort at the Oval against one of the strongest teams in the county championship served partially to redeem the visitors' reputation after the dismal batting in the previous match at Stoke-on-Trent.

Although Staffordshire did not enjoy 'first-class' status, it possessed one of the greatest bowlers in the entire history of cricket. Sydney Barnes combined the new techniques of swerve and spin with a remarkably consistent mastery of pace and flight.[151] A tall 'fast-medium' bowler, he used to great effect the bounce afforded by the improved pitches of the day. 'I cannot believe that any bowler has ever lived who shared Barnes's power of making a cricket ball bounce on a hard wicket, bounce as though a ball of red-hot fire!' Cardus declared.[152] A famously tough-minded competitor, Barnes was also a fierce stickler for his rights as a professional cricketer. Notably, he chose to play most of his cricket in Staffordshire rather than kow-tow to the whims of the amateur administrators who ran the first-class counties.[153]

The Indians had the misfortune to run into the 'most difficult bowler in England' at the top of his game.[154] They were decimated twice in the space of a single day's cricket in which Barnes displayed his peerless versatility as a bowler. In the first innings, on a slow, rain-affected pitch, he maintained a perfect line and length as the Indians were dismissed for a paltry seventy-four runs. 'The greatness of the bowling lay almost more than anything else in the fact that there was for the batsman no release from the tension of this alert defence, no single loose ball to hit,' noted one reporter.[155] The visitors' second innings 'was memorable for one of the finest pieces of bowling that even Barnes has done'. As the wicket hardened under a warm sun, he 'made the ball turn first one way and then the other in a way that was simply unplayable'.[156] 'Right-hand leg break bowling of the pace which he attained made even old followers of cricket open their eyes in astonishment,' wrote another observer.[157] The Indians were bowled out for fifty-seven in just eighty minutes. His masterly display yielded Barnes the remarkable match figures of fourteen wickets for twenty-nine runs.

★   ★   ★

Power relations were also in play off the cricket pitch. As we have seen, the MCC had drawn up the schedule for the Indian cricketers' tour. The fixture list was arranged to suit the convenience of the county clubs that were to host the Indians. Significantly, the visitors were deliberately pitted against the strongest teams from the very outset. Save for the match against Staffordshire, all the 'second-class' games were bunched together in the second half of the tour.

It is not clear how much of a say the Indian organizers of the tour had in the schedule that was foisted on the players. Sewell claimed that their views had been duly considered and declared that 'out of their own mouths they stand condemned if they grumble at their lot'.[158] Given the unequal power relations, however, the Indians had no choice but to go along with the decisions of the MCC. At the same time, the public statements of the team management suggest that the Indians were deeply unhappy about their match schedule. Indeed, J.M. Divecha repeatedly cited the 'bad arrangement of the programme' as a factor in the Indians' unbroken run of defeats at the outset.[159] 'We were completely outclassed at a period of the tour which gave us no time to harden our condition and firm up,' he later told reporters.[160] It was a view shared by others in the Indian side. Their fixtures, Baloo observed, 'were not arranged with a due regard to the entirely new conditions under which the team had to play'.[161]

Interestingly, an encounter between Divecha and Lord Harris highlights the power dynamics between the sporting representatives of the rulers and the ruled. 'After losing 7 or 8 matches,' the Parsi team manager revealed, 'I had a chat with Lord Harris about the arrangement of the fixtures and expressed my view of the awkward method adopted by pitting first class counties against us at first.'[162] The ex-Governor of Bombay was utterly unsympathetic, 'holding that as the purpose of the tour was purely educational, much more benefit would be derived from matches with the best counties than from matches with weaker sides'.[163] As Divecha pointed out, however, 'no team could go on playing day after day losing games without losing heart and becoming disorganized'.[164]

The schedule of the Indian cricketers allowed them no rest between games. Indeed, only once between the start of their tour on 1 June and the match at Leicestershire on 13 July did the visitors get a break of more than two days. In his interviews, the Parsi manager cited the unremitting schedule as a factor in the Indians' poor showing at the outset. 'The programme was too ambitious,' he explained, 'inasmuch as we were not acclimatised at the beginning of the tour and unaccustomed to play six days in a week and travelling to the next centre immediately after a three days' fixture.'[165] As a consequence, the Indian team 'had gone stale and had deteriorated through overstrain'.[166] 'At times,' he added, 'it was difficult for me to complete a team.'[167] Indeed, according to Vithal's autobiography, on one occasion Divecha himself had to take to the field as a substitute for an indisposed player.[168]

While the Indian management complained about the schedule, English commentators and the publicists of the imperial cricketing establishment blamed the visitors' troubles on internal power struggles within the team. A fortnight into the tour, Anglo-Indian newspapers in India began to dwell on the 'apparent lack of cohesion in the Indian cricket team'.[169] The English sporting correspondent of the *Madras Mail* reported that 'the strong Parsee element in the eleven is already making something of a dead set against the other people on the side'. This journalist claimed that at the nets the Parsi bowlers had deliberately ignored Jayaram. 'It is rather petty, and if this is typical of the sect, it is a pity that there are any Parsees in the team at all,' he declared.[170] 'Small wonder that the Indian cricket team is failing to win matches if it goes into the field deliberately insulting the susceptibilities of probably its best all-round man in Jayaram and its only wicket-keeper in Seshachari,' thundered an enraged Madras civilian.[171] But the allegations also drew a furious response from a Bombay Parsi. Writing to the *Times of India*, one J.M. Bharucha invited readers to visit the Excelsior Cinematograph, 'where in the Indian cricket team film Parsi bowlers are seen bowling to Messrs Baloo and Pai'. If the Parsi bowlers could bowl to 'their rivals, the Bombay Hindu cricketers', he asserted, there was no reason for them to avoid doing so to Jayaram. 'It is jealousy only and nothing else to belittle the Parsis who have subscribed half of the funds for sending the Indian XI to England,' declared this irate letter writer.[172] The controversy also prompted Divecha to deny strenuously the allegations levelled against the Parsis.[173]

However, it is fairly clear that the first Indian team did not bond together in the manner that its promoters had hoped. 'It is a matter of common knowledge,' one newspaper later claimed, 'that the members of this team quarrelled even on the steamer!'[174] Proximity, then, appears to have deepened, rather than diminished, the friction between the Indian cricketers. In particular, the Parsi and Hindu cricketers from Bombay were unable to overcome their longstanding mutual antipathy despite being thrown together for a prolonged period of time in a foreign land. There was, in other words, a palpable absence of 'communitas' (to use a term favoured by anthropologists) among the players. Perhaps dietary preferences were a factor in exacerbating these internal differences, for it may have curtailed the possibilities of sociability off the field. Notably, the Brahmin cricketers were vegetarians, whereas the rest of the team comprised meat eaters. The Parsis, in particular, did not hide their disdain for the dietary fastidiousness of their Brahmin teammates. Take, for instance, Divecha's explanation for Pai's frequent breakdowns during the tour: 'He is a vegetarian and in Great Britain meat must be eaten if one is to keep fit.'[175]

Kanga's elevation to the captaincy also caused the tensions off the field to spill over onto it. His tactical decisions—chopping and changing the team in an arbitrary fashion, constantly fiddling with the batting order, and curious field placements—appears to have alienated the team's Hindu and Muslim cricketers. At the same time, Vithal's autobiography also suggests that there was some resentment among the Hindu and Parsi players about the selection of Shafqat Hussein.[176] The Aligarh bowler was no longer the force he had been in his prime; moreover, he had become a liability in the field. According to Vithal, on one occasion a furious Kanga reprimanded Shafqat for fluffing a simple catch. To the captain's astonishment, the bowler retorted angrily that he possessed only one functioning eye. Incredibly, none of the Hindu and Parsi players had previously known about his disability. This startling revelation, it appears, intensified his teammates' resentment about Shafqat's inclusion in the touring party.[177]

Only one Indian player ended the first half of the tour with his reputation enhanced. Palwankar Baloo established beyond any doubt that he was the greatest Indian bowler of his generation. Statistics, that ubiquitous yardstick of sporting achievement, offer incontrovertible proof of his success. By the time the Indians arrived in Leicester, Baloo had sent down 334 overs—more than any other player in the side—and was their leading wicket taker with sixty victims in eleven matches. Significantly, in many of these games, Baloo had only one crack at the opposition. On five occasions, he had a haul of five wickets or more in an innings: against Oxford, 5-87; Cambridge, 8-103; Lancashire, 7-83; Staffordshire, 6-35; Kent, 5-109; and Northamptonshire, 6-58. And four times he narrowly missed out on this honour, with figures of 4-96 against the MCC, 4-74 against Warwickshire, 4-100 against Surrey, and 4-127 against Yorkshire.

The ageing Baloo's bowling feats are remarkable considering that this was his first experience of English playing conditions. Moreover, if we go by Sewell's account, it would appear that he might have even had more wickets but for poor captaincy and field placement. According to the Englishman, Baloo 'was taken off when bowling very well indeed, and lost wickets through having his field in all sorts of incredible positions'.[178] Sewell also pointed out how in favourable conditions at Old Trafford, Kanga chose to open the attack with Warden and Bulsara despite 'ample proof' that Baloo was 'by a very long way his best bowler'.[179] Stray remarks in Vithal's autobiography also suggest that Baloo was not entirely happy with the manner in which he was treated by Kanga. On one occasion, the bowler asked the captain for a specific field placement and was brusquely turned down. The very next ball a catch landed on the very spot where Baloo had wished to station a fielder. According to Vithal, his brother chose quietly to carry on bowling rather than remonstrate with his skipper.[180] 'Balu's slow ball and his indefatigable uncomplaining disposition will long be remembered by all

Figure 21. The Indian cricketers at Hove, Sussex, August 1911.
Standing (left to right): J.S. Warden, Palwankar Baloo, an English host, H.F. Mulla, and M.D. Pai.
Seated (left to right): M.D. Bulsara, Salamuddin Khan, K. Seshachari, H.D. Kanga, Prince Shivaji Rao, J.M. Divecha, and R.P. Meherhomji.
Seated on the ground (left): Palwankar Shivram; (right): Syed Hasan. Courtesy of the Roger Mann Picture Library.

who have played against the native team,' declared Sewell.[181] But the Dalit stalwart's best was yet to come.

VI

'The most unfortunate county this year is Leicestershire,' remarked the *Manchester Guardian* a few days before their match against the visiting Indians. 'They have frequently played a really fine game, and yet they have sustained twelve defeats and have yet to score their first victory.'[182] The Indian cricketers, at the mid-point of their tour, thus encountered a team with an identical track record. Like the Indians, Leicestershire too had problems off the pitch. But their difficulties stemmed from the club's precarious financial position. Four years earlier, matters had reached such a pass that there was even talk of disbanding the club. 'There have been recurring deficits for several seasons which have placed great difficulties in the way of the committee,' reported the *Manchester Guardian* in September 1907.[183] As often was the case, such predictions of doom instantly rallied the club's supporters and active measures were devised to boost its finances. 'Leicestershire as the result of a successful bazaar, start the year free from debt,' noted the same newspaper in April 1911. 'A sign of revival is the organization of a cricket week at Leicester in July.'[184] The county's match against the visiting Indians was to be the highlight of this newly invented sporting occasion.

'Whatever may have been their failings in their twelve engagements prior to visiting the County Ground, Leicester, yesterday, the All-Indians, as they are termed, gave us then as pleasing an exhibition of cricket as we could wish to witness,' reported a local newspaper after the first day of the match.[185] Batting first on a friendly pitch, the Indians got off to a flying start. Kanga, recovering from a hand injury, and Meherhomji put on a brisk opening partnership of 178 runs. The Indian captain went on to make 163, and his team ended the day on 431-9. The following morning, the Indians' innings ended on 481, with Shivram falling short of his century by fifteen runs. It was his first notable score since the match against Warwickshire.

When the Indians took to the field, Baloo and Salamuddin bamboozled the Leicestershire batsmen, taking five wickets apiece. 'Each man bowled intelligently, and seldom sent down a ball for hitting purposes,' wrote one correspondent.[186] Bowled out for 283, Leicestershire had to endure the ignominy of the 'follow on'. Another magnificent bowling performance from Baloo, who took six wickets for ninety-three runs, enabled the Indians to get rid of the home side for 248 in their second innings. The Indians knocked off the fifty-one runs required to win the match for the loss of three wickets. The local press was quick to congratulate the Indians on their first victory. 'It was a capital performance, as it was brought about by all-round good cricket and play quite superior to much that has been seen at Ayleston Road this season,' declared the *Leicester Daily Post*.[187] But the head-line in another newspaper best summed up the visitors' triumph: 'A HULLA-BALLOO!', declared the *Star*.[188]

Their comprehensive triumph over Leicestershire galvanized the Indian cricketers. In the very next match, they prevailed over Somerset in a nail-biting finish at Taunton. Once again, there were some outstanding performances on the Indian side. On the opening day, Salamuddin (6-64) and Baloo (4-48) bowled out Somerset for 157. A chanceless century by the muscular Bajana, who had played on this ground before, enabled the Indians to take a lead of thirty-nine runs. Somerset fared much better in their second innings, with Baloo for the first time proving ineffectual with the ball. Set a target of 265, the Indians appeared 'doomed to defeat' on the final day when they lost their sixth wicket for 102.[189] At this stage, Baloo walked out to join his brother Shivram. The Palwankar siblings proceeded to put together a rollicking partnership of 116 in a little over an hour. 'They played delightful cricket, and hit powerfully on both sides of the wicket,' wrote one reporter.[190] When Baloo was dismissed after scoring an entertaining half-century, the visitors were forty-seven runs short of the target. Shafqat Hussein quickly followed Baloo back to the pavilion. Bulsara then offered Shivram dogged support as the latter reached his century. But the portly Parsi departed with the Indians still twenty-two runs adrift. Shivram and Syed Hasan now whittled away at the target amidst mounting tension. With one run required to level the scores, Shivram edged a ball to the slips, but the catch was put down. Fittingly, it was the Dalit batsman from Bombay who struck the winning runs. Praising the centurion, one newspaper noted that 'Shivram batted splendidly and fairly won the match for his side'.[191] For the second successive time, the Palwankars had carried the Indian team to victory.

Buoyed by their consecutive victories, the Indian cricketers inflicted crushing defeats on their next two opponents. Representative cricket at Lincolnshire and Durham was deemed 'second class', and the Indians proved too strong for both counties. 'Since the turning point of the tour at Leicester the Indian team seems incapable of doing anything but win matches,' declared Sewell in his weekly report.[192] These decisive victories owed much to the strivings of Baloo, Shivram, and Salamuddin. Against Lincolnshire at Sleaford, Shivram scored 175 and helped the Indians post a score of 463-6. Salamuddin and Baloo easily got rid of the Lincolnshire batsmen both times in the match to leave the Indians winners by an innings. Against Durham at Sunderland, Salamuddin scored eighty-five in the first innings took five wickets in the second innings, as his team coasted to a seven-wicket victory.

The following match, against Northumberland at Newcastle-on-Tyne, was notable for the non-appearance of the Indian team's premier bowler for the first time since the beginning of their tour. Baloo's tireless bowling efforts in the previous weeks had aggravated his synovitis. At Newcastle, however, a fine all-round performance by Warden made up for his absence.

The bespectacled Parsi, who had struggled during the first part of the tour, shone with both bat and ball against Northumberland. Along with Meherhomji, he scored a century in the Indian first innings and then proceeded to take eleven wickets in the match. Notwithstanding Warden's magnificent performance, however, the Indians lost by one wicket. Sobered by this unexpected defeat, they journeyed north to commence the Celtic leg of their cricket tour.

VII

The history of cricket in Scotland furnishes interesting parallels with its career in colonial India. In both contexts, English men of arms introduced the game in the first half of the eighteenth century. In India, it was sailors moored off the Gulf of Khambat who were said to have played the game as early as 1721. In Scotland, this activity was the pastime of soldiers stationed in the country after the Jacobite Rebellion in 1745.[193] As in colonial India, moreover, it was in the second half of the nineteenth century that the game began to acquire deeper roots in Scotland. Cricket north of the border received a fillip with the appearance in 1849 of the peripatetic All England eleven, which played against a twenty-two of Scotland.[194] Significantly, during the late nineteenth century, the same institutions that had propelled the expansion of cricket in England also played an important role in entrenching it in Scotland: the public schools, the universities, and recreational clubs supported by the aristocracy in the country and the newly rising middle classes in the towns. By 1911, notwithstanding the undisputed popular supremacy of football, cricket had secured a devoted following in Scotland.[195]

Like their Indian counterparts, Scottish cricket promoters also sought greater recognition from the imperial establishment at Lord's. Yet, much to their frustration, this was not really forthcoming. 'It has been suggested in some quarters that the best eleven that Scotland could produce might be equal to giving the average English county a fairly good game, and that Caledonia stern and wild should be graciously permitted to collect a side to take part in the County Championship,' wrote one correspondent in 1911. 'Caledonia,' he drily added, 'has been pardonably stern and wild at such an insinuation of national debility.'[196] Scottish promoters thus regarded the visit of the Indian cricketers as an opportunity to showcase the progress of cricket in their country.

The visitors travelled to Scotland at a time when many others were undertaking the same journey. 'With the advent of August there has been an unprecedented rush to the North,' remarked one Scottish newspaper. 'Train and motor car gave evidence daily of the enormous number spending a holiday in the Highlands.'[197] Perhaps the Indians too wished that they were on vacation, for they had begun to chafe at their relentless schedule. 'Unaccustomed to such a series of matches they are in schoolboy language "fed up" with the tour,' reported Sewell.[198] The performance of the tourists in the three matches that they played in Scotland suggests that the view was not unfounded.

The Indians first took on North of Scotland, a team comprising club cricketers from the Highland league, at Inverness. The match commenced in 'brilliant sunshine', with the visiting team being led on to the field by 'four boy bag-pipers playing "Highland Laddie" while the spectators raised hearty cheers'.[199] But the home supporters had little to celebrate once play began. Seshachari, in charge of the Indian team because Kanga had opted out, won the toss and invited the home side to bat first. North of Scotland was unable to cope with Warden's wiles and subsided for 158. In their reply, the Indians scored 401-4, with Meherhomji and Salamuddin scoring centuries. The Scottish team fared even worse the second time it went into bat and lost the match by an innings. 'No respectable London club XI would ever lose a match to the North of Scotland XI, who did not play in kilts but looked as though they might just as well have done so,' sneered Sewell.[200] With the match done and dusted inside two days, the visitors took time off to visit the famous battle site of Culloden.

The Indian cricketers faced a far stiffer challenge in their next game at Mossilee, a few miles uphill from the border town of Galashiels, against an all-amateur team representing the recently formed Scottish Cricket Union. Batting first, the Indian batsmen caved in easily against the swerve of a fast bowler named John Ferguson and the googlies of Bruce Lockhart, a Cambridge undergraduate who had claimed ten wickets against them in the match at Fenners. A sterling bowling performance by Warden and Baloo prevented their opponents from securing an unassailable lead. But the visitors' defeat seemed a foregone conclusion when their batting collapsed again in the second innings. Luckily for the Indians, rain on the final day prevented this embarrassing outcome. However, it was clear to many observers that the Indian players were no longer focused on cricket. 'I never saw such a bored lot. They all seem dead sick of cricket,' one Scottish cricketer told Sewell after this match.[201] The only Indian player to elicit unstinted praise was Palwankar Baloo, who had taken to the field despite his synovitis and a strained back. 'Old Balu as all our people call him is very popular wherever he goes, and everyone is sorry that this injury may have the effect of preventing him getting his hundred wickets,' remarked Sewell.[202]

The Indians' final fixture proved to be the most exciting of the three matches they played in Scotland. Their encounter against the Scottish Counties at Perth was a low-scoring thriller. The Indians went in first and were bowled out for 165, with Meherhomji being the only one to score a fifty. Another superb bowling display by Warden and Baloo restricted the home side to 210. A fine knock of eighty-one by Jaya Ram allowed the Indians to set their opponents a target of 174. Although Baloo was unable to bowl in the second innings, the Indians established an early ascendancy over their opponents. When their sixth wicket fell with only ninety-one runs on the board, it looked as if the Scots would lose the match. The Indian players now 'commenced to show a keenness that they had not before exhibited in the field'.[203] However, the Scottish batsmen kept their nerve and slowly began to chip away at the target. Excitement among the spectators began to escalate as the home side advanced towards victory. When the Scottish team eventually won the match, 'there was a burst of enthusiasm such as has seldom been equalled on the North Inch'.[204] The players from both teams were raucously cheered off the field as a local band struck up 'Will ye no come back again?'[205]

★   ★   ★

By the time the Indian cricketers had discharged their obligations in Scotland, matters were on the boil south of the border, where the unremitting heatwave was accompanied by flaring tempers in parliament and violent protests on the streets. Luckily for the visitors, the next stage in their tour took them across the Irish Sea to Belfast, which had not yet been transformed into the hotbed of political protest that it was very shortly to become.

Cricket in Ireland, as in Scotland and India, was an alien import associated with imperial power.[206] It had come to the country with the British army towards the end of the eighteenth century. At this time, the English game 'was confined essentially to the military, the gentry and members of the viceregal or Chief Secretary's staff and household'.[207] In the half-century that followed the union in 1801, there developed a flourishing cricket culture in cities like Dublin, Cork, and Belfast as well as in smaller garrison towns. The game was rooted in the culture of the Anglo-Irish gentry in the countryside as well as the town-dwelling middle classes. In particular, it was nurtured in public schools and universities catering to this Anglo-Irish elite. More surprisingly, cricket also emerged as a site of sociability between elites and plebeians in city and countryside alike. Equally, its appeal cut across the deeply entrenched religious divide and the game flourished in places that would later come to be seen as 'strongholds of Gaelic sports'.[208] Indeed, one historian has suggested that by 1860 'cricket had probably become the most popular sport in Ireland'.[209]

But the picture was very different half a century later. By the end of the Edwardian era, many observers regarded with deepening gloom the future of Irish cricket. Their funereal mood can be gleaned from an essay on 'Cricket in Ireland' by a contributor to Pelham Warner's *Imperial Cricket*, whose publication was timed to coincide with the 1912 Triangular tournament featuring England, Australia, and South Africa. 'It is impossible to take a cheerful view of the future of cricket in Ireland,' wrote its author Ernest Ensor. 'For nearly a century the game has been played strenuously by the Anglo-Irish,' he elaborated, 'but they have failed altogether as missionaries, and have not succeeded in attracting the country people to the game. It remains exotic.'[210] According to Ensor, one of the key factors that militated against the growth of cricket in Ireland was that 'the real Irish do not like and do not understand games'. This was a result, he argued, of the Irish lack of 'self-restraint, obedience, unselfishness'. 'If all people in Ireland could learn to practice the hum-drum virtues necessary for cricket, many Irish difficulties would be solved,' Ensor declared.[211]

This was racist discourse masquerading as reasoned analysis. The decline of cricket in Ireland was scarcely the outcome of innate defects in the Irish character. On the contrary, institutional and social factors—notably, the absence of a central organizing body and prolonged rural conflict— were responsible for its diminishing vitality during the late nineteenth century.[212]

At the same time, the palpable lack of enthusiasm for the colonizer's sport was by no means an inevitable outcome of the rise of Irish cultural nationalism. Indeed, the growth of nationalist ideology did not necessarily entail the eclipse of cricket in the island. Leading Irish nationalists had played the game in school and college. This is not so surprising given that they were mostly drawn from the ranks of the middle classes and had thus been

exposed to the game at a formative stage in their lives. Cricket also continued
to be played wherever it had entrenched itself in the cultural life of labourers and peasants. This was, for instance, the case in County Kilkenny, where
'the sport had spread beyond the big houses and was played in every town
and village'.[213]

Nonetheless, it is undeniable that the formation of the Gaelic Athletics
Association in 1884 hastened the Irish repudiation of cricket. The new body
was part of a vigorous movement that sought to reject English cultural
imports in favour of authentically Irish artefacts and practices.[214] Cricket
now came to be seen by the cultural nationalists as a sport tainted by its
association with a foreign ruling class and hence, to be boycotted in favour
of traditional Gaelic recreational activities. But conversely, the sport retained
a tenacious hold in those northern counties where it was symbolically
charged with pro-Union sentiments. Such was the case in Belfast, where the
Indians arrived to take on the Northern Cricket Union of Ireland.

Their encounter with the Ulstermen turned out to be the most extraordinary of the visitors' tour. Batting first on a perfect pitch in glorious sunshine, the Indians got off to a good start with Meherhomji playing a series
of 'crisp square cuts and lovely off-drives' that enthralled the spectators.[215]
The Parsi opening batsman narrowly missed out on his century, but notched
up his thousandth run of the tour. Jayaram and Salamuddin also played
entertaining cricket as the Indians posted a total of 324. The Ulster team
began their reply at 4.30 p.m. Less than an hour later the entire team had
been dismissed for twenty-six. 'It was an object lesson in batting weakness
that was most humiliating to Northern cricket,' remarked one stunned
observer.[216] The chief destroyers were Baloo and Salamuddin. The former's
Barnes-like bowling figures are worth noting: five wickets for nine runs off
9.2 overs. Following on, the home side was reduced to 15-5 by the close of
play. The last wicket of the day was claimed by Baloo; fittingly, it was his
hundredth of the tour. The next morning, neither of the Indian wicket
takers was given the ball so as to prolong the match. But the remaining Irish
batsmen were unable to cope with Bulsara and Warden and were bowled
out for sixty-five.

In order to mollify irate spectators, the organizers hastily arranged a festival match between the same teams. But this was scarcely a consolation for
supporters of Irish cricket who had looked forward to the main contest with
great anticipation. 'Cricketers in the future will tell how the native gentlemen from the Indian empire made 324 against our best bowling, but how

these same gentlemen captured fifteen of our best batsmen at a cost of 41 runs,' lamented one Irishman after the first day's play. 'Needless to say, the feeble batting of what was considered the strongest batting which the Northern Union could select came as an unpleasant surprise to Belfast cricketers. On both days the wicket from the batsmen's point of view, was as near perfect as possible,' rued another local correspondent after witnessing the Irish debacle.[217]

The Indians' final fixture of their Celtic sojourn was equally distinctive, but for its setting rather than the play. The visitors went by train from Belfast to the north County Wicklow town of Bray, where they took part in a match at the Woodbrook estate of one of Britain's richest businessmen. Country house cricket was a uniquely late Victorian and Edwardian phenomenon, which did not survive the First World War.[218] But in its heyday, it was an integral part of British cricketing culture. Its defining feature was that the leading aristocrat or notable of an area put together a team comprising local worthies and specially invited guests against another club or one of the many wandering elevens of the period. These weekend matches were staged on the grounds of the aristocratic house, watched by a mixed crowd of men and women, with the host providing lavish entertainment throughout the proceedings. The quality of the cricket and the settings in which it was played tended to vary. But the fixtures were important occasions in the social calendar and participation in them was a key marker of status. Significantly, the players were usually amateur, though it was not unusual for the odd professional to be included in the host's team.

Unlike many other patrons of country house cricket, Stanley Herbert Cochrane was not an aristocrat. His father had made his millions as one half of the business firm of Cantrell and Cochrane, which sold mineral water and ginger ale in different parts of the world. The firm's advertisements boldly proclaimed the global appeal of its products:

> The popping of Cantrell and Cochrane's corks is heard in the bungalows of the British cantonment in the Far East, and its sparkle is familiar to the Vice-Regal entourage up in the hot season refuge of the Anglo-Indians at Simla. Dons and seignorinas quaff this liquid boon in the tropical climes of South America; the West Indies welcome it as a treasure; Africa's 'sunny fountains' are out-rivaled in their very habitat by its gleam; the Antipodes have taken this gift of the Mother Empire with gratitude.[219]

Inheriting a vast fortune after his father's death in 1904, Cochrane set about pursuing his passion for cricket. At Woodbrook, he spent £1,000 'shipping hundreds of tons of clay from Nottingham to ensure a top-class playing surface'.[220] The estate, noted Ernest Ensor, was equipped 'admirably in every way that it is perfectly suitable for a Test match'. Cochrane also 'engaged a staff of six or seven English professionals' and proceeded to challenge 'all Irish clubs'.[221] Nor did he rest content with inviting local teams. Both the Australians and South Africans on their visits to Britain played cricket matches at Woodbrook. It was in keeping with this tradition that the All-India team became Cochrane's guests.

Once again, the Indians played in 'intense' heat that would have been 'unbearable but for the light, but refreshing, breeze which wafted across the ground from the sea'.[222] The visitors lost the toss and, as usual, Baloo and Salamuddin took most of the wickets as the home side chalked up 278. In their reply, the Indian batsmen struggled against the bowling of Aubrey Faulkner, the famed googly exponent from South Africa, who had been invited to play for Cochrane's team. Only Jayaram, Shivram, and Warden countered the South African's wiles with any degree of confidence. Chasing a target of 255 in the second innings, after yet another fine bowling performance by Baloo and Salamuddin, the Indians lost the match by thirty-six runs.

★   ★   ★

The Indian cricket team's return to England coincided with the dramatic, blood-spattered climax of the labour protest that had convulsed Britain for weeks. In mid-August, barely days after the great London dock strike and the riots in Liverpool, railway workers had begun to strike in different centres. On 15 August 1911, the major railway unions issued an ultimatum calling for an immediate resolution of their outstanding issues. The government's peremptory rejection of this demand signalled the start of a nation-wide railway strike two days later. The workers' action, reported *The Times*, 'took effect in widely varying degrees on different lines and in different localities', but the overall result was a 'complete paralysis of the railway services'.[223] The scale of the general strike, and the violence that accompanied it, alarmed the government and a speedy truce was agreed with the railway unions on 19 August. The move was no doubt hastened by the news of a horrific incident the previous day at Llanelli in South Wales. When a train carrying blacklegs was attacked by striking railway workers, the troops in charge of the area shot dead two men and injured scores of others. Enraged mobs responded by rampaging through the town, ransacking shops and torching vehicles.'Bullets and bayonets, riot, pillage, fire and a great explosion marked the last phase of the strike,' reported the *Daily Mail*.[224]

Meanwhile, the Indian cricketers travelled from Belfast to Brighton to play their penultimate first-class fixture against Sussex. The scene of Ranji's most thrilling batting exploits, the Brighton ground held great symbolic significance for the visitors. Interestingly, they were bolstered by the reappearance in their ranks of Prince Shivaji Rao, who had previously turned out for them against Surrey at the Oval. The game itself turned out to be a low-scoring contest, not least because of the reappearance of traditional English weather conditions. Bowling first on a rain-affected pitch, the Indians dismissed the home side for 158, with Bulsara unexpectedly emerging as the main wicket taker. Baloo experienced one of his rare failures with the ball; but a catch he took in the slips was rated by many as 'the smartest seen at Brighton' that season.[225] Going into bat on a tricky pitch, the Indians struggled against the fast swerve and leg spin of the Sussex bowlers. Although the aggressive Mulla and the dogged Shivram put up a fight, their team was bowled out for 138. Once again, the Indian bowlers brought their team back into contention. Sussex were shot out for 149 in

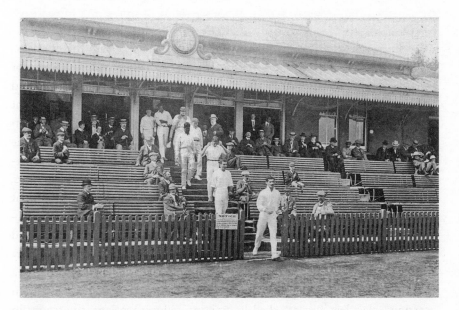

Figure 22. Led by H.D. Kanga, the Indian cricket team takes the field against Sussex County Cricket Club, Hove, August 1911. Courtesy of the Roger Mann Picture Library.

their second innings, with Warden and an ailing Baloo taking nine wickets between them. The last day's play was 'full of incident'.[226] Requiring 170 to win, the Indians appeared to be on top when the century mark was reached for the loss of only three wickets. But two quick run-outs turned the tide in favour of Sussex. A fighting innings from Salamuddin was unable to prevent the Indians from losing the match by ten runs.

It was entirely in keeping with their illogical schedule that the Indian cricketers were forced to return to the west coast for the final match of their long tour. Bristol was yet another venue with historic significance for the Indians: the home turf of the greatest English cricketer of the Victorian age as well as the most entertaining batsman of the Edwardian era. The awe-struck Indians had already met the legendary W.G. Grace at Catford during their match against Kent. But the match against Gloucestershire offered them their first sighting of Gilbert Jessop. The home side won the toss and elected to bat, but a rain delay at the outset meant that it was late afternoon when the great man walked out to bat. The Indians, noted one correspondent, 'must have felt keenly interested in the famous cricketer as he took his stand at the wickets. They were anxious to see him bat—this had been openly said—but they did not want too many runs from him'.[227] As it turned out, Jessop was in a curiously subdued mood and took forty minutes to score twenty-four runs. 'The Indian players must have been very surprised at this form, having, no doubt, anticipated hitting of the hurricane order,' noted the match report.[228] The rest of the Gloucestershire batsmen did not distinguish themselves and a fine bowling performance by Warden, who took eight wickets, allowed the Indians to restrict the home team to 252.

When it was their turn to bat, the Indians put on a display that would have gratified Jessop. The Parsi opening duo of Kanga and Meherhomji gave the visitors a good start with a flawless century partnership. The latter, in particular, played a dazzling array of shots and scored his first century against one of the recognized teams in the county championship. The remaining batsmen made useful contributions, the most noteworthy being a fluent eighty-eight by Shivram. As a result, the Indians were able to take a lead of 112 on the first innings. Chastened by the leather hunt they had been subjected to, the Gloucestershire batsmen played with greater resolve in the second innings. Set an improbable 268 to win on the final afternoon, the Indians soon found themselves in desperate straits when their sixth wicket fell with the score on forty-six. Yet again, it was

a Palwankar who came to their rescue: a fighting innings by Baloo
ensured a face-saving draw for his team.

VIII

As the shadows lengthened at Bristol on the final afternoon of the Indians'
tour, public attention across the country was riveted on Northampton,
where a team of underdogs was about to overturn the established order of
English cricket. The last Saturday of August 1911 was the opening day of a
county match between Northamptonshire and Warwickshire. A late summer fixture between these two teams in a normal year would scarcely have
merited the attention of cricket watchers. But the summer of 1911 had been
anything but normal and it was on the basis of this match that the fate of the
county championship was about to be decided that year. With fifteen victories in nineteen games and a winning percentage of 72.63, Warwickshire, for
long one of the weakest first-class counties, was assured of the imaginary
trophy if it defeated the home team.[229] By close of play on the first day, the
leaders had virtually sealed the fate of the match. After bowling out
Northamptonshire for seventy-three, Warwickshire secured a commanding
lead. Two days later, their team conclusively won the match by an innings
and thirty-three runs and were crowned the kings of English cricket.

'Warwickshire, once despised and forlorn, are champions,' exulted the
Birmingham Gazette.[230] Even *The Times*, not given to outbursts of enthusiasm, admitted that 'a more astonishing and at the same time more creditable
result has never been seen in the whole history of county cricket'.[231] When
the Warwickshire team returned to Birmingham's New Street Station, 'the
city turned out to welcome the champions'.[232] 'The team was driven in
taxi-cabs decorated with the county colours to the Grand Hotel, where an
informal reception was held,' reported one newspaper. 'The streets were
everywhere lined with people, and the progress to the hotel was marked by
the wildest enthusiasm on the part of the thousands of spectators.'[233]
'Birmingham, which cared nothing for cricket, has become cricket-mad,'
marvelled a local newspaper.[234]

For some observers, Warwickshire's triumph was symbolic of the unusual
summer of 1911. 'A season which in the all-important weather has been
utterly unlike its immediate predecessors was bound to produce notable
changes in the character of the game and the position of the counties,'

remarked the *Manchester Guardian*. The paper pointed to Warwickshire's 'dramatic transformation' as proof of the 'higher class of play' that had marked that summer's county cricket: 'Last year they were third from the bottom, today they are at the head, and they are there as the result of consistently good play.'[235] However, others drew a different conclusion from this unexpected outcome. 'The championship has been revolving in a circle, as if the honours were the exclusive property of a small corporation,' declared the *Athletic News*. Warwickshire's victory would 'by the force of example encourage those who have been unfortunate to take heart in the fight. It is not for the good of the game that the prizes should be monopolised'.[236]

One wonders what the Indian cricketers, as they prepared to depart British shores, would have made of that sentiment.

10

Beyond the Boundary

I

On 6 December 1909, there took place a well-attended dinner at the Authors' Club in London. The chief guest that evening was F.S. Jackson and the topic for discussion was 'Imperial Cricket'. Before the proceedings began, the chairman read out a letter from Sir Arthur Conan Doyle, who was unable to attend the event, but wrote that 'the guest, the company, and the subject would be all equally to my taste'. Jackson began his speech by stressing how it was 'vital to our existence as a great Empire that the bonds with our people across the seas should be drawn as closely as possible together'. Cricket, he noted, was spreading through the empire 'at a most extraordinary rate'. After pointing to the firm hold the game had established in Australasia and South Africa, the future Governor of Bengal drew his audience's attention to the 'probability of a team coming over from India consisting of Hindoos, Mahomedans, and Parsees'. For this Yorkshireman, 'it was an awful prospect to think of an Indian team coming over here composed of eleven Ranjis'.[1]

As we have seen, however, the Indian cricket team that eventually arrived in Britain struggled to make a mark on the imperial playing fields. Nonetheless, Jackson's remarks show how sporting tours in the age of empire carried symbolic meanings that went beyond the boundary. The Indian cricket tour was the latest in a series of politically charged sporting visits from the colonies to the United Kingdom in the Edwardian era. The decade leading up to the arrival of the Indians had seen journeys to the imperial centre by three Australian cricket teams (1902, 1905, and 1909), the legendary 'All Blacks' team from New Zealand (1905), three South African cricket teams (1901, 1904, and 1907), the first Springbok rugby team (1906–7), and two West Indian cricket teams (1900 and 1906). Many observers saw such visits as a valuable means of forging fraternity within the empire. One writer declared:[2]

> Colonial Conferences and Parliaments of Premiers are all very well in their way, but it is the sympathies of the common people as expressed in the football and cricket fields that draws heart to heart. And so it is that every visit to this country of Australians, South Africans, Parsees, and West Indians welds another link in the chain that binds us all together.

Significantly, the Indian cricketers' visit, coinciding as it did with the coronation, became an occasion for public reflections on the Raj. As the representatives of Britain's most valuable colonial possession, these sporting tourists were viewed through the lens of imperial fraternity, loyalism, and the 'civilizing mission'. At the same time, the response to the tour in sections of the press generated dissonances that undercut the goodwill that its publicists hoped to promote. And although the Indian cricketers were no longer regarded as curiosities on the sporting field, Orientalist assumptions about their playing skills inflected the reporting of their matches. However, while the visitors were received with great cordiality at every centre they visited, the popular attendance at their matches belied the high expectations that the tour's organizers had entertained at the start of the long, hot summer of 1911.

II

The visits of colonial sportsmen to Britain were an occasion for their hosts to affirm the role of sport in strengthening the bonds of empire. From the outset of the Indian cricketers' tour, British commentators highlighted the imperial significance of their venture. This had much to do with the fact that their presence was acknowledged by the new king-emperor. Although George V was unable to keep his promise to watch the Indians play at Lord's, the Prince of Wales and his brother attended the match as the monarch's representatives. It was a gesture that was widely reported in the British press and, at one stroke, elevated the political significance of the tour. 'Apart from the Delhi Durbar and the part played by India in the Coronation festivities our Oriental Dominion this year claims attention in a fashion that is likely to make a special appeal to the ordinary sport-loving Englishman. For the first time a team of cricketers thoroughly representative of the Dependency is visiting this country,' noted one newspaper.[3]

Some observers swiftly appropriated the first Indian cricket team as a *British* imperial project to unite on the sporting field an ancient land riven by mutually warring castes and communities. 'For many years,' claimed a writer in *Health and Strength*,

> *Englishmen have deemed* [my italics] that a representative team should come over here, but there have always been difficulties in the matter of caste, etc. Anyhow, it has at last been found possible to persuade Mohammedan, Hindu, and Parsee to join forces and come over to England to show us what advances the game has made throughout our Indian Empire.

Naturally, this account chose to extoll Lord Harris, 'who, when he went to Bombay, gave a great impetus to the game by personally playing with the natives'. Indeed, the writer even took recourse to fiction to sustain his dubious assertion. In this version of events, confronted with 'a tremendous outcry' in the Indian press about his support for the game, Harris declared: 'All men are equal on the cricket field.' 'So now, a dozen years after this courageous defiance of convention, Lord Harris's example has borne fruit,' the writer claimed. Moreover, the team itself, he assured his readers, was 'carefully selected by Captain Greig, the brilliant Hampshire batsman'.[4] Unsurprisingly, there was no scope in this narrative for the first Indian cricket team to be anything other than an imperial initiative.

Others regarded the visiting Indian cricketers as an example of this uniquely Anglo-Saxon sport's innate capacity to generate fraternity. 'The present team from our Indian Empire is made up of Hindoos, Mohammedans, Sikhs, and Parsees, and affords an excellent example of the unifying influence of cricket all over the world,' noted an editorial in one newspaper.[5] Pelham Warner reiterated the same theme:

> There is a case in point of the extraordinary power the game has over its votaries in this matter of sinking all prejudices and dislike, real or imaginary, in the tour in the United Kingdom of a team from India composed of men of all castes and creeds. I make so bold as to say that this travelling and living together of natives of various castes and creeds will have far-reaching effect in India.[6]

These remarks also echoed similar comments by Edward Sewell:

> The peculiar characteristics of our national game for creating good fellowship for starting and cementing lifelong friendships, and for bringing bodies together which hitherto had been asunder as the poles, have never had a finer chance of asserting themselves than during the next three months. Time was when a Parsee cricketer merely smirked when you spoke of a Mahometan or

a Hindu cricketer. Such a being was not on his map at all, non-existent. Since then the followers of Zoroaster have crossed swords with those of Mahomet. The gentle Hindu has also come along since the day when the Parsee XI was all powerful on the Bombay maidan, and triangular tournaments have taken place at that salubrious spot. Thus does the West once again take its lead from the East.[7]

For yet others, the Indian cricket tour showed that athletic games in general were a valuable instrument of imperial soft power. 'There are not many links which unite Europeans and Orientals,' averred J.E.C. Welldon, the dean of Manchester (and formerly the bishop of Calcutta and headmaster of Harrow). 'May it not be hoped that games such as cricket and football, which have done so much to create a sympathetic feeling between Great Britain and her colonies, may help to bridge the gulf, which must always to some extent spread, between Europeans and natives in India?'[8]

Some observers highlighted the composition of the Indian cricket team, with its mixture of 'princes as well as less exalted players', as an example of the unique bifurcation of political sovereignty in India. 'How many Birmingham folk,' asked one widely read daily in that city, 'are conscious that there are really two Indias—that there are more than 62 ½ millions of Indians who are not British subjects at all?' This other India, noted the *Birmingham Daily Mail*, was ruled by 'princes and chiefs, who acknowledge fealty to the British Government as the dominant and protecting Power in India'. The visit of an Indian cricket team led by a princely captain was thus seen as an occasion for 'ordinary Englishmen to appreciate the great distinction that has to be made between the two Indias'.[9]

Much of the early press coverage of the tour centred on the princely participants in this historic cricket tour. 'These Indians are very distinguished and picturesque folk whatever the value of their cricket may be,' remarked the *Birmingham Gazette*. The paper went on to describe these royal cricketers for the benefit of its readers:

> First and foremost there is the 'skipper' of the All-Indian team—His Highness Maharajadhiraja Bhupinder Singh Bahadur of Patiala. He is a full-blooded Indian noble whose ancestor Phul, the successor of Baryam, held high office in the court of the Emperor Baber in 1526. His Highness enjoys a salute of seventeen guns and is entitled to be received and visited by the Viceroy. The All-India team also includes Prince Sivaji Rao Gaekwar of Baroda. He is not of course, *the* Gaekwar of Baroda, who is a mighty Indian potentate. The cricketing prince is the younger son of Sir Sayaji Rao, who, by the way, is now in London for the Coronation. There is yet another Prince with the team, the

son and heir of Colonel, his Highness Maharaja Sir Nripendra Narayan Bhup Bahadur of Kuch Behar. He comes of the same Rajput stock from which Ranjitsinhji is descended, a stock described by Colonel Tod as 'the Normans of India.'[10]

The inclusion of Prince Hitendra Narayan in this list (presumably because he had played for Somerset the previous year) suggests that the press was happy to embellish reality to arouse public interest in the Indian cricketers' tour.

As its captain, the Maharaja of Patiala received most of the media attention that was directed at the Indian team in Britain. A number of accounts stressed Bhupinder Singh's status as a key ally of the Raj. 'He comes of an old fighting stock that has always been loyal to British rule,' pointed out the *Manchester Guardian*.[11] An old India hand sought to enlighten the public at home about the crucial role played by Bhupinder's ancestors in shoring up British rule in north India during the rebellion of 1857. In a letter to the *Daily Mail*, the former civil servant and Liberal politician William Plowden reminded readers that

Among the many distinguished Indian princes now in England none has more claims on the consideration of the people of this country than the young Maharajah of Patiala. His love of sport, not unusual among his compatriots of similar age and rank, and specially his appearing here captaining an Indian cricket team, in addition to a remarkably good polo team, will bring him much in evidence, and those who are brought into touch with him will fully appreciate the simplicity and geniality of his character. But it is as the descendant of Maharajah Narendur Singh, the ruler of the Pattiala principality in the troublous times of 1857, that his claim on the British people are most conspicuous. Had it not been for the loyal example set by Narendur Singh on May 13, 1857, the strong Sikh battalion, 1,600 men, Sikhs officered entirely by Sikhs, employed by us as military police at Ambala and Loodhiana, would have joined the mutinous Pandehs of the Bengal army, bringing a most hostile influence against us, not only in the Cis Sutlej, where the regiment was quartered, but also in the Trans-Sutlej and the Manjha, the great recruiting ground of our Sikh regiments. But for the action of the Maharajah of Pattiala, the brilliant example he set to the other great chiefs of the Cis-Sutlej—Jheend and Nabha— and his influence on Ranjeet Singh's old regiment, which as was afterwards known, was waiting to learn what the Sikh chiefs of the Cis-Sutlej would do, we should have had the warlike populations of the Punjab on our backs, and advance against Delhi would have been impossible. Under God's Providence it is to the Maharajah of Pattiala we owed our ability to break the neck of the great Indian Mutiny before reinforcements from England reached India.[12]

★ ★ ★

Fraternity and loyalism were not the only lenses through which contemporaries viewed the Indian cricketers' tour. As with the Parsi cricketing visits a quarter of a century earlier, some also held up their visit as proof of the success of the British 'civilizing mission' in the subcontinent. 'India has adopted many English institutions but to none perhaps except the umbrella, the beloved companion of both the babu and the ryot, has it taken more warmly than to cricket,' remarked one writer in the *Manchester Guardian*. 'The Maidan of Calcutta on a winter day looks like an English park. There are cricket pitches in abundance and, as in England, any group of urchins who can get possession of a stick and a ball will play happily with imaginary wickets.'[13]

Moreover, as we have seen, the Indian cricket tour was seen by its imperial promoters as an educational enterprise. In keeping with the idea of sport as pedagogy, the organizers in Britain drew up a challenging tour schedule to test the stamina and skill of the Indian cricketers. Being pitted at the outset against superior opponents, it was argued, would help improve the colonial visitors' standards of play and thereby, make them better cricketers. It was a view shared by many in the British press. 'The promoters knew well enough that Indian cricket was much below the standard of first-class cricket in England,' remarked the *Athletic News*, 'but they undoubtedly did a wise thing when they suggested that a strong programme should be arranged.'[14] 'They came over to learn something about cricket, and they will go back with plenty of illustrations of how it should be played,' agreed 'Free Critic' in the *Umpire*.[15]

The portrayal of the Indian cricketers as pupils stood in stark contrast to the way teams from the self-governing dominions were represented in the late Edwardian era. From their very first visit to the Mother Country in 1878, the white Australian cricketers had conclusively established that they were a force to reckon with on the sporting field. As a result, they were treated as equals when they toured Britain. The Australian cricketers, one writer remarked, were 'foemen worthy of our best willow blades'.[16] This was also the case with the first 'All Blacks' rugby team, whose performances had shown that these colonial sportsmen had little to learn from their metropolitan hosts. Likewise, after their sporting visits in 1906 and 1907, the South Africans too came to be seen as worthy opponents in rugby and cricket.

Significantly, many in Britain believed that it was the hosts who had much to learn from their overseas kinsmen. 'During visits of foreign teams we find that however good we may previously have thought ourselves there are others just as good if not better,' wrote one English commentator in 1909. 'These tours help to broaden our views and that most certainly assists the game generally by inducing a more generous spirit of the deeds of the visiting team, whether it be from Australia, South Africa, or America.' On the cricket pitch, this writer argued, both the Australians and South Africans had 'taught us something'. The Australians had shown 'the value of fast break-bowling' and 'how to place the field'; the South Africans 'showed us the real efficacy of good "googlie" bowling which we before only half suspected, and had regarded only as freak bowling, a passing fancy which would retire from the game with its inventor'.[17]

Unlike the sporting teams from the dominions, the Indian cricketers were not seen to pose a challenge on the field of play. The imperial hosts could thus adopt a tone of paternal indulgence towards these unthreatening colonial visitors. 'They have come over without any attempt at booming themselves, and the consequence is they are in need of a little advertisement,' wrote 'Old Shako' in the *Daily News* at the start of their tour. 'The point I wish to emphasise is that if they are losing matches the public must not stay away on that account. Their cricket is excellent in spirit, if it does not prove to be so in the result.'[18]

Before long, however, the poor showing of the Indian cricketers began to attract sharp criticism in some quarters. 'So far the Indians have not won a first-class match, and it must be admitted that they are hardly better than some of our second-class counties,' declared one newspaper in late June.[19] Some went further and suggested that the visitors were not even 'the equals of a second-class county team'.[20] Others felt that the Indians 'have obviously quite a lot to learn ere they can be regarded as competent to tackle the full strength of our leading counties with any real hope of success'.[21] 'The peninsula cannot yet send us a great team, in spite of the fact that they once sent us a great—some say the greatest—cricketer,' concluded yet another disappointed critic.[22]

The plight of the Indian cricket team also moved one letter writer in the *Daily Mail* to wonder if 'it would be more encouraging to our visitors, and also make some of the games more interesting, if the stronger counties turned out purely amateur teams in opposition to them?'[23] 'The Chiel', a British correspondent writing in the *Madras Mail*, was far more scathing:

> The mournful procession known as the tour of the Indian cricket team wends its weary way gladdening the hearts of English bowlers with an eye on the analyses table. As the date approached for the arrival of the 'Urri Whatfors', as

someone has nicknamed Mr. Kanga's team, bowlers might be seen smacking their chops in the vicinity of the players' dressing rooms, and eyeing each Indian much after the manner in which a panther having discovered a goat tied with rope to a tree lies and gloats after making the fatal final rush. The plain truth must now be told that the rupees spent on giving these estimable gentlemen a sight of the Coronation, and of the pavilions of the United Kingdom, would have been much better spent in having a good English team out to India.[24]

For some critics, the fault lay not so much with the Indian team as the promoters of the tour. 'There is no doubt that our dusky visitors were absurdly and deliberately over-praised, by men who should have known the truth, before they arrived,' averred one newspaper. 'What has been the result? People looked for a good team, and saw a side which failed again and again in every department of the game.'[25] Others blamed the unreasonably taxing schedule for the Indian cricket team's failures. The London correspondent of the *Times of India* reported that 'the opinion has become firmly established that a less ambitious programme ought to have been arranged for their tour'. 'That they have come here to learn from their opponents rather than with the expectation of winning a lot of games is generally appreciated but it must be rather depressing for them to be outclassed in match after match,' he remarked.[26]

As the defeats piled up, questions also began to be raised about the MCC's decision to award 'first-class' status to matches featuring the Indian cricketers. 'Ought the Indians' matches to count as first-class?' queried the Reverend Holmes in the columns of *Cricket*. 'It is ridiculous for a first-class county to play full strength against them,' he griped.[27] A similar sentiment about the colonial visitors was voiced by the cricket correspondent of the *Sheffield Daily Telegraph*, who agreed that it was 'more and more apparent that the first-class qualification bestowed on them was a mistake'.[28]

Such remarks appeared unwarranted and unfair to more sympathetic observers. 'Failure should not be jeered at,' admonished the editor of *Cricket*. The Indian cricketers, he argued, were 'here to learn'. 'On the testimony of those who have played against them in their own country they possess considerable ability, which a tour like this is likely to develop. But a section of the Press persists in judging them by the standard of Australian and South African teams, and setting them down as duffers,' he lamented.[29] Rebutting their critics, this influential commentator argued that the Indian cricketers' performance had by no means been 'so weak as to justify an objection to the M.C.C.'s decision that their matches with first-class sides should rank as first-class'.[30] 'Old Shako' in the *Daily News* similarly took umbrage at the suggestion that the English first-class counties should field only amateurs against the Indian cricket team. 'In short,' he wrote, 'to please some people, we should insult our visitors by patronising them, and at the same time destroy one of the main objects of the tour—its educational mission.'[31] For, he contended, 'we should not teach them a great deal if we brought the quality of the opposition down to their present level'.[32]

The Indian cricketers, for their part, found highly useful the pedagogical rhetoric of their imperial hosts. Aware that they faced an uphill task, they drew on the idea of their cricket tour as a learning exercise to manage the expectations of the metropolitan audience. Homi Kanga made this amply clear in a newspaper interview at the very outset of their tour. 'It is true,' he said, 'that we want to win all our matches if we can. But it is the educational side which is the more important. We have men who can assimilate things, and who can teach the younger men when they get back.'[33] And as the Indians lost time and again in the first weeks of the tour, Kanga and Divecha repeatedly stressed the educational character of their tour in order to negate criticism in the British press. Moreover, aware of the powerful hold of amateurism in Britain's elite sporting culture, they highlighted their own status as cricketers who played for pleasure rather than profit. 'Our team,' Divecha told one newspaper, 'is a purely sporting team. There is no monetary side to it. We are out for experience, for completing our education.'[34]

As a result, the Indians won over the British press by the 'sporting' way in which they accepted their reverses. 'These Indian cricketers are a bright lot of boys, all good natured, anxious to learn and anxious to do their best in somewhat trying circumstances. Their defeats they regard philosophically and with the saving grace of humour,' gushed one reporter.[35] 'Whatever differences of opinion may prevail as to the wisdom of placing the matches with the All-Indian team in the first-class rank, all sportsmen will admire the philosophical spirit in which our Eastern visitors have so far accepted their continuous defeats,' agreed 'Old Ebor' in the *Yorkshire Evening Post*. Nor was this all. If a result of the tour, he reflected, 'is to increase—as it well may—the respect which the British and Indian races feel for each other, will the tour, with all its losses, have been undertaken in vain? Thoughtful men will give only one answer to that question'.[36]

These words were penned a few days before the Indians broke their run of defeats at Leicester. The news of their subsequent triumphs was greeted with pleasure by the sporting press in Britain. 'The Indian cricketers have at last got into their stride, and have recently been winning matches with as much regularity as they previously lost them,' said the *Athletic News*. 'We rejoice in their success, for it cannot fail to have a good effect.' The paper also declared that the Indian cricket team was 'a far better one than has generally been supposed'.[37] Similar sentiments were also expressed in other newspapers. 'During the past twenty-four hours,' reported the English cricket correspondent of the *Times of India* after the tourists' consecutive wins at Leicester and Taunton, 'I have heard many expressions of genuine pleasure that the Indians, after ten consecutive defeats have struggled out of the rut to such good purpose as to defeat two first-class counties.' Even more praiseworthy, he pointed out, was their stoicism in the face of adversity. Throughout their 'rather protracted period of failure, they never became in the least dispirited, they held bravely to the contention that they had come to England to be educated in cricket, and expected to be chastised in the course of learning'.[38] Thus, by playing the role of exemplary pupils, who uncomplainingly accepted the punishment meted out to them, the Indian cricketers succeeded in defanging their critics.

III

A group of Australian Aboriginals was the first non-white cricket team to tour Britain. This pioneering venture featured a remarkable cast of thirteen indigenous cricketers drawn from the Wimmera region of western Victoria. Coached and captained by Charles Lawrence, a former Surrey player who was part of the first English cricket tour of Australia, the Aboriginal team arrived in Britain in the summer of 1868. Advertised by the tour's promoters as the sporting representatives of a 'Stone Age' race that was on the verge of becoming extinct, these cricketers aroused a great deal of curiosity among the British press and public. The Aboriginal visitors took part in a gruelling schedule of forty-seven matches that lasted from May to October 1868. The team acquitted itself reasonably, winning fourteen matches and losing the same number against opposing sides that, for the most part, were just below 'first-class' standard. It also possessed in its ranks two cricketers—Johnny Mullagh and Johnny Cuzens—who were rated highly by their opponents. On the whole, however, the visitors' proficiency in cricket aroused mixed reactions. Instead, it was their display of indigenous martial prowess that amazed the critics and attracted the crowds. The tour's white managers had cannily sought to tap into the British public's growing appetite for spectacles involving exotic racial imports. On the final day of every cricket match, therefore, they included a variety of events that showcased the Aboriginals' astonishing skills with a variety of weapons. The 'sham fights' with spears that the team members staged in their specially designed costumes—'black skin-tight leggings and short drawers of opossum skin'—kept the turnstiles busy that summer. The Aboriginal team also put on boomerang displays that mesmerized the crowds. Another electrifying performance involved one of their players, Dick-a-Dick, armed with little more than a club and a shield, parrying cricket balls repeatedly flung at him by spectators standing at a short distance. The visitors also injected a martial touch into their cricket, taking to the field with a loud war cry. Accentuating the 'primitivist elements' of Aboriginal culture and emphasizing their racial difference yielded the tour's white promoters handsome profits. But it also reinforced the widespread tendency in late Victorian Britain to regard any non-whites playing the game as a curiosity.[39]

Two decades later, the touring Parsi cricketers in late Victorian Britain did not venture to showcase any sporting skills other than cricket. But they too were viewed as unnatural exponents of this Anglo-Saxon game. 'Among the curiosities of modern cricket, second only in interest to the tour of aboriginal Australians many years ago,' wrote one English journalist in 1888, 'must be reckoned the tours in England of Parsee amateurs from the Presidency of Bombay.' This writer reflected the popular consensus when he remarked that 'it would be mere affectation to pretend that any cricket interest attaches to their doings. No doubt a good many people will go to see them play from curiosity to ascertain for themselves how a purely Eastern race acquit themselves at a game which is almost the exclusive property of the Anglo-Saxons'.[40]

The Indian cricket tour of Britain in 1911 was the last by a non-white team before the outbreak of the First World War. However, by the time they visited the country, an important shift had taken place in British popular attitudes towards the cricketing aptitude of non-white races. The metropolitan public could no longer take it for granted that the latter would be mere curiosities on the cricket field. A major reason for this change in popular perceptions was undoubtedly the dramatic cricketing career of Ranjitsinhji. His dazzling feats with the bat disrupted prevailing assumptions about cricket and race in late Victorian Britain. Unlike the Australian Aboriginals and the Bombay Parsis, the Indian prince's cricketing ability could neither be doubted nor disparaged. Indeed, it was apparent to everyone who watched Ranji that his playing skills were far superior to that of most Englishmen. In disturbing the fundamental racial assumption that yoked together cricket and English identity, Ranji presented his white audience with a fundamental conundrum. If cricket was an 'Anglo-Saxon' game, how was it that a native from India was able to outshine Englishmen at it? One index of the importance accorded to this question in the imperial public sphere was the reams of newsprint devoted to analysing Ranji's physical attributes, bodily deportment, and style of play.[41] Even though the Indian Prince had not been seen on an English cricket ground since the summer of 1908, many in Britain yearned for yet another glimpse of his magic. Indeed, some writers even believed that 'if this wizard of the bat were to return into our midst and voluntarily walk out to the wicket, he would once more expose our inferiority, his forty years notwithstanding'.[42]

Unsurprisingly, then, there was universal regret that Ranji was unable to lead the first Indian cricket tour of Britain. 'It is a great pity his Highness the Jam Sahib of Nawanagar was not able to captain the team,' lamented one newspaper. 'His presence, his wonderful skill, and his still more wonderful knowledge of the game would have enormously strengthened the cricketing quality of the side.' 'Ranji,' the paper added, 'would not only have "electrified" the crowd as he did on so many occasions, but he would have instilled the fullest possible confidence in every member of the team in regard to their cricketing prowess.'[43] Moreover, as *The Times* presciently noted in its preview of the cricket season, the Jam Saheb's 'tremendous skills as a batsman will very likely lead the public to be on the lookout to see if his mantle may not have fallen on the others of his race'.[44] Indeed, for the cognoscenti and the crowd alike, the principal attraction of the Indian cricket tour of Britain was the possibility that it might yield another 'Ranji'.

Several candidates presented themselves for this role over the course of that summer. One 'potential Ranji' identified by the metropolitan press was Prince Shivaji Rao of Baroda. 'He can be an excellent bat, especially against good bowling, and the way he places a ball on the middle stump round to square leg with the least possible amount of energy—merely a shake of the wrists—is reminiscent of the Jam of Nawanagar at his best,' enthused the *Manchester Guardian*.[45] A sentiment echoed by *Athletic News*, which believed that the prince possessed 'the polished grace of the Oriental cricketer'.[46] However, not all were convinced that Shivaji Rao was ready as yet to fill Ranji's shoes. 'His batting shows not a little genius, but it is surely premature to compare him, as some newspapers have done, with Ranjitsinhji,' cautioned *Cricket.* 'In the field he is not, at present, particularly agile, while his running between wickets could be improved.'[47] Moreover, the prince was said to be mercurial at the wicket. 'One day he will bat like a consummate artist; the next he will shape like a mere beginner,' grumbled the *Bystander.*[48]

Prior to his arrival in the country, Bhupinder Singh, too, was viewed as a future Ranji. Informing its readers that the Indian prince was 'known among Anglo-Indians as Ranji the Second', one paper claimed that he held 'the record of having secured twenty-one runs in eight minutes against the Bombay Parsees'.[49] However, after watching him on the field for the first time at Oxford, others were reminded of another English cricket icon. A headline in the *Daily Express* ran: 'New Prince of Cricket—Maharaja Who Looks Like W.G.' The accompanying story noted that 'while he is at the wicket he bears an extraordinary likeness to Dr. W.G. Grace. His figure is the figure of the Prince of Cricket, his dark beard from a distance lends colour to the likeness, and there were many on the ground yesterday who commented on the fact'.[50] But it was hard to shake off the shadow of the Jam Saheb, and this writer found himself reminiscing about the 'days when Prince Ranjitsinhji was among us'. His description of Bhupinder's batting was no doubt calculated to evoke memories of Ranji: 'The ball comes from his bat quicker than the eye can follow it. In fact, there are times when one hardly realises that the prince has moved, such is the rapidity with which he makes his strokes.'[51]

Their erratic appearances during the Indian tour meant that neither Shivaji Rao nor Bhupinder Singh was able to live up to their billing as the next Oriental cricketing wizard. The metropolitan press turned, therefore, to the commoners in the team in its quest for intimations of Oriental magic. Mistry's dazzling batting at Lord's drew the inevitable comparisons with Ranji. 'Whatever the amount of success destined to attend the efforts of the Indian Team,' declared one writer after the Lord's match, 'most certain it is that in Major Keki Manikji Mistri the side possesses a brilliant batsman who is worth a place in almost any side.'[52] But some observers were also quick to note that this left hander had his own distinctive style. 'From Indian batsmen one expects flicks of the wrist and fine cutting,' noted the *Times*, 'but one was surprised to see that Major Mistri's strength lay as much in really powerful driving as in anything else.'[53] After the Parsi batsman disappeared from the tour, the press proceeded to identify Meherhomji and Shivram as possible contenders for the title of the 'second Ranji'.

But as the weeks passed, the British media grew increasingly frustrated in its search for the next Oriental magician. 'One unconsciously judges Indian cricket by "Ranji's" standard,' remarked the *Manchester Guardian*, 'but with the exception of the batting of Shivram, which was faintly reminiscent of the willowy wrist play that "Ranji" used to delight us with, there was nothing to recall the great Indian cricketer.'[54] The *Leeds Mercury* was more astringent, declaring that none of the Indian cricketers was 'worthy, in a cricket sense, to black "Ranji's" boots; no one, indeed, who stood out above his fellows in a combination of mediocrities'.[55]

★   ★   ★

The British press did not only view the Indian cricketers in relation to the absent Ranji. They also evaluated the merits of individual players according to contemporary cricketing standards. Thus regarded, too, these colonial sporting pupils were found wanting. Interestingly, press reports did not, by and large, seek recourse to explicitly racist ideas in describing and assessing the Indian players. References to race in media representations of the colonial visitors mostly consisted of casual allusions to their skin colour—'dusky' being the favoured adjective—and the predictable invocation of prevailing stereotypes about the wristy, but impulsive, Oriental.

Of the three principal cricketing skills, it was the quality of their bowling that critics found most praiseworthy about the Indians. In this art, according to the *Birmingham Gazette*, the visitors had 'nothing to learn from us'.[56] Although Warden and Salamuddin occasionally drew praise for their efforts, it was the indefatigable Palwankar Baloo who consistently impressed observers. Without exception, English commentators were quick to laud his subtle modulations of pace and flight. After his first appearance at Oxford, *The Times* noted that of all the Indian bowlers, Baloo 'seemed to be the most difficult, as he changes his pace cleverly'.[57] 'Among the bowlers Baloo is quite first-rate,' stated the *Manchester Guardian*. 'He has a complete mastery of spin and break, and he varies his pace and length very cleverly.'[58] 'Baloo is unquestionably a fine bowler. His length is generally excellent, and he turns them from the leg, as so many left-handers do,' agreed the *Staffordshire Advertiser*.[59] The comment is particularly interesting as this reporter watched Baloo and Barnes bowl in the same match. That he could hold his own against a man universally regarded as one of the all-time greats is perhaps the most irrefutable testimony of this remarkable Dalit bowler's prowess. But it was not simply Baloo's command over his craft that attracted comment; critics were equally impressed by his staggering capacity to bowl for long spells throughout that hot summer. According to the *Athletic News*, he gave 'the impression that he could bowl and bowl without becoming tired'.[60]

On the other hand, the abject display of the Indian batsmen against the English first-class counties drew a great deal of criticism. This is not surprising given the inflated public expectation at the outset that they would play like Ranji. Even Sewell, who was otherwise cautious in sizing up the visitors, had unwittingly fuelled such comparisons. 'The batting is, as usual with natives of India, noticeable for wrist-work and eye-work. This was so remarkable in the play of Ranjitsinhji, and is merely typical of the race,' he wrote at the start of their tour.[61] But as the Indian batsmen began to flail against the fast-pace swerve and googlies of English bowlers, the press repeatedly castigated them for capitulating feebly against their opponents. 'It has been a charge against the All India Team during their tour in this country that their batting has shown a lack of backbone,' cavilled the *Yorkshire Post*.[62] 'The side as a whole battled like a well-coached public school eleven in a rather poor year,' was the damning verdict of another newspaper.[63]

It was regarded as a self-evident truth by many in the metropolitan press that 'the discipline of self-restraint' was the defining feature of English cricket. Moreover, 'real cricket' was seen to call for 'continuous self-denial for the sake of the side'.[64] Some observers saw the Indians' desperate batting tactics in the early encounters as evidence that they did not possess the calm temperament of Anglo-Saxon cricketers. After watching them struggle, one correspondent felt that 'they lacked the power to remain cool in a crisis'. 'The Indians, regarded collectively, are the quickest starters in England at the present time,' remarked this writer, and advised them to cultivate 'the power of restraint'.[65] Yet when the Indian batsmen played circumspectly after the debacle at Lord's, they were criticized for their lack of manly initiative. 'Their batting was very unenterprising and painfully tedious,' complained one reporter. 'Talk about the slowness of the batting having done much to decrease interest in county cricket, why the Indians would, with their tactics, do much to kill the game in a very short time,' exclaimed another critic.[66] Yet other commentators were critical of the Indian batmen's lack of 'co-operation and understanding' at the crease.[67] 'The playing batsman on more than one occasion stood at his wicket watching the ball, while his colleague was vainly calling him for a run,' noted the *Manchester Guardian*.[68]

However, press opinions about the Indian batting changed considerably by the end of their tour. Jack Hobbs was one of the first English observers to predict that the Indian team possessed 'batsmen who are far above the ordinary, and given the best plumb wickets they ought to make a great number of runs'.[69] Less than two weeks later, their strong batting performance at Leicester amply bore out the Surrey professional's assessment. After watching Kanga and Meherhomji bat, a local reporter wrote that both men 'revealed batting qualities of an exceedingly high standard'. 'They cut, drove, and hit to leg with all the skill of our greatest masters of the game,' observed this writer. As the Indian batsmen began to redeem themselves, such comments became more frequent in the press. 'We have seen many worse batsmen than Meherhomji and Jaya Ram representing England in her contests with the strength of the Antipodes,' remarked one journalist.[70] 'There was no uncertainty in the batting,' noted a local Bristol newspaper after the Indians had piled up runs against Gloucestershire. 'Moreover,' it added, 'their timing was so accurate that the ball was rarely lifted, and very few chances were given.'[71]

What about the Indians' fielding? 'Temperaments differ according to nationality and the same abstract qualities are expressed in different ways in different countries. But the index of a cricketer is common to all lands and we know quite well what we mean as a smart and alert fieldsman,' declared the *Sportsman*. These remarks were made in the context of the 1906 West Indian cricket tour of England and were pointedly directed at some of the allegedly 'listless' black players in the side.[72] Similar criticism was voiced about the Indian cricketers. 'It has come as a huge surprise to me to learn that the fielding of the All-India team is their weakest point,' reported 'Free Critic' after their first match at Oxford.[73] But a deeper perusal of the match reports reveals that assessments of the Indian cricketers' fielding were bewilderingly contradictory. For instance, the *Manchester Guardian* commented after their match at Old Trafford that the Indian fielders did not 'anticipate a stroke and run into meet the ball' and that their throwing was 'both feeble and inaccurate'. 'Occasionally a smart bit of ground fielding and a good throw in would be seen, but on the whole the work was very poor, and the number of catches missed would have broken the hearts of bowlers who were not philosophers or inured to disappointment,' agreed the *Leeds Mercury* after the visitors' poor showing at Hull.[74] On the other hand, the *Birmingham Gazette* observed that the Indians possessed

as clever a body of fielders as will be found in this or any country. Whether running in, full tilt or waiting for the ball to come to them, they pick up remarkably well, and with a continuous action they pick and thrown in, a feature of their work which does not give the batsmen much chance to get a run for the throw.[75]

'The visitors fielded magnificently, and the clever manner in which they saved boundary hits was a fine object lesson to English players,' echoed a local newspaper after the Indians' match against Lincolnshire at Sleaford.[76] One observer tried to reconcile the inconsistencies by suggesting that the Indian fielding was 'curiously bad and good'. 'Their long, supple fingers pick the ball up off the turf with great ease, but their catching in the air is not so safe,' explained this journalist.[77] But it is more likely that the quality of Indians' fielding was a matter of attitude and not aptitude. In other words, the visitors fielded well when the state of the match enthused them, and badly when the relentless schedule dampened their ardour for the game.

IV

If the representations of the first Indian cricket team in the metropolitan press were decidedly mixed, the same cannot be said for its social reception in Britain. As with their Parsi predecessors, the Indian cricketers were warmly welcomed wherever they went. The MCC, their principal hosts in Britain, organized a grand dinner in honour of the team at Lord's on 9 June. The event was attended by powerful figures within the British establishment as well as the Indian princes who had arrived in London for the coronation. Lord Desborough, who presided over the occasion, toasted the visiting cricketers and declared that 'such a tour would do immense good to India'.[78] Similar events in honour of the visitors were also organized by their hosts at other venues.

Interestingly, the visit of these colonial sportsmen was accorded greater significance in Wales, Scotland, and Ireland. These countries viewed the visit of the Indian team as a recognition of their own status within the empire of cricket. The local authorities in all three nations held formal public events to welcome the visitors. Thus, the team was given 'a civic reception by the Lord Mayor of Cardiff at the City Hall'.[79] When they played the North of Scotland Cricket League at Inverness, the Lord Provost extended the Indians a welcome 'in the name of the town' and presided over a lunch in their honour at the Alexandra Hotel. His toast 'was enthusiastically pledged with Highland honours, the company singing "For they are jolly good fellows"'.[80] Likewise, the Corporation at Perth organized a dinner for the visitors at the town's Royal George Hotel. One contemporary berated the civic authorities at Galashiels for not following suit. 'It is a great honour to have the Indians at Galashiels,' noted this enthusiast on the eve of their visit, 'and we consider it was the least the Town Council could have done to honour the visit by entertaining the Indians to a banquet. Perhaps it is not yet too late for this to be done.'[81] The historical record is silent on whether the authorities acted on the suggestion.

The Indian cricketers were also the honoured guests of wealthy patrons during their Celtic sojourn. In Scotland, the whiskey magnate A.T. Bell lavished hospitality on them, personally chauffeuring them around the 'beauties of Loch Rannoch'. The visitors also tried their hand at golf at the links on the North Inch and the Island of Moncrieffe.[82] Similarly, Stanley Cochrane arranged sight-seeing trips for the Indians after their visit to his Woodbrook estate.

The involvement of former imperial officials was another noteworthy feature of the public reception accorded to the visiting Indian cricketers. Lord Harris, the ex-Governor of Bombay, came out of retirement to lead the Kent side against the Indian cricket team. His friend Lord Hawke, who travelled frequently to the subcontinent on hunting expeditions, did likewise when the Indians played against Yorkshire. Another Raj official, the controversial Sir Andrew Fraser, who had served as the Lieutenant-Governor of Bengal at the time of the Swadeshi movement, was the chief guest at a lunch arranged by the Scottish Cricket Union at Galashiels. In his speech, Fraser welcomed the Indians to Scotland 'as a Scotsman who had spent a good deal of his life in India'.[83]

But it was Edward Sewell who perhaps played the most crucial role in the Indian cricket tour of Britain. This former Anglo-Indian became the self-appointed intermediary between the visitors and the British public. Sewell contacted the Indian cricketers as soon as they arrived in the country. Indeed, he swiftly commandeered Jayaram and Syed Hasan to play for his club in a friendly fixture. As we have seen, he also played for the Indian team against Hampstead CC. Importantly, Sewell's writings on the Indian cricket tour shaped public perceptions of the venture both in Britain and in India. In his regular reports on the Indians' doings he sought to dispel what he regarded as metropolitan ignorance about the subcontinent. For instance, he gleefully assailed the misconception in some sections of the British press that the team consisted entirely of Parsis. Moreover, whereas his British contemporaries spoke of the Indian team as comprising 'Hindoos,

Muhammadans and Parsees', Sewell furnished a detailed caste and sectarian profile of the team.[84] He also used his experience as an old Indian hand to convey the discombobulation of the tourists in England. Thus, commenting on the Indian cricketers' apparent distaste for British food, Sewell wrote:

> Our tiffins don't suit our visitors. I don't wonder it in some cases. Pai, for instance has mourned for the departed curry-bhat ever since he left Bombay. He cannot make bat and ball meet on salmon mayonnaise and the rather sawdusty sort of *murghi* which disgraces most of our cricket lunch tables so well as he can on a course of the right sort of curry made with fresh *masala* and genuine ghee. I can sympathise with him. It took me more than a couple of months to get used to the change of diet when I returned from India so I am not in the least surprised that the eye and various *etceteras* do not answer the helm in his case. All these things count a great more than can be put on paper.[85]

However, there was another aspect to Sewell's involvement with the touring side that was less amusing to its Indian backers. His friendship with the South Indian cricketers in the team had quickly alerted this ex-Madras official to its internal dissensions. Using this information, Sewell repeatedly began to insinuate that the Parsi management of the Indian team was deliberately ill-treating the Hindu players. In particular, in his weekly letters to the *Times of India*, he dwelt on the manner in which Jayaram and Pai had been arbitrarily dropped from the team. Their exclusion, he hinted, were 'explicable only on one ground which I need not mention'.[86] The ridicule he heaped on the Indian team's Parsi management forced. Framjee Patel to write to Sewell, who promptly informed his readers that he was 'delighted to hear that my notes are appreciated in the right quarter'. 'If in my view a little too much attention has been paid to the merits of the Parsi members of the team and not enough to those of the Hindu it is unfair to the latter not to mention it,' Sewell crowed.[87] But others would have been justified in discerning in his remarks the inveterate British tendency to stir up trouble between the subjects of the Raj.

V

'That there is a great "boom" in cricket this season there can be no denying,' wrote the cricket correspondent of the *Daily Mail* in June 1911. 'One has only to visit Lord's or the Oval to observe this, and the enthusiasm is not confined to London only, for in the Midlands and the North the county

cricket matches are drawing splendid "gates".'[88] 'There can be no doubt that
cricket, the spectacle, has struck another flood-tide,' confirmed the London
correspondent of the *Times of India* a few weeks later. 'Once again is it
sailing proudly on a wave of public approbation. All over the country, the
attendances this season have been considerably larger than for several years
past.' Indeed, noted the same writer, the 'Varsity match' between Oxford and
Cambridge that summer 'obtained its share of the general increase of
patronage' and attracted on each day 'something like 10,000 spectators'.[89]
Given these propitious circumstances, to what extent did the first Indian
cricket team prove a draw at the turnstiles?

Newspaper accounts offer impressionistic estimates of the attendance at
the Indians' matches and, occasionally, provide snippets about the social
composition of the spectators. Fortuitously, however, we have a more
substantial source in the form of the financial statement of the 1911 Indian
cricket tour of Britain. This fascinating document, which was published in
the Bombay newspapers a few months after the end of the tour, provides
detailed information on the share of the gate receipts that the visitors
received for every match.[90] In instances where their hosts had guaranteed
the Indian team a minimum amount, the figures in the financial statement
are in themselves no guide to the match attendance. But where the Indians
had not been offered such a guarantee, their share of the total receipts offers
a rough idea of how many spectators might have turned up at the ground
to watch the visitors. Used in conjunction with the press reports, this information allows us to assess more accurately the popular reception of the first
Indian cricket team in Britain.

The evidence to hand suggests a variable picture of the crowd attendance
at the matches featuring the Indian cricket team. The visitors' first two
fixtures, at Oxford and Cardiff, were reported to have attracted a 'large'
crowd. The financial statement of the tour reveals that the Indians received
£30 and £50 respectively for these matches. It is not clear if these sums
were guaranteed to the visitors beforehand or if they were a half-share of
the total receipts at the turnstiles. The neat roundness of the figures would
suggest the former. But if we assume that the money that the Indians
received for both matches represented 50 per cent of the gate receipts, the
total match attendance would have been approximately 2,400 at Oxford
and 4,000 at Cardiff.[91]

The opening day of the Indians' match against the MCC, the most
important of their tour, attracted a much larger crowd. 'Tempered by the

occasion and the extremely pleasant afternoon,' noted the *Sportsman*, 'there was a capital attendance at Lord's, the Indian community now in England for the coronation festivities mustering in force, and many of them lending an air of picturesqueness by their turbans and long, bright-coloured garb.'[92] The 'most striking figure', reported the *Manchester Guardian*, 'was a mighty Indian wearing a sort of flowered dressing gown of cream and gold, gorgeously lined with tinted silk of crimson lake.'[93] Nyayapati Ramanujaswami, one of the Indians present at the ground that day, thought that the turnout was substantial, but not 'so large as I had expected'.[94] As we have seen, the Indian cricketers gave their supporters very little cause for cheer. The sole exception was Mistry, whose brilliant innings 'roused the crowd to a high pitch of enthusiasm'.[95]

After their poor performance at the headquarters of cricket, there was a perceptible dip in the public attendance at the Indians' matches against the major first-class counties. There were no more than a few hundred spectators at Edgbaston, Old Trafford, Northampton, Hull, and Taunton. Both Lancashire and Yorkshire had given the Indian organizers a match guarantee of £100 and, thus, incurred a heavy financial loss on the fixtures featuring the visitors. Kent, too, lost money on account of the guarantee of £100 that Lord Harris had offered the Indians, even though the press reports estimated a respectable turnout of 'four or five thousand spectators' at this match.[96] The low turnout at other first-class venues can be seen from the measly sums that the Indians received as their half-share of the gate receipts: £22 at Edgbaston, £21 at Northampton, £17 at Taunton, and £29 at Bristol.[97]

To a large extent, the Indians' early reverses dampened public interest in their matches. But their experience was not unique in this regard; first-class county teams that found themselves at the bottom of the points table swiftly found spectators voting with their feet. 'The fact is that the public will not go to see a losing or an unattractive team,' the *Sheffield Telegraph* noted. The paper pointed to the 'renewed interest' in cricket at Edgbaston as evidence that 'success and brilliance are the qualities required to gladden the financial heart'.[98]

Other factors, too, played a part in the poor turnout at the Indians' matches against the strong first-class counties. The absence of Ranji and the disappearance of the Maharaja of Patiala and Mistry diminished public interest in the team. Moreover, the Indian cricketers made no attempt to feed the metropolitan appetite for Oriental exotica. 'The spectators were disappointed with the appearance of our visitors from India,' reported a Hull newspaper after the opening day of the visitors' match in that city. 'They had expected to have seen turbans and other fanciful Oriental headgear and costumes, and were disappointed when they appeared in the regulation flannels.'[99] But the attendance at this match was also affected by factors that were not of the Indians' making. The decision of the local organizers to hike the admission price from six pence to one shilling was said to have generated popular discontent. 'The attendance was very disappointing and there is no doubt that Hull people are not likely to be induced to pay the admission charged for what is really friendly cricket,' noted the same paper.[100]

Interestingly, the very next match between the Indians and the Leicestershire team not only attracted a substantial crowd but also made a profit for the organizers. The hosts had not offered the colonial visitors a guarantee for this match and the Indians received £43 as their share of the gate receipts.[101] This would suggest a turnout of approximately 3,500 spectators, which tallies with the attendance figures mentioned in press reports. The increased turnout for this game was undoubtedly because it had been scheduled as part of the newly introduced 'Leicester Cricket Week'. To boost its finances, the county club had organized a variety of social entertainments alongside the cricket: a torchlight 'military tattoo', a bohemian concert, a pantomime show, a 'motor cycle gymkhana', and a lacrosse match.[102] These variety shows were designed to lure the spectators to the ground to watch the main cricketing fixture of the week, which pitted the home side against the touring Indian cricket team. A similar outcome also attended the penultimate fixture of the Indians' tour at Brighton. As at Leicester, the visitors were scheduled as part of a week-long cricket festival in this fashionable sea resort. The closely contested game saw a fair turnout, and the gate receipts awarded to the Indians suggests that approximately 2,800 spectators watched this match.

The Indian cricketers attracted a bigger crowd when they played against the second-class counties. For instance, their match against Durham at Sunderland attracted 'a large attendance of spectators who cordially welcomed the visitors'. Newspaper reports estimated that around 4,000 spectators watched this match, which accords with the £47 that the Indians received as their share of the total takings. Similarly, their visit to Newcastle was said to have 'aroused much interest', and the opening day of their match against Northumberland attracted around 3,000 spectators.[103] The overall match attendance yielded the Indians £53 by way of gate receipts. Likewise, their fixture with Lincolnshire was eagerly anticipated, with one local observer noting that it would 'give an impetus to cricket in the Sleaford district'.[104] There was thus a large attendance to greet the Indians on the opening day of the match.

Notably, too, the Indian cricketers drew crowds in the Celtic countries, where cricket was by no means the most popular sport. Going by the local newspapers it would appear that there was great public interest in the visitors' matches in Scotland.[105] Impressionistic estimates in the match reports suggest that between 2,000 and 4,000 spectators watched them at every venue. An interesting feature of the game at Galashiels was the presence of a 'large number of Indians', mostly students, 'who had come from Edinburgh and elsewhere to witness their compatriots trying their skill against Scotland's chosen eleven'.[106]

The tourists had been given a pre-match guarantee of £50 for their matches against North of Scotland and the Scottish Union. The latter match at Galashiels only generated £47 in earnings and thus resulted in a financial loss for its organizers.[107] This triggered a controversy with some newspapers alleging that the choice of Galashiels as a venue had affected the profitability of the fixture. However, the organizers of the match countered by pointing out that it was the rain-affected final day that had dampened the collections.[108] On the other hand, A.T. Bell and his associates at Perth had much reason to celebrate. Scottish Counties not only emerged victors in the thrilling encounter with the Indians, but also made over £100 in gate receipts. The Indians received £53 as their share of the total earnings for this match.

A similar story also repeated itself when the Indian cricket team travelled to Ireland. 'The visit of the All-Indian Team to the North of Ireland is the principal cricketing event of the present season, and lovers of the great summer pastime naturally regarded it as such,' reported the *Belfast Evening News*.[109] The Indians had been given a pre-match guarantee of £50 for their match against the Northern Cricket Union. The press reports suggest that the match at Belfast was watched by a large crowd, but it is not clear if the organizers made a profit. There was an equally good turnout for their next engagement at Stanley Cochrane's Woodbrook estate. For this game, the Indians received £75, which suggests that this was a guaranteed amount. At any rate, it is unlikely that their affluent host was unduly bothered about the financial profitability of the match.

Figure 23. A section of the crowd at the match between All India and Sussex County Cricket Club, Hove, 1911. Note the 'Welcome India' banner in the background. Courtesy of Marylebone Cricket Club Library.

Judged by the available audience figures for the Edwardian era, the turnout at the Indians' matches was hardly impressive. Venues that staged tests between England and Australia often attracted crowds of up to 75,000 spectators per match. First-class contests between famous rivals like Lancashire, Yorkshire, and Surrey also tended to generate match attendances in excess of 50,000. Yet it would be unfair to judge the Indian cricketers by these exceptional standards. By the end of the 1900s, most first-class county matches drew far smaller crowds. Public interest in any particular match, as we have seen, was highly contingent on a county's place in the annual championship, the weather, and the presence of 'star' players. Because the English first-class teams did not accrue any points for these matches, there was little competitive interest in the encounters with the Indians. The absence of Ranji and the team's early reverses served to dilute further the public appeal of the colonial visitors. Viewed against this backdrop, the first Indian cricket team in Britain did not fare abysmally.

VI

'In conclusion,' wrote Edward Sewell in his final report on the Indian cricket tour, 'the team was popular wherever it went. That much I have learnt from various people who were present or playing against the visitors.'[110] Although their performance on the pitch had been mixed, the members of the first Indian cricket team were universally acknowledged by their hosts as 'true sportsmen' and 'keen learners'. A final public gesture by Homi Kanga and J.M. Divecha sought to reaffirm the Indian cricketers' image as exemplary colonial pupils. On 1 September 1911, the two Parsis sent the following letter to the editor of The Times:

> Before leaving at the close of the season we wish to express on behalf of the 'All-Indian Cricket Team' our sincere thanks to the captains, the managing committees, and the members of all the counties we had the privilege of playing with for the warm welcome and cordial treatment they uniformly extended to us. It was, of course, not in any spirit of rivalry or competition on equal terms that the project of our tour was originally conceived; the main idea was an educational one, and the experience we have gained here has amply justified it, and will serve in future to direct our efforts to attaining a higher standard of proficiency on the cricket field. For enabling us to achieve

this object we owe a debt of gratitude to Lord Harris, Lord Hawke, the Marylebone Cricket Club, and its energetic secretary, Mr. Lacey, without whose assistance we should never have been able to carry out the elaborate programme of this tour. Permit us this opportunity of thanking yourself and the British Press generally for the impartial criticism and generous recognition of our play, and also the public for the encouragement they gave us.[111]

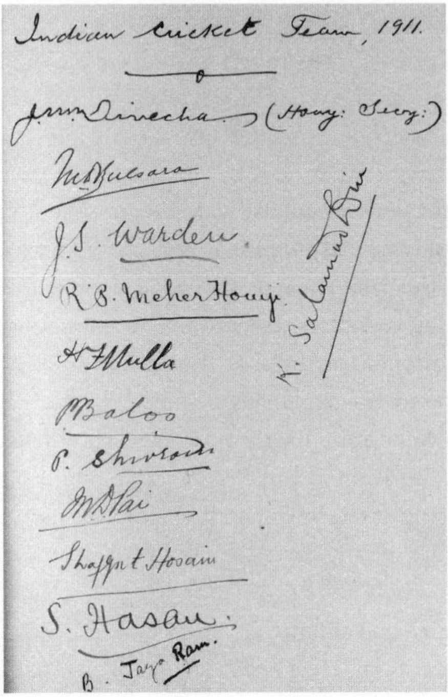

Figure 24. Autographs of the 1911 All-India cricket team. The signatures were discovered in the autograph book of Amy Logan, whose family had theatrical connections in late nineteenth-century Edinburgh. Courtesy of Reverend David Logan, Church of Scotland.

11

Ends and Beginnings

I

The members of the first Indian cricket team sailed together to Britain, but they did not return as a single group. First to arrive back in Bombay, in late August, was the Maharaja of Patiala and his entourage. Bhupinder Singh told the waiting reporters that he was 'unfeignedly sorry that he was unable to turn out oftener for the side which he took Home in such good hopes'.[1] But he offered no explanation as to why he had abandoned the tour. The Maharaja left immediately in a special train to Patiala, where a 'magnificent reception' awaited him.[2] Led by the chief officials of the state, a large crowd gathering at the 'beautifully decorated' railway station to greet the prince. Bhupinder was escorted to his Moti Bagh palace in a gilded carriage, accompanied by a large procession of 'richly caparisoned elephants, horses, artillery, cavalry and infantry'.[3]

On 15 September 1911, eleven members of the Indian cricket team returned to Bombay on board the P&O liner *S.S. Salsette*. 'All of them were in the pink of condition with the exception of two, who had evidently suffered somewhat from sea-sickness,' noted one reporter. The players were 'quite unanimous in their recognition of the magnificent hospitality accorded them in the Old Country'.[4] In his press interviews, J.M. Divecha highlighted the benefits of their tour. The visit had offered the Indian cricketers 'fine opportunities of studying the methods of play of the foremost batsmen and bowlers at Home'. Politically, too, much good had come out of the venture. 'To the large majority of the British public, India was little more than a geographical expression,' Divecha declared. Hence, the tour 'had done something to bring India more vividly before the eyes of the public there'. The Parsi manager was equally sanguine about the Indian team's performance in Britain. He highlighted the adversities that the team had to confront over the course of their three-month sojourn in the imperial metropolis: the unhelpful schedule, the constant travel and play, the remarkable heat wave, the unfamiliar playing conditions, and the absence of their captain and best batsman for the better part of the tour. In these circumstances, he told his interlocutors, the Indian team had acquitted itself 'fairly well and under more favourable conditions it could have beaten all of the weaker of the first-class counties as well as all the second-class counties'.[5]

Palwankar Baloo, the hero of the hour, was notably more critical in his assessment of the Indian performance. The most successful bowler on the tour revealed to reporters, eager to record every word, that 'he did not look upon the result of the tour as satisfactory'.[6] Baloo offered a clear-eyed assessment of the reasons for the Indian team's disappointing showing. The absence of Ranji and Prince Hitendra Narayan from the original team, and the disappearance of Bhupinder Singh and Keki Mistry once it got to Britain, had weakened the batting. The late withdrawal of Maneck Chand, the fastest bowler in the country—'who could have come off wonderfully well on the fast, dry wickets they met with at Home'—had deprived the Indians of a potentially lethal spearhead. The eldest Palwankar also dwelt on the power dynamics that underpinned cricketing encounters between the colonizers and the colonized. Thus, 'the bad arrangement of the programme' had been a major factor in the poor performance of the Indians at the outset of the tour. It would have been 'much better', Baloo said, 'if the first big matches had been interspersed with a few second-class fixtures, so that at the beginning in place of the monotonous series of heart-rending reverses they could have had some successes to cheer then up'. On the cricket pitch, too, 'the Indian batsmen were quite at sea with the express deliveries of the English fast bowlers and equally so with the googlies'.[7]

Baloo, noted one reporter, 'was modest about his own prowess with the ball'.[8] Instead of dwelling on his extraordinary feats, he chose to praise his fellow bowlers. It was left to Seshachari to acknowledge the contribution of his teammate. Baloo, he told interviewers, 'had been man of the side' and the team 'could not have got on without him'.[9] Nor was the Tamilian wicket keeper the only one to applaud the Dalit bowler. The remarkable feats of the Palwankar brothers had transformed them into public heroes. The day after the Indian team's return to Bombay, a ceremony was held at the Hindu Gymkhana to honour the players who had represented the community. Ironically, Baloo and Shivram, who were treated with disdain when they set out for London, now received special tokens of honour 'in appreciation of their services to the team'.[10] Baloo was presented with a gold medal, while his brother received a silver cup. The Palwankar brothers were also the guests of honour at a public ceremony organized by representatives of the so-called 'Depressed Classes' in Bombay. Notably, the address on this occasion was presented by a young man named Bhimrao Ambedkar, future leader of the Dalit masses and the principal architect of independent India's constitution.[11]

The last Indian cricketer to return to Bombay was the team's stand-in captain Homi Kanga, who arrived in his hometown in the spring of 1912. Shortly thereafter, he presented a report on the tour to its organizers. Kanga expressed his satisfaction at the 'cordial welcome' that the team had received from the British public. He also praised his teammates for having 'discharged their duty on the Cricket Field in a way that did credit to themselves and to those who worked for them'.[12] There were warm words of praise for the team's manager. 'On Mr. Divecha fell the greatest burden of the tour for the carrying out of the whole scheme,' he wrote, 'which besides involving an exercise of considerable tact and judgement, involved the considerable labour of carrying on a voluminous correspondence in connection with the railway journeys, hotel accommodation, etc.' But before signing off, Kanga made known his displeasure about one matter pertaining to the tour:

> I have read in two Gujarati papers the results of several interviews given by some of the members of the team, on their return, to the reporters of those papers. It is true that every member of the team has a right to find out causes of effects in his own way and to form an opinion of his own on matters relating to the success of the enterprise. Some of them, however, have made certain statements, which, I am sorry to find, are quite irrelevant to the merits of the case and are attacks on other members of the team in the disguise of criticism, which I myself deprecate and which, I hope, your Committee will join me in deprecating.[13]

Kanga's report was submitted to the final meeting of the 'Indian Cricket Team for England Committee', which took place at the Tata headquarters in Navsari Buildings on 10 April 1912.[14] An audited statement of the tour receipts and expenses was also presented and approved at the meeting. The receipts totalled Rs. 61,643 (consisting of the guarantee money raised in India plus the gate receipts in England), while the expenditure amounted to Rs. 49,475. The organizers resolved to return the outstanding balance of

Rs. 12,168 to the guarantors of the venture. That done, the attendees at the meeting unanimously agreed to dissolve the 'Indian Cricket Team for England Committee'.[15]

★ ★ ★

The return of the first national cricket team attracted a great deal of coverage in the Indian press. Some observers expressed their disappointment at the outcome of the tour. 'It must be regretfully acknowledged,' said the *Hindu*, 'that judging by the performances of the team, the best cricket in India is only second class.'[16] 'Our national cricket team has returned from England with the confession that it had to learn much and teach little,' agreed the *Indian Spectator*. It advised its readers to 'forget the early defeats, and congratulate the team on its later triumphs'.[17] Others were more inclined to regard the tour as a success. 'Although this attempt looked, in the beginning, like fighting the lion in its own den,' declared the *Hindoo Patriot*, 'the results of the many matches that were played show that the Indian team was equally good.'[18] 'They have, moreover,' added the *Hindi Punch*, 'established good fellowship all round. They have been on freedom's soil where caste is powerless and lessons in the art of give and take are learnt sooner and remembered longer.'[19]

Interestingly, the European-owned newspapers, not known for acknowledging the aspirations of the colonized, were mostly sympathetic in their assessment of the Indians' performance. 'The Indian cricketers' tour has come to an end and they can look back upon their record with justifiable pride,' opined the *Bombay Gazette*.[20] Other Anglo-Indian newspapers too concurred that the team had acquitted itself creditably. 'They lacked the assistance of some of the strongest Indian players; they were more or less hampered by unfamiliar conditions; and they commenced with a series of defeats which admittedly damped their spirits to a considerable extent. Thus handicapped, they are entitled to all the more credit for their later victories,' remarked the *Statesman*.[21] There was general agreement, too, that the tour had been a successful educational exercise. One European newspaper even looked ahead to an Indian cricket tour of imperial Britain in the not too distant future, when 'perhaps the visitors' last messages would be redolent more of the magnanimity of victory than the education of defeat'.[22]

In the long run, however, the aims and hopes that lay behind the organization of the 1911 Indian tour of Britain were overtaken by the political events that occurred in the subcontinent in its aftermath. The years immediately following the end of the First World War witnessed an irreparable fracture in relations between rulers and ruled. Indian nationalists had hoped that India's handsome contribution to the war effort would be recognized and rewarded by the British with a new round of substantive political reform. Much to their chagrin, however, the political concessions that were embodied in the Montagu-Chelmsford reforms of 1918 were nullified by the refusal of the Raj to roll back war-time restrictions on civil liberties. Under the leadership of Mahatma Gandhi, Indian nationalists organized country-wide demonstrations against the draconian Rowlatt Act, which extended the emergency measures introduced by the colonial state during the war years. The brutality of the British response to this protest movement was powerfully symbolized by the massacre at Amritsar on 13 April 1919.

These developments inaugurated a new phase in the history of Indian nationalism. For the generation of Indian politicians who came of age in the interwar years, empire and nation increasingly came to represent mutually exclusive entities. Now, nationalist visions of India's future contemplated the end of British rule over the subcontinent. The first casualties of the new era were the ageing generation of Anglophile Indian moderates, who had sought to reconcile their patriotism with membership of the British Empire. As the political tapestry of the Raj swiftly unravelled, the first Indian cricket tour of Britain was shorn of the symbolic meanings with which it had once been freighted.

II

The singularity of the attempt to forge a national team became apparent immediately after the end of the tour. Within days of their return, the cricketers who had played side by side for India were pitted against each other in teams that were constituted on the basis of religious identity. The year 1912 saw the entry of the Muslims into Bombay's premier cricket competition, which had hitherto featured the Europeans, Parsis, and Hindus. Community trumped nation, and it was not until 1926–7, when the first MCC team came to the subcontinent, that an All-India team once again took to the cricket field. Five more years went by before a composite team travelled to Britain, in the summer of 1932, to play the first official test matches in India's cricketing history.

In the meantime, the Bombay Quadrangular became the most popular sporting tournament in colonial India.[23] However, there was a significant shift in the balance of power among its participants. The Europeans and Parsis ceased to dominate these cricketing contests. Frequent defeats against Indian teams steadily diminished the aura of sporting invincibility that had once surrounded the Europeans. The Parsis, too, regularly went down to their Hindu and Muslim opponents. Gradually, a new sporting rivalry came to the fore in the Quadrangular. The increasingly fractious relations between Hindus and Muslims had an impact on the cricket pitch. Matches featuring the two communities began to generate intense collective emotions in a polarized political climate. On both sides, victory in the cricketing arena was feverishly touted as evidence of a community's vigour and unity; conversely, defeat was interpreted as an outcome of internal debility and discord.[24]

The sectarian organization of the sport was by no means the only cause of strife. As the nationalist movement acquired a mass base in the interwar years, contests between Indian and European cricket teams came to be infused with anti-colonial sentiments.[25] In turn, the sporting representatives of the Raj grew ever more petulant in their everyday encounters with local teams. Significantly, the Indo-British coalition that had made possible the first Indian cricket team had fragmented by the mid-1920s. Indeed, European commercial interests in Bengal now tried to reassert their control over a sport that had long been dominated by Bombay's cosmopolitan Indian elites.[26]

Caste, too, became a source of discord on the cricket field.[27] From 1912 onwards, there was a strong clamour every year among Hindu fans for Palwankar Baloo to be made captain of their team in the Quadrangular tournament. But the leaders of the Hindu Gymkhana chose to ignore this popular demand. Worse still, they contrived to find ways of slighting their best bowler. Repeatedly denied the captaincy, Baloo was even forced to fight for his place in the Hindu team.

The year 1920 was a particularly eventful one in the history of modern India. Mahatma Gandhi took charge of the Indian National Congress and launched the Non-Cooperation Movement against the colonial government. Simultaneously, the Palwankar brothers embarked on their own protest against the selection committee of the Hindu Gymkhana. When Baloo was dropped from that year's Quadrangular, and their own claims on the captaincy ignored, Shivram and Vithal chose to withdraw from the Hindu team.[28] In a letter published in the *Bombay Chronicle*, the Palwankars pointed to the flagrant caste bias that had denied them the captaincy. Denouncing the selectors' decision as 'unsportsmanlike in the extreme', the two brothers made it clear that they felt 'very strongly the covert or overt insult levelled at us as belonging to the so-called depressed class'.[29] Their remarks resonated with a wide section of the Hindu public, which 'approved of Gandhi's wider struggle against Untouchability'.[30] The Hindu Gymkhana, too, was forced to undo the damage wrought by its selection committee. The Palwankar trio was recalled for the Hindus' final fixture against the Parsis. Towards the closing stages of this match, Baloo captained his team on the field. It was the last time he appeared in the tournament that had made him famous across India.[31]

III

Palwankar Baloo's stupendous achievements on the cricket field paved the way for his entry into politics. In April 1926, he entered the Bombay Municipal Corporation as a government nominee.[32] He also began to interest himself in the social and political problems confronting his caste.[33] Six years later, he was a protagonist in a riveting political drama. In August 1932, the British government granted separate electorates to the 'Depressed Classes' in Indian legislatures. Dr B.R. Ambedkar, the brilliant lawyer who had emerged as the most influential Dalit representative, was a staunch advocate of this policy. Gandhi, on the other hand, sternly opposed this move. On 20 September, the Congress leader began an indefinite fast at Yeravada prison in protest against the government's decision. As Gandhi's condition began to deteriorate, public pressure began to mount on Ambedkar to save the Mahatma's life. Baloo, who had strong congress sympathies, was one of the many public leaders who called for a compromise. More importantly, he was one of the two negotiators whom Ambedkar nominated for his parleys with Gandhi.[34] But four and a half years later, Baloo and Ambedkar once again found themselves on opposite sides of the political fence. The Congress cannily fielded the famous bowler against its most implacable foe in the 1937 provincial elections in Bombay. Ambedkar won a tight race by a little over 2,000 votes.[35]

For Baloo, the disappointment of electoral defeat is likely to have paled in comparison with the sorrow induced by the death, 'after a brief illness', of Shivram in January 1939.[36] This Palwankar, unlike his elder brother, had kept a low profile after he retired from cricket. He worked until the end of his life for the GIP Railway in Bombay. But while he was alive, Shivram continued to retain links with the game that had brought him fame, playing for his office club and briefly coaching the students of the city's Wilson College.

His brother's death may have been partly responsible for Baloo's gradual withdrawal from the public arena. But his colleagues and fans had not entirely forgotten the great man. In October 1945, some months after his seventieth birthday, the *Bombay Chronicle* carried a long article on Baloo by his erstwhile teammate D.B. Deodhar.[37] Ironically, a quarter of a century earlier, this Poona Brahmin had been one of the protagonists in the controversy over the captaincy of the Hindu side in the Bombay Quadrangular. Now, however, Deodhar recalled his former teammate with a respect bordering on reverence. 'P. Baloo who was in the height of his cricket glory and greatness forty years ago and whose skill in his art still remains unsurpassed,' he declared, 'was to my mind the first and greatest of cricketers who can be called "Self made." No other cricketer then and now had to fight so hard against the difficulties and dangers, inflicted by both man and nature.' Baloo's example, Deodhar noted, was 'inspiring and hopeful for young Indian cricketers, who have little facilities and who have to depend upon themselves to build up the game'.[38] In recognition of the Dalit cricketer's political significance, the *Chronicle* article featured a photograph of Baloo and Ambedkar seated side by side.

Three years after Deodhar's heartfelt eulogy, Palwankar Vithal published his autobiography. Here, he recounted the tales of his eldest brother's glory days. By now, Baloo himself had completely retreated into the shadows. But his death on 4 July 1955 at Bombay's King Edward Memorial Hospital triggered an outpouring of public tributes. The funeral at the Santa Cruz crematorium was attended by cricketers and politicians alike, among them Dalit representatives in parliament and the Bombay Legislative Assembly.[39] 'P. Baloo has gone on, to join the truly mighty array of Indian cricketers who are no more. It is our national misfortune that the young of today know nothing about the men who made Indian cricket much of what it is,' wrote the popular radio commentator A.F.S. ('Bobby') Talyarkhan. 'Cricket will miss Baloo, but always remember him.'[40]

IV

For the Palwankars, cricket became a resource in their stirring struggle for dignity and justice. Indian elites, on the other hand, continued to regard the imperial game as a route to power and prestige. This was certainly the case with Maharaja Bhupinder Singh, for whom sport was an important instrument in furthering his political interests.[41]

After his first visit to the imperial metropolis, the position of the Patiala prince became more secure than it had been prior to his departure. His conduct reassured the ruling establishment in London that he had the makings of a reliable ally. When King George V arrived in Delhi for the grand *durbar* in the winter of 1911, the Maharaja was accorded a prominent part in the royal ceremonies.[42] Prolonged exposure to the imperial high table gave Bhupinder the confidence to exert his authority in Patiala's internal administration. But this caused some disquiet among the British spies stationed at his court. In February 1912, they reported that the prince had taken to wearing a 'diamond crown made in England, just like the crown of European kings'. Local European officials also circulated rumours that the Maharaja was 'playing the absolute devil, seducing respectable girls and so on; that the honour of women is not safe in Patiala'. Fortunately for Bhupinder, the local political agent sided with him. 'He has been most careful of his reputation since his return from England,' C.H. Atkins reassured his superiors.[43]

The First World War marked a turning point in Bhupinder's political career. Patiala was at the forefront of the Indian contribution to the British war effort. The state was generous in providing its imperial overlords with men, money, and materials throughout the conflict.[44] Bhupinder was 'an enthusiastic recruiter for the British Indian army'.[45] In return for his services, the Maharaja was chosen by the Viceroy to represent the princely states at the 1918 Imperial War Conference in London.[46] In the following decade, Bhupinder also played a prominent part in Indian princely politics. From its founding in 1921, he became an important figure in the Chamber of Princes.[47] Ironically, Bhupinder's fiercest rival in this forum was Maharaja Ganga Singh of Bikaner, his mentor during the 1911 Indian cricket tour of Britain.

Yet, even as he strutted the political stage in India and abroad, the whiff of scandal constantly hung over Bhupinder. Within Patiala and outside, there were frequent allegations about his sexual misdemeanours, profligate lifestyle, and autocratic ways. Notwithstanding their internal misgivings, the colonial authorities disregarded the rumours. In 1930, however, the government was forced to take notice of the Maharaja's doings after the nationalist All-India States People's Conference published a searing 'indictment of Patiala'.[48] The widely publicized pamphlet fiercely castigated Bhupinder's misrule and accused him of a variety of crimes, ranging from financial malfeasance to the torture and murder of political opponents. The British government instituted an official inquiry that was designed to give the Maharaja an easy ride. Bhupinder was swiftly exonerated of all the charges levelled against him.[49] As one colonial official in the Political Department noted, 'We cannot afford to see a state of [the] importance & position of Patiala crack'.[50]

In extricating himself from this pickle, Bhupinder expended much of the political capital he had accumulated during the 1920s. His subsequent dealings with the British authorities were marked by acrimony. Weakened politically, the Maharaja began to chafe at the government's renewed interference in his internal affairs. At the same time, Bhupinder also began to oppose the government's plans for a federation comprising the princely states and British Indian provinces. Relations between Lord Willingdon, the Viceroy, and the Maharaja became deeply strained by the mid-1930s.[51]

Buffeted by strong political headwinds, Bhupinder used cricket to regain influence in imperial affairs. He made his first move in November 1931, offering to fund the All-India cricket tour of Britain that was scheduled to take place the following summer. Bhupinder's daring attempt to hijack the venture did not go down well with the Viceroy, who 'bitterly opposed' the Maharaja's involvement in the proposed tour. But Patiala's generous offer proved irresistible to the recently formed Board of Control for Cricket in India (BCCI). In January 1932, cricketers from all over India arrived to take part in the selection trials that were organized at Patiala and Lahore under the Maharaja's personal supervision. Rather pointedly, no Europeans were invited to take part in these matches.[52] Shortly afterwards, the forty-year-old Bhupinder ensured that his acolytes made him captain of the Indian team. As in 1911, the representation was on 'communal' lines: there were seven Hindus, four Muslims, four Parsis, and three Sikhs in the squad.[53]

Bhupinder's triumph was short-lived. A few weeks after his appointment as captain had been announced, the Maharaja stepped down from the position and withdrew from the tour.[54] According to one of Bhupinder's biographers, Lord Willingdon prevailed on London 'to overrule Patiala's decision to lead the 1932 team to England'.[55]

The next round in the cricketing battle between the proconsul and the prince occurred when Douglas Jardine's MCC team toured the subcontinent in the winter of 1933–4. At Delhi, the visitors included the Maharaja in their team as he was a member of the club. The Viceroy and his wife tried to persuade the English captain to drop the Patiala prince from the MCC side. Jardine proved unyielding and Bhupinder played for the tourists.[56] Once again, Willingdon had his revenge. When Bhupinder put himself forward for the captaincy of the Indian team that was due to take on the MCC a few weeks later, the Viceroy promptly scuttled the idea.[57]

The Maharaja was nothing if not resilient. Even the Viceroy of India could not prevent him from using his considerable resources to dominate the BCCI. In March 1934, he was elected president of the recently formed Cricket Club of India (CCI), which sought to discharge in the Indian context the role that the MCC performed in imperial cricket. Four months later, at a board meeting in Simla, Bhupinder announced that he would donate the gold cup for a new national cricket championship organized on territorial lines. His only stipulation was that the trophy be named after Ranji, who had died the previous year.[58] In November 1935, Bhupinder also sponsored a tour of the subcontinent by a side calling itself 'His Highness the Maharaja of Patiala's Team of Australian cricketers'.[59] The tour, which was arranged by the prince's trusted aide Frank Tarrant, was intended to serve as a preparation for the next visit by an Indian cricket team to Britain.

But in sport as in politics, Bhupinder's actions galvanized his rivals. The European interests that sought to reassert their control over Indian cricket did not take well to his growing dominance of the BCCI. The Maharaja also had to contend with a new Indian rival, who was more congenial to the Viceroy. The Maharajkumar of Vizianagaram had emerged as an ambitious cricket impresario in the early 1930s. Importantly, the England-educated 'Vizzy' had assiduously courted Lord Willingdon during his frequent visits to Delhi.[60] In August 1934, he prevailed on the BCCI to name the national cricket championship after Willingdon and even donated a trophy for this purpose. Bhupinder worked behind the scenes to get the board to reverse its decision; the Viceroy was forced to award the 'Ranji trophy' to the first winners of the new competition.[61] Two years later, however, it was Vizzy who outsmarted the Maharaja and seized control of the All-India cricket team that travelled to Britain in the summer of 1936.[62]

By this time, Bhupinder Singh's waning influence over Indian cricket mirrored his increasingly beleaguered position in the political domain. But there was one last moment in the limelight before the final fadeout. As president of the CCI, the Maharaja oversaw the construction of a state-of-the-art stadium in Bombay. Bhupinder worked closely on this scheme with the resourceful Anthony de Mello, one of the founders of the BCCI. The two men cannily persuaded the Governor of Bombay to throw his weight behind the project. Lured by the prospect of 'immortality', Lord Brabourne ensured that the CCI acquired at a throwaway price a site measuring 90,000 square yards.[63] Despite his indifferent health, Bhupinder attended the inauguration ceremony of the Brabourne Stadium on 7 December 1937.[64] 'Now, I can die a happy man,' he is said to have remarked on his return to Patiala.[65] Shortly afterwards, the Maharaja fell ill and never recovered. He died on 23 March 1938 in the Moti Bagh palace, surrounded by the inmates of his legendary seraglio.

V

Celebrity, sporting or otherwise, is a function of public visibility. Unlike Palwankar Baloo and Bhupinder Singh, most of the individuals who first represented India on the cricket field were swiftly forgotten after the end of their playing days. Their post-cricket lives have left only the faintest of traces in the historical record. For information about these Indian cricketers, we have to rely mostly on their obituaries in contemporary newspapers and sporting publications. A few—notably, Shafqat Hussain, Syed Hasan, and Maniksha Bulsara—were not even accorded that sign of public recognition.

The first to merit a press obituary was Kilvidi Seshachari, who unexpectedly died of pneumonia at Calcutta's Medical College Hospital on 25 January 1917. His last first-class match for the Hindus was in the Bombay Quadrangular of 1912. Thereafter, Seshachari restricted himself to occasional appearances for the cricket team put together by his employer, the Maharaja of Natore. 'He was a thorough sportsman in the true sense of the expression, a real friend and a gentleman who will be missed by all,' noted 'Extra Cover' in the *Englishman*.[66]

The other south Indian Brahmin in the first Indian cricket team also hung up his boots soon after the end of the 1911 tour. Thereafter, B. Jayaram devoted himself to his official duties in the Mysore State's Geological Department. On a visit to Bangalore in February 1934, Edward Sewell visited his old friend 'at his estate at an unspellable place reached along an unmentionable road'. He reported that Jayaram, now retired, had taken to 'growing papayas and several fruit I had never heard of in his small Eden on the salubrious Mysore plateau'. The two men 'had a long crack about old times, chatting about men we had played with and against from Grace downwards'. 'He still looked good for another hundred with or without a dentist's aid,' remarked Sewell.[67] It was not to be: Jayaram died, aged sixty-four, in December 1936.

Mukund Pai retired from the game in the same year as Palwankar Baloo. After 1921, Pai retained his links, 'in an advisory capacity', with Hindu cricket in Bombay. At a special ceremony held in August 1935, he was made an honorary member of the Hindu Gymkhana for his services to club and community. Only two other cricketers before him had been accorded this coveted distinction: Baloo and Shivram.[68] The 66-year-old Pai died of 'heart failure' at his home in the Chikalwadi neighbourhood of Bombay on 5 August 1948. 'He leaves behind [a] wife, a son, three daughters, relatives and friends to mourn his loss,' stated the terse notice in the *Times of India*.[69]

By this time, all but one of the Parsi cricketers in the first Indian cricket team were also dead. The first to succumb was Manikji Bajana, who died of colon cancer on 28 April 1927 at the Mildmay Mission Hospital in London. He had spent the preceding sixteen years in Britain, having settled down in the country after the end of the 1911 Indian cricket tour. His impressive batting performance against Somerset prompted the county to hire Bajana. The Parsi was a popular figure at Taunton, where he quickly acquired the nickname 'Pyjamas'.[70] In 1915, he married Dadie Hicks, a London resident, and the couple lived in the city's Bayswater area. A man of 'independent means', Bajana tried his hand at different businesses. Until 1920, he dealt in antiques. When that venture failed, he became a commission agent.[71]

In contrast to the peripatetic Bajana, Jehangir Warden returned to a settled existence in his home town. He continued to represent the Parsis in the Bombay Quadrangular until his retirement from the game in 1924. Thereafter, he became a respected umpire in local cricket. Off the field, Warden was a cricket coach at St Xavier's College in the early 1920s. The experience appears to have prompted him to pen a book entitled *Knotty Cricket Problems Solved* (1923).[72] He died in Bombay—a few days past his forty-third birthday—on 16 January 1928. Warden's compatriot Hormusji

Mulla also lived and worked his entire life in the same city. An expert in income-tax law, he became a partner in his family firm, Messrs Mulla and Mulla. In 1938, Hormusji was appointed as the solicitor to the Government of India at Bombay. He had been in this position for less than two years when he died in January 1940.[73] We do not know how Rustomji Meherhomji occupied his time after his cricketing days had ended. The press notice of his death in November 1943 is frustratingly telegraphic.[74]

Homi Kanga fared better in death than many of his Indian teammates. His role as a prominent cricket administrator kept him in the public eye long after the others had been consigned to oblivion. News of his demise on 29 December 1945 was greeted with sorrow by the cricket community.[75] In a tribute to Kanga in the *Bombay Chronicle*, D.B. Deodhar recalled his stellar performances on the 1911 Indian cricket tour of Britain. He praised the departed cricketer for being 'always generous, open and straight forward even to his opponents on and off the field'. But above all, it was Kanga's cosmopolitan civility in the face of the 'unseemly and unhealthy rivalry' fostered by sectarian cricket that the veteran Poona cricketer sought to highlight. 'Men like him who are citizens of the world could take part in the communal matches and yet rise above them,' reflected Deodhar.[76]

The oldest member of the famed Parsi batting triumvirate outlived his compatriots. Remarkably, a few weeks after his fifty-second birthday, Keki Mistry captained the second 'All-India' team that took the field at Bombay against Arthur Gilligan's touring MCC side in December 1926.[77] The Parsi stalwart scored a 'great and courageous' half-century.[78] The following year, Mistry captained the Parsis for the last time in the Bombay Quadrangular. 'The Colonel is getting on in years but he has not lost much of his vigour and nought of his judgment,' marvelled one observer.[79] As a trusted aide of Bhupinder, Mistry continued to be involved in Indian cricket in the following decade.[80] But after the death of the Maharaja, he kept a low profile. The 'Grand Old Man' of Indian cricket died in Bombay on 22 July 1959.[81] In his obituary, 'Bobby' Talyarkhan, who had watched the dapper Parsi batsman in his pomp, recalled the memory.

> I can see Mistry coming out to bat—the snowwhite sun-topee, the spotless flannels, with shirt sleeves buttoned at the wrist. The gait of a man who wanted to hurry out there to the middle, to look for runs, to get them. These were the batsmen whose joyful practice produced the theories of later times. And it's all gone now. So is the great Indian cricketer.[82]

The youngest member of the first Indian cricket team lived the longest. After he finished his law degree at Aligarh, Salamuddin Khan returned to Jullunder before finding employment in Bhopal. The move happened at the initiative of his Aligarh contemporary Nawab Hamidullah Khan, the ruler of this princely state.[83] The lanky Pathan continued to play cricket, regularly turning out for the Hamidia Club in Bhopal until the late 1920s.[84] There was even a rare cricketing appearance for his *alma mater* when Arthur Gilligan's MCC side visited Aligarh in February 1927.[85] In the following decades, Salamuddin Khan made a name for himself as a legal luminary, eventually becoming the chief justice of Bhopal. And it was in the same town that he breathed his last on 2 June 1975.[86]

A year before his death, the retired judge presided over a dinner at his residence. On this occasion, he regaled his guests with stories about the first Indian cricket tour of Britain. One featured the young Prince of Wales (the future King Edward VIII), who 'unable to fathom Jehangir Warden's left-arm wiles from the pavilion tried to play Warden at the nets with bat in hand'. But, recalled the raconteur, the prince 'did not even "see" Jehangir's deliveries'.[87] Salamuddin's 'roar of laughter' points to the hidden transcript that lies beyond the historian's grasp. It suggests that, for all their public displays of deference, these colonial cricketers did not always comport themselves as docile pupils.

VI

More than four decades after the death of its last surviving member, the first Indian cricket team and its tour of Britain is seen as a curiosity. As the context that once lent it meaning has entirely receded from collective memory, the event has been divested of its historical significance. For many writers, India's career in international cricket dates from its formal recognition as an independent test-playing nation in 1947.[88] The 1911 tour is viewed as a part of the sport's fuzzy prehistory in the subcontinent. Ironically, the venture has come to be associated primarily with Maharaja Bhupinder Singh, who is widely regarded as its quixotic moving spirit. Few today are even aware that this was a collective project that in its time galvanized many sections of the Indian public.

Arguably, too, the project to fashion the first national team anticipated, in more ways than one, the future of Indian cricket. In mirroring the country's social diversity, the 1911 Indian cricket team inaugurated a new register in which the nation came to be imagined. 'Team India' is now a potent national symbol with an unparalleled popular appeal. Equally, the middle classes still form the core constituency of Indian cricket, providing the bulk of the game's players and followers in the subcontinent. Moreover, the nexus of money and power that made possible the first Indian team continues to flourish, forming the basis of the country's global dominance as a cricketing superpower. Now, as then, the elites who control the sport seek to exploit the game's popularity for their own ends. Although the days of lordly cricketing aristocrats are long past, the 'superstar culture' that began with Ranjitsinhji remains a pervasive feature of Indian cricket to this day. And, finally, while sporting encounters between England and India no longer carry the symbolic charge they once did, present-day rivalries within the postcolonial commonwealth of cricket testify to the enduring charisma of what was once the imperial game.

Notes

PREFACE

1. Edmund Blunden, *Cricket Country* (London, 1944).
2. Sonia Orwell and Ian Angus (eds), *The Collected Essays, Journalism and Letters of George Orwell, Volume III: As I Please, 1943–1945* (London, 1968), pp. 47–50.
3. Jeffrey Hill and Anthony Bateman, 'Introduction', in Jeffrey Hill and Anthony Bateman (eds), *The Cambridge Companion to Cricket* (Cambridge, 2011), p. 3. See also Anthony Bateman, 'Cricket pastoral and Englishness', in Hill and Bateman (eds), *The Cambridge Companion to Cricket*, pp. 11–25.
4. See, in this context, Mike Marquesee, *Anyone but England: Cricket and the National Malaise* (London, 1994); Jack Williams, *Cricket and England: A Cultural and Social History of the Inter-War Years* (London, 1999); and Anthony Bateman, *Cricket, Literature and Culture* (Farnham, 2009).
5. James Pycroft, *The Cricket-Field: Or, The History and the Science of Cricket* (Boston, MA, 1859), p. 25.
6. Neville Cardus, *English Cricket* (London, 1945), p. 4.
7. Ashis Nandy, *The Tao of Cricket: On Games of Destiny and the Destiny of Games* (Delhi, 2000), p. 1.
8. https://www.economist.com/the-economist-explains/2014/02/04/why-indians-love-cricket. Accessed on 12 September 2018.
9. Quoted in Rajdeep Sardesai, *Democracy's XI: The Great Indian Cricket Story* (New Delhi, 2017), p. 8.
10. I have found especially useful Arjun Appadurai's insight that an 'imperial class regime' comprising local and British elites developed around cricket in colonial India. Arjun Appadurai, 'Playing with Modernity: The Decolonization of Indian Cricket', in Arjun Appadurai and Carol A. Breckenridge (eds), *Consuming Modernity: Public Culture in a South Asian World* (Minneapolis, MN, 1995), pp. 28–30.
11. Nandy, *The Tao of Cricket*, pp. 1–2.
12. In this context, see the important arguments in Appadurai, 'Playing with Modernity', pp. 24–5. Appadurai's schematic account draws much of its empirical evidence from Richard Cashman, *Patrons, Players, and the Crowd: The Phenomenon of Indian Cricket* (Delhi, 1979).
13. Ramachandra Guha, *A Corner of a Foreign Field: The Indian History of a British Sport* (London, 2002), p. xv.

14. According to one estimate, there were 187 'international' cricket tours between 1859 and 1914. See, 'A Guide to International Tours before the Great War', *Cricket Quarterly*, II (1964), pp. 219–22. After cricket, rugby was the other significant imperial team sport in the late Victorian and Edwardian era. But rugby tours were organized less frequently and took place primarily between Britain and its white settler colonies in the southern hemisphere. Football, on the other hand, never quite became 'an imperial game'. Richard Holt, *Sport and the British: A Modern History* (Oxford, 1989), p. 226.

15. E.B.V. Christian, 'Cricket and the Empire: A Parallel', *Cricket: A Weekly Record of the Game* (hereafter *Cricket*), XIII: 361 (7 June 1894), p. 183.

16. T.N. Harper, 'Empire, Diaspora and the Languages of Globalism, 1850–1914', in A.G. Hopkins (ed.), *Globalization and World History* (London, 2002), pp. 141–66.

CHAPTER I

1. Amalendu Guha, 'More about the Parsi Seths: Their Roots, Entrepreneurship and Comprador Role, 1650–1918', *Economic and Political Weekly*, 19, 3 (21 January 1984), pp. 117–32.

2. Dosabhai Framji Karaka, *History of the Parsees* (London, 1884), 2 vols., I, p. xxi.

3. A.M. Vicziany, 'Bombay Merchants and Structural Changes in the Export Community, 1850 to 1880', in K.N. Chaudhuri and Clive Dewey (eds), *Economy and Society: Essays in Indian Economic and Social History* (Delhi, 1976), pp. 105–46; Rajnarayan Chandavarkar, *The Origins of Industrial Capitalism in India: Business Strategies and the Working Classes in Bombay, 1900–1940* (Cambridge, 1994), pp. 21–71.

4. Douglas E. Haynes, *Rhetoric and Ritual in Colonial India: The Shaping of a Public Culture in Surat City, 1852–1928* (Berkeley, CA: California University Press, 1991), p. 114.

5. Jesse S. Palsetia, *Jamsetjee Jejeebhoy of Bombay: Partnership and Public Culture in Empire* (Delhi, 2015), pp. 97–133.

6. Lakshmi Subramanian, *Three Merchants of Bombay: Business Pioneers of the Nineteenth Century* (New Delhi, 2012), p. 89.

7. *The Times of India* (hereafter *TOI*), 6 November 1915, p. 11.

8. Karaka, *History of the Parsees*, II, p. 295. Such declarations of loyalty did not mean that the Parsis were abject in their dealings with their foreign rulers. On the contrary, affirmations of the larger imperial bond enabled the Paris intelligentsia to assail the lapses of the colonial authorities in Bombay.

9. *Minister's Magazine*, June 1899, p. 616. Quoted in T.M. Luhrmann, *The Good Parsi: The Fate of a Colonial Elite in a Postcolonial Society* (Cambridge, MA, 1996), p. 113.

10. Luhrmann, *The Good Parsi*, p. 117.

11. J.R.B. Jejeebhoy, 'The Sporting Parsi', in H.D. Darukhanawala, *Parsis and Sports and Kindred Subjects* (Bombay, 1935), pp. 15–18.

12. Darukhanawala, *Parsis and Sports*, pp. 60–97; Luhrmann, *The Good Parsi*, pp. 119–20.

13. J.M. Framjee Patel, *Stray Thoughts on Indian Cricket* (Bombay, 1905), p. 2.

14. Manekji Kavasji Patel, *History of Parsee Cricket: Being a Lecture Delivered at the Framji Cowasji Institute under the Presidency of Dr Blaney on the 10th December 1892* (Bombay, 1892), p. 1.

15. Jivanji Jamshedji Modi, *The Game of Ball-Bat: Chowgân Gui among the Ancient Persians as Described in the Epic of Firdausi* (Bombay, 1890), p. 1. Another writer, Ardeshir Sorabji Camdin, asserted: 'It is not surprising that the sons of Roostum and Zal should triumph over their antagonists on the cricket-field, inasmuch as cricket, of course in a rude form, was the national game of the ancient Persians as narrated in Shah Nameh or the Book of Kings'. As evidence he offered the following tale: 'When Alexander the Great, on ascending the throne, discontinued the payment of one thousand gold eggs, which his father Philip used to pay as a tribute to Darius Codomanus, the latter was very wroth, and regarding Alexander as a mere child, despatched the following message with one of his chieftains who carried in his hands a *ball*, a *bat*, and a vessel containing the seeds of sesamum: "Thou art still a child, so play with this *bat* and *ball*, and the Persian army, innumerable as the seeds of sesamum, will invade Macedonia."' Quoted in Patel, *History of Parsee Cricket*, pp. 3–4. Yet others also saw in contemporary Parsi games such as 'Gooye-i-bazi'—played with a stick and a ball—'the germ of cricket'. Ibid., pp. 5–6.

16. Patel, *History of Parsee Cricket*, p. 7.

17. Framjee Patel, *Stray Thoughts*, p. 5.

18. Shapoorjee Sorabjee, *A Chronicle of Cricket amongst Parsees, and the Struggle: Polo versus Cricket* (Bombay, 1897), p. 8.

19. D.E. Wacha, *Shells from the Sands of Bombay: Being My Recollections and Reminiscences* (Bombay, 1920), p. 82.

20. Framjee Patel, *Stray Thoughts*, p. 1.

21. Patel, *History of Parsee Cricket*, p. 13. The Parsi youths were encouraged by British soldiers stationed in Bombay. One of them was Henry Havelock, better known for his role in the siege of Lucknow during the Great Uprising of 1857. Ibid., p. 14.

22. Framjee Patel, *Stray Thoughts*, p. 6.

23. The two clubs had contrasting careers: Orient CC folded up after two years, whereas Zoroastrian CC was in existence for almost half a century, surviving 'many ups and downs that freaks of Dame Fortune could inflict'. Sorabjee, *Chronicle*, p. 25.

24. Guha, *A Corner of a Foreign Field*, p. 14. 'The reason,' according to one Parsi chronicler, 'was that during those days the history of Greece was generally taught in the schools that had the least pretence to afford very high or classical education. The youths naturally were very much led away by the mighty exploits of the Greek gods and their youthful fancy kept these names vividly uppermost in their minds.' Sorabjee, *Chronicle*, p. 11. The same source also tells us that there were 'several different clubs bearing the same name, but distinct one from another living at shorter or longer intervals of time between one another. Thus, there have been 3 Marses, 3 Alberts, 4 Prince of Wales, 2 Juveniles, 3 Spartans, 2 Jupiters, 2 Cyruses, 2 Persians, 4 Baronets, &c'. Ibid., p. 28.

25. Interestingly, some clubs on the Bombay *maidan* were apparently organized along occupational lines. For instance, the 'Lawyers' Cricket Club', comprising articled clerks working for government solicitors, was 'open to other lawyers' clerks only'. Sorabjee, *Chronicle*, p. 12.

26. Framjee Patel, *Stray Thoughts*, p. 8.

27. Sorabjee, *Chronicle*, pp. 10–11.

28. Framjee Patel, *Stray Thoughts*, p. 10.

29. Sorabjee, *Chronicle*, p. 15.

30. Ibid., p. 22.

31. Ibid., p. 13.

32. Ibid., pp. 13–14.

33. Ibid.

34. Patel, *History of Parsee Cricket*, p. 17.

35. Sorabjee, *Chronicle*, pp. 30–1.

36. Framjee Patel, *Stray Thoughts*, p. 15; Sorabjee, *Chronicle*, p. 31.

37. *TOI*, 5 January 1877, p. 2. This was Parsee CC's second match against the same team; they had lost the first encounter. *TOI*, 1 January 1877, p. 3.

38. *TOI*, 2 April 1877, p. 3.

39. *Daily News*, 6 February 1877, p. 5.

40. Quoted in *TOI*, 29, May 1877, p. 3.

41. *TOI*, 8 August 1877, p. 3.

42. *Bombay Gazette* (hereafter *BG*), 8 August 1877, p. 2; *TOI*, 8 August 1877, p. 3.

43. *BG*, 8 August 1877, p. 2.

44. *TOI*, 2 October 1877, p. 3.

45. Framjee Patel, *Stray Thoughts*, p. 17.

46. Sorabjee, *Chronicle*, p. 33.

47. Patel, *History of Parsee Cricket*, pp. 21–2.

48. *TOI*, 25 September 1889, p. 5.

49. Ibid.

50. *TOI*, 5 December 1877, p. 3. Katrak's 'peculiar' bowling action attracted much comment among European observers. According to an account that found its way into the *London Evening Standard*: 'He retires about ten paces, sets his right arm in motion, then walks forward a little, increasing the pump-handle action of his arm the while, and when about four paces off the wicket he runs, his arm by this time going at a tremendous rate, and then delivers the ball as if he were angry with it and bent upon annihilating somebody.' Quoted in the *Salisbury Times*, 24 November 1877, p. 6.

51. Sorabjee, *Chronicle*, pp. 32–3.

52. *TOI*, 10 December 1877, p. 3.

53. Framjee Patel, *Stray Thoughts*, p. 16.

54. *BG*, 2 October 1877, p. 2. On the other hand, another contemporary took it for granted that the Parsi cricketers would seek to exhibit themselves as exotica: 'People [in England] will of course go to see them, as they play in their national costume, the novelty of which alone will attract crowds, so I suppose we must

say that the tour will be a success. Yes, a success, inasmuch as the annual tour of the Clown Eleven and the One Arm *v*. One Leg match are successes, financially.' *TOI*, 30 March 1878, p. 3.

55. Homi K. Bhabha, *The Location of Culture* (Abingdon, 2004), pp. 121–31.

56. Ibid., p. 125.

57. *Bell's Life in London and Sporting Chronicle* (hereafter *Bell's Life*), 9 March 1878, p. 10.

58. *Daily Telegraph*, 24 April 1878, p. 5.

59. *Daily News*, 8 December 1877, p. 6.

60. Quoted in *Monmouthshire Merlin and South Wales Advertiser*, 26 April 1878, p. 7.

61. *Daily Telegraph*, 24 April 1878, p. 5.

62. *Bell's Life*, 14 September 1878, p. 12.

63. *Sheffield and Rotherham Independent*, 6 June 1878, p. 5.

64. *Aberdeen Journal*, 14 June 1878, p. 8.

65. *TOI*, 1 November 1878, p. 3.

66. Sorabjee, *Chronicle*, p. 35.

67. Parsi Cricketers, *A Reply to a Malicious Attack in the 'Rast Goftar' Newspaper against the Propriety of Parsi Cricketers Going to England to Play against English Clubs* (Bombay, 1878), pp. 3–4.

68. Ibid., pp. 6–10.

69. Ibid., pp. 14–15.

70. Ibid., pp. 17–20.

71. Ibid., p. 24. Had they undertaken the visit, the Parsi cricketers declared, the English press would undoubtedly have praised them 'even more than the Australians because they would have been impressed by their small build and agility. On top of that the Australians are Christians while the Parsis are a completely different religious community!' Ibid., p. 25. Such statements suggest that the Parsi cricketers saw themselves as part of a wider imperial sporting world. Moreover, their arguments indicate a sharp awareness on the part of these Indian sportsmen that their chief attraction to the British public lay in their novelty.

72. *TOI*, 1 November 1878, p. 3.

73. Ibid.

74. Sorabjee, *Chronicle*, pp. 35–6.

75. Ibid., pp. 68–124.

76. Guha, *A Corner of a Foreign Field*, p. 20.

77. Sorabjee, *Chronicle*, pp. 69–71.

78. Ibid., pp. 74–6; Guha, *A Corner of a Foreign Field*, pp. 23–4.

79. Sorabjee, *Chronicle*, p. 77.

80. Guha, *A Corner of a Foreign Field*, pp. 24–5.

81. Sorabjee, *Chronicle*, p. 77; Guha, *A Corner of a Foreign Field*, pp. 27–8.

82. Sorabjee, *Chronicle*, pp. 83–4.

83. Ibid.

84. Ibid., pp. 95–6.

85. Ibid., p. 97.

86. *TOI*, 15 September 1884, p. 5.

87. Sorabjee, *Chronicle*, p. 82. Indeed, when the Bombay government had overturned its own resolution the previous year and ruled in favour of the European polo players, the *Rast Goftar* had urged the cricketers to 'keep on agitating and send petition after petition to Government in support of their contention'. Quoted in *TOI*, 4 June 1883, p. 3.

88. *Rast Goftar*, 27 September 1885, quoted in Guha, *A Corner of a Foreign Field*, p. 27.

89. Sorabjee, *Chronicle*, p. 79.

90. *TOI*, 4 June 1883, p. 5.

91. *TOI*, 4–11 June 1883, *passim*.

92. Shortly after these letters appeared in *TOI*, a meeting of the entire Parsee CC was held at which it was resolved that 'this matter be dropped altogether' and that in future any internal differences be 'settled among themselves' and not aired in the press. *TOI*, 11 June 1883, p. 3.

93. *TOI*, 5 June 1883, p. 5.

94. *TOI*, 9 June 1883, p. 5.

95. *TOI*, 5 June 1883, p. 5.

96. *TOI*, 7 June 1883, p. 5.

97. Sorabjee, *Chronicle*, pp. 122–4. See also Guha, *A Corner of a Foreign Field*, pp. 52–77.

98. Here, there arose by 1888 a gleaming pavilion, largely funded by a 'handsome donation' from Jamsetji Nusserwanji Tata. Vasant Raiji, *India's Hambledon Men* (Bombay, 1986), p. 81. 'We earnestly hope the institution will gradually kindle in the Parsees, especially the upper and middle classes, a genuine love of manly sports which, in course of time, will evolve a better type of men physically, and even to some extent morally, than what we find at present,' remarked one Parsi newspaper. *Rast Goftar and Satya Prakash*, 26 February 1888, p. 240.

99. Sorabjee, *Chronicle*, p. 40.

100. Kathryn Hansen, 'Parsi Theatre and the City: Locations, Spectators, and Patrons of the Parsi Theatre in 19th-Century Bombay', in *SARAI Reader 02: The Cities of Everyday Life* (Delhi, 2002), pp. 40–9.

101. Sorabjee, *Chronicle*, pp. 40–1.

102. But three members of the squad—Pestonji Dinshaw Dastur, Burjorji Balla, and Dinshaw Dadabhai Khambatta—were from Karachi.

103. *TOI*, 15 March 1886, p. 4. Interestingly, the Bombay Gymkhana allowed the Parsi cricketers to play some practice matches on their own ground, and the club's players even participated in these. *Cricket*, V: 116 (6 May 1886), p. 98.

104. Framjee Patel, *Stray Thoughts*, p. 32; An English Sportsman, 'Parsis and Sport', *Parsi*, 1: 9 (September 1905), p. 356.

105. *TOI*, 15 April 1886, p. 4.

106. Framjee Patel, *Stray Thoughts*, p. 32.

107. *TOI*, 19 April 1886, p. 3.

108. *Cricket*, V: 114 (22 April 1886), p. 73.

109. *Bristol Mercury*, 10 May 1886, p. 3.

110. *Sheffield and Rotherham Independent*, 15 May 1886, p. 3.

111. The simultaneous arrival of the two overseas cricket teams prompted one Bristol newspaper to reflect on this 'Indo-Colonial invasion'. Noting that it was 'remarkable to find them playing cricket at all', the paper welcomed the Parsis as the 'representatives of a brilliant nationality', whose playing techniques would be 'sufficiently embarrassing to a generation mostly trained upon the fashionable slow round'. *Western Daily Press*, 16 March 1886, p. 5.

112. *Illustrated Sporting and Dramatic News*, 16 January 1886, p. 442.

113. *Illustrated Sporting and Dramatic News*, 6 March 1886, p. 643. See, in this context, Peter Lamont and Crispin Bates, 'Conjuring Images of India in Nineteenth-Century Britain', *Social History*, 32: 3 (August 2007), pp. 308–24.

114. *Daily News*, 24 April 1886, p. 6. On the inauguration of the Indian and Colonial Exhibition, see *Penny Illustrated Paper* (hereafter *PIP*), 1 May 1886, pp. 274–5; *Times*, 5 May 1886, p. 11. See also Arindam Datta, 'The Politics of Display: India 1886 and 1986', *Journal of Arts and Ideas*, 30: 1 (1997), pp. 115–45; Peter H. Hoffenberg, *An Empire on Display: English, Indian, and Australia Exhibitions from the Crystal Palace to the Great War* (Berkeley, CA, 2001).

115. *Sporting Life* (hereafter *SL*), 29 May 1886, p. 2.

116. Framjee Patel, *Stray Thoughts*, p. 33.

117. *SL*, 26 May 1886, p. 4.

118. They made little impression on the Victorian giant, who dismissively remarked that the visitors 'met with very little success, even against second- and third-rate clubs'. W.G. Grace, *Cricket Reminiscences and Personal Recollections* (London, 1980), p. 192.

119. *Cheltenham Chronicle*, 5 June 1886, p. 3.

120. *Derby Express*, 16 June 1886, p. 4.

121. *Scottish News*, quoted in *TOI*, 6 July 1886, p. 7. Even *Wisden* did not think it 'worthwhile to print any of the scores'. Quoted in Jonathan Rice (ed.), *Wisden on India: An Anthology* (London, 2011), p. 6.

122. *Nottingham Daily Express*, 12 July 1886, p. 7.

123. Sorabjee, *Chronicle*, pp. 44–5.

124. *TOI*, 20 March 1888, p. 5. Only two players from the first Parsi cricket team to tour Britain made the second journey. One of these was Sorabji Harvar, who played for the Zoroastrian CC. All we know of this cricketer is that he was an 'excellent fielder, and a fair bat, but a bad judge of a run'. We know more about his talented teammate Jalbhai Merwanjee Morenas, who died in 1892 at the young age of twenty-eight. A product of the Fort High School in Bombay, 'his name had become a terror in all local matches'. After completing his education, Morenas moved to Baroda in the mid-1880s, where he served as the private secretary to the ruler of the petty principality of Wadhan. He was one of the few players in the first Parsi cricket tour of Britain to impress the game's connoisseurs. At Lord's against the MCC, recalled one writer, 'he skied over the boundary three successive balls from the redoubtable W.G. Grace, and the latter was so much struck with the feat, that he congratulated the young cricketers and presented him with his photo'. *TOI*, 30 May 1892, p. 3. His participation

in these ventures clearly meant a great deal to Morenas, for he kept a bulging scrapbook comprising newspaper clippings from both tours. The scrapbook is currently in the possession of the distinguished poet Keki Daruwalla. I am grateful to Mr Daruwalla for allowing me to peruse this valuable source.

125. See, for instance, *Kaiser-e-Hind*, 19 February 1888, p. 200; *Rast Goftar and Satya Prakash*, 25 March 1888, p. 364.

126. *SL*, 8 June 1888, p. 4.

127. *Cricket*, VII: 189 (2 August 1888), p. 313.

128. Framjee Patel, *Stray Thoughts*, p. 45.

129. Visiting the Houses of Parliament was clearly *de rigueur* for Indian visitors to the imperial metropolis. In 1888, the Parsi cricketers visited the Houses of Parliament 'through the courtesy of the Hon. Chandos Leigh'. *Cricket*, VII: 182 (14 June 1888), pp. 201–2; *Sheffield Evening Telegraph*, 7 June 1888, p. 2.

130. *Cricket*, V: 130 (12 August 1886), p. 341.

131. *Cricket*, VII: 182 (14 June 1888), pp. 201–2.

132. *BG*, 23 April 1886, p. 4.

133. *TOI*, 23 April 1886, p. 4.

134. 'Second Visit of a Parsee Cricket Team to England', *Cricket*, VII: 173 (12 April 1888), p. 61.

135. *BG*, 23 April 1886, p. 4.

136. *Cricket*, VII: 192 (23 August 1888), p. 353.

137. *Morning Post*, 28 September 1888, p. 4.

CHAPTER 2

1. *Morning Post*, 1 November 1889, p. 3; *Standard*, 1 November 1889, p. 1.

2. *The Times*, 1 November 1889, p. 11.

3. *The Times*, 15 October 1892, p. 10; Lord Hawke, *Recollections and Reminiscences* (London, 1924), pp. 270–83.

4. Cecil Headlam, *Ten Thousand Miles through India and Burma: An Account of the Oxford University Authentics' Cricket Tour with Mr K.J. Key in the Year of the Coronation Durbar* (London, 1903), p. 5.

5. The Parsis of Bombay were the only Indians to be accorded a fixture against the first visiting English team. The next set of English cricketing visitors to the subcontinent took part in a match against a 'native team' at Madras and twice took on the Parsi cricketers of Bombay. The Oxford University Authentics played against the Parsi and the Hindu cricket teams at Bombay as well as a team comprising Muslim college students at Aligarh.

6. *Standard*, 14 November 1889, p. 5.

7. Peter Wynne-Thomas, *The Complete History of Cricket Tours at Home and Abroad* (London, 1989).

8. 'A few years ago English cricketers hardly concerned themselves with what their brother cricketers were doing in foreign climes to keep up the traditions of the game, except when Australia was concerned. But touring teams have awakened an interest in the cricket of South Africa, India, Canada, the

United States, and the West Indies,' noted one observer in August 1897. *Cricket*, XVI: 461 (12 August 1897), p. 341.

9. Wynne-Thomas, *Complete History*, p. 13.

10. David Frith, *The Trailblazers: The First English Cricket Tour of Australia, 1861–62* (London, 1999), pp. 3–10; also see Warwick Frost, 'Heritage, Nationalism, Identity: The 1861–62 England Cricket Tour of Australia', *International Journal of the History of Sport*, 19: 4 (December 2002), pp. 55–69.

11. Wynne-Thomas, *Complete History*, p. 14.

12. For details, see Wynne-Thomas, *Complete History*, pp. 23–33; Holt, *Sport and the British*, pp. 229–30. See also A.W. Pullin ('Old Ebor'), *Alfred Shaw Cricketer: His Career and Reminiscences* (London, 1902).

13. In this context, see also Derek Birley, *The Willow Wand: Some Cricket Myths Explored* (London, 2000), pp. 80–7.

14. Richard Holt, 'The Amateur Body and the Middle-Class Man: Work, Health and Style in Victorian Britain', *Sport in History*, 26: 3 (2006), p. 352.

15. Norman Baker, 'Whose Hegemony? The Origins of the Amateur Ethos in Nineteenth Century English Society', *Sport in History*, 24: 1 (2004), pp. 1–16.

16. James Bradley, 'The MCC, Society and Empire: A Portrait of Cricket's Ruling Body, 1860–1914', in J.A. Mangan (ed.), *The Cultural Bond: Sport, Empire, Society* (London, 1992), pp. 27–46.

17. 'Lord Harris', *Cricket*, II: 35 (5 July 1883), pp. 213–14; Lord Harris, *A Few Short Runs* (London, 1921); James D. Coldham, *Lord Harris* (London, 1983).

18. Scyld Berry and Rupert Peploe, *Cricket's Burning Passion: Ivo Bligh and the Story of the Ashes* (London, 2006), p. 6.

19. *Cricket*, III: 79 (25 December 1884), pp. 489–90.

20. 'Lord Hawke', *Strand Magazine*, 10 (July 1895), p. 65; Owen Conway, 'Lord Hawke at Home', *Windsor Magazine* (1898), reproduced in David Rayvern Allen (ed.), *Cricket's Silver Lining, 1864–1914: The 50 Years from the Birth of Wisden to the Beginning of the Great War* (London, 1987), pp. 239–45; Hawke, *Recollections*; James P. Coldham, *Lord Hawke: A Cricketing Legend* (London, 2003).

21. P.F. Warner, *Long Innings: The Autobiography of Sir Pelham Warner* (London, 1951), p. 41.

22. Lord Hawke, 'Introduction', in P.F. Warner (ed.), *Imperial Cricket* (London, 1912), p. 2.

23. Warner, *Long Innings*; Gerald Howat, *Plum Warner* (London, 1987).

24. P.F. Warner, *Cricket in Many Climes* (London, 1900), p. vii.

25. John Darwin, *The Empire Project: The Rise and Fall of the British World-System* (Cambridge, 2009), p. 147.

26. Ibid., p. 244.

27. Richard Cashman, 'Symbols of Imperial Unity: Anglo-Australian Cricketers, 1877–1900', in Mangan (ed.), *The Cultural Bond*, pp. 128–41. See also Keith A.P. Sandiford, *Cricket and the Victorians* (Aldershot, 1994), p. 157.

28. Bernard Hall, Richard Parry, and Jonty Winch, 'More than a Game', in Bruce Murray and Goolam Vahed (ed.), *Empire and Cricket: The South African Experience 1884–1914* (Pretoria, 2009), p. 5.

29. Jonty Winch, 'Guardians of the Game: The Role of the Press in Popularising the 1888/89 Tour and Establishing the South African Cricket Association', in Murray and Vahed (ed.), *Empire and Cricket*, p. 48. William Milton, the principal organizer of this tour, subsequently went on to become Cecil Rhodes' parliamentary private secretary. Hall et al., 'More than a Game', pp. 5–6. Interestingly, as prime minister of the Cape Colony, Cecil Rhodes not only offered his support for the first South African cricket tour of England in 1894 but was also one of those responsible for the exclusion from the team of 'Krom' Hendricks, a 'coloured' fast bowler. Jonty Winch, '"I could a Tale Unfold": The Tragic Story of "Old Caddy" and "Krom" Hendricks', in Murray and Vahed (eds), *Empire and Cricket*, pp. 63–80.

30. Dean Allen, 'Cricket's "Laird": James Logan', in Murray and Vahed (eds), *Empire and Cricket*, pp. 141–58.

31. Dean Allen, 'Logan's Golden Age: Cricket, Politics and Empire, 1888–1910', unpublished PhD thesis, University of Brighton (2008), p. 188.

32. Aviston D. Downes, '"Flannelled Fools"? Cricket and the Political Economy of the West Indies c. 1895–1906', *International Journal of the History of Sport*, 17: 4 (2000), pp. 59–80; Geoffrey Levett, 'The "White Man's Game"? West Indian Cricket Tours of the 1900s', *International Journal of the History of Sport*, 34: 7–8 (2017), pp. 599–618. Dr R.B. Anderson, the Tobago-based organizer of the first English cricket tour of the Caribbean in 1895, told an interviewer in Britain that the tour would not only 'mark an epoch in the history of the game out there', but also prove beneficial 'from a social and, probably, an economic point of view'. Moreover, he added, 'the ignorance of stay-at-home Englishmen about the West Indies is something appalling. Instead of regarding it as a great health resort...people in this country seem to regard it as a special manufactory for ague and malarial fevers'. *Cricket*, XIV: 383 (11 April 1895), p. 49.

33. Warner, *Cricket in Many Climes*, p. 271.

34. Headlam, *Ten Thousand Miles*, p. 167.

35. Ibid., p. 7. Interestingly, however, when Lord Hawke's team visited Madras, an entrance fee was charged for those wishing to watch the game from enclosures. *Madras Mail*, 1 December 1892, p. 501.

36. Headlam, *Ten Thousand Miles*, p. 7.

37. Hawke, *Recollections*; Guha, *A Corner of a Foreign Field*, pp. 63–9.

38. Headlam, *Ten Thousand Miles*, p. 6.

39. In the nineteenth century, the British who lived in India were called 'Anglo-Indians'; individuals of British–Indian descent were categorised as 'Eurasians'.

40. Hawke, *Recollections*, p. 271. When Lord Hawke's men travelled from Madras to Bangalore, one newspaper informed its readers that 'the Madras Railway Company had placed at their disposal what is popularly known as the "Wedding Saloon"'. 'Whether the journey up to Bangalore in a carriage to which are attached so many tender associations will end in an appropriate manner or not it is, of course, impossible to say,' it added. Quoted in *Bangalore Spectator*, 6 December 1892, p. 2. As it happened, the visitors easily won both their matches in the city.

41. Headlam, *Ten Thousand Miles*, pp. 19–20.

42. Ibid., pp. 98–9.

43. Lord Hawke, 'The Late Lord Harris', *John Wisden's Cricketers' Almanack for 1933* (London, 1933), p. 229.

44. *BG*, 20 December 1892, p. 5.

45. Quoted in *TOI*, 30 December 1892, p. 5. See also Guha, *A Corner of a Foreign Field*, pp. 64–5.

46. Headlam, *Ten Thousand Miles*, p. 76.

47. Ibid., p. 49.

48. Ibid., p. 9.

49. Ibid.

50. *Madras Weekly Mail*, 1 December 1892, p. 501.

51. Ibid.

52. Coldham, *Lord Hawke*, p. 89.

53. *Madras Weekly Mail*, 1 December 1892, p. 501.

54. *Englishman* (*Weekly Summary*), 18 January 1893, p. 16.

55. For instance, during their stay in Bombay, the Oxford University Authentics were made honorary members of the Yacht Club, the Byculla Club, and the Bombay Club. Headlam, *Ten Thousand Miles*, pp. 26–7.

56. Ibid., p. 66.

57. 'Lord Hawke's Team in India: By One of the Team', *Cricket Field*, II: 26 (25 February 1893), p. 22.

58. Headlam, *Ten Thousand Miles*, p. 232.

59. Coldham, *Lord Hawke*, p. 90.

60. Ibid., p. 91.

61. Headlam, *Ten Thousand Miles*, p. 232.

62. *Cricket Field*, I: 24 (31 December 1892), p. 431.

63. *Cricket Field*, II: 26 (25 February 1893), p. 22.

64. Ibid., p. 23.

65. Headlam, *Ten Thousand Miles*, p. 75.

66. Ibid., p. 203.

67. John Strachey, *India* (London, 1888).

68. Headlam, *Ten Thousand Miles*, p. 4.

69. Ibid., p. 93.

70. Ibid., pp. 94–6.

71. See, in this context, David Gilmour, *The Ruling Caste: Imperial Lives in the Victorian Raj* (London, 2007), pp. 145–8.

72. Elizabeth Kolsky, *Colonial Justice in British India: White Violence and the Rule of Law* (Cambridge, 2011).

73. Headlam, *Ten Thousand Miles*, p. 94.

74. Ibid., pp. 102–3.

75. Ibid., p. 169.

76. Ibid., p. 168.

77. Clement Scott, 'Cricket Etiquette in India', *Wheel of Life* (1899), reproduced in Allen, *Cricket's Silver Lining*, p. 88.

78. Ibid., p. 89.

79. Ibid., pp. 89–90.

80. *Daily Telegraph*, 21 January 1893, p. 8.

81. Patel, *History of Parsee Cricket*, pp. 34–5.

82. Ibid., p. 36.

83. Ibid., pp. 36–7.

84. Framjee Patel, *Stray Thoughts*, p. 53.

85. *TOI*, 31 January 1890, p. 5.

86. Framjee Patel, *Stray Thoughts*, p. 59.

87. Philip Trevor ('Dux'), *The Lighter Side of Cricket* (London, 1901), pp. 269–70.

88. Ibid.

89. *BG*, 1 February 1890, p. 5.

90. *TOI*, 4 February 1890, p. 5.

91. Quoted in *Bombay Gazette Overland Summary* (hereafter *BGOS*), 7 February 1890, p. 3.

92. *BG*, 1 February 1890, p. 4.

93. *TOI*, 1 February 1890, p. 5.

94. Quoted in *TOI*, 5 February 1890, p. 5.

95. Framjee Patel, *Stray Thoughts*, p. 59.

96. Ibid.

97. Quoted in *TOI*, 5 February 1890, p. 6.

98. Ibid.

99. *TOI*, 10 February 1890, p. 3.

100. *TOI*, 25 August 1890, p. 5.

101. Ibid., p. 5.

102. Ibid.

103. *TOI*, 25 August 1890, p. 4.

104. Framjee Patel, *Stray Thoughts*, p. 59.

105. Ibid., pp. 62–9.

106. Ibid., p. 70.

107. Ibid.

108. *BG*, 16 December 1892, p. 6.

109. *TOI*, 21 December 1892, p. 5.

110. Patel, *History of Parsee Cricket*, pp. 47–9.

111. *SL*, 23 December 1892, p. 3.

112. Scott, 'Cricket Etiquette', pp. 88–9.

113. Quoted in *TOI*, 30 December 1892, p. 3.

114. Ibid.

115. Hawke, *Recollections*, pp. 272–3.

116. Quoted in *BG*, 16 January 1893, p. 7.

117. *Liverpool Mercury*, 26 December 1892, p. 4.

118. Framjee Patel, *Stray Thoughts*, p. 74.

119. *TOI*, 30 December 1892, p. 5.

120. *BG*, 2 January 1893, p. 5.

121. Lord Harris, Governor of Bombay, to Baron Wenlock, Governor of Madras, 31 December 1892, Harris Collection, Mss Eur D592/12, India Office Records (hereafter IOR), Asia, Pacific, and Africa Collections (hereafter APAC), British Library (hereafter BL).
122. Framjee Patel, *Stray Thoughts*, p. 75.
123. Hawke, *Recollections*, p. 273.
124. Quoted in *TOI*, 10 January 1893. See also *Civil and Military Gazette*, 30 January 1893, p. 6.
125. *BG*, 28 December 1892, p. 6.
126. Ibid.
127. *BG*, 4 January 1893, p. 5.
128. *BG*, 5 January 1893, p. 5.
129. *BG*, 6 January 1893, p. 5.
130. *BG*, 9 January 1893, p. 5.
131. Ibid.
132. News of the incident also made its way into the imperial public sphere. An editorial in *Cricket Field* went so far as to describe the action of the Parsi cricketers as 'little short of a blow to human progress'. *Cricket Field*, II: 26 (25 February 1893), p. 18.
133. *BG*, 11 March 1893, p. 6. See also *TOI*, 23 March 1893, p. 6.
134. Quoted in *TOI*, 12 January 1893, p. 5.
135. *BG*, 11 February 1893, p. 4.
136. Ibid.
137. Patel, *History of Parsee Cricket*, p. 58.

CHAPTER 3

1. Quoted in *Cricket*, XV: 438 (26 November 1896), p. 472.
2. Headlam, *Ten Thousand Miles*, p. 168.
3. Framjee Patel, *Stray Thoughts*, p. 163.
4. Cashman, *Players, Patrons and the Crowd*, p. 24.
5. *Bristol Mercury*, 28 September 1898, p. 7.
6. Framjee Patel, *Stray Thoughts*, pp. 49–69.
7. Sorabjee, *Chronicle*, p. 29; see also Guha, *A Corner of a Foreign Field*, p. 16.
8. Sorabjee, *Chronicle*, p. 29.
9. Guha, *A Corner of a Foreign Field*, pp. 60–3.
10. Appadurai, 'Playing with Modernity', pp. 25–31.
11. *Pall Mall Gazette*, 6 October 1898, p. 9.
12. See, in this context, Satadru Sen, *Migrant Races: Empire, Identity and K.S. Ranjitsinhji* (Manchester, 2004).
13. File R/C. 8. 1884 78/2, Crown Representative's Records (hereafter CRR): Western India States Agency (hereafter WISA), 1884, IOR/R/2/708/8, APAC, BL; Simon Wilde, *Ranji: The Strange Genius of Ranjitsinhji* (London, 1999), pp. 9–22.

14. Sen, *Migrant Races*, p. 21.

15. Wilde, *Ranji*, pp. 22–5.

16. Ibid., pp. 25–82.

17. *Strand Magazine*, 12 (July 1896), p. 251.

18. Sen, *Migrant Races*, p. 31.

19. Ibid., pp. 29, 44–5.

20. Ibid.

21. *Athenaeum*, 21 August 1897, p. 251.

22. Sen, *Migrant Races*, pp. 30–2.

23. *Cricket*, XIV: 397 (18 July 1895), pp. 273–4. See also Wilde, *Ranji*, pp. 62–9; Sen, *Migrant Races*, p. 17.

24. Wilde, *Ranji*, pp. 64–5; Sen, *Migrant Races*, pp. 17, 41. For an account of Naoroji's career as a British parliamentarian, see Dinyar Patel, *Naoroji: Pioneer of Indian Nationalism* (unpublished ms, forthcoming), chapter 6.

25. *Cricket*, XV: 423 (18 June 1896), p. 219.

26. *Daily Mail*, 11 September 1896, p. 7.

27. Ibid.

28. 'Natives of India as Cricketers', *Nilgiri News*, reprinted in *Cricket*, XV: 438 (26 November 1896), p. 472.

29. Sen, *Migrant Races*, pp. 45–51.

30. Roland Wild, *The Biography of Colonel His Highness Shri Sir Ranjitsinhji* (London, 1934), pp. 25–7; Wilde, *Ranji*, pp. 44–51; Sen, *Migrant Races*, pp. 83–6.

31. Wilde, *Ranji*, pp. 61–2; Sen, *Migrant Races*, p. 52.

32. Wilde, *Ranji*, p. 62.

33. Ibid., p. 97.

34. Ibid., p. 99.

35. File 1896–1901, 'Jamnagar – Ranjitsingji's file', CRR: WISA, Political Agent, Kathiawar—Halar Pranth, Confidential Files, 1896–1901, IOR/R/2/575/12, APAC, BL. See also Wilde, *Ranji*, pp. 100–2.

36. Ibid., p. 107.

37. Sen, *Migrant Races*, pp. 53–7.

38. Wilde, *Ranji*, p. 98; Sen, *Migrant Races*, pp. 58–61.

39. Wilde, *Ranji*, pp. 98–9. For a fictional recreation of Ranji's stay in Patiala, see Ian Buruma, *Playing the Game* (New York, 1991).

40. File R/C 469, 'Nawanagar State', CRR: WISA, List C: Confidential Files, 1906–11, IOR/R/2/741/263, APAC, BL; File 1896–1901, 'Jamnagar – Ranjitsingji's file', CRR: WISA, Political Agent, Kathiawar—Halar Pranth, Confidential Files, 1896–1901, IOR/R/2/575/12, APAC, BL. See also Wilde, *Ranji*, pp. 107–9.

41. File 1896–1901, 'Jamnagar – Ranjitsingji's file', CRR: WISA, Political Agent, Kathiawar—Halar Pranth, Confidential Files, 1896–1901, IOR/R/2/575/12, APAC, BL.

42. Letter from the Governor-General of India in Council, Calcutta, to Lord George F. Hamilton, Secretary of State for India, London, 2 February 1899, File 1896–1901, 'Jamnagar – Ranjitsingji's file', CRR: WISA, Political Agent, Kathiawar—Halar Pranth, Confidential Files, 1896–1901, IOR/R/2/575/12,

APAC, BL. However, Curzon and his officials were disinclined 'to recommend that the settlement of the succession should now be disturbed'. Ibid.

43. Quoted in *Cricket*, XVIII: 505 (27 April 1899), p. 91.

44. Framjee Patel was related to Ardeshir Patel, the manager of the 1886 Parsi cricket tour of England, as well as D.H. Patel, the captain of that pioneering team.

45. *SL*, 25 November 1897, p. 4; *Homeward Mail*, 27 November 1897, p. 1582; *Daily Mail*, 7 December 1897, p. 6; *Standard*, 7 December 1897, p. 8; *TOI*, 29 December 1897, p. 4.

46. *TOI*, 26 November 1898, quoted in *The Age* (Melbourne), 28 December 1898, p. 5; *TOI*, 22 February 1899, p. 6.

47. *Cricket*, XVIII: 505 (27 April 1899), p. 91.

48. For their views on the Indian cricket tour, see *Daily Mail*, 17 November 1898, p. 3.

49. *SL*, 17 December 1898, p. 8.

50. *Cricket*, XVIII: 505 (27 April 1899), p. 91.

51. *TOI*, 9 November 1899, p. 4.

52. *TOI*, 26 November 1898, quoted in *The Age* (Melbourne), 28 December 1898, p. 5.

53. Quoted in *TOI*, 31 March 1899, p. 5.

54. *Daily Mail*, 2 February 1899, p. 5; *TOI*, 3 February 1899, p. 11.

55. *TOI*, 31 March 1899, p. 5.

56. Alan Ross, *Ranji* (London, 1988), p. 62.

57. Sen, *Migrant Races*, pp. 46–8.

58. Quoted in *Cricket*, XVIII: 505 (27 April 1899), p. 92.

59. Ibid.

60. Quoted in *Cricket*, XIX: 533 (12 April 1900), p. 59.

61. Ibid.

62. *Cricket*, XIX: 549 (2 August 1900), pp. 305–6.

63. Quoted in *TOI*, 22 January 1903, p. 6.

64. Ibid.

65. *Cricket*, XIX: 549 (2 August 1900), p. 305.

66. Quoted in *TOI*, 27 January 1903, p. 5.

67. *TOI*, 28 January 1903, p. 8.

68. *BGOS*, 31 January 1903, p. 7.

69. Quoted in *TOI*, 23 February 1903, p. 8.

70. Ibid.

71. *Athletic News and Cyclists' Journal* (hereafter *Athletic News*), 12 January 1902, p. 6. To support his contention, Sewell publicized a letter in the *Civil and Military Gazette* from 'A Parsi Flannelled Fool', who reported that 'this blunder of the authorities concerned has evoked a good deal of dissatisfaction among the native cricket circles'. The letter writer went on to deplore 'the colour prejudice' that had vitiated 'a game whose object in this land is to establish harmonious relations between the rulers and the ruled'. *Athletic News*, 26 January 1903, p. 4.

72. See, for example, *TOI*, 1 September 1897, p. 4.

73. *BGOS*, 27 April 1901, p. 6.

74. Headlam, *Ten Thousand Miles*, p. 227.

75. Ibid., pp. 227–8.

76. Ibid., pp. 228–9.

77. Ibid.

78. Quoted in *TOI*, 17 March 1903, p. 6.

79. Raiji, *India's Hambledon Men*, pp. 80–1.

80. Anandji Dossa, '75 Years' Life of Eternal Joy: Parmanand Jivan', in *P.J. Hindu Gymkhana Platinum Jubilee Souvenir, 1894–1969* (Bombay, 1969).

81. W.D. Begg, *Cricket and Cricketers* (Ajmer, 1929), pp. 228–9; J. Naoomal, 'Cricket in Karachi', in Syed M.H. Maqsood (ed.), *Who's Who in Indian Cricket* (Delhi, 1940), pp. 72–3.

82. Naoomal, 'Cricket in Karachi', p. 73.

83. Begg, *Cricket and Cricketers*, pp. 231–3.

84. Naoomal, 'Cricket in Karachi', p. 73; 'Karachi Bohra Gymkhana: A Short History', *Sports Mirror, Special Souvenir for Jamshedi Nawroze and Republic Day of Pakistan*, Karachi, 23 March 1964; Begg, *Cricket and Cricketers*, pp. 225–7.

85. Naoomal, 'Cricket in Karachi', pp. 73–4.

86. Edward Docker, *History of Indian Cricket* (Delhi, 1976), p. 7.

87. S.R. Jagannathan, 'Father of Madras Cricket', in Suri and Raja (compiled), *Buchi Babu (Father of Madras Cricket) and His Sporting Clan* (Madras, 1993), p. 13.

88. M. Suryanarayan, 'Living in Old Mylapore', in Suri and Raja, *Buchi Babu*, pp. 7–11; C. Ramaswamy, *Ramblings of a Games Addict* (Madras, 1966), pp. 5–12; 'A Great Cricketer's Reminiscences: Leaves from the Late Mr B. Subrahmaniam's Diary', in *The Madras Cricket Association, Silver Jubilee Souvenir, 1930–1955* (Madras, 1956), pp. 45–7.

89. C. Ramaswami, 'Buchi Babu, All-Rounder', in Suri and Raja, *Buchi Babu*, pp. 39–42. On Ranji's visit to Madras, see, *TOI*, 28 April 1898, p. 6; *TOI*, 29 April 1898, p. 5; *TOI*, 2 May 1898, p. 3.

90. S.P. Sarbadhikary, 'Bengali Cricket in Calcutta: Some Little Known Facts of Interest and Importance', *Calcutta Municipal Gazette*, XIX: 6 (6 January 1934), pp. 289–90; Boria Majumdar, 'A Case of Indian Exceptionalism: Bengali Middle-Class Patronage of Sport in Colonial Bengal', in Sanjay Joshi (ed.), *The Middle Class in Colonial India* (Delhi, 2010), p. 285.

91. See, in this context, Satadru Sen, *Disciplined Natives: Race, Freedom and Confinement in Colonial India* (Delhi, 2012), pp. 107–31.

92. *Graphic*, 17 November 1900, p. 747.

93. Cashman, *Patrons, Players and the Crowd*, pp. 27–8; Docker, *History*, pp. 7–8.

94. Richard Cashman has highlighted the cosmopolitan character of the Patiala cricket team that took the field that year: W. Brockwell (Surrey professional), K.M. Mistry (Parsi, Bombay), Prince Ranjitsinhji (English test player, Rajput), Maharaja of Patiala (Sikh), B. Billimoria (Parsi, Bombay), Badesi Ram (Hindu), Arthur Priestley (English amateur), J.T. Hearne (Middlesex professional), Mehta (Parsi, Karachi), Manzoor Mahomed (Muslim), and Williams (European/Anglo-Indian). Cashman, *Patrons, Players and the Crowd*, p. 29.

95. Begg, *Cricket and Cricketers*, pp. 65–79, 86–136, 188–99, 216–22; Cashman, *Players, Patrons and the Crowd*, pp. 24–47.
96. See Cashman, *Players, Patrons and the Crowd*, p. 25; Guha, *A Corner of a Foreign Field*, pp. 106–7.
97. Begg, *Cricket and Cricketers*, pp. 204–11; Docker, *History*, pp. 8–9; Cashman, *Players, Patrons and the Crowd*, p. 39.
98. Cashman, *Players, Patrons and the Crowd*, p. 40; Begg, *Cricket and Cricketers*, pp. 212–14; Boria Majumdar, 'Maharajas and Cricket: Self, State, Province and Nation', *International Journal of the History of Sport*, 22: 4 (July 2005), pp. 641–6.
99. *TOI*, 11 February 1903, p. 4.
100. *TOI*, 18 February 1903, p. 9. But interestingly, some observers noted that the European newspapers in Calcutta had 'not done anything whatever to forward the interests of the scheme, which they seem to have left severely alone'. *Cricket*, XXII: 649 (31 December 1903), p. 476.
101. Quoted in *TOI*, 23 April 1903, p. 3.
102. *TOI*, 29 April 1903, p. 5.
103. *BGOS*, 13 June 1903, p. 7.
104. *TOI*, 29 April 1903, p. 5.
105. Quoted in *TOI*, 27 January 1903, p. 5.
106. Ibid.
107. Ibid.
108. Ibid.
109. *TOI*, 17 March 1903, p. 6.
110. Quoted in *TOI*, 18 February 1903, p. 9.
111. *BGOS*, 28 March 1903, p. 11.
112. *BGOS*, 4 April 1903, p. 20.
113. Ibid.
114. *TOI*, 17 June 1903, p. 5.
115. *BGOS*, 4 April 1903, p. 20.
116. *BGOS*, 11 July 1903, p. 6; see also *BGOS*, 18 July 1903, p. 10.
117. *BGOS*, 18 July 1903, p. 10.
118. *BGOS*, 26 September 1903, pp. 5–6.
119. *BGOS*, 7 November 1903, p. 10.
120. *BGOS*, 28 March 1903, p. 11.
121. *TOI*, 11 February 1903, p. 4.
122. *BG*, 8 December 1903, p. 4.
123. *Cricket*, XXII: 649 (31 December 1903), p. 476.
124. *BG*, 8 December 1903, p. 4.
125. Ibid.
126. *TOI*, 8 June 1928, p. 12.
127. Ibid.
128. Ibid. As might be expected of an account penned long after the event, 'Old Timer' got key facts wrong. For instance, the decision to abandon the tour was made by a majority of eight to five, and no casting vote had been required.

129. *BG*, 27 January 1904, p. 6.

130. *BG*, 28 January 1904, p. 4.

131. Ibid.

132. *Athletic News*, 4 April 1904, p. 4.

133. *Athletic News*, 16 April 1904, p. 4.

134. *BGOS*, 30 January 1904, p. 20.

135. *TOI*, 25 January 1904, p. 9.

136. *TOI*, 11 February 1903, p. 4.

137. *BG*, 8 December 1903, p. 4.

138. Quoted in *BGOS*, 26 December 1903, p. 9.

139. *TOI*, 25 January 1904, p. 9.

140. Ibid.

141. Quoted in *Athletic News*, 15 February 1904, p. 4.

142. *BG*, Monday, 22 February 1904, p. 7.

143. *BG*, 28 January 1904, p. 4.

144. Ibid.

CHAPTER 4

1. *TOI*, 1 October 1909, p. 7.

2. The details of the Wyllie murder are drawn from contemporary newspapers.

3. *Manchester Guardian* (hereafter *MG*), 12 July 1909, p. 9.

4. *Observer*, 11 July 1909, p. 9.

5. *MG*, 12 July 1909, p. 7; *The Times*, 12 July 1909, p. 4.

6. *MG*, 24 July 1909, p. 9.

7. *The Times*, 24 July 1909, p. 4.

8. *The Times*, 18 August 1909, p.7; *MG*, 18 August 1909, p. 12; *Daily Mirror*, 18 August 1909, p. 4.

9. James Campbell Ker, *Political Trouble in India 1907–1917* (Calcutta, 1917; reprinted 1973), pp. 5–10; Sumit Sarkar, *The Swadeshi Movement in Bengal, 1903–1908* (Delhi, 1973; revised edition, 2011).

10. Sumit Sarkar, *Modern India, 1885–1947* (London, 1989), p. 112.

11. Ibid., pp. 125–37.

12. *Amrita Bazar Patrika* (hereafter *ABP*), 29 January 1906, p. 9.

13. Sarkar, *Modern India*, pp. 115–25.

14. Ibid., pp. 123–5.

15. Partha Chatterjee, *The Black Hole of Empire: History of a Global Practice of Power* (Delhi, 2012), p. 285.

16. Sarkar, *Swadeshi Movement*, pp. 286–343, 395–418.

17. Ker, *Political Trouble in India*, pp. 123–33, 140–51, 290–1; Sedition Committee, 1918, *Report* (Calcutta, 1918), pp. 31–5; Sarkar, *Modern India*, pp. 123–5; Sarkar, *Swadeshi Movement*, pp. 407–10.

18. Sedition Committee, 1918, *Report*, p. 6.

19. 'Disturbances in Bombay in connection with the trial of Mr Bal Gangadhar Tilak', *Proceedings of the Government of Bombay, Judicial Department* (September 1908), no. 38, Maharashtra State Archives, Mumbai.

20. Ker, *Political Trouble in India*, pp. 155–77; Nicholas Owen, 'The Soft Heart of the British Empire: Indian Radicals in Edwardian London', *Past and Present*, 220 (August 2013), pp. 143–84; Harald Fischer-Tine, 'Indian Nationalism and the "World Forces": Transnational and Diasporic Dimensions of the Indian Freedom Movement on the Eve of the First World War', *Journal of Global History*, 2: 3 (November 2007), pp. 325–44.

21. For biographical information about Krishnavarma, see Ganeshi Lal Verma, *Shyamji Krishnavarma, the Unknown Patriot* (New Delhi, 1993) and Indulal Yajnik, *Shyamji Krishnavarma: Life and Times of an Indian Revolutionary* (Bombay, 1950).

22. Ker, *Political Trouble in India*, pp. 155–9, Sedition Committee, 1918, *Report*, p. 5.

23. Sachindra Lal Ghosh, 'India House and Madan Lal Dhingra', in Arun Chandra Guha (ed.), *The Story of Indian Revolution* (Bombay, 1972), p. 92.

24. Ker, *Political Trouble in India*, p. 156.

25. Owen, 'The Soft Heart of the British Empire', p. 149.

26. Ker, *Political Trouble in India*, pp. 157–8.

27. Quoted in A.M. Shah, 'The *Indian Sociologist*, 1905–14, 1920–22', *Economic and Political Weekly* (August 2006), pp. 3436.

28. Ker, *Political Trouble in India*, p. 157.

29. Ker, *Political Trouble in India*, p. 158; Sedition Committee, 1918, *Report*, p. 5.

30. Ker, *Political Trouble in India*, pp. 158–9; Dhananjay Keer, *Savarkar and His Times* (Bombay, 1950).

31. Ker, *Political Trouble in India*, p. 159.

32. Keer, *Savarkar*, pp. 29–34; Owen, 'The Soft Heart of the British Empire', pp. 149–50.

33. Ker, *Political Trouble in India*, p. 160.

34. Ibid., p. 163.

35. On Pandurang Bapat, see Ker, *Political Trouble in India*, p. 364. In the French capital, Bapat met Hemchandra Kanungo, a member of the Calcutta Anushilan Samiti who had also travelled to the city for the same purpose. The duo succeeded in procuring a Russian bomb-making manual from a man whom they only knew as 'PhD'. Keer, *Savarkar*, p. 36; Sarkar, *Swadeshi Movement*, pp. 406–7. In January 1908, Kanungo returned to Calcutta with his deadly new expertise and set in motion the chain of events that culminated in the ill-fated actions of Khudiram Bose and Prafulla Chaki. Keer, *Savarkar*, p. 38.

36. Ker, *Political Trouble in India*, p. 165; Ghosh, 'India House', pp. 94–5.

37. Rozina Visram, *Asians in Britain: 400 Years of History* (London, 2002), pp. 158–9.

38. *MG*, 24 July 1909, p. 9; *The Times*, 24 July 1909, p. 4.

39. Ker, *Political Trouble in India*, p. 163.

40. Keer, *Savarkar*, pp. 49–50. There were good reasons why they chose the political *aide-de-camp* for the Secretary of State for India. Curzon Wyllie had set his

sights on Savarkar, about whose 'seditious activities' he had steadily gathered information. On the basis of this evidence, he had written to the Benchers of Gray's Inn, dissuading them from calling Savarkar to the bar. See, Owen, 'The Soft Heart of the British Empire', pp. 158–9. Curzon Wyllie had also begun to work on a scheme to set up a government-sponsored student hostel to rival India House. Simultaneously, he had stepped up surveillance of India House, even contacting French intelligence for the purpose. See, Visram, *Asians in Britain*, p. 159. Madan Lal too had felt the subtle pressure of Curzon Wyllie's moves against India House. In April, the young Punjabi student had received a letter from the Englishman, inviting him to a meeting at the India Office. Wyllie had contacted Madan Lal at the behest of his elder brother Kundan Lal Dhingra, who had grown increasingly concerned about his sibling's connections with Indian radicals in London. See, *The Times*, 24 July, p. 4; *MG*, 12 July 1909, p. 7; *MG*, 24 July 1909, p. 9.

41. *The Times*, 12 July 1909, p. 4; *MG*, 12 July 1909, p. 7; *The Times*, 24 July 1909, p. 4; *MG*, 24 July 1909, p. 9.
42. Ker, *Political Trouble in India*, p. 165.
43. *The Times*, 3 July 1909, p. 8; *MG*, 3 July 1909, p. 9.
44. *PIP*, 10 July 1909, p. 19.
45. *The Times*, 6 July 1909, p. 5; see also *The Times*, 17 July 1909, p. 10.
46. *Daily Express*, 5 July 1909, p. 1.
47. Ibid.
48. *PIP*, 10 July 1909, p. 19.
49. *Daily Telegraph*, 3 July 1909, p. 12.
50. J.D. Rees, *The Fortnightly Review*, 86: 512 (August 1909), pp. 272–3.
51. Mohamed Ali, *Some Thoughts on the Present Discontent* (Bombay, 1907), pp. 21–3.
52. Ibid., p. 41.
53. Framjee Patel, *Stray Thoughts*, pp. 159–75.
54. Ibid., p. 165.
55. Ibid., p. 174.
56. *TOI*, 12 October 1918, p. 7.
57. *BGOS*, 25 June 1910, p. 8.
58. Framjee Patel, *Stray Thoughts*, pp. 157–8.
59. Ibid., p. 157.
60. Quoted in *TOI*, 31 March 1906, p. 2.
61. *Cricket*, XXV: 722 (14 June 1906), p. 193.
62. Ibid.
63. Ibid.
64. *Sportsman*, 11 June 1906, p. 2.
65. *TOI*, 14 July 1906, p. 11.
66. File 1906, No. 1573, 'Nawanagar Succession', CRR: WISA, Cutch, Kathiawar and Mahi Kantha Agencies: Bombay Government Confidential Files, 1906, IOR/R/2/676/20, APAC, BL.

67. File 1906, 'Ranjitsinhji's claim to the Nawanagar Gadi', CRR: WISA, Political Agent, Kathiawar-Halar Pranth, Confidential Files, 1906, IOR/R/575/15, APAC, BL.

68. File 1906, No. 1573, 'Nawanagar Succession', CRR: WISA, Cutch, Kathiawar and Mahi Kantha Agencies: Bombay Government Confidential Files, 1906, IOR/R/2/676/20, APAC, BL.

69. *ABP*, 17 December 1906, p. 4.

70. *Homeward Mail*, 20 August 1906, p. 1031.

71. *Cricket*, XXV: 738 (29 November 1906), p. 451.

72. *Indian Spectator*, 14 August 1898, p. 647.

73. *BGOS*, 5 October 1901, p. 9.

74. See, *TOI*, 9 October 1902, p. 4; *TOI*, 14 October 1901, p. 4.

75. Headlam, *Ten Thousand Miles*, pp. 35–6.

76. *BGOS*, August 1902, p. 6.

77. *Kaiser-i-Hind* (hereafter *KIH*), 21 May 1905, p. 9; TOI, 8 May 1906, p. 3.

78. *TOI*, 15 May 1905, p. 5; *KIH*, 21 May 1905, p. 9.

79. Quoted in *TOI*, 25 May 1905, p. 6.

80. *KIH*, 21 May 1905, p. 9.

81. Quoted in *TOI*, 25 May 1905, p. 6.

82. *TOI*, 29 September 1905, p. 8.

83. *TOI*, 17 February 1906, p. 11.

84. *Indian Social Reformer*, XVI: 26 (25 February 1906), p. 301.

85. *TOI*, 8 May 1906, p. 3.

86. *TOI*, 21 May 1906, p. 5.

87. Ibid.

88. *TOI*, 29 March 1907, p. 1A.

89. Ibid.

90. *TOI*, 28 May 1907, p. 5.

91. *Cricket*, XXVI: 755 (4 July 1907), p. 256.

92. *KIH*, 26 May 1907, p. 8.

93. *TOI*, 9 July 1907, p. 9.

94. *TOI*, 23 August 1907, p. 7.

95. *Tribune*, 21 August 1909, p. 5. 'It was not unusual,' one cricketer recalled more than a quarter of a century later, 'for the police to intervene and take control of the situation, often of the grounds, after the completion, or even during the progress, of important fixtures between Hindu and Parsi Clubs. I have recollections, as a small boy, of having witnessed more than one scene of this kind from the pavilion of one of the leading Gymkhanas.' Indeed, he added, it was 'not unusual, in the first decade of this century, to find a couple of lathis carefully stored in the kit-bag, along with the gear, as a matter of pure precaution.' B.N. Kagal, 'Communal Cricket', in Maqsood (ed.), *Who's Who in Indian Cricket*, p. 25.

96. *BG*, 30 September 1909, p. 5.

97. Bruce Murray, 'Abe Bailey and the Foundation of the Imperial Cricket Conference', *South African Historical Journal*, 60: 3 (2008), p. 389.

98. Murray, 'Abe Bailey', pp. 375–96; Patrick Ferriday, *Before the Lights Went Out: The 1912 Triangular Tournament* (Hove, 2011), pp. 87–105.

99. Murray, 'Abe Bailey', pp. 386–8.

100. Ibid., pp. 388–9.

101. Richard Parry and Dale Slater, 'The Googly, Gold and the Empire: The Role of South African Cricket in the Imperial Project, 1904–1912', in Murray and Vahed (eds), *Empire and Cricket*, p. 239; see also Geoff Levett, 'Constructing Imperial Identity: The 1907 South African Cricket Tour of England', in Murray and Vahed (eds), *Empire and Cricket*, pp. 241–58.

102. *The Times*, 9 December 1907, p. 7.

103. Rowland Bowen, Cricket: A History of Its Growth and Development throughout the World (London, 1970), p. 150; Jon Gemmell, ' "The Springboks Were Not a Test Side": The Foundation of the Imperial Cricket Conference', *Sport in Society: Cultures, Commerce, Media, Politics*, 14: 5 (June 2011), p. 705.

104. Murray, 'Abe Bailey', p. 390; Ferriday, *Before the Lights Went Out*, 91–7.

105. Parry and Slater, 'Googly', p. 237. See also Murray, 'Abe Bailey', pp. 382–6.

106. *The Times*, 4 February 1908, p. 11; *SL*, 4 February 1908, p. 1.

107. *The Times*, 6 March 1908, p. 13; *SL*, 6 March 1908, p. 4; Murray, 'Abe Bailey', p. 391.

108. *The Times*, 30 May 1908, p. 6.

109. Murray, 'Abe Bailey', pp. 391–2; Ferriday, *Before the Lights Went Out*, pp. 97–8.

110. *The Times*, 8 July 1908, p. 15.

111. *The Times*, 14 July 1908, p. 15.

112. Murray, 'Abe Bailey', 392; see also Ferriday, *Before the Lights Went Out*, pp. 98–102.

113. Indeed, as early as March 1908 he had urged the South African Cricket Association 'to press for the creation of the Imperial Board of Control as soon as possible'. Murray, 'Abe Bailey', pp. 390–2.

114. Ibid., pp. 392–3.

115. *TOI*, 4 May 1908, p. 5.

116. *Tribune*, 16 May 1908, p. 1.

117. *TOI*, 20 September 1909, p. 6.

118. *TOI*, 1 October 1909, p. 7.

119. Ibid.

120. Quoted in *TOI*, 6 October 1911, p. 8.

121. On one memorable occasion in December 1892, he captained a team of eleven Tatas against the Parsi Gymkhana. *TOI*, 20 December 1892, p. 3.

122. *Bombay Chronicle* (hereafter *BC*), 16 June 1919, p. 10.

123. *Capital*, 25 May 1911, p. 1200.

124. Like others of their ilk, the Tatas too were opposed to the rise of militant nationalism and supported the 'moderate' wing of the congress. Indeed, Ratan Tata backed Gopal Krishna Gokhale's initiative in creating a Servants of India Society, designed as a counterpoise to the secret societies that advocated the cult of the bomb. See, Ramachandra Guha, *Gandhi before India* (London, 2013), pp. 385–7.

125. Murray, 'Abe Bailey', p. 384, Ferriday, *Before the Lights Went Out*, p. 88.

126. Murray, 'Abe Bailey', pp. 384–5.

127. Ibid., p. 387.

128. See also Guha, *Gandhi before India*, pp. 385–7 .

129. *TOI*, 1 December 1909, p. 5.

130. *BGOS*, 18 June 1910, p. 17.

131. *BGOS*, 25 June 1910, p. 8.

132. Minutes of MCC Committee, 8 November 1909, MCC Library, Lord's.

133. *BG*, 28 February 1910, p. 6.

134. *BG*, 25 June 1910, p. 8.

CHAPTER 5

1. *TOI*, 2 March 1911, p. 5.

2. Extra Cover, *The Indian Cricketers' Tour of 1911* (hereafter, *The Indian Cricketers' Tour*) (Bombay, 1911), p. 16.

3. *BG*, 14 December 1909, p. 6.

4. *Cricket*, XXVIII: 829 (21 December 1909), p. 473. During the course of 1910, newspapers reported that a Ceylonese team would participate in the trial matches in Bombay in the winter of 1910. Indeed, one local European cricketer was reported to have declared that 'were the Ceylonese to prove their mettle against the crack Indian teams...he will do all in his power to persuade the Marylebone Club, of which he is a member, to guarantee support to a Ceylonese team to visit England five years hence'. Quoted in *Cricket*, XXIX: 849 (4 August 1910), p. 311.

5. *Tribune*, 13 September 1910, p. 3. Applauding this suggestion, the editor of the *Tribune* asserted that no 'hole and corner method of selection will be tolerated by the country if the team is to be styled the All India Team'. 'We cannot afford to build hopes on the captaincy of Ranji or anyone else when no inter-provincial contests have been instituted to bring the best of Indian players together and to create in them by means of frequent contests enough interest and enthusiasm to bring out the highest professional skill,' he observed. *Tribune*, 13 September 1910, p. 1.

6. *BG*, 10 October 1910, p. 4.

7. *BG*, 2 December 1910, p. 3.

8. *TOI*, 21 November 1910, p. 7.

9. *BG*, 2 March 1911, p. 4; *TOI*, 3 March 1911, p. 5; *Cricket*, XXX: 862 (30 March 1911), p. 39.

10. In his survey of the game published in 1905, Framjee Patel noted how in a number of Indian cities and towns, school cricket was 'progressing rapidly' and was 'heartily taken up by the intelligent classes'. Framjee Patel, *Stray Thoughts*, p. 131.

11. See, for instance, Jamshed Dinshaw Antia, *Elphinstone College Tours* (Bombay, 1913).

12. P.N. Polishwalla, *Indian Cricket Annual of 1926* (Bombay, September 1926), pp. 36–42.

13. *TOI*, 8 June 1910, p. 5.

14. *TOI*, 6 March 1911; *BG*, 6 March 1911, p. 7.

15. *The Parsi*, I: 1 (January 1905), p. 15.

16. *The Parsi*, I: 3 (April 1905), pp. 124–5.

17. The 1911 census recorded 52,435 Parsis in Bombay city, out of a total population of 9,72,892. Leela Visaria, 'Demographic Transition among Parsis, 1881–1971, I: Size of Parsi Population', *Economic and Political Weekly*, 9: 41 (12 October 1974), pp. 1735–41.

18. *TOI*, 9 September 1910, p. 8; *TOI*, 28 October 1910, p. 6; *TOI*, 15 February 1911, p. 7.

19. Framjee Patel, *Stray Thoughts*, p. 87; *Cricket*, XVIII: 508 (18 May 1899), p. 129; *BG*, 2 March 1911, p. 4.

20. *Cricket*, XVIII: 508 (18 May 1899), p. 129. On one memorable occasion in November 1898, Ranji and Mistry shared a mammoth 376-run partnership for Patiala against the Amballa Gymkhana. According to one European account, Rajinder Singh 'laid wagers with members of his staff that Ranji wouldn't make as many runs as Mistry'. As it turned out, Ranji exceeded Mistry's score of 255 by two runs. The Maharaja of Patiala 'marked his appreciation and affection by presenting the successful batsman with a magnificent set of jewelled studs'. Vasant Raiji, 'Pioneers of Indian Cricket: Colonel K.M. Mistry', in Anandji Dossa and Mohandas Menon (eds), *Association of Cricket Statisticians of India, Cricket Yearbook 1989–1990* (Bombay, 1989), p. 19.

21. Framjee Patel, *Stray Thoughts*, p. 87.

22. *Cricket*, XVIII: 508 (18 May 1899), p. 129.

23. Quoted in *BG*, 15 January 1909, p. 8.

24. Framji Patel, *Stray Thoughts*, p. 90.

25. *The Parsi*, I: 10 (October 1905), p. 1905, p. 419.

26. Framjee Patel, *Stray Thoughts*, p. 95.

27. *The Parsi*, I: 9 (September 1905), p. 441–2.

28. *The Parsi*, I: 10 (October 1905), p. 377.

29. Framjee Patel, *Stray Thoughts*, p. 95.

30. Popularly known as 'the Middlesex Second Eleven', the Hampstead CC took pride in the fact that 'it counted amongst its distinguished members men who had played for England against the Colonies and also men who had played for the Colonies against the Old Country'. Frederick 'Demon' Spofforth, Pelham Warner, and Andrew Stoddart, among others, were some of the prominent figures who represented the club during the Edwardian era. *Hampstead and Highgate Express*, 9 March 1901, p. 7.

31. Framjee Patel, *Stray Thoughts*, p. 97; *BG*, 15 September 1910, p. 5.

32. *BG*, 2 March 1911, p. 4; *TOI*, 31 December 1945, p. 10.

33. Framjee Patel, *Stray Thoughts*, p. 97.

34. *BG*, 15 January 1909, p. 8.

35. Extra Cover, *The Indian Cricketers' Tour*, pp. 20–1.

36. *Cricket*, NS, 1: 30 (14 December 1912), p. 593.

37. *BG*, 2 March 1911, p. 4.

38. *TOI*, 9 August 1959, p. 10.

39. *TOI*, 3 March 1911, p. 5. 'I am sure there will be no two opinions as regards the different players selected by the Committee with the exception of Mr H.F. Mulla,' declared one letter writer in *BG*. 'I do not see any reason why the Committee did not select Mr Talpade or some other better man in place of Mr Mulla.' *BG*, 4 March 1911, p. 5. Perhaps such reservations stemmed from a perception that this young Parsi batsman 'wavers between slogging and stonewalling, and naturally very often comes to grief'. *BG*, 15 September 1910, p. 5.

40. The reserve Parsi player in that list, M.D. Parekh, did not travel to Britain with the Indian cricket team. Like a number of Parsi cricketers, Parekh was an all-rounder, who turned out regularly for the Baronet CC, the Parsi Gymkhana, and the GIP Railway team.

41. Begg, *Cricket and Cricketers*, p. 132.

42. A.A. Thompson, *Cricket My Happiness* (London, 1956), p. 110.

43. *MG*, 24 May 1911, p. 10.

44. A. Rahman, 'Cricket in Rampur State', in Maqsood (ed.), *Who's Who in Indian Cricket*, p. 39.

45. *Illustrated Sporting and Dramatic News*, 19 July 1913, p. 1012.

46. *Leader*, 18 December 1910, p. 7; *BG*, 19 December 1910, p. 6. For details of their tour, see Ziauddin Ahmad, *Muhammadan Anglo-Oriental College, Aligarh, Calendar, 1911–12* (Aligarh, 1911), p. 26.

47. Ahmad, *Muhammadan Anglo-Oriental College*, p. 97; S.K. Bhatnagar, *History of the MAO College Aligarh* (Aligarh Muslim University, 1969), p. 72; Safi Ahmad Kakorwi (ed.), *Morison's History of the MAO College Aligarh* (Lucknow, 1988), pp. 19–20.

48. David Lelyveld, *Aligarh's First Generation: Muslim Solidarity in British India* (Princeton, NJ, 1978), p. 254.

49. Lelyveld, *Aligarh's First Generation*, pp. 254–5.

50. Ibid., p. 255; see also *TOI*, 6 September 1899, p. 4.

51. Syed Ali Hasan, 'Mr Beck and MAO Cricket Club', *Muhammadan Anglo-Oriental College Magazine* (hereafter *MAOC Magazine*), New Series, VII: 14 (15 November 1899), pp. 4–6.

52. *TOI*, 14 November 1884, p. 3. The team visited Meerut, Amritsar, Lahore, Jullunder, and Delhi, winning six out of the seven matches that it played. See also Lelyveld, *Aligarh's First Generation*, p. 255.

53. *TOI*, 14 November 1884, p. 3. It is said that once the game had taken off in Aligarh the founder 'used to sit the whole day long and witness the matches, and always had the same anxiety about the result as the players had'. Akhtar Hasan, 'Cricket in Aligarh'; Maqsood (ed.), *Who's Who in Indian Cricket*, p. 56.

54. Lelyveld, *Aligarh's First Generation*, p. 255.

55. Bhatnagar, *History of the MAO College*, pp. 151–2.

56. Lelyveld, *Aligarh's First Generation*, p. 256.

57. Ibid., p. 256.

58. Ibid., pp. 255–61.

59. *TOI*, 14 November 1884, p. 3.

60. Guha, *A Corner of a Foreign Field*, p. 43.

61. *TOI*, 29 October 1894, p. 4.

62. Muhammed Ali, 'Leaves from the Diary of Mr Prince-Rez or a week at an Indian College', *MAOC Magazine*, NS, 6: 6 (June 1898), p. 243.

63. Hasan, 'Cricket in Aligarh', p. 56.

64. Bhatnagar, *History of the MAO College*, p. 360.

65. Lelyveld, *Aligarh's First Generation*, p. 292.

66. Ibid.; Kakorwi, *Morison's History*, p. 30.

67. Lelyveld, *Aligarh's First Generation*, p. 293.

68. For an account of this tour, see *MAOC Magazine*, NS, 5: 2 (February 1897), pp. 51–60.

69. Ibid., pp. 52–3.

70. Ibid., p. 58.

71. *MAOC Magazine*, NS, 6: 1 (January 1898), pp. 4–11; *MAOC Magazine*, NS, 6: 2 (February 1898), pp. 52–3; *MAOC Magazine*, NS, 6: 7 (July 1898), pp. 304–5.

72. Rudyard Kipling, *Kim* (Oxford, 1998), p. 164; see also Peter Oborne, *Wounded Tiger: The History of Cricket in Pakistan* (London, 2014), p. 54.

73. *MAOC Magazine*, NS, IX: 6–7 (June–July 1901), pp. 52–3.

74. *Homeward Mail*, 1 July 1901, p. 818; *MAOC Magazine*, NS, IX: 6–7 (June–July 1901), pp. 32–7; *MAOC Magazine*, NS, IX: 8–10 (October–December 1901), pp. 14–16.

75. *MAOC Magazine*, NS, IX: 8–10 (October–December 1901), pp. 3–4.

76. Headlam, *Ten Thousand Miles*, p. 171.

77. Ibid., pp. 173–4.

78. Ibid., p. 174.

79. *BG*, 23 December 1903, p. 5; *BG*, 28 December, p. 6; *BG*, 29 December 1903, p. 5; *BG*, 30 December 1903, p. 5.

80. *BG*, 28 December 1903, p. 6.

81. *BG*, 31 December 1903, p. 5; *BG*, 1 January 1904, p. 5.

82. In August 1902 *Cricket* ran a feature on him, in which he was described as a batsman with 'a splendid eye' and a powerful drive 'which he makes without any apparent effort'. *Cricket*, XXI: 610 (7 August 1902), pp. 321–2. See also *MAOC Magazine*, NS, X: 1 (January 1902), pp. 1–6; *Sportsman*, 2 September 1902, p. 4; *Tatler*, 23 July 1902, 56, p. 158; *MAOC Magazine*, NS, X: 8–9 (October–November 1902), p. 22.

83. *Indian People*, 12 March 1905, p. 155.

84. *BG*, 7 March 1905, p. 4.

85. *TOI*, 2 March 1907, p. 8; *TOI*, 25 March 1907, p. 5; *TOI*, 11 April 1907, p. 7; *TOI*, 7 May 1908, p. 6; *TOI*, 7 June 1909, pp. 7–8; *TOI*, 26 July 1909, p. 6. On the strife in the college, see Bhatnagar, *History of the MAO College*, pp. 187–209.

86. Bhatnagar, *History of the MAO College*, pp. 226–41; Lelyveld, *Aligarh's First Generation*, pp. 327–48.

87. *BG*, 28 December 1903, p. 6. His contemporaries spelt this Aligarh cricketer's name in a bewildering variety of ways.

88. Ibid.

89. *BG*, 27 December 1910, p. 6.

90. Palwankar Vithal, *Mazhe Krida-Jeevan* (Bombay, 1948), pp. 33–5.

91. *Cricket*, XXX: 883 (2 September 1911), p. 485.

92. *BG*, 2 March 1911, p. 4.

93. On cricket at Government College, Lahore, see Osman Samiuddin, *The Unquiet Ones: A History of Pakistan Cricket* (Delhi, 2014), pp. 16–35, and Oborne, *Wounded Tiger*, pp. 60–2.

94. *Aligarh Magazine*, IX: 9–10 (October–December 1901), pp. 14–16.

95. Begg, *Cricket and Cricketers*, pp. 138–41.

96. *BG*, 21 December 1903, p. 4; *BG*, 28 December 1903, p. 6.

97. *BG*, 31 December 1903, p. 5.

98. Begg, *Cricket and Cricketers*, pp. 138–41.

99. Begg, *Cricket and Cricketers*, p. 70.

100. *Indian Social Reformer*, XVI: 25 (18 February 1906), p. 293.

101. *BG*, 9 February 1906, p. 5.

102. Ibid.

103. *BG*, 5 February 1906, p. 3.

104. *Indian Social Reformer*, XVI: 25 (18 February 1906), pp. 292–3; see also Guha, *A Corner of a Foreign Field*, pp. 110–14.

105. Guha, *A Corner of a Foreign Field*, pp. 81–98; 123–47.

106. *Indian Social Reformer*, XVI: 25 (18 Februrary 1906), p. 293.

107. Geo. W. Briggs, *The Chamars of India* (Calcutta and London, 1920), p. 11, 20.

108. Ibid., pp. 224–5.

109. Ibid., p. 20.

110. Eleanor Zelliot, *Ambedkar's World: The Making of Babasaheb and the Dalit Movement* (New Delhi, 2013), p. 33.

111. Ibid.

112. Rosalind O'Hanlon, *Caste, Conflict and Ideology: Mahatma Jotirao Phule and Low Caste Protest in Nineteenth-Century Western India* (Cambridge, 1985), p. 275.

113. Vithal, *Mazhe Krida-Jeevan*.

114. Ibid., pp. 11–12.

115. Ibid., p. 12.

116. Guha, *A Corner of a Foreign Field*, p. 89.

117. Vithal, *Mazhe Krida-Jeevan*, pp. 12–13.

118. Ibid., p. 13.

119. Ibid., p. 13.

120. Ibid., p. 14.

121. Ibid., p. 14.

122. Ibid.

123. Ibid., p. 15.

124. *BC*, Weekly Edition, 14 October 1945, p. 7.

125. Vithal, *Mazhe Krida-Jeevan*, p. 22.

126. *TOI*, 16 October 1933, p. 3.

127. *BG*, 2 March 1911, p. 4.

128. M.E. Pavri, *Parsi Cricket* (Bombay, 1901), p. 164.

129. *BC*, Weekly Edition, 14 October 1945, p. 7.

130. Vithal, *Mazhe Krida-Jeevan*, p. 16.

131. Quoted in *BC*, 6 July 1955, p. 8.

132. Vithal, *Mazhe Krida-Jeevan*, p. 15.

133. Alluding to this episode, P. Vithal stated in his autobiography that the Parsi slow bowler A.H. ('Johnny') Mehta eventually availed of the opportunity and travelled to Britain in place of his brother, Vithal, *Mazhe Krida-Jeevan*, p. 17.

134. Vithal, *Mazhe Krida-Jeevan*, pp. 29–30; Guha, *A Corner of a Foreign Field*, pp. 96–7.

135. Vithal, *Mazhe Krida-Jeevan*, p. 18.

136. Between 1907 and 1911, Baloo also took a total of forty-two wickets for the Hindus in the 'Triangular' tournament featuring the Europeans and the Parsis. Vasant Raiji and Mohandas Menon, *Story of the Bombay Tournament: From Presidency to Pentangular, 1892–93 to 1945–46* (Bombay, 2006), p. 22.

137. *BC*, 6 July 1955, p. 8.

138. *BC*, 6 July 1955, p. 8. A fifth brother, Krishna, was also said to have been a promising sportsman but, like Ganpat, he died young. Vithal, *Mazhe Krida-Jeevan*, pp. 23.

139. According to Vithal, the brothers had own specialisms as hockey players: Baloo was a centre forward, Shivram was inside right, Ganpat, inside left, and Vithal, right full-back. In this sport, as with their cricket, they played with perfect 'understanding'. Vithal, *Mazhe Krida-Jeevan*, pp. 21–2.

140. Vithal, *Mazhe Krida-Jeevan*, pp. 22–3; *Cricket*, XXX: 883 (2 September 1911), p. 485.

141. Vithal, *Mazhe Krida-Jeevan*, p. 23.

142. *BG*, 2 January 1905, p. 3.

143. Ibid.

144. Vithal, *Mazhe Krida-Jeevan*, p. 34.

145. Ibid., pp. 24–7.

146. Ibid., p. 27.

147. Ibid., p. 35. Pandharpur is a prominent pilgrimage site in southeastern Maharashtra, home to a famous temple dedicated to the Hindu deity Vitthal (popularly known as 'Vithoba' and regarded as an incarnation of Lord Vishnu) and his consort Rukmini.

148. Ibid.

149. *Madras Mail*, 30 January 1917, p. 6.

150. *Cricket*, XXV: 723 (21 June 1906), pp. 209–10. Nor is there any record of Seshachari in the Dulwich College Archive. Personal communication with Calista Lucy, Keeper of the Archive, Dulwich College, 7 September 2017.

151. *Cricket*, XXV: 723 (21 June 1906), pp. 209–10.

152. For a useful biographical account, see Norman P. Grubb, *C.T. Studd: Cricketer and Pioneer* (Cambridge, 2014).

153. *Cricket*, XXV: 723 (21 June 1906), pp. 209–10.

154. *Cricket*, XXI: 610 (7 August 1902), p. 330.

155. Ibid.

156. *Cricket*, XXV: 723 (21 June 1906), p. 210.

157. *BG*, 2 March 1911, p. 4.

158. *Cricket*, XVII: 472 (31 March 1898), pp. 33–4.

159. Ibid.

160. Ibid.

161. Ibid.

162. Begg, *Cricket and Cricketers*, p. 282.

163. Ramachandra Guha, *The Last Liberal and Other Essays* (Ranikhet, 2004), p. 35.

164. *Athletic News*, 5 January 1903, p. 6.

165. *Sportsman*, 6 January 1903, p. 4.

166. *Athletic News*, 12 January 1903.

167. *Athletic News*, 5 January 1903, p. 6.

168. *Evening Standard and St James's Gazette*, 3 July 1909, *Special Four-Page Supplement*, p. 2.

169. Ibid.

170. *BG*, 2 March 1911, p. 4.

171. *Cricket*, NS, 1: 29 (16 November 1912), p. 574.

172. *Cricket*, NS, 1: 29 (16 November 1912), p. 574; *TOI*, 26 August 1935, p. 10.

173. *Cricket*, NS, 1: 29 (16 November 1912), p. 574.

174. *BG*, 30 December 1903, p. 5; *Cricket*, NS, 1: 29 (16 November 1912), p. 574.

175. *TOI*, 1 March 1907, p. 7.

176. *BG*, 2 March 1911, p. 4.

177. *TOI*, 29 October 1935, p. 13.

178. *Cricket*, XXIX: 834 (21 April 1910), p. 76.

179. *Cricket*, XXX: 866 (6 May 1911), p. 130.

CHAPTER 6

1. There is no agreement on the number of princely states. According to the 1909 *Imperial Gazetteer of India*, there were 693 states in this category. But in 1929 the Indian States Committee 'reduced the number to 562'. Barbara N. Ramusack, *The Indian Princes and Their States: The New Cambridge History of India*, III: 6 (Cambridge, 2004), p. 2.

2. Manu Bhagavan, *Sovereign Spheres: Princes, Education and Empire in Colonial India* (Delhi, 2003); Ramusack, *Indian Princes and Their States*; Waltraud Ernst and Biswamoy Pati, *India's Princely States: People, Princes and Colonialism* (London, 2007); Aya Ikegame and Andrea Major, 'Princely Spaces and Domestic Voices: New Perspectives on the Indian Princely States', *Indian Economic and Social History Review*, 46:3 (2009), pp. 293–300.

3. Diwan Jarmani Dass, *Maharaja: The Lives, Loves and Intrigues of the Maharajas of India* (Delhi, 2007).

4. K. Natwar Singh, *The Magnificent Maharaja: The Life and Times of Maharaja Bhupinder Singh of Patiala, 1891–1938* (Delhi, 2008); Barbara N. Ramusack, 'Sir Bhupinder Singh, 1891–1938', *Oxford Dictionary of National Biography*, https://doi.org/10.1093/ref:odnb/35408.

5. *BG*, 31 March 1910, p. 4.

6. Ibid.

7. P.S.V. Fitzgerald, Agent to the Governor, Kathiawar, to Sir Steyning W. Edgerley, Chief Secretary, Government of Bombay, 20 October 1906, File 1906, No. 1573, 'Nawanagar Succession', CRR: WISA, Cutch, Kathiawar and Mahi Kantha Agencies: Bombay Government Confidential Files, 1906, IOR/R/2/676/20, APAC, BL. See also Wilde, *Ranji*, pp. 169–73.

8. File 1906, No. 1573, 'Nawanagar Succession', CRR: WISA, Cutch, Kathiawar and Mahi Kantha Agencies: Bombay Government Confidential Files, 1906, IOR/R/2/676/20, APAC, BL; File R/C 469, 'Nawanagar State', CRR: WISA, List C: Confidential Files, 1906–11, IOR/R/2/741/263, APAC, BL.

9. *TOI*, 11 March 1907, p. 7; *TOI*, 12 March 1907, p. 7; *The Times*, 13 March 1907, p. 5; Wild, *Biography*.

10. 'Nawanagar: Claims against the Jam Sahib', Political and Secret Department, Subject File 3370/1908, 1908–12, IOR/L/PS/10/157, APAC.

11. Wild, *Biography*, pp. 110–11.

12. For instance, in November 1909 he was quick to turn down a request from the Hindu Gymkhana in Bombay to lead their team in the annual Triangular contests with the Presidency and the Parsis. *TOI*, 2 November 1909, p. 5.

13. His studious silence only served to fuel the rumours that continuously circulated about his participation in the tour. Framjee Patel and his associates, for their part, realized that the public speculation about Ranji's involvement would only serve to increase public interest in the venture. It was only in the early months of 1911 that they finally acknowledged that Ranji would not be a part of the first Indian cricket team to travel to Britain.

14. *TOI*, 21 October 1909, p. 5.

15. *Cricket*, II: 56, New Series (20 September 1913), p. 626.

16. *ABP*, 7 June 1911, p. 9.

17. *TOI*, 23 November 1910, p. 5.

18. *BG*, 5 May 1911, p. 5.

19. 'Death of His Highness Sir Rajinder Singh, Maharaja of Patiala', Office of Political Agent, Phulkian States, Proceedings of the Foreign Department (Secret Branch), Government of India, File F-5/A-1-1-1900, pp. 1–43, National Archives of India (hereafter NAI), New Delhi.

20. *Sanatan Dharm Gazette* (Lahore), November 1900, *Selections from the Vernacular Newspapers Published in the Punjab*, XIII: 49 (1900), pp. 650–1, para. 17, IOR/L/R/5/184, APAC.

21. 'Political Control of the Phulkian States: Patiala Succession', note by J.M. Douie, Officiating Chief Secretary to Government, Punjab and Its Dependencies, 14 November 1900, para. 8, Proceedings of the Foreign Department (Secret Branch), Government of India (January 1901), NAI, New Delhi.

22. File A I A 58–67 1894, CRR: Political Department (hereafter PD), Internal Branch, Confidential 'A' Proceedings, 1893, IOR/R/1/1/969, APAC, BL.

23. *Civil and Military Gazette*, 14 April 1893, File A I A 58–67/1894, CRR: PD, Internal Branch, Confidential 'A' Proceedings, 1893, IOR/R/1/1/969, APAC, BL.

24. File A I A 58–67/1894, CRR: PD, Internal Branch, Confidential 'A' Proceedings, 1893, IOR/R/1/1/969, APAC.

25. 'His Highness Maharaja-Dhiraja Sir Bhupindar Singh, Mahindar Bahadur, G.C.I.E., G.B.E, Maharaja of Patiala', 1918, Political and Secret Department Memoranda: Section D, IOR/L/PS/D234, APAC, BL.

26. 'Narrative of Certain Punjab Native States: Patiala', Proceedings of the Foreign Department (Secret Branch), Government of India (January 1901), NAI, New Delhi; *Memoranda on the Native States of India, Furnished by the Local Political Officers* (Simla, 1905), pp. 264–5; W.L. Conran and H.D. Craik (revised and corrected), *Chiefs and Families of Note in the Punjab* (Lahore, 1910), Vol. II, pp. 393–8; *Punjab State Gazetteers: Phulkian States: Patiala, Jind and Nabha with Maps. Compiled and Published under the Authority of the Punjab Government, 1904* (Lahore, 1909).

27. Note by J.B. Wood, Secretary, Foreign Department, Government of India, 24 November 1910, File S I June 1911, nos. 11–12, CRR: PD, Internal Branch Secret Proceedings, 1910–11, IOR/R/1/1/433, APAC, BL.

28. File A I A 58–67/1894, CRR: PD, Internal Branch, Confidential 'A' Proceedings, 1893, IOR/R/1/1/969, APAC, BL.

29. Sir W. Mackworth Young, Lieutenant-Governor, Punjab, to Lord Curzon, Viceroy of India, 15 November 1900, Letter no. 182, Curzon Collection (July–December 1900), IOR, Mss Eur F111/202, APAC, BL.

30. Bhupinder's return to Patiala appears to have been hastened by fears that he was being brought up as a 'Hindu' at the Dholpur court. File Con B I A 57–66/1898, CRR: PD, Internal Branch, Confidential 'B' Proceedings, 1897–98, IOR/R/1/1/1056, APAC, BL.

31. In February 1900, the nationalist *Tribune* listed a litany of complaints against Rajinder's rule: the financial condition of the state was 'not satisfactory', the personal expenditure of the Maharaja was 'too heavy a charge on the revenue', firms had begun to frequently complain about the non-payment of dues, villagers were constantly petitioning 'complaining of the exactions of the Maharaja's officials', and the laxity in the administration was borne out by the 'great delay in answering correspondence and attending to official business'. *Tribune*, 13 February 1900, p. 2.

32. Lord George Hamilton, Secretary of State for India, to Lord Curzon, Viceroy of India, 2 February 1899, Letter No. 4, Curzon Collection (January–June 1899), IOR, Mss Eur F111/158, APAC, BL.

33. 'Political Control of the Phulkian States', File S 1 November 1900, nos. 11–15, CRR: PD, Internal Branch Secret Proceedings, 1900, IOR/R/1/1/251, APAC, BL.

34. 'Minute by His Excellency the Viceroy on the Appointment of a Political Agent to the Phulkian States', 11 October 1900, File S 1 November 1900, nos. 11–15, CRR: PD, Internal Branch Secret Proceedings, 1900, IOR/R/1/1/251, APAC, BL.

35. The Viceroy's view put him at odds with the Lieutenant Governor of Punjab, who agreed with Curzon about the need for a political agent but resisted the transfer of his powers over the Phulkian States to the government of India. In particular, Sir Mackworth Young advocated caution in dealing with Rajinder. A precipitate attempt to appoint a political agent, he feared, might prompt the Patiala ruler to do 'something desperate—something which will be much worse politically than his drinking'. Sir W. Mackworth Young, Lieutenant-Governor, Punjab, to Lord Curzon, Viceroy of India, 21 October 1900, Letter no. 154, Curzon Collection (July–December 1900), IOR, Mss Eur F111/202, Vol. II, APAC, BL.

36. 'Death of His Highness Sir Rajinder Singh, Maharaja of Patiala', Office of Political Agent, Phulkian States, Proceedings of the Foreign Department (Secret Branch), Government of India, File F-5/A-1-1-1900, pp. 1–43, NAI, New Delhi.

37. J.M. Douie, Officiating Chief Secretary, Government of Punjab and Its Dependencies, to Secretary, Government of India, Foreign Department, 20 November 1900, Proceedings of the Foreign Department (Secret Branch), Government of India, File F-5/A-1-1-1900, NAI, New Delhi.

38. Lord Curzon, Viceroy of India, to Lord George Hamilton, Secretary of State for India, 3 January 1901, Letter no. 1, Curzon Collection (January–June 1901), IOR, Mss Eur F111/160, APAC, BL.

39. Sir Walter Lawrence to Lord Curzon, 10 April 1903, Letter no. 111, Curzon Collection (January–June 1903), IOR, Mss Eur F111/207, APAC, BL.

40. 'Political Control of the Phulkian States: Patiala Succession', note by J.M. Douie, Officiating Chief Secretary to Government, Punjab and Its Dependencies, 14 November 1900, para. 4, Proceedings of the Foreign Department (Secret Branch), Government of India (January 1901), NAI, New Delhi.

41. Sir W. Mackworth Young, Lieutenant-Governor, Punjab, to Lord Curzon, 9 December 1900, Letter no. 206, Curzon Collection (July–December 1900), IOR, Mss Eur F111/202, APAC, BL.

42. H.S. Barnes, Secretary, Government of India, Foreign Department, to the Chief Secretary, Government of the Punjab, 2 January 1901, para. 8, Proceedings of the Foreign Department (Secret Branch), Government of India, File F-5/A-1-1-1900, pp. 1–43, NAI, New Delhi.

43. Natwar Singh, *Magnificent Maharaja*, p. 49.

44. E.D. Maclagan, Chief Secretary, Government of the Punjab, to S. Harcourt Butler, Secretary, Government of India, Foreign Department, 19 December 1908, File S I February 1911, nos. 1–6, CRR: PD, Internal Branch Secret Proceedings, 1908–10, IOR/R/1/1/425, APAC, BL.

45. Stefan Collini, 'The Idea of "Character" in Victorian Political Thought', *Transactions of the Royal Historical Society*, Fifth Series, 35 (1985), pp. 29–50.

46. M.W. Fenton, Chief Secretary, Government of the Punjab, to S. Harcourt Butler, Secretary, Government of India, Foreign Department, 5 July 1909, File S I February 1911, nos. 1–6, CRR: PD, Internal Branch Secret Proceedings, 1908–10, IOR/R/1/1/425, APAC, BL.

47. E.D. Maclagan, Chief Secretary, Government of the Punjab, to S. Harcourt Butler, Secretary, Government of India, Foreign Department, 19 December 1908, File S I February 1911, nos. 1–6, CRR: PD, Internal Branch Secret Proceedings, 1908–10, IOR/R/1/1/425, APAC, BL.

48. J.M. Douie, Officiating Chief Secretary, Government of Punjab, to Lieutenant-Colonel Stuart-Beatson, Inspector-General, Imperial Service Troops, Umballa Cantonment, 5 December 1900, Proceedings of the Foreign Department (Secret Branch), Government of India, File F-5/A-1-1-1900, pp. 1–43, NAI, New Delhi.

49. Major C. Powney Thompson, Political Agent, Phulkian States and Bahawalpur, to M.W. Fenton, Chief Secretary, Government of the Punjab, 14 August 1909, File S I February 1911, nos. 1–6, CRR: PD, Internal Branch Secret Proceedings, 1908–10, IOR/R/1/1/425, APAC, BL.

50. Note by Sir Louis W. Dane, Lieutenant-Governor, Punjab, 16 September 1909, Proceedings of the Foreign Department, Government of India (February 1911), File S I February 1911, nos. 1–6, CRR: PD, Internal Branch Secret Proceedings, 1908–10, IOR/R/1/1/425, APAC, BL.

51. Quoted in S.R. Ashton, *British Policy towards the Indian States* (London, 1982), p. 37.

52. Barbara Ramusack, *Indian Princes and Their States*, pp. 117–18.

53. Ashton, *British Policy*, pp. 42–5.

54. S. Harcourt Butler, Secretary, Government of India, Foreign Department, to M.W. Fenton, Chief Secretary, Government of the Punjab, 27 September 1909, File S I February 1911, nos. 1–6, CRR: PD, Internal Branch Secret Proceedings, 1908–10, IOR/R/1/1/425, APAC, BL.

55. Ibid.

56. Ibid.

57. 'Extract from the Diary of the Political Agent, Phulkian States and Bahawalpur, for the Period Ending 18 December 1909', File S I February 1911, nos. 1–6, CRR: PD, Internal Branch Secret Proceedings, 1908–10, IOR/R/1/1/425, APAC, BL.

58. 'Extract from the Diary of the Political Agent, Phulkian States and Bahawalpur, for the Period Ending 27 January 1910', File S I February 1911, nos. 1–6, CRR: PD, Internal Branch Secret Proceedings, 1908–10, IOR/R/1/1/425, APAC, BL.

59. 'Confidential Note on Patiala Affairs', Lieutenant-Colonel C.M. Dallas, Political Agent, Phulkian States and Bahawalpur, 21 May 1910, File S I February 1911, nos. 1–6, CRR: PD, Internal Branch Secret Proceedings, 1908–10, IOR/R/1/1/425, APAC, BL.

60. Sir Louis W. Dane, Lieutenant-Governor, Punjab, to Sir James R Dunlop Smith, Private Secretary to the Viceroy, 4 January 1910, File S I February 1911, nos. 1–6, CRR: PD, Internal Branch Secret Proceedings, 1908–10, IOR/R/1/1/425, APAC, BL.

61. S. Harcourt Butler, Secretary, Government of India, Foreign Department, to E.D. Maclagan, Chief Secretary, Government of the Punjab, 17 February 1910,

File S I February 1911, nos. 1–6, CRR: PD, Internal Branch Secret Proceedings, 1908–10, IOR/R/1/1/425, APAC, BL.

62. J.B. Wood, Officiating Secretary, Government of India, Foreign Department, to E.D. Maclagan, Chief Secretary, Government of the Punjab, 6 April 1910, File S I February 1911, nos. 1–6, CRR: PD, Internal Branch Secret Proceedings, 1908–10, IOR/R/1/1/425, APAC, BL.

63. E.D. Maclagan, Chief Secretary, Government of the Punjab, to S. Harcourt Butler, Secretary, Government of India, Foreign Department, 12 May 1910, File S I February 1911, nos. 1–6, CRR: PD, Internal Branch Secret Proceedings, 1908–10, IOR/R/1/1/425, APAC, BL.

64. S. Harcourt Butler, Secretary, Government of India, Foreign Department, to Lieutenant-Colonel A.F. Pinhey, Private Secretary to the Viceroy, 30 May 1910, File S I February 1911, nos. 1–6, CRR: PD, Internal Branch Secret Proceedings, 1908–10, IOR/R/1/1/425, APAC, BL.

65. Lieutenant-Colonel C.M. Dallas, Political Agent, Phulkian States and Bahawalpur, to E.D. Maclagan, Chief Secretary, Government of the Punjab, 28 June 1910, File S I February 1911, nos. 1–6, CRR: PD, Internal Branch Secret Proceedings, 1908–10, IOR/R/1/1/425, APAC, BL.

66. Maharaja of Patiala, to the Political Agent, Phulkian States and Bahawalpur, 30 June 1910, File S I February 1911, nos. 1–6, CRR: PD, Internal Branch Secret Proceedings, 1908–10, IOR/R/1/1/425, APAC, BL. See also Proceedings of the Home Department (Political Branch), Government of India (September 1910), no. 6, NAI, New Delhi.

67. 'Measures Taken in the Patiala and Certain Other Native States for the Discouragement of Sedition', File S I September 1910, nos. 2–4, CRR: PD, Internal Branch Secret Proceedings, 1909–10, IOR/R/1/1/416, APAC, BL.

68. *Sheffield Daily Telegraph*, 4 April 1910, p. 6.

69. E.D. Maclagan, Chief Secretary, Government of the Punjab, to S. Harcourt Butler, Secretary, Government of India, Foreign Department, 11 May 1910, File S I September 1910, nos. 2–4, CRR: PD, Internal Branch Secret Proceedings, 1909–10, IOR/R/1/1/416, APAC, BL.

70. Secretary, Government of India, Foreign Department, to E.D. Maclagan, Chief Secretary, Government of the Punjab, 13 June 1910, File S I September 1910, nos. 2–4, CRR: PD, Internal Branch Secret Proceedings, 1909–10, IOR/R/1/1/416, APAC, BL.

71. 'Confidential Note on Patiala Affairs', Lieutenant-Colonel C.M. Dallas, Political Agent, Phulkian States and Bahawalpur, 21 May 1910, File S I February 1911, nos. 1–6, CRR: PD, Internal Branch Secret Proceedings, 1908–10, IOR/R/1/1/425, APAC, BL.

72. Lieutenant-Colonel C.M. Dallas, Political Agent, Phulkian States and Bahawalpur, to E.D. Maclagan, Chief Secretary, Government of the Punjab, 28 June 1910, File S I February 1911, nos. 1–6, CRR: PD, Internal Branch Secret Proceedings, 1908–10, IOR/R/1/1/425, APAC, BL.

73. J.B. Wood, Officiating Secretary, Government of India, Foreign Department, to H.P. Tollinton, Officiating Chief Secretary, Government of the Punjab, 8 July 1910,

File S I February 1911, nos. 1–6, CRR: PD, Internal Branch Secret Proceedings, 1908–10, IOR/R/1/1/425, APAC, BL.

74. Maharaja of Patiala, to Lieutenant-Colonel C.M. Dallas, Political Agent, Phulkian States and Bahawalpur, 28 July 1910, File S I February 1911, nos. 1–6, CRR: PD, Internal Branch Secret Proceedings, 1908–10, IOR/R/1/1/425, APAC, BL.

75. H.P. Tollinton, Officiating Chief Secretary, Government of the Punjab, to J.B. Wood, Officiating Secretary, Government of India, Foreign Department, 4 September 1910, File S I February 1911, nos. 1–6, CRR: PD, Internal Branch Secret Proceedings, 1908–10, IOR/R/1/1/425, APAC, BL.

76. Ibid.

77. C.H. Atkins, Political Agent, Phulkian States and Bahawalpur, to H.P. Tollinton, Officiating Chief Secretary, Government of Punjab, 10 September 1910, File S I February 1911, nos. 1–6, CRR: PD, Internal Branch Secret Proceedings, 1908–10, IOR/R/1/1/425, APAC, BL.

78. S. Harcourt Butler, Secretary, Government of India, Foreign Department, to H.P. Tollinton, Officiating Chief Secretary, Government of the Punjab, 20 September 1910, File S I February 1911, nos. 1–6, CRR: PD, Internal Branch Secret Proceedings, 1908–10, IOR/R/1/1/425, APAC, BL.

79. Sir Louis W. Dane, Lieutenant-Governor, Punjab, to C.H. Atkins, Political Agent, Phulkian States and Bahawalpur, 19 October 1910, File S I February 1911, nos. 1–6, CRR: PD, Internal Branch Secret Proceedings, 1908–10, IOR/R/1/1/425, APAC, BL.

80. Telegram from Sir Louis W. Dane, Lieutenant-Governor, Punjab, to the Private Secretary to the Viceroy, 22 October 1910, File S I February 1911, nos. 1–6, CRR: PD, Internal Branch Secret Proceedings, 1908–10, IOR/R/1/1/425, APAC, BL.

81. The Patiala Imperial Service Troops, which had been created in 1887, comprised 1,200 infantry men and a 600-strong cavalry regiment. Its soldiers had been deployed in frontier campaigns in the 1890s and were widely regarded as a well-trained unit. *Memoranda on the Native States*, p. 265; Conran and Craik, *Chiefs and Families of Note in the Punjab*, II, p. 397.

82. Major E.J.M. Molyneux, Inspecting Officer, Punjab Imperial Services Cavalry, to Major-General F.H.R. Drummond, Inspector-General, Imperial Service Troops, 18 October 1910, File S I February 1911, nos. 1–6, CRR: PD, Internal Branch Secret Proceedings, 1908–10, IOR/R/1/1/425, APAC, BL.

83. 'Note by Minto', 24 October 1910, File S I February 1911, nos. 1–6, CRR: PD, Internal Branch Secret Proceedings, 1908–10, IOR/R/1/1/425, APAC, BL.

84. Telegram from Private Secretary to the Viceroy, to the Lieutenant-Governor of the Punjab, 24 October 1910, File S I February 1911, nos. 1–6, CRR: PD, Internal Branch Secret Proceedings, 1908–10, IOR/R/1/1/425, APAC, BL.

85. Ibid.

86. *Tribune*, 6 November 1910, p. 5; *TOI*, 7 November 1910, p. 8.

87. *ABP*, 4 November 1910, p. 6; *Tribune*, 5 November 1910, p. 4; *TOI*, 5 November 1910, p. 10; *Leader*, 6 November 1910, p. 4.

88. Cashman, *Patrons, Players and the Crowd*, p. 32. See also Anthony de Mello, *Portrait of Indian Sport* (London, 1959), p. 126.

89. *BGOS*, 20 November 1909, p. 10.

90. M.W. Fenton, Chief Secretary, Government of the Punjab, to S. Harcourt Butler, Secretary, Government of India, Foreign Department, 12 June 1909, File S I February 1911, 1–6, CRR: PD, Internal Branch Secret Proceedings, 1908–10, IOR/R/1/1/425, APAC, BL.

91. M.W. Fenton, Chief Secretary, Government of the Punjab, to S. Harcourt Butler, Secretary, Government of India, Foreign Department, 5 July 1909, File S I February 1911, 1–6, CRR: PD, Internal Branch Secret Proceedings, 1908–10, IOR/R/1/1/425, APAC, BL.

92. *Vilayat*: literally, foreign land; at this time, the term principally meant Britain and Europe.

93. Note by J.B. Wood, Officiating Secretary, Government of India, Foreign Department, 17 June 1910, File S I February 1911, nos. 1–6, CRR: PD, Internal Branch Secret Proceedings, 1908–10, IOR/R/1/1/425, APAC, BL.

94. C.H. Atkins, Political Agent, Phulkian States and Bahawalpur, to M.W. Fenton, Chief Secretary, Government of the Punjab, 1 January 1911, File S I June 1911, nos. 11–12, CRR: PD, Internal Branch Secret Proceedings, 1910–11, IOR/R/1/1/433, APAC, BL.

95. C.H. Atkins, Political Agent, Phulkian States and Bahawalpur, 'Unofficial Report on Patiala Affairs for the Month of December 1910', 31 December 1910, File S I June 1911, nos. 11–12, CRR: PD, Internal Branch Secret Proceedings, 1910–11, IOR/R/1/1/433, APAC, BL.

96. C.H. Atkins, Political Agent, Phulkian States and Bahawalpur, to M.W. Fenton, Chief Secretary, Government of the Punjab, 1 January 1911, File S I June 1911, nos. 11–12, CRR: PD, Internal Branch Secret Proceedings, 1910–11, IOR/R/1/1/433, APAC, BL.

97. M.W. Fenton, Chief Secretary, Government of the Punjab, to J.B. Wood, Secretary, Government of India, Foreign Department, 9 January 1911, File S I June 1911, nos. 11–12, CRR: PD, Internal Branch Secret Proceedings, 1910–11, IOR/R/1/1/433, APAC, BL.

98. 'There are undoubtedly a certain number of Chiefs who will come to England in any case,' wrote Viceroy Hardinge to the Secretary of State. But he insisted that 'all my Council are very strong in their opinion as to the undesirability of any Chiefs or representatives going to England for the Coronation other than the military deputation'. Lord Hardinge, Viceroy of India, to Earl of Crewe, Secretary of State for India, Letter No. 4, 8 December 1910, Crewe Collection, IOR, Mss Eur Photo Eur 469, APAC, BL.

99. M.W. Fenton, Chief Secretary, Government of the Punjab, to J.B. Wood, Secretary, Government of India, Foreign Department, 9 January 1911, File S I June 1911, nos. 11–12, CRR: PD, Internal Branch Secret Proceedings, 1910–11, IOR/R/1/1/433, APAC, BL.

100. Ibid.

101. J.B. Wood, Secretary, Government of India, Foreign Department, to M.W. Fenton, Chief Secretary, Government of the Punjab, 12 January 1911, File S I June 1911, nos. 11–12, CRR: PD, Internal Branch Secret Proceedings, 1910–11, IOR/R/1/1/433, APAC, BL.

102. Ibid.

103. C.H. Atkins, Political Agent, Phulkian States and Bahawalpur, 'Unofficial Report on Patiala Affairs for the Month of January 1911', 2 February 1911, File S I June 1911, nos. 11–12, CRR: PD, Internal Branch Secret Proceedings, 1910–11, IOR/R/1/1/433, APAC, BL.

104. M.W. Fenton, Chief Secretary, Government of the Punjab, to the Secretary, Government of India, Foreign Department, 17 March 1911, File S I June 1911, nos. 11–12, CRR: PD, Internal Branch Secret Proceedings, 1910–11, IOR/R/1/1/433, APAC, BL.

105. 'Copy of a Letter Dated the 1st March, from the Political Agent, Phulkian States and Bahawalpur, to the Chief Secretary to the Government of the Punjab', Proceedings of the Foreign Department (Secret Branch), Government of India (June 1911), no. 11, NAI, New Delhi.

106. M.W. Fenton, Chief Secretary, Government of the Punjab, to the Secretary, Government of India, Foreign Department, 17 March 1911, File S I June 1911, nos. 11–12, CRR: PD, Internal Branch Secret Proceedings, 1910–11, IOR/R/1/1/433, APAC, BL.

107. Note by Lieutenant-Colonel Sir A.H. McMahon, Secretary, Government of India, Foreign Department, 24 March 1911, File S I June 1911, nos. 11–12, CRR: PD, Internal Branch Secret Proceedings, 1910–11, IOR/R/1/1/433, APAC, BL.

108. Lieutenant-Colonel Sir A.H. McMahon, Secretary, Government of India, Foreign Department, to Lieutenant-Colonel Sir James R. Dunlop Smith, Political Aide-de-Camp to His Majesty's Secretary of State for India, India Office, London, 13th April 1911, File S I June 1911, nos. 11–12, CRR: PD, Internal Branch Secret Proceedings, 1910–11, IOR/R/1/1/433, APAC, BL.

109. C.H. Atkins, Political Agent, Phulkian States and Bahawalpur, 'Report on Patiala Affairs for the Month of March 1911', 6 April 1911, File S I June 1911, nos. 11–12, CRR: PD, Internal Branch Secret Proceedings, 1910–11, IOR/R/1/1/433, APAC, BL.

110. Ibid.

111. *Tribune*, 19 April 1911, p. 1.

112. C.H. Atkins, Political Agent, Phulkian States and Bahawalpur, 'Report on Patiala Affairs for the Month of March 1911', 6 April 1911, File S I June 1911, nos. 11–12, CRR: PD, Internal Branch Secret Proceedings, 1910–11, IOR/R/1/1/433, APAC, BL.

113. *Tribune*, 12 May 1911.

114. *TOI*, 1 May 1911, p. 5.

115. Extra Cover, *The Indian Cricketers' Tour*, p. 38.

116. *Madras Times* (Overland Edition), 11 May 1911, p. 7.

117. *TOI*, 5 May 1911, p. 5.

118. *TOI*, 5 May 1911, p. 5; *BG*, 5 May 1911, p. 6.
119. *Indian Nation*, 19 June 1911, p. 287.
120. *TOI*, 5 May 1911, p. 5. The first images of the Indian cricket team appeared on the morning of their departure. *TOI*, 6 May 1911, p. 7.
121. *TOI*, 5 January 1910, p. 10.
122. *TOI*, 5 May 1911, p. 5.
123. Ibid.
124. Ibid.
125. These words were not new: Patel was recycling them from his own book, written six years earlier, on the history of Indian cricket. See, Framjee Patel, *Stray Thoughts*, p. 175.
126. *TOI*, 5 May 1911, p. 5; *Tribune*, 10 May 1911, p. 3.
127. *BG*, 5 May 1911, p. 4.
128. *TOI*, 6 May 1911, p. 8.
129. *Capital*, 11 May 1911, p. 1086.
130. *BG*, 6 May 1911, p. 8; *Tribune*, 9 May 1911, p. 4.
131. Extra Cover, *The Indian Cricketers' Tour*, p. 37.
132. Vithal, *Mazhe Krida-Jivan*, p. 17.
133. *TOI*, 8 May 1911, p. 5; *BG*, 8 May 1911, p. 3.
134. Although the Palwankar brothers did not say anything at the time, Vithal later revealed in his autobiography that they had both been deeply stung by this public insult. See, Vithal, *Mazhe Krida-Jivan*, pp. 17–18.

CHAPTER 7

1. *SL*, 22 May 1911, p. 7.
2. *TOI*, 10 June 1911, p. 7.
3. *TOI*, 15 April 1910, p. 14.
4. *Daily Mail*, 22 May 1911, p. 9.
5. *SL*, 22 May 1911, p. 7.
6. *TOI*, 10 June 1911, p. 7.
7. Extra Cover, *The Indian Cricketers' Tour*, pp. 35–6.
8. *SL*, 23 May 1911, p. 6.
9. Edwin Pugh, *The City of the World: A Book about London and the Londoner* (London, 1912), pp. 10–11.
10. *TOI*, 10 May 1911, p. 6.
11. Geoffrey Levett, 'Sport and the Imperial City: Colonial Tours in Edwardian London', *London Journal*, 35: 1 (March 2010), p. 51.
12. Ibid.
13. Jonathan Schneer, *London 1900: The Imperial Metropolis* (London, 2001), pp. 19–28; Jerry White, *London in the Twentieth Century* (London, 2008), p. 8.
14. M.H. Port, *Imperial London: Civil Government Building in London 1851–1915* (London, 1995), 233–51.
15. Schneer, *London 1900*, pp. 18–19; White, *London in the Twentieth Century*, pp. 9–10.
16. Schneer, *London 1900*, p. 19.

17. Ibid., p. 28.
18. David Gilbert and Felix Driver, 'Capital and Empire: Geographies of Imperial London', *GeoJournal*, 51 (2000), p. 28.
19. *Illustrated London News*, 20 May 1911, p. 15.
20. Henry James, *English Hours* (Oxford, 1981), p. 95.
21. Arthur H. Beavan, *Imperial London* (London, 1901), pp. 234–6; Port of London Authority (henceforth PLA), *London, Port of Empire* (London, 1914); Stephen Inwood, *City of Cities: The Birth of Modern London* (London, 2005), pp. 21–3.
22. Karl Baedeker, *Baedeker's London and Its Environs: Handbook for Travellers* (Leipzig, London, and New York, 1911), p. 144.
23. PLA, *London*, p. 64.
24. White, *London in the Twentieth Century*, p. 110.
25. *Evening Standard*, 25 January 1911. Quoted in Ben Looker, *Exhibiting Imperial London: Empire and the City in Late Victorian and Edwardian Guidebooks* (London, 2002), p. 15.
26. S. Satthianadhan, *A Holiday Trip to Europe and America* (Madras, 1897), quoted in Visram, *Asians in Britain*, p. 116.
27. E.V. Lucas, *A Wanderer in London* (London, 1906), p. 221.
28. Antoinette Burton, *At the Heart of the Empire: Indians and the Colonial Encounter in Late-Victorian Britain* (London, 1998), p. 177.
29. *Hindoo Patriot*, 6 July 1911, p. 3.
30. Ker, *Political Trouble in India*, p. 167, 177; Keer, *Savarkar*, pp. 63–8; Janaki Bakhle, 'Savarkar (1883–1966), Sedition and Surveillance: The Rule of Law in a Colonial Situation', *Social History*, 35: 1 (February 2010), pp. 51–75; Fischer-Tine, 'Indian Nationalism', pp. 332–3.
31. Visram, *Asians in Britain*, p. 85; Hillary J. Shaw, *The Consuming Geographies of Food: Diet, Food Desserts and Obesity* (London, 2014), p. 43.
32. *Graphic*, 27 May 1911, p. 790.
33. *Daily Mail*, 25 May 1911, p. p. 6.
34. *TOI*, 2 June 1911, p. 6.
35. *Daily Mail*, 25 May 1911, p. 6.
36. *MG*, 24 May 1911, p. 8.
37. *The Times*, 15 May 1911, p. 11.
38. *Tribune*, 4 July 1911, p. 2.
39. *Tribune*, 8 July 1911, p. 5.
40. *Hindoo Patriot*, 30 June 1911, p. 6.
41. *MG*, 28 May 1911, p. 5.
42. *Observer*, 28 May 1911, p. 15.
43. *The Times*, 12 June 1911, p. 7.
44. *MG*, 14 June 1911, p. 6.
45. *The Times*, 24 June 1911, p.9.
46. *The Times*, 13 May 1911, p. 11.
47. *MG*, 14 May 1911, p. 6.
48. *The Times*, 5 May 1911, p. 7.
49. Ibid.

50. Timothy Mitchell, 'The World as Exhibition', *Comparative Studies in Society and History*, 31: 2 (1989), 217–36.

51. *Observer*, 14 May 1911, p. 6.

52. See, in this context, Mark Freeman, 'Splendid Display; Pompous Spectacle: Historical Pageants in Twentieth Century Britain', *Social History*, 38: 4 (2013), pp. 423–55.

53. Deborah Ryan, 'Staging the Imperial City', in Felix Driver and David Gilbert (eds), *Imperial Cities: Landscape, Display and Identity* (Manchester, 1999), pp. 117–35.

54. *The Times*, 8 June 1911, p. 6.

55. *The Times*, 5 May 1911, p. 7.

56. Susan Fielding, 'London 1911: Celebrating the Imperial', *Revues.org*, 11 (2011), pp. 1–11.

57. *The Times*, 3 March 1911, p. 9.

58. *Daily Express*, 16 May 1911, p. 1.

59. Ian C. Fletcher, 'Introduction: New Perspectives on the First Universal Races Congress of 1911', *Radical History Review*, 92 (Spring 2005), p. 99.

60. Ibid.

61. *The Record of the Proceedings of the First Universal Races Congress Held at the University of London, July 26–29, 1911* (London, 1911), p. 2.

62. G. Spiller (ed.), *Papers on Inter-Racial Problems Communicated to the First Universal Races Congress Held at the University of London, July 26–29, 1911* (London, 1911).

63. *The Crisis: A Record of the Darker Races*, II: 5 (September 1911), p. 202.

64. *MG*, 27 July 1911, p. 6.

65. Susan D. Pennybacker, 'The Universal Races Congress, London, Political Culture, and Imperial Dissent, 1900–1939', *Radical History Review*, 92 (Spring 2005), p. 106.

66. Ibid., p. 104.

67. *Leader*, 9 July 1910, p. 3.

68. *Indian Social Reformer*, quoted in *Homeward Mail*, 8 August 1910, p. 1000.

69. *Leader*, 29 July 1910, p. 3; *BG*, 22 November 1910, p. 4.

70. *ABP*, 22 December 1910, p. 1.

71. *Kala Paani*: literally, 'Black Water'; here, refers to oceanic travel.

72. *Hindi Punch*, 12 February 1911, p. 14; *Hindi Punch*, 12 February 1911, p. 19.

73. *Hindi Punch*, 26 March 1911, p. 21.

74. *TOI*, 30 September 1910, p. 9.

75. File No. 4285, Public and Judicial Department, IOR/L/PJ/6/1121, APAC, BL.

76. T. Ramakrishna, *My Visit to the West* (London, 1915); N. Ramanujaswami, *My Trip to England, 1911* (Madras, 1912).

77. Burton, *At the Heart of the Empire*, pp. 1–71, pp. 152–92; Julie F. Codell, 'Reversing the Grand Tour: Guest Discourse in Indian Travel Narratives', *Huntington Library Quarterly*, 70: 1 (March 2007), pp. 173–89; Visram, *Asians in Britain*, pp. 105–22.

78. Tamson Pietsch, 'A British Sea: Making Sense of Global Space in the Late Nineteenth Century', *Journal of Global History*, 5: 3 (November 2010), pp. 423–46.

79. Ramakrishna, *My Visit to the West*, pp. 11–12.

80. Ramanujaswami, *My Trip to England*, pp. 12–13.
81. Ibid., p. 34.
82. Ramakrishna, *My Visit to the West*, p. 22.
83. Ibid., p. 29.
84. Ramanujaswami, *My Trip to England*, p. 88.
85. Ibid., p. 89.
86. Ramakrishna, *My Visit to the West*, p. 24.
87. Ramanujaswami, *My Trip to England*, pp. 68–9.
88. Ibid., p. 70.
89. Ramakrishna, *My Visit to the West*, p. 5.
90. Ramanujaswami, *My Trip to England*, pp. i–iii.
91. Ibid., p. 112.
92. Ibid., pp. 63–4.
93. Ibid., p. 48.
94. Ibid., p. 62.

CHAPTER 8

1. *The Times*, 24 February 1911, p. 15; *Health and Strength*, VIII: 23 (10 June 1911), p. 571; 'Festival of Empire', *History Today* (August 2002), pp. 2–3; Erik Nielsen, *Sport and the British World, 1900–1939: Amateurism and National Identity in Australasia and Beyond* (Basingstoke, 2014), pp. 114–15.
2. On Jack Johnson's legendary career and times, see Theresa Runstedtler, *Jack Johnson, Rebel Sojourner: Boxing in the Shadows* (Berkeley, CA, 2012) and Geoffrey C. Ward, *Unforgivable Blackness: The Rise and Fall of Jack Johnson* (London, 2005).
3. Runstedtler, *Jack Johnson*, p. 74.
4. Ibid., pp. 78–100.
5. *MG*, 8 June 1911, p. 5; *Sheffield Daily Telegraph*, 13 June 1911, p. 11.
6. *MG*, 23 June 1911, p. 8.
7. Runstedtler, *Jack Johnson*, p. 106.
8. *TOI*, 6 May 1911, p. 7.
9. *The Times*, 29 April 1911, p. 15. On the history of racquets, see J.R. Atkins, *The Book of Racquet: A Practical Guide to the Game and Its History and to the Different Courts in Which It Is Played* (London, 1872).
10. A.R. Winsloe, *Rackets in India* (Bombay, 1930), p. 4.
11. Major-General S.H. Sheppard, 'Foreword', in Winsloe, *Rackets in India*, p. v.
12. According to one account of sport in colonial India, 'custom long decreed that a military station was incomplete without its racquet court'. F.R. Aflalo, *Sportsmen's Book for India* (London, 1904), p. 518.
13. *TOI*, 25 June 1935, p. 12.
14. Winsloe, *Rackets in India*, p. 8; Darukhanawala, *Parsis and Sports*, pp. 225–6.
15. Darukhanawala, *Parsis and Sports*, pp. 225–6.
16. Ibid.; see also *TOI*, 25 June 1935, p. 12.
17. *TOI*, 26 February 1902, p. 8.

18. Ibid.
19. *The Times*, 29 April 1911, p. 15. Remarkably, Latham was also simultaneously the world champion in tennis. *Observer*, 6 May 1945, p. 8.
20. Quoted in *TOI*, 20 February 1903, p. 9.
21. *TOI*, 3 January 1903, p. 5; *TOI*, 30 May 1903, p. 8.
22. *TOI*, 30 May 1903, p. 8.
23. Ibid.
24. Ibid.
25. *TOI*, 13 June 1903, p. 11.
26. Ibid.
27. *TOI*, 16 June 1903, p. 6; *The Times*, 25 May 1903, p. 12.
28. *Yorkshire Telegraph and Star*, 29 May 1903.
29. *TOI*, 3 February 1904, p. 5; *TOI*, 4 June 1903, p. 3.
30. *TOI*, 3 February 1904, p. 5; *Times*, 2 June 1903, p. 10; *TOI*, 4 June 1903, p. 3.
31. *The Times*, 4 May 1903, p. 10.
32. *MG*, 17 July 1903, p. 4.
33. Ibid.
34. *The Times*, 26 December 1910; *MG*, 23 January 1911, p. 3.
35. *The Times*, 2 June 1909, p. 18.
36. *Observer*, 22 May 1910, p. 13; *The Times*, 29 April 1911, p. 15.
37. *Observer*, 15 January 1911, p. 12. *MG*, 26 January 1911, p. 3.
38. *MG*, 2 February 1911, p. 3.
39. *TOI*, 17 October 1910, p. 9; *TOI*, 2 February 1911, p. 5.
40. *TOI*, 2 February 1911, p. 5.
41. *TOI*, 4 February 1911, p. 7.
42. *TOI*, 2 February 1911, p. 5.
43. *The Times*, 20 March 1911, p. 14.
44. *The Times*, 10 April 1911, p. 12.
45. *Observer*, 30 April 1911, p. 19; *TOI*, 20 May 1911, p. 7.
46. *New York Times*, 30 April 1911, p. 8.
47. *TOI*, 20 May 1911, p. 7.
48. *MG*, 30 April 1911, 19.
49. *Daily Mail*, 1 May 1911, p. 4.
50. *SL*, 1 May 1911, p. 1.
51. *MG*, 30 April 1911, p. 19; *The Times*, 1 May 1911, p. 15.
52. *MG*, 14 May 1911, p. 16.
53. *Daily Mirror*, 1 May 1911, p. 14.
54. *The Times*, 1 May 1911.
55. *Sheffield Daily Telegraph*, 1 May 1911, p. 6.
56. *Daily Mirror*, 13 April 1911, p. 14.
57. *MG*, 25 May 1911, p. 5.
58. *SL*, 24 May 1911, p. 6.
59. S. Mazumdar, *Strong Men over the Years: A Chronicle of Athletes* (Lucknow, 1942), p. 65; Joseph S. Alter, 'Gama the World Champion: Wrestling and Physical Culture in Colonial India', *Iron Game History* (October 1995), p. 5.

60. John Rosselli, 'The Self-Image of Effeteness: Physical Education and Nationalism in Nineteenth-Century Bengal', *Past and Present*, 86 (February 1980), p. 141.

61. Rosselli, 'The Self-Image of Effeteness'; Carey A. Watt, *Serving the Nation: Cultures of Service, Association and Citizenship* (New Delhi, 2005); Rosalind O'Hanlon, 'Military Sports and the History of the Martial Body in India', *Journal of the Economic and Social History of the Orient*, 50: 4 (2007), pp. 490–523.

62. Joseph S. Alter, 'Subaltern Bodies and Nationalist Physiques: Gama the Great and the Heroics of Indian Wrestling', *Body and Society*, 6: 2 (2000), pp. 45–72; and Alter, *Gama*, p. 3.

63. Graeme Kent, *The Strongest Men on Earth: When the Muscle Men Ruled Show Business* (London, 2012), pp. 235–40.

64. *Daily News*, 19 January 1892, p. 5.

65. Graham Noble, 'The Lion of the Punjab: Gama in England, 1910', *In Yo: Journal of Alternative Perspectives on Martial Arts and Sciences*, 1–IV (May 2002), p. 3. Accessed on 9 April 2013 at http://ejmas.com/jalt/jaltart_noble_0502.htm; see also Mazumdar, *Strong Men*.

66. Alter, *Gama*, p. 4. But according to another source, it was Madho Singh—a reputed wrestler and a friend of Gama's father—who took care of the young boy and trained him as fighter. Mazumdar, *Strong Men*, p. 64.

67. Alter, *Gama*, p. 5.

68. Ibid.

69. Mazumdar, *Strong Men*, pp. 52–8.

70. *Health and Strength*, VI: 20 (14 May 1910), p. 521.

71. *MG*, 28 January 1908, p. 10; *MG*, 29 January 1908, p. 10; *Health and Strength*, IV: 5 (1 February 1908), p. 104.

72. *Health and Strength*, VI: 6 (5 February 1910), pp. 126–33; *The Times*, 25 February, p. 21; *The Times*, 21 June 1910, p. 19; *The Times*, 19 December, p. 18; *The Times*, 20 December 1910, p. 17.

73. Edward Hitchcock and R.F. Nelligan, *Wrestling: Catch-as-Catch-Can Style* (New York, 1912).

74. *The Times*, 16 February 1910, p. 20.

75. *MG*, 3 May 1910, p. 14.

76. *SL*, 1 July 1910 p. 6.

77. Quoted in *SL*, 1 July 1910, p. 6.

78. *Daily Mail* (Hull), 13 June 1910, p. 8; *The Times*, 21 June 1910, p. 19; *Health and Strength*, VII: 2 (9 July 1910), p. 39. On the Japanese wrestlers in London, see *Health and Strength*, VI: 20 (14 May 1910), pp. 522–3.

79. *Health and Strength*, VII: 5 (30 July 1910), p. 131; *Health and Strength*, VII: 6 (6 August 1910), p. 154; *SL*, 6 August 1910, p. 1; *SL*, 8 August 1910, p. 1.

80. Kent, *Strongest Men*, pp. 248–9.

81. *SL*, 23 July 1910, p. 8.

82. *SL*, 6 August 1910, p. 1.

83. *Health and Strength*, VII: 6 (6 August 1910), p. 154.

84. *The Times*, 9 August 1910, p. 14.

85. *Daily Mail* (Hull), 8 August 1910, p. 6.

86. *Health and Strength*, VII: 11 (10 September 1910), p. 253.

87. *The Times*, 9 August 1910, p. 14.

88. Ibid.

89. Ibid.

90. *SL*, 9 August 1910, p. 2.

91. *Health and Strength*, VII: 7 (13 August 1910), p. 178.

92. *SL*, 1 September 1910, p. 2.

93. Ibid.

94. *SL*, 6 September 1910, p. 1.

95. Ibid.

96. Daily Mail (Hull), 6 September 1910, p. 8.

97. *SL*, 5 September 1910, p. 1.

98. *TOI*, 30 September 1910, p. 7.

99. *Daily Mail* (Hull), 6 September 1910; see also *Health and Strength*, VII: 12 (17 September 1910), p. 277.

100. *Health and Strength*, VII: 12 (17 September 1910), p. 271.

101. Sir Athol Oakley, *Blue Blood on the Mat* (Chichester, 1996), pp. 18–19; Kent, *Strongest Men*, pp. 278–9.

102. *SL*, 22 February 1908, p. 7.

103. *The Times*, 12 September 1910, p. 15; *SL*, 12 September 1910, p. 6; *Sportsman*, 12 September 1910, p. 7; *Health and Strength*, VII: 12 (17 September 1910), pp. 271–6.

104. *Observer*, 11 September 1910, p. 8.

105. *The Times*, 19 September 1910, p. 14.

106. *SL*, 19 September 1910, p. 6; *Sportsman*, 19 September 1910, p. 3.

107. *SL*, 12 September 1910, p. 6.

108. *Health and Strength*, VII: 13 (24 September 1910), pp. 303–4.

109. *Yorkshire Telegraph and Star*, 27 September 1910, p. 6; see also *Health and Strength*, VII: 15 (8 October 1910), p. 359.

110. *SL*, 15 May 1911, p. 8.

111. Ibid.

112. *SL*, 17 May 1911, p 6.

113. *SL*, 19 May 1911, p 7; *Health and Strength*, VIII: 21 (27 May 1911), p. 515–17.

114. *SL*, 24 May 1911, p. 6.

115. Ibid.

116. *SL*, 17 May 1911, p 6.

117. Ibid.

118. *SL*, 19 May 1911, p. 7.

119. *SL*, 17 May 1911, p 6.

120. *SL*, 23 May 1911, p. 4.

121. *SL*, 25 May 1911, p. 6.

122. Ibid.

123. Ibid.

124. *SL*, 20 May 1911, p. 8; *SL*, 24 May 1911, p. 6.

125. *SL*, 25 May 1911, p. 6; *Health and Strength*, VIII: 22 (3 June 1911), pp. 541–7.

126. *SL*, 25 May 1911, p. 6.

127. Ibid.

128. *The Times*, 25 May 1911, p. 17.

129. *SL*, 26 May 1911, p. 6.

130. *The Times*, 11 July 1911, p. 14.

131. Ibid. According to another report, Cherpillod repeatedly called Ahmed Baksh a 'cochon' (pig) as he tried vainly to extricate himself from the latter's unyielding grip. *Health and Strength*, IX: 2 (8 July 1911), p. 32.

132. *MG*, 11 July 1911, p. 5.

133. *The Times*, 11 July 1911, p. 14.

134. *Health and Strength*, IX: 3 (15 July 1911), p. 60.

135. *Courier and Argus*, 22 August 1911, p. 7; *Sunday Star* (Washington), 27 August 1911, Part 5, p. 4.

136. *SL*, 2 June 1911, p. 7; *Health and Strength*, VIII: 23 (10 June 1911), p. 570.

137. See Mazumdar, *Strong Men*.

138. *SL*, 2 June 1911, p. 7.

139. *Health and Strength*, VIII: 22 (3 June 1911), pp. 541–2.

140. Saint Nihal Singh, 'The Story of India's Hercules', *Indian Review* (June 1912), pp. 478–82; Saint Nihal Singh, 'The Indian Hercules: The Amazing Feats of Professor Rama Murti Naidu', *Strand Magazine*, 50 (1915), pp. 691–7.

141. Saint Nihal Singh, 'The Story of India's Hercules', p. 478.

142. Ibid.

143. Saint Nihal Singh, 'The Indian Hercules', p. 695.

144. Ibid.

145. Saint Nihal Singh, 'The Story of India's Hercules', pp. 478–9.

146. Saint Nihal Singh, 'The Indian Hercules', p. 695; Saint Nihal Singh, 'The Story of India's Hercules', p. 479.

147. Saint Nihal Singh, 'The Story of India's Hercules', p. 479.

148. Saint Nihal Singh, 'The Indian Hercules', p. 695; Saint Nihal Singh, 'The Story of India's Hercules', p. 479.

149. See Rosselli, 'The Self-Image of Effeteness', pp. 144–5.

150. Rosselli, 'The Self-Image of Effeteness', p. 145.

151. Saint Nihal Singh, 'The Indian Hercules', p. 695.

152. Saint Nihal Singh, 'The Story of India's Hercules', p. 479.

153. Saint Nihal Singh, 'The Indian Hercules', p. 695.

154. On Eugen Sandow's visit to India in 1905, see Carey A. Watt, 'Cultural Exchange, Appropriation, and Physical Culture: Eugen Sandow in Colonial India', *International Journal of the History of Sport*, 33: 16 (2016), pp. 1921–42.

155. Saint Nihal Singh, 'The Story of India's Hercules', p. 479.

156. Saint Nihal Singh, 'The Story of India's Hercules', p. 480; Saint Nihal Singh, 'The Indian Hercules', p. 694.

157. Saint Nihal Singh, 'The Story of India's Hercules', p. 480.

158. *TOI*, 29 February 1908, p. 11.

159. Saint Nihal Singh, 'The Story of India's Hercules', p. 480.

160. Saint Nihal Singh, 'The Indian Hercules', pp. 695–6.

161. Saint Nihal Singh, 'The Story of India's Hercules', p. 478.

162. Saint Nihal Singh, 'The Indian Hercules', p. 694. 'No less than 110 medals have been awarded him by those who have witnessed and admired his wonderful feats of strength,' noted Nihal Singh in 1912. Saint Nihal Singh, 'The Story of India's Hercules', p. 478.

163. Saint Nihal Singh, 'The Story of India's Hercules', p. 478.

164. See, for instance, *Tribune*, 1 February 1911, p. 5.

165. Saint Nihal Singh, 'The Indian Hercules', p. 695.

166. Mazumdar, *Strong Men*, p. 42.

167. Saint Nihal Singh, 'The Indian Hercules', p. 697.

168. Saint Nihal Singh, 'The Indian Hercules', p. 697.

169. Saint Nihal Singh, 'The Indian Hercules', p. 692.

170. Mazumdar, *Strong Men*, p. 42.

171. Watt, 'Cultural Exchange', pp. 1928–31.

172. Ibid., p. 1928, p. 1931.

173. Ibid., p. 1931.

174. Saint Nihal Singh, 'The Indian Hercules', p. 691.

175. *Health and Strength*, VIII: 23 (10 June 1911), p. 570.

176. *Tribune*, 31 January 1911, p. 5.

177. *Health and Strength*, IX: 1 (1 July 1911), p. 2. See also *Tribune*, 16 July 1911, p. 5.

178. *Health and Strength*, IX: 1 (1 July 1911), p. 3.

179. Ibid.

180. Ibid.

181. Ibid.

182. Ibid.

183. *Tribune*, 16 July 1911, p. 5.

184. Saint Nihal Singh, 'The Indian Hercules', p. 695.

185. *ABP*, 20 July 1911, p. 4.

186. *Tribune*, 1 October 1911, p. 6.

187. Mazumdar, *Strong Men*, p. 48.

188. See, for instance, *The Times*, 31 July 1911, p. 12.

189. *MG*, 21 August 1911, p. 3.

190. Ibid.

191. *ABP*, 31 July 1911, p. 6.

192. See Tony Mason, 'Football on the Maidan: Cultural Imperialism in Calcutta', in Mangan (ed.), *The Cultural Bond*, pp. 142–53; Kausik Bandyopadhyay, '1911 in Retrospect: A Revisionist Perspective on a Famous Indian Sporting Victory', *International Journal of the History of Sport*, 21: 3–4 (June–September 2004), pp. 363–83; Dwaipayan Sen, 'Wiping the Stain of the Field of Plassey: Mohun Bagan in 1911', *Soccer and Society*, 7: 2–3 (April–July 2006), pp. 208–32.

193. Extra Cover, *The Indian Cricketers' Tour*, p. i.

CHAPTER 9

1. Leonard Woolf, *An Autobiography* (Oxford, 1980), Vol. 2: 1911–1969, pp. 5, 20.

2. Siegfried Sassoon, *The Weald of Youth* (London, 1942), p. 117. See also Juliet Nicholson, *The Perfect Summer: Dancing into Shadow, England in 1911* (London, 2006), pp. 123–47.

3. Charles Harding, 'The Summer of 1911', *Nature*, 87: 2189 (12 October 1911), pp. 489–90; *Athenium*, 4387 (25 November 1911), p. 667. See also Charles Harding, 'The Abnormal Summer of 1911', *Quarterly Journal of the Royal Meteorological Society*, 38: 161 (January 1912), pp. 1–32.

4. Mike Kendon and John Prior, 'Two Remarkable British Summers: "Perfect" 1911 and "Calamitous" 1912', *Weather*, 66: 7 (July 2011), p. 180.

5. Ibid.

6. *Daily Mail*, 22 July 1911, p. 3.

7. *TOI*, 7 August 1911, p. 9.

8. *Daily Mail*, 8 July 1911, p. 5.

9. *Daily Mail*, 15 July 1911, p. 5.

10. *Daily Mail*, 6 June 1911, p. 3.

11. *MG*, 31 July 1911, p. 9.

12. *MG*, 17 July 1911, p. 10.

13. George Dangerfield, *The Strange Death of Liberal England* (London, 2008).

14. Standish Meacham, '"The Sense of an Impending Clash": English Working-Class Unrest before the First World War', *American Historical Review*, 77: 5 (December 1972), p. 1343.

15. Dangerfield, *Strange Death*, pp. 37–120; David Brooks, *The Age of Upheaval: Edwardian Politics, 1889–1914* (Manchester, 1995); David Powell, *The Edwardian Crisis: Britain, 1901–14* (London, 1996); Walter L. Arnstein, 'Edwardian Politics: Turbulent Spring or Indian Summer?', in Alan O'Day (ed.), *The Edwardian Age: Conflict and Stability 1900–1914* (London, 1979), pp. 60–78; Peter Clarke, 'The Edwardians and the Constitution', in Donald Read (ed.), *Edwardian England* (London, 1982), pp. 40–55; Asa Briggs, 'The Political Scene', in Simon Nowell-Smith (ed.), *Edwardian England, 1901–14* (London, 1964), pp. 43–102.

16. Nicholson, *Perfect Summer*, p. 189.

17. *Daily Express*, 10 August 1911, p. 1.

18. *Daily Mail*, 9 August 1911, p. 5.

19. *The Times*, 15 June 1911, p. 9.

20. *Daily Mail*, 15 June 1911, p. 5.

21. Quoted in *PIP*, 30 September 1911, p. 430.

22. *Graphic*, 26 August 1911, p. 299. See also Dangerfield, *Strange Death*, pp. 190–3; G.D. Searle, *A New England: Peace and War 1886–1918* (Oxford, 2004), pp. 445–6.

23. George Askwith, deployed as a trouble shooter by the Board of Trade, recalled how one ship owner spoke of 'a revolution'. In Hull, he heard a town councillor 'remark that he had been in Paris during the Commune and had never seen anything like this'. George Ranken Askwith, *Industrial Problems and Disputes*

(London, 1920), pp. 149–50. After a tour of the East End during the dock strike, one writer invoked the spectre of the failed workers' uprising in St Petersburg six years earlier, which 'ended with the sabring of the strikers on the memorable Red Sunday that reddened the snow in front of the Winter Palace'. *Daily Mail*, 11 August 1911, p. 4.

24. Searle, *A New England*, p. 443.

25. Bowen, *Cricket*; Patrick Morrah, *The Golden Age of Cricket* (London, 1967); David Frith, *The Golden Age of Cricket* (London, 1978); George Plumptre, *The Golden Age of Cricket* (London, 1990).

26. John Arlott, 'An Innings at Hove', in David Rayvern Allen, *Arlott on Cricket* (London, 1985), pp. 84–6; John Arlott, *Alletson's Innings* (London, 1958).

27. Marquesee, *Anyone but England*, p. 74.

28. Plumptre, *Golden Age*, pp. 7–8.

29. Neville Cardus, *English Cricket*, p. 61.

30. Ibid., p. 71.

31. Sandiford, *Cricket and the Victorians*, pp. 136–7; Plumptre, *Golden Age*, pp. 31–2.

32. Cardus, *English Cricket*, pp. 61–3.

33. Between 1895 and 1910, there were fifty-four totals of over 600. Plumptre, *Golden Age*, p. 29.

34. John Arlott, 'Sport', in Simon Nowell-Smith (ed.), *Edwardian England, 1901–14* (London, 1964), p. 479.

35. Quoted in Gerald Brodribb, *The Croucher: A Biography of Gilbert Jessop* (London, 1974).

36. Ibid., pp. 27–8.

37. Ibid. Some of Jessop's batting performances entered the folklore of English cricket. None more so than the legendary 'Jessop's Match' at the Oval in August 1902. This was the fifth and final test of a sensational series between England and Australia. England had already lost the Ashes, following their narrow defeat at Old Trafford in an enthralling contest. Jessop, who had been left out of that match, was recalled for the Oval test and played one of the most scintillating innings in the history of the game. Needing 263 runs to win in the second innings, England had lost half their side with less than fifty runs on the board when the Gloucestershire man walked in to bat. On a spiteful wicket, Jessop put the Australian attack to the sword, scoring 104 in seventy-seven minutes off eighty balls. England famously scraped home by one wicket in a tense final session played out in fading light. Ibid., pp. 5–20.

38. Bowen, *Cricket*, pp. 167–9.

39. Ibid., p. 142.

40. Meacham, '"The Sense of an Impending Clash"', p. 1362.

41. Plumptre, *Golden Age*, pp. 67–86.

42. Arlott, 'Sport', p. 478.

43. Home Gordon, 'The Problems of Contemporary Cricket', *Fortnightly Review*, 90: 535 (July 1911), p. 175.

44. Marquesee, *Anyone but England*, p. 90.

45. Sydney H. Pardon (ed.), *John Wisden's Cricketers' Almanack for 1911* (London, 1911), p. 179.

46. Marquesee, *Anyone but England*, pp. 27–54.

47. Keith Sandiford and Wray Vamplew, 'The Peculiar Economics of English Cricket before 1914', *International Journal of the History of Sport*, 3: 3 (1986), pp. 313–14; Wray Vamplew, *Pay Up and Play the Game: Professional Sport in Britain* (Cambridge, 1988), pp. 119–21.

48. Vamplew, *Pay Up and Play the Game*, pp. 59–61, 119–21.

49. Ibid., pp. 91–2; Sandiford and Vamplew, 'Peculiar Economics', pp. 312–13, 322–3.

50. E. V. Lucas, 'Hambledon Redivivus', *The Times*, 4 September 1908, in Marcus Williams (ed.), *Double Century: 200 Years of Cricket in The Times* (London, 1985), p. 147.

51. Philip Trevor, *The Problems of Cricket* (London, 1907).

52. Ibid., p. 147.

53. Ibid., p. 87.

54. Ibid., p. 155.

55. Ibid., p. 241.

56. Ibid., p. 253.

57. Home Gordon, 'The Past Cricket Season', *Badminton Magazine of Sports and Pastimes*, 30 (1910), p. 434.

58. *Illustrated Sporting and Dramatic News*, 22 January 1910, p. 858.

59. Sydney H. Pardon (ed.), *John Wisden's Cricketers' Almanack for 1910* (London, 1910), p. 173.

60. Sandiford and Vamplew, 'Peculiar Economics', pp. 313–24.

61. Vamplew, *Pay Up and Play the Game*, pp. 87–99, 115–24.

62. P. F. Warner, 'The End of the Cricket Season', *Badminton Magazine of Sports and Pastimes*, 35 (1912), p. 398. Quoted in Sandiford and Vamplew, 'Peculiar Economics', p. 320.

63. *MG*, 13 April 1911, p. 3.

64. *The Times*, 8 May 1911, p. 13.

65. *MG*, 14 May 1911, p. 16.

66. *MG*, 14 May 1911, p. 16.

67. *Daily Mail*, 15 May 1911, p. 11.

68. *Daily Mail*, 17 May 1911, p. 6.

69. *Globe*, 27 May 1911, p. 5.

70. *The Times*, 22 May 1911, p. 18.

71. *Daily News*, 22 May 1910, p. 10.

72. *MG*, 21 May 1911, p. 17.

73. Ibid.

74. *PIP*, 3 June 1911, p. 723.

75. Quoted in Extra Cover, *The Indian Cricketers' Tour*, pp. 44–5.

76. *Evening News*, 23 May 1911, p. 5.

77. *Daily News*, 24 May 1911, p. 10.
78. *Daily News*, 29 May 1911, p. 10.
79. *Illustrated Sporting and Dramatic News*, 3 June 1911, p. 640.
80. Sewell, 'Letter No. II', in Extra Cover, *The Indian Cricketers' Tour*, p. 97.
81. *Illustrated Sporting and Dramatic News*, 3 June 1911, p. 640.
82. Sewell, 'Letter No. I', in Extra Cover, *The Indian Cricketers' Tour*, p. 95.
83. Lieutenant-Colonel Sir James Dunlop Smith, Political Aide-de-Camp to the Secretary of State for India, to James Du Boulay, Private Secretary to the Viceroy of India, 21 August 1911, File Con B I A 5 1912, CRR: PD, Internal Branch, Confidential 'B' Proceedings, 1911, IOR/R/1/1/1098, APAC, BL.
84. Roger Fulford, 'The King', in Simon Nowell-Smith (ed.), *Edwardian England, 1901–14* (London, 1964), pp. 1–42; J.B. Priestley, *The Edwardians* (London, 1970), pp. 9–35.
85. Jamie Camplin, *The Rise of the Plutocrats: Wealth and Power in Edwardian England* (London, 1978), 238–51; Erika Diane Rappaport, *Shopping for Pleasure: Women in the Making of London's West End* (Princeton, NJ, 2000), pp. 142–77.
86. Sophie Campbell, *The Season: A Summer Whirl through the English Social Season* (London, 2013).
87. 'Coronation of King George', report by Lieutenant-Colonel Sir James Dunlop Smith, Political Aide-de-Camp to the Secretary of State for India, Political and Secret Department Memoranda: Section D, 11 November 1911, IOR/L/PS/18/D199, APAC, BL.
88. Ibid.
89. Lieutenant-Colonel Sir James Dunlop Smith, Political Aide-de-Camp to the Secretary of State for India, to James Du Boulay, Private Secretary to the Viceroy of India, 21 August 1911, File Con B I A 5 1912, CRR: PD, Internal Branch, Confidential 'B' Proceedings, 1911, IOR/R/1/1/1098, APAC, BL.
90. Ibid.
91. *Daily Mail*, 26 May 1911, p. 7; *The Times*, 26 May 1911, p. 7; *Sheffield Daily Telegraph*, 26 May 1911, p. 7.
92. *Tatler*, 7 August 1918, p. ii.
93. *Athletic News*, 29 May 1911, p. 1; *St Andrews Citizen*, 3 June 1911, p. 3; *Graphic*, 3 July 1911, p. 833.
94. 'Coronation of King George', Report by Lieutenant-Colonel Sir James Dunlop Smith, Political Aide-de-Camp to the Secretary of State for India, Political and Secret Department Records, Memoranda: Section D, 11 November 1911, IOR/L/PS/18/D199, APAC, BL.
95. Ibid.
96. Ibid.
97. Ibid.
98. Lieutenant-Colonel Sir James Dunlop Smith, Political Aide-de-Camp to the Secretary of State for India, to James Du Boulay, Private Secretary to the Viceroy of India, 21 August 1911, File Con B I A 5 1912, CRR: PD, Internal Branch, Confidential 'B' Proceedings, 1911, IOR/R/1/1/1098, APAC, BL.

99. Marquess of Crewe, Secretary of State for India, to Lord Hardinge, Viceroy of India, 9 June 1911, Letter No. 35, Crewe Collection, IOR, Mss Eur Photo Eur 469, APAC, BL.

100. Lord Hardinge, Viceroy of India, to Marquess of Crewe, Secretary of State for India, 29 June 1911, Letter No. 46, Crewe Collection, IOR, Mss Eur Photo Eur 469, APAC, BL.

101. Nicholson, *Perfect Summer*.

102. *Tribune*, 13 June 1911, p. 2.

103. *Bystander*, 12 July 1911, p. 64.

104. Lieutenant-Colonel Sir James Dunlop Smith, Political Aide-de-Camp to the Secretary of State for India, to James Du Boulay, Private Secretary to the Viceroy of India, 21 August 1911, File Con B I A 5 1912, CRR: PD, Internal Branch, Confidential 'B' Proceedings, 1911, IOR/R/1/1/1098, APAC, BL.

105. *MG*, 4 March 1911, p. 8.

106. Sewell, 'Letter No. I', in Extra Cover, *The Indian Cricketers' Tour*, p. 93.

107. *MG*, 9 June 1911, p. 6.

108. *Daily Mirror*, 29 May 1911, p. 5. See also *Daily Express*, 3 June 1911, p. 5; *Sheffield Daily Telegraph*, 9 June 1911, p. 6.

109. *Athletic News*, 12 June 1911, p. 5.

110. *Lincolnshire Echo*, 27 May 1911, p. 5.

111. *Courier and Argus*, 2 June 1911, p. 6; *The Times*, 2 June 1911, p. 15.

112. *Globe*, 5 June 1911, p. 5; *Daily News*, 2 June 1911, p. 2.

113. *Birmingham Daily Gazette*, 2 June 1911, p. 7; *Week and Sports Special* ('*Green Un*', Sheffield), 10 June 1911, p. 1.

114. *Oxford Journal Illustrated*, 7 June 1911, p. 14.

115. *MG*, 9 June 1911, p. 6.

116. *MG*, 9 June 1911. See also *Sheffield Daily Telegraph*, 9 June 1911, p. 6.

117. *Sportsman*, 12 June 1911, p. 1.

118. Sewell, 'Letter No. VII', in Extra Cover, *The Indian Cricketers' Tour*, p. 115.

119. *Observer*, 2 April 1911, p. 14; *Health and Strength*, VIII: 14 (8 April 1911).

120. Sewell, 'Letter No. VII', in Extra Cover, *The Indian Cricketers' Tour*, p. 115.

121. *Globe*, 25 May 1911, p. 3.

122. *Tatler*, 17 May 1911, p. 169.

123. *Sketch*, 21 June 1911, p. 349.

124. *Sketch*, 26 July 1911, p. 71.

125. *Englishman*, 27 July 1911, p. 4.

126. *Illustrated Sporting and Dramatic News*, 5 May 1923, p. 429.

127. *Sunderland Daily Echo*, 28 June 1911, p. 3.

128. *Sketch*, 26 July 1911, p. 71.

129. Ibid.

130. *Sphere*, 19 August 1911, p. 202.

131. *The Times*, 17 July 1911, p. 14.

132. Lieutenant-Colonel Sir James Dunlop Smith, Political Aide-de-Camp to the Secretary of State for India, to James Du Boulay, Private Secretary to the

Viceroy of India, 21 August 1911, File Con B I A 5 1912, CRR: PD, Internal Branch, Confidential 'B' Proceedings, 1911, IOR/R/1/1/1098, APAC, BL.

133. Ibid.

134. Ibid.

135. Extra Cover, *The Indian Cricketers' Tour*, p. 1.

136. Ibid., p. 155.

137. Ibid.

138. *Yorkshire Evening Post*, 11 July 1911, p. 6.

139. Cardus, *English Cricket*, pp. 76–7.

140. Plumptre, *Golden Age*, p. 34.

141. Ibid.

142. Ibid.

143. Parry and Slater, 'The Googly, Gold and Empire', pp. 221–40.

144. *TOI*, 4 June 1909, p. 6.

145. *Athletic News*, 19 June 1911, p. 1.

146. *Observer*, 21 May 1911, p. 17.

147. *Birmingham Gazette and Express*, 16 June 1911, p. 6.

148. Extra Cover, *The Indian Cricketers' Tour*, p. 150.

149. *Athletic News*, 12 June 1911, p. 5.

150. Ibid.

151. See also *Tatler*, 18 June 1913, p. 138.

152. Leslie Duckworth, *S.F. Barnes: Master Bowler* (London, 1967), pp. 20–1.

153. Duckworth, *Barnes*, pp. 48–67.

154. Sewell, 'Letter No. VI', in Extra Cover, *The Indian Cricketers' Tour*, p. 112.

155. *Staffordshire Advertiser*, 1 July 1911, p. 3.

156. Ibid.

157. *TOI*, 15 July 1911. See also Extra Cover, *The Indian Cricketers' Tour*, p. 61.

158. *Illustrated Sporting and Dramatic News*, 3 June 1911, p. 640.

159. Extra Cover, *The Indian Cricketers' Tour*, p. 149.

160. Ibid., p. 155.

161. Ibid., p. 153.

162. Ibid., p. 156.

163. Ibid., pp. 149–50.

164. Ibid., p. 150.

165. Ibid., pp. 154–5.

166. Ibid., p. 156.

167. Ibid., p. 150.

168. Vithal, *Mazhe Krida Jeevan*, p. 36.

169. *TOI*, 27 June 1911, p. 5.

170. *Madras Mail*, 21 June 1911, p. 6.

171. Quoted in *TOI*, 27 June 1911, p. 5.

172. *TOI*, 28 June 1911, p. 4.

173. Extra Cover, *The Indian Cricketers' Tour*, p. 151.

174. *KIH*, 17 September 1916, p. 22.

175. Extra Cover, *The Indian Cricketers' Tour*, p. 150.

176. Vithal, *Mazhe Krida Jeevan*, pp. 33–4.

177. Ibid.

178. Sewell, 'Letter No. XIII', in Extra Cover, *The Indian Cricketers' Tour*, p. 134.

179. Sewell, 'Letter No. V', in Extra Cover, *The Indian Cricketers' Tour*, p. 109.

180. Vithal, *Mazhe Krida Jeevan*, pp. 160–1.

181. Sewell, 'Letter No. XIII', in Extra Cover, *The Indian Cricketers' Tour*, p. 134.

182. *MG*, 10 July 1911, p. 4.

183. *MG*, 12 September 1907, p. 11.

184. *MG*, 13 April 1911, p. 3.

185. *Leicester Daily Post*, 14 July 1911, p. 6.

186. *Leicester Daily Post*, 15 June 1911, p. 6.

187. *Leicester Daily Post*, 17 July 1911, p. 4.

188. *Week and Sports Special* ('*Green Un*', Sheffield), 15 July 1911, p. 6.

189. *Daily News*, 20 July 1911, p. 8.

190. *Western Daily Press*, 20 July 1911, p. 9.

191. *Daily News*, 20 July 1911, p. 8.

192. Sewell, 'Letter No. X', in Extra Cover, *The Indian Cricketers' Tour*, p. 124.

193. N.G.R. Mair, 'Scotland', in E.W. Swanton and John Woodcock (eds), *Barclays World of Cricket: The Game from A to Z* (London, 1980), p. 510; Richard Penman, 'The Failure of Cricket in Scotland', *International Journal of the History of Sport*, 9: 2 (August 1992), p. 302.

194. John Lang, 'Cricket across the Border', in Warner (ed.), *Imperial Cricket*, pp. 230–3; Mair, 'Scotland', p. 510.

195. Penman, 'The Failure of Cricket in Scotland', pp. 302–5.

196. *TOI*, 26 August 1911, p. 7.

197. *Inverness Courier*, 4 August 1911, p. 5.

198. Sewell, 'Letter No. XII', in Extra Cover, *The Indian Cricketers' Tour*, p. 129.

199. *Evening Telegraph and Post*, 31 July 1911, p. 1; *Inverness Courier*, 1 August 1911, p. 5.

200. Sewell, 'Letter No. XI', in Extra Cover, *The Indian Cricketers' Tour*, p. 128.

201. Sewell, 'Letter No. XII', in Extra Cover, *The Indian Cricketers' Tour*, p. 129.

202. Sewell, 'Letter No. XII', in Extra Cover, *The Indian Cricketers' Tour*, p. 129.

203. *Perthshire Courier*, 15 August 1911, p. 4.

204. *Scotsman*, 10 August 1911, p. 5.

205. *Perthshire Courier*, 15 August 1911, p. 4; *Evening Telegraph and Post*, 9 August 1911, p. 3.

206. On the history of Irish cricket, see G. Siggins, *Green Days: Cricket in Ireland, 1792–2005* (Stroud, 2005). For an overview of Irish sport in general, see, William Murphy, 'Associational Life, Leisure and Identity since 1740', in Eugenio F. Biagini and Mary E. Daly (eds), *The Cambridge Social History of Modern Ireland* (Cambridge, 2017), pp. 383–401; and Liam O'Callaghan, 'Sport and the Irish: New Histories', *Irish Historical Studies*, 41: 159 (2017), pp. 128–34.

207. Stanley Bergin and Derek Scott, 'Ireland', in Swanton and Woodcock (eds), *Barclays World of Cricket*, p. 508.

208. Jon Gemell, 'Naturally Played by Irishmen: A Social History of Irish Cricket', *Sport in Society*, 12: 4–5 (May–June 2009), p. 452.

209. Ibid., p. 451. See also Sean Reid, 'Identity and Cricket in Ireland in the Mid-Nineteenth Century', *Sport in Society*, 15: 2 (March 2012), pp. 147–64.

210. Ernest Ensor, 'Cricket in Ireland', in Warner (ed.), *Imperial Cricket*, p. 243.

211. Ibid., pp. 243–4.

212. Reid, 'Identity and Cricket in Ireland', pp. 147–64.

213. Gemmell, 'Naturally Played by Irishmen', pp. 454–5.

214. Ibid., pp. 452–5. See also Patrick F. McDevitt, 'Muscular Catholicism: Nationalism, Masculinity and Gaelic Team Sports, 1884–1916', *Gender and History*, 9: 2 (August 1997), pp. 262–84.

215. *Northern Whig*, 12 August 1911, p. 3.

216. Ibid.

217. Ibid.

218. Plumptre, *Golden Age*, pp. 156–70.

219. Quoted in Ger Siggins, 'Sir Stanley Cochrane and the Irish Dream', *Irish Daily Mail*, 30 August 2012, https://www.cricketeurope.com/DATABASE/ARTICLES5/articles/000021/002175.shtml.

220. Ibid.

221. Ensor, 'Cricket in Ireland', pp. 253–4.

222. *Irish Times*, 14 August 1911, p. 5.

223. *The Times*, 19 August 1911, p. 7.

224. *Daily Mail*, 21 August 1911, p. 5.

225. *TOI*, 9 September 1911, p. 7.

226. Ibid.

227. *Western Daily Press*, 25 August 1911, p. 9.

228. Ibid.

229. *Athletic News*, 28 August 1911, p. 1.

230. *Birmingham Gazette and Express*, 30 August 1911, p. 4.

231. *The Times*, 11 September 1911, p. 10.

232. *Birmingham Gazette and Express*, 30 August 1911, p. 4.

233. *Gloucester Citizen*, 30 August 1911, p. 5.

234. *Birmingham Gazette and Express*, 30 August 1911, p. 4.

235. *MG*, 7 September 1911, p. 3.

236. *Athletic News*, 28 August 1911, p. 1.

CHAPTER 10

1. *SL*, 7 December 1909, p. 6.

2. *Berkshire Chronicle*, 15 May 1907, p. 6.

3. *Birmingham Daily Mail*, 13 June 1911, p. 3.

4. *Health and Strength*, 10 June 1911, p. 571.

5. *Birmingham Daily Mail*, 15 June 1911.

6. P.F. Warner, 'The Benefit of Cricket', *TOI*, 23 June 1911, p. 5.

7. *Illustrated Sporting and Dramatic News*, 3 June 1911, p. 640.

8. *MG*, 2 August 1911, p. 4.

9. *Birmingham Daily Mail*, 13 June 1911, p. 3.

10. *Birmingham Gazette and Express*, 15 June 1911, p. 4.

11. *MG*, 4 March 1911, p. 8.

12. *Daily Mail*, 15 June 1911, p. 4.

13. *MG*, 10 May 1911, p. 3.

14. *Athletic News*, 12 June 1911, p. 5.

15. *Umpire*, 25 June 1911, p. 10.

16. *Berkshire Chronicle*, 15 May 1907, p. 6.

17. *TOI*, 4 June 1909, p. 6.

18. *Daily News*, 29 May 1911, p. 10.

19. *Week and Sports Special* ('*Green Un*', Sheffield), 24 June 1911, p. 1.

20. *Umpire*, 25 June 1911, p. 10.

21. *Leeds Mercury*, 11 July 1911.

22. *Umpire*, 18 June 1911, p. 10.

23. *Daily Mail*, 27 June 1911, p. 9.

24. *Madras Mail*, 20 July 1911, p. 4.

25. *Week and Sports Special* ('*Green Un*', Sheffield), 15 July 1911, p. 1.

26. *TOI*, 8 July 1911, p. 7.

27. *Cricket*, XXX: 876 (15 July 1911), p. 339.

28. *Sheffield Daily Telegraph*, 17 July 1911, p. 3.

29. *Cricket*, XXX: 876 (15 July 1911), p. 339.

30. Ibid.

31. *Daily News*, 12 June 1911, p. 8.

32. Ibid.

33. Extra Cover, *The Indian Cricketers' Tour*, p. 37.

34. *Birmingham Gazette*, 16 June 1911, p. 6.

35. Ibid.

36. *Yorkshire Evening Post*, 10 July 1911, p. 6.

37. *Athletic News*, 31 July 1911, p. 1.

38. *TOI*, 5 August 1911, p. 7.

39. On the Aboriginal cricket tour, see John Mulvaney and Rex Harcourt, *Cricket Walkabout: The Australian Aboriginal Cricketers on Tour 1867–68* (London, 1988); Ashley Mallet, *Lords' Dreaming: The Story of the 1868 Aboriginal Tour of England and Beyond* (London, 2002); Greg Ryan, '"Handsome Physiognomy and Blameless Physique": Indigenous Sporting Tours and British Racial Consciousness, 1868 and 1888', *International Journal of the History of Sport*, 14: 2 (1997), pp. 67–81; and David Sampson, 'Culture, "Race" and Discrimination in the 1868 Aboriginal Tour of England', *Australian Aboriginal Studies*, 2 (2009), pp. 44–60.

40. Quoted in *TOI*, 25 June 1888, p. 6.

41. Satadru Sen, *Migrant Races*, pp. 40–1.

42. *Daily News*, 22 May 1911, p. 10.

43. *Birmingham Gazette and Express*, 15 June 1911, p. 4.

44. *The Times*, 13 April 1911, p. 13.

45. *MG*, 4 June 1911, p. 15.

46. *Athletic News*, 8 May 1911, p. 5.

47. *Cricket*, 20 May 1911, p. 168.

48. *Bystander*, 31 May 1911.

49. *Longford Journal and Midland Times*, 25 March 1911, p. 5.

50. *Daily Express*, 3 June 1911, p. 5.

51. Ibid.

52. *Cricket*, XXI: 872 (17 June 1911), p. 252.

53. *The Times*, 9 June 1911, p. 12.

54. *MG*, 21 June 1911, p. 3.

55. *Leeds Mercury*, 12 July 1911, p. 6.

56. *Birmingham Gazette and Express*, 16 June 1911, p. 6.

57. *The Times*, 2 June 1911, p. 15.

58. *MG*, 21 June 1911, p. 3.

59. *Staffordshire Advertiser*, 1 July 1911, p. 3.

60. *Athletic News*, 12 June 1911, p. 5.

61. *Illustrated Sporting and Dramatic News*, 3 June 1911, p. 640.

62. *Yorkshire Post*, 12 July 1911, p. 10.

63. *Manchester City News*, 24 June 1911, p. 9.

64. *MG*, 4 April 1909, p. 13.

65. *TOI*, 1 July 1911, p. 7.

66. *Umpire*, 25 June 1911, p. 10.

67. *MG*, 21 June 1911, p. 3.

68. *MG*, 20 June 1911, p. 4.

69. *India*, 7 July 1911, p. 3.

70. *Northern Whig*, 12 August 1911, p. 3.

71. *Western Daily Press*, 26 August 1911, p. 9.

72. *Sportsman*, 14 June 1906, p. 3; also see, in this context, Geoffrey J. Levett, 'Playing the Man: Sport and Imperialism, 1900–1907', Unpublished PhD thesis, University of London (2014), p. 196.

73. *Umpire*, 4 June 1911, p. 12.

74. *Leeds Mercury*, 11 July 1911, p. 6.

75. *Birmingham Gazette and Express*, 16 June 1911, p. 6.

76. *Sleaford Gazette and South Lincolnshire Advertiser*, 29 July 1911, p. 8.

77. *MG*, 21 June 1911, p. 3.

78. *TOI*, 7 July 1911, p. 5.

79. Extra Cover, *The Indian Cricketers' Tour*, p. 52.

80. *Inverness Courier*, 1 August 1911, p. 5.

81. *Southern Reporter*, 3 August 1911, p. 3.

82. Sewell, 'Letter No. XIII', in Extra Cover, *The Indian Cricketers' Tour*, p. 133.

83. *Border Telegraph*, 8 August 1911, p. 3.

84. *Sheffield Daily Telegraph*, 25 May 1911, p. 11.

85. Sewell, Letter VII, in Extra Cover, *The Indian Cricketers' Tour*, pp. 116–17.

86. Sewell, 'Letter V', ibid., p. 109.

87. Sewell, 'Letter IX', ibid., p. 121.

88. *Daily Mail*, 14 June 1911, p. 6.

89. *TOI*, 22 July 1911, p. 7.

90. *BG*, 2 April 1912, p. 3.

91. At this time, spectators usually paid six pence as the admission price for a county cricket match (although at some grounds they were charged more for access to stands that offered greater comfort and more amenities).

92. *Sportsman*, 9 June 1911, p. 1.

93. *MG*, 9 June 1911, p. 6.

94. Ramanujaswami, *My Trip to England*, p. 62.

95. *Evening News*, Thursday, 8 June 1911, p. 5.

96. *Sportsman*, 4 July 1911, p. 1.

97. *BG*, 2 April 1912, p. 3.

98. *Sheffield Telegraph*, 25 August 1911, p. 6.

99. *Daily Mail* (Hull), 10 July 1911, p. 8.

100. *Daily Mail* (Hull), 11 July 1911, p. 8.

101. *BG*, 2 April 1912, p. 3.

102. *Leicester Daily Mercury*, 8 July 1911, p. 2; *Leicester Daily Mercury*, 15 July 1911, p. 2.

103. *Newcastle Evening Mail*, 27 July 1911, p. 8.

104. *Lincolnshire Echo*, 4 March 1911, p. 4.

105. *Inverness Courier*, 1 August 1911, p. 5; *Aberdeen Daily Journal*, 1 August 1911, p. 5.

106. *Border Telegraph*, 8 August 1911, p. 4.

107. *Border Telegraph*, 8 August 1911, p. 3.

108. *Southern Reporter*, 10 August 1911, p. 3.

109. *Belfast Evening News*, 12 August 1911, p. 6.

110. Sewell, Letter XV, in Extra Cover, *The Indian Cricketers' Tour*, p. 142.

111. *The Times*, 5 September 1911, p. 11.

CHAPTER 11

1. Extra Cover, *The Indian Cricketers' Tour*, p. 147.

2. *Tribune*, 26 August 1911, p. 5.

3. *Tribune*, 31 August 1911, p. 5.

4. *BG*, 16 September 1911, p. 7.

5. Ibid.

6. Ibid.

7. Ibid.

8. Ibid.

9. *Madras Weekly Mail*, 21 September 1911, p. 273.

10. *BG*, 20 March 1912, p. 6.

11. Guha, *A Corner of a Foreign Field*, p. 121.

12. *BG*, 12 April 1912, p. 6.

13. Ibid.

14. *BG*, 2 April 1912, p. 3.

15. Ibid.

16. Quoted in Extra Cover, *The Indian Cricketers' Tour*, p. 177.

17. *Indian Spectator*, 23 September 1911, p. 1.

18. *Hindoo Patriot*, 8 September 1911, p. 3.

19. *Hindi Punch*, 17 September 1911, p. 20.

20. Quoted in Extra Cover, *The Indian Cricketers' Tour*, p. 173.

21. *Statesman*, 21 September 1911, p. 2.

22. Quoted in Extra Cover, *The Indian Cricketers' Tour*, p. 183.

23. Vithal, *Mazhe Krida-Jivan*, pp. 59–65; Ramachandra Guha, 'Cricket and Politics in Colonial India', *Past and Present*, 161 (November 1998), pp. 160–5. Such was the popular appeal of this 'carnival of cricket' that it spawned a host of imitators in other cities. Similar tournaments sprang up in Karachi (1916), Nagpur (1919), Secunderabad (1922), Lahore (1922), Ahmedabad (1926), and Kalyan (1926). Raiji and Menon, *Story of the Bombay Tournament*, pp. 98–101.

24. Guha, *A Corner of a Foreign Field*, pp. 189–318.

25. Ibid., p. 176.

26. Docker, *History*, pp. 12–14.

27. See Ramachandra Guha, 'Cricket and Caste: The Heroic Struggles of the Palwankar Brothers', in Dilip Menon (ed.), *Cultural History of Modern India* (New Delhi, 2006), pp. 1–31; Guha, *A Corner of a Foreign Field*, pp. 123–86.

28. Vithal, *Mazhe Krida-Jivan*, pp. 88–90.

29. *BC*, 3 December 1920, p. 5.

30. Guha, *A Corner of a Foreign Field*, p. 143.

31. Ibid., pp. 144–5.

32. *TOI*, 3 March 1926, p. 12.

33. *BC*, 8 January 1930, p. 10; *TOI*, 8 January 1930, p. 13.

34. The outcome was the famous 'Poona Pact', which gave the 'Depressed Classes' more seats in return for relinquishing the demand for separate representation. Guha, *A Corner of a Foreign Field*, pp. 194–6.

35. Guha, *A Corner of a Foreign Field*, pp. 238–44. It was not his first electoral defeat. In November 1933, Baloo contested the municipal elections in Bombay. Intriguingly, he chose to stand as a candidate of the Hindu Mahasabha, a right-wing organization that was ideologically opposed to the Congress. The move did not pay off and he lost to his principal Parsi rival. Ibid., pp. 210–11.

36. *TOI*, 30 January 1939, p. 12; Vithal, *Mazhe Krida-Jivan*, p. 23.

37. *BC*, Weekly Edition, 14 October 1945, p. 7.

38. Ibid.

39. *Hindu*, 6 July 1955, p. 8.

40. *BC*, 6 July 1955, p. 8.

41. On the other hand, Bhupinder's two princely cricketing rivals in 1911 did little of note thereafter. Shivaji Rao of Baroda died of pneumonia in November 1919; Prince 'Hitty' of Cooch Behar succumbed to influenza the following winter. See, *TOI*, 27 November 1919, p. 7; *TOI*, 13 November 1920, p. 16.

42. None was more pleased than James Dunlop Smith, who noted in his diary that 'the lad is keeping up the reputation he made in England'. Quoted in Natwar Singh, *Magnificent Maharaja*, p. 70.

43. File Con B I A 6 1913, CRR: PD, Internal Branch, Section A, Confidential 'B' Proceedings, 1912–13, IOR/R/1/1/1105, APAC, BL.

44. *Patiala and the Great War: A Brief History of the Services of the Premier Punjab State, Compiled from Secretariat and Other Records* (London, 1923).

45. Ramusack, 'Sir Bhupinder Singh'.

46. Ibid.

47. He was elected Chancellor of this advisory body in 1926 and served a four-year term. Thereafter, he held the post of Chancellor on two further occasions (1933–35; 1937–8). Ibid.

48. All-Indian States' People's Conference, *Indictment of Patiala: being a report of the Patiala Enquiry Committee appointed by the Indian States' People's Conference* (Bombay, 1930).

49. Ramusack, *Indian Princes and Their States*, p. 120; Ian Copland, *The Princes of India in the Endgame of Empire* (Cambridge, 1997), pp. 81–2; Natwar Singh, *Magnificent Maharaja*, pp. 209–35.

50. Note by Harold Wilberforce-Bell, Agent to the Governor-General, Punjab, 31 December 1929. Quoted in Ramusack, *Indian Princes and Their States*, p. 120.

51. Copland, *The Princes of India*, pp. 127–43; Natwar Singh, *Magnificent Maharaja*, pp. 209–35.

52. Docker, *History*, p. 43.

53. *TOI*, 5 February 1932, p. 9.

54. *TOI*, 3 March 1932, p. 3.

55. Natwar Singh, *Magnificent Maharaja*, p. 266.

56. Docker, *History*, p. 66.

57. 'You know that I appreciate as much as anyone, all you have done to encourage cricket in this country, but I cannot honestly say that I think it would be right to captain this side and it surprises me much that you think you ought to,' Willingdon privately admonished Bhupinder. Quoted in Natwar Singh, *Magnificent Maharaja*, pp. 267–8.

58. de Mello, *Portrait of Indian Sport*, pp. 142–3; Docker, *History*, pp. 83–6.

59. Mike Coward, *Cricket beyond the Bazaar* (Sydney, 1990), pp. 89–113; Docker, *History*, pp. 96–108.

60. Docker, *History*, p. 42; Mihir Bose, *A History of Indian Cricket* (London, 1990), 65–8. He flattered the Viceroy by funding the construction of a 'magnificent' pavilion at Delhi's new Ferozeshah Kotla cricket ground. *TOI*, 11 February 1933, p. 18.

61. Docker, *History*, pp. 92–5; Bose, *A History*, p. 92–4.

62. Docker, *History*, pp. 108–10; Bose, *A History*, pp. 96–101.

63. de Mello, *Portrait of Indian* Sport, pp. 262–74; Vasant Raiji and Anandji Dossa, *CCI and the Brabourne Stadium 1937–1987* (Bombay, 1987), pp. 11–28. See also the newspaper clippings in the Brabourne Collection, IOR, Mss Eur F97/76–77, APAC, BL.

64. *TOI*, 8 December 1937, p. 15.

65. Quoted in Natwar Singh, *Magnificent Maharaja*, p. 270.

66. Quoted in *Madras Mail*, 30 January 1917, p. 6.

67. *TOI*, 13 February 1934, p. 5.

68. *TOI*, 26 August 1935, p. 10.

69. *TOI*, 7 August 1948, p. 2.

70. David Foot, *Sunshine, Sixes and Cider: A History of Somerset Cricket* (London, 1986), p. 62.

71. The information about Bajana's occupation is drawn from his death certificate. I am deeply grateful to Edward Kelvin Storey for generously sharing this document and his research on Manikji Bajana. Personal communication, 3 May 2012.

72. Vasant Raiji, *Cricket Memories: Men and Matches of Bygone Days* (Bombay, 2010), p. 29.

73. *TOI*, 9 January 1940, p. 3.

74. *TOI*, 15 November 1943, p. 2.

75. *BC*, Weekly Edition, 30 December 1945, p. 13; *TOI*, 31 December 1945, p. 6.

76. *BC*, Weekly Edition, 20 January 1946, p. 6.

77. *TOI*, 3 November 1926, p. 13.

78. *TOI*, 20 December 1926, pp. 13, 18.

79. *TOI*, 21 November 1927, p. 14.

80. See, for instance, *TOI*, 9 December 1935, p. 6; *TOI*, 1 November 1937, p. 11.

81. *TOI*, 23 July 1959, p. 10.

82. *TOI*, 25 July 1959, p. 10.

83. *TOI*, 9 June 1975, p. 6.

84. See, for instance, *TOI*, 23 November 1927, p. 6; *TOI*, 26 November 1927, p. 17.

85. *TOI*, 21 February 1927, p. 15.

86. *TOI*, 5 June 1975, p. 8.

87. 'Early Flashes of Indian Cricket', Berry Sarbadhikary File, II, October–December 1974, Anandji Dossa Collection, Cricket Club of India, Mumbai.

88. Sujit Mukherji, *Playing for India* (New Delhi, 1988); S. Giridhar and V.J. Raghunath, *From Mumbai to Durban: India's Greatest Tests* (New Delhi, 2016).

Bibliography

MANUSCRIPT SOURCES

India Office Records, Asia, Pacific and Africa Collections, British Library, London

Crown Representative Records (IOR/R/1)
Native Newspaper Reports (L/R/5)
Political and Secret Department Records (IOR/L/P&S)
Private Office Papers (IOR/L/PO)
Proceedings of the Government of India and of its Presidencies and Provinces (IOR/P)
Public and Judicial Department Records (IOR/L/P&J)
Residency Records (IOR/R/2)

Marylebone Cricket Club, Lord's, London

Minutes of the MCC Committee, 1909–11

Government of India, National Archives of India, New Delhi

Proceedings of the Foreign Department
Proceedings of the Home Department (Political)

Government of Bombay, Maharashtra State Archives, Mumbai

Records of the Judicial Department and the General Department

Cricket Club of India, Mumbai

Anandji Dossa Collection

PRIVATE PAPERS

India Office Records, Asia, Pacific and Africa Collections, British Library, London

Brabourne Collection (Mss Eur F 97)
Crewe Collection (Mss Eur Photo Eur 469)
Curzon Collection (Mss Eur F 111)
Dunlop Smith Collection (Mss Eur F166)
Hardinge Collection (Mss Eur E389)
Harris Collection (Mss Eur D 592)
Morley Collection (Mss Eur D 573)
Willingdon Collection (Mss Eur F93)

OFFICIAL PUBLICATIONS

Conran, W.L. and H.D. Craik, *Chiefs and Families of Note in the Punjab. A Revised Edition of 'The Punjab Chiefs', By Sir Lepel H. Griffin and of the 'Chiefs and Families of Note in the Punjab' by Colonel Charles Francis Massy*, 2 vols, Lahore: Civil and Military Gazette Press, 1910.

Ker, James Campbell, *Political Trouble in India, 1907–1917*, Calcutta: Superintendent Government Printing, India, 1917; reprint, Delhi: Oriental Publishers, 1973.

Memoranda on the Native States of India, Furnished by the Local Political Officers, Simla, Government Central Printing Office, 1905.

Punjab State Gazetteers: Phulkian States: Patiala, Jind and Nabha with Maps. Compiled and Published under the Authority of the Punjab Government, 1904, Lahore, 1909.

Sedition Committee, 1918, *Report*, Calcutta: Superintendent Government Printing, India, 1918.

Selections from the Records of the Government of India, Foreign Department: Correspondence between His Excellency Lord Minto and Certain Ruling Chiefs Regarding Measures to Be Taken for the Suppression of Sedition, and Extracts from Speeches during His Excellency's Recent Tour, Calcutta: Superintendent Government Printing, India, 1910.

NON-OFFICIAL PUBLICATIONS

All-Indian States' People's Conference, *Indictment of Patiala: Being a Report of the Patiala Enquiry Committee Appointed by the Indian States' People's Conference*, Bombay: Indian States' People's Conference, 1930.

Patiala and the Great War: A Brief History of the Services of the Premier Punjab State, Compiled from Secretariat and Other Records, London: Printed for private circulation by the Medici Society, 1923.

The Times, India and the Durbar, A Reprint of the Indian Articles in the 'Empire Day' Edition of The Times, May 24th, 1911, London: Macmillan and Co., 1911.

Universal Races Congress, *The Record of the Proceedings of the First Universal Races Congress Held at the University of London, July 26–29, 1911*, London: P.S. King and Son, 1911.

NEWSPAPERS AND JOURNALS

India

Amrita Bazar Patrika (Calcutta)
Bangalore Spectator
Bengalee (Calcutta)
Bombay Chronicle
Bombay Gazette
Bombay Gazette Overland Summary
Calcutta Municipal Gazette
Capital (Calcutta)

Civil and Military Gazette (Lahore)
Cricket Times
Economic and Political Weekly
Empire (Calcutta)
Englishman (Calcutta)
Hindi Punch (Bombay)
Hindoo Patriot (Calcutta)
Hindu (Madras)
Indian Cricket (Bombay)
Indian Nation (Calcutta)
Indian People (Allahabad)
Indian Planters' Gazette and Sporting News (Calcutta)
Indian Social Reformer (Madras/Bombay)
Indian Spectator (Bombay)
Kaiser-e-Hind (Bombay)
Kesari (Poona)
Leader (Allahabad)
Madras Mail
Madras Times
Madras Weekly Mail
Mahratta (Poona)
Muhammadan Anglo-Oriental College Magazine (Aligarh)
Parsi (Bombay)
Pioneer (Allahabad/Lucknow)
Rast Goftar and Satya Prakash (Bombay)
Statesman (Calcutta)
Times of India (Bombay)
Tribune (Lahore)

United Kingdom

Aberdeen Daily Journal
Athenaeum (London)
Athletic News and Cyclists' Journal
Badminton Magazine of Sports and Pastimes
Belfast Evening News
Belfast Evening Telegraph
Bell's Life in London and Sporting Chronicle
Berkshire Chronicle
Birmingham Daily Gazette
Birmingham Daily Mail
Birmingham Gazette and Express
Border Telegraph (Galashiels)
Bristol Mercury
Bystander (London)

Cambridge Daily News
Cardiff Citizen
Cheltenham Chronicle
Courier and Argus (Dundee)
Cricket: A Weekly Record of the Game
Cricket and Football Field
Cricket Field
Cricket Quarterly
Cricketer Annual
Crisis: A Record of the Darker Races
Daily Dispatch (Manchester)
Daily Express (London)
Daily Mail (Hull)
Daily Mail (London)
Daily Mirror (London)
Daily News (London)
Daily Telegraph (London)
Derby Express
Dundee Courier
Edinburgh Evening News
Evening Mail (Newcastle)
Evening News (London)
Evening Standard and St James's Gazette (London)
Evening Telegraph and Post (Dundee)
Evening Telegraph and Star (Sheffield)
Fortnightly Review
Globe (London)
Gloucester Citizen
Graphic (London)
Hampstead and Highgate Express
Health and Strength (London)
Homeward Mail from India, China, and the East
Illustrated London News
Illustrated Sporting and Dramatic News (London)
India (London)
Inverness Courier
Irish Daily Mail (Dublin)
Irish Times (Dublin)
Isis (Oxford)
Leeds Mercury
Leicester Daily Mercury
Leicester Daily Post
Lincolnshire Echo
Liverpool Mercury

Longford Journal and Midland Times (Longford)
Manchester City News
Manchester Guardian
Monmouthshire Merlin and South Wales Advertiser (Newport)
Morning Post (London)
Northern Whig (Belfast)
Nottingham Daily Express
Observer (London)
Oxford Journal Illustrated
Pall Mall Gazette (London)
Penny Illustrated Paper (London)
Perthshire Courier (Perth)
Referee (London)
Salisbury Times
Scotsman (Edinburgh)
Sheffield and Rotherham Independent
Sheffield Daily Telegraph
Sketch (London)
Sleaford Gazette and South Lincolnshire Advertiser
Southern Reporter (Selkirk)
Sporting Life (London)
Sportsman (London)
St Andrews Citizen
Staffordshire Advertiser (Stafford)
Standard (London)
Strand Magazine
Sunderland Daily Echo
Tatler (London)
Taunton Echo
The Times (London)
Umpire (Manchester)
Week and Sports Special ('Green Un', Sheffield)
Western Daily Press (Bristol)
Windsor Magazine
Yorkshire Evening Post (Leeds)
Yorkshire Post (Leeds)
Yorkshire Telegraph and Star (Sheffield)

United States of America

New York Times
Sunday Star (Washington)

Australia

Age (Melbourne)

CRICKET ALMANACS, SOUVENIRS, AND YEARBOOKS

Chinoy, Rustom Framroze (compiled), *History of the Young Zoroastrian Cricket Club, 1867–1967*, Bombay: Publisher unknown, 1968.

Cricket Association of Bengal: Silver Jubilee Souvenir (1929–54), Calcutta: Cricket Association of Bengal, 1956.

Cricket Chat: Gleanings from 'Cricket', Portraits and Biographies of Eminent Cricketers, London: 'Cricket' Office, 1886–8.

Dossa, Anandji and Mohandas Menon (compiled and ed.), *Association of Cricket Statisticians of India, Cricket Yearbook 1989–1990*, Bombay: Marine Sports, 1989.

John Wisden's Cricketers' Almanack, London: John Wisden & Co., 1880–1940.

Maqsood, Syed M.H. (ed.), *Who's Who in Indian Cricket*, Delhi: Published by the author, 1940.

Maqsood, Syed M.H. (ed.), *Who's Who in Indian Cricket, 1942–43*, Delhi: Caxton Press, 1943.

P.J. Hindu Gymkhana Platinum Jubilee Souvenir, 1894–1969, Bombay: P.J. Hindu Gymkhana, 1969.

Polishwalla, P.N., *Indian Cricket Annual of 1926*, Bombay: Published by the author, 1926.

Polishwalla, P.N., *School and College Cricket in India*, Bombay: K. Ida & Co., 1921.

Raiji, Vasant and Anandji Dossa, *CCI and the Brabourne Stadium 1937–1987*, Bombay: Cricket Club of India, 1987.

Ramaswami, K.S. (ed.), *Mysore State Cricket Association, Silver Jubilee Souvenir, 1934–1959*, Bangalore: Mysore State Cricket Association, 1959.

Sports Mirror, Special Souvenir for Jamshedi Nawroze and Republic Day of Pakistan, Karachi, 23 March 1964.

The Madras Cricket Association, Silver Jubilee Souvenir, 1930–1955, Madras: Madras Cricket Association, 1956.

The Madras Cricket Club, 1848–1968, Madras: Madras Cricket Club, 1969.

PERIOD WORKS

Aflalo, F.R., *Sportsmen's Book for India*, London: Horace Marshall and Son, 1904.

Ahmad, Ziauddin, *Muhammadan Anglo-Oriental College, Aligarh, Calendar, 1911–12*, Aligarh: Published by the author, 1911.

Ali, Mohamed, *Some Thoughts on the Present Discontent*, Bombay: Bombay Gazette Steam Press, 1907.

Antia, Jamshed Dinshaw, *Elphinstone College Tours*, Bombay: Fort Printing Press, 1913.

Askwith, George Ranken, *Industrial Problems and Disputes*, London: John Murray, 1920.

Atkins, J.R., *The Book of Racquets: A Practical Guide to the Game and Its History and to the Different Courts in Which It Is Played*, London: Frederick Warne, 1872.

Baedeker, Karl, *Baedeker's London and Its Environs: Handbook for Travellers*, Leipzig, London, and New York: Karl Baedeker; T. Fisher Unwin; Charles Scribner's Sons, 1911.

Beavan, Arthur H., *Imperial London*, London: J.M. Dent & Co., 1901.

Begg, W.D., *Cricket and Cricketers*, Ajmer: Begg & Co., 1929.

Briggs, Geo W., *The Chamars of India*, Calcutta and London: Association Press and Oxford University Press, 1920.

Darukhanawala, H.D. (ed. and compiled), *Parsis and Sports and Kindred Subjects*, Bombay: Published by the author, 1935.

Ensor, Ernest, 'Cricket in Ireland', in P.F. Warner (ed.), *Imperial Cricket*, London, 1912.

Extra Cover, *The Indian Cricketers' Tour of 1911*, Bombay: D.E. Taraporevala, Sons & Co., 1911.

Framjee Patel, J.M., *Stray Thoughts on Indian Cricket*, Bombay: Times Press, 1905.

Grace, W.G., *Cricket Reminiscences and Personal Recollections*, London: Hambledon Continuum, 1980.

Harris, Lord, *A Few Short Runs*, London: Murray, 1921.

Hawke, Lord, *Recollections and Reminiscences*, London: Williams and Norgate, 1924.

Headlam, Cecil, *Ten Thousand Miles through India and Burma: An Account of the Oxford University Authentics' Cricket Tour with Mr K.J. Key in the Year of the Coronation Durbar*, London: J.M. Dent & Co., 1903.

Hitchcock, Edward and R.F. Nelligan, *Wrestling: Catch-as-Catch-Can Style*, New York, 1912.

Jeejeebhoy, J.R.B. (ed.), *Some Unpublished and Later Speeches and Writings of the Hon. Sir Pherozeshah Mehta*, Bombay: Commercial Press, 1918.

Jeejeebhoy, J.R.B., 'The Sporting Parsi', in H.D. Darukhanawala (ed. and compiled), *Parsis and Sports and Kindred Subjects*, Bombay: Published by the author, 1935.

Karaka, Dosabhai Framji, *History of the Parsees*, 2 vols, London: Macmillan, 1884.

Kipling, Rudyard, *Kim*, London: Macmillan & Co., 1901; reprint, Oxford: Oxford University Press, 1998.

Lang, John, 'Cricket across the Border', in P.F. Warner (ed.), *Imperial Cricket*, London, 1912.

Lucas, E.V., *A Wanderer in London*, London: Methuen & Co., 1906.

Modi, Jivanji Jamshedji, *The Game of Ball-Bat: Chowgân Gui among the Ancient Persians as Described in the Epic of Firdausi*, Bombay: Education Society's Press, 1890.

Parsi Cricketers, *A Reply to a Malicious Attack in the 'Rast Goftar' Newspaper against the Propriety of Parsi Cricketers Going to England to Play against English Clubs*, Bombay: Published by the authors, 1878.

Patel, Manekji Kavasji, *History of Parsee Cricket: Being a Lecture Delivered at the Framji Cowasji Institute under the Presidency of Dr Blaney on the 10th December 1892*, Bombay: J.N. Petit Parsi Orphanage Captain Printing Press, 1892.

Pavri, M.E., *Parsi Cricket*, Bombay: J.B. Marzban & Co., 1901.

Port of London Authority, *London, Port of Empire*, London: Port of London Authority, 1914.

Pugh, Edwin, *The City of the World: A Book about London and the Londoner*, London: Thomas Nelson & Sons, 1912.

Pullin, A.W., *Alfred Shaw Cricketer: His Career and Reminiscences*, London: Cassell & Co., 1902.

Pycroft, James, *The Cricket-Field: Or, The History and the Science of Cricket*, Boston: Mayhew & Baker, 1887.

Ramakrishna, T., *My Visit to the West*, London: T. Fisher Unwin, 1915.

Ramanujaswami, N., *My Trip to England, 1911*, Madras: Ananda Press, 1912.

Sorabjee, Shapoorjee, *A Chronicle of Cricket amongst Parsees, and the Struggle: Polo versus Cricket*, Bombay: Published by the author, 1897.

Spiller, G. (ed.), *Papers on Inter-Racial Problems Communicated to the First Universal Races Congress Held at the University of London, July 26–29, 1911*, London: P.S. King and Son, 1911.

Strachey, John, *India*, London: Kegan Paul, Trench & Co., 1888.

Trevor, Philip, *The Lighter Side of Cricket*, London: Sampson Low, Marston & Co., 1901.

Wacha, D.E., *Shells from the Sands of Bombay: Being My Recollections and Reminiscences*, Bombay: K.T. Anklesaria, 1920.

Warner, P.F., *Cricket in Many Climes*, London: William Heinemann, 1900.

Warner, P.F. (ed.), *Imperial Cricket*, London: London and Counties Press Association, 1912.

Warner, P.F., *Long Innings: The Autobiography of Sir Pelham Warner*, London: Harrap, 1951.

Wild, Roland, *The Biography of Colonel His Highness Shri Sir Ranjitsinhji*, London: Rich & Cowan, 1934.

Winsloe, A.R., *Rackets in India*, Bombay: Times of India Press, 1930.

SECONDARY SOURCES

Articles and Books

Allen, David Rayvern (ed.), *Cricket's Silver Lining, 1864–1914: The 50 Years from the Birth of Wisden to the Beginning of the Great War*, London: Willow Books, William Collins Sons & Co., 1987.

Allen, Dean, 'Cricket's "Laird": James Logan', in Bruce Murray and Goolam Vahed (eds), *Empire and Cricket: The South African Experience 1884–1914*, Pretoria: Unisa Press, University of South Africa, 2009, 141–58.

Alter, Joseph S., 'Gama the World Champion: Wrestling and Physical Culture in Colonial India', *Iron Game History* (October 1995): 3–9.

Alter, Joseph S., 'Subaltern Bodies and Nationalist Physiques: Gama the Great and the Heroics of Indian Wrestling', *Body and Society*, 6: 2 (2000): 45–72.

Appadurai, Arjun, 'Playing with Modernity: The Decolonization of Indian Cricket', in Arjun Appadurai and Carol A. Breckenridge (eds), *Consuming Modernity: Public Culture in a South Asian World*, Minneapolis, MN: Minnesota Press, 1995.

Arlott, John, *Alletson's Innings*, London: Epworth Press, 1958.

Arlott, John, 'An Innings at Hove', in David Rayvern Allen, *Arlott on Cricket*, London: Guild Publishing, 1985, 84–6.

Arnstein, Walter L., 'Edwardian Politics: Turbulent Spring or Indian Summer?', in Alan O' Day (ed.), *The Edwardian Age: Conflict and Stability 1900–1914*, London: Macmillan, 1979, 60–78.

Ashton, S.R., *British Policy towards the Indian States*, London: Curzon Press, 1982.

Baker, Norman, 'Whose Hegemony? The Origins of the Amateur Ethos in Nineteenth Century English Society', *Sport in History*, 24: 1(2004): 1–16.

Bakhle, Janaki, 'Savarkar (1883–1966), Sedition and Surveillance: The Rule of Law in a Colonial Situation', *Social History*, 35: 1 (February 2010): 51–75.

Bandyopadhyay, Kausik, '1911 in Retrospect: A Revisionist Perspective on a Famous Indian Sporting Victory', *International Journal of the History of Sport*, 21: 3–4 (June–September 2004): 363–83.

Bateman, Anthony, *Cricket, Literature and Culture*, Farnham: Ashgate, 2009.

Bateman, Anthony, 'Cricket Pastoral and Englishness', in Jeffrey Hill and Bateman (eds), *The Cambridge Companion to Cricket*, Cambridge: Cambridge University Press, 2011, 11–25.

Berry, Scyld and Rupert Peploe, *Cricket's Burning Passion: Ivo Bligh and the Story of the Ashes*, London: Methuen, 2006.

Bhabha, Homi K., *The Location of Culture*, Abingdon: Routledge, 2004.

Bhagavan, Manu, *Sovereign Spheres: Princes, Education and Empire in Colonial India*, Delhi: Oxford University Press, 2003.

Bhatnagar, S.K., *History of the MAO College Aligarh*, Aligarh: Aligarh Muslim University, 1969.

Birley, Derek, *The Willow Wand: Some Cricket Myths Explored*, London: Aurum Press, 2000.

Blunden, Edmund, *Cricket Country*, London: Collins, 1944.

Bose, Mihir, *A History of Indian Cricket*, London: Andre Deutsch, 1990.

Bowen, Rowland, *Cricket: A History of Its Growth and Development throughout the World*, London: Eyre and Spottiswoode, 1970.

Bradley, James, 'The MCC, Society and Empire: A Portrait of Cricket's Ruling Body, 1860–1914', in J.A. Mangan (ed.), *The Cultural Bond: Sport, Empire, Society*, London: Routledge, 1992, 27–46.

Briggs, Asa, 'The Political Scene', in Simon Nowell-Smith (ed.), *Edwardian England, 1901–14*, London: Oxford University Press, 1964, 43–102.

Brodribb, Gerald, *The Croucher: A Biography of Gilbert Jessop*, London: London Magazine, 1974.

Brooks, David, *The Age of Upheaval: Edwardian Politics, 1889–1914*, Manchester: Manchester University Press, 1995.

Burton, Antoinette, *At the Heart of the Empire: Indians and the Colonial Encounter in Late-Victorian Britain*, Berkeley, CA: University of California Press, 1998.

Buruma, Ian, *Playing the Game*, New York: Farrar, Straus and Giroux, 1991.

Campbell, Sophie, *The Season: A Summer Whirl through the English Social Season*, London: Aurum Press, 2013.

Camplin, Jamie, *The Rise of the Plutocrats: Wealth and Power in Edwardian England*, London: Constable, 1978.

Cardus, Neville, *English Cricket*, London: Collins, 1945.

Cashman, Richard, *Patrons, Players, and the Crowd: The Phenomenon of Indian Cricket*, New Delhi: Orient Longman, 1979.

Cashman, Richard, 'Symbols of Imperial Unity: Anglo-Australian Cricketers, 1877–1900', in J.A. Mangan, ed., *The Cultural Bond: Sport, Empire, Society*, London: Frank Cass, 1992, 128–41.

Chandavarkar, Rajnarayan, *The Origins of Industrial Capitalism in India: Business Strategies and the Working Classes in Bombay, 1900–1940*, Cambridge: Cambridge University Press, 1994.

Chatterjee, Partha, *The Black Hole of Empire: History of a Global Practice of Power*, Delhi: Permanent Black, 2012.

Clarke, Peter, 'The Edwardians and the Constitution', in Donald Read (ed.), *Edwardian England*, London: Croom Helm, 1982, 40–55.

Codell, Julie F., 'Reversing the Grand Tour: Guest Discourse in Indian Travel Narratives', *Huntington Library Quarterly*, 70: 1 (March 2007): 173–89.

Coldham, James D., *Lord Harris*, London: George Allen and Unwin, 1983.

Coldham, James P., *Lord Hawke: A Cricketing Legend*, London: Tauris Parke, 2003.

Collini, Stefan, 'The Idea of "Character" in Victorian Political Thought', *Transactions of the Royal Historical Society*, Fifth Series, 35 (1985), 29–50.

Copland, Ian, *The Princes of India in the Endgame of Empire*, Cambridge: Cambridge University Press, 1997.

Dangerfield, George, *The Strange Death of Liberal England*, New York: Harrison Smith and Robert Haas, 1935; reprint, London: Serif, 2008.

Darwin, John, *The Empire Project: The Rise and Fall of the British World-System*, Cambridge: Cambridge University Press, 2009.

Dass, Jarmani, *Maharaja: The Lives, Loves and Intrigues of the Maharajas of India*, Delhi: Hind Pocket Books, 2007.

Datta, Arindam, 'The Politics of Display: India 1886 and 1986', *Journal of Arts and Ideas*, 30: 1 (1997): 115–45.

de Mello, Anthony, *Portrait of Indian Sport*, London: P.R. Macmillan, 1959.

Deodhar, D.B., *I Look Back: An Autobiography*, Madras: Sport and Pastime, 1966.

Docker, Edward, *History of Indian Cricket*, Delhi: Macmillan, 1976.

Downes, Aviston D., '"Flannelled Fools"? Cricket and the Political Economy of the West Indies c. 1895–1906', *International Journal of the History of Sport*, 17: 4 (2000): 59–80.

Duckworth, Leslie, *S.F. Barnes: Master Bowler*, London: Hutchinson & Co. and Cricketer, 1967.

Dwaipayan, Sen, 'Wiping the Stain of the Field of Plassey: Mohun Bagan in 1911', *Soccer and Society*, 7: 2–3 (April–July 2006): 208–32.

Ernst, Waltraud and Biswamoy Pati, *India's Princely States: People, Princes and Colonialism*, London: Routledge, 2007.

Ferriday, Patrick, *Before the Lights Went Out: The 1912 Triangular Tournament*, Hove: Von Krumm Publishing, 2011.

Fielding, Susan, 'London 1911: Celebrating the Imperial', *Revues.org*, 11 (2011): 1–11.

Fischer-Tine, Harald, 'Indian Nationalism and the "World Forces": Transnational and Diasporic Dimensions of the Indian Freedom Movement on the Eve of the First World War', *Journal of Global History*, 2: 3 (November 2007): 325–44.

Fletcher, Ian C., 'Introduction: New Perspectives on the First Universal Races Congress of 1911', *Radical History Review*, 92 (Spring 2005): 99–102.

Foot, David, *Sunshine, Sixes and Cider: A History of Somerset Cricket*, London: David and Charles, 1986.

Freeman, Mark, 'Splendid Display; Pompous Spectacle: Historical Pageants in Twentieth Century Britain', *Social History*, 38: 4 (2013): 423–55.

Frith, David, *The Golden Age of Cricket*, London: Lutterworth Press, 1978.

Frith, David, *The Trailblazers: The First English Cricket Tour of Australia, 1861–62*, London: Boundary Books, 1999.

Frost, Warwick, 'Heritage, Nationalism, Identity: The 1861–62 England Cricket Tour of Australia', *International Journal of the History of Sport*, 19: 4 (December 2002): 55–69.

Gemell, Jon, 'Naturally Played by Irishmen: A Social History of Irish Cricket', *Sport in Society*, 12: 4–5 (May–June 2009): 447–63.

Gemmell, Jon, '"The Springboks Were Not a Test Side": The Foundation of the Imperial Cricket Conference', *Sport in Society: Cultures, Commerce, Media, Politics*, 14: 5 (June 2011): 701–18.

Ghosh, Sachindra Lal, 'India House and Madan Lal Dhingra', in Arun Chandra Guha (compiled and ed.), *The Story of Indian Revolution*, Bombay: Allied Publishers, 1972.

Gilbert, David and Felix Driver, 'Capital and Empire: Geographies of Imperial London', *GeoJournal*, 51: 1/2 (2000): 23–32.

Gilbert, Martin, *Servant of India: A Study of Imperial Rule from 1905 to 1910 as Told through the Correspondence and Diaries of Sir James Dunlop Smith*, London: Longmans, 1966.

Gilmour, David, *The Ruling Caste: Imperial Lives in the Victorian Raj*, London: Pimlico, 2007.

Giridhar, S. and V.J. Raghunath, *From Mumbai to Durban: India's Greatest Tests*, New Delhi: Juggernaut, 2016.

Grubb, Norman P., *C.T. Studd: Cricketer and Pioneer*, Cambridge, 2014.

Guha, Amalendu, 'More about the Parsi Seths: Their Roots, Entrepreneurship and Comprador Role, 1650–1918', *Economic and Political Weekly*, 19: 3 (21 January 1984): 117–32.

Guha, Ramachandra, *A Corner of a Foreign Field: The Indian History of a British Sport*, London: Picador, 2002.

Guha, Ramachandra, 'Cricket and Caste: The Heroic Struggles of the Palwankar Brothers', in Dilip Menon (ed.), *Cultural History of Modern India*, New Delhi: Social Science Press, 2006, 1–31.

Guha, Ramachandra, 'Cricket and Politics in Colonial India', *Past and Present*, 161 (November 1998): 155–90.

Guha, Ramachandra, *Gandhi before India*, London: Penguin, 2013.

Guha, Ramachandra, *The Last Liberal and Other Essays*, Ranikhet: Permanent Black, 2004.

Hall, Bernard, Richard Parry, and Jonty Winch, 'More than a Game', in Bruce Murray and Goolam Vahed (eds), *Empire and Cricket: The South African Experience 1884–1914*, Pretoria: Unisa Press, University of South Africa, 2009, 3–17.

Hansen, Kathryn, 'Parsi Theatre and the City: Locations, Spectators, and Patrons of the Parsi Theatre in 19th-Century Bombay', *SARAI Reader 02: The Cities of Everyday Life*, Delhi: Centre for the Study of Developing Societies, 2002: 40–9.

Harding, Charles, 'The Abnormal Summer of 1911', *Quarterly Journal of the Royal Meteorological Society*, 38: 161 (January 1912): 1–32.

Harding, Charles, 'The Summer of 1911', *Nature*, 87: 2189 (12 October 1911): 489–90.

Harper, T.N., 'Empire, Diaspora and the Languages of Globalism, 1850–1914', in A.G. Hopkins (ed.), *Globalization and World History*, London: Pimlico, 2002, 141–66.

Haynes, Douglas E., *Rhetoric and Ritual in Colonial India: The Shaping of a Public Culture in Surat City, 1852–1928*, Berkeley, CA: University of California Press, 1991.

Hill, Jeffrey and Anthony Bateman, 'Introduction', in Jeffrey Hill and Anthony Bateman (eds), *The Cambridge Companion to Cricket*, Cambridge: Cambridge University Press, 2011, 1–10.

Hoffenberg, Peter H., *An Empire on Display: English, Indian, and Australia Exhibitions from the Crystal Palace to the Great War*, Berkeley, CA: University of California Press, 2001.

Holt, Richard, *Sport and the British: A Modern History*, Oxford: Oxford University Press, 1989.

Holt, Richard, 'The Amateur Body and the Middle-Class Man: Work, Health and Style in Victorian Britain', *Sport in History*, 26: 3 (2006): 352–69.

Howat, Gerald, *Plum Warner*, London: Unwin Hyman, 1987.

Ikegame, Aya and Andrea Major, 'Princely Spaces and Domestic Voices: New Perspectives on the Indian Princely States', *Indian Economic and Social History Review*, 46: 3 (2009): 293–300.

Inwood, Stephen, *City of Cities: The Birth of Modern London*, London: Macmillan, 2005.

James, Henry, *English Hours*, Oxford: Oxford University Press, 1981.

Kakorwi, Safi Ahmad (ed. and annotated), *Morison's History of the MAO College Aligarh*, Lucknow: Markaz-e-Adab-e-Urdu, 1988.

Keer, Dhananjay, *Savarkar and His Times*, Bombay: A.V. Keer, 1950.

Kendon, Mike and John Prior, 'Two Remarkable British Summers: "Perfect" 1911 and "Calamitous" 1912', *Weather*, 66: 7 (July 2011): 179–84.

Kent, Graeme, *The Strongest Men on Earth: When the Muscle Men Ruled Show Business*, London: Robson Press, 2012.

Kolsky, Elizabeth, *Colonial Justice in British India: White Violence and the Rule of Law*, Cambridge: Cambridge University Press, 2011.

Lamont, Peter and Crispin Bates, 'Conjuring Images of India in Nineteenth-Century Britain', *Social History*, 32: 3 (August 2007): 308–24.

Lelyveld, David, *Aligarh's First Generation: Muslim Solidarity in British India*, Princeton, NJ: Princeton University Press, 1978.

Levett, Geoffrey, 'Constructing Imperial Identity: The 1907 South African Cricket Tour of England', in Bruce Murray and Goolam Vahed (eds), *Empire and Cricket: The South African Experience 1884–1914*, Pretoria: Unisa Press, University of South Africa, 2009, 241–58.

Levett, Geoffrey, 'Sport and the Imperial City: Colonial Tours in Edwardian London', *London Journal*, 35: 1 (March 2010): 39–57.

Levett, Geoffrey, 'The "White Man's Game"? West Indian Cricket Tours of the 1900s', *International Journal of the History of Sport*, 34: 7–8 (2017): 599–618.

Looker, Ben, *Exhibiting Imperial London: Empire and the City in Late Victorian and Edwardian Guidebooks*, London: Centre for Urban and Community Research, 2002.

Luhrmann, T.M., *The Good Parsi: The Fate of a Colonial Elite in a Postcolonial Society*, Cambridge, MA: Harvard University Press, 1996.

McDevitt, Patrick F., 'Muscular Catholicism: Nationalism, Masculinity and Gaelic Team Sports, 1884–1916', *Gender and History*, 9: 2 (August 1997): 262–84.

Mair, N.G.R., 'Scotland', in E.W. Swanton and John Woodcock (eds), *Barclays World of Cricket: The Game from A to Z*, London: HarperCollins, 1980, 510–13.

Majumdar, Boria, 'A Case of Indian Exceptionalism: Bengali Middle-Class Patronage of Sport in Colonial Bengal', in Sanjay Joshi (ed.), *The Middle Class in Colonial India*, Delhi: Oxford University Press, 2010, 278–96.

Majumdar, Boria, 'Maharajas and Cricket: Self, State, Province and Nation', *International Journal of the History of Sport*, 22: 4 (July 2005): 641–6.

Mallet, Ashley, *Lords' Dreaming: The Story of the 1868 Aboriginal Tour of England and Beyond*, London: Souvenir Press, 2002.

Marquesee, Mike, *Anyone but England: Cricket and the National Malaise*, London: Verso, 1994.

Mason, Tony, 'Football on the Maidan: Cultural Imperialism in Calcutta', in J.A. Mangan (ed.), *The Cultural Bond: Sport, Empire, Society*, London: Frank Cass, 1992, 142–53.

Mazumdar, S., *Strong Men over the Years: A Chronicle of Athletes*, Lucknow: Oudh Printing Works, 1942.

Meacham, Standish, '"The Sense of an Impending Clash": English Working-Class Unrest before the First World War', *American Historical Review*, 77: 5 (December 1972).

Mitchell, Timothy, 'The World as Exhibition', *Comparative Studies in Society and History*, 31: 2 (1989): 217–36.

Morrah, Patrick, *The Golden Age of Cricket*, London: Eyre and Spottiswoode, 1967.

Mukherji, Sujit, *Playing for India*, New Delhi: Orient Longman, 1988.

Mulvaney, John and Rex Harcourt, *Cricket Walkabout: The Australian Aboriginal Cricketers on Tour 1867–68*, London: Macmillan, 1988.

Murphy, William, 'Associational Life, Leisure and Identity since 1740', in Eugenio F. Biagini and Mary E. Daly (eds), *The Cambridge Social History of Modern Ireland*, Cambridge: Cambridge University Press, 2017, 383–401.

Murray, Bruce, 'Abe Bailey and the Foundation of the Imperial Cricket Conference', *South African Historical Journal*, 60: 3 (2008): 375–96.

Murray, Bruce and Goolam Vahed (eds), *Empire and Cricket: The South African Experience 1884–1914*, Pretoria: Unisa Press, University of South Africa, 2009.

Muthiah, S., *The Spirit of Chepauk, the MCC Story: A 150-Year Sporting Tradition*, Chennai: Eastwest Books, 1998.

Nandy, Ashis, *The Tao of Cricket: On Games of Destiny and the Destiny of Games*, Delhi: Oxford University Press, 2000.

Nicholson, Juliet, *The Perfect Summer: Dancing into Shadow, England in 1911*, London: John Murray, 2006.

Nielsen, Erik, *Sport and the British World, 1900–1930: Amateurism and National Identity in Australasia and Beyond*, Basingstoke: Palgrave Macmillan, 2014.

Noble, Graham, 'The Lion of the Punjab: Gama in England, 1910', *In Yo: Journal of Alternative Perspectives on Martial Arts and Sciences*, 1–4 (May 2002).

O'Callaghan, Liam, 'Sport and the Irish: New Histories', *Irish Historical Studies*, 41: 159 (2017), 128–34.

O'Hanlon, Rosalind, *Caste, Conflict and Ideology: Mahatma Jotirao Phule and Low Caste Protest in Nineteenth-Century Western India*, Cambridge: Cambridge University Press, 1985.

O'Hanlon, Rosalind, 'Military Sports and the History of the Martial Body in India', *Journal of the Economic and Social History of the Orient*, 50: 4 (2007): 490–523.

Oakley, Athol, *Blue Blood on the Mat*, Chichester: Summersdale, 1996.

Oborne, Peter, *Wounded Tiger: A History of Cricket in Pakistan*, London: Simon and Schuster, 2014.

Orwell, Sonia and Ian Angus (eds), *The Collected Essays, Journalism and Letters of George Orwell, Volume III: As I Please, 1943–1945*, London: Secker and Warburg, 1968.

Owen, Nicholas, 'The Soft Heart of the British Empire: Indian Radicals in Edwardian London', *Past and Present*, 220: 1 (August 2013): 143–84.

Palsetia, Jesse S., *Jamsetjee Jejeebhoy of Bombay: Partnership and Public Culture in Empire*, Delhi: Oxford University Press, 2015.

Penman, Richard, 'The Failure of Cricket in Scotland', *International Journal of the History of Sport*, 9: 2 (August 1992): 302–15.

Pennybacker, Susan D., 'The Universal Races Congress, London, Political Culture, and Imperial Dissent, 1900–1939', *Radical History Review*, 92 (Spring 2005): 103–17.

Pietsch, Tamson, 'A British Sea: Making Sense of Global Space in the Late Nineteenth Century', *Journal of Global History*, 5: 3 (November 2010): 423–46.

Plumptre, George, *The Golden Age of Cricket*, London: Queen Anne Press, Macdonald, 1990.

Port, M.H., *Imperial London: Civil Government Building in London 1851–1915*, New Haven, CT: Yale University Press, 1995.

Powell, David, *The Edwardian Crisis: Britain, 1901–14*, London: Palgrave, 1996.

Priestley, J.B., *The Edwardians*, London: Heinemann, 1970.

Raiji, Vasant, *Cricket Memories: Men and Matches of Bygone Days*, Bombay: Ernest Publications, 2010.

Raiji, Vasant, *India's Hambledon Men*, Bombay: Tyeby Press, 1986.

Raiji, Vasant and Mohandas Menon, *Story of the Bombay Tournament: From Presidency to Pentangular, 1892–93 to 1945–46*, Mumbai: Ernest Publications, 2006.

Ramaswamy, C., *Ramblings of a Games Addict*, Madras: Sremati, 1966.

Ramusack, Barbara N., 'Sir Bhupinder Singh, 1891–1938', *Oxford Dictionary of National Biography*.

Ramusack, Barbara N., *The Indian Princes and Their States: The New Cambridge History of India*, III: 6, Cambridge: Cambridge University Press, 2004.

Rappaport, Erika Diane, *Shopping for Pleasure: Women in the Making of London's West End*, Princeton, NJ: Princeton University Press, 2000, 142–77.

Reid, Sean, 'Identity and Cricket in Ireland in the Mid-Nineteenth Century', *Sport in Society*, 15: 2 (March 2012): 147–64.

Rice, Jonathan (ed.), *Wisden on India: An Anthology*, London: Bloomsbury, 2011.

Ross, Alan, *Ranji: Prince of Cricketers*, London: Pavilion Books, 1988.

Rosselli, John, 'The Self-Image of Effeteness: Physical Education and Nationalism in Nineteenth-Century Bengal', *Past and Present*, 86 (February 1980): 121–48.

Runstedtler, Theresa, *Jack Johnson, Rebel Sojourner: Boxing in the Shadows*, Berkeley, CA: University of California Press, 2012.

Ryan, Deborah, 'Staging the Imperial City', in Felix Driver and David Gilbert (eds), *Imperial Cities: Landscape, Display and Identity*, Manchester: Manchester University Press, 1999, 117–35.

Ryan, Greg, '"Handsome Physiognomy and Blameless Physique": Indigenous Sporting Tours and British Racial Consciousness, 1868 and 1888', *International Journal of the History of Sport*, 14: 2 (1997): 67–81.

Samiuddin, Osman, *The Unquiet Ones: A History of Pakistan Cricket*, Delhi: Harper Sport, 2014.

Sampson, David, 'Culture, "Race" and Discrimination in the 1868 Aboriginal Tour of England', *Australian Aboriginal Studies*, 2 (2009): 44–60.

Sandiford, Keith A.P., *Cricket and the Victorians*, Aldershot: Scolar Press, Ashgate, 1994.

Sarbarbadhikary, Berry, *Indian Cricket Uncovered*, Calcutta: Illustrated News, 1945.

Sardesai, Rajdeep, *Democracy's XI: The Great Indian Cricket Story*, New Delhi: Juggernaut, 2017.

Sarkar, Sumit, *Modern India, 1885–1947*, Delhi: Macmillan, 1983; revised edition, London: Macmillan, 1989.

Sarkar, Sumit, *The Swadeshi Movement in Bengal, 1903–1908*, Delhi: Permanent Black, 2010.

Sassoon, Siegried, *The Weald of Youth*, London: Faber and Faber, 1942.

Satadru, Sen, *Migrant Races: Empire, Identity and K.S. Ranjitsinhji*, Manchester: Manchester University Press, 2004.

Schneer, Jonathan, *London 1900: The Imperial Metropolis*, New Haven, CT: Yale University Press, 2001.

Searle, G.D., *A New England: Peace and War 1886–1918*, Oxford: Oxford University Press, 2004.

Sen, Satadru, *Disciplined Natives: Race, Freedom and Confinement in Colonial India*, Delhi: Primus Books, 2012.

Shah, A.M., 'The *Indian Sociologist*, 1905–14, 1920–22', *Economic and Political Weekly*, 41: 31 (5–11 August 2006): 3435–9.

Shaw, Hillary J., *The Consuming Geographies of Food: Diet, Food Desserts and Obesity*, London: Routledge, 2014.

Siggins, G., *Green Days: Cricket in Ireland, 1792–2005*, Stroud: History Press, 2005.

Singh, K. Natwar, *The Magnificent Maharaja: The Life and Times of Maharaja Bhupinder Singh of Patiala, 1891–1938*, Delhi, 2008.

Subramanian, Lakshmi, *Three Merchants of Bombay: Business Pioneers of the Nineteenth Century*, New Delhi: Penguin, 2012.

Suri and Raja (compiled), *Buchi Babu (Father of Madras Cricket) and His Sporting Clan*, Madras: Published by the author, 1993.

Thompson, A.A., *Cricket My Happiness*, London: Sportsmans Book Club, 1956.

Verma, Ganeshi Lal, *Shyamji Krishnavarma, the Unknown Patriot*, New Delhi: Government of India Publications Division, 1993.

Vicziany, A.M., 'Bombay Merchants and Structural Changes in the Export Community, 1850 to 1880', in K.N. Chaudhuri and Clive Dewey (eds), *Economy and Society: Essays in Indian Economic and Social History*, Delhi: Oxford University Press, 1976, 105–46.

Visaria, Leela, 'Demographic Transition among Parsis, 1881–1971, I: Size of Parsi Population', *Economic and Political Weekly*, 9: 41 (12 October 1974): 1735–41.

Visram, Rozina, *Asians in Britain: 400 Years of History*, London: Pluto Press, 2002.

Vithal, Palwankar, *Mazhe Krida-Jeevan*, Bombay: Bharti Prakashan, 1948.

Ward, Geoffrey C., *Unforgivable Blackness: The Rise and Fall of Jack Johnson*, London: Pimlico, 2005.

Watt, Carey A., 'Cultural Exchange, Appropriation, and Physical Culture: Eugen Sandow in Colonial India', *International Journal of the History of Sport*, 33: 16 (2016): 1921–42.

Watt, Carey A., *Serving the Nation: Cultures of Service, Association and Citizenship*, New Delhi: Oxford University Press, 2005.

White, Jerry, *London in the Twentieth Century*, London: Vintage Books, 2008.

Wilde, Simon, *Ranji: The Strange Genius of Ranjitsinhji*, London: Aurum Press, 1999.

Williams, Jack, *Cricket and England: A Cultural and Social History of the Inter-War Years*, London: Frank Cass, 1999.

Williams, Marcus (ed.), *Double Century: 200 Years of Cricket in The Times*, London: Willow Books, 1985.

Winch, Jonty, 'Guardians of the Game: The Role of the Press in Popularising the 1888/89 Tour and Establishing the South African Cricket Association', in Bruce Murray and Goolam Vahed (eds), *Empire and Cricket: The South African Experience 1884–1914*, Pretoria: Unisa Press, University of South Africa, 2009, 45–60.

Winch, Jonty, '"I Could a Tale Unfold": The Tragic Story of "Old Caddy" and "Krom" Hendricks', in Bruce Murray and Goolam Vahed (eds), *Empire and Cricket: The South African Experience 1884–1914*, Pretoria: Unisa Press, University of South Africa, 2009, 63–80.

Woolf, Leonard, *An Autobiography*, 5 vols, London: Hogarth Press, 1960–9; reprint, 2 vols, Oxford: Oxford University Press (paperback edition), 1980.

Wynne-Thomas, Peter, *The Complete History of Cricket Tours at Home and Abroad*, London: Hamlyn, 1989.

Yajnik, Indulal, *Shyamji Krishnavarma: Life and Times of an Indian Revolutionary*, Bombay: Lakshmi Publications, 1950.

Zelliot, Eleanor, *Ambedkar's World: The Making of Babasaheb and the Dalit Movement*, New Delhi: Navayana Publishing, 2013.

Unpublished Theses and Manuscripts

Allen, Dean, 'Logan's Golden Age: Cricket, Politics and Empire, 1888–1910', Unpublished PhD thesis, University of Brighton, 2008.

Levett, Geoffrey J., 'Playing the Man: Sport and Imperialism, 1900–1907', Unpublished PhD thesis, University of London, 2014.

Patel, Dinyar, *Naoroji: Pioneer of Indian Nationalism*, Unpublished ms.

Text Acknowledgement

Walter Benjamin, Reprinted by permission of HarperCollins Publishers Ltd © 1992
Walter Benjamin

Index